Help!

HAZEL EVANS

Help!

How and where to find the answer

to your every problem

MACMILLAN

First published 1996 by Macmillan

an imprint of Macmillan Publishers Ltd
25 Eccleston Place, London SW1W 9NF
and Basingstoke

Associated companies throughout the world

ISBN 0 333 64178 7

1 3 5 7 9 8 6 4 2

A CIP catalogue record for this book is available from
the British Library.

Printed and bound in Great Britain by
Mackays of Chatham plc, Chatham, Kent

CONTENTS

This book is for my grandchildren
Christie, Jessie, Isabelle and William

Introduction

Why write this sort of book? The answer is simple – the days of the 'nanny' welfare state are over, and with constant cut-backs in government funding we are being thrown more and more on our own resources. Small wonder, then, that the Citizens' Advice Bureau, most people's first port of call, is overloaded, handling almost eight million queries a year. At the same time, the family whom we might turn to for advice and support tends to be scattered these days and it is sometimes difficult to find anyone who can help you.

What I have tried to do in this book is to offer help for almost every problem or situation that life may throw at you. The book has been written alone, without a team of researchers, because I wanted to put myself in the shoes of someone faced with a particular problem. I was in for a lot of surprises. Government departments come in for a great deal of stick, but ringing them as an ordinary citizen I found they were manned by genuinely helpful, courteous people who were eager to be of assistance.

Then there are the support groups which are proliferating. At their best they work brilliantly, giving not just information, but sympathy and support too. During the course of a year I rang thousands of groups. Some had recorded helplines which sometimes sprang surprises: ringing one for rape victims, I got a message saying there was no one there for three weeks as they had gone to the international women's conference in Beijing!

How to use this book

When ringing a helpline remember that telephone numbers prefixed with 0800 are free, those prefixed with 0345 are charged at your local rate, whatever part of the country you phone from, while 0891 calls are charged at a higher rate than normal.

If you are writing in for information, remember that these groups are usually run by volunteers and depend on public contributions for funds, so it is only courteous to enclose a stamped addressed envelope.

The tremendous growth in the numbers of support groups over the last few years is bound to continue. If your group has not been mentioned in this edition of

Help! please write and give us details. While every possible care has been taken to make sure that the information in the book is accurate, the government, in particular, keeps moving the goal posts and new legislation may be enacted between the writing and publishing of the book.

HAZEL EVANS

London and Provence, 1996

ACKNOWLEDGEMENTS AND THANKS

It would take an enormous amount of space to list all of the people who have helped me. I would especially like to thank all the support groups and organizations which gave me particular help: the National Council for Civil Liberties, one of the best-organized groups I came across; also the Commission for Racial Equality; National Debtline; Parents Aid; the NSPCC; the National Consumer Council; the Portia Trust; the Office of Fair Trading and the Automobile Association to name just a few. While compiling *Help!* I have read literally thousands of booklets and leaflets to glean information. If I have inadvertently quoted directly from yours without acknowledging it, my apologies.

Particular thanks to Gwen Riddle of Barclays Bank, Keith Crane of the DSS in Leeds and the lady who mans the pensions helpline in Newcastle. A book like this is out-of-date almost before it is printed, but thanks to Roger Fowler who meticulously checked all the names, addresses and phone numbers.

Finally, special thanks go to my friend Martin Pring of Walworth School who showed me what real life is like out there, and to the NHS's Mariano (Mr Martinez-Tenorio), a splendid Spaniard who runs the plaster room at the Chelsea and Westminster Hospital. Ironically, I broke my wrist while compiling the disabled section of the book. Mariano not only made me laugh but plastered my wrist so that I could still use the computer and, more important, hold 'just a little glass of red wine'!

1

EMERGENCIES

RAISING THE ALARM IN AN EMERGENCY

- Ring 999.
- Speak clearly.
- Say which service you want: the fire brigade, an ambulance if someone has been injured, fire, police, mountain rescue, coastguard or air-sea rescue.
- Describe the incident as clearly as possible.
- Say what has happened.
- Say where it has happened.
- Say if anyone is hurt, how badly and whether the person is trapped.
- Give the injured person's approximate age.
- Do not hang up until you are told to do so.

IF YOU HAVE, OR WITNESS, A CAR ACCIDENT

A serious accident

- Warn approaching traffic. Stand well away from the accident scene to allow for the speed of approaching traffic, road layout and weather conditions. Use red warning triangles if you have them.
- Assess the conditions. How many people and vehicles are involved? Is anyone trapped in the wreckage? Is there any danger of fire (if so, ban smoking and disconnect vehicles' batteries). Find out if anyone present has first-aid training.
- Summon help. Check if anyone has a mobile phone. If not, send someone to locate a telephone in a house nearby, or coin box. If on a motorway get someone to drive to the next emergency telephone. Ask for the police, give the exact location, the types of vehicles involved and an estimate of the number of injured. The police will call the other services.

An accident involving minor injury

- If anyone is injured you must call the police.
- You must produce your insurance certificate within 24 hours, at your local police station.
- Make an accurate record of the accident on the spot, record the names, addresses and statements of witnesses.
- Do not admit liability at this stage. Say as little as possible, especially as you may be suffering from shock.

A damage-only accident

- You must stop and give information to anyone who has 'reasonable grounds' for asking it: your name, address, the car's registration number and details of your insurance.
- Inform your insurance company even if you are not planning to make a claim. This need not jeopardize your no-claims bonus.
- If only your own car is damaged and it is your fault, you need not tell the police. Whether you claim on your insurance depends on the level of the damage.
- If your car and/or the other car have minor damage and it is not clear who is at fault, do not admit liability. Exchange names and addresses and decide between you whether or not to make an insurance claim. If names and addresses are not exchanged you should report the incident to the police within 24 hours.
- If there is serious damage to either car you should tell the police.
- If you have damaged anyone's car or property and cannot find the owner you should also call the police.

NB If you suspect that the other driver in an accident, however slight, has broken the law – is drunk or possibly driving a stolen vehicle, call the police as a safeguard.

If you are involved in any accident that might involve an insurance claim

- Make a map of the scene showing the road layout, the positions of the vehicles and how far they were from each other. Make a note of the position and length of any relevant skid-marks.
- Make a note of anything that might obstruct either driver's view, a sharp bend, parked vehicles or trees.
- If you have a camera with you, take photographs of the scene.

The Law Society has now set up an Accident Line. If you suffer injury in a road, work or other accident, you can find out, free of charge, if you are entitled to compensation: ring 0500 192939.

If you kill or injure an animal on the road

You must stop if you kill or injure a dog, horse, sheep, cattle, pig, donkey, mule or goat. Technically you do not have to stop for a cat if you kill it outright, but if there is a reasonable chance of saving it then you must stop and get help under the 1911 Protection of Animals Act which says you must not cause an animal unnecessary suffering. Summon help from the police if necessary to get a vet. Tell the police only if the damage or injury is serious. Legally you must give your name and address to anyone who has reasonable grounds for wanting them.

IF YOU ARE ARRESTED

The police must say that you are under arrest and tell you why. They must also tell you that you have a right to remain silent and that anything you do say may be taken down and used as evidence against you. If this happens to you, deal with it this way:

- Say as little as possible, admit nothing at this stage.
- Demand to see your solicitor or a duty solicitor in private. If you do not have a solicitor, you should ask the police to phone for a duty solicitor whose services are free.
- Say you want to telephone your family or a friend to tell them what has happened. You have a right to do this. Say as little as possible to them over the phone, as you may be overheard.
- Demand to keep all your property (they may ask you to empty your pockets and your handbag) except anything that could be construed as an offensive weapon or something that would help you to escape or commit an offence such as scissors or penknife.

The police have a right to

- Search you, if they have not already done so.
- Take your fingerprints if you are over the age of 14. They cannot, however, take urine or blood samples without your consent. Any samples must be taken by a doctor. They also cannot photograph you at this stage.

- Deny you your telephone call to relatives or friends if they think you are sending them a warning as a member of a gang.
- Question you as much as they like. This is sometimes done on the nice-nasty principle, with one detective adopting a bullying tone and the other one claiming to be your friend.

The police must destroy fingerprints and photographs if you are not charged or if you are found not guilty. You have the right to ask to see this done or to be shown evidence that it has been done.

If you are detained

The police cannot detain you for more than 24 hours without charging you, unless you are thought to have committed a serious offence such as manslaughter, rape or murder, in which case a senior officer can extend this. Whatever the cause, you cannot be held without a charge for more than 96 hours without being taken before a magistrate's court.

   If the police refuse you bail – to let you out on certain conditions – they have to bring you before a magistrate's court within 24 hours of your arrest (48 hours if it is over the weekend).

If you are charged

- The police officer will read out formally the crime with which you are charged.
- He must then give you a copy of the charge sheet and a notice of your legal rights.
- You may then probably be released, pending a court case which may not come up for several months.
- If the offence you are charged with is more serious, and if the police think you will re-offend or abscond, they can remand you in custody until the case is tried.
- If you are remanded on bail, you have to find sureties (people who will agree to pay a certain sum of money into court if you abscond before the trial). You may also have to report to the police station once a week pending the trial.

IF YOU ARE BURGLED

If you come home and see signs of a break-in before you enter the house:
- Do not go in or call out – the intruder might still be inside.
- Go to a neighbour's house or use your mobile or car phone to call the police.

- If you do go indoors, do not touch anything until the police have had a chance to look around and, possibly, look for fingerprints.
- Once inside the house make a detailed list of all property that has been stolen. Include serial numbers and model numbers and photographs if you have them.
- Give the investigating officer as much information as possible, no matter how trivial it may seem – suspicious persons in the vicinity or anyone you suspect might be involved.

IF YOU ARE MUGGED

- Protect yourself first – your possessions can be replaced, your health cannot.
- Think first about getting away from your attacker. Fight back only as a last resort – you may be injured fighting back.
- Make as much noise as possible – scream, shout and run to the nearest busy, well-lit place you can find.
- Report everything to the police as soon as you can. Every little piece of information, no matter how tiny, really does help. Do not feel embarrassed if you have been indecently assaulted or raped. If you are a woman, ask to speak to a female officer (*see* **If you have been raped**, *page 7*).

If you are mugged, have your bag stolen or are indecently assaulted on the railway or underground, you should report the incident immediately to the **transport police**. (Grab a station employee and ask him to take you to the transport police.)

The transport police will make a report on the incident, interview any witnesses, start investigations and allocate you an investigating officer. If it is a serious crime, they will call in the CID. Tell the police about any injuries and any loss or damage that has occurred because of the crime.

If your possessions are covered by insurance you must report the crime to the police, however little chance you think you have of getting your goods back. Many insurance policies will not pay out otherwise. You must also tell the police at this stage that you want compensation if the offender is convicted. If the offender is convicted, the prosecution will ask for compensation on your behalf in the court – something you cannot do directly.

NB If you are injured through a crime of violence you may be eligible for compensation whether or not the offender is caught. Ask for a copy of the leaflet *Victims of Crimes of Violence: A Guide to the Criminal Injuries Compensation Scheme* from the police, a Citizens' Advice Bureau or the Criminal Injuries Compensation Board (*see page 458*). The police may also put you in touch with Victim Support at this stage (*see page 459*).

WHAT TO DO AFTER A BAG SNATCH

Bank or building society

Ring them immediately, report the loss of your cheque book, cheque guarantee card and cashpoint card.

Credit cards

Ring the credit card companies at once and tell them the cards have been stolen, then confirm in writing within 7 days. Most companies have a 24-hour lost card replacement service:

- Access 01701 352255
- Barclaycard 01604 230230
- Diners 01252 516261
- American Express 01273 696933
  Remember to report the loss of building society cards, store cards, car rental or petrol company cards to the appropriate firms.

Driving licence

Apply for a duplicate licence at once on form D.1 obtained from a Post Office. This will cost £6 but you are breaking the law if you drive without being able to produce a licence.

Keys

Get the locks changed on both the house and the car, especially if your address was in your bag. This is expensive but it is better than allowing a thief to have access to both; 24-hour locksmiths can be found via the police or Yellow Pages.

Library tickets

A thief could use them to steal books from the library and you would be liable for any books taken out and not returned. Contact the library at once.

Pension/benefit books

Tell the DSS at once, as well as the Post Office where you draw your pension. The DSS can arrange an emergency loan until your new books arrive.

Receipts for repairs/dry cleaning

Inform the shops at once and arrange to collect the items before the thief does.

Season tickets

Contact the bus or rail station at once. A duplicate rail season ticket can be issued at the station where you got the original for £5. If you have a special senior citizen's travel card, tell the transport company concerned at once.

Uncashed cheques, giros and money orders

If they are made out to you, tell the people who issued them at once. They may be able to stop payment and send you another order.

Drugs/medicines

If there are potentially dangerous tablets in your bag or wallet, let the police know at once. If it were found by children they could mistake the pills for sweets.

IF YOU HAVE BEEN RAPED

Either go immediately to the police station nearest the scene of the incident or phone and they will send someone to your home. Remember, the sooner you report the assault, the more likely the police are to find the person who raped you. Take a friend or relative with you if you want to. The police will want to know:

- Where and when the rape took place, your name, age and address and a description of the person who assaulted you.
- If a car was involved; try to remember the colour, the model and the registration number.

Do not wash or change your clothes – go to the police station as you are. You may destroy valuable evidence by washing or changing. Do not take anything away from the scene where the attack happened, especially if it was indoors; there may be fingerprints around. Try not to touch anything, the police may find some clues. They will be looking for fingerprints, semen stains, articles of clothing or weapons.

The police may also want to take your fingerprints so that they can eliminate yours from any other prints they find. Your prints will be destroyed after this has been done, and you can ask to be present when this happens. You will be asked to give as detailed a description as possible of your attacker. You may also be asked to look at photographs to see if you can identify anyone. You may also be asked to talk to a police artist so he can draw an impression of what you think the person looks like.

Give the police every detail. It may be distressing or embarrassing to talk about, but this is important.

After reporting the assault the police will ask you to be examined by a doctor who is specially trained in this work. The examination is to make sure that you get any medical help you need, but also to look for evidence. You should be able to choose whether you have a male or female doctor. The doctor will probably also want to take small samples, such as swabs from your vagina, and perhaps from your rectum or your mouth, depending on the nature of the attack. These samples are collected for evidence and might help identify the attacker.

The clothes you were wearing at the time of the assault may also be sent away to a laboratory to be examined, then kept as evidence. In addition, the police may want to take photographs of any bruises, cuts or other injuries you have suffered.

The police will appoint an officer, either male or female, to chaperone you, in other words to look after your interests. The officer will keep in touch with you and tell you what is happening, contact a support group for you if you wish and make a hospital appointment for you if you want one. Remember, that if the police find someone and the case comes to trial, your anonymity is guaranteed by law if you are female or under 18 years old. The law forbids newspapers to publish anything that might identify you. Also, as a general rule, you should not be asked about your previous sexual history in court.

Being raped is a traumatic experience. Get some counselling from an appropriate support group (*see page 19*).

IF YOU WITNESS A CRIME

- If you see anyone acting suspiciously in your neighbourhood, call the police at once. Do not draw attention to yourself when you do so, as this might frighten the suspect away. Instead go into a shop, a neighbour's house or get into your car to use a mobile phone to call the local police station.
- Make a careful note of anything you notice about the person concerned, including height, age and what the person is wearing.
- Note the registration numbers of any cars in the immediate area in case they are used for a getaway.

The success of the *Crimewatch* programme on BBC TV shows how much help the public can be in bringing criminals to book. Ring Crime Stoppers on 0800 555111.

IF YOU HAVE TO DEAL WITH SUDDEN DEATH

If you have any reason to believe the person might still be alive, contact the emergency services immediately – you might save a life.

How to tell if someone is dead

- See if there is a pulse. Using two fingers (not your thumb) feel either at the wrist or inside the arm by the elbow. The pulse may be faint if the person is fat, suffering from heart disease or has taken drugs.
- Hold a mirror to the person's mouth – if it clouds over the person is still breathing.
- Look at the eyes to see if there is any movement or reaction. Touch the eyeball gently with your finger if you feel you are able to do so. A bluish complexion and dark mauve lips usually means that the person is dead, but extreme cold conditions or tranquillizers can sometimes produce the same effect.

- Look to see if the person is carrying a donor card – organs such as kidneys, liver and heart can only be used if someone is brain-stem dead and is on a ventilator, but it is possible that tissue such as cornea, skin or bone could be used if not.
- Phone the police if the death is suspicious, otherwise phone your doctor.

ILLNESS OR SUDDEN DEATH ABROAD

If you become ill in an EC country, you can get emergency treatment free via form E111, which is available at your Post Office. If you do not have one with you, it can be back-dated. However, you may have to pay a small daily charge for a hospital stay or for procedures like X-rays and laboratory tests.

Sudden death abroad

- If you are on a package holiday, your tour operator should be able to organize the repatriation of the body. Contact your tour representative immediately, telling him who the next of kin is, and where the body needs to be sent.
- Contact the local British Consulate. It can contact next of kin for you and give you advice on procedures. In certain countries, usually in hotter climates, it is not possible to repatriate the body and it will have to be buried there.

The body, if it is to be flown back to this country, will go as air freight. Airlines are not bound to refund passenger tickets that are not used due to death, but in most circumstances they will.

IF YOU HAVE A FIRE

- Never try to tackle a fire yourself unless it is very small.
- Shut the door to the room where the fire is – never open a shut door if you suspect there is a fire behind the door.
- Call 999 from a neighbour's telephone to get the fire brigade, do not stay inside your own house.

If something catches fire on the cooker

- Leave it where it is.
- Do not douse it with water – this will cause the flames to spread.
- Smother the flames – jam a lid, a metal tray or anything to hand on top of the flames. Or drop a damp bath towel over the fire.
- Do not go near the pan for at least half an hour – the flames may leap up again if you take the cover off.

If your chimney catches fire

- Throw a bucket of water over the fire in the grate.
- Phone the fire brigade even if you think the fire has gone out.

If someone's clothes catch fire

- Knock the person to the ground and roll him in a rug or carpet to smother the flames.
- Phone for the ambulance.

If your car catches fire

- If moving, stop the vehicle as soon as it is safe to do so.
- Turn off the ignition and get everyone out as fast as possible. Make sure they stand well away from the car and safely away from passing traffic.
- Call the fire brigade.
- If the fire is a small one in the engine, release the bonnet but do not lift it. Use a fire extinguisher, if you have one, to direct a blast between the bonnet and the car body.
- If you think the flames are out, lift the bonnet carefully and disconnect the battery. Stand by to make sure the fire does not start up again.

GAS LEAKS

If you smell gas

- Turn off all gas appliances.
- Call the Gas Board's emergency line; it is in the phone book.

If the smell persists

- Turn the gas off at the meter.
- Open all doors and windows.
- Do not strike a match anywhere in the house. And do not switch on any electrical item – the switch itself makes a small spark which could ignite the gas.

If you can still smell gas

- Go and stand out in the garden or in the street well away from the building, as there might be an explosion.
- If the Gas Board has not arrived at this point, make a 999 call to the police.

SEVERE GALE WARNINGS

If a severe storm is forecast

- Move your car to somewhere in the open, away from unsafe buildings or large trees.
- Put large objects like wheelbarrows, bicycles and ladders that might be in the garden, indoors or under cover.
- Make sure all doors and windows are shut and securely fastened.
- Turn off the electricity and gas if a really bad storm is forecast.

After the storm

- If there is any sign of damage, call the fire brigade.
- Avoid damaged trees, roofs, walls and anything that might topple over or fall to the ground.

FLOODS

A domestic flood

- Call the plumber.
- If you suspect a burst pipe, turn off the water at the stopcock.
- Open all the hot and cold taps to empty the pipes.
- Bind rags tightly round the leak if you can locate it, put something underneath to catch the water.
- If you have a frozen pipe that is likely to burst but is still intact, thaw it out gently using a hair-dryer, a hot-water bottle or towels soaked in hot water. Never use a blow torch or naked flame.
- If the leak is serious, water may get into the electricity circuits and your plumbing might be 'live'. Switch off the electricity and get someone in to check it.

If flooding is forecast

- Move as much as you can from the ground floor to the first floor, giving priority to valuable items and pieces of electrical equipment. Include food, warm clothing, a battery-operated radio and a torch. Take vital personal papers such as your passport, insurance policies and your phone book.
- If you are given sandbags, put them in front of doors and air bricks. If you have time to make some of your own, garden soil in sacking or wrapped in old clothes or a rolled-up rug is better than nothing.

- Turn off the electricity, gas and water at the mains. Do not forget to shut down the stopcocks on washing machines and boilers.
- Seal the lid of the seat of the downstairs lavatory in place with rope and insulating tape to try to stop water overflowing from it.
- Move your car to high ground if there is any nearby.
- Telephone the police or emergency services if necessary, to alert them to your predicament.

Dealing with flood damage

- Determine whom you need to contact to make a claim; look for an emergency helpline number. If there is one, phone it. The company may send a tradesman to do the repairs.
- If flood damage occurs, arrange for temporary repairs to prevent further damage. Put plastic sheeting or tarpaulin over storm-damaged roofs to stop more rain coming in.
- Flood waters may make the building unsafe. Doors and windows may swell and floors may bulge. If you cannot get back into your house, force entry by a window rather than a door; you will do less damage that way.
- Do not switch on the electricity. Get it checked by an Electricity Board official to make sure it is safe.
- When the water recedes, take up floor coverings and wash walls and floors with a disinfectant solution.
- Leave doors and windows, and built-in cupboards open for moist air to escape.
- Contact your insurers as soon as possible. The company may insist on sending an assessor before you can do any work.
- Keep receipts for any work carried out, as these will form part of your claim.
- Keep any damaged items, as the insurance company will want to see them.
- Keep rooms heated. It is important to get warm air circulating. Lift one or two floorboards to increase under-floor draughts. Pull furniture away from walls. Oil hinges and locks to prevent them from seizing up.
- Wait at least 6 months before redecorating, laying carpets or floor covering, even though the floorboards may look and feel dry before this. Check under floorboards after 6 and 12 months for signs of dry rot. If you find any, get expert advice at once.

LOST KEYS

Many keys are stolen, rather than lost, when the owner puts them in the front door, goes inside the house carrying parcels or luggage, returns to retrieve them and finds they are missing. If this is the case, or if you have lost your keys together with something that gives your address:

- Leave someone in the house while you search for them.
- Phone an emergency locksmith (Yellow Pages has listings) and stand guard in the house while you wait for the locksmith to arrive.
- Phone the police to make sure that the keys have not been handed in before the locks are changed.

IF YOU LOSE YOUR PASSPORT

- If you lose your passport in this country, report the matter to the police, then contact the Passport Office (*see page 18*) and fill in an application form for a new one.
- If you lose your passport abroad, and know what has happened to it – it fell in the sea, for instance – contact the consular section of your nearest British Consulate or High Commission which will issue you with travel documents to get you back home.
- If your passport is stolen abroad, contact the local police immediately as well as the British Consulate.

STRANDED PENNILESS ABROAD

In really dire circumstances the British Consul will advance money to you in order to get home against a sum deposited in the UK by relatives, usually at the local police station. Otherwise, Western Union (*see page 19*) have an international money transfer service that sends money world-wide within minutes of it being paid by cash or credit card in the UK.

BASIC FIRST AID

The St John Ambulance Brigade has a fast first-aid guide (*see page 18*). Get a copy and keep it by your first-aid kit.

Unconsciousness

- Lay the person on his back.
- Tilt the head back, lift the chin upwards and open the mouth. Clear out any obstructions, such as food or vomit. Make sure the tongue is not blocking the airways.

If the victim is breathing and has a pulse
- Turn the person onto his side, cross and bend one leg over the other, bend the outer arm up.
- Turn the head to one side and tilt it back so that the chin juts forward. This is known as the **recovery position**.

If the victim is not breathing
- Get someone to dial 999 for an ambulance.
- Pinch the end of the nose firmly. Tilt the head back to open the airways.
- Take in a deep breath and place your lips firmly around theirs to form a seal.
- Blow into the mouth so that the chest rises.
- Let it fall, then breath in again.
- Give a minimum of 10 breaths this way.

Choking

- Do not put your fingers down anyone's throat, get the person to cough.
- Bend the person over and slap the back between the shoulder blades.

If this does not work
Stand behind the person, encircle their middle with your arms at waist level. Make a fist with one hand, put it thumb uppermost between the navel and breastbone. Clasp it with your other hand and jerk both hands upwards pushing in at the same time. This is known as the **Heimlich manoeuvre**.

If a small baby is choking
- Hold the baby upside down and slap his back between the shoulder blades. Do not attempt to treat a baby by the Heimlich manoeuvre.

Burns and scalds

- If clothing is stuck to the skin do not attempt to remove it.
- Hold the area under cold running water if possible, if not, place in a bowl, or use a gentle shower spray.
- Continue for at least 10 minutes.
- Cover the area with cling-film or a plastic sandwich bag.
- Do not put cream on a burn or scald, the doctor will have to take it off before treatment, causing the victim more pain.

Electric shock

- Turn off the power, or pull out the plug. **Do not** touch the victim until you have done so.

- If it is not possible to turn the power off for some reason, use something non-conductive, like a wooden broom, to push the victim away from what he has touched.
- If he is not breathing, follow the steps for unconsciousness (*see page 13*).
- If he is breathing, put him in the recovery position (*see page 14*) and check him for burns and treat.

Bleeding wounds

- Wearing surgical gloves if possible (*see page 16*, **First Aid Kit**) press on the wound with a pad of cloth. If it is a large gash, press the edges together.
- If possible, lift the limb above the heart and hold or support it that way.
- Send for a doctor. If you have to move the victim, bandage the wound as tightly as possible with anything clean to hand.

Broken bones

- If it is anything other than a broken arm or wrist, try not to move the victim, call for an ambulance instead.
- If necessary, support the broken limb using cushions, padding, a rolled-up sweater or anything similar.

Heart attack/stroke

- Call 999 for an ambulance.
- If the victim is unconscious try to resuscitate him (*see* **Unconsciousness**).
- If conscious, do not lay the victim down, prop him in a half-sitting position.
- Loosen clothing around waist and neck.
- If the victim has had a suspected heart attack, get him to chew an aspirin.

Poisoning

If you suspect someone has taken poison either in a suicide attempt or by accident, remember that it is not likely to take effect immediately, you have time to act.

- Phone 999.
- Try to find out what the person has taken. Look for a bottle, if possible.
- Do **not** try to make the person sick, do not give him an emetic (salt water, for instance). If the person is sick, save a sample to give the ambulance crew.
- If the person's mouth is burning, give a little milk or water.
- Phone the local poison information centre.

Local poison information centres
Belfast 01232 240503
Birmingham 0121 554 3801
Cardiff 01222 709901
Dublin 0001 379966
Edinburgh 0131 2929 2477
Leeds 01532 430715
London 0171 635 9191
Newcastle 0191 232 1525

Typical household poisons
Bleach, Cleaning fluids and dishwasher powders, Turpentine and white spirit, Herbicides and other garden products, Polishes, Alcohol in very young children

Poisonous plants, indoor
Castor oil plant, Datura, Dieffenbachia, Oleander, Poinsettia

Poisonous plants, outdoor
Broom, Bryony, Buckthorn, Buttercups, Cherry laurel, Cowbane, Cuckoo pint, Daffodil bulbs, Daphne mezerium, Deadly nightshade, Dog's mercury, Foxglove, Fungi (including Death cap mushroom), Hellebores, Hemlock, Henbane, Holly, Hyacinth bulbs, Ivy, Laburnum, Lupin, Lily-of-the-valley, Marsh marigold, Meadow saffron, Mistletoe, Monkshood, Pokeweed, Potato leaves, stems and sprouts, Privet, Ragwort, Rhododendron, Rhubarb leaves, Snowberries, Water iris, Wood anemone, Woody nightshade, Yew

A BASIC FIRST AID KIT

Keep a first aid kit in the house and in the car. It should contain
• Scissors.
• Safety pins.
• Disposable surgical-style gloves.
• Medicated wipes.
• Sterile dressings.
• Eye pad.
• Cling-film to put over burns and scalds.
• A bottle of sterile water.
You do not need creams or antiseptic lotions. Cleanse wounds with plain or salt-water.

IF SOMEONE IN YOUR FAMILY GOES MISSING

Each year a quarter of a million people go missing. From a family man who is running away from responsibility, to a child who has quarrelled with his parents, they leave behind someone desperate to know where they are and that they are safe.

- Look to see if the missing person has left a diary or address book. Check out the phone numbers in it. Once you have contacted everyone who might know where the person is – family, friends or work colleagues – call the police.
- Contact the Missing Persons helpline on 0181 392 2000 and the Police Missing Persons Bureau on 0500 700 700. Currently, it only deals with those under 19 and over 65, people who are considered to be at risk, those who are ill or are feared to have come to some harm. Also contact the Salvation Army on 0171 383 2772. It is worthwhile contacting organizations like Centrepoint (*see page 493*).
- If a child has run away, remember it is not an offence to leave home without parental consent. Under the Children Act, in the London area at least, if a child leaves home, the police have no power to take the child into custody or to the police station unless the child can be considered in need of police protection or is arrested, although the police may tell the parents where the child is. Other police authorities may have different guidelines.
- Hire a private investigator if you wish, but remember that anyone can become a private detective, they do not need a licence.

IF YOUR CHILD IS ABDUCTED

If your child disappears and you suspect your ex-partner

- Contact the police, ask that a port alert be made in case your ex-partner tries to take the child abroad. If there is 'real and imminent danger' of the child being abducted, the police are obliged to alert all airport and seaport authorities. Give the police as many details as you can: full names, addresses, dates of birth and personal descriptions. Provide them with photographs. If you can guess where they may be going, give the police details.
- Get in touch with your solicitor immediately. He can get an emergency court order preventing the child being taken out of the country. This order can be made out of court hours. Or he can have the child made a ward of court.

If your child has disappeared and you do not know who has taken it

- Ring the police immediately. Give a description of the child, what clothing he was wearing and provide the police with all the photographs you can.

- Ring parents, friends, neighbours and anyone who may have had contact or seen your child.

IF YOU ARE FEELING SUICIDAL

- Do not stay on your own. If possible, go round and see someone, or move in temporarily with someone. Tell them how you feel.
- Phone the Samaritans. Their national helpline number is 0345 909090.
- See your doctor as soon as you can. Tell him that you are suffering in this way. He should be able to arrange for you to be taken into a hospital voluntarily for the time being or put you in touch with a support group.
  See also **Depression,** *page 39.*

EMERGENCIES: HELP DIRECTORY

Accident

- Automobile Association, Fanum House, Basingstoke, Hants RG21 2EA, (01256 20123). The AA has a freephone breakdown service on 0800 887766, 0345 887766 for mobile phone users.

First aid

- *St John Ambulance First Aid Guide* is available from Hascombe Enterprises Ltd, 17 Albemarle Street, London W1X 3HA, (0171 409 7518)

Missing passport

- Passport Office, Clive House, 70 Petty France, London SW1H 9HD, (0171 799 2728). Report your passport lost or stolen to this office.

Missing people

- Missing Persons Helpline, 0181 383 2772
- Police Missing Persons Bureau, 0500 700 700
- Salvation Army, 105–109 Judd Street, King's Cross, London WC1H 9TS, (0171 383 2772). The Salvation Army have a tracing service and can help to find missing relatives. Write initially to the above address.

Rape, sexual abuse

• If you have been raped or sexually abused and you need to talk to someone urgently, ring the Samaritans or call the Victim Support line on 0171 735 9166. They will put you in touch with a local group.

Sending money abroad

• Western Union, MT Consumer Service, 3 King Street Cloisters, Hammersmith W6 0GY. Western Union has a hotline on 0800 833 833 for urgent cash transfers and a credit card hotline on 0800 866866.

Suicidal feelings

• Samaritans, 10 The Grove, Slough, Berks SL1 1QP, (01753 532713). The Samaritans has 183 local branches throughout the country giving round-the-clock confidential help to people who feel suicidal or desperate. They now have a national helpline number: 0345 909090. They can also be contacted on the internet on Jo@Samaritans.org or Samaritans@anonpenct.fi

2

HEALTH

YOU AND YOUR DOCTOR

Your doctor is a key person in your life, someone you should be able to consult freely, in confidence, and in whom you have faith. Your GP is also the gateway to all the help you might need from the National Health Service, whether it is the services of a chiropodist or an operation by a top surgeon. So, choose carefully before you sign up. Many people are frightened or intimidated by their doctor, seeing their GP as a god-like figure who always knows best. But doctors are human and some of them are better at dealing with people than others. Above all, they too can make mistakes.

Your doctor and the NHS

We all think of NHS treatment as free, but in fact we all pay for it with our taxes, so we have the right to complain if we are not getting the services we want. A great deal has changed since the early days of the NHS; cuts have been and are continuing to be made in all areas, putting doctors under a great deal of stress and pressure. Many doctors' practices are now fundholding, which means they administer their own budgets and have to make uncomfortable decisions about which patients should get expensive treatment, which are urgent cases and which are not. For all its faults, the NHS is still very good at dealing with emergencies of all kinds, acute illnesses and urgent operations. Where it does fall down is in dealing with non-urgent conditions and minor out-patient problems – in short, the overloaded, underfunded system has difficulty in coping with non-emergency treatment of all kinds.

Your rights as a patient

The Patients' Charter, issued by the Ministry of Health, says you have the following rights.
- To receive health care on the basis of clinical need, regardless of your ability to pay, your lifestyle or any other factor. Clinical need is the key word here – someone else has to decide that you have this need; you cannot do it yourself.

- To be registered with a GP and to be able to change your GP easily and quickly if you want to. However, the GP of your choice does not have to accept you and does not have to give a reason. And, while you are entitled to treatment at the surgery you register with, you have no automatic right to see your own particular doctor every time.
- To receive emergency medical care at any time through your GP or the emergency ambulance service, hospital accident and emergency departments. Any GP can and must provide emergency treatment, if necessary, even if you are not registered with him.
- To be referred to a consultant acceptable to you, when your GP thinks it necessary, and to be referred for a second opinion if you and your GP agree that this is desirable. You have no automatic right to a second opinion. If your GP will not arrange one, you will either have to pay for it yourself or change your doctor.
- To be given a clear explanation of any treatment proposed, including any risks and alternatives, before you decide whether you will agree to the treatment. However, a doctor can withhold information if he thinks it would damage your health (or would cause you anxiety). Remember, you can refuse treatment or stop treatment at any time, even if it threatens your life. Ultimately, you are responsible for your own body.
- To have access to your health records and to know that those working for the NHS are under a legal duty to keep their contents confidential. You are also entitled to see the medical records of your children who are too young to make decisions for themselves. However, your GP is entitled to discuss your case with other health workers.
- To choose whether or not you wish to take part in medical research or training. If you do not want students to watch you being examined or treated, tell your doctor, who must go along with your wishes. You, on the other hand, have the right to bring someone with you when you are consulting the doctor.

How to find a doctor

Go to your public library or main Post Office and ask to see the local directory of family doctors. This will give the sex of each GP, whether they speak any other language apart from English, what their specialities are, also whether they offer maternity or other services. Or contact your local Family Health Services Authority (FHSA).

The best way to choose a doctor is on personal recommendation. Ask around as you shop and when you take the children to school – ask everybody. Some doctors are better with babies and small children than others, some are particularly good with elderly people, and so on. Some may be good but have no 'bedside manner'. Many practices have a woman doctor on staff, others do not.

Visit a likely practice and ask if it has a leaflet giving the names and qualifications of the doctors, and any services or clinics the practice might offer, such as mother and baby clinics. Find out what the surgery hours are and whether there is an appointment system – just looking round the waiting room will give you a general impression of the surgery. Waiting rooms with crude strip lighting, plastic-covered benches and tired old magazines tend to increase stress and apprehension while you are waiting. Sometimes just a lick of paint would make all the difference.

Find out what the receptionists are like. Are they approachable? Receptionists at most surgeries are in the unenviable state of being the meat in the sandwich between patients who can be anything from tiresome to downright abusive, and doctors who make unrealistic demands on them. Added to that is the increasing burden of record-keeping and form-filling. But they should nevertheless be pleasant and sympathetic.

How to register with a doctor
Go to the surgery and take your NHS medical card with you. If you are accepted, fill in Part A of your card and hand it to the GP. The Family Health Services Authority will then send you an updated one. If you have lost your card ask the FHSA for a replacement, giving your name, address, date of birth and details of your last GP. Meanwhile, register without it, filling in a form supplied by the surgery. Children under 16 must be registered by their parents. Different members of a family can be registered with different GPs. You can transfer to another GP for special services like maternity care if your own surgery does not provide it.

How to get a temporary/emergency doctor
If you are going to be in another area for three months or less, you can register as a temporary patient with a local GP and still stay on the list of your doctor back home.

Problems with registering
If the doctor of your choice refuses to accept you, he must give you any treatment you need while you find someone else. Send your medical card to the FHSA with a note, giving his name and that of any doctors with whom you would prefer not to be registered. The FHSA will then find a GP who will accept you. If you are without a doctor, your local FHSA must find you one within two working days.

Changing your doctor
You do not have to give a reason for changing your doctor or say that you are leaving. The process is quick and easy; you simply go along to the new GP of your choice with your medical card and register. If you have a problem, contact the FHSA. You can expect them to send you a list of doctors within two working days, together with details on how to change doctors. Your GP has the right to take you off his list without giving you a reason, although he must tell the FHSA, who will

notify you. However, he has to continue to treat you, if necessary, for seven days after you have been notified. If you have changed your GP, you can expect your local FHSA to send your medical records to your new GP quickly – usually within two working days for urgent cases and up to six weeks for all other cases.

Health checks

You are entitled to a health check within 28 days of joining your new surgery. This includes measurement of your height, weight and blood pressure, a urine test and enquiries about your lifestyle – how much you drink, whether you smoke and how much exercise you take. The doctor should discuss the results of the tests with you. However, he need not do this if 'it is not in your interests' (if it would cause you anxiety). Anyone between the ages of 16 and 74 who has not seen their GP in the last three years is entitled to ask for a health check at any time, and if you are over 74 you should be offered a yearly health check in the surgery or at your own home, if you prefer.

Consulting your doctor

Doctors allocate 7-8 minutes to each patient, so if you are bringing along a second member of the family with a problem, ask the receptionist to allocate you extra time.

- Smile as you walk in through the door, doctors are only human and will respond to a cheerful face.
- Explain what the problem is briefly and clearly. Write out a list of what you want to say and ask beforehand.
- Listen carefully to what the doctor says about your condition and write a note of it as you leave the surgery.
- Ask the doctor to explain what he means if you do not understand. Get him to write down any important instructions. Ask when he wants to see you again.

If you are not happy about the treatment the doctor is offering, be brave and ask if there are any other methods that can be used. Remember that you and your doctor are in partnership, working together to cure whatever is wrong with you.

Refusal

A doctor can refuse to give you treatment if:

- You do not have your medical card with you and he does not believe you are registered with him.
- If the doctor does not think you need treatment.
- If there is an appointment system and you have not made an appointment.

Telephoning your GP

If you have a busy job and find it difficult to get to the surgery, a non-urgent complaint might be dealt with over the phone. Find out from the surgery when it is convenient to ring (most doctors set aside certain times for this). You can then discuss with him whether or not it is necessary for you to come in, and get some guidance, at the same time, on what action to take.

Urgent appointments

If you need to see your GP urgently, but not in an emergency, either ring or go to the surgery and ask to be seen that day, even if an appointment is not available. The doctor must then decide if you do need urgent treatment or whether you could wait without risk to your health. If it is agreed that your case is urgent, you cannot insist on seeing your own GP; you must see whoever is available.

Waiting times

If the doctor refers you to a consultant or for an operation, ask what the likely waiting time is. If it is very long, ask if it is possible to see another consultant or go to another hospital. If your GP is part of a fund-holding practice, he can refer patients to any hospital he likes. If not, he has to first get permission from his District Health Authority. If you are waiting for an operation and your nearest hospital has a long waiting list, you can find out the waiting times in other parts of the country by phoning the National Waiting List Helpline on 0181 983 1133. Ring and tell them what operation you need; they will tell you which areas have the shortest lists and give you details of the hospitals.

Home visits

You cannot insist that a GP visits you at home. A doctor will only do it if he thinks your medical condition requires it. And it is up to the GP to decide how urgent the visit is. If you need a visit from a nurse, your doctor will arrange it for you. If you are over 75, however, you are entitled to an annual home visit and health check. If you become seriously ill after a GP has refused a home visit, then he could be in breach of his contract or could be found to have been negligent.

HOW TO COMPLAIN

Under the Patients' Charter you have the right to have any complaint about NHS services investigated and to receive a full and prompt written reply. If you have a complaint concerning your GP, contact your local FHSA within 13 weeks of the incident. The FHSA may settle it informally or hold a formal hearing at which the GP may be given a warning and/or have pay deducted. If you are unsure of your ground, talk to the local Community Health Council first. If a doctor has behaved unprofessionally, by excessive drinking or sexual harassment, for instance, you can complain to the General Medical Council, who will investigate the case.

How to proceed

- Make a note, as soon as you can, of what went wrong, then write to the authority concerned.
- Allow a reasonable time for the investigation.
- If you are dissatisfied with the authority's explanation or the handling of the case, write to the Health Service Commissioner (*see page 96*). Enclose copies of all the relevant papers connected with the case.

Complaining about hospital treatment

If you have a complaint about treatment in hospital or by the community health services, you should contact the District Health Authority. If it is a specialist hospital, you should get in touch with the Special Health Authority in your area.

Compensation

To get compensation or damages you have to prove negligence in a legal action and will need professional advice. In this case contact Action for Victims of Medical Accidents (*see page 95*).

DRUGS AND MEDICINES

NHS prescriptions are free if you are:
- Under 16 (or 19 in full-time education).
- A woman of 60 or over, a man of 65 or over.
- Pregnant or have had a baby in the last 12 months.
- Suffering from certain medical conditions or a permanent disability which leaves you home-bound, for instance.
- A disabled war or service pensioner.
- On income support or family credit or a low income (ask your Social Services office). This applies to your partner as well.

The doctor may prescribe a generic drug, that is, one that is called by its proper medical name, or a branded drug which will contain almost the same ingredients as the generic drug, but may have another name given to it by the manufacturer. So, if you have high blood pressure and have been used to taking the branded drug Inderal, you may find yourself being given propranolol instead, which is its generic name. When the doctor hands you a prescription, make sure that you are told:
- How often and when the medicine should be taken.
- For how long you should take it.

- Whether or not there may be side effects.
- When he wants to see you again.

Under EC regulations, the prescription bottle must list:

- The brand name of the drug, if there is one.
- Its proper generic name.
- How many tablets are in the bottle.
- A use-by date.
- What complaint the drug is for.
- What active ingredients it contains.
- A safety warning if it could, for instance, cause drowsiness.
- The name and address of the company selling the drug.
- Details of how it should be stored.
- A symbol, usually of an adult with or without a child or baby, showing who can take the drug safely.

This information may be on the label, or, in the case of branded drugs, may be in a leaflet inside the box. Doctors can only issue prescriptions for drugs on the NHS Prescribed Drugs list. In an emergency, however, your GP may give you drugs needed for immediate treatment, for which there is no charge.

Saving money

Prescription charges are now quite high, so if you have to pay them, check with the chemist to determine whether the actual cost of the drug is less than the prescription charge. If so, buy it direct from the chemist as if it was a private prescription. If you need regular prescriptions, cut down on payments by applying at the local Post Office for a discounted yearly season ticket.

Buying medicines without a prescription

Powerful drugs are only obtainable on prescription. But if you go into a chemist's to buy other, over-the-counter medicines, the assistant should ask you:

- Who the medicine is for.
- What the symptoms are.
- How long you have suffered with the symptoms.
- Whether you have seen a doctor.
- What you think caused the condition.
- Whether you are taking any other medicines or herbal remedy.
- Whether you are pregnant.

The assistant is not being nosy, he is obliged by the chemist's code of practice to ask these questions to make sure that he is not giving you something that might do you harm.

Painkillers

These are the most common drugs that we buy for ourselves.

Aspirin is the cheapest and most popular painkiller and is good for bringing down a high temperature. It is also good for inflammation. It should not be taken by anyone who suffers from indigestion as it can cause stomach ulcers or bleeding. Aspirin should never, ever be given to children.

Paracetamol is a relatively safe choice of painkiller, but it will not help if you have inflammation.

Codeine is a good choice of painkiller if you have a cough, but if you have any kind of breathing problem you should avoid it.

PRIVATE MEDICINE: PAYING FOR TREATMENT

One way to avoid the inevitable queues to see consultants and to receive hospital treatment is to pay for private treatment via one of the private health insurers. You will not necessarily get better quality care than on the NHS, but you will get seen promptly and surgery done more quickly. You can also choose when and where you go into hospital.

When is it worth paying?
- If you are self-employed and need to keep fit in order to earn money. Tiresome chronic conditions that involve long waits for treatment on the NHS can be tackled right away if you have health insurance.
- If you work for a company that offers to pay part of your health insurance premiums.

How much will I have to pay?
This is worked out according to your age and your medical history. There is a banded scale of charges, depending on the hospital you opt for and where you live. In London, for instance, hospital charges are higher than the rest of the country. With some companies, you can volunteer to pay an excess, or the first £100 or more, of your claims and therefore pay a much lower yearly subscription. Enquire whether the company you are considering has this facility. You can also get good deals with family membership, insuring children cheaply. People over 60 may be able to get tax relief on their premiums.

Will they accept me?
Each company has its own set of rules but by shopping around you will be able to find someone to take you – at a price. Some companies will not take on anyone over 55, for instance, or someone with a long-standing history of, say, hypertension. But if you persist, you will find others that will.

How does it work?
If you need an operation or specialist treatment and the NHS waiting list is long, you go through your GP in the usual way, saying you want to consult a specialist

privately. Alternatively you can pay to go to a private doctor – although some GPs have both private and NHS practices. Your doctor should then help you choose a surgeon or consultant in the private sector.

What is not covered

- Private health insurance will not normally cover a routine visit to a private GP, or an ordinary check-up or screening. It also does not cover routine visits to dentists or opticians.
- You will also have to pay for your own medicines in full. You cannot consult a private doctor and get an NHS prescription.

Also excluded are such treatments as:

- Cosmetic treatment.
- Health hydros, nature cure clinical establishments.
- Normal pregnancy and childbirth.
- Treatment of infertility, including IVF.
- Vasectomy and sterilization.
- Regular or long-term renal dialysis.
- Aids and related conditions.
- Alleviation of chronic or incurable conditions.
- Nursing home or geriatric care.

You may also have to pay extra if you choose a hospital that is in a more expensive band than the one for which you are covered. You may not be able to get all your costs back if the surgeon you choose charges fees that are higher than the company is willing to reimburse – some companies have a maximum pay-out figure. Before embarking on treatment, ask how much the whole process will cost, then contact your insurance company to make sure it will foot the bill.

Settling the bill

Most insurance companies settle bills directly with hospitals and clinics but in some cases you might be asked to pay for your treatment and then recoup it from the company.

HOSPITALS

More than a million people in this country are waiting for an operation at any given time. Hospitals are now being accused of running up impressive numbers of patients treated and trying to adhere to the Patients' Charter by treating more minor operations at the expense of people needing major surgery. There are also stories of patients being sent home too soon, only to have to return – which pushes up the statistics again as they then count as a new admission.

New and expensive advances in treatment for serious conditions which at one time would have been fatal, plus an ageing population, means that there is just not enough money to go round. Someone has to decide who gets priority, hence the worry that some hospitals may refuse to perform heart surgery on heavy smokers, or in some cases, use old age as a cut-off point for overloaded services like physiotherapy. Worrying, too, is the fact that the contract system between GPs and hospitals limits the choice of consultants for a particular condition. If you have a particular problem and need surgery, it would pay you to press your GP to ask his local administrative committee for an Extra Contractual Referral (ECR) to see the right specialist.

In theory, you should be able, within reason, to choose which hospital you go to. But in practice, your GP is likely to have an arrangement with one particular hospital. Almost all NHS hospitals are now run as self-governing trusts and some are more efficient than others. Although improvements have been made in waiting times, popular operations like those for cataracts and hip replacements usually attract waiting times of 18 months. It is worthwhile persuading your GP to shop around and try to find a shorter wait (*see page 24*). If your GP is a fundholder, he is more likely to be able to do this and you are likely to be dealt with more quickly.

If you are referred to a specialist as an outpatient you should expect to be seen within 13 weeks, but the waiting time can stretch to 26 weeks. Having got there, you should not have to wait more than 30 minutes beyond the time of your appointment. Under the Patients' Charter, your operation should not be cancelled on the day you are due to go into hospital or after you have gone in, but this can happen – if the hospital has to deal with a sudden emergency, for instance.

Accident and Emergency

In most hospitals today, if you go to what used to be called the casualty department, and is now call Accident and Emergency, the first person you are likely to see is the triage nurse. She is there to assess your situation and she will put you into one of three categories:

- Emergency status – you will be seen right away for conditions like heart attack or serious injuries.
- Possibly life-threatening status – you should be seen within five minutes for fractures, chest pains and the like.
- Minor status – you are supposed to be seen within 45 minutes but can sometimes wait for hours.

If you are admitted to hospital, you should now get a bed within two hours. If you want to discuss something with the nurse and you do not want to be overheard, you have the right to ask to go somewhere private to do so.

SEEING A SPECIALIST

If your doctor has referred you to a specialist, be prepared for two long waits under the NHS – the first for an appointment, the second when you get to the clinic.

- Do your homework. Have the story of your illness worked out as succinctly as possible. Write down all the salient points you want to make and questions you want to ask.
- Find out as much as you can about your medical problem and the medical jargon attached to it. You will find it easier, then, to understand what the surgeon is talking about. Look it up in a medical dictionary in your local reference library.
- Bring along any medicines you are taking or make a list of their names.
- Take a book or magazine with you, even if you find yourself going over the same paragraph again and again, it is better than staring at the other patients, wondering what is wrong with them.
- Do not take lots of carrier bags or shopping with you. You may be sent for X-rays or blood tests and will have to cart them along with you.
- Wear clothes that are easy to get on and off, since you may find yourself dressing and undressing several times, if you are sent for tests.
- You have a right to ask how long it may be before you are seen, when you check in at the reception desk.
- Take someone with you, if you feel more comfortable doing so.
- Have a notebook and pen at the ready so that you can write down what the specialist says. Do not be afraid to ask him to repeat himself or to ask him questions if you do not understand. Or get him to write down the details for you.
- Remember that if you do not feel happy about what has happened, you can ask for a second opinion, although this may not be granted.

GOING INTO HOSPITAL

You have certain hospital rights under the Patients' Charter. You can expect all staff you meet to wear name badges. You can also expect the NHS to respect your privacy, dignity, religious and cultural beliefs at all times and in all places. For example, meals should suit your dietary and religious needs. Staff should ask you whether you want to be called by your first or last name and respect your preference.

Single-sex wards

You cannot demand to go into a single-sex ward, although the NHS, mindful of the uproar about mixed wards, is doing its best to segregate the sexes. Under the Patients' Charter, except in emergencies, you have the right to be told before you go into hospital whether you will be going into a ward for both men and women or not, though in all cases you can expect single-sex washing and toilet facilities. If you do not want to go into a mixed-sex ward, you will be faced with the choice of delaying your admission until single-sex accommodation is available. In an emergency, if you are in intensive care or need specialist nursing or observation, you may have no option but to go into a mixed-sex ward.

Going in

If you are going into hospital, the specific hospital should send you a leaflet telling you how to get to it, what the visiting hours are and what you should bring. Apart from basics like nightclothes and washing items, bring a good supply of reading matter – lying in a hospital bed can be extremely boring. Find out whether the hospital has a library trolley, a hospital shop and a mobile telephone trolley so you know what facilities are going to be available. Delegate the job of phoning to find how you are to one member of the family, get that person to pass it on to the rest. Answering telephone calls takes up a lot of the nurses' valuable time.

TAKING YOUR CHILD TO HOSPITAL

If your child is admitted to hospital you can expect him or her to be cared for in a children's ward under the supervision of a consultant paediatrician. Exceptionally, when a child has to be admitted to a ward other than a children's ward, you can expect a named consultant paediatrician to be responsible for advising on your child's care. If your child is admitted to hospital without prior notice, a bed must now be found for him within two hours. If you take your child to Accident and Emergency, he should be seen immediately, in a separate area specially for children. Under the new draft Children's Charter, a child going into hospital must be told the names of the nurses looking after him, and must be given choices over food and what to wear. He is also allowed to bring in some personal possessions. Teenage children should be offered a choice between staying in a children's ward or an adult ward.

If your child has to be admitted to hospital, perhaps for a minor operation, ask the ward sister if you can bring the child for a visit beforehand so that the ward is not frightening and unfamiliar when the day comes.

- Prepare the child by telling him in advance that he is going in. Find hospital stories to read and play dressing-up games.

- Tell your child that the doctors are going to make him better, and that there will be other children to play with. Promise a toy as a present perhaps, when it is all over.
- Assure your child that you will be there as much as you can. In many hospitals parents are allowed almost unlimited access, and may well be permitted to stay overnight with the child.
- When you take your child in, go armed with biscuits, something to read, and something to drink if you do stay there overnight. Have a phone card handy.
- If your child is having an operation, explain it as simply as possible. Tell your child about the anaesthetic that will send him to sleep, and that when he wakes up, it will all be over. Explain, too, that this is the reason why he is not allowed to eat or drink anything beforehand.
- Reassure your child that he will soon be well enough to get up and to play with other children in the ward and after that he will be coming home. But do not give definite times or dates.

YOU AND YOUR OPERATION

Is your operation really necessary? A report on routine surgery – tonsils, hysterectomies, gall bladder and prostate operations – published recently by the Department of Health shows that surgeons in some areas are said to be twenty times more likely to operate than colleagues elsewhere, and that many small operations are preventive rather than a curative. In some areas, hysterectomies are carried out on four women out of ten, against five in a hundred in other areas where drugs or hormone therapy are offered instead. If your condition is not life-threatening and you are unhappy at the idea of having an operation, it pays to ask for a second opinion.

Your operation

If yours is a fairly routine operation, then you should phone the hospital to make sure that a bed is available for you when the date comes up. You will have to sign a consent form before you have an operation, agreeing to the anaesthetic and the treatment. You will probably have been told not to eat or drink for a set number of hours beforehand.

On arrival at hospital, you will have any necessary last-minute tests, then undress and put on a surgical gown. The anaesthetist will see you, probably to ask you if you have any allergies or health problems. You will be given a pre-med, which may be an injection or tablets, to make you feel drowsy. You will also have an identification tag put on your wrist or ankle. At this stage, the surgeon may pay you a brief visit.

Next, a nurse will arrive with a hospital porter and you will be lifted onto a trolley and wheeled into the anaesthetic room where you will be given an injection and asked to count to ten – by which time you will have drifted off into unconsciousness. The next thing you will know is waking up in the recovery room, probably alongside several other people in various stages of coming round. You could find a glucose drip in your arm to speed up your recovery and you could have an oxygen mask over your face, but that is less usual. You may feel sick and you could have a sore throat, both are normal side-effects of the anaesthetic.

DAY SURGERY

More and more so-called routine operations – over two million a year – are now done by day surgery. These usually take no longer than half an hour to perform. Done on a production-line basis, they cut down waiting lists as surgeons can pack more people in. You go in in the morning and come out in the afternoon. It does not sound quite so frightening since it is a case of minimum fuss, but little or no care afterwards – you are responsible for yourself. One-third of all operations are now being done this way.

Which procedures qualify for day surgery?

Abortion, Amputation of toes/small fingers, Bladder biopsy, Cataracts, Circumcision, Corneal transplants, Cosmetic nose surgery, Cyst removal, Ear correction, Ear wax removal, Endometrial ablation/resection, Fibroid removal, Ganglia removal, Hernia repair, Impacted wisdom teeth, Kidney drainage, Larynx biopsy, Laser surgery, Middle ear drainage, Nasal polyp removal, Ovarian biopsy, Removal of ovarian cysts, Small skin grafts, Tattoo removal, Tubal sterilization, Urethral dilitation, Vasectomy. A number of operations on children are on this list including hernias, undescended testes, tongue tie, toe fusion correction and grommets in the ears.

If you are offered day surgery
- Do not rush into agreeing, however persuasive the consultant is. Think things over first, especially if you live alone.
- Do not agree if you are over 65 and in rather poor health. Do not agree if you live more than an hour's drive from the hospital or do not have a phone.

Questions you should ask
- Who is going to operate on me? It could be anyone from a junior registrar, fresh out of medical school, to a consultant.

- How painful will it be and will I be given something for the pain afterwards?
- What will the after-effects be and how long will they last?
- Will the hospital report to my GP? Good hospitals will keep in touch with the GP concerned.
- Will I be properly checked and given instructions on what to do, before being sent home?
- Will I be kept in overnight if I do not feel well enough to go home?

Before the operation

There are a number of ways you can make life easier for yourself in the event of day surgery. For a start, stock up with convenience foods beforehand so that you have something easy to prepare. You may not feel like going out at first. It would be wise to take someone with you and have someone to collect you, or organize a mini-cab beforehand. Even with a local anaesthetic you may feel disoriented. You will need someone to keep an eye on you for 24 hours afterwards.

Do not drive yourself to and from the hospital however minor the operation. You could feel drowsy after the anaesthetic and you may do damage with the exertion of driving. It is wise to wait 48 hours afterwards before attempting to drive. In some operations, hernia for instance, you will not be able to drive for about a fortnight.

On the day, do not eat or drink anything for at least six hours beforehand – the hospital should tell you this. Turn up on time or you may miss your place in the operating queue. Come armed with a book, magazine, knitting or something else to do, since you may be in for long waits in or out of a hospital bed.

When you have day surgery

- You are checked to make sure you are fit for the operation.
- You are then put into a theatre gown.
- You are taken directly into the operating theatre – no pre-medication is given.
- You are given an anaesthetic, usually via an injection, then operated on.
- After the operation, you are taken into the recovery room under the supervision of a nurse.
- Once you have come round, you are taken into a ward to have a sleep, then offered something to eat and drink.
- You are then checked to see that you are fit to be discharged.

YOU AND YOUR DENTIST

The good news about dentists is that their equipment is getting better and better – the equivalent of a road drill with which they used to attack our teeth has turned into a far more sensitive instrument with a shrill whine. The bad news is that it does not pay them to have a bedside manner – the faster they can put us through under the NHS, the more they earn. There are stories too that dentists are striking off thousands of NHS patients because it is no longer worthwhile treating them. In fact, according to the British Dental Association, two out of five dentists are not taking on new NHS patients.

You are entitled to free NHS dental care if:

- You are under 18 years old.
- You are under 19 and still in full-time education.
- You are pregnant or have had a baby in the last 12 months.
- You or your partner are on income support or family credit.
- You or your partner have a certificate for full help with NHS services.
- You have dentures that need repair.

If you have a low income, you may be able to get help with dental costs – ask your social security office or dentist for form AG1 for more details.

Registering with a dentist

If you have difficulty finding an NHS dentist in your area, contact your Family Health Services Authority (FHSA) for their list of dentists. You can ask them to help you find one, and in that case, expect a response to your request within five working days. Remember too that dentists are now allowed to advertise, so you could start your search by looking in your local Yellow Pages.

If you are registered with a dentist, you have the right to receive advice in an emergency, and treatment, if he considers it necessary. Your dentist should offer you a two-year continuing care contract and then let you know the expected cost of your NHS treatment before this begins. He should then repair or replace, free of charge, any NHS-allowed work on your teeth that goes wrong within twelve months. The contract is renewable for another two years after each course of treatment. You will be asked to sign a dental estimate form before your dentist starts NHS treatment and to sign again once your treatment is finished.

If you are not enrolled in a contract, your dentist is not legally required to ask you if you want NHS or private treatment, or to tell you that he has changed from NHS to private work, so you should ask before treatment starts. You may find that the particular type of treatment you want – a crown for cosmetic reasons, for instance – may not be available under the NHS, so check first. Private dental charges are at least double those on the National Health Service.

How to cut dental charges

- Look after your teeth. Brush teeth and gums at least twice a day. Clean between your teeth using dental floss or a small special brush – ask your dentist about it.

- Go for regular check-ups – the cost of a check-up is only half the amount charged for a filling.
- Get as much work done as possible while you are pregnant and in the following 12 months. Treatment is free.
- Use a fluoride toothpaste, which helps prevent tooth decay, says the British Dental Association.
- Avoid too many sweet things, particularly if they are sticky. If you must eat toffees, clean your teeth immediately afterwards.

Dental insurance

You can take out dental health insurance under two different schemes. Under the capitation plan, you pay a monthly premium to your dentist for an individual private continuing care contract. Ask your dentist about this. Or you can take out an individual insurance plan through one of the big health insurers. Both these schemes can be worthwhile if you and your family have problem teeth.

Scared of the dentist?

Being frightened of dentistry is called *odontophobia*. Few of us like going to the dentist and some of us are positively terrified. Some dentists are more sympathetic than others, but unfortunately the NHS militates against sympathetic treatment – dentists say that if they are dealing with someone nervous, it can take up to half an hour to do one filling. The best way to find a sympathetic dentist is to ask around among friends and family.

Find a dentist who is caring and willing to listen. You will find dentists who advertise that they welcome nervous patients in your local Yellow Pages, but some are better than others, so it is worthwhile asking around. Your doctor may also be able to suggest someone. The British Dental Association suggests that you phone a number of dentists, explain you are nervous and ask what treatments they offer and see what response you get.

- Make an appointment for a check-up first. Move on at your own pace.
- Make the appointment for first thing in the morning so you do not worry about it all day.
- Take a friend with you if you feel it would help.
- Tell your dentist what you are frightened of – the drill, injections or pain. If you have had a bad experience before, tell him about it.
- Ask him what can be done about it. He may offer special techniques to relax or sedate you. In serious cases hypnosis can help and so can 'relative analgesia', the so-called happy gas, a mix of nitrous oxide and oxygen which makes you drowsy and happy but not unconscious.
- Ask him what he proposes to do to you if you feel that understanding this will help.

- If you are still worried, contact a local self-help group like those run by the Phobics Society (*see page 137*).

Your dentist – how to complain

If you need complicated treatment – a dental bridge, perhaps – your dentist will have to get permission from the Dental Practice Board for this to be done on the NHS. If the Board turns you down, you or your dentist can appeal to your local Family Practitioner Committee (Health Board in Scotland and Health and Social Services Board in Northern Ireland).

If you wish to complain about NHS treatment given by your dentist, you must do so in writing within six months of completion of the treatment. Contact your local Family Practitioner Committee. If you are accusing your dentist of 'serious professional misconduct' – misleading you into taking private treatment, giving you excessive treatment or behaving badly – you should complain to the Registrar of the General Dental Council (*see page 114*).

If you want compensation for bad treatment, then you may need to sue your dentist for negligence, in court. You must make your claim within three years. Contact your Community Health Council in the first instance (Local Health Council in Scotland, District Committee in Northern Ireland). You may also need to see a solicitor.

YOU AND YOUR OPTICIAN

Competition is intense in the eye business. Despite the fact that few people qualify for free NHS sight tests, many opticians now offer free eye tests if you buy your spectacles from them – it pays to shop around. You qualify for free eye tests under the NHS if you are:
- Under 16.
- Under 19 and still in full-time education.
- Receiving income support or family credit.
- Receiving a disability working allowance, with savings under £8,000.
- On a low income – enquire at the DSS about this.
- Diabetic.
- Eligible for NHS complex lens vouchers.
- Registered blind or partially sighted.
- A glaucoma sufferer.

If you think you qualify, ask your optician for form AG1 or get one from your local Post Office or Social Security office.

Your eye test

If you are having your eyes tested, you should tell the optometrist the reason for your visit – headaches or poor vision, for instance. You may be asked what medicines you are taking. If you already wear glasses or contact lenses, you should bring them with you, along with your old prescription if you have one. You should also tell the optometrist if you are using a VDU (visual display unit or computer) screen in connection with your work. After a certain age, you should have your eyes tested for possible glaucoma, a condition that can cause blindness if it is not treated. This is done by puffing a short burst of air against each eye – a technique that is a little startling but in no way painful. It is now possible to perform eye tests on babies in hospital with a process called Video Refraction, which uses a video camera and a flash.

Prescriptions

Having had your eyes tested, the optician will give you a prescription if you need spectacles or contact lenses. Under certain circumstances, you may qualify for help from the NHS, in which case your optician will give you a voucher. This voucher does not have to be used to buy spectacles on the spot – you can take it to another optician. For further details about the voucher system, see leaflet G11, available from your local social security office. You may also be able to get a small frame supplement. You qualify for a voucher if you are:

- Under 16.
- Under 19 and still in full-time education.
- Receiving income support or family credit.
- On a low income – see above.
- Receiving a disability working allowance with savings under £8,000.

Contact lenses

These are not usually available under the NHS. If you are considering investing in contact lenses, ask your optician:

- The price and check how many after-care visits are included.
- Whether he is willing to give you a refund if you find you cannot cope with your lenses, and whether there is a time limit on this.
- If there is a replacement scheme – most people lose one of their lenses sooner or later.

Laser eye surgery

Most short-sighted people have more than an 80 per cent chance of having perfect vision with the help of laser eye surgery. It takes less than a minute to have Photo

Refractive Keratectomy (PRK), followed by 24 hours of discomfort and pain, then blurred vision for a week or so. This treatment, which is relatively new, is expensive and not available on the NHS. You need to be over 21 to have the treatment and experiments are going on to try to treat long-sightedness with laser therapy as well. Take advice from your GP or optician on whether or not the treatment is right for you, and ask for the name of a reputable clinic.

STATES OF MIND

Anxiety

We all get anxious from time to time. While classic depression causes the whole body system to slow down, anxiety causes the fight or flight response to be activated – the muscles tense, the heart beats more quickly, the person breaks out into a sweat, the mouth goes dry and adrenalin is generated. These are normal bodily responses to a crisis, but if a person is in a state of permanent anxiety, then health can be jeopardized. There is also a clinical condition called anxiety neurosis, which means the victim may keep going to check that the car will start, where the front door key is and other sorts of repetitive neurotic behaviour; this needs professional help. What can you do if someone around you is suffering from abnormal anxiety?

- Talk to the person and try to get to the roots of his fears.
- Get him to relax.
- Persuade him to laugh, even if he has to force it. Get him to try even if he says he has nothing to laugh at. Join in with the person; the very ridiculousness of the situation may make him smile. Laughter relaxes those tautened muscles keyed up by anxiety. It has been found that laughter releases endomorphins, natural painkillers produced by the body, and that it also helps boost the immune system.
- If the anxiety persists, get the person to see a counsellor and/or a doctor – this condition can often be alleviated by drugs.

Depression

Depression is suffered by most of us from time to time, sometimes with good reason, sometimes for no reason at all. It may be triggered off by some event in our lives – redundancy, divorce, bereavement or stress. Most people who suffer from depression get better, but some people remain in this debilitating state, unable to think straight, unable to make decisions and irrational in their behaviour.

In this country, one person in twenty suffers from depression. Many people fear that they will lose their jobs, their friends and even their families if they admit they are ill. Depression is often masked by a smiling face put on for the outside world. Inside the sufferer feels isolated, miserable, sad and full of anxiety, cut off from life, seeing it in black and white instead of colour. While men are more likely to commit suicide, twice as many women – one in five – suffer from depression.

A depressive personality sees 'through a glass darkly' as St Paul said, viewing himself in a distorted mirror. He may be obsessive or a perfectionist who falls short of his own high standards. But sometimes a cheerful, energetic person may suddenly have what is popularly called 'a nervous breakdown' without any warning. If it gets out of hand the person may even become suicidal. You can become depressed, after a debilitating illness like the flu. It is now realized that lack of sunlight can trigger off depression in some people (*see* **SAD**, page *135*). Another cause of depression can be rage which has been internalized, rather than expressed. People who are unable to express their very natural anger may 'bottle it up' and are therefore at risk of becoming depressed.

Are you suffering from depression?
Some of the tell-tale signs of depression include:
• Having negative thoughts all the time.
• Hating yourself.
• Feeling that other people hate you.
• Lassitude, feeling that nothing is worth doing.
• Hating being with people, hating being alone.
• Mulling over the same things obsessively.
• Feeling numb, thinking nothing.
• Feeling tired.
• Sleep problems.
• Bingeing on food.
• Smoking too much.
• Drinking too much.

Helping yourself out of depression
Depression is sometimes confused with unhappiness. But the difference is clear – if something bad or sad has happened to us and other people are able to cheer us up, then we are unhappy. If we are depressed, then no one will be able to lift our mood. Unhappy people, in the end, deal with what has happened and recover their normal balance, while depressed people have more difficulty.

If your depression is caused by anger over some situation, do not try to hide your feelings. Recognize that you are angry and learn how to deal with it. Join an assertiveness class or decide to be more honest with people about the way you feel. Take some physical exercise to deal with unexpressed anger.

- Carry on working if it makes you feel better, but do not be afraid to get a doctor's certificate if you cannot cope.
- Do some kind of physical work or exercise. You will find it will lift your mood.
- Accept any help that is offered. Do not feel that you are being weak in doing so.
- Avoid watching violent, depressing or downright disturbing TV programmes late at night, otherwise you will go to bed with your mind seething. Soft lights and sweet music are better.
- Make a list of all the things you have achieved in life; it will make you feel better about yourself.
- Counselling is good if the depression arises out of an event in your life. If the depression is severe and there is no known reason, then drugs may be the only answer. Some menopausal women with depression have found it has been lifted magically by HRT. A short stay in hospital is sometimes suggested for someone who is severely depressed.

How to support someone with depression

Helping someone over the hurdle of depression can make your relationship stronger but you run the risk of feeling depressed too, if your attempts to help are rejected.

- Show the person affection, tell them you love and care for them.
- Listen to what they have to say sympathetically.
- Encourage them to work out what changes they might make in their life to make them feel better. Encourage them to join a support group (*see page 136*).
- Do not blame the person – they feel guilty enough already. Avoid telling them to 'pull themselves together'.
- Praise any small steps towards recovery, be encouraging.
- Do not do too much for them, get them to make the phone call to a counsellor or to a support group.
- Contact a support group yourself. An organization such as Depressives Anonymous (*see page 136*) will give you help and guidance on handling the situation.
- Do not neglect yourself and your own needs. Depressives tend to drag down the people around them. You need a break from time to time or you will be drawn into the net.

Stress

See also **Employment,** *page 353.*

Suicidal feelings

It can be terrifying to realize that someone near to you is suicidal. A strong wish to die may seem to be the ultimate way out for people whose problems have become overwhelming and who find living gives them emotional pain. Suicide is the ultimate self-destructive act and fortunately only a few carry it to its final conclusion. Many more people may injure themselves or take overdoses because they feel they cannot go on with life as it is.

A sudden personal crisis may trigger things off – being left by a partner or having huge business debts. There may be feelings of loneliness and isolation or unbearable pressures at work. For other people the feelings of despair mount over the years as their self-esteem becomes more and more battered. The thought of death can be very appealing in this situation. Many of us have these feelings but do not act on them but a minority of people will. Suicide is more common among men than women and increases in age. Suicides among men under 25 have doubled in the last ten years. Every year one girl in 100 attempts to kill herself. Relationship problems are often the cause with girls, while drug problems and unemployment are the reasons for young men. Certain groups are more likely to kill themselves – Asian women between the ages of 15 and 24 have a three times higher than national suicide rate, often associated with family problems.

Most suicides do give some advance warnings; they may not say so specifically but talk about ending their misery. It is reckoned that 40 per cent of people who do succeed in killing themselves have made previous attempts.

Warning signs

- A sudden marked change in the person's behaviour. It could be for the better – he may be unusually calm and quiet.
- Talks in a pessimistic or negative way.
- Talks of feeling lonely and isolated.
- Talks about suicide. Do not believe that people who talk about killing themselves never do so. Almost everyone who has taken their own life has, in fact, spoken about it at some time or other.
- Coming out of severe depression. Often someone who is really depressed lacks the energy to organize his own end. In the early days of recovery he should be watched.
- Not able to wash or change clothes.
- Drinking heavily.
- Signs of irritability, depression, a feeling of hopelessness and confusion. Dying seems the easy way out of a hopeless situation.
- May express feelings of uselessness.
- Some people may deliberately hurt themselves by cutting or burning themselves or running in front of traffic. They may do this in a state of emotional distress, while not necessarily aiming to die.

How to handle it

All suicide threats should be taken seriously, even if the victim has made them before. The popular idea that it is only a 'cry for help' may be true, but you cannot be sure. If someone is really determined to commit suicide it may not be possible to stop him, even if he is put into hospital.

Even if someone is determined to take his own life, it is still worthwhile talking things over and examining every option.

- Do not let the person depress you too. You are not going to be able to wave a magic wand and make him better, in the end he has to do that himself.
- Get the person to talk. However fearful you are that he may kill himself, it is vital that you keep the lines of communication open. Bring the subject out into the open. Be there. Be around, listen to him.
- Get help. Persuade the suicidal person to talk to someone else about it or join a support group.
- Talk to the doctor about it, even if you cannot get the would-be suicide to come with you. It might be possible to get anti-depressants for them.
- Above all, watch the person carefully without him realizing it. Look upon him as a small child whom you would not leave to his own devices.
- If you are really worried, contact the doctor by phone.

Keep large quantities of drugs locked up. Having to organize the method of suicide may give the person enough time to change his mind, while a bottle of lethal pills to hand may make him act on impulse. Remember, everyday items like aspirin and paracetamol can be fatal if taken in large enough doses and may not have any effect immediately.

Hypochondria

Undue anxiety about your health is called hypochondria. All of us have mild attacks of this condition, either by seeing something in a medical dictionary, then thinking we have it, or worrying unduly about some symptom, then haunting the doctor's surgery. But a real hypochondriac would not dare go to the doctor in case he has some terrible illness. He may feel physically unwell most of the time and worry a great deal.

The best way to help a hypochondriac is to take him totally seriously, but at the same time get him to realize that he is worrying unduly about his health. Do not suggest that he sees the doctor unless you suspect something is really wrong – being sent for tests may well make things worse. If the condition persists, persuade him to join a group that tackles phobias (*see page 137*).

ME

Myalgic encephalomeylitis or ME has had a bad press. Even now the medical profession is divided between those who recognize it as a genuine physical disease and those who think it is all in the mind. People who have this debilitating condition are often branded as work-shy, neurotic, lacking concentration and sometimes lose their jobs. ME is sometimes called Yuppie Flu. It very often does start with flu-like symptoms and sometimes the victim is thought to have glandular fever. So far there is no explanation and no known cure for this condition which can affect children as young as eight years old.

If you are suffering from ME you will certainly experience deep fatigue, insomnia, lack of concentration and muscle pain. It often starts with a headache. All your GP can do at this point is to treat the symptoms. At the moment only one person in five can expect to recover completely, but progress is slow. Learning to live with ME means learning to slow down and take life at a more leisurely pace. It helps to join a support network like the ME Association (*see page 123*).

Panic attacks

We all get panic attacks at some time, before we have to go to an interview or make a speech. But when the attacks arrive for no reason whatsoever, then help may be needed. If you suffer from a panic attack you may feel dizzy and faint, sweat profusely, shake and feel sick. Terror washes over you in waves, you may have palpitations, which can make you feel scared and as if you are having a heart attack. It can happen in a crowded place, on an unaccustomed journey or even at home.

Panic attacks can be brought on by overwork, not working or some traumatic event like the loss of a partner. Panic attacks are an indication that your feelings of anxiety have gone into overdrive.

Hyperventilation can often be the cause of the actual physical symptoms. This happens when you breathe too fast, filling up your lungs with oxygen and lowering the carbon dioxide level in your blood. You feel breathless because your lungs cannot take any more oxygen and the low carbon dioxide level triggers off dizziness, and sometimes, pins and needles and numbness. At the same time your body releases adrenaline. How do you cope with hyperventilation? Lower the oxygen level in your lungs by breathing in and out of a paper bag or put your hand over your mouth, breathing in the air you have exhaled. Do it several times and you should immediately feel calmer. If you feel faint, take something sugary, preferably glucose, sit down and put your head between your legs for a moment. Then take your mind off the subject by doing something on which you have to concentrate very hard – even if it is only threading a small needle. In the long-term try taking up meditation or yoga, both of which will help you to live a calmer life.

If the attacks persist, see your GP. He may prescribe beta-blockers, anti-depresssants or a course of therapy to tackle the problem.

Post-traumatic stress

Lockerbie ... Hillsborough ... disasters of this kind never leave our memories, but what about those who were actually there? Post-traumatic stress has finally been recognized as a condition and, what is more, one that needs treatment. Smaller-scale disasters in our own lives bring the same reactions – parents who have lost a child in an accident, or someone who survives a car crash when their friend is killed.

If something distressing like this has happened to you, you are almost bound to suffer a stress reaction, especially if the experience was life-threatening. You may find yourself feeling guilty at having survived, to a point where you feel that you, too, ought to die. You may well have flash-backs, panic attacks, nightmares and physical manifestations like migraine and stomach upsets. If you think you are suffering from this kind of stress you should seek professional help immediately. You need to talk to someone. Apart from counselling, group therapy is said to be of great help (*see page 127*).

MENTAL ILLNESS

Mental illness is a broad label for disturbances in the way we think and feel and act. We all suffer from anxiety and depression and mood swings from time to time – but sometimes these go beyond being a condition and become an illness. Contrary to popular belief, however, mentally ill people as a whole are no more violent than the rest of us, though, as with the whole of the general public, there are always a few dangerous individuals.

What causes mental illness?

Many factors may be involved. It can be caused by a number of things including brain damage, possibly after birth or pregnancy complications, or there may be genetic factors and a tendency which runs in the family. On rare occasions, a head injury or an accident can cause mental illness, and stress or a sudden change in lifestyle can push some people over the edge. Scientists also think that in some instances, the changes are chemical and occur in the transmitter substances, the switching system of the brain.

Dealing with mental illness

Although people may feel sorry for someone who has a physical illness, those who are mentally disturbed may provoke fear rather than sympathy. As a result people tend to shy away from sufferers because they behave in unpredictable and embarrassing ways. Families tend to close ranks around the sufferer, ashamed of the secret. They may admit that a relative has had a nervous breakdown or suffers from their nerves, but would not say that the person was mentally disturbed as such.

As most of us now know, mentally ill patients are now sent out to live in the community under the new care in the community policy, instead of being locked up in mental hospitals. Care in the community should be backed by day hospitals, day centres, hostels and group homes, but due to underfunding, these facilities are very thin on the ground and where they do exist, patients have to be encouraged to use them. Increasingly, the burden of caring for the mentally ill is falling upon families and friends. If someone in your family develops a mental illness like schizophrenia or manic depression, you will be faced with problems you never dreamed of. Mental illness of any kind affects the whole family.

Who looks after the mentally ill these days?

The psychiatrist
He is a trained doctor who then takes a further six or more years training in psychiatry. However well-qualified he might be, his ability to communicate with you will depend on your one-to-one relationship. It is important that you have a good rapport with your psychiatrist. Some psychiatrists will be good communicators, others not so good. The rapport you have is a very personal and individual sort of thing. A good psychiatrist will be able to take a dispassionate look at the situation. He will ask a lot of questions to assess the condition of the patient and then decide on and mastermind the treatment to be given.

The clinical psychologist
He probably has had no formal medical training but will have a degree in psychology and three years of special training on top of that. He will be there to assess the progress of the patient and offer advice on how to handle him. The clinical psychologist does not prescribe medication.

The community psychiatric nurse
A conventional nurse who has had training in psychiatry, she (or he) acts as a go-between between the psychiatrist and the family. She will visit and supervise the administering of any medication prescribed to the patient. She will also offer some support to the family.

The social worker
A social worker may also become involved, primarily to counsel the family but also to advise on benefits and rights, and what other things might be done. The social worker should have had some training in mental health work. To get a social worker assigned to you, ring the local Social Services department.

Community psychiatric nurse
More specialist nurses are being allocated to the community and there may be one in your area. This nurse supervises medication, if necessary, and offers general support. Ask your local Health Authority if there is one in your area.

Treatment

Initially, treatment will be given by your GP, but if he feels it necessary he will refer the patient to a psychiatrist, which may involve a wait. If there is a crisis, however, a psychiatrist might make a home visit. Either way, he will want to see the patient on his own, then talk to you. The psychiatrist may prescribe drugs as a first stage. There is a huge spectrum of drugs available (including a relatively new drug clozapine), to treat mental illness. These range from the very powerful to mild but addictive pills like Valium. Tranquillizers are used largely to calm down schizophrenics, while anti-depressants are often used for manic depression. Both sorts are given to make the patient feel and behave better quickly, while other methods of treatment are worked out for him.

Anti-depressants take time to work – it can be months before the patient is 'balanced out'. It is vital to stick to the instructions for taking the pills; you may have to use all your powers of persuasion to get the sufferer to continue to take tablets that do not seem to be doing any good. There are new laws now under the Mental Health Act, which ensure that patients who refuse or neglect to take their medication can be recalled to hospital. Both anti-depressants and tranquillizers are dangerous mixed with alcohol, which should be cut back or discontinued (ask the doctor). One group of anti-depressants, now prescribed less and less, has a disastrous effect of suddenly raising blood pressure, which could result in a stroke, if they are mixed with certain commonplace foods such as cheese, Marmite or chocolate. So if your doctor gives you a list of banned products, take it very seriously.

Electroconvulsive therapy (ECT)

Shock treatment is not used as much as it was, but can be very successful for manic depression. This is seldom done without the consent of the patient – you are asked to sign a consent form. But it can be used in certain circumstances against the patient's will, usually in acute situations. But the hospital has to get the consent of a second doctor. The treatment is given under anaesthetic. An electric current goes through the brain via electrodes attached to the patient's head, causing the equivalent of an epileptic fit. A muscle relaxant is given to stop the patient from twitching violently and, perhaps, hurting himself. After ECT, the patient may feel confused and have a short-term loss of memory. Anyone having it as an out-patient must be accompanied by a relative or friend to see him home safely.

Group therapy

This is being used more and more in day centres; patients get together to talk over their problems with each other and trained staff.

Counselling and psychotherapy

Patients have individual sessions with psychologists, psychiatrists, psychotherapists or trained hospital staff.

Schizophrenia

It is believed that more than 200,000 people in this country suffer from schizophrenia, a serious mental illness. Many uninformed people think it gives you split personalities – like Jekyll and Hyde – but that is a different condition altogether. Schizophrenia is a condition where the functions of the mind become jumbled in a cocktail of memory, emotion and sensation that gets out of hand. Schizophrenics live in an unreal world, one in which they have hallucinations, delusions and fixations – they may hear voices, for instance. In some cases, if the person is suffering from paranoid schizophrenia, he may become convinced that he has enemies and that people are conspiring to harm him.

It can start suddenly with a bout of paranoia or come on gradually, and it affects men and women equally. It may well begin during the sufferer's teenage years. The sufferer may start by complaining that people are always looking at him or talking about him. This may be accompanied by total negativity. The sufferer does not want to join in anything or go anywhere. At other times he may appear perfectly normal, but inevitably work or study is affected. Natural tensions within the household tend to make it worse.

Schizophrenics are treated with a cocktail of drugs, some of which, unfortunately, have nasty side-effects – symptoms similar to those of Parkinson's disease, for instance – that need still more medication. The drugs also tend to slow the person down, for they work by depressing the communication network in the brain, damping down communication between cells. This helps get rid of the hallucinations so many schizophrenics suffer.

Manic Depression

A manic depressive is someone who is subject to violent mood swings, switching from the symptoms of classic depression to being hyped-up, erratic and irritable with anyone who cannot understand his ideas or keep up with him or who tries to curb his activities. If the case is severe the sufferer may have a persecution complex coupled with delusions. Someone who has manic depression may experience a lack of sex drive or lose interest in sex altogether, though the situation will improve once he begins to get better. The sufferer may change his eating habits, eating too much or not eating enough. Weeks of depression and hopelessness are contrasted with huge surges of energy, when the person can be found cleaning the house in a fury, firing off memos in the office and suffering from sleeplessness.

Once it is diagnosed, manic depression can be controlled very successfully by drugs such as Lithium. The important thing is to persuade the patient to keep up the course of treatment even if he feels better. Most manic depressives find that joining a support group helps them recover their self-confidence (*see page 137*).

How to cope with the symptoms of mental illness

Delusions

It is tiring and exasperating coping with a sick friend or relative suffering from delusions.

- Do not try and talk the sufferer out of it.
- Agree with the person, but keep your own point of view. If she says that the man next door has a machine which is making the TV go wrong, tell her that you know she thinks that is happening, but that as far as you are concerned the TV seems to be working all right. Never argue with the person or you will then have joined the other side.

If the sufferer is telling complete strangers or friends of the family about the delusions try to deter him or her by saying 'let's keep that as our secret'. Above all, keep quiet and calm. Do not let the person see that he or she has upset you – this is easier to write about than to do!

Restlessness

Some schizophrenics and many manic depressives go through phases when they can become erratic and restless, pacing up and down and unable to sit and relax. This is very nerve-wracking for the family who feel they should be around to keep an eye on the sufferer. The best way to deal with this is to organize shifts. Agree with the sick person that he is upset, then try to persuade him to do some activity such as reading or watching TV to take his mind off it.

Lack of hygiene

In a severely depressed state, the sick person may cling to one set of clothes and refuse to bathe. Sometimes it is possible to retrieve clothing while the person is asleep – if he can be persuaded to get into pyjamas. Persuasion will have to be used to get the sufferer to wash and shave. Do not make a big issue out of it, but persuade him to keep minimum standards, explaining that everyone else does.

If the sufferer will not see the doctor

Mentally ill people are often reluctant to see a doctor for fear that they might be sent away to hospital as a result. If coaxing and persuasion do not work, see your GP yourself and tell him what is happening and describe the symptoms. If necessary, he may make a house call to assess the situation. Try to establish a good relationship with the psychiatrist or whoever is treating the patient. If a crisis arises, do not go to the casualty department of your local hospital where you will be stuck with a long wait. For occasions like this contact the nearest Crisis Intervention Centre; get their number from your doctor.

Violence

Anticipation is vital if you suspect that the mentally ill person may act violently towards you. It is a good idea to devise some kind of signalling system with your neighbours if something goes wrong, for you may not be able to phone the police yourself.

If you feel the atmosphere is getting tense, if the person is trying to pick a fight, remove yourself from the scene. Get out of the house, taking with you anyone else in the family who might be attacked. Do not try to reason with the sufferer, or answer back, just get out. Sometimes you can persuade the person to go out instead. If you are trapped, do not let yourself get backed into a corner of the room, try to work your way towards the door. Keep a large heavy piece of furniture, like a table, between you so that he cannot reach you. (Anyone who lives with a potentially violent person should put ornaments and anything throwable out of sight.)

If you can escape, phone the police or get a neighbour. Technically, the police cannot do anything unless you have been attacked, but the sight of the police may calm the patient down. Do not make a habit of calling the police, however, or they may not take your call seriously when you most need them. If this kind of scenario is happening, you should be in constant touch with a psychiatric clinic or hospital. Take action as soon as you can. A situation like this needs professional help.

What happens if the sufferer needs to be committed or cannot manage his affairs?
See **Legal,** *page 451.*

What about your children?

Children are amazingly resilient and can cope with the most bizarre lifestyle if one parent is calm and reassuring. It is best to tell them that mummy or daddy is sick, and that if you are upset at times or cannot give them all the attention they would like, it is because you are having to help their other parent.

Children of, say, 12 or more can be very adept at coping with a mentally ill parent – often better at dealing with them than the partner. Get the family to close ranks, surround the children with normal relatives and friends so that the irrational behaviour of one parent is diffused and there are familiar people around.

Looking after yourself

Try to remain tolerant and calm even if you are feeling drained and distressed. Keep up your outside interests, if you can, and try not to be drawn totally into the sufferer's distorted, dark world. If you feel you must keep an eye on the person, try not to be too obvious in stalking him. Try to build up a support system of friends and relatives to talk things over.

Benefits
If mental illness has made you or a relative unable to work, there are benefits that can be applied for (*see* **Disabled,** *page 66*).

ALTERNATIVE MEDICINE

Interest in alternative medicine is growing fast. Since 1991, GPs have been allowed to recommend some treatments on the NHS. Complementary healers now work in many hospitals or hospices, although they are not allowed, under the code of practice of the Confederation of Healing Organizations, to diagnose, use manipulation, prescribe drugs or interfere in a medically prescribed routine. Complementary, fringe or unorthodox medicine, as it is sometimes called, covers a mix of ways of diagnosing and treating illnesses which are separate from conventional scientific medicine. As a result a number of widely different kinds of treatment from near mumbo-jumbo, cosmetic to near scientific are lumped together under one blanket title. Some of the treatments are available on the NHS but in most cases you will have to pay for them.

Alternative treatments

Acupuncture
A well-known technique that involves inserting small needles into specific points on the body to improve the flow of energy which in turn is supposed to prevent and treat disease and disability. It is based on the theory that energy in the body is distributed along 12 channels, or meridians, and sometimes needs balancing. Acupressure and electro-acupuncture, which uses a small electric current via needles inserted into the body, both operate on the same principles.

Alexander Technique
A system whereby you improve your posture and the habitual ways of moving and holding your body, while adjusting your mental and physical attitudes towards life. You are also made aware of which habitual patterns of movement create unnecessary tension in your body.

Aromatherapy
A popular therapy which uses highly concentrated essential oils, which have been extracted from plants for both cosmetic and healing purposes. Essential oils are massaged into the skin to treat physical or emotional tension and to enhance or uplift your mood. They are also vaporized and used in a wide range of health and beauty treatments.

Autogenic Training

A treatment for stress that instils positive ideas into your subconscious by the use of repetition. You repeat instructions to yourself over and over again.

Ayurvedic medicine

A form of Indian medicine based on Vedic texts treating the body and the patient's way of life as a whole.

Bach Flower Remedies

Concentrated flower essences, preserved in liquid, are used to balance your emotional state and physical well-being.

Biodynamics, Biofeedback

A counselling-based therapy which aims to release psychological blocks, inhibitions and body tensions. It is sometimes used to lower high blood pressure. Biofeedback uses the same basic principles, but in this case you treat yourself via a machine called an electromyograph. This machine translates electric impulses in muscles into signals, showing the onset of tension, which can be seen or heard. Biofeedback has been found to be helpful to migraine sufferers.

Chiropractice

A technique to restore movement and release trapped nerves, especially in the spine, by a mix of massage and sharp thrusts of manual force. More vigorous than osteopathy.

Colonic irrigation

A form of enema which washes out the bowels thoroughly to remove toxins.

Colour therapy

The use of energies of specific colours, channelled through the hands to your body, through touch or with the use of coloured lights. The aim is to rebalance the body by restoring the energy of the body so that it may heal itself.

Diathermy

An electromagnetic healing therapy which sends pulses of magnetic energy deep into the body tissues to warm and heal them.

Faith/spiritual healing

The use of psychic energy and/or prayer to heal. This includes prayer and spiritual healing, and absent healing given to patients who are at a distance from the healer.

Herbalism

One of the most ancient forms of medicine which is being used increasingly to treat a number of ailments that baffle conventional medical science. There are several schools of herbal medicine and Chinese herbalists are particularly sought after in this country. Herbal remedies, however innocent they may seem, contain powerful, even toxic ingredients and it is dangerous to mix them or to prescribe them for yourself. Seek advice from a qualified practising herbalist.

Holistic medicine

A way of treating the 'whole' person mixing conventional medicine with alternative therapies and psychotherapy.

Homeopathy

A well-known healing system which treats your symptoms by giving you minute doses of substances which cause the same symptoms in someone healthy. Homeopathic healers often use biochemic remedies and also Bach flower remedies – extracts of flowers which tackle the emotional roots of a disease.

Hydrotherapy

Treating discomfort or disease with water is popular in Europe, using mineral waters, thermal springs, special pools or mud.

Hypnotherapy

Hypnosis, for most of us, means putting someone in a trance so that they act irrationally, making complete fools of themselves. Nine out of ten of us can be hypnotized quite easily, and we can even learn to hypnotize ourselves. Hypnotic suggestion is also used to treat illness, stress and mental problems. By harnessing the mind to help heal the body, it is a very good way to treat phobias and addictions such as smoking. It has even been found to help in severe cases of irritable bowel syndrome.

There has been a lot of publicity about recovered memory, the recall, usually under hypnosis, of some former trauma in childhood that has been repressed for years. This usually turns out to be some form of abuse. Past memories can come flooding back naturally under therapy but it is also alleged by some people in the medical profession that these memories can be implanted, that the patient is 'helped' by the therapist to recall something that never, in fact, happened.

Hypnotic regression is a dangerous technique, and the resulting 'memories' can cause unimaginable misery, split families and often make the patient extremely unhappy. Another problem arises when therapeutic revelations involve the law. In the United States, a therapist who hears anything during the session that contravenes the law must report it to the authorities. This has not happened, so far, in this country, but well may. Think very carefully before embarking on this kind of therapy and if you do go down that road, always use an accredited therapist (*see page 100*).

Iridology

A method of diagnosing disease by observing the marks, colours and patterns of the iris in the eye.

Kinesiology

Often used to detect allergies, kinesiology investigates illness via the muscles which are tested to diagnose different kinds of disfunction. This is done usually by putting gentle pressure on the arm. The reaction of the muscle then suggests the reason for ill health.

Meditation

A method of relaxing, calming and clearing the mind, sometimes achieved by repeating a word that has no meaning, over and over again. It is often good for headaches, migraine and high blood pressure. You need to learn how to meditate. There are organizations that can help you, as well as many books on the subject.

Naturopathy

Also known as a nature cure, this therapy encourages the body's own capacity to heal itself. Medicines are seldom given.

Nutritional therapy

The treatment of disease by special diets and the use of food supplements as medicines. These may include fasting, macrobiotic diet, veganism or vegetarianism.

Osteopathy

A technique to restore the correct movement and function of your muscles and bones by leverage, 'manual articulation' and rhythmic stretching. Apart from aiding physical conditions such as backache, it can sometimes help tension, headaches and stress. Cranial osteopaths apply pressure to the bones of the skull for treatment of certain specific conditions.

Psychotherapy

As more and more of us want someone to talk to and are willing to pay for it, psychotherapy has become the boom business of the nineties. Although not an alternative medicine per se, psychotherapy is used to treat a number of psychosomatic illnesses as well as being used as treatment for emotional and relationship problems. But virtually anyone can set themselves up as a therapist – you do not need a licence to do so. You can call yourself a counsellor or a psychotherapist and start up a lucrative business right away. Professional listener would be a more honest way to describe some of them.

There is no doubt that there is a lot of valuable help to be had from talking things through, but do not hand over your mind to someone who is untrained. If you decide to go outside the NHS and pay for private counselling, look for someone who is accredited by The British Association of Counselling, United Kingdom Council of Psychotherapy or British Psychological Society. Treatment takes time and can be very expensive. It may not necessarily solve your problems but it may give you a better understanding of your situation, so that you can make choices.

Radiesthesia

Using pendulums and other instruments to focus psychic power to diagnose disease. Homeopathic treatment usually follows.

Recovered memory

This therapy is hitting the headlines as this book goes to press. The technique involves delving into a patient's past and releasing memories, some of which may be unpleasant, in order to expurgate them. This is done by asking questions, or by hypnotic regression (*see* **Hypnotherapy**, *page 53*).

Reflexology

Massage of certain reflex points of the feet to treat other parts of the body. Reflexologists target certain parts of the foot to deal with tension and other imbalances in the body.

Relaxation techniques

Methods of relaxation which have to be learned that release muscle tensions, soothe the mind and body.

Shiatzu

Oriental massage, especially finger massage, is used to improve the flow of energy around the body in order to prevent disease or disability. Like acupuncture, it uses the median points of the body and pressure is applied with the fingers instead of with needles.

Siddha medicine

A form of Indian medicine on Ayurvedic lines, practised by the people of southern India.

Unani medicine

A form of traditional Indian medicine combined with ancient Arab techniques.

Zone therapy

Another name for reflexology, see above.

COSMETIC SURGERY

More than 60,000 people a year have plastic surgery for cosmetic purposes – you can now have your entire face and body reshaped. And it is said that 20 per cent of these procedures end up being treated by the NHS because the surgery has gone wrong in some way. Of course, there are excellent surgeons, but unfortunately this is a branch of medicine which is open to exploitation. While it is illegal to operate without a medical licence, any qualified doctor can carry out plastic surgery, whether or not he has the specialist training and experience in this branch of medicine. The sad thing is that you often end up paying more for unqualified treatment than you would if you went through your own GP.

How to find someone qualified? Contact an organization like the British Association of Aesthetic Plastic Surgeons, at the Royal College of Surgeons (*see page 112*). They will send you a list of qualified surgeons throughout the country and also the NHS hospitals at which they practise. This association can also advise on laser treatments, collagen implants and liposuction. If you want cosmetic surgery and are prepared to pay for it, it is now possible to raise a loan, in strict confidence, to spread the payments over a number of months (*see page 112*).

Plastic surgery on the NHS

It is possible to have cosmetic surgery done under the NHS but first it has to be proved that the disfigurement affects you psychologically. Breast reconstruction after a mastectomy is one such instance. But if you are worried about the size of your nose you are very unlikely to get it corrected free of charge unless, perhaps, it has become a genuine phobia. You have to tell your GP how your problem is affecting your life. For NHS treatment you will need a letter of referral from your GP to consult a surgeon – some surgeons ask for this even for private treatment.

Face-lift or rhitidectomy

This procedure is done to defeat the effects of gravity and rejuvenate an ageing face. It is designed to correct a sagging jaw-line, drooping corners of the mouth, the deeper smile lines and the loose skin of the neck. It does not eliminate fine wrinkles. It can also be combined with other operations, to correct the eyes, perhaps. The operation takes 2–3 hours; the skin is cut, leaving scars above the ears, beyond the hairline, in front and behind the ear. Then the skin of the temples, the cheeks and neck is pulled upwards and backwards and surplus skin cut away.

You will find that your hairline starts higher up after the operation and you will feel discomfort afterwards, rather than pain. You need to be in hospital for one or two days and you will have temporary bruising which should fade completely within 2-3 weeks. However, it will take 2-3 months for your face to settle down completely. A face-lift has no effect on fine creasing around the lips and will not last for ever. Your skin will continue to age at the same rate but you will have 'saved' several years and will always look younger than your real age.

Otoplasty

This operation corrects protruding ears. It is usually done on children, but must not be performed below the age of six, because the cartilage of the ears is too weak hold the repair. The operation, which is often performed on the NHS, is done from behind the ear so that scars are well-hidden. The patient needs to wear a dressing to protect the ears for the first ten days after the operation and the ears can be sore and tender for up to three months afterwards.

Nose reduction or reshaping

This is not usually done on anyone under the age of 16, since our noses are still growing before that age. This operation needs a lot of planning – you and your surgeon must be quite sure what shape you want to end up with. In reduction rhinoplasty, no incision is made in the outside skin – instead cuts are made inside the nostrils. First the bridge is cut back, then the two sides of the nose are cut where they join the cheekbone and brought together. The natural elasticity of your skin then shrinks to fit the smaller frame. Sometimes the nostrils are narrowed as well. If the nose needs shortening then the cartilage which forms the tip of the nose is also cut back.

Having your nose done results in some bruising and swelling, particularly around the eyes, which may last up to three weeks. You may have to wear a splint over your nose.

Blepharoplasty

Eyelid surgery takes out the loose skin which collects in folds in the upper lids and can even obstruct our sight as we get older. Surplus skin is removed together with any surplus slackened muscle and protruding fat. This operation is often performed at the same time as a face-lift. It will leave you with scars in the fold in the upper lid and just below the lash-line of the lower lid. You will also have bruised and swollen eyes for up to three weeks.

Breast reduction

Known as reduction mammaplasty, this operation removes excess tissue from the breasts, leaving scars around the nipples and down to a fold under the breast. It is not advisable to take the contraceptive pill for up to six weeks beforehand and it is unlikely that you will be able to breast-feed afterwards. You will have to stay home for at least a fortnight after the operation and you should not do any chores during that time, especially those that involve lifting. It will take at least a month for you to recover fully.

Breast augmentation

This operation is mainly done for vanity, although there are some women who feel their lives are ruined because they are not well-endowed enough. Incisions are made under the armpit, around the nipple or in the lower fold of the breast, and mushroom shaped implants of silicone jelly and/or salt solution are inserted. Silicone implants have caused some women torment and have been very successful in others. They are currently banned in America, Canada and Japan after horrifying side-effects, mainly from operations done before 1993, and a number of women in this country are also involved in litigation.

There may be a limit to the size to which your breasts can be enlarged. You will be given a general anaesthetic for the operation and have to stay in hospital for at least 24 hours, possibly with drainage tubes on either side of your breasts. The after-effects of this operation can be painful for the first two days. You should not do any domestic chores until your stitches are removed, or drive. You will need two to three weeks off work and you should avoid strenuous exercise at that time.

Liposuction

Often advertised as a minor procedure, which it is not, this operation can only tackle small defined areas at a time and is not a cure for obesity although it can smarten up your shape. Once you are over 40, however, you may be too old to have it done. The elasticity tends to go from your skin and it may not tighten up as it should afterwards, leaving unsightly lumps and folds.

Under anaesthetic a small cut is made in your skin over the area to be treated. A metal tube attached to a vacuum pump is inserted into the incision and it 'hoovers' the tunnels of excess fat out from underneath, leaving blood vessels and nerves untouched. You can expect considerable bruising after liposuction, which will certainly be uncomfortable and probably painful. The discoloration will last for about a month, but residual lumpiness and swelling will last up to six months. You may also feel some numbness and the incisions will leave scars. Afterwards the fat cells should not return, so your new shape should remain.

Liposuction does not remove cellulite. If you have liposuction done on your stomach you may have to have surplus skin removed as well (abdominoplasty) which could leave you with large unsightly scars and, possibly, numbness in the lower part of your stomach. If you are contemplating liposuction it is vital to find an experienced cosmetic surgeon to do the job or you may have problems afterwards.

Is surgery for you?

Why do you feel you need plastic surgery? There might be a very good reason or you may simply be dissatisfied with your looks. Many people have it done because they are frightened of looking old. But even the best face-lift only lasts for a finite length of time. Sometimes it is not surgery you want, but counselling to make you happier in the skin you already have – *bien dans son peau*, as the French say. Every time you smile, you give your face an instant temporary lift, so why not do that more often instead!

Other cosmetic treatments

Collagen injections

These are used to eliminate wrinkles on the face and lips. Collagen is injected into the skin underneath the length of each line so that its bulk brings the depth of that line to the surface. It usually needs to be repeated every 6-12 months as the wrinkles tend to reappear when the collagen is absorbed.

Dermabrasion, chemical peeling

Rubbing away the surface of the skin by derabrasion and painting on an acid solution – called chemical peeling – can cause the skin to tighten up and the wrinkles to flatten for a while. But if you are particularly concerned about frown lines and crows' feet around the eyes, you may need to have a brow lift instead.

Laser treatment

This treatment is now done in clinics throughout the country. Your local cosmetic surgeon will be able to give you details. Lasers, especially vascular specific lasers, can be used to eliminate scars, birthmarks, benign moles and even brown liver spots which signify old age. They can also be used to almost eliminate – certainly fade – tattoos, and to reduce broken veins on the face.

   Used in sessions that last only minutes, laser guns which look like pocket torches, beam concentrated rays onto the skin and are worth considering by anyone who has a disfigurement – a port-wine birthmark for instance – and feels sensitive about it. All you feel is a prickling sensation. But the treatments should be taken with caution because they can cause scarring. It is therefore important to go to a good clinic. The latest development in laser technology is the high energy ultra-pulse laser, developed in the USA, which can be used to 'resurface' the skin, soften frown lines and wrinkles and minimize acne scars. The skin may take up to a week to heal and be red after treatment for up to three months, so will need covering temporarily with make-up.

Electrolysis

Facial hair tends to increase in women after the menopause when oestrogen levels dip. It can also be hereditary. The easiest way to remove it is to weaken the growth by bleaching it or using a depilatory cream. You can also have it waxed but shaving will leave you with stubble. Never attempt to pull hairs out with tweezers – you may get more coarse growth on the site. If unwanted hair is a real problem then consider having it permanently removed by electrolysis. An electric current is sent down a very fine needle which is placed into each hair follicle in turn. Sometimes this is combined with heat to speed up the process. There is a certain amount of pain at the time, but it is over quickly.

Camouflage

The right make-up can do a great deal to camouflage facial blemishes. There are specialists who now work with theatrical make-up houses to devise camouflage creams that you can blend, like an artist, to get the right skin tones (*see page 112*).

LIFE-THREATENING ILLNESSES

Cancer

Cancer spreads fastest in the young. The older you are, the slower its rate of development. Very old people may well have cancer without knowing it because its progress has become so slow. The good news is that patients who develop this disease are now living four times as long as they did twenty years ago.

Many people feel that they bring cancer on themselves by having some kind of emotional trauma. The latest research tends to disprove this theory. Doctors now think that many cancers are caused by an inherited gene which predisposes us to the illness, regardless of dietary influences, or, as far as we know, emotional upset. Others, lung cancer for instance, as all smokers now know, can be as a result of our lifestyle. One thing we do know is that people with a positive attitude have the best recovery rate.

The possibilities of cures for cancer, which is not one, but a whole family of diseases, look bright. Experiments are going on with a form of gene therapy, which seems promising. And new powerful drugs like paclitaxel, derived from yew trees, hold out hope for breast cancer sufferers, with tests to pin-point high-risk women on the way. Cancer vaccines to help the immune system tackle the disease are on trial in the USA. And an instant dipstick test is now being developed to detect bladder cancer at an early stage.

Speed is of the essence in dealing with this disease. The sooner it is treated the greater the likelihood of a complete cure. If you suspect something is wrong, you should see your GP immediately. Be persistent, even if he says nothing is amiss, make a nuisance of yourself, ask to see a specialist, ask for a second opinion – it is your life and you know your body better than anyone else.

To be told that you have cancer can be a devastating experience. Many people fear the treatment as much as the disease itself. Hospitals are often too busy to spend time on explanations and compassion. Hospital staff simply do not have time to talk. Often, when going in for treatments like radiography and chemotherapy, which can make you feel ill and out of sorts, you are treated like a car going in for repairs rather than someone with a life-threatening condition. No wonder patients often feel a mix of despair and anger. This is where support networks comes in. On page *109* you will find listings of groups who will help and encourage you and your family at this difficult time.

Recent research has shown that treatment for cancer is very patchy in this country, with specialist surgeons few and far between. And this is reflected in the results. So it pays to be persistent and insist that you are sent to a centre of excellence. The National Cancer Alliance (*see page 110*) has now compiled a directory of cancer specialists throughout the country. It will also give advice on the best treatments available.

Breast cancer

One woman in twelve may develop breast cancer, but the good news is that more and more are recovering completely, thanks to early treatment. Today the operation is often no more than a simple small incision to have a lump removed – you may only stay in overnight. And remember that nine out of ten lumps found are completely benign.

Detection

To catch cancer at its earliest possible stage, examine your breasts once a month.

- Undress, sit in front of the mirror and look at your breasts. Look for any changes in shape, any swellings, dimpling of the skin or alteration in your nipples. There is no evidence, by the way, that cancer can be caused by a bump or a bruise.
- Raise both arms above your head and check your breasts again. It is quite normal for one breast to be larger or higher than the other.
- Lie down and run your hand over each breast in turn, keeping your fingers straight and close together. Using moderately firm pressure, slide your hand over the breast, starting under the arm, moving across above the nipple towards the centre of your chest. Do the same thing over the nipple and then below it, until you have examined the whole breast. Do not pinch the skin as you may then feel lumpy tissue which is perfectly normal.
- Have breast screening when it is offered to you. Women over the age of 50 should have a mammogram every three years. Updated equipment now means that the mammogram machine does not pinch you painfully as it once did.

Breast pain

Seven out of ten women have painful breasts on occasion, often at certain times of the month. Then their breasts may be hard and inflamed. Mastalgia, as this condition is called, is thought to be caused by fluctuations in hormone levels in those with extra sensitive breast tissue. It can cause unnecessary anxiety and depression – I should know, since I suffered from it for thirty years.

This distressing situation – sometimes you feel as if your breast is on fire – can often be treated by balancing your hormones, or changing the Pill, if you take it. In some cases the doctor may prescribe tamoxifen, the drug that is used for breast cancer. It is being used experimentally to treat breast pain, although recent reports indicated that it could have side-effects. Many women find that taking oil of evening primrose brings some relief and that vitamin B6 also has beneficial effects. Others have found their condition improved if they cut down on animal fats and caffeine in their diet. A well-fitting bra can also help alleviate the discomfort. It is said that 80 per cent of the female population wear the wrong-sized bras – go to a store that has a fitting service.

Prostate and testicular cancer

The fourth most common cancer in this country after lung, breast and colon cancer, is that of the prostate, the gland tucked away below the bladder that produces seminal fluid to carry the sperm. There are plans to bring in some form of screening for this type of cancer. However, few men are likely to get it under the age of 45 – half the reported cases involve men over 75.

In middle age, any problem with the prostate is most likely to be an enlargement of the gland making it difficult for sufferers to urinate or forcing them to make many trips to the lavatory during the night. This is simply treated with antibiotics or, sometimes, with minor surgery. If you are having difficulty starting or ending urination, producing a weak stream, have pain or are passing blood, go and see your GP. If it is prostate cancer and is caught early, it can be treated without any worry about impotence and you can still father a child.

Testicular cancer can be detected with a simple regular early warning check.
- Cup your scrotum and testicles in your hand to check any change in size or weight.
- Using both hands, roll each testicle between your thumb and fingers to see if you can feel a new lump or bump.

If you find anything unusual, go and see your doctor at once. It can then be treated very successfully – over 90 per cent of men who develop this condition can now expect to be cured.

Heart conditions

Coronary heart disease kills as many people as cancer does. Every three minutes, someone in this country dies of it. And it is only just being recognized as the number one killer of women as well as men, causing one in four deaths. In fact as many women under 65 die from coronary heart disease as they do from breast and cervical cancer combined. Hormone replacement therapy seems to reduce the risk, but there is still a question mark hanging over whether or not it could trigger off breast cancer.

Women in this country have the highest rate of heart disease in the world – ten times higher than Japanese women. However, men are still three times as likely to get coronary heart disease as women are until after the menopause, when the figures even out. Until now women have had a hard time having heart disease diagnosed, with the average GP telling them that they have indigestion or it is their hormones. Doctors are now being educated to think otherwise, but if, as a woman, you suspect that you may have CHD, as it is called, do not be fobbed off – it is better to make a fool of yourself than to suffer.

Heart disease – how to cut the risks

There are many ways in which we can help ourselves avoid heart disease.

- Stop smoking. Smokers have twice the risk of heart attack as non-smokers and women smokers who are on the pill have the highest risk of all.
- Cut down on saturated fats (red meat, dairy products), salt and sugary foods. Replace those fats with oils like sunflower, soya, olive oil and low-fat spreads. Switch to semi-skimmed milk, white meats and fish. Avoid crisps and other snacks. Remember that cakes and biscuits are high in saturated fats too.
- Take exercise. But check it out with your doctor first. Exercise will strengthen your heart and keep your blood pressure down. It should make you slightly out of breath. If you do not want to go to a gym or health club, try walking, swimming or cycling. You should do it for at least twenty minutes, three times a week.
- Check your weight and blood pressure regularly.
- If your family has a history of heart disease get your cholesterol level checked.
- Drink sensibly. Find out your limits (*see* **Alcohol,** *page 89*).
- Avoid stressful situations as much as possible.
- Contact your doctor if you have unexpected chest pains, a pain running down your arm, especially 'indigestion' in the chest that comes and goes.

Signs of a heart attack

- Crushing or gripping pain in the middle of the chest.
- Pain spreading up to the jaw or down the left arm.
- Feeling of faintness, breaking out in a sweat.
- Pallor of the skin.

Symptoms like this that last for up to ten minutes, especially after exertion, then go away, could signify angina, a related condition that can be kept under control with drugs.

High blood pressure

One in seven people may get high blood pressure at some time or other, sometimes as the result of stress, sometimes from narrowing of the arteries. If it tends to run in the family, you should have regular check-ups. Very high blood pressure can lead to heart disease or a stroke. Fortunately it can be treated with drugs, but a lot can be done by amending your lifestyle with measures similar to those for heart disease, above.

- Keep your weight down. The more kilos you put on, the more likely you are to get high blood pressure.

- Try to limit the amount of alcohol you take. A drink now and then can relax you, too much can send your blood pressure soaring.
- Cut down on salt if your blood pressure has shown a rise. Replace it with herbs and spices.
- Exercise as much as you can. Walking is good for you and swimming is an excellent way to keep fit.
- Stop smoking, it raises your blood pressure.
- Avoid stressful situations. Start out early if you are catching a train or plane. Try not to have confrontational arguments.

Stroke

In the UK one person in every 250 over the age of 65 is likely to have a stroke. But they are less likely to die from it than someone who has one in middle age. Strokes can also attack children and teenagers in rare circumstances. A stroke occurs when the blood supply to the brain is interrupted. This can be caused by:
- A clot of blood forming on the wall of a brain artery. This is called cerebral thrombosis.
- A clot is swept into the artery of the brain depriving it of oxygen. This is called a cerebral embolism.
- A blood vessel in the brain bursts. This is more common in younger people.

Warnings
- Slurred speech.
- Sudden pins and needles or non-functioning of an arm or a leg. If they come and go, these can be signs of transient ischaemic attacks – TIAs in the trade – which can be controlled by drugs but may be a warning that you are likely to suffer a stroke later on.

Signs of a stroke
Depending on the severity of the stroke you could suffer from:
- Loss of speech.
- Paralysis.
- Loss of feeling in a limb.
- Sudden abnormal behaviour.
- Vision disturbance.
- Face distortion.

Sometimes one side of the body becomes paralysed. Right-handed people who have a right-sided stroke may also lose their speech. In some circumstances, the victim may have difficulty swallowing or lose control over bowels and bladder, and they may become unconscious.

To have a stroke can be a devastating, frightening experience but with modern medicine, more and more people are surviving. You may have to come to terms with some kind of lost function and learn new ways to live with the damage. But a tremendous amount can be done with intensive speech therapy and physiotherapy – it is vital to get the right treatment. It is also important to keep moving. Even a couple of days in bed can lead to long-term stiffness. Contact a support network such as the Stroke Association (*see page 120*).

AIDS

Mistakenly called 'the gay plague', AIDS (Acquired Immune Deficiency) is no respecter of gender. It is spread mainly in two ways: by unprotected casual sex and via shared hypodermic needles. HIV (Human Immuno-Deficiency Virus) is the first stage of this disease, when you are usually unaware of the fact that anything is wrong with you. Many people diagnosed as HIV-positive have not developed AIDS, even after ten years. If the person develops full-blown AIDS, however, this is because the body's immune system has broken down, leaving the victim open to a whole range of illnesses – the opening stages are often mistaken for glandular fever. The AIDS virus is carried mainly in bodily fluids such as blood, semen and vaginal fluids.

You cannot catch AIDS from
- A lavatory seat.
- Crockery or cutlery used by a carrier.
- Shaking hands with someone who has the disease, or breathing in the same air as them.

You can catch AIDS from
- Unprotected sex with someone who has the disease, especially during anal intercourse. The skin of the anus is relatively fragile, and easily broken.
- Sharing a razor or toothbrush with an AIDS carrier, if it is infected with the sufferer's blood.
- Coming into contact with blood from the wound of someone with the disease, particularly if you have broken skin.
- Sharing hypodermic needles, or by having your ears pierced, a tattoo, or acupuncture treatment using needles that have been used by an AIDS carrier.
- By transfusions of contaminated blood. After a number of haemophiliacs were affected by AIDS when given infected blood, all donated blood in this country is now screened against the disease. But having an emergency transfusion overseas, especially in a Third World country, does carry a risk.

A simple blood test can tell you whether you are HIV-positive or not. At the present there is no cure for AIDS, although there may soon be one. Meanwhile, there is a National AIDS Helpline (0800 567 123) which gives free confidential advice, 24 hours a day, every day of the year. There are also telephone numbers for the following languages on certain days of the week

- Welsh language, daily, 10 am–2 am, 0800 37 11 31
- Cantonese, Tuesday, 0800 28 24 46
- Bengali, Tuesday, 0800 37 11 32
- Punjabi, Wednesday, 0800 37 11 33
- Gujerati, Wednesday, 0800 37 11 34
- Urdu, Wednesday, 0800 37 11 35
- Hindi, Wednesday, 0800 37 11 36
- Arabic, Thursday, 0800 28 24 47

DISABLEMENT

Many of us find ourselves temporarily disabled by accident or illness – one in four families, worldwide has someone who is disabled in some way or other, at any one time.

Permanently disabled people are not ill. They may have been ill, have had an accident, have lost their sight or hearing or have a mental handicap, but the disability is what they are left with afterwards. They could be someone who is unable to walk, or to walk very far, they may be unable to do certain jobs and they may need some kind of special housing. Our attitude towards disabled people is curious. We tend to focus on the disability, not the person. Yet disabled people's aspirations are the same as the rest of us, their emotions are the same. They learn to get round their problem. We have to do the same.

It is a fact that many people think that because someone is in a wheelchair, is deaf or blind that he or she is incapable of thinking for themselves – the 'does he take sugar?' syndrome. When I was stuck in a wheelchair after an accident, I found people talking over my head as if I did not exist.

How to help someone who is disabled

Ask the person what help he wants. Most disabled people like to be independent and 'helping' them may have just the opposite effect. Dragging a blind person across the road without checking that he actually wants to cross it, shouting loudly at a deaf person who may well be wearing a hearing aid, or speaking across the head of someone in a wheelchair may not be help, but be a humiliation and hindrance. So ask first.

Disablement – your rights

Cuts to the Community Care budgets hit the disabled badly. There are two main allowances you can claim, and remember that if you are caring for someone who is disabled, you may be able to claim an allowance – get leaflet FB31 from your local Social Security Office to find out. Keep in mind that now, for the first time, disabled people can take an employer to court for discrimination.

The Disability Living Allowance

The DLA, as it is called, is a tax-free benefit for people who need help with personal care, with getting around or both. It is not dependent on National Insurance contributions or affected by any savings or, usually, by any income you and your partner may have. It is usually ignored as income when assessing Income Support. It is also only available to people under 65 – over that age you qualify for an Attendance Allowance instead.

To get DLA you must normally have needed help for at least three months and be likely to need it for at least a further six months. There are special rules for people with terminal illness – contact the Benefits Agency about this. It is divided into two components:

- **The care component** This is given if you need help with personal care because you are ill or disabled. This includes such things as washing, dressing, and, if you are over 16, preparing a cooked main meal. You can claim this even if no one is actually giving you the care you need.
- **The mobility component** This concerns you if you need help with getting around, if you cannot walk at all or have difficulty in walking because you are ill or disabled. You can claim this even if you can walk but need someone with you to make sure you are safe or to help you find your way around most of the time.

The Disability Working Allowance

This is a tax-free, income-related benefit for people aged 16 or over who are working 16 hours a week or more and have an illness or disability which limits their earning capacity. To claim it you must be getting a Disability Living Allowance, Attendance Allowance or some other benefit like a War Disablement Pension or Incapacity Benefit. You can get DWA if you are self-employed but you will not get it if you are on a training scheme.

To get DWA you have to sign a form asserting that you can pass a disability test. This is the hot potato as far as benefits are concerned, based on stricter medical criteria than before, with assessments on your ability to perform certain tasks. In the first instance, you fill in and sign a declaration about your condition, then, when you come to renew your claim, you may also have to fill in a self-assessment form and provide confirmation of your condition from your doctor or specialist.

You may be asked to have a medical test, in some circumstances. There are bizarre stories of people who are well enough to turn up for an interview being refused. Remember that if you are told you do not qualify, you have a right to be given an explanation of why that decision has been reached.

You can claim DWA by post. Get a claim pack from a Social Security Office, Jobcentre or Citizens' Advice Bureau. There are also a wide range of services available and equipment that can be borrowed; get leaflet HB 5 *Equipment and Services* from a Social Security Office.

Getting around

We should all be aware of the practical problems that disabled people face in their daily lives. Steep slopes, high pavements and tall steps are all hazards for the disabled. Going to the cinema can be even more of a problem since cinemas seldom have car parks and often the films are shown in an auditorium up a steep flight of steps. Obstacles on the pavement can cause problems not just for the wheelchair-bound but for somebody who cannot see very well. Rubbish sacks dumped outside the door, gratings and inspection plates not replaced properly by workmen are all hazards that have to be faced.

Heavy doors can be difficult to yank open even for those who are perfectly able-bodied. But if you are in a wheelchair, and if you have little strength in your arms it becomes a nightmare. There are stories of people being able to barge in through heavy doors in their wheelchairs but then be unable to get out again. Toilet facilities are another hazard. New buildings have to have access and facilities, if it is 'reasonable and practical'. But in many older buildings it is an impossibility. Pubs rarely have toilets that can be used by the wheelchair-bound.

Public transport

Travel by train can be a nightmare. Many stations have steps but no lift. If you have to travel in the guard's van – and many trains do not have other doors wide enough to take a wheelchair – then you are in for a dismal trip. No eating is allowed and if you have someone with you, there will be nowhere for them to sit. There have been stories of wheelchair-bound people being forgotten in the guard's van and shunted into a siding. Other stories of people having to abandon their luggage at the station because there is no one to carry it.

British Rail are suitably contrite about this, but say that disabled passengers should let their local station know 48 hours in advance, and tell a friend or relative which train they are travelling on just in case they do not arrive as expected. Waiting for the bus can be a problem for the frail since many bus stops are without seats and still more without shelters. You may get free travel, but getting yourself in and out of the bus can be a hazard because of the height of the platform.

By car

Disabled people need to pass the same driving test as the rest of us, in a suitably adapted car, if necessary. You must tell the DVLA about your disability when you apply for a provisional licence and they could insist that you drive an adapted vehicle. If you are having to re-learn to drive after a disability, try to find an instructor who is experienced at teaching disabled people, (*see page 133*).

You may get state benefit to help pay for a car and/or to adapt it. If you are told you do not qualify you have a right to be given an explanation of why they came to their decision. A change of car can cause problems if you have a disabling condition like arthritis. Some car companies (Ford, for instance) are now making a disabled driver's version of popular models. Adaptions to cars can include: push/pull hand controls instead of pedals, including a hand-operated clutch; a ball on the steering wheel making it easier to turn; swivel seats and adapted handbrakes for people who have a disabled arm; and winches to hoist a wheelchair on board.

If you are buying a car you might keep these points in mind. Make sure that:
- The door sill is not too high and the door is wide enough for you to get in.
- That you can easily use the door handle.
- Once in, make sure you can open and close the door with ease and that there is enough space for your legs at the back as well as at the front?
- Is the seat comfortable? If not, can it be adjusted easily?
- Can you get out of the car without difficulty?
- Can you fasten and unfasten the seat belt?
- Can you work all the controls with ease?
- Can you lift and shut the boot lid, and if you have a wheelchair, is the space inside large enough to take a fold-up wheelchair?

Drivers who are disabled are now penalized by tax rules. One in ten drivers has some kind of disability which could affect their handling of the car unless the car was adapted. Now if you have to have your car specially converted, that cost goes on to the taxable value of the car. If you travel by car regularly, either as a driver or a passenger, and belong to one of the big car organizations such as the AA, you may be eligible for a priority car breakdown service and a discount, especially if you have a special parking badge. It is well worth while making enquiries.

Getting petrol may be a problem if the garage is a self-serve one. Car parking is supposed to be made easier by having a special disabled sticker. But, as I've found driving around with a disabled friend, the general public is quite blatant about parking in those special spaces, resulting in a long, sometimes painful walk to the supermarket or theatre entrance. And now there is a thriving trade in stolen orange disabled car badges too.

At the bank

Most cash machines in the wall are too high for the wheelchair-bound to use. And if you are blind or partially sighted, after having located a machine with difficulty it is almost impossible to use unless you are accompanied by somebody sighted.

Cashiers' counters are also usually too high. Consider switching to one of the new telephone banks instead. Then you only need to go to a branch to draw cash. The Post Office causes similar problems – stamp machines are often out of reach and counters are usually too high, especially if you need to sign something or fill in forms.

Stores and supermarkets

Goods are often out of reach at supermarkets and there are seldom any seats where disabled customers can rest. In the stores, changing rooms are unlikely to be wide enough to take a wheelchair. And though many of the big shops have escalators, not all of them have lifts. If you do not have someone to accompany you, telephone the store concerned and arrange for a member of staff to meet you and help you with your shopping. Many supermarkets, Sainsbury's, for instance, have special facilities for the disabled.

Benefits and services

There are special benefits and services available for blind and partially sighted people. Get large-print leaflet FB 19 from your local Social Security Office or ask for the information on audio cassette.

Deafness

People tend to be patronizing to deaf people. Whereas the blind get plenty of sympathy, deaf people are often thought of as stupid, and in many ways, feel more isolated by their disability. Someone in a social setting who is trying desperately to follow a conversation that they cannot quite hear is likely to have an expression on their face that could be taken as stupidity.

Many things can cause deafness, especially in later life. If you are not hearing as well as you used to, your first stop is your GP. The cause may be something as simple as an excess of wax or you could have an infection. If that is not the case you may be referred to an ear, nose and throat (ENT) specialist. If there is no cure, you will probably be offered a hearing aid.

There are two sorts of deafness. Straightforward deafness means that the person simply cannot hear; the hearing lacks sensitivity. This is called conductive deafness – everything sounds muted – and often comes with old age. This situation can certainly be helped by a hearing aid. By far the cheapest kind of aid looks like personal stereo. Called binaural amplifiers, they consist of headphones and a pack that looks like a personal stereo. The volume of the headphones can be adjusted and they can be plugged into loop sound systems that are installed for the deaf in some cinemas and theatres.

But just as distressing is a lack of discrimination in hearing, called sensori-neural loss. This is when you can hear but you have lost the ability to discriminate between the person who is talking to you and general background noise – this is highlighted in busy places like pubs. If you lack hearing discrimination, then a hearing aid, which is basically an amplifier, will not help. Instead it will make your situation worse. Indeed an old-fashioned ear trumpet would be much better.

A test has now been worked out to isolate the problem and measure your degree of hearing discrimination. Audiology clinics throughout the country should soon be using it. With that, there is hope that hearing aid design will be improved to take in this kind of problem hearing.

Hearing aids

There are various types of deafness. Some people cannot hear words in high frequencies – like those found in the voices of small children. Other people can hear sounds of speech but not the actual words. A hearing aid will amplify sounds and should be available to you on the NHS if your doctor feels that you need one. A hearing aid does not magically restore your hearing to its former level. Your first impression will be that it makes all sounds, including background ones, rather loud. Hearing aids work best in quiet surroundings and when you are talking to one or two people at a time. The NHS has a range of almost 20 hearing aids, most of which fit behind the ear. To get a more sophisticated in-the-ear model, you may have to pay. If you are buying a hearing aid for yourself, make sure that it has a special setting that takes loop systems, which are being installed in many places like churches, theatres, cinemas. All NHS aids have this facility.

Buying a hearing aid

Only a registered dispenser can sell you something called a hearing aid. If it is called something other than that, then the seller does not have to be registered – a point to watch. If you decide to buy one privately, you may be tempted by advertisements which lead to you believe that with one of these aids your troubles will be over. But you need to exercise caution.

- If you fill in a form, you will probably get a visit at home from the firm's representative. If you do not want this, state so clearly on the form.
- If you are buying a concealed aid that tucks behind or in the ear, be sure to try it out before you buy; it may not fit your ear.
- Make sure that if you are buying a concealed aid that you can use its controls – they can be fiddly to work, especially if you have arthritic fingers.
- Make sure that you can return it after a trial period; read the small print carefully before parting with any cash.
- If you are in doubt, buy it under a credit scheme, then the Consumer Credit Act will give you the legal period of at least seven days to cancel if you change your mind. This only works if you signed the agreement in your own home, face-to-face with a representative, and not at the firm's showroom (*see page 393*).

Implants

Profoundly deaf children can show signs of deep anger and violence out of sheer frustration at feeling excluded from what is going on. There is hope that many young children for whom an ordinary hearing aid will not work and who would have grown up in a world of silence will be able to hear. This is thanks to a bionic ear, a tiny electrical device which is implanted in the cochlear or inner ear in children under the age of five, so that they can hear sounds of speech. The work is being done at the Nottingham Paediatric Cochlear Implant Group.

A receiver is implanted in the bone behind the ear with a series of electrodes placed within the cochlea. Fixed by magnets to the receiver is a tiny transmitter which stimulates the hearing nerve directly, by-passing the damaged area. Signals go to a microphone fitted behind the ear which collects the sounds and sends them to a speech processor which the child carries like a personal stereo. The sounds are not perfect, but as a result, most will be able to communicate without using sign language or lip-reading and will also be able to understand simple conversation, and even use the phone.

Other aids

Apart from hearing aids, there are a number of devices to make life easier in the home for a deaf person.

- You can get a telephone with an amplified handset, so you can turn the volume up, or get a device to link up with your hearing aid. Ask British Telecom for information.
- You could fit indoor extensions to the doorbell so you can hear it in other rooms of the house. Or you could have a system of flashing lights instead.
- If you cannot turn up the sound sufficiently on the radio and TV, you could install a home loop system to link up with your hearing aid.
- Consider going to lip-reading classes to help you understand people better. Most adult education institutes run them.

Ask your local Social Services department for help, or contact the Royal National Institute For Deaf People (*see page 114*).

How to help a deaf person

About 17 per cent of people in the UK have some kind of hearing loss, so you are certain to have to talk to a deaf person from time to time. The National Association of Deafened People suggests that before you speak to a deaf person:

- Attract the person's attention by calling or waving or by tapping him on the shoulder.
- Make sure he can see your full face, not just a side view and do not turn away while talking. The person may be lip-reading.
- If he wears a hearing aid, turn off background noise such as TV and radio, or move away from noisy machinery.

- It is better that you are both at the same level, either both sitting or standing.
- Do not get too close – the ideal distance is about a metre. Position yourself so that the light from a window or lamp is on your face.
- Make eye contact.
- Do not speak too fast but do keep a natural rhythm of speech. Speak clearly, but do not exaggerate.
- Pause briefly at the end of each sentence to give him time to work out what you have said.
- Speak up a little but do not shout – it distorts your face.
- Keep your hands away from your face and do not smoke or eat so he can watch your mouth.
- It is a good idea to write down names, addresses and numbers that are difficult to lip-read accurately.

Loss of sight

Loss of sight is one of the commonest disabilities in this country – one person in 60 is at the very least partially sighted. Most of us think of someone who is blind as living in a world of total darkness. In fact very few people live in a black world; only 18 per cent of blind people see nothing. Most people have some perception of light and dark, others have enough sight to be able to make out colours, shapes and lines, and it is for people like these that many large galleries are putting Braille labels alongside the pictures – causing some mirth for ordinary people who wonder how blind people would ever come to look at paintings.

People with white canes are not necessarily totally blind but they may still need help. If the person has a white cane with red bands, this signifies that he has both impaired sight and hearing. The same goes for a guide dog with a red and white harness.

Things are getting better for the blind. Among the improvements on the way there is a move to put medicines in packs with labels in Braille. Sound loops now being installed in theatres, cinemas and concert halls are useful for blind people too. Sweden, in conjunction with NEC, the Japanese electronics giant, is currently experimenting with an innovative system of magnetic markers in tiles, doors and open spaces where there are no apparent walls or gutters to guide blind people. The markers send out a signal which is picked up by a battery-operated white cane. The signal makes the cane vibrate gently, alerting its user to the fact that an object is near. They are also working on the idea of using electric speakers to give information about location as the blind person passes over antennae on the pavement.

If you or any member of your family is suffering from any degree of visual impairment, your first stop is the Customer Services Department of the Royal National Institute for the Blind (*see page 107*). This organization, founded over a hundred years ago by a surgeon who had to give up work because he lost his sight, can put you in touch with a vast network of organizations and local support groups, including people who can provide very sophisticated special equipment to make life easier. They can also help you by:

- Training or retraining you, aiming to help you to compete for jobs on equal terms with fully sighted people.
- Improving your quality of life by designing and selling products such as Braille watches, special kitchen equipment, even board games.
- Supplying talking book players on free loan, with volunteers to service them if they go wrong.
- A library of talking book cassettes available in Asian languages as well as English sent through the post in special wallets, so you do not have to parcel them up to send them back – postage is free.
- A phone number (0181 903 6668) for up-to-the-minute information on new books.

The RNIB will also help over benefit rights, housing, health and social services. It also has a useful book on tape, in Braille and in conventional form called *You and Your Sight – Living with a Sight Problem*. It covers subjects such as day-to-day home life, work, adapting your home and has details of more than 60 organizations that can help. The tape and Braille editions can be ordered from Customer Services (*see page 107*).

How to help a blind person
Some advice from the Royal National Institute for the Blind:

- When you go up to a blind or partially sighted person, say hello and say who you are. Address him by name if you know it, or touch him lightly on the arm so he knows you are speaking to him. Do not feel embarrassed if you say 'nice to see you' when you meet them, blind people use the phrase too.
- Before you leave, say you are about to go. Otherwise he might go on talking to an empty space.
- If you are serving food to a blind person on a regular basis, treat the plate like a clock and place the food on it that way every time you serve it. So, meat is at 6 o'clock, potatoes at 12 o'clock and so on.

Guiding a blind person
- If you think the person needs help, first ask. If you are guiding someone, offer your arm so that he may hold it just above the elbow. Keep your guiding arm relaxed and walk either side by side or half a pace ahead of him so he can feel from your movements when to turn or stop.
- When you reach a kerb, stop and tell your companion whether it is a 'kerb up' or 'kerb down'. Use a crossing if there is one, do not take risks.
- Always lead a blind person from in front, never push him in front of you.

- Give him plenty of room to skirt round obstacles.
- Do watch out for hazards at head height like overhanging trees, especially if the person is taller than you.
- Do explain changes in ground surface, if you are walking from a pavement onto grass or gravel, and point out paving slabs and road surfaces that are uneven.
- If you are going up stairs or steps, put the blind person on the side with the handrail.
- If you are using an escalator, tell the blind person whether he is going to go up or down. Guide him to the moving hand-rail, get him to negotiate the first step onto the escalator himself, then move ahead of him on the escalator so that you are there to help him off.
- Always go through a doorway with the blind person on the hinge side.
- Never back a blind person into a seat. Guide him to it, describe it to him and place his grip hand on the back, arm or seat so he can feel his way into it.
- Lead a blind person onto a train or bus, point out any wider than average gaps between train and platform or high platforms on a bus.

Equipment for the disabled – what is available?

Whether your disability is temporary or a way of life, there are an increasingly large number of aids to help you.

Walking
Walking sticks should have a rubber tip at least 4cm (1½in) in diameter in order to grip the ground. Keep the tip clean or it may become slippery and replace it when it gets smooth. Tips can be bought from any chemist that sells surgical aids. Many people find a T-shaped handle better than a curved one. It is useful to have an elastic loop around the handle, or a leather thong which goes around your wrist, so the stick dangles from your arm if you are holding on to a banister or opening a door.

In the home, screw spring clips to places like the edge of a dining table, so that you can clip the stick into place while you eat, and alongside the bath and lavatory. Buy two sticks, keep one downstairs and one up so you do not have the danger of tripping on your stick while tackling the stairs.

If you need more stability, choose a special metal stick that ends in three or four widely splayed legs. It will stand up of its own accord, but you cannot use it on the stairs.

Walking or Zimmer frames are much more stable than sticks but do take up a lot of room. They should have rubber tips on the legs to prevent them slipping and some models have wheels on the front legs for people who find them difficult to lift. There are also folding versions, versions that can be used on the stairs and for people who are only able to use one hand. Experiment first, if you can, by using a tea trolley, to see if a frame will help you. Consider another alternative: fit casters on the legs of an ordinary wooden chair instead of a frame downstairs in the house. The seat can then also be used as a 'tray' to carry things.

Wheelchairs

Many people refuse to 'take to a wheelchair' because they feel that it is an admission of defeat, but it is something to help you get around, nothing more.

- Hire before you buy to make sure that it is right for you.
- Find out what options are available.
- Try manoeuvring, try the brakes to make sure you can use them easily. If not you may need a brake extender.

The basic wheelchair has a straight back and fixed arms but you can get a version with an adjustable back for those people who cannot sit up straight. Apart from the basic type, there are a huge variety of models to choose from. There are chairs for people who have lost either or both legs, for people who can only use one hand, small models for children and adjustable ones. You can also get them with elevated leg rests for people who must keep their legs up. There are chairs with detachable arms making it possible to transfer from the wheelchair to the toilet, into the car and into bed with minimum fuss.

The chair is propelled by hand using the metal hand-rims that circle the drive wheels. If you have a weak grip, you can get a version with rubber-tipped projections. If you cannot propel the wheelchair yourself, consider using a battery-powered chair with power that lasts up to eight hours at a time. You can also find versions with a wheelchair narrower, a gadget that narrows the chair temporarily to squeeze through narrow openings.

Helping someone in a wheelchair

Pushing a wheelchair is like pushing a pram – but heavier. Stairs and kerbs can be a problem – though I have seen someone in a wheelchair go down an escalator to my astonishment; the helper turned the chair backwards.

- If you are going down a steep kerb, make sure both back wheels touch the ground at the same time. It is often easier to turn the chair round and get it down back first.
- If you are pushing up a steep kerb, put your foot on the tipping lever and tip the chair backwards so that the front wheels lift onto the top of the kerb first.
- You need two people to lift a chair up the stairs. Never attempt to do it alone. It is often better to lift the person up the stairs and then follow with the chair.

The British Red Cross has a useful free leaflet called *Using a Wheelchair* (*see page 132*).

Reading

If you cannot hold a book with ease, consider buying a bookstand.

You can get versions like music stands that stand on the floor, others that are suitable to fit on a bed. If your fingers are weak try wearing a rubber thimble or holding a soft rubber to turn the pages. If you are unable to use your hands, it is possible to use a special mouth-stick, but consult your GP, or possibly your dentist first – it may need special fitting to avoid damage to your teeth. You can also get battery-operated automatic page turners.

If you are bed-ridden and cannot sit up, you may find it difficult to hold a book. Ask about prismatic glasses which make it possible for you to read while lying down. Another aid to reading in bed is a personal reading lamp that clips onto a book; you often see them advertised in mail-order catalogues.

More and more books are now available on cassette which you can borrow from the library. If you do not have a machine for playing back cassettes, the local Social Services may help. It is also possible to buy or hire a microfilm projector for filmed books which you can use from a bedside or chairside switch. It projects the pages of the book onto the ceiling or the wall so that it is possible to read while lying in bed.

Writing

People whose fingers may not work well, will find felt tip pens easier to use than ballpoints and 3B pencils easier than the usual HB. If gripping is more difficult, try pushing a soft foam hair roller over the barrel of the pen to make it easier to grasp. If you use a typewriter or computer and only have the use of one hand you can re-train yourself to type with one hand. If you use a computer, there are versions that are voice-activated.

Telephoning

There are all kinds of aids around to help anyone who has difficulty using the phone. You can get lightweight head-sets, and something called a Callmaker which works on smart cards, or a push-button telephone with pre-programmed essential numbers – ideal for people who have difficulty seeing. For the deaf there are amplifiers, second earpieces and flashing lights to take the place of the phone bell. If your voice is weak you can get a voice amplifier – contact British Telecom for its booklet, *Aids for the Elderly and Disabled*.

Adapting your home

Whether you become disabled or have someone in your household who has a disability or is very elderly and frail, there are many ways in which you can adapt the house to make things more comfortable.

The entrance

Whether someone is wheelchair-bound or walks with difficulty, the easiest way to make entry possible is to build a ramp over existing steps. It can be made from wooden planking or something more permanent, but remember that the gradient should never be less than 3.6m (12ft) in length for every 30cm (1ft) rise. In winter you could cover it with jute matting to make it non-slip in times of snow and ice. If you live in an area where snow and frosts are common, it might pay to build a canopy over it too. The width is important as well. It should be wider than a wheelchair – 75cm (30in) is the minimum width to allow for, but 90cm (3ft) is better.

Opening the front door may be a struggle for some people. It is possible to get rubber-handled levers to fit round doorknobs. If you have to open the door with a Yale key, try pushing a piece of dowelling or metal tube through the hole in the top of the key to give you increased leverage when you turn it.

Stairs

Not everyone wants to live in a bungalow, but stairs are often a real hazard for anyone who is disabled. Fortunately there are plenty of ways to help. It pays to put rubber stair treads down which make going up and down easier and it goes without saying that carpeting should not be worn and frayed. For those who can walk, a second bannister rail on the opposite side to the first one will give added help. Think about extending it by about 45cm (18in) both top and bottom to give extra support when stepping onto or off the stairs.

Stair lifts, which are widely advertised, are the best solution for anyone who can only negotiate the stairs with difficulty. They cost a great deal but sometimes the local authority will provide a grant; and it is possible in some circumstances to hire them. A stair lift is usually a seat which can be fixed or folding, which travels up and down the staircase on tracks either on the stairs themselves or on the wall, which takes up less space.

Floors

Thick carpeting makes using a wheelchair very fatiguing – cork or wooden flooring is best. Loose rugs are dangerous, if you must have them, fit them with grippers or double-faced adhesive tape. Retrieving things that have been dropped on the floor or leaning across to pick up something can be a real problem if you have difficulty in getting up or bending down. You can buy reachers, some of which are designed like giant scissors, others have a trigger which makes them look rather like a long-handled tree pruner. You can also get them with a magnetic tip.

Furniture

Make sure the furniture is the right height. Tables and chairs can be raised easily by putting wooden blocks on the bottom of the legs. If you have difficulty in standing up from a sitting position, you can buy armchairs with adjustable spring-assisted seats that lift you up.

There are all sorts of accessories available for beds – side rails to help in getting up or a freestanding trapeze to help transfer an invalid into a wheelchair. A simple piece of thick rope, fixed to the bottom of the bed, will help someone who has difficulty in sitting up. You pull on it to help hoist you up. Then there are beds that tilt, and those with built-in back rests. You can see if one would be useful by constructing a make-shift back support by tipping a chair upside down and putting a pillow on its back.

Getting around

You can get useful grab rails installed by the local authority free of charge. They are particularly useful in the bathroom, lavatory or by the side of short sets of stairs. There is also a range of bath seats, some of which fit across the top. The toilet can be made higher by simply fitting a special plastic moulded seat which adds height. There are many other home aids to discover. Find out about the large selection of items for the kitchen and gadgets to help you put on your clothes. You can even get specially adapted children's equipment for disabled parents.

Depression after disablement

Sudden disablement after an illness or an accident can leave you feeling bitter, with a tendency to look back to better times in the past. If your disablement is permanent then the future can seem unthinkable.

- Remember that inside you are just the same person.
- Do not suffer in silence. Do not continually moan, but unload your feelings onto a good friend. Join a support network. Above all, do not bottle things up. Suffering in silence never helped anyone.
- Fight for all the aids you can muster to make life easier. There are a lot of things you can borrow, free, from the British Red Cross and other similar organizations.
- Look to the future, use the enforced time to home in on some interest you have been meaning to take up – learning to paint, perhaps, writing poetry or building up a music library.
- Avoid getting overtired, exhaustion frequently triggers off depression. You may find you have to work that much harder at things because of your disability, so pace yourself, conserve your strength and get plenty of sleep.
- If you are house-bound, you may find yourself feeling unexpectedly lonely and isolated, even if you have family around you. So call up your friends and get them to come round. Be bright and good company, and you will be sure they will come back.
- Keep in touch with the outside world by radio or TV, do not isolate yourself.
- Do not be in pain, which is tiring and debilitating. If the medication you have been given is not working, tell your GP.

ADDICTIONS

Who is an addict?

An addict is someone who goes on drinking, taking drugs or smoking cigarettes even though he knows his habit is causing problems to himself, his friends and family. However, addictive behaviour is quite normal and not a disease, according to latest findings in the USA; it only becomes a problem when it gets out of hand.

Someone likely to become an addict is a person who cannot bear reality and will use anything to alter his perception of life. It is interesting to note that people with real problems are less likely to become addicts than those who have not. And more people continue to die every year from the effects of alcohol and tobacco than drugs.

It is possible to get off an addiction to drugs, including drink and tobacco, and stay off. Each year thousands of people do it. But the addict has to choose. Drugs that are addictive are usually those that affect mood, and that, of course, is why people take them – to feel better.

Are you an addict?

- Are you in control? Could you have a bottle of drink, some drugs or a packet of cigarettes in the home without using it? If you do not touch it, are you preoccupied with the fact that it is there?
- Do you take your drug openly or do you hide bottles and packets?
- Do you find it difficult to think of anything but your next drink or 'fix'?
- Are your friends or family worried about your habit? Are they beginning to say things about it?
- Do you get touchy if they make remarks about your habit?
- Are your friends beginning to drop you?
- Is your health, personal life, social life, work or finances affected by your habit?
- Do you drink, smoke more than you used to?
- Do you have memory lapses?
- Do you cadge extra cigarettes, extra drinks at parties?
- Do you tend to lose control after one dose?
- Do you feel remorse about your behaviour the morning after?
- Are you using alcohol/drugs continuously? Does it affect your work?
- Do you use drink/drugs to get you started in the morning?
- Do you do things under the influence that you wouldn't otherwise do?

Addiction is progressive, like a cancer. The sooner you turn back, the easier it will be to stop. Do not put it off, start today. If you found a cancerous lump, you would act quickly. Do not say, 'I'll quit tomorrow', start now. It may be that a sharp shock will start you on the road to recovery, nearly being run over, crashing the car or leaving the bath running. Get help: Narcotics or Alcoholics Anonymous will help you. And anonymous is the key word. There you will meet fellow addicts who have given up. You will mix with people who have discovered a way to get off and stay off. If there is no Narcotics Anonymous in your area, the AA will help.

Recreational drugs

There will always be people who take these regularly and many more people will experiment with them. These drugs can do permanent damage to some people and not to others, as their effects vary from person to person. The body builds up a tolerance to many drugs, making you need more and more of a drug to get the same effect. If you do become addicted, then finding the money to buy supplies of the drug may turn a perfectly law-abiding person into a criminal. Although not technically addictive, cannabis and Ecstasy are the most popular, easily bought drugs. It is estimated that three million people in Britain smoke cannabis or 'pot'. And more and more people have tried Ecstasy, the newer designer drug, sometimes with tragic results. On the hard drug front, there are now over a hundred thousand registered heroin addicts.

A-Z of recreational drugs

Acid or LSD, once linked with the hippies of the 70s, is usually taken as a pill or a tab (a small square of blotting paper soaked in the drug). Acid is a hallucinagenic drug whose effects last about 8 hours. It heightens feelings and sharpens sensations; everything looks different and you may well hallucinate. It can leave you feeling paranoid, with the shakes, and people with some inherent mental problem can be pushed over the edge by a 'bad trip'. The long-term danger is its effect on the brain: you may experience 'flashbacks' and relive a previous trip without taking further doses of the drug.

Amphetamines are in fact a range of drugs which come either as a powder that is 'snorted' (inhaled through the nose), or in pill form. They can also be injected. Once addicted to them, they are very difficult to give up. Known as 'speed', the drug literally speeds up your nervous system giving you extra energy. People on amphetamines tend to talk and move faster, the pupils of the eyes are dilated and their palms feel sweaty. The effects last 3–4 hours and it takes a couple of days to recover. After the ups come the downs – deep depression and lethargy which is difficult to shake off follows.

Amyl/Butyl nitrate is a liquid which is inhaled from a bottle. It used to be used to treat angina because it makes the heart pump fast and lowers the blood pressure and makes you feel dizzy – you may even black out. You may be silly and giggly too. It is used in the club scene, largely by gays, and is claimed to heighten sexual arousal. It is highly dangerous to anyone with low blood pressure or a heart condition. The downside, when the effect of the drug begins to wear off, is headaches, sickness, hot flushes and blackouts.

Anabolic steroids are derived from testosterone, the male hormone, and although not illegal, are taken mainly by sportsmen and fitness freaks to improve performance and increase aggression. They are often circulated at gyms and health clubs. These steroids are usually taken as pills but can be injected. Some steroids available on the gym scene are for veterinary purposes and are highly dangerous to use.

Danger signs are abnormal muscle development, pimples and increased 'maleness' – deep voice, more hair. They promote the build-up of muscle tissue and are believed to damage the liver and the heart. They also stunt the growth of adolescents and are thought to bring a diminished sex drive and low sperm count in men. Women's breasts may shrink and facial and body hair growth will increase. Anabolic steroids should not be confused with corticosteroid drugs which are often prescribed by doctors for conditions like arthritis.

Barbiturates are sedatives which calm people down and in high doses act as sleeping pills. Withdrawal symptoms include seizures and delirium. They are not used as much now by addicts as they used to be, but many older women who still have them on prescription may unwittingly misuse them.

Cannabis, also called 'pot' and 'hash', is usually smoked but can be made up into cakes or tea. It is mildly intoxicating and relaxing. It can make you feel in a pleasant frame of mind and makes you more aware of your surroundings. It is also known as a gateway drug, one that may lead someone into an illicit environment when other drugs will be offered them.

Like alcohol, it affects your ability to drive. It can also affect your short-term memory and make you lethargic. Although there has been a lot of talk about cannabis being legalized, fines for using this particular drug have recently been increased. If you suspect someone is using cannabis, look for butt-ends of 'joints' (hand rolled cigarettes) and the sickly sweet smell, as well as bloodshot eyes, dilated pupils and unaccustomed talkativeness. There is a risk of bronchitis and lung cancer, partly because the leaves or resin are often mixed with tobacco.

Cocaine, or coke, is a powerful stimulant that is usually snorted, but it is occasionally injected. It is a very expensive white powder and one of the hardest of the so-called hard drugs. It is said to give you self-confidence and energy, make you excitable and is often taken by people with stressful high-speed jobs, since it cuts down your need for food or sleep. It is very addictive, and the euphoria wears off quickly. For those who use it casually, the after-effects are like a hangover, with headache, dehydration and depression, and if you become addicted, the withdrawal symptoms can be terrible – breathing difficulties, sweats and sickness. Long-term, the user is likely to get nose ulcers and may suffer from convulsions. The user will probably lose weight too. Side-effects include paranoia, hallucinations and a sudden rise in blood pressure which could fuel a stroke or a heart attack. Cocaine users can also be involved in violent crimes, stealing to fuel their habit. Signs of use, apart from finding the crystalline white powder or crystals, are folded wraps of paper, the sudden appearance of a mirror and old-fashioned razor blades and straws to use for sniffing.

Crack is a cheaper, smokeable kind of cocaine that has been chemically treated and is often adulterated with baking soda and other sorts of powders to make it go further. It is usually smoked in a pipe or in tin foil. It acts quicker than straight cocaine, giving an extreme high which does not last very long – only 10-12 minutes in fact.

It has similar effects to cocaine and is said to enhance sexual desire. Like cocaine, it is extremely easy to get addicted to it and as the effects wear off, extreme tiredness and depression set in. There is a danger of lung damage and crack smokers risk heart failure through the toxic action of the drug. Signs of use: crack is usually smoked through a pipe, so the sudden appearance of one should raise alarm bells.

Ecstasy is a 'designer', laboratory-made drug, otherwise known as MDMA, that comes in pills or capsules that are often sold at 'raves', clubs and pop festivals. Some pills that claim to be Ecstasy may in fact be a far more potent and dangerous cocktail of several different drugs including crude heroin. Ecstasy is said to give you an instant feeling of energy and euphoria and friendliness to all around you. It is also claimed to heighten your senses while having sex.

It may often cause diarrhoea, nausea and sweating. If you have overdosed you are likely to get fits of anxiety and be unable to sleep. Since the pink, brown or yellow tablets are swallowed, there is no equipment you are likely to come upon, but anyone on Ecstasy is likely to have an excessive thirst, be restless, unable to sleep and appear unco-ordinated. It is known to cause liver and possibly brain damage, is highly dangerous to anyone with high blood pressure or a heart condition. It is a particularly dangerous drug for anyone with epilepsy or mental illness of any kind. There have been a number of well-publicised deaths among young people recently.

Heroin, or smack, is a white powder that comes from the opium poppy and is a derivative of morphine which is often used in medicine. It costs a great deal of money and is usually dissolved in water and injected just under the skin, a practice that is called 'shooting up' or the more serious 'mainlining' which involves injecting into a vein. Occasionally it is heated and inhaled through a straw.

Why do people get hooked on heroin? It is said to give users a feeling of great pleasure, security, self-confidence and freedom from pain or anxiety. Indeed, another derivative of the opium poppy, morphine, is used in medicine to prevent pain. Genuine addicts need a dose two or three times a day. Finding the money to pay for the habit often leads to crime and prostitution. It is extremely addictive and has dreadful withdrawal symptoms – sweats, clammy skin, breathing difficulties and cramps. It also makes menstruation irregular. Heroin users often share needles with others, and run the risk, that way, of catching HIV and hepatitis. They also find they need more and more of it to get the same effect and end up by overdosing.

Signs of use include the paraphernalia of heroin taking – paper wraps, syringes and needles, blackened pieces of tinfoil, a belt, tie or string to act as a tourniquet to find a vein and bent spoons. The user will have bloodstains on his clothing and bedding and needle marks on the hands or arms, but occasionally legs or feet, and the pupils of the eyes will be very small. An addict will also stop looking after himself and suffer from malnutrition and poor hygiene. Trying to get someone off heroin is not a job for an amateur, professional help will be needed.

Solvents Solvent abuse does not just mean sniffing glue but other substances that give off a vapour – lighter fuel, petrol, nail varnish remover, anti-freeze, typewriter correction fluid, deodorant, even shoe dye. Because all these things are relatively cheap to buy, solvent abuse is particularly attractive to children. And it is difficult to control because it is almost impossible to prove that a child who goes into a shop to buy lighter fuel is going to sniff it, not hand it over to a parent. However, from the legal point of view, it is an offence for a shopkeeper to supply anyone under the age of 18 with any of these substances, knowing that they are intending to use it to become intoxicated.

Solvent abuse tends to make the sniffer giddy, euphoric and, in excess, causes hallucinations. It has the same effect as alcohol or anaesthetics. Lighter fuel, in particular, can cause sniffers to be sick and choke on their vomit and can also cause heart failure. Some sniffers put their heads into plastic bags which heightens the effect and which might also suffocate them. Solvent vapours have a quick effect and disappear within between five minutes and half an hour. Afterwards the sniffer may have a mild hangover, mainly a headache, for up to a day.

Solvents are very dangerous because they can cause death through heart failure, especially aerosol gases and cleaning fluids, while aerosol gases squirted straight into the mouth can suffocate. In the long term they can cause brain damage, kidney and liver failure.

How to spot a drug user
Look out for:
- Cardboard filter or a cannabis cigarette.
- A machine for hand-rolling cigarettes or a switch to rolling their own.
- The sudden use of room fresheners – a desire to leave windows open, although

this could be for ordinary smoking. The undeniable sickly sweet smell of cannabis is difficult to disguise.
• Canisters in strange places – dry cleaning fluid, lighter fuel.
• The paraphernalia needed for cocaine and heroin – see above.
The person himself, if on hard drugs, will have a pallid skin tone, and will almost certainly be thin. He may avoid looking at you directly and any sudden change in behaviour needs watching.

Getting someone off drugs

If you are a friend, partner or parent of an addict you probably feel a mix of fear, guilt and anger. 'Where did we go wrong?' is the question we all ask. People around addicts often withdraw from the social scene too and spend fruitless hours searching for a cure. First you have to face up to several truths.

It is not your fault Do not blame yourself. Addicts can be very manipulative and often try to shift the blame onto family and friends.

You cannot control the person You are wasting your time trying to make an addict promise not to take whatever he is addicted to. Throwing away supplies, nagging, threatening and bullying won't work either. Neither does asking the doctor, the vicar or a social worker to have a serious talk with the person.

Do not help the person The addict has to suffer the consequences of what he is doing and hit rock bottom before he comes round to freeing himself of his plight. Do not pay off his debts or fines, do not find him a job or a home. Do not take the person to the doctor, however painful it may be to stand back and watch him suffer. What you need to do is to create a crisis. Say 'I love you, I care about you but unless you do something about your drinking, I'm going to leave/cut off your pocket money/evict you. If you will take treatment, however, I'll support you all the way'. Say, in effect, that if he wants help you will help him, but if he wants to stay with his habit then he is on his own.

Stick to your commitment Do not say 'unless you do something you'll have to leave home', then back down if he regresses.

Do not stay silent about things that distress you Say 'I was very angry last night when you came in stoned and upset your sister/smashed up the TV/left the gas on'. Say it in the morning when the person has quietened down, not at the time.

Do not get into an argument But show that you cannot be pushed around. Express your feelings firmly and quietly. Do not back down.

The family often suffers more than the addict. Anyone high on drugs is out of touch with reality. You are not, it is all too real. You need to:
• Get on with your own life.
• Learn to become detached, the more you do it the easier it becomes.
• Rebuild outside relationships if you have neglected them. You need all the friends you can get.

- Do not allow yourself to be pulled into addiction yourself, leaning on tranquillizers, for instance, to cope with the situation.
- Join a support group (*see page 115*). Meet other people who have been through the same experience.
- Do not become so engrossed that you neglect the other members of the family.
- Do not waste time trying to understand the addict – focus your mind on something positive like treatment prospects.

Children and drugs

The very word 'drugs' strikes a chill in the heart of parents – the image of a hollow-cheeked junkie crouched in a shop doorway flashes in front of their eyes, along with a pathetic silhouette on the TV screen confessing to the addiction. Fortunately, the proportion of teenagers who end up this way is minute. It is true, though, that many young people are going to experiment with drugs however much you try to stop them, faced as they are with a growing array of substances.

It is reckoned that about a third of young people, by the time they reach twenty, will have experimented with something. And most of them will not have bought the drugs in the first place, but been handed them by friends. 'Legal' drugs, solvents for sniffing, for example, are cheap and easily found. Hard drugs like heroin, crack or cocaine are very expensive and are not likely to be tried by teenagers but those in their twenties.

Drugs are thought to be fun, exciting and above all, illicit, making them seem a daring and interesting thing to do. Drug-taking spans all segments of society, middle-class children in private schools are just as tempted as those who are deprived. What is new, however, is the fact that drug-taking is starting at an earlier age. By the time they become teenagers, the problem intensifies – it is estimated that in the northeast, 70 per cent of 15–16 year olds have been offered drugs and of those, half will have tried them. Because of the concern these statistics provoke, the government is planning to give lessons on drugs awareness to children as young as five. Teachers are going to be appointed as counsellors for children who get into trouble with drugs.

At their worst, drugs can be seen as a way of escape from a life which the child feels is unbearable. Peer pressure – the opinion of their fellow schoolmates – is also a major factor in drug-experimentation. The trouble is that many of the symptoms of drug-taking are the same as those exhibited by any teenager – mood swings, bad exam results and staying out late.

Drug-testing kits

It is now possible to buy a home drug-testing kit which can be used to make secret checks to see if someone has been taking drugs. One kit analyses hair samples which will show if drugs have been taken in the preceding weeks. The other, which is cheaper, tests urine but in that case needs the co-operation of the child concerned in providing a sample. However, drug support groups and agencies condemn the practice of spying on a child in this way as they feel that it breaks the instinctive trust that a child has in its parents and makes them feel betrayed. Some parents have found that openly having the kit and doing the test in front of the child acts as a deterrent or gives them a fright.

Is your child taking drugs?
There are a number of warning signs related to drug-taking.
- School work deteriorates.
- No longer takes part in things he used to enjoy.
- Seems restless and irritable, with sudden outbursts of temper and mood swings.
- Seems to have made a new group of friends and stays out a great deal.
- Spends excessively or tries to borrow or even steal money.
- Personal appearance deteriorates, shows no interest in clothes and has a disinclination to wash.
- Excessively tired without any obvious reason why.
- Appetite seems to have gone.
- Look out for the excessive use of scent or after-shave (to hide the smell of drugs, especially cannabis). He may wear sunglasses to hide dilated or constricted pupils.
- Solvent users suffer from tiredness, forgetfulness and lack of concentration.

Many of these pointers could be put down simply to general teenage behaviour but taken together, there might be cause for alarm.

How to handle the situation
- Do not be confrontational. Aggression on your part will probably be met with fire. Do you smoke? Is your sideboard covered with gin bottles – he will be quick to point out that those, too, are drugs.
- Stay calm. However you feel, try not to react too violently. Listen to what he has to say, good communication is essential. It is vital to show your child that you love him. Set a good example in using your drugs – alcohol, painkillers – in a responsible way.
- Talk to them about the problem, point out that it is illegal and he could end up in trouble with the police. It could seriously damage his health both now and in the future. Point out that he does not know what he is actually taking – most drugs are contaminated with other products.
- Try to find out why your child has used drugs. He may well be taking drugs, not because he has a personal problem, but simply because he is bored or because drugs make him feel grown-up.
- If necessary phone a support network or a drugs helpline (*see page 115*).

What if your child is caught?

Most first-time offenders, including those under 17 hauled before a juvenile court, are likely to be fined. If it is a very minor case – a cannabis cigarette found in a blazer pocket, for instance, they may receive nothing more than a caution from the police. Regular offenders face heavy punishment – both prison and fines. Traffickers, quite rightly, face penalties up to life imprisonment.

The legal aspect

If your child or a member of your family brings drugs into the home you could face legal action. You can be prosecuted if it can be proved that they are sharing 'illegal substances' with friends or family under your roof. However, the law does not expect you to 'grass' on your child or family, but it is your duty in law to hand over any illegal drugs you find to the police or, more practically, to destroy them. The Home Office has now set up Drugs Prevention Units throughout the country, providing information and advice. It would consider funding you if you wanted to set up a local anti-drugs campaign.

Everyday drugs

Whether we know it or not, most of us take in a drug as part of our daily diet. **Caffeine** is an essential ingredient in tea, coffee, chocolate and some soft drinks like colas. It makes you feel more alert and stimulates the mind. Caffeine is also present in some headache pills. Too much caffeine, say in a constant supply of strong black coffee, can make you jumpy, stop you from sleeping and give you indigestion It also raises the blood pressure so anyone suffering from hypertension should keep their consumption down to sensible levels.

Medicinal drugs

Tranquillizers

In the past few years it has been realized that you can become addicted to prescription drugs given for anxiety and depression At one time doctors handed out Valium – the best-known tranquillizer – like sweets. Today doctors are much more cautious. The most widely used tranquillizers now are Diazepan, Temazepan and Librium, and the sleeping tablet Mogadon. Designed to reduce stress, help you sleep and free you from anxiety, they can cause drowsiness which is dangerous if you drive. They are also very difficult to give up, particularly if they are used as sleeping pills. Taking more than the prescribed dose will make you zombie-like.

These drugs are designed to be taken for only a few weeks at a time, to help a patient cope with or get over a specific case of tension or anxiety. But it is all too easy to become dependent on them, though doctors now are much more careful about giving repeat prescriptions. Taken with alcohol they can be fatal and it is all too easy to overdose, forgetting whether you have taken your pill or not.

It is very easy to become dependent on tranquillizers and if you take them over a long period, then stop, you may suffer withdrawal symptoms as uncomfortable as those from conventional drugs – the shakes, confusion, irritability, a return of anxiety and the inability to perform the most simple daily routines.

Prozac
This new drug is an anti-depressant that is said to make people happy and confident, with a feeling of joie de vivre. It is one of a new range of 'mood brighteners' – Paxil and Noloft are two other brand names. There is a danger that this 'happy pill' may become a recreational drug on the black market and be bought by people who are not clinically depressed but just want to feel better artificially.

HRT
Recent research at St Thomas's Hospital, London, has shown that some women may become addicted to hormone replacement therapy (HRT), taking up to seven times the proper dose of pills or using many more than one skin patch at a time. Some claimed that they needed larger and larger doses to eliminate hot flushes and other menopausal symptoms. It is suspected that some others are taking large doses in an effort to keep looking young. It is also thought that some women may develop a resistance to HRT in the same way that heroin addicts do. Not only is it dangerous to exceed the dose the doctor has prescribed, but 'drying out', if you have to come off the HRT, can be as unpleasant an experience as withdrawing from some illegal drugs.

Drink and tobacco – the social drugs

The so-called social drugs cause far more early deaths than drugs of an illicit nature – it is reckoned that one hundred thousand people die each year from diseases related to smoking against a mere 97 for people who died from taking too many opiates – heroin for instance – and no deaths at all are recorded from the direct misuse of cannabis.

Alcohol
See also **Drinking and driving, Legal,** page 43.
Alcohol is one of the most ancient drugs and is probably the only one to be mentioned in the Bible. Over 90 per cent of us drink it in some form or other. In small doses it makes you feel relaxed, uninhibited and more confident. In short, it is a social lubricant and helps you forget your worries because it depresses the nervous system. Alcohol is absorbed into the blood-stream and takes effect in five or ten minutes. The result can last for several hours.

How much effect a drink has depends on how much you take, how fast you drink and whether you have eaten anything. Other factors include your weight, your personality and the situation in which you find yourself. People who drink regularly can tolerate more alcohol than those who are not used to alcohol. Women absorb alcohol faster than men because their bodies contain less water, which dilutes the effect of the drink.

A unit of alcohol is roughly half a pint of beer or a small glass of wine. Four units will make most men feel uninhibited and relaxed, while double that could slur their speech and make them clumsy. In the case of women, roughly half the number of units will have the same effect. The official safe limits are 3 to 4 units a day for men, and 2 to 3 units a day for women. Drinking 50 units a week, if you are a man, and 35 units a week, if you are a woman, is definitely dangerous.

Getting drunk does not give you self-confidence. It does not make you taller, better-looking, sexier or more sophisticated. In large quantities, drink turns you into a repetitive bore at the best, aggressive and violent at worst. You may also end up in the arms of someone you would not touch with a barge-pole if you were sober. Drink makes people more violent than any of the so-called hard drugs and it is extremely addictive. Alcohol also makes you sick, gives you a headache and hangover. Drinking way over the limits over a period of time can give you liver disease, heart disorders and brain damage. Sudden withdrawal from drink is as bad as from other strong drugs, giving you sweating, anxiety, trembling and in some cases, delirium and convulsions.

Signs of alcoholism
- Discovery of bottles and cans, both empty and full.
- Undeniable sour smell of drink on the breath.
- Reddened blood-shot eyes.
- Sudden uninhibited behaviour.
- Aggression.
- Slurred speech.
- Unsteadiness.
- Nausea.
- Unconsciousness.

Alcoholics risk having accidents – walking in front of traffic, falling down stairs, setting themselves on fire and drowning. They may even cause someone else's death by drinking – driving or jay-walking. In large quantities, alcohol reduces the sex drive and contributes to infertility. In the long-term, liver damage is the main worry but less well known is that it makes you susceptible to several cancers, including those of the mouth and throat; pancreatitis; gastritis; and duodenal disorders. It also raises the blood pressure, increasing the likelihood of strokes.

There are outright alcoholics, heavy drinkers, problem drinkers and bout drinkers – people who can go for a week or more without a drink and then take off on a binge.

An alcoholic in the family

Your social life and your relationships with the outside world will be affected by having an alcoholic in your family, and you will have an increasing sense of isolation as a family. Nobody wants to believe there is a problem and to keep the peace, many families join in the conspiracy that the drinker is not, in fact, drinking heavily. It starts as a social atmosphere. You go out and socialize, then your partner begins to behave badly after a few drinks. As a result you stop going out and have people come to your home instead. But the same situation crops up again and you simply stop inviting anyone over.

Dealing with a problem drinker

A real alcoholic needs professional help. If you have one in your family, you may feel guilty, thinking that it is your fault because you connived with them. It is not. You cannot control the problem, nor can you cure it. Criticizing, nagging, threatening and sympathizing do not work. Neither does the dangerous practice of drinking heavily yourself to keep up with the alcoholic. The only person who can help a really heavy drinker is the drinker himself. He has to want to change. Joining a support group such as AA (*see page 97*) can help. You, in turn, could get help in handling the situation from Al-Anon (*see page 97*).

Getting yourself off heavy drinking

- If you are longing for a drink, create a deliberate delay. Do something else, wait for half an hour. The craving might then be gone.
- Do not put yourself in a high-risk situation. If friends are going out for a drink and you feel you might be tempted to slide, refuse the invitation.
- Alternate low-alcohol or non-alcoholic drinks with what you usually imbibe. Pace yourself.
- Try not to get into a drinking 'school' where each person buys a round. You are bound to drink more that way.
- If you drink spirits and drink at home, buy a pub measure for the bottle. Home measures are usually more generous.
- Do not offer to help buy the drinks for the office party or any other similar occasion. You will be tempted to do some beer or wine-tasting.
- Do not blame others. Do not dump your lack of will-power onto parents, the stress of work or your partner. In the end the buck stops with you.
- Do not use alcohol as a crutch. Using drink as a medicine when we feel tense, depressed or lacking in confidence is all too easy to do. 'Dutch courage' is the first step to addiction.
- Above all, do keep trying to cut down and give up. If you have a relapse, start over again.

If you can go out for a drink with friends and stay on mineral water then you have made a great step forward and have the right to feel proud of yourself. But if it is a day when you are not feeling okay, then stay away.

What to do if your child comes home drunk

Teenage drinking in on the increase. One of the main worries today is that a child who goes to a 'rave' may mix alcohol and a designer drug like Ecstasy with disastrous results. Ecstasy causes excessive dehydration but taking a great deal of liquid with it can have fatal results, as has been demonstrated in several tragic cases recently.

- Make sure he has not taken Ecstasy. Get some water into him to dilute the alcohol in the blood. Fizzy drinks speed up the intake of alcohol and in the same way, sparkling water will dilute it faster than still water.
- Do not try to discuss the subject with your child while he is drunk. Wait until he has sobered up.
- Be a good sensible role model if you can. Children from families who either drink in excess or totally abstain are the ones that are most likely to succumb.

Tobacco

Nicotine is one of the most addictive drugs of all; it leaves your blood system within minutes of taking that first puff and makes you crave for more. Tobacco is a stimulant. Smokers say that tobacco reduces stress, relieves monotony and tastes good after meals. But if you care about the environment then bear in mind that trees are cut down and burned to cure tobacco – and the average smoker gets through one tree per fortnight.

Few smokers will deny that they do actually smoke, but most heavy smokers lie – even to themselves – about the actual number of cigarettes they have in any one day. The signs of a heavy smoker are obvious: his or her hair, clothes and skin will be saturated with the smell of tobacco, their fingers and teeth will be nicotine-stained and their breath will smell.

This year it is predicted that just under fifty thousand women and over seventy thousand man will die from smoke-related illnesses. Smoking is now well-publicised as increasing the likelihood of heart disease, stroke, bronchitis and emphysema, thrombosis, and cancers – particularly of the lung, but also of the cervix, kidneys and bladder. Smoking mothers are much more likely to give birth to premature or underweight babies. It is illegal to sell tobacco products to children under the age of 16, but many tobacconists ignore this.

Giving up smoking

It *is* possible to give up smoking. Over the last 15 years, ten million people, more than 1,000 a day, have succeeded in doing so. But there is no point in trying unless you really want to do so. The Health Education Authority says that it should be done in stages.

Preparing to stop

- Make a list of the reasons why you want to stop smoking and keep it with you. These will probably include: health, money, fear of cancer, being nagged by partner and anti-social behaviour.
- Do not attempt to stop smoking if you are under any special kind of stress, you will only make things worse.
- You are going to have to depend on will-power to see you through. Will-power can be built up like muscle power, start doing just that by putting a cigarette back in the packet when you plan to have a smoke.
- Prepare yourself for the fact that you will have withdrawal symptoms at first. Legislate for things to do that will distract you – organize visits to the cinema and other places where smoking is forbidden when you begin to give up.
- Analyse your habits, make a note of when you have your first cigarette and change the situation. If you normally have one with a cup of coffee, switch to tea or orange juice.
- Work out whether it is best to stop over the weekend or at work and pencil in a date.
- Do not tell everyone what you are planning to do. If you do relapse then they will be quick to remind you of your promise. Instead, surprise them.
- The day before you give up, get rid of all cigarettes, ashtrays and lighters.

Stopping

- Plan to get through just one day at a time without smoking. Mark the days off on a calendar and watch them mount up.
- From day one on, drink plenty of orange juice or take vitamin C tablets. It will help your body to get rid of the nicotine more quickly.
- Put all the money you would have spent on cigarettes in a special piggy bank and count it from time to time. Six months off cigarettes could be the price of a holiday.
- Keep yourself busy, find something to do on those occasions when you would have relaxed with a cigarette. If you need to do something with your hands and find yourself reaching for a cigarette, fiddle with something else.
- If you need to put something in your mouth, make yourself a hot drink or chew sugar-free chewing gum until the craving passes.
- When you feel tired and tempted to give up, get out your list of reasons why you are stopping, and look at it.
- As with dieting, you may find you have some so-called friends who will do their best to get you to have a cigarette. Maybe they cannot stop themselves and do not want you to succeed, or maybe they are just being mischievous. Avoid them for the time being.

- Do not be tempted to have 'just one cigarette', the craving will return. Instead phone a helpline (*see page 135*). If you do have a relapse, stop smoking again right away. The longer you leave it, the more difficult it will be to give up again.
- Remind yourself that you are not trying to give up smoking but that you are now a non-smoker.

Finally the day will come when you wake up and realize you have not thought about cigarettes for 24 hours. When you go into a place where someone is smoking and it repels you, then you know you have won through!

Diet drugs

Thousands of women may be putting their health at risk by taking addictive (and unknowingly dangerous) drugs to help them diet. It is unlikely that you will get them from your GP, but many people, desperate to lose weight, are tempted by unregulated diet clinics which will prescribe them. Combined with a drastic diet, their effects are even more lethal. The General Medical Council (the governing body for GPs) has very strict guidelines for their use, but has no legal right to enforce their rulings. It has no jurisdiction over slimming clinics which frequently advertise their services. Drugs that should only be prescribed by your GP or a similarly qualified person include:

- Tenuate Dospan.
- Duromine.
- Ionamin.
- Bendrofluazide.

These drugs may be properly prescribed for other purposes, quite safely.

Addictive diet drugs

Appetite suppressants These amphetamine-like drugs persuade the brain that your body does not need food. The downside is that they can cause insomnia, depression and, in extreme cases, psychosis and hallucinations.

Diuretics Used perfectly properly for some conditions such as hypertension, these drugs help reduce fluid in your body. But they also flush out essential minerals, in particular potassium, from your system and need to be carefully prescribed.

Gambling

Before the arrival of the National Lottery, it was illegal to advertise gambling but this legal protection no longer exists. Gambling is basically a form of entertainment and now more and more people are being incited to join in – indeed it is said that some people are now totally addicted to scratch cards which promise instant excitement.

An addiction to gambling is so overpowering that it totally preoccupies the mind. Many people find it impossible to resist the impulse despite attempts to stop, fantasizing that this week's win will overcome last week's losses. It is reckoned that at any one time there are almost two million gamblers in this country. Addictive gambling can disrupt and damage family and working life. Over eighty thousand gamblers are so addicted to their habit that they are in danger of ruining themselves financially, borrowing at excessive rates, tipping over into crime and even committing suicide. Anti-depressants are being used to try to treat this condition because it is thought that there may be a link between gambling and depression. There are also experiments being conducted, using drugs, to try and damp down the 'highs' that gamblers experience.

Meanwhile, if you have a gambler in the family or feel you are tempted to go over the top yourself, many of the suggestions for dealing with other addictions apply (see above). Joining a support group such as Gamblers Anonymous – look for your nearest branch in the Phone Book – can be of great help.

HEALTH: HELP DIRECTORY

Health, General

- Health information line Freefone 0800 665544.
- Action for Victims of Medical Accidents, Bank Chambers, 1 London Road, London SE23 3TP, (0181 291 2793). Advises patients who think they have a claim after medical treatment. If it thinks you have a case, it will refer you to a special list of solicitors and find someone to give an independent medical opinion on your condition.
- Chief Executive of the NHS, Department of Health, Richmond House, 79 Whitehall, London SW1A 2NS, (0171 210 4850). The office to complain to if you feel you are being denied a right under the Patients' Charter.
- College of Health, St Margaret's House, 21 Old Ford Road, London E2 9PL, (0181 983 1225). Has a helpline on 0181 983 1133 for patients on waiting lists. Should be able to suggest alternative hospitals that can cope with your case more quickly.
- Health Rights Ltd, Unit 405, Brixton Small Business Centre, 444 Brixton Road, London SW9 8EJ, (0171 501 9856). An organization that may be able to help you with your rights vis-à-vis the NHS.

- Health Service Commissioner, Church House, Great Smith Street,
London SW1 3BW, (0171 276 3000). This commissioner is the equivalent of an
ombudsman. Contact him if you are not happy about the way your complaint
against a doctor or hospital has been handled.
- National Association for Patient Participation, 50a Wallasey Village,
Wallasey L45 3NL, (0151 677 9616), Runs a number of self-help groups
throughout the country encouraging patients to work towards better care from
their GPs.
- Patients Association, 8 Guildford Street, London WC1N 1DT, (0171 242 3460).
An independent but government-aided organization that advises patients and
their families over their rights. It can, for instance, tell you how to complain
about aspects of the service you have had.
- The UK Central Council for Nursing, Midwifery and Health Visiting, 23
Portland Place, London W1 3AF, (0171 637 7181). Contact this office if you
have a complaint concerning nurses, midwives or health visitors.
- Women's Health, 52–54 Featherstone Street, London EC1Y 8RT,
(0171 251 6580). An information, advice and support centre specializing in
women's health. It can put you in touch with local support and contact groups
and has a number of useful leaflets on women's health issues.

You and your dentist
See Dental problems (*page 114*).

Agoraphobia

See Phobias (*page 137*).

AIDS

AIDS Care, Education and Training, 27a Carlton Drive, London SW15 2BQ,
(0181 780 0400). A Christian-based charity with a round-the-clock team of
doctors and nurses throughout the country providing care in the home for AIDS
sufferers.
- AIDS Education and Research Trust, 11 Denne Parade, Horsham, West Sussex
RH12 1JD, (01403 210202). Has an information service for the public.
- Body Positive, 51b Pilbeach Gardens, London SW5 9EB, (0171 373 9124). A
self-help group and centre for people affected by HIV and AIDS which runs a
helpline, visits hospitals and counsels victims. Also runs a support group for
prisoners, and will occasionally give financial help.
- Catholic AIDS Link, PO Box 646, London E9 6QP, (0181 986 0807). Gives
support in every way – emotional, spiritual and financial – to HIV and AIDS
sufferers. Holds a regular support group and religious services.

- CRUSAID, Livingstone House, 11 Carteret Street, London SW1H 9DJ,
  (0171 976 8100). Set up mainly as a fund-raising organization for AIDS
  sufferers, it does have a special fund for people in desperate need because of
  AIDS.
- Lantern Trust, 72 Honey Lane, Waltham Abbey, Essex EN9 3BS,
  (01992 714900). Works with carers of HIV/AIDS sufferers in London and all
  parts of the country. It also runs an information service.
- London Lighthouse, 111–117 Lancaster Road, London W11 1QT,
  (0171 792 1200). A residential centre that gives help, counselling and support
  to people affected by, or concerned with, HIV and AIDS. It also offers
  convalescent care and runs a hospice.
- Positively Woman, 347–349 City Road, London EC1V 1LR, (0171 713 0222). A
  support organization for women who are HIV-positive or affected with AIDS,
  especially mothers or those who have children who are AIDS sufferers.
  Counselling is available over the phone and in person. This organization also
  gives practical and financial support.
- Terence Higgins Trust, 52–54 Gray's Inn Road, London WC1X 8JU,
  (0171 242 1010). This well-known organization has a helpline for anyone
  worried about or suffering from AIDS, and a one-to-one 'buddy' service,
  people who work personally with AIDS victims. Can give help and advice on
  all aspects of the disease whether legal, financial or medical.

Albinos

- Albino Fellowship, 16 Neward Crescent, Prestwick, Ayrshire KA9 2JB,
  (01292 470336). Advice and support group for anyone who is an albino or has
  an albino child. It campaigns against prejudice from the public and publishes a
  regular newsletter.

Alcohol problems

- Accept Services UK, 724 Fulham Road, London SW6 5SE, (0171 371 7477).
  This organization has a day centre for alcoholics and their families. Offers
  counselling and has a drinkwatchers group for people who want to cut down
  their level of drinking.
- Al-Anon Family Groups UK & Eire, 61 Great Dover Street, London SE1 4YF,
  (0171 403 0888). This organization has a round-the-clock telephone service to
  help families, including teenage children, with a drink problem in the family.
- Alcoholics Anonymous, General Service Office, PO Box 1, Stonebow House,
  Stonebow, York YO1 2NJ, (0171 352 3001). With over 2,000 groups throughout
  Britain, AA offers support to anyone trying to overcome a serious drinking
  habit. The helpline, above, is manned from 10am to 10pm daily.

- Alcohol Recovery Project, 68 Newington Causeway, London SE1 6DF, (0171 403 3369). This London-based organization runs four counselling centres for people with drink problems, one of which is for women only. It also has a series of 'dry' hostels, one for women and children.
- Drinkline, 7th Floor, Weddel House, 13–14 West Smithfield, London EC1A 9DL, (0171 332 0150). Has a helpline on 0171 0202 for the London area, 0345 320202 for the rest of the country, giving help with alcohol problems. It operates from 9am to 11pm Monday to Friday, 6pm to 11pm at weekends.
- National Council for Social Aid, 59 Catherine Place, London SW1E 6DY, (0171 630 7046). Helps provide hostels and homes for young men and women, ex-prisoners, especially alcoholics.
- Turning Point, New Loom House, 101 Back Church Lane, London E1 1LU, (0171 702 2300). With regional offices in Manchester and the Midlands, Turning Point runs a counselling service, telephone advice services and rehabilitation centres for people with drink problems, and their families. The centre is manned by volunteers who have been through the same problems. Also works with people who have learning disabilities and with drug addicts.
- United Kingdom Alliance, 176 Blackfriars Road, London SE1 8ET, (0171 928 1538). This organization offers care to people who have drink problems, referring them to places that can help and treat them. It is also a pressure group which campaigns for stricter control of licenses and licensing hours and against exploitation of alcohol.

See also
Association for Prevention of Addiction Ltd (*page 115*).
Richmond Fellowship (*page 117*).
Salvation Army (*page 18*).
Teen Challenge UK (*page 117*).

Alternative and complementary medicine

- Institute for Complementary Medicine, PO Box 194, London SE16 1QZ, (0171 237 5165). Gives information on complementary medicine of all kinds.

Acupuncture
- The Association of Western Acupuncture, 112 Conway Road, Colwyn Bay, Clwyd LL29 7LL, (01492 534328). Can put you in touch with a local member of the association.
- British Acupuncture Council, Suite D, Park House, 206–8 Latimer Road, London W10 6RE, (0181 964 0222), The Council keeps a register of qualified practitioners throughout the country.

- British Medical Acupuncture Society, Newton House, Newton Lane, Lower Whitley, Warrington, Cheshire WA4 4JA (01925 730727). Has a list of acupuncturists who are also doctors.
- The Traditional Acupuncture Society, 1 The Ridgeway, Stratford-upon-Avon, Warwickshire CV37 9JL, (01789 298798). Has a list of members practising five-element traditional Chinese acupuncture.

Alexander Technique
- Alexander Teaching Centre, 188 Old Street, London EC1V 9BP, (0171 250 3038). The centre has a list of qualified members who practise the technique.
- The Society of Teachers of the Alexander Technique, London House, 266 Fulham Road, London SW10 9EL, (0171 351 0828). Has a list of fully qualified teachers throughout the country.

Aromatherapy
- London School of Aromatherapy, Ground Floor, 93 Fortress Road, London NW5 1AG, (0171 267 6717). Has a list of qualified aromatherapists.

Ayurvedic Medicine
- International Society of Ayurvedic Medicine, PO Box 3043, Barnet, Herts EN4 0QZ. Can give you a list of practitioners using Ayurvedic medicine.

Chiropractic Therapy
- British Chiropractors' Association, 5 First Avenue, Chelmsford, Essex CM1 1RX, (01245 353078). Has a list of qualified chiropractors throughout the country.
- Chiropractic Advancement Association, PO Box 1492, Trowbridge, Wilts BA14 9YZ, (01722 415027). Has an advice and help service for patients.

Colour therapy
- Aetherius Society, 757 Fulham Road, London SW6 5UU, (0171 736 4187). A New Age mission offering colour healing, spiritual healing and absent healing.

Faith/spiritual healing
- British Alliance of Healing Associations, 23 Nutcroft Grove, Fetcham, Leatherhead, Surrey KT22 9LD, (01372 373241). Is the central association for spiritual healing associations throughout the country and can put you in touch with local healers and societies.
- Centre for Attitudinal Healing, PO Box 2023, London W12 9NY, (0181 549 2529). Offers classes on all aspects of attitudinal healing.
- Churches Council for Health and Healing, St Marylebone Parish Church, Marylebone Road, London NW1 5LT, (0171 486 9644). A Christian organization

which has an information centre and a wide range of publications on the subject of healing through prayer.

- Harry Edwards Spiritual Healing Sanctuary Trust, Burrows Lea, Shere, Guildford, Surrey GU5 9QG, (01483 202054). Offers a service of spiritual healing both personally and long distance.
- National Federation of Spiritual Healers, Old Manor Farm Studio, Church Street, Sunbury-on-Thames, Middx TW16 6RG, (01932 783164). Can give information and put you in touch with a spiritual healer in your locality who uses prayer, meditation or laying-on of hands.
- Seekers Trust, The Close, Addington, West Malling, Kent ME19 5BL, (01732 843589). A Christian-based group which holds retreats and prayer groups for people in need of spiritual healing.
- Spiritualists' Association of Great Britain, 33 Belgrave Square, London SW1X 8QB, (0171 235 3351). Has a healing support group and can put you in touch with a spiritualist who practises healing.
- Spiritualists' National Union, Redwoods, Stansted Hall, Stansted, Essex CM24 8UD, (01279 816363). Can give you a list of spiritual healers in your area.
- White Eagle Lodge, New Lands, Brewells Lane, Rake, Hampshire GU33 7HY, (01730 893300). Runs a series of lodges practising Christian healing, both by direct contact and in the patient's absence.

Holistic medicine

- British Holistic Medical Association, Rowland Thomas House, Royal Shrewsbury Hospital South, Shrewsbury, Shropshire SY3 8XF, (01743 261155). Can supply self-help tapes on holistic medicine and lists of local practitioners.

Homeopathy

- British Homeopathic Association, 27a Devonshire Street, London W1N 1RJ, (0171 935 2163). Has a list of homeopathic doctors throughout the country.
- The Faculty of Homeopathy, The Royal Homeopathic Hospital, Great Ormond Street, London WC1N 3HR, (0171 837 9469). Can put you in touch with a fully qualified homeopathic doctor. The hospital itself provides in- and out-patient facilities within the NHS and can give details of other hospitals in Glasgow, Liverpool, Bristol and Tunbridge Wells.
- The Dr Edward Bach Centre, Mount Vernon, Sotwell, Wallingford, Oxon OX10 0PZ, (01491 834678). Prepares and supplies Bach Flower Remedies and gives help and advice on the subject. Has books and information leaflets.

Hypnotherapy

- Association for Applied Hypnosis, 33 Abbey Park Road, Grimsby, South Humberside DN32 0H2, (01472 347702). Has a list of qualified members who subscribe to its code of practice.

- Association of Qualified Curative Hypnotherapists, 10 Balaclava Road, Kings Heath, Birmingham B14 7SG, (0121 444 5435). Can put you in touch with one of its members who obey the Association's code of practice.
- British Hypnotherapy Association, 1 Wythburn Place, London W1H 5WL, (0171 723 4443). Has a register of qualified hypnotherapists throughout the country subscribing to its code of practice, and can give information on hypnotherapy.
- National Council of Psychotherapists and Hypnotherapy Register, 24 Rickmansworth Road, Watford, Herts WD1 7HT, (01590 644913). Can put you in touch with a local member. Has its own code of practice.
- National Register of Hypnotherapists and Psychotherapists, 12 Cross Street, Nelson, Lancs BB9 7EN, (01282 699378). Watchdog for standards in the profession, this organization can put you in touch with a hypnotherapist or psychotherapist.
- The National School of Hypnosis and Psychotherapy, 28 Finsbury Park Road, London N4 2JX, (0171 359 6991). Can put you in touch with practitioners in hypnotherapy or psychotherapy who subscribe to its code of practice.

Meditation
- School of Meditation, 158 Holland Park Avenue, London W11 4UH, (0171 603 6116). Holds introductory talks for anyone wanting to know more about meditation.
- Transcendental Meditation National Office, Mentmore Towers, Mentmore, Leighton Buzzard LY7 0QH, (01296 662366). Disciples of the Maharishi, it can put you in touch with one of its network of Transcendental Meditation Centres throughout the UK. Ring freephone 0800 269 303 for general information and details of courses.
- Guild of Health Ltd, Edward Wilson House, 26 Queen Anne Street, London W1M 9LB, (0171 580 2492). Holds meditation and relaxation groups and a prayer network, all with health in mind.

Naturopathy
- British Naturopathic and Osteopathic Association, Frazer House, 6 Netherhall Gardens, London NW3 5RR, (0171 435 8728). Can tell you where to find a qualified practitioner.

Osteopathy
- British and European Osteopathic Association, 70 Galahad Road, Bromley, Kent BR1 5DT, (0181 850 1785). Has a list of members throughout the UK subscribing to its code of practice.
- The British Osteopathic Association, 8–10 Boston Place, London NW1 6QH, (0171 262 5250). Has a list of members who comply with its code of practice and that of the General Medical Council.

- The College of Osteopaths, 111 Thorkhill Road, Thames Ditton, Surrey KT7 0UW, (0181 398 3308). Has members throughout the UK subscribing to its code of practice.
- Cranial Osteopathic Association, 478 Baker Street, Enfield, Middx EN1 3QS, (0181 367 5561), Has a list of osteopaths qualified in cranial osteopathy.
- The General Council and Register of Osteopaths Ltd, 56 London Street, Reading, Berks RG1 4SQ, (01734 576585). Has a full membership list and a code of practice.
- The Osteopathic Clinic, 8–10 Boston Place, London NW1 6KH, (0171 262 1128). Has a list of medical practitioners practising osteopathy.

Psychotherapy
- British Association of Psychotherapists, 37 Mapesbury Road, London NW2 4HJ, (0181 452 9823). Can put you in touch with a psychotherapist in your area and offer a clinical service.

See also Hypnotherapy (*page 100*).

Reflexology
- Chiltern Institute of Reflexology, 193 Tring Road, Aylesbury, Bucks HP20 1JH, (01296 24854). Can give you the names of reflexologists in your area.
- International Institute of Reflexology, 32 Coppetts Road, Muswell Hill, London N10 1JY, (0181 444 6354). Has a register of reflexologists.

Relaxation techniques
- The Relaxation Society, 84 Herbert Gardens, Willesden, London NW10 3BU, (0181 969 6704). Can give you a list of members.

Shiatsu
- Shiatsu Society, 5 Foxcote, Wokingham, Berks RG11 3PG, (01734 730836). Can give full information on Shiatsu and put you in touch with practitioners throughout the country.
- Community Health Foundation, East-West Centre, London EC1 9FR, (0171 251 4076). Gives advice on diet and runs courses on healthy eating. Also has a clinic which does Shiatsu massage, Tai Chi, aromatherapy, yoga and holistic massage.
- The Shiatsu Society, 19 Langside Park, Kilbarchan, Renfrewshire PA10 2EP, (01505 704657). Has a list of registered practitioners throughout the UK.

Unani medicine
- The School of Oriental Herbal Medicine, 446 East Park Road, Leicester LE5 5HH, (0116 273 4633). Can put you in touch with practitioners of Unani medicine.

See also Association of Ayurvedic Practitioners (*page 99*).

Allergies

- Food and Chemical Allergy Association, 27 Ferringham Lane, Ferring-by-Sea, West Sussex BN12 5NB, (01903 241178). Gives practical help and advice to allergy sufferers.
- Medic-Alert Foundation, 12 Bridge Wharf, 156 Caledonian Road, London N1 9UU, (0171 833 3034). Worth belonging to if you suffer from a serious allergy. For a modest cost, the Foundation gives allergy sufferers a special disc to wear, so that police, ambulance, medical services can call its register and find out what allergy the person has.

See also Diet (*page 115*).

Alopecia

See Hair loss (*page 119*).

Amputation

See The Disabled (*page 127*).

Ankylosing spondylitis

- National Ankylosing Spondylitis Society, 5 Grosvenor Crescent, London SW1X 7ER, (0171 235 9585). Administers a network of local groups throughout the country giving advice and information to sufferers. Also sells a cassette tape and a home video of exercises that can help.

Anorexia

- Eating Disorders Association, Sackville Place, 44 Magdalen Street, Norwich NR3 1JE, (01603 621414). A countrywide network of support groups for sufferers and their families, mainly through telephone helplines. It also has a newsletter. Ring to find your local group. Has a youth helpline on 01603 765050.
- Montreux Counselling Centre, Box 5460, Victoria, British Columbia V8R 6S4, Canada, (001 604 598 3076). This centre has had spectacular success in treating people with anorexia.
- Overeaters Anonymous, PO Box 19, Stretford, Manchester M32 9EB, (0161 762 9348). Offers counselling, help, treatments for anyone with an eating disorder, countrywide.

- Single Concern Group, PO Box 4, High Street, Goring-on-Thames RG8 9DN, (01491 873195). Also known as Person-to-Person and Future Friends, this organization runs a help service and phone line which includes help for people with eating disorders.
- Women's Therapy Centre, 6 Manor Gardens, London N7 6LA, (0171 263 6200). Provides one-to-one or group therapy on a number of women's issues, including anorexia and bulimia, and can put you in touch with someone in your area who can help.

See also First Steps to Freedom (*page 137*).

Apert syndrome

- Apert Syndrome Support Group, Fullers Barn, The Green, Milton Keynes, Bucks MK6 8AN, (01908 608557). A support group for patients, especially during and after surgery.

Arthritis

- Arthritis and Rheumatism Council, Copeman House, St Mary's Court, St Mary's Gate, Chesterfield, Derby S41 7TD, (01246 558033). The Council has a leaflet on Lupus, a painful disease of the joints that affects young women. Send a large SAE with a 30p stamp for a copy.
- Arthritis Care, 18 Stephenson Way, London NW1 2HD, (0171 916 1500). Freephone helpline 0800 289170. Help in every way to improve the quality of life for arthritis sufferers. There are support branches all over the country. Has holiday hotels, self-catering units and a residential home and makes grants for equipment, etc. Also has a branch for young people called Young Arthritis Care.
- Horder Centre for Arthritis, St John's Road, Crowborough, East Sussex TN6 1XP, (01892 665577). Offers treatments to alleviate pain of arthritis and specialized nursing care. Has a unit for joint replacements and physiotherapy centre.
- Lady Hoare Trust for Physically Disabled Children, 4th Floor, Mitre House, 44–46 Fleet Street, London EC4Y 1BN, (0171 583 1951). Concerns itself with caring for children suffering from juvenile chronic arthritis or similar diseases, and their families, with the help of special workers.
- Lupus UK, 51 North Street, Romford, Essex RM1 1BA, (0108 731251). Has a range of support groups giving both practical and financial help to sufferers from the form of arthritis called systemic lupus erythematosus.
- Raynaud's and Scleroderma Association Trust, 112 Crewe Road, Alsager, Cheshire ST7 2JA, (01270 872776). Acts as an information exchange between patients suffering from this particular form of arthritis.

Arthrogryposis

- Arthrogryposis Group, The Oaks, Common Mead Lane, Gillingham, Dorset SP8 4SW, (01747 822655). Counsels children suffering from this condition and their families.

Asbestosis

- Society for the Prevention of Asbestosis and Industrial Diseases, 38 Drapers Road, Enfield, Middx EN2 8LU, (01707 873025). Helps people who are ill or disabled through asbestosis and other industrial diseases.

Asthma

- British Lung Foundation, 6th Floor, New Garden House, Hatton Garden, London EC1N 8JR, (0171 831 5831). Runs an information service on breathing problems, including asthma.
- Invalid Children's Aid Nationwide, Barbican City Gate, 1–3 Dufferin Street, London EC1Y 8NA, (0171 374 4422). Runs an information service and special school for severely asthmatic children.
- National Asthma Campaign, Providence House, Providence Place, London N1 0NT, (0171 226 2260). With branches all over the country, this organization helps asthmatics to understand their condition and to control it. Also has leaflets and information sheets on the condition. Runs an asthma helpline on 0345 010203.

Autism

See Children (*page 267*).

Back problems

- National Back Pain Association, 16 Elmtree Road, Teddington, Middx TW11 8ST, (0181 977 5474). Has useful leaflets, cassettes and booklets for back-pain sufferers. The latest, called *Help Yourself to a Better Back*, tells you how to avoid back injury and how to get better if you suffer from it.
See also Pain (*page 126*).

Blindness/sight problems

- Action for Blind People, 14 Verney Road, London SE16 3DZ, (0171 732 8771). This group helps both blind people and those who are partially sighted, organizing training, accommodation, grants and benefits, and holidays as well.

- Baha'i Service for the Blind, 14 Chishill Road, Heydon, Royston, Herts SG8 8PW, (01763 838309). Has books in Braille and tapes of Baha'i teachings, and produces a magazine on tape for Baha'i followers.
- British Blind Sport, Heygates Lodge, Elkington, Northants NN6 5NH, (01372 462214). Works with visually handicapped people to give them sporting opportunities.
- British Retinitis Pigmentosa Society, PO Box 350, Buckingham MK18 5AS, (01280 860363). A support group bringing together and helping sufferers from this condition.
- British Wireless for the Blind Fund, Gabriel House, 34 New Road, Chatham, Kent ME4 4QR, (01634 832501). Lends radios, cassette players and, now, TV sound receivers to blind people from the age of 8 upwards who cannot afford their own.
- CALIBRE, Aylesbury, Bucks HP22 5XQ, (01296 432339). This is a free lending library of books on cassette for people who are unable to read conventional books.
- Feminist Audio Books, 52–54 Featherstone Street, London EC1Y 8RT, (0171 251 2908). Runs a tape library for the blind or partially sighted which includes feminist and lesbian books.
- Free Tape Recorded Library for the Blind, 105 Salusbury Road, London NW6 6RH, (0171 624 8844). Has a free lending library of books on cassette.
- Gift of Thomas Pocklington, 20 Lansdowne Road, London W11 3LL, (0171 727 6426). A trustee-administered organization which cares for the blind in residential homes and sheltered accommodation. At the moment these are in London, Birmingham and Plymouth.
- Guide Dogs for the Blind Association, Hillfields, Burghfield, Reading, RG7 3YG, (01734 835555). A charity which trains and provides guide dogs for the blind.
- Guild of Methodist Braillists, 29 Brookfield Lane, Churchtown, Gloucester GL3 2PR, (01452 714390). A service for blind Methodists providing the Bible and other material in Braille.
- Henshaw's Society for the Blind, John Derby House, 88–92 Talbot Road, Manchester M16 0GS, (0161 872 1234). Working mainly in the north of England and in north Wales, the society provides support and training for the blind and the partially sighted and runs residential, nursing and holiday homes.
- Incorporated Association for Promoting the General Welfare of the Blind. 37–55 Ashburton Grove, London N7 7DW, (0171 609 0206). The Association runs workshops and accommodation for the blind, in London and Luton.
- International Glaucoma Association, c/o King's Healthcare, Denmark Hill,

London SE5 9RS, (0171 737 4000). Has information on glaucoma, a condition that causes blindness but which is preventable.

- Living Paintings Trust, Silchester House, Silchester, Reading, Berks RG7 2LT, (01734 700776). This organization makes 'feelie', tactile versions of famous paintings, complete with a taped guide for the blind.
- Mobility Aid and Guide Dog Alliance, 1 Palmer Road, Carlisle CA2 7NE, (01228 39523). This organization trains guide dogs and their owners. Also deals in other aids for those who cannot see.
- National Federation of Families with Visually Impaired Children, Queen Alexandra College, 49 Court Oak Road, Harborne, Birmingham B17 9TG, (0121 428 5038). Backs a series of parent support groups throughout the country. Also puts parents in touch with others in a similar situation, runs family weekends and has an information service.
- National Library for the Blind, Cromwell Road, Bredbury, Stockport, Cheshire SK6 2SG. Sends Braille books free of post to registered blind people. It also produces large print books.
- National Music for the Blind, 2 High Park Road, Churchtown, Southport, Mersyside PR9 7QL, (01704 28010). This organization has an extensive music library and lends out discs and tapes to blind or partially sighted people. You pay a single fee for this service, the cost depends on your age.
- Partially Sighted Society, Queen's Road, Doncaster, South Yorks DN1 2NX, (01302 323132). This society helps people who are partially sighted with an information and advice service. There are local groups all over the country.
- Royal National Institute for the Blind, 224 Great Portland Street, London W1N 6AA, (0171 388 1266). The Institute gives help to blind and partially sighted people in every way, with an extensive talking book and Braille library, residential homes, advice on education and careers. Also runs colleges for blind students and care homes for the elderly.
- Sense, 11–13 Clifton Terrace, Finsbury Park, London N4 3SR, (0171 272 7774). This is a special support group for parents whose children are deaf/blind as a result of rubella (German measles) in pregnancy. Gives support and advice and practical help in centres and homes, holidays for children afflicted with this condition and respite breaks for their carers.
- St Dunstan's Working for Men and Women Blinded in the Services, PO Box 4XB, 12–14 Harcourt Street, London W1A 4XB, (0171 723 5021). Helps ex-servicemen and women in every way, visiting them, helping them find jobs, supplying equipment, talking books. Also helps them with accommodation and puts them in touch with local clubs.
- Talking Newspaper Association of the United Kingdom, National Recording Centre, Heathfield, East Sussex TN21 8DB, (01435 866102). Turns newspapers

and magazines into cassettes for blind people. Membership is £15 per annum; in return members receive cassettes by post.

- Torch Trust for the Blind, Torch House, Hallaton, Market Harborough, Leics LE16 8UJ, (01858 555301). Has a library of Christian literature on tape and in Braille, which it loans out to the blind. Also runs correspondence courses for young blind people.
- Vision Aid, 22a Chorley New Road, Bolton BL1 4AP, (01204 531882). Works with families of blind or partially sighted children, offering support, counselling and advice over the phone. Also loans out toys, games and educational equipment.
- Vision Homes Association, 1D Tollgate Road, Ludlow, Shropshire SY8 1TQ, (01584 877166). Helps young mentally handicapped adults who are also partially sighted, through a series of local support groups and an information service. Also has accommodation for young adults.

See also
Disabled Section (*page 127*).
Jewish Care (*page 128*).
National Deaf-Blind League (*page 113*).
Sue Ryder Foundation (*page 110*).

Brain damage

- Association for Brain Damaged Children and Adults, Clifton House, St Paul's Road, Foleshill, Coventry CD6 5DE, (01203 711888). An association which deals with victims in the Coventry area.
- Brain Damage Research Trust, 6 Court Lane, London E21 7DR, (0181 299 1327), May be able to help you with contact numbers.

See also Head injury (*page 119*).

Breast cancer

See also Cancer (*page 109*).
- Breast Cancer Care Helpline, London 0171 867 1103, Glasgow 0141 3531050, Edinburgh 0131 2210407, Free Helpline (London only) 0500 245345. This service also counsels husbands and families of breast cancer victims.
- Breast Care and Mastectomy Association of Great Britain, 15–19 Britten Street, London SW3 3TZ, (0171 867 1103). Runs a helpline for women facing breast surgery. Also has information on the latest forms of treatment available.

- Cancerkin, Royal Free Hospital, Pond Street, London NW3 2QG, (0171 794 0500). Gives full support to women with breast cancer and their families, with clinics, relaxation sessions and emotional support. Patients need to be referred by their GP.

Brittle bone disease

- Brittle Bone Society, 112 City Road, Dundee DD2 2PW, (01382 817771). Gives help, advice, financial support and information on how to live with a brittle bone condition.

Bronchitis

See British Lung Foundation (*page 105*).

Bulimia nervosa

See Anorexia (*page 103*).

Cancer

- BACUP, British Association of Cancer Patients, 3 Bath Place, Rivington Street, London EC2A 3JR. This organization gives out medical information via the phone or its publications on various aspects of cancer. It has a medical information line on 0800 181199 for patients out of London and one for the London area on 0171 613 2121. Ring its counselling service on 0171 696 9000.
- BACUP Scotland, 30 Bell Street, Glasgow G1 1LG, (0141 553 1553). See above.
- Bristol Cancer Help Centre, Grove House, Cornwallis Grove, Clifton, Bristol BS8 4PG, (0117 974 3216). Has day and residential courses for cancer patients with advice on medication, relaxation and healing.
- Cancer Care Society, 21 Zetland Road, Redland, Bristol, Avon BS6 7AH, (0117 942 7419). Gives information and counselling on the various forms of cancer. Also has some holiday homes for sufferers.
- Cancer Laryngectomy Trust, 10 Brant Avenue, Illingworth, Halifax, West Yorks HX2 8DL, (01422 244165). Helps people who have had surgery for cancer of the throat, both from a practical and social point of view.
- Cancer Link, 17 Britannia Street, London WC1X 9JN, (0171 833 2451). An organization with self-help groups all over the country that gives full emotional support and information to people with cancer, and their families. A call to its helpline, above, will put you in touch with one of over 500 self-help groups throughout the country. Call 0131 22875557 if you live in Scotland, 0171 713 7867 for information in Asian language. Also has a helpline for young people with cancer, and their families, on 0800 591028.

- Cancer Relief Macmillan Fund, Anchor House, 15–19 Britten Street, London SW3 3TZ, (0171 351 7811). Cares for cancer sufferers from the time of diagnosis on. Macmillan nurses will visit patients in their homes, there are also day centres and help for those in financial need. It has a leaflet called *Help*, giving addresses, telephone numbers, helplines, etc.
- Dr Jan de Winter Cancer Prevention Foundation, 6 New Road, Brighton, East Sussex BN1 1UF. Runs a clinic for scanning, ultrasound, mammograms and smear tests for anyone worried they might have cancer. People who are unable to pay are tested free of charge.
- Edward's Trust, Edward House, 87–89 Stirling Road, Edgbaston, Birmingham B16 9BD, (0121 455 6257). Supports families with children suffering from cancer, leukaemia, with financial help, information, etc. It also has a bereavement counselling service.
- Malcolm Sargent Cancer Fund for Children, 14 Abingdon Road, London W8 6AF, (0171 937 4548). Gives practical help and support to children under 21 who have cancer, leukaemia or Hodgkin's disease. It runs holiday homes for sufferers and their families.
- Marie Curie Cancer Care, 28 Belgrave Square, London SW1X 8QG, (0171 235 3325). Has centres throughout the UK giving hospice and day care, and nurses to visit patients in their own homes.
- National Cancer Alliance, PO Box 579, Oxford OX4 1LB, (01865 793 566). Send an SAE for information on services and specialists. It has a directory of cancer specialists throughout the country and also gives advice on treatments available.
- New Approaches to Cancer, 5 Larksfield, Egham, Surrey TW20 0RB, (01784 433610), Has a network of cancer-help centres throughout the UK, encouraging people to use complementary medicine alongside conventional treatment in the fight against cancer.
- Radiotherapy Action Group Exposure, 24 Lockett Gardens, Trinity, Salford M3 6BJ, (0161 839 2927). Counsels and supports cancer survivors who are suffering from side-effects of radiotherapy.
- Rainbow Centre for Children with Cancer and Life-Threatening Illness, PO Box 604, Bristol BS99 1SW, (0117 9853343). Provides total help and support to children suffering from cancer or other life-threatening illnesses, and their families, in their homes or in hospital.
- Sue Ryder Foundation, Cavendish, Sudbury, Suffolk CO10 8AY, (01787 280252). Famous for its homes all over Britain not only for cancer sufferers but for the physically handicapped, Huntington's Chorea, the mentally ill and the elderly.
- Teenage Cancer Trust, Kirkman House, 54a Tottenham Court Road, London

W1P 9RF, (0171 436 2877). Can give information and help on cancer
treatments throughout the country.
- Tenovus Cancer Information Centre, PO Box 88, College Buildings, Courtenay
  Road, Splott, Cardiff CF1 1SA, (0800 526527). Admin 0222 619846. Runs a
  nationwide helpline staffed by trained nurses. Also has a screening unit and
  counselling centre for people in Wales.

See also
Breast cancer (*page 108*).
Hodgkin's disease (*page 121*).
Leukaemia (*page 122*).

Cerebral palsy

Scope, Spastics Society, 12 Park Crescent, London W1N 4EQ, (0800 626216).
Devoted to the care of people with this particular impairment, Scope, which has
branches all over the country, has a telephone helpline (above) and runs a
counselling and information service as well as schools, educational and
residential centres.
- SOS, 12 Park Crescent, London W1N 4EQ, (0171 637 9681). Runs two
  residential homes for people with cerebral palsy and works with children with
  this disability. It is part of Scope (formerly the Spastics Society).

Cleft palate

- CLAPA, 1 Eastwood Gardens, Kenton, Newcastle-upon-Tyne, (0191 285 9396).
  A self-help group that gives information and advice on the latest ways to treat
  this condition.

Coeliac disease

- Coeliac Society of the United Kingdom, PO Box 220, High Wycombe, Bucks
  HP11 2HY, (01494 437278). An information service for coeliacs – people with
  an allergy to protein in wheat or those who suffer from dermatitis
  herpetiformis.

Colostomy

- British Colostomy Association, 15 Station Road, Reading, Berks RG1 1LG,
  (01734 391537). The British Colostomy Association reassures and gives
  practical help to people who face having, or have had, a colostomy operation.
  It has a telephone helpline and will answer queries by post.

- Charity for Incontinent and Stoma Children, 51 Anderson Drive, Darvel, Ayrshire KA17 0DE, (01560 322024). Counsels and helps the families of children who have had a colostomy, ileostomy or urostomy. It also gives advice on chronic incontinence.

Cosmetic help

- British Association of Aesthetic Plastic Surgeons, c/o Royal College of Surgeons, Lincoln's Inn Fields, London WC2A 3PF, (0171 405 2234). The organization to contact if you are planning cosmetic surgery. It has a range of useful leaflets on the subject. Send a large SAE with a first-class stamp for its list of fully accredited plastic surgeons.
- British Association of Skin Camouflage, c/o Mrs Jane Goulding, 25 Blackhorse Drive, Silkstone Common, Barnsley, South Yorkshire S75 4SD, (01226 790744). Send a large SAE for information on services in your locality.
- The British Red Cross, 9 Grosvenor Crescent, London SW1X 7EJ, (0171 235 5454). It has a cosmetic camouflage programme for people with severe burns, birthmarks or vitiligo. Ring your local branch and ask to speak to the beauty care officer. You need to be referred by your GP.
- Changing Faces, 1 & 2 Junction Mews, Paddington, London W2 1PN, (0171 706 4232). Works with people with facial disfigurement throughout the country, counselling them and giving them advice on what help and treatment is available.
- Disfigurement Guidance Centre, PO Box 7, Cupar, Fife KY15 4PF, (01337 870281). Has a number of publications including a skinlaser directory, giving details of up-to-date treatment at private and NHS clinics.
- First Medical Finance Ltd, Sovereign House, 91–93 Buckingham Palace Road, London SW1W 0RS, (0171 828 2000). Will give unsecured loans to cover cosmetic surgery. To apply by telephone ring freefone 0800 61 45 49.
- Let's Face It, Support Network for the Facially Disfigured, 10 Wood End, Crowthorne, Berks RG11 6DQ, (01344 774405). Supports and counsels people with facial disfigurement, visiting them in hospital, and helps them by phone and by post.

Crohn's disease

- Crohn's in Childhood Research Association, Parkgate House, 356 West Barnes Lane, Motspur Park, Surrey KT3 6NB, (0181 949 6209). Runs support groups throughout the country for parents of children with this disease.
- National Association for Colitis and Crohn's Disease, 98a London Road, St Albans, Herts AL1 1NX, (01727 844296). Runs groups throughout the country giving help and personal support to sufferers with this condition.

Cystic fibrosis

- Cystic Fibrosis Research Trust, Alexandra House, 5 Blyth Road, Bromley, Kent BR1 3RS, (0181 464 7211). Gives families advice over schools, employment for young people with cystic fibrosis, and also helps over housing and holidays. Has 300 local support groups and useful booklets, films and videos.

Deafness, hearing difficulties

- Breakthrough Trust for Deaf-Hearing Integration, The Hall, Peyton Place, London SE10 8RS, (0181 853 5661). Helps to integrate deaf people, especially the elderly or those who are house-bound, into the community and gives them support and advice. It has an electronic phone service which sends out news bulletins daily.
- British Deaf Association, 38 Victoria Place, Carlisle CA1 1HU, (01228 48844). Can give financial help to deaf people in need. It also helps over education via grants and scholarships and runs holiday trips abroad.
- Council for the Advancement of Communication with Deaf People, Pelaw House, School of Education, University of Durham, Durham DH1 1TA, (0191 374 3607). Keeps a register of trained people who are skilled in communicating with the deaf.
- Friends for the Young Deaf, East Court Mansion, Council Offices, College Lane, East Grinstead, West Sussex RH19 3LT, (01342 323444). Works nationally with young deaf people improving their self-confidence and their quality of life via volunteers throughout the UK.
- Hearing Dogs for the Deaf, Training Centre, London Road, Lewknor, Oxon OX9 5RY, (01844 353898). Works in a similar way to Guide Dogs for the Blind, training and supplying specially trained dogs for deaf people, alerting them to sounds like the telephone, door bell etc.
- LINK The British Centre for Deafened People, 19 Hatfield Road, Eastbourne, East Sussex BN21 2AR, (01323 638230). Runs assessments and residential courses for people who have become deaf during their adult life, and for their families.
- National Association of Deafened People, 103 Heath Road, Widnes, Cheshire WA8 7NU, (0151 424 3977). A support, back-up and information service for deaf people which publishes a regular newsletter and campaigns on members' behalf.
- National Deaf-Blind League, 18 Rainbow Court, Paston Ridings, Peterborough, Cambs PE4 7UP, (01733 573511). Offers support to people who are both deaf and blind, helping them in times of illness, lending out equipment, organizing holidays and social functions for them.

- National Deaf Children's Society, 15 Dufferin Street, London EC1Y 8PD, (0171 250 0123). Helps deaf children and their families in every way with counselling, practical advice. It also helps with hearing-aids and specialist equipment and runs holidays for them.
- Royal Association in Aid of Deaf People, 27 Old Oak Road, Acton, London W3 7HN, (0181 743 6187). A complete back-up for deaf people, fighting for their rights, providing interpreters where necessary, and equipment. Also has a tinnitus helpline on 0345 090210.
- Royal National Institute for Deaf People, 105 Gower Street, London WC1E 6AH, (0171 387 8033) (Textline 0171 383 3154). Provides a wide range of services for deaf people, helping them over their rights. Also has residential care for the deaf.
- SIGN Campaign for Deaf People, 21 Stratton Road, Beaconsfield, Bucks HP9 1HR, (01494 680308). Helps improve the quality of life for young deaf people by encouraging them to live in the community rather than in institutions, counselling and watching over them when they do so. It has two projects at the moment, one in London and one in Manchester.
- Sympathetic Hearing Scheme, 7–11 Armstrong Road, London W3 7JL, (0181 740 4447). A support service for deaf people who have difficulty hearing in public places such as theatres, cinemas, banks and shops.

See also
Disabled (*page 127*).
British Tinnitus Association (*page 139*).

Dental problems

- British Dental Health Foundation, Eastlands Court, St Peter's Road, Rugby, Warwicks CV21 3QP, (01788 546365). Runs a helpline for anyone who is worried about visiting the dentist on 0788 546365.
- British Society of Medical and Dental Hypnosis, 17 Keppel View Road, Kimberworth, Rotherham, South Yorks S61 2AR, (0709 554 5580). Has a list of qualified doctors and dentists who use hypnotherapy within the framework of orthodox medicine and who subscribe to the General Medical Council code of practice.
- The General Dental Council, 37 Wimpole Street, London W1M 8DQ, (0171 486 2171). The people to contact if you are accusing your dentist of serious professional misconduct.

Depression

See States of Mind (*page 136*).

Diabetes

- British Diabetic Association, 10 Queen Anne Street, London W1M 0BD,
  (0171 323 1531). Has wide ranging services for diabetics – literature, videos,
  on the subject. Also runs special holidays for diabetic children.
- Diabetes Foundation, 177a Tennison Road, London SE25 5NF,
  (0181 656 5467). Has a round-the-clock helpline run by doctors giving general
  help and advice to diabetics and the families of diabetic children.

Diet, nutrition

- Society for the Promotion of Nutritional Therapy, PO Box 47, Heathfield, East
  Sussex TN21 8ZX, (01435 867007). The Society is able to put you in touch
  with a practitioner in your area using nutritional therapy.
- Vegan Society, 7 Battle Road, St Leonards-on-Sea, East Sussex TN37 7AA,
  (01424 427393). Can give you information on the vegan way of eating
  including nutritional help.
- Vegetarian Society of the United Kingdom, Parkdale, Dunham Road,
  Altrincham, Cheshire WA14 4QG, (0161 928 0793). Can put you in touch with
  local vegetarian groups and also has a large number of publications on sale.
- Women's Nutritional Advisory Service, PO Box 268, Lewes, East Sussex
  BN7 2QN, (01273 487366). Gives help and advice on nutrition for women,
  especially those suffering from PMT or having difficulties with the
  menopause.

Disability, disabled

See Practical health problems (*page 127*).

Drugs, drug and solvent dependence

- ADFAM National, 5th Floor, Epworth House, 25 City Road, London
  EC1Y 1AA, (0171 638 3700). Runs a national helpline (above) for families and
  friends of drug users.
- The Advisory Council on Alcohol and Drug Education, 1 Hulme Place, The
  Crescent, Salford, Manchester M5 4QA, (0161 745 8925). Provides support for
  parents and carers on the subject of drug and alcohol abuse.
- Association for the Prevention of Addiction Ltd, 67–69 Cowcross Street,
  Smithfield, London EC1M 6BP, (0171 251 5860). Works with people addicted
  to drugs or drink by offering help, advice and information. Also provides
  needles and works with HIV sufferers.
- Cocaine Anonymous, c/o Matey, PO Box 2EY, London W1A 2EY,
  (0171 284 1123). Offers help to cocaine and crack users. Also has a recorded
  message giving dates and places across the country where addicts can get
  help.

- Committee Against Drug Abuse, 231 Old Kent Road, London SE1 5LU, (0171 231 1528). A centre which helps addicts by providing needle exchanges, detoxing and counselling. Also gives legal advice and help with housing and referrals to GPs or hospital clinics.
- Community Drugs Project, 39 Manor Place, London SE17 3BB, (0171 703 0559). Counsels drug users and offers needle exchanges. Also gives help and advice on the safer use of drugs and on safer sex.
- Drug Aid, 1 Neville Street, Cardiff CF1 8LP, Phone 01222 383313, their 24-hour telephone helpline, if you or your family have drug problems.
- Drugline Ltd, 9a Brockley Cross, London SE4 2AB, (0181 692 4975). Helps drug addicts by telephone counselling and interviews. Also makes visits to prisons and hospitals.
- Families Anonymous, Unit 37, The Doddington and Rollo Community Association, Charlotte Despard Avenue, London SW11 5JE, (0171 498 4680). Gives support and help to the families and friends of drug addicts. Also runs a telephone helpline.
- Hungerford Drug Project, 32a Wardour Street, London W1V 3HJ, (0171 437 3523). Runs a drop-in centre and a telephone help service, counselling people who have drug problems, and their friends and families.
- Institute for the Study of Drug Dependence, Waterbridge House, 32–36 Loman Street, London SE1 0EE, (0171 928 1211). A useful place to contact if you have a query over drugs or drug addiction. It runs an information service on the subject on 0171 803 4720.
- Life for the World Trust, Wakefield Building, Gomm Road, High Wycombe, Bucks HP13 7DJ, (01494 462008). A Christian-based organization which counsels people who are trying to kick the drug habit. It uses group therapy, Bible teaching and encourages addicts to take up a sport or a craft.
- Lifeline, 101–103 Oldham Street, Manchester M4 1LW, (0161 839 2054). Has a number of publications for drug users, runs a needle exchange service and support for families of users.
- Narcotics Anonymous, UK Service Office, PO Box 1980, London N19 3LS, (0171 272 9040). Works in the same way as Alcoholics Anonymous, helping people to give up drugs. Holds regular meetings where people who have kicked the habit can talk to those who are trying to give it up. It also works with those who have alcohol problems.
- National Children's Bureau, 8 Wakeley Street, London EC1V 7QE, (0171 843 6000). Has information on solvent sniffing. It has two books, *Soluble Problems* and *Sniffing Solutions*.
- National Drugs Helpline, PO Box 5000, Glasgow G12 9BL, (Freephone 0800 776600). The Department of Health has a number of brochures on drug and solvent abuse. These booklets are available in a number of languages other

than English including Arabic, Urdu, Bengali, etc. It also has leaflets for
children from 8–12 and 13–18 years old. Contact them at the free round-
the-clock helpline number above. The Central Drugs Prevention Unit on
0171 217 8631 has teams throughout the country working in the community,
helping and funding anti-drugs campaigns.
- Parent Line, Endway House, The Endway, Hadleigh, Essex SS7 2AN,
  (01702 554782). Gives support and assistance to families of drug users via its
  helpline on 01702 559900.
- Parents/Partners and Drugs, 1 Maidenhead Road, Stratford-upon-Avon, Warks
  CV37 6XR, (0789 261376). Founded by people who, in the past, have had to
  deal with drug problems in their families, this group has an information pack
  to help families and friends of drug users.
- The Promise Counselling Centre, 2a Cromwell Place, London SW7 2JE,
  (0171 581 8222). A counselling and recovery treatment centre for drug users
  who cannot kick the habit and, separately counsels their families.
- Release, 388 Old Street, London EC1V 9LT, (0171 729 9904). This organization
  works with drug abusers who get on the wrong side of the law, with help over
  legal problems and, in the case of arrest, emergency aid. It has an emergency
  helpline on 0171 603 8654 which is particularly useful if someone has been
  arrested for a drug offence.
- Re-Solv, The Society for the Prevention of Solvent and Volatile Substance
  Abuse, 30A High Street, Stone, Staffs ST15 8AW, (01785 817885). Can give you
  information on glue-sniffing and solvent abuse in general. It has videos and
  booklets and can tell you of your nearest support group.
- Richmond Fellowship, 8 Addison Road, London W14 8DL, (0171 603 6373). A
  Fellowship which concerns itself with all kinds of problems connected with
  mental health. It works with people who are recovering from drug addiction
  and has accommodation and workshops all over the country to help them.
- SCODA, The Standing Conference on Drug Abuse, Waterbridge House, 32–36
  Loman Street, London SE1 0EE, (0171 928 9500). It runs a national freephone
  helpline for anyone with drug problems on 0800 776600.
- Scottish Drugs Forum, 5 Oswald Street, Glasgow G1 4QR, (0141 221 1175).
  Will refer you to centres in Scotland that can help.
- Shaftesbury Square Hospital, 116–120 Great Victoria Street, Belfast BT2 7BG,
  (01232 329808). Helps drug users and their families in Northern Ireland.
- Solvent Abuse Resource Group, 28 Penny Street, Blackburn, Lancs BB1 6HL,
  (01254 677493). Counsels people who are hooked on solvents.
- Teen Challenge UK, Teen Challenge Centre, Penygroes Road, Gorslas, Llanelli,
  Dyfed SA14 7LA, (01269 842718). Runs places where young people with
  problems can meet, and a residential centre for young men and women
  suffering from drug problems.

- Welsh Office Drugs Unit, Welsh Office, Cathays Park, Cardiff CF1 3NQ, (01222 825111). Offers a similar service in Wales.

Dyslexia

See Special needs (*pages 267, 345*).

Eczema

- National Eczema Society, 163 Eversholt Street, London NW1 1BU, (0171 388 40970). Helps eczema sufferers and their families with advice and information via groups throughout the country.

Emphysema

See British Lung Foundation (*page 123*).

Endometriosis

- Endometriosis Society, 50 Westminster Palace Gardens, 1–7 Artillery Row, London SW1Q 1RL, (0171 222 2776). A support group for sufferers with this condition. It has an evening helpline above, from 7 pm to 10 pm.

Epilepsy

- British Epilepsy Association, Anstey House, 40 Hanover Square, Leeds LS3 1BE, (0113 243 9393). Gives help, information and support to people with epilepsy via a network of groups. Has a freephone helpline on 0800 309030.
- David Lewis Centre, Mill Lane, Warford, Alderney Edge, Cheshire SK9 7UD, (01565 872613). Has an assessment service for both children and adults suffering from epilepsy.
- National Society for Epilepsy, Chalfont St Peter, Gerrards Cross, Bucks SL9 0RJ, (01494 873991). Working from the centre, the Society offers help and support to sufferers and their families, as well as assessment and residential care.
- St Piers Lingfield, St Piers Lane, Lingfield, Surrey RH7 6PW, (01342 832243). A special residential school and hospital for children with all kinds of special needs, including epilepsy and learning problems. It also has a Further Education Unit helping older children.

Facial disfigurement

See Cosmetic help (*page 112*).

Feet, problems with

- Sole-Mates, 46 Gordon Road, London E4 6BU, (0181 524 2423). Has a matching-up service for people who have one foot larger than the other. It can also supply single shoes.

Glaucoma

- International Glaucoma Association, Kings College Hospital, Denmark Hill, London SE5 9RS, (0171 737 3265). Gives help and advice over the phone or by post to those suffering from glaucoma.

Growth problems

- Restricted Growth Association, PO Box 18, Rugeley, Staffs W515 2GH, (01889 576571). Counsels and helps adults, and the families of children who have not grown to their expected size.

Haemophilia

- Haemophilia Society, 123 Westminster Bridge Road, London SE1 7HR, (0171 928 2020). Gives support, back-up, help and advice to haemophiliacs via local groups throughout the country.

Hair loss

- Hairline International, 39 St John's Close, Knowle, Solihull, West Midlands B93 0NN, (01564 775281). Also known as the Alopecia Patient's Society, this organization gives support to people who are losing, or have lost, their hair. It does this via telephone counselling, concessions on the price of wigs and a regular newsletter giving up-to-date details of research.

Handicaps

See Disabled (*page 127*).

Head injury

- Action for Dysphasic Adults, 1 Royal Street, London SE1 7LL, (0171 261 9572). A support group for people suffering from difficulty with speech or loss of speech after head injuries or stroke.
- Children's Head Injury Trust, c/o Neurosurgery, The Radcliffe Infirmary, Woodstock Road, Oxford OX2 6HE, (01865 224786). Has support groups throughout the country for families of children who have suffered serious head injury.

- Headway (National Head Injuries Association Ltd), 7 King Edward Court, King Edward Street, Nottingham NG1 1EW, (0115 924 0800). Has more than 100 support groups throughout the country to help people suffering from head injuries and their families. It also runs assessment centres and residential homes.

See also
Association for Brain Damaged Children and Adults (*page 108*).

Heart problems, stroke

- British Cardiac Patients Association, 'Belmont', 30 Perne Road, Cambridge CB1 3RT, (01223 247431) helpline. Offers support and advice to all heart patients and their families, especially those who are waiting for, or have just had, heart surgery. Known as The Zipper Club, it also organizes social activities via local groups. It has a telephone helpline (*see above*).
- British Heart Foundation, 14 Fitzhardinge Street, London W1H 4DH, (0171 935 0185). Educates the general public and helps and encourages those suffering from heart disease with the loan of special equipment.
- Chest, Heart and Stroke Association, CHSA House, 123–127 Whitecross Street, London EC1Y 8JJ, (0171 490 7999). Specializes in helping stroke sufferers; and in Scotland and Northern Ireland also help with more general heart conditions.
- Heart Line Association, Rossmore House, 26 Park Street, Camberley, Surrey GU15 3PL, (01276 675655). A support system for parents of children with heart conditions which operates via local self-help groups.
- Stroke Association Community Services, William Moon Lodge, The Linkway, Brighton BN1 7EJ, (01273 562690). Counsels and gives practical help to stroke sufferers who have been left with speech or mobility problems. It works via volunteers throughout the country.

Hepatitis B

- Group B Hepatitis Group, Basement Flat, 7a Fielding Road, London W14 0LL, (0171 244 6514). A counselling and telephone helpline service for sufferers of hepatitis B.

Herpes

- Herpes Association, 41 North Road, London N7 9DP, (0171 607 9661). Has a telephone helpline on 0171 609 9061, giving information, advice and counselling to sufferers or those who suspect they have herpes. It also answers queries by post.

High blood pressure

See Heart problems (*page 120*).

HIV (Human Immuno-deficiency Virus)

See AIDS (*page 96*).

Hodgkin's disease

• Hodgkin's Disease Association, PO Box 275, Haddenham, Aylesbury, Bucks HP17 8JJ, (01844 291479). Offers advice and support to sufferers of Hodgkin's disease and non-Hodgkin's lymphoma and their families via local groups and through a telephone helpline on 01844 291500. It can also lend out videos, tapes and books on the subject.
See also Cancer (*page 109*).

Hormone replacement therapy (HRT)

See Menopause (*page 123*).

Hydrocephalus

See Spina bifida (*page 135*).

Hypertension

See Heart problems (*page 120*).

Ileostomy

• Ileostomy Association of Great Britain and Ireland, Amblehurst House, Black Scotch Lane, Mansfield, Notts NG18 4PF, (01623 28099). Counsels, advises and helps people who have had an ileostomy (bladder removed) with literature, equipment and general information.
See also Incontinence (*below*).

Incontinence

• The Charity for Incontinent and Stoma Children, 51 Anderson Drive, Darvel, Ayrshire KA17 0DE, (01560 322024). Gives practical help, support and advice to families with a child who has permanent bowel or bladder problems, perhaps after surgery.
• Chartered Society of Physiotherapy, 14 Bedford Row, London WC1R 4ED, (0171 242 1941). Has a useful leaflet on coping with incontinence. Send an SAE for a copy.

- Enuresis Resource and Information Centre, 65 St Michael's Hill, Bristol BS2 8DZ, (0117 9264920). Gives information and advice to sufferers and their families.

Irritable bowel syndrome

- IBS Network, c/o Wells Park Health Project, 1a Wells Park Road, London SE26 6JE, (0181 291 3332). Helps sufferers from irritable bowel syndrome via support groups and introductions to fellow victims.

Kidney problems

- British Kidney Patient Association, Bordon, Hants GU35 9JP, (01420 472021). Gives help and advice and sometimes financial aid to kidney patients and their families. Also runs two holiday centres where patients can have dialysis while taking a break away from home.
- National Federation of Kidney Patients' Associations, 6 Stanley Street, Worksop, Notts S81 7HX, (01909 487795). Helps kidney patients to help themselves. Can give advice over holiday places where dialysis can be made available.

Laryngectomy

- National Association of Laryngectomy Clubs, Ground Floor, 6 Rickett Street, London SW6 1RU, (0171 381 9993). Supports and helps, via the post or over the phone, people who have had their larynx removed. Will also visit patients in hospital both before and after their operations.

Leukaemia

- Cancer and Leukaemia in Childhood Trust (CLIC), 12–13 Kings Square, Bristol B52 8JH, (0117 924 8844). Works with children suffering from cancer and leukaemia and their families, offering grants, accommodation and somewhere for the families to stay near their child in hospital.
- Childhood Cancer and Leukaemia Link, 36 Knowles Avenue, Crowthorne, Berks RG45 6DU, (01344 750319). Help and information service for parents of children with cancer or leukaemia.
- Elimination of Leukaemia Fund, 17 Venetian Road, London SE5 9RR, (0171 737 4141). Has an information service on leukaemia.

See also

Cancer (*page 109*).

Malcolm Sargent Cancer Fund for Children (*page 110*).

Lung diseases

- British Lung Foundation, New Garden House, 78 Hatton Garden, London EC1N 8JR, (0171 831 5831). Has an information service for sufferers of diseases of the chest and lungs, such as bronchitis.

Lupus

See Arthritis (*page 104*).

ME (Myalgic encephalomyelitis)

- Action for ME, PO Box 1302, Wells, Somerset BA5 2WE, (01749 670 799). Has a 24-hour information line on 0891 122 976. Send an SAE for free information pack.
- ME Association, Stanhope House, High Street, Stanford le Hope, Essex SS17 0HA, (01375 642 466). Has an advice and information pack, please send an SAE.

Meniere's disease

- Meniere's Society, 98 Maybury Road, Woking, Surrey GU21 5HX, (01483 740597). Gives support, help and information to sufferers from this condition via local groups throughout the country.

Meningitis

- National Meningitis Trust, Fern House, Bath Road, Stroud, Glos GL5 3TJ, (01453 751738). Gives information and help to sufferers and their families via support groups throughout the country. It has a 24-hour support line on 0345 538118.

Menopause

- Amarant Trust, Grant House, 56–60 St John Street, London EC1M 4DT, (0171 490 1644). Runs menopause clinics throughout the country, offering counselling and advice including help and information over Hormone Replacement Therapy.
- Women's Health Concern, PO Box 1629, London W8 6AU, (0171 938 3932). Counsels and offers information by post and over the phone to women suffering from gynaecological problems including those connected with the menopause, and advises them on the use of Hormone Replacement Therapy.

Mental handicaps

- Christian Concern for the Mentally Handicapped, PO Box 351, Reading, Berks RG1 7AL, (01734 508781). A Christian-based organization which has several residential homes in this country for mentally handicapped people.
- MENCAP 117–123 Golden Lane, London EC1Y 0RT (0171 454 0454). Works on behalf of, mentally handicapped children and adults.
- Mental Health Foundation, 37 Mortimer Street, London W1N 7RJ, (0171 580 0145). Masterminds the funding of self-help groups of people with mental disorders and their families. Contact in writing to see if you qualify for a grant.

See also

Children with Special Needs and Special Educational Needs (*pages 267, 345*).

Metabolic diseases

- Research Trust for Metabolic Diseases in Children, Golden Gates Lodge, Weston Road, Crewe, Cheshire CW1 1XN, (01270 250221). Works to put families of children with metabolic diseases in touch with each other for mutual support. Also makes grants where necessary and has a round-the-clock phone service on 01270 626834.

Migraine

- British Migraine Association, 178a High Road, Byfleet, Surrey KT14 7ED, (01932 352468). A support group for people suffering from migraine, it keeps up to date on the latest research and new treatments on offer. Send an SAE for details of help and advice it can give.
- Migraine Trust, 45 Great Ormond Street, London WC1N 3HZ, (0171 278 2676). An information and advice service for migraine sufferers, it also runs a number of self-help groups.

Miscarriage

- Miscarriage Association, c/o Clayton Hospital, Northgate, Wakefield WF1 3JS, (01924 200799). Runs a series of groups throughout the country supporting women who are threatened with, or have suffered, a miscarriage.

See also National Childbirth Trust (*page 216*).

Motor neurone disease

- Motor Neurone Disease Association, PO Box 246, Northampton NN1 2PR, (01604 250505). A support service with offices around the country for sufferers of motor neurone disease and their families. It offers counselling, information and advice. It loans out equipment and gives small grants to help with nursing.

Multiple sclerosis

- ACT, Alliance for Cannabis Therapeutics, PO Box CR14, Leeds LS7 4XF, (Fax 0113 2371000). A patients' organization which have found that taking a small amount of cannabis is useful in helping control MS. They are campaigning for it to be made available on a doctor's prescription. For information please send four first-class stamps.
- Federation of MS Therapy Centres, Unit 4, Murdock Road, Bedford MK41 7PD, (01234 325781). Has centres throughout the country which offer therapy to sufferers. It also has a telephone counselling line on 0171 222 3123.
- Multiple Sclerosis Society of Great Britain and Northern Ireland, 25 Effie Road, Fulham, London SW6 1EE, (0171 610 7171). Has a network of 360 branches throughout the country that help and support people suffering from this disease, and a helpline on 0171 371 8000. It also has holiday facilities and homes for short stays and can give grants for special equipment.

Munchausen's syndrome

- Munchausen's Syndrome Self-Help Group, 22a Tankerville Road, London SW16 5LL, (0181 679 4324). Offers help and counselling to people who are addicted to medical treatment and hospitals. It has a helpline, above.

Muscular dystrophy

- Muscular Dystrophy Group, 7–11 Prescott Place, London SW4 6BS, (0171 720 8055). Has branches all over the country offering support and information for sufferers from the disease.

Osteoporosis

- National Osteoporosis Society, PO Box 10, Radstock, Bath, Avon BA3 3YB, (01761 432472). Gives support, information and advice by phone or through the post to those who either suspect they are suffering from, or actually have, osteoporosis. It also issues a regular newsletter with the latest research news and has some useful leaflets on diet and on the subject in general.

See also Menopause (*page 123*).

Pain

- National Back Pain Association, 16 Elmtree Road, Teddington, Middx TW11 8ST, (0181 977 5474). Has an information pack which it will send on receipt of a donation of £2.50 to the association.
- Pain Concern UK, PO Box 318, Canterbury, Kent CT4 5D, (01227 264 677). The main self-help support group for sufferers. Has a helpline on 01227 264 677.
- Pain Management Unit, St Thomas's Hospital, London SE1 7EH, (0171 922 8107). Has a chronic pain helpline on 01227 264677 which operates from Monday to Friday, 10am to 4pm.
- Pain Research Institute, Rice Lane, Liverpool L9 1AE, (0151 632 0662). Has leaflets on pain and audio programmes on pain management. Phone at the above number for details.
- The Pain Society, 9 Bedford Square, London WC1B 3RA, (0171 636 2750). Can give help and information on the management of pain, and has a leaflet giving details of pain clinics throughout the country.
- Painwise UK, 33 Kingsdown Park, Whitstable, Kent CT5 2DT, (01277 277886). Has a helpline, above, for people with chronic pain. Also has a useful booklet *Self Help Pain Management*.

Parkinson's disease

- Parkinson's Disease Society of the UK Ltd, 22 Upper Woburn Place, London WC1H 0RA, (0171 383 3513). Gives support, information and advice to sufferers from Parkinson's disease and their families.

Phobias

See States of mind (*page 136*).

Polio

- British Polio Fellowship, Ground Floor, Unit A, Eagle Office Centre, The Runway, South Ruislip, Middx HA4 6SE, (0181 842 1898). Works for the welfare of polio sufferers of all ages, giving advice and counselling. Also runs special holiday and residential homes.

Post-natal depression

See Depression (*page 136*).

Post-traumatic stress

- Ticehurst House Hospital, Ticehurst, Wadhurst, Sussex TN5 7HU, (01580 200391). This hospital runs a special centre for people suffering from post-traumatic stress. Contact it for information.

Practical health problems

Disabled/handicapped, General
- British Home and Hospital for Incurables, Crown Lane, London SW16 3JB, (081 670 8261). Takes care of the severely disabled and chronically sick, encouraging them to take up interests and hobbies that will improve their quality of life.
- British Limbless Ex-Service Men's Association, 185–187 High Road, Chadwell Heath, Essex RM6 6NA, (0181 590 1124). Helps ex-servicemen who have lost a limb or an eye while in the Forces or their widows. It has a network of branches all over the country giving advice over pensions, helping financially. It also runs two homes in the north of England and in Scotland.
- Caring and Sharing Trust, Cottons Farmhouse, Whiston Road, Cogenhoe, Northants NN7 1NL, (01604 891487). Helps handicapped people and their families, especially those living in the country. Runs holiday projects and also helps elderly people.
- Catholic Handicapped Fellowship, 2 The Villas, Hare Law, Stanley, Co. Durham DH9 8DQ, (01642 823080). Works with Catholic churches throughout the country organizing activities for handicapped people, including short-stay care, transport to church services.
- Disability Alliance, 1st Floor East, Universal House, 88–94 Wentworth Street, London E1 7SA, (0171 247 8776). Has a welfare rights telephone advice line on 071 247 8763. Also publishes a *Disability Rights Handbook* to income benefits and aids for £8.95 plus postage, £5 if you are on benefit.
- Disabled Christians Fellowship, 211 Wick Road, Brislington, Bristol BS4 4HP, (0117 983 0388). A Christian-based support group for disabled people including those in their teens and twenties. It has a pen-friends section and organizes special holidays.
- Disabled Housing Trust, Norfolk Lodge, Oakenfield, Burgess Hill, West Sussex RH15 8SJ, (01444 239123). Has sheltered housing complexes and residential homes in several sites throughout the country giving specialist accommodation for disabled people and their families.
- Disablement Information and Advice Line, Park Lodge, St Catherine's Hospital, Tickhill Road, Balby, Doncaster, Yorks DN4 8QN, (01302 310123). Gives information and advice by phone on every aspect of being disabled.

- Dogs for the Disabled, Frances Hay House, Banbury Road, Bishops Tachbrook, Leamington Spa CV33 9UQ, (01926 651179). This organization trains and provides dogs for people who are disabled but not blind or deaf.
- Greater London Association of Disabled People, 336 Brixton Road, London SW9 7AA, (0171 274 0107). Has an information service for disabled people in the London area.
- Habinteg Housing Association Ltd, 10 Nottingham Place, London W1M 3FL, (0171 486 3519). A special housing association that concentrates on providing specially designed homes for the wheelchair bound.
- Handidate Dating Agency, The Wellington Centre, 52 Chevalier Street, Ipswich, Suffolk IP1 2PB, (01473 226950). This is a contact and dating service for people with disabilities.
- Independent Living Alternatives, Ashford Offices, Ashford Passage, Ashford Road, London NW2 6TP, (0181 450 4055). Works in the London area running a counselling service. Gives advice and information to disabled people who want to live independently, not in an institution.
- Invalids at Home, 17 Lapstone Gardens, Kenton, Harrow, Middx HA3 0EB, (0181 907 1706). Aims to help as many long-term invalids as possible to stay at home rather than in an institution. It makes discretionary grants which are administered through local social workers.
- Jewish Care, Stuart Young House, 221 Golders Green Road, London NW11 9DQ, (0181 458 3282). A support group working in London and the Home Counties that works with the physically and visually handicapped, also the mentally ill and their families, with residential and day care centres and personal counselling.
- Leonard Cheshire Foundation, Leonard Cheshire House, 26–29 Maunsel Street, London SW1P 2QN, (0171 828 1822). Famous for its network of homes for the mentally and physically disabled, the Foundation also has a team which will visit the disabled in their homes, and runs a hotel for disabled people at Sandringham, Norfolk.
- National Association for Limbless Disabled, 31 The Mall, London W5 2PX, (0181 579 1758). Has a service giving help and information to people who have lost a limb.
- National Listening Library, 12 Lant Street, London SE1 1QH, (0171 407 9417). A postal library on tapes for people with physical and mental disabilities of all kinds. Also loans out cassette players. It includes a range of books on tape for children. There is a subscription of £25 a year, but there is also help for those who can't afford that.
- 'Not Forgotten' Association, 158 Buckingham Palace Road, London SW1W 9TR, (0171 730 2400). Acts on behalf of disabled ex-servicemen and

women, by lending TV sets to the housebound and those in homes and
hospitals. Also organizes concerts, holidays and outings for them.
• Queen Elizabeth's Foundation for Disabled People, Leatherhead Court,
  Leatherhead, Surrey KT22 0BN, (01372 842204). Offers residential care and
  further education for physically handicapped school-leavers. There is a
  training college, an assessment centre, and it tries to place students in
  employment. Also has a holiday home and a day centre for the physically
  handicapped.
• Shaftesbury Society, 16 Kingston Road, London SW19 1JZ, (0181 542 5550).
  Once known as the Ragged School, the Society now works with disabled
  people or those with learning difficulties in the inner cities. Also helps the
  poor and those who are homeless.
• WinVisible: Women with Visible and Invisible Disabilities, King's Cross
  Women's Centre, 71 Tonbridge Street, London WC1H 9DZ, (0171 837 7509).
  Offers advice and support for women with mental as well as physical
  disabilities, that is to say, victims of rape, racism or discrimination of any
  kind.

See also
Field Lane Foundation (*page 314*).
Outsiders Club (*page 204*).
Royal British Legion, Employment (*page 371*).
Lady Hoare Trust for Physically Disabled (*page 104*).

Disabled, sports and pastimes
• Artsline, 54 Chalton Street, London NW1 1HS, (0171 388 2227). Telephone
  information and advice service gives information and advice about leisure and
  arts activities available to the disabled in the Greater London area.
• Association for Swimming Therapy, 26 Stone Grove, Edgware, Middx HA8
  7UA, (0181 958 1642). An organization that can put you in touch with a
  network of clubs who teach swimming to handicapped people.
• British Ski Club for the Disabled, Springmount, Berwick St John, Shaftesbury,
  Dorset SP7 0HQ, (01747 828515). Organizes training classes on dry slopes and
  skiing holidays for the disabled and their carers.
• British Sports Association for the Disabled, Mary Glen Haig Suite, Solecast
  House, 13–27 Brunswick Place, London N1 6DX, (0171 490 4919). Works with
  the Sports Council to organize sports events for disabled people.
• British Wheelchair Sports Foundation, Guttman Sports Centre, Harvey Road,
  Stoke Mandeville, Bucks HP21 9PP, (01296 84848). Based at Stoke Mandeville,
  and working with people who are paralysed, the Foundation finances and runs
  the Guttman Sports Centre, and the Olympic village alongside it.

- Conquest, (Society for Art for the Physically Handicapped), 3 Beverley Close, East Ewell, Epsom, Surrey KT17 3HB, (0181 393 6102). Gives information and help, holds art classes and exhibitions for disabled artists.
- Crypt Foundation, Forum, Stirling Road, Chichester, West Sussex PO19 2EN, (01243 786064). Works with young disabled artists with short-term residential care.
- Disabled Photographers' Society, PO Box 41, Wallington, Surrey SM6 9SG, (0181 647 3179). Lends cameras and equipment such as wheelchair stands to disabled members, also to schools, hospitals and centres for people with disabilities. Holds an annual exhibition of members' work.
- Grand National Archery Society, Liaison Officer for the Disabled, Pine Lodge, Haverbrakes Road, Haverbrakes, Lancaster LA1 5BJ, (01524 381902). Can give help and information for anyone who is disabled and wants to take up archery.
- Great Britain Wheelchair Basketball Association, 104 London Road, Chatteris, Cambs PE16 6SF, (01354 695560). Runs a network of wheelchair basketball clubs throughout the country and also national teams.
- Handicapped Anglers Trust, Hazelthorpe, Stalisfield, Faversham, Kent ME13 0DY, (01233 714127). Helps disabled people to take up angling, and makes special boats for their use.
- Jubilee Sailing Trust, Test Road, Eastern Docks, Southampton, Hants SO14 3GG, (01703 631388). Runs adventure sailing holidays for people who are handicapped on a specially designed ship.
- Music for the Disabled, 2 Wendy Crescent, Guildford, Surrey GU2 6RP, (01483 67813). An entertainment group who arrange for musicians to play to disabled as therapy, and to work with severely disabled and mentally handicapped children.
- National Association of Swimming Clubs for the Handicapped, The Willows, Mayles Lane, Wickham, Hants PO17 5ND, (01329 833689). Can put disabled people in touch with their local swimming club. It also runs galas throughout the country and a camping holiday every year for club members.
- Riding for the Disabled Association, Avenue R, National Agricultural Centre, Kenilworth, Warwicks CV8 2LY, (01604 858160). Can put disabled people who want to ride in touch with their local group.
- Shape London, 356 Holloway Road, London N7 6PA, (0171 700 0100). Works with disabled people, including the deaf, in the London area, in the arts and also with the elderly, giving them a chance to join in with dance and music productions. Also runs a ticket scheme for seats for theatres and concerts in the capital.

- Society for Horticultural Therapy, Goulds Ground, Vallis Way, Frome, Somerset BA11 3DW, (01373 464782). Gives advice to disabled people who want to garden, with projects throughout the country and demonstration plots.
- Uphill Ski Club of Great Britain, 12 Park Crescent, London W1N 4EQ, (0171 636 1989). Has a ski school in the Cairngorms, Scotland, offering winter sports for the disabled.

Disabled, holidays

- BREAK, 20 Hooks Hill Road, Sheringham, Norfolk NR26 8NL, (01263 823170). Provides holidays and short-term care for people, both children and adults, who have severe learning difficulties, especially through handicaps.
- Camping for the Disabled, 20 Burton Close, Dawley, Telford, Salop TF4 2BX, (01743 761889). This organization gives information and advice on camping for disabled people. It also organizes camping weekends in Britain for the physically handicapped and has lists of accessible camp-sites both in the UK and in France.
- Disaway Trust, 2 Charles Road, London SW19 3BD, (0181 543 3431). Runs holidays for disabled people over the age of 16 in this country and abroad. Helpers can also be accommodated at half the holiday cost.
- English Heritage, Iveagh Bequest, Kenwood, Hampstead Lane, London NW3 7JR, (0181 348 1286). Has a free guide listing nearly 100 historic landmarks that are accessible to disabled and partially sighted people. It gives access, parking and other facilities and says whether wheelchairs, tape tours or braille guides are available. Copies available in local libraries, and English Heritage sites.
- Handihols, 12 Ormonde Avenue, Rochford, Essex SS4 1QW, (01702 548257). Runs a holiday house-swop and hospitality service for disabled people and their families.
- Holiday Care Service, 2nd Floor, Imperial Buildings, Victoria Road, Horley, Surrey RH6 7PZ, (01293 774535). Runs a holiday information and support service which can give details of suitable holidays for people with specific disabilities. Has *Accessible Accommodation Regional Guides* covering the whole of the UK at 50p each.
- MENCAP Holiday Services, 119 Drake Street, Rochdale OL16 1PZ, (01706 54111). Runs adventure and special care holidays, also guest-house holidays for mentally handicapped children and grown-ups in England and Wales.
- Peter le Marchant Trust, Colston Bassett House, Colston Bassett, Nottingham NG12 3FE, (01509 265590). Operates boats on the Norfolk Broads and other inland waterways that are adapted for the physically or mentally handicapped. The Trust runs holidays and day trips and lets out boats for a small charge to handicapped people or terminally ill people and their families.

- Scout Holiday Homes Trust, Baden-Powell House, Queen's Gate, London SW7 5JS, (0171 584 7030) F 581 9953. Although a Scout-based organization, the Trust offers cheap holidays on chalet and caravan sites all over the country for handicapped children who are not necessarily Scouts and their families.
- Trengweath Trust, Erme House, Station Road, Plymouth, Devon PL7 3AU, (01752 346861). Has special programmes in school holidays for brothers and sisters of disabled children in Devon and Cornwall, and a training scheme for parents of children under five, so they can learn from the experts how to care for and treat their child.
- Winged Fellowship Trust, Angel House, 20–32 Pentonville Road, London N1 9XD, (0171 833 2594). Organizes holidays for the disabled with or without a helper, at specially built centres both in Britain and abroad, with outings, entertainments. Has a programme of special interest holidays covering things like photography, crafts, music and drama.
- Young Disabled on Holiday, 33 Longfield Avenue, Heald Green, Cheadle, Cheshire SK8 3NH, (0161 499 3639). Works with disabled people aged 18–35, organizing holidays for them.

Disabled, aids and equipment

- Association for Spinal Injury Research, Rehabilitation and Re-integration, Royal National Orthopaedic Hospital, Brockley Hill, Stanmore, Middx HA7 4LP, (0181 954 0701). Helps patients and ex-patients of the Royal National Orthopaedic Hospital over specialist wheelchairs and other equipment they might need.
- British Red Cross Society, 9 Grosvenor Crescent, London SW1X 7EJ, (0171 235 3241). Has a series of publications on subjects ranging from home-made aids to how to push a wheelchair.
- Disabled Living Centres Council, 1st Floor, Winchester House, 11 Cranmer Road, London SW9 6EJ, (0171 820 0567). Has 39 centres throughout the country which can help you find all kinds of equipment from stair lifts to jar openers.
- Disabled Living Foundation, 380–384 Harrow Road, London W9 2HU, (0171 289 6111). Has a useful information service by phone or by post regarding special clothing, for example, for incontinence, special shoes and all kinds of equipment for the disabled, from eating and drinking aids, bed hoists to clothing and wheelchairs. A display of what's available can be seen at the above address.
- Keep Able Foundation, 2 Capital Interchange Way, Brentford, Middx TW8 0EX, (0181 994 6614). The foundation runs a support group to try and improve the quality of life for those people who are severely disabled after accident or illness.

- Mobility Trust, 50 High Street, Hungerford, Berks RG17 0NE, (01488 686335). A very helpful organization who will give help over equipment of all kinds for the disabled. In cases of exceptional need, will give loans and grants.
- Research Institute for Consumer Affairs, 2 Marylebone Road, London NW1 4DF, (0171 935 2460). Works rather like the Consumers' Association but for the disabled and the elderly, testing products and equipment and choosing the best in each category. Will answer general queries from the public, and has a useful leaflet *Equipment for an Easier Life*, enclose an SAE.
- Royal Association for Disability and Rehabilitation, RADAR, Unit 12, City Forum, Lonson EC1V 8AF, (0171 250 3222). Co-ordinates the work of most groups working with the disabled. It has a number of useful publications including *Made to Measure*, a booklet which gives advice on converting your home for someone who is disabled.
- Spinal Injuries Association, Newpoint House, 76 St James's Lane, London N10 3DF, (0181 444 2121). Gives a support and counselling service to paraplegics and other people disabled with spinal injuries. Also helps in a practical way by putting new wheelchair users in touch with other more experienced ones. It has specially adapted caravans and boats for hire.
- Wireless for the Bedridden, 159a High Street, Hornchurch, Essex RM11 3YB, (01708 621101). A charitable organization providing radio and TV sets for disabled or invalid people who are housebound, and also for the elderly poor.

Disabled, transport/disabled drivers
- Banstead Mobility Centre, Damson Way, Fountain Drive, Carshalton, Surrey SM5 4NR, (0181 770 1151). Can put you in touch with special driving instructors for the disabled.
- Community Transport Association, Highbank, Halton Street, Hyde, Cheshire SK14 2NY, (0161 351 1475). Runs an information and advice service for community transport groups, but will try to help people who have transport difficulties because they are disabled or elderly and frail.
- Disabled Drivers' Association, Ashwellthorpe, Norwich NR16 1EX, (050841 449). Helps disabled drivers, or those who would like to drive, through local clubs throughout the UK.
- Disabled Drivers' Motor Club Ltd, Cottingham Way, Thrapston, Northants NN14 4PL, (01832 734724). An information and support service that is worth joining if you are a disabled driver.
- Mobility Information Service, National Mobility Centre, Unit 2a, Atcham Estate, Shrewsbury SY4 4UG, (01743 761889). Has a round-the-clock information service on mobility for disabled people and will answer queries by post. Will also assess your ability to drive. Has listings of instructors for disabled drivers, and a service giving a list of attended pump filling stations

and eating places that are accessible to wheelchair travellers, bed and breakfast etc.

- TRIPSCOPE, Pamwell House, 160 Pennywell Road, Bristol, Avon BS5 0TX, (0181 994 9294) London, (0117 941 4094) Bristol, Gives information and advice on travel over the phone to disabled or elderly people, their families and their friends.

Pre-menstrual tension

- National Association for Pre-menstrual Syndrome, PO Box 72, Sevenoaks, Kent TN13 1XQ, (01732 459378). Essentially a pressure group to make people more aware of the condition of PMT, it also gives advice via its telephone information helpline on 01732 741709.

Pre-eclampsia

See Conception (*page 216*).

Psoriasis

- Psoriasis Association, 7 Milton Street, Northampton NN2 7JG, (01604 711129). Has a series of support groups throughout the country counselling and helping sufferers.

Repetitive strain injury

See RSI, Disabled (*see below*).

Rheumatism

See Arthritis (*page 104*).

RSI (Repetitive Strain Injury)

- Repetitive Strain Injury Association, Chapel House, 152–156 High Street, Yiewsley, West Drayton, Middx UB7 7BE, (01895 431134). A support group which gives information and advice to sufferers from RSI. Has a useful set of leaflets.

Schizophrenia

See page 48.

Seasonal Affective Disorder

* SAD Association, PO Box 989, London SW7 2PZ (01904 422630). A support
  group for sufferers.

Senile dementia

See Alzheimer's disease (*page 286*).

Sickle cell anaemia

* Hackney Sickle Cell Support Group, c/o Sickle Cell and Thalassaemia
  Information Centre, St Leonard's Hospital, Nuttall Street, London N1 5LZ,
  (0171 301 3462). Runs an information service and gives help and support to
  sufferers and their families, and arranges outings for children suffering from
  the disease.
* Sickle Cell Society, 54 Station Road, London NW10 4UA, (0181 961 7795).
  Gives counselling and, if necessary, financial help to sufferers and organizes
  social events and holidays for children.

Smoking problems

* ASH, Action on Smoking and Health, 109 Gloucester Place, London W1H 3PH,
  (0171 935 3519). Acts mainly as a pressure group, fighting for the rights of the
  non-smoker.
* QUIT, National Society of Non-Smokers, Victory House, 170 Tottenham Court
  Road, London W1P 0HA, (0171 388 5775). Runs a quit-smoking line on
  0171 487 3000, giving encouragement and help to people who want to give up
  smoking.

Spastics

See Cerebral palsy (*page 111*).

Spina bifida

* Association for Spina Bifida and Hydrocephalus, 42 Park Road, Peterborough
  PE1 2UQ, (01733 555988). Gives aid and support to people suffering from
  spina bifida and hydrocephalus, aiming to improve their quality of life via a
  nationwide network of helpers.

Spinal injury

- Spinal Injuries Association, Newpoint House, 76 St James's Lane, London N10 3DF, (0181 444 2121). Has a counselling helpline, above, for people with spinal injuries. It also has books on sexuality for spinally injured people.
See also Disabled (*page 127*).

Stammering

- British Stammering Association, 15 Old Ford Road, London E2 9PJ, (0181 983 1003). Help and support for people who stammer. It has a pen- and phone-friend network, a library of publications on the subject and information about specialist therapies.
See also Michael Palin Centre (*page 264*).

States of mind

Cults, problems with
- The British Cult Information Centre, BCM CULTS, London WC1N 3XX, (0181 651 3322). Can give details of cults in this country and advise anyone who is worried about a friend or relative's addiction to a cult.
- Deo Gloria Outreach, Selsdon House, 212–220 Addington Road, South Croydon, Surrey CR2 8LD, (0181 651 6428). Can give help and advice on the subject of cults.
- FAIR, Family Action Information Rescue, BCM Box 3535, PO Box 12, London WC1N 3XX, (01892 538313). Can give help and advice if you are worried about involvement with a cult. It acts as a referral agency and publishes a quarterly newsletter.
- Information Network Focus on Religious Movements, Houghton Street, London WC2A 2AE, (0171 955 7654). Runs an information service on religious cults of all kinds.

Counselling
- British Association of Counselling, 1 Regent Place, Rugby CV21 2PJ, (01788 578328). Has a list of local counsellors all over the country and information on how to select one for your particular problem, also what to expect at the first meeting.

Depression
- Association for Post-natal Illness, 25 Jerdan Place, London SW6 1BE, (0171 386 0868). A support group with helpers all over the country for women who are suffering from post-natal depression.

- Depression Alliance, PO Box 1022, London SE1 7QB, (0171 721 7672). Gives information and support via a network of local groups. Send an SAE for information, it does not run a helpline.
- Depressives Anonymous, 36 Chestnut Avenue, Beverley, North Humberside HU17 9QU, (01482 860619). Gives help and support to people suffering from depression. It has a pen-friend club and can recommend useful reading matter.
- Fellowship of Depressives Anonymous, 36 Chestnut Avenue, Beverley, North Humberside HU17 9QU, (01482 860619). Has a network of self-help groups giving information and support.
- Manic Depression Fellowship, 8–10 High Street, Kingston-upon-Thames, Surrey KT1 1EY, (0181 974 6550). Helps sufferers of manic depression and their relatives via a network of local groups.
- Meet-a-Mum Association, Cornerstone House, 14 Willis Road, Croydon, Surrey CR0 2XX, (0181 665 0357). Mothers counsel and support women suffering from post-natal depression and mothers everywhere who are feeling lonely.

See also
Single Concern Group (*page 204*).
Samaritans (*page 19*).

Phobias
- First Steps to Freedom, 22 Randall Road, Kenilworth, Warwicks CV8 1JY, (01926 851608). Has a helpline, above, and pen-friend service. Offers advice, counselling to sufferers from anxiety, obsessional disorders and phobias.
- Pax, 4 Manorbrook, London SE3 9AW, (0181 318 5026). It has an information and advice service for phobia sufferers and those who have anxiety and panic attacks. Also runs an agoraphobia information service and has numerous tapes and books on sale. It will also put you in touch with a fellow-sufferer.
- Phobics Society, 4 Cheltenham Road, Chorlton-cum-Hardy, Manchester M21 9QN, (0161 881 1937). A support group for sufferers from all kinds of phobias, anxiety and compulsive disorders. Has a range of leaflets and can put you in touch with fellow phobics. It also has telephone helplines.
- Triumph Over Phobia, PO Box 1831, Bath BA1 3YX, (01225 3303533). Send a SAE for self-help information.

Schizophrenia
- National Schizophrenia Fellowship, 28 Castle Street, Kingston-upon-Thames, Surrey KT1 1SS, (0181 547 3937). Supports and helps people suffering from schizophrenia and their families via a network of self-help groups. It also has an advisory and information service.

- SANE, 2nd Floor, 199–205 Old Marylebone Road, London NW1 5QP, (0171 724 6520). An organization that supports and counsels people suffering from schizophrenia and their families. Has a telephone helpline on 0171 724 8000.
- Schizophrenia Association of Great Britain, Bryn Hyfryd, The Crescent, Bangor, Gwynedd LL57 2AG, (01248 354048). This association is conducting research into the causes of schizophrenia and needs volunteer patients and families to help.

General

- Arbours Association, 6 Church Lane, London N8 7BU, (0181 340 7646). Helps people in emotional distress with counselling at its crisis centre. Also has rehabilitation communities.
- Befrienders International, 23 Elysium Gate, 126 New Kings Road, London SW6 4LZ, (0171 731 0101). An umbrella organization which includes groups who counsel people who are suicidal or in emotional despair. Also has a useful contact list.
- Clinical Theology Association, St Mary's House, Church Westcote, Oxford OX7 6SF, (01993 830209). A Christian-based organization that can put you in touch with a local counsellor or personal growth group.
- Ex-Services Mental Welfare Society, Broadway House, The Broadway, London SW19 1RL, (0181 543 6333). Helps ex-servicemen and women who are suffering from mental illness with long-stay homes, treatment centres and assessment. It also handles their claims for disablement pensions etc.
- Guideposts Trust Ltd, Two Rivers, Station Lane, Witney, Oxon OX8 6BH, (01993 772886). Has residential homes and nursing homes, also day-care centres for people who have been living in mental hospitals and are being released into the community.
- International Stress Management Association, The South Bank Unit, South Bank University, LPSS, 103 Borough Road, London SE1 0AA, (0171 928 8989). Can give information and advice on the best ways to tackle stress, particularly if it is work-related.
- Matthew Trust, London SW6 3AG, (0171 736 5976). Helps people who are mentally ill, also those who have been in long-stay mental hospitals.
- Mental After-care Association, 25 Bedford Square, London WC1B 3HW, (0171 436 6194). Offers help to the mentally ill in all sorts of ways via day centres, homes, and general information.
- MIND, National Association for Mental Health, Granta House, 15–19 Broadway, Stratford, London E15 4BQ, (0181 519 2122). Has an information service and many books and pamphlets on the subject of mental health via its London headquarters and many centres throughout the country. It has an information line on 0181 522 1728.

- Philadelphia Association, 4 Marty's Yard, 17 Hampstead High Street, London NW3 1QW, (0171 794 2652). This organization runs two therapeutic homes for the mentally ill.
- Psychiatric Rehabilitation Association, Bayford Mews, Bayford Street, London E8 3SF, (0181 985 3570). Helps and counsels the mentally disturbed and helps them get back into a working life via day centres, courses to give them work experience. It also has some accommodation.
- Sons of Divine Providence, Westminster House, 25 Lower Teddington Road, Hampton Wick, Kingston-upon-Thames, Surrey KT1 4HB, (0181 977 5130). A Catholic-based organization that provides residential care for those who are mentally disabled or elderly.
- Unwind Self-Help by Mail, 'Melrose', 3 Alderlea Close, Gillesgate, Durham DH1 1DS, (0191 3842056). Gives hope and encouragement to people in mental despair via a self-help and contact club which publishes a regular magazine.
- Women's Therapy Centre, 6–9 Manor Gardens, London N7 6LA, (0171 263 6200). Gives sessions of psychotherapy to women, either solo or in groups, at a reasonable price.

See also

Association for Post-natal Illness, Post-natal depression (*page 136*).
Carr-Gomm Society Ltd (*page 204*).
Family Welfare Association (*page 274*).
International Stress Management Association (*page 138*).
Outsiders Club (*page 204*).
Portal Christian Rehabilitation Centres (*page 164*).
Portia Trust (*page 461*).
Psychiatric Rehabilitation Association (*page 138*).
Samaritans (*page 19*).
Servite Houses (*page 313*).
Shape London (*page 130*).
Society of St Vincent de Paul (*page 494*).
Sue Ryder Foundation (*page 110*).
Turning Point (*page 98*).
United Response (*page 346*).

Stroke

See Heart problems/stroke (*page 120*).
See also Action for Dysphasic Adults, Head injury (*page 119*).

Teeth, tooth problems

See Dental Problems (*page 114*).

Tinnitus

- British Tinnitus Association, 14–18 West Bar Green, Sheffield S1 2DA, (01142 796 600). Offers information, help and support for tinnitus sufferers and sets up local support groups.
- The Royal National Institute for Deaf People (*page 114*) has a tinnitus helpline on 0345 090210.

Toxoplasmosis

- Toxoplasmosis Trust, 61–71 Collier Street, London N1 9BE, (0171 713 0663). Helps victims and their families of this disease which can cause epilepsy, deafness and brain damage, but which can be treated by antibiotics when diagnosed in time during pregnancy. It runs an advice service on the subject for expectant mothers and has a helpline on 0171 713 0599.

Tracheotomy

- Tracheotomy Patients Aid Fund, 70 Medway, Crowborough, East Sussex TN6 2DW, (01892 652820). Supports, advises and informs people who have had a tracheotomy and who are living on ventilators. It can supply equipment so that the patient can live at home, rather than in hospital, working via their doctor.

Ulcerative colitis

See Crohn's disease (*page 112*).

Urostomy

- Urostomy Association, 'Buckland', Beaumont Park, Danbury, Essex CM3 4DE, (01245 224294). A support group for people who have had a urinary diversion. It will visit patients at home or in hospital to talk over practical aspects such as marital and social problems, housing and welfare. There are also self-help groups throughout the country.

See also The Charity for Incontinent and Stoma Children, Incontinence (*page 121*).

Vaccine damage

- Association of Parents of Vaccine-damaged Children, 2 Church Street, Shipston-on-Stour, Warwicks CV36 4AP, (01608 661595). The organization to contact if your child has suffered damage after vaccination and you feel you have a claim against the authorities.

Vasectomy

See Birth control (*page 149*).

Vegetarianism/veganism

See Diet (*page 115*).

Vitiligo

- Vitiligo Society, 19 Fitzroy Square, London W1P 5HG, (0171 388 8905). A support group for people suffering from this skin disease, offering advice and information.

See also Cosmetic help (*page 112*).

Weight problems

- Overeaters Anonymous, PO Box 19, Stretford, Manchester M32 9EB, (0161 762 9348). Gives information and support to people with weight problems via group meetings throughout the UK. The above number gives contact telephone numbers for London and the rest of the country.

See also

Anorexia (*page 103*).

Diet (*page 115*).

3

SEX

SEXUAL PROBLEMS WITH YOUR PARTNER

A happy, fulfilling sex life is a bonus that we may take for granted until something goes amiss. It may not be until problems arise, perhaps, that we realize what an important factor it is in our lives.

Many people embark on a relationship with great expectations and enthusiasm only to find themselves or their partners flagging, for various reasons. Few people realize, for instance, the effect that the arrival of children can have on your sex life. First of all, there is the all-pervading fatigue and lack of stimulus involved in looking after a small child all day. Then there are the wretched sleepless nights and the early morning visits from toddlers clambering into your bed. Small wonder that, for many couples at this stage in their lives, sex tends to be one of the last things on their minds. But it is very important to make time to make love, even though it will require planning and effort.

If serious difficulties arise – if one partner is keener than the other, for instance – most problems can be overcome by compromise and by talking freely to each other. If the problem cannot be resolved and you feel awkward discussing the situation with your GP, it might be worth seeking help from a counsellor or psychosexual medical practitioner (*see page 162*). You may well find it easier to talk to a qualified stranger about what is wrong than someone you know.

Orgasm

In order to have an orgasm – whether you are a man or a woman – you must freely 'let go'. This may be exactly the opposite of how you conduct the rest of your life, where you feel you are in control most of the time. Some people find letting go difficult and, as a result, find orgasm difficult to achieve. It can lead to a number of problems. The trouble is that, once you've had a disastrous sexual encounter, it is hard to think of trying again, for fear of failure. The more you love the person concerned, the harder the pressure to please them, and therefore the more difficult the situation becomes.

Premature ejaculation

Most men suffer from this common problem at some time in their lives, often during teenage years. It happens when the man ejaculates either before he enters the woman's vagina, often if his penis is touched, or immediately he puts his penis into the vagina. A man in this situation simply cannot stop his ejaculation, because it is a reflex response. He is not likely to get much pleasure out of it, and he may feel humiliated at his lack of control.

All kinds of factors, from intense erotic feelings to stress, can cause this problem on a temporary basis. If it goes on, the situation can result in distress for both partners and will certainly leave the man's partner frustrated. Sometimes the reason is psychological, sometimes it comes from lack of confidence. Some people find using a thick condom helpful because it dulls the sensitivity of the penis somewhat. Others find that matters are improved if the woman sits on top of the man during intercourse.

If your partner has this problem, try squeezing just below the head of his penis between thumb and forefinger, firmly but gently for a count of 10 when he has the urge to ejaculate. Repeat the process until you are both ready for him to come.

Impotence

Failure to achieve an erection, or to be able to maintain it, is a situation that affects almost all men at some time or other. There may be many reasons, the most common of which are too much drink, stress or fatigue or, perhaps, simply not fancying the woman you are with.

Men are not sex machines, although many films and videos may give that impression. Sometimes you may simply not feel up to making love to someone, or, if you are with someone for the first time you may suffer from performance anxiety, worrying that you are not going to be able to satisfy her. Unfortunately, a woman who is trying to help in this situation can be seen as demanding, which will only make matters worse.

This problem may afflict men of all ages. A mix of performance anxiety and, in some cases, guilt over infidelity to their partner may also result in impotence. Worry that they are unable to 'get it up' makes matters worse, triggering off a vicious cycle which affects performance.

If the problem persists, then it could have a physical cause. It is now believed that some men who have had a vasectomy develop a form of impotence over the years, due to the operation's effect on their testosterone levels. If this is the case then it can be swiftly remedied by taking testosterone in the form of a pill. Conditions such as multiple schlerosis, diabetes, blood pressure problems and prostate trouble can affect you, especially if you are on certain drugs. Sometimes just changing the medication will do the trick. If you have had an operation of any

144 – SEX   HELP!

kind relatively recently, this may cause problems too.

If there is no medical or physical reason why you should suddenly become impotent, then counselling or therapy can sometimes help. In this type of treatment, you and your partner are often discouraged from having penetrative sex for a time while you relearn the pleasures of simply touching and caressing one another instead.

Vaginismus

This distressing condition, which occurs when the muscles of the vagina literally seize up and go into spasm, is far more prevalent than many people realize. Sometimes it is discovered early on when a teenage girl tries to use tampons and fails.

Vaginismus can be a quite involuntary tension in that area of your body, caused by negative thoughts about sex instilled into you as a child – perhaps your parents taught you that sex was 'dirty'. Many women with this problem feel that their vaginas are unattractive or that they are somehow anatomically inadequate. An unfounded fear of venereal disease or AIDS can also be a reason. In a few very rare instances it is necessary to have surgery to remove or stretch the hymen, but often psychotherapy can cure the situation by encouraging the patient to relax and to give up control, to feel and handle herself. It will also assure her that, far from being hostile, her vagina is a warm and welcoming place, and that if it is elastic enough to take the head of a baby during birth, it cannot possibly be too small for a penis.

Frigidity

Like impotence, frigidity can strike anyone at any time of life. Some women have never had an orgasm, others find, after years of happy sex, that they cannot climax any more. It can also, very rarely, have an hormonal cause, and may arise after going on the Pill. I have even heard of one woman who became temporarily frigid after her much-loved father died; she felt that he was watching her from heaven when she and her husband made love.

Urged on by some of the raunchier women's magazines, women now have very high expectations of their sex lives, Sex, at its best, can be such a joyous experience that it is small wonder that the woman who realizes she is missing out feels like someone who is banned from joining an exclusive club.

Making love not only involves thinking of your partner's needs but also letting yourself go, and the inability to do just that can cause problems. You have to learn to trust your partner and to enjoy yourself. Sometimes it is difficult to give up control – and to have an orgasm you have to do just that. Sometimes women who feel they are slow to 'come' will switch off deliberately and fake orgasm instead. If you find yourself suddenly frigid, reassure yourself that nothing is wrong – buy a vibrator from a sex shop or through the post if you are unable to touch yourself and give yourself a climax.

Masturbation

The Victorians believed that masturbation led to all kinds of disastrous conditions including blindness – but, then, until 1861, views on anything other than conventional sex were so narrow that both homosexuality and bestiality were punishable by death.

Almost all children go through a masturbatory stage and find at an early age that handling their genitals gives them pleasure. Most men and women masturbate from time to time. Masturbation also has a place in normal sexual relationships between couples. It may also be the only way to get sexual relief, without involving someone else, in a marriage that is on the rocks, when the partners are not sleeping together.

TEENAGERS AND SEX

The best sex education is assimilated gradually over the years, as a child asks questions of its parents. The worse kind is no education at all, leaving the child to discover the facts of life via information from their friends which may at the best be scant and smutty, and at the worst incorrect. State schools now have to provide their pupils with some sex education. Find out what your child is being taught on this subject and how far the teaching goes.

Try to talk to your child about sex without making a big deal of it – thrusting a book in his hand, then running away is just not good enough, though a simple handbook on puberty may be a useful aid.

Girls are usually better informed about sex than boys – their mothers will have prepared them for the start of periods. Many parents are more concerned about a girl becoming pregnant than they are about their son making someone pregnant. When you are talking to a child about the facts of life, you should build birth control into the conversation as a matter of course. Your child should know:

• How a baby is conceived.
• About birth control.
• About sexually transmitted diseases.
• About AIDS in particular.

You will also want to talk about the dangers of being promiscuous and the problems and responsibilities of unwanted pregnancy.

If you suspect that your child is experimenting with sex, then there is no point in reading him the riot act. You have to accept what is inevitable and teach him to be responsible about it. A girl should be taken to a Family Planning Clinic if she is shy about going to the family GP. In the case of a boy, make sure he knows where and how to get a packet of condoms and has the money to buy them.

Teenage pregnancy

The prospect of teenage pregnancy is a fear that lurks in the back of every mother's mind. There may be many reasons why your daughter becomes pregnant. Some girls think that they will be lucky and refuse to believe it could happen to them. Many more think it is impossible the first time. Or, as I once heard, because they 'did it standing up with their clothes on'. Or they may have been using the withdrawal method (*see page 148*). Then there is yet another group who actually want to become pregnant – so that they can leave school or a job they hate. A girl may also get herself pregnant deliberately in the hope that the father will marry her – an idea not confined to teenagers, of course. Some girls become pregnant because they want someone all of their own to love.

BIRTH CONTROL

These are the basic methods of birth control.

The contraceptive pill

The most widely used form of birth control, the pill is prescribed free of charge on the NHS. There are three main types of pill – the combined pill and the triphasic pill are both taken for 21 days out of 28 days, while the progestogen-only (or mini pill) is taken continuously. This mini, low-dose pill is slightly less effective but still very safe (although some brands have been withdrawn because of other problems). It is the only kind that can be taken if you are breast-feeding.

For safety reasons women over the age of 35, especially if they smoke, are now advised to discontinue the pill. Your doctor may decide not to prescribe it if you have a history of thrombosis or migraine, or in some cases if you smoke heavily.

The pill may not be reliable if you take it 12 hours late. In the case of the low-dose pill, you should use other methods if you take it more than 3 hours late. With either pill, if you have a severe stomach upset or bad diarrhoea, you may 'lose' your dose and you should take other precautions for the time being. Taking the pill can cause weight gain, headaches, loss of sexual desire and depression.

Progestogen implant

An implant is a small soft tube that is inserted under the skin of your inner upper arm and stays put for up to five years. It releases a small steady amount of progestogen into your blood stream. The implant has to be put in under a local anaesthetic and there may be some bruising or swelling for a day or two afterwards. You can also feel it under your skin. The advantage of the implant is that you do not have to remember to take the pill, but it can cause irregular periods at first, with occasional breakthrough bleeding between them.

Progestogen injection

It is possible to have an injection of progestogen which will stop ovulation for two or three months. It often causes your periods to become irregular or stop altogether, and your fertility will take up to a year to return to normal once you stop. Weight gain is sometimes a side-effect of this method of birth control.

The condom

The condom (or sheath) is worn by the man over his penis so that his sperm cannot enter his partner. Easily available and if properly worn, can be very reliable but not as safe as the pill. Many men dislike using condoms because they say it lessens the sensation in their penis. Widely available without prescription over the counter, often in machines in pub and public lavatories, look for condoms that have the BSI Kitemark on the packet and check on their expiry date. A condom is the best method of contraception to use for casual encounters since it helps protect against AIDS and other sexually transmitted diseases.

There is also a female condom available which has about the same success rate as the more common male version. It is a soft polyurethene sheath that is pushed into the vagina to line it and protect the area just outside. Like the male condom, it helps prevent you from catching sexually transmitted diseases, but it is vital that the penis goes inside the condom, and not between the condom and the wall of the vagina. Many condoms, both male and female versions, come spermicidally lubricated.

The cap and the diaphragm

The diaphragm is a flexible rubber dome that you cover with spermicidal gel and insert into your vagina so that it covers the cervix, before having sex. It must be left in place for at least 6 hours afterwards, and it needs to be specially fitted in the first instance by a professional and checked every 12 months or so, particularly if you gain or lose a lot of weight, have a baby, a miscarriage or an abortion. The cap, which is smaller, fits over the cervix and is held in place by suction. Some women find it difficult to put in place, and retiring to the bathroom to fit it may spoil the spontaneity of a sexual encounter. It provides some but very little protection against AIDS and other similar diseases. The cap, the diaphragm and the condom can all be made more effective if used with spermicidal gels, foams or pessaries. The latter, used on their own, however, are only 25 per cent effective.

The coil or IUD

Less popular than it used to be, this plastic device is inserted into the uterus through the cervix by a doctor. Threads are attached to the device and hang down into the vagina as an indication that the device is still in place. An IUD is usually used by a woman who has already had at least one child. It stays in place until the doctor decides it needs to be replaced, usually every three to five years. It is almost, but not quite as reliable as the pill. Newer versions have a progestogen hormone which prevents the lining of the womb from thickening and therefore reduces heavy periods and stomach cramps which sometimes occur with the older variety.

The coil is usually prescribed for women who have completed their family. If you are younger, there is an increased risk of pelvic infection which can lead to infertility. Some doctors believe that it encourages the likelihood of an ectopic pregnancy – when a foetus develops in a fallopian tube – and it is a risk to consider. Some women have heavier and more painful periods while using the coil. It is, however, almost as safe and reliable as the pill.

The morning-after pill

This method of contraception is usually only prescribed in an emergency and is not very reliable – the failure rate could be up to one in three. You take a tablet, known as PC4, for up to four days after intercourse as prescribed by your doctor. The drug, a cocktail of hormones, tricks the body into believing it is not pregnant, making the womb reject any fertilized egg.

The morning-after pill cannot be taken on a regular basis, since it is a fairly drastic treatment and it tends to cause nausea and vomiting. It must also be taken very soon after intercourse. This causes problems since many slip-ups of this kind occur at weekend parties and you may have to wait until Monday to get to the doctor's surgery. After taking this pill your proper period may arrive on time, a little early or a little late. You should be given a follow-up appointment, which you should keep, especially if your next period is late or unusually light. If you have any pain or unusual bleeding, see the doctor at once.

Withdrawal (coitus interruptus)

Withdrawal – where the man withdraws his penis from the vagina just before he ejaculates – is probably the oldest form of contraception of all. It is very unsafe because sperm may leak into the vagina before he actually comes; however, many couples use it, usually because their religion bans them from using any other method.

The natural method

The natural method is the only one allowed officially by the Roman Catholic Church, but it is being used increasingly by people with no religious denomination. To be successful it involves a combination of calendar, temperature and mucus inspection methods combined with an awareness of ovulation pains and cervical palpation. The Natural Family Planning Service (*see page 162*) says that if you are properly trained in what is known as the Simto-thermal method, it can be 98 per cent effective, but you must be taught how to use it first.

Female sterilization

Up to half of all couples over the age of 40 now choose sterilization as their contraceptive method, according to the Family Planning Association. It is now more popular than the pill with that age group. Sterilization is the ultimate form of birth control for women, but you should be absolutely sure that you never want to become pregnant again before taking this step because it is irreversible. There have been stories of women wanting to conceive again after a marriage break-up, or, more tragically, after the loss of children. The operation is performed by sealing off or cutting the fallopian tubes under an anaesthetic. You may have to stay overnight in hospital and you will need a few days to recuperate.

Male sterilization

Vasectomy or male sterilization is the most final and extreme kind of birth control for men when they and their partners decide they do not want any more children. The tubes that carry the sperm are cut, so that when the man ejaculates there are none present in his semen. You have to use contraception for a month or so after a vasectomy until you are given the all-clear (two consecutive negative sperm tests). There may be some bruising after the operation and a few days' rest is needed. But like female sterilization, you must be very certain that this is the option for you, since it is reversible only in a few cases.

ABORTION

The Roman Catholic Church preaches the clear doctrine that abortion is a sin, while the Anglican Church and the Jewish faith are ambivalent on the subject.

Sikhs and some Hindus are opposed to abortion, as are Buddhists and Muslims. Whatever your personal views on abortion, everyone must agree that the current situation, where it is possible to have an abortion legally, is a vast improvement on the days before the 1967 Act, when almost the same number of women who now have abortions, had them illegally, often dying dreadful deaths from severe bleeding or blood poisoning.

No one in this country can have an abortion simply on demand. Nobody can force you to have an abortion, either. Ordinarily, your abortion has to be recommended by your doctor and another doctor – usually a gynaecologist or, less frequently, a psychiatrist. A number of agencies – the British Pregnancy Advisory Service is one good example – will help you through the legal and medical hurdles (*see page 161*). If your doctor has a strongly held belief that abortion is wrong – he may be a practising Catholic – he may try to dissuade you, and may not recommend you to the second doctor. If he cannot dissuade you, you would have to go to another doctor – this is where one or other of the support groups can help (*see page 161*).

An abortion is defined as the termination of a pregnancy up to the 24th week, although abortions are rarely done as late as this. A miscarriage is actually known as an abortion in medical circles, but in this case it is called a spontaneous abortion. When it is done by a doctor it is called a therapeutic abortion.

Experiments with a new French form of pill featuring the drug Mifepristone have been going on for some time. This pill virtually causes a home abortion; rather than preventing pregnancy, like the contraceptive pill, it dislodges the fertilized egg after it has been implanted in the womb. If it proves to be safe and is put on the market it could eliminate the need for many surgical abortions.

Do I qualify?

A woman can decide to have her pregnancy terminated whether or not the father of the child agrees. He has no legal rights. In England, Wales and Scotland, but not in Northern Ireland, you can be given an abortion on the following grounds.

Your life is at risk if the pregnancy goes ahead

This could mean that you have heart or blood-pressure problems, disease of the liver or kidneys, a life-threatening illness such as cancer or TB. (However, many women with cancer have courageously decided to go ahead and have their babies even though it could endanger their lives.) The main concerns are whether the pregnancy would accelerate the disease or lead to a situation where doctors could not continue treating you for your condition – giving chemotherapy or radiotherapy for instance.

*The pregnancy (and resulting child) might injure your mental or physical health, or
that of any existing children*

In general, doctors must decide whether having the child would cause injury to
your mental or physical health. Quite apart from severe mental disorders or
mental handicaps, this definition includes mental illness, such as severe
depression or distress which may arise because of the situation. This reason is
most frequently cited.

This might include a young mother who simply could not cope with the arrival
of another child at this stage, in which case the health of existing children might
also suffer. It might include someone who has no partner, no job and is homeless.
This rule is the one that applies to victims of incest or rape.

*If the child was born, he or she would suffer from some physical or mental
abnormality*

This is one of the most distressing and sad reasons for seeking abortion and
would apply to anyone who was carrying a foetus suffering from a condition such
as spina bifida or Down's syndrome. It also applies if you are HIV positive or have
AIDS, and do not want to take the risk of passing the virus on to your child.

Chorionic villus sampling, done in the early stages of pregnancy, shows if there
is the likelihood of a chromosome defect in the foetus which is likely to result in
an hereditary disease. Amniocentesis tests, which also pick up defects, are done
later, usually at 16 weeks, and mainly on older mothers. If a defect is found,
having an abortion at this late stage in the pregnancy can be particularly
harrowing. Unfortunately, once you are over the age of 35, your risk of having a
deformed or handicapped baby increases somewhat.

You and your partner have to make up your minds whether or not it is fair to
bring a handicapped child into the world, and also whether you feel your
relationship and that with any other children can take the strain of bringing up the
child. It is a terrible decision to have to make, and perhaps unbiased counselling
would be of some help (*see page 162*).

What happens?

Most abortions are done before the end of the 12th week, when you are about
three months pregnant. An abortion during the first trimester of the pregnancy
takes less than ten minutes, it is usually done under a general anaesthetic and no
overnight stay in hospital is necessary unless complications arise. There are two
methods of abortion widely used during this period: the first is a D & C (dilatation
and curettage, a common operation when the cervix is dilated and the uterus
scraped); the second is suction. If anything is left in the womb after suction then it
is removed by scraping or curettage with a special scalpel. A small suction device
on the end of a small tube is inserted through the vagina, into the womb where it

sucks out the contents including the foetus and placenta. The operation is very similar to a D & C.

After the 13th week, when it is difficult to stretch the cervix artificially without damaging it, different procedures are used. You may be given prostaglandin, a hormone that is produced naturally by the body at the end of a full-term pregnancy and stimulates labour. To facilitate an abortion, prostiglandin is administered either as a vaginal gel or an infusion into the womb, which causes the uterus to contract, inducing labour and the delivery of the foetus.

If you are having an abortion because of foetal abnormality, the doctor will usually inject an irritant into the sac around the foetus which will then cause you to give birth.

Having an abortion this way, like having a baby, takes several hours. The foetus is almost always born dead but may show some signs of life which do not continue for long – a distressing situation, however, for both the mother and the nursing staff.

Post-abortion blues

Even if you are relieved to no longer be pregnant, it is quite natural to have feelings of regret, depression and even guilt. Some of these feelings will be caused by hormonal fluctuations as your body rapidly tries to assimilate the fact that you are no longer pregnant. If you have had a late abortion, have felt the baby move or perhaps even started to produce milk, you are more likely to feel depressed. It is vital to get some counselling to help you through this painful time (*see page 162*).

SEXUALITY

The human animal is capable of a wide range of sexual practices and experiences, some of which are accepted without comment; others may, in some societies, cause surprise and even censure.

Homosexuality

Nobody knows what makes one person homosexual and another one not. Despite a lot of high-minded theories, it has not yet been proved that it is caused by your genes, by your hormones or by having a parent you hated. It is highly unlikely, too, that you can be seduced into become gay by another person.

During the teenage years a child may become confused or upset by what appear to be homosexual feelings. Most of us go through a stage, usually during adolescence, when we get a 'crush' on someone of the same sex. And we should all realize that we are quite capable of loving someone of the same sex and delighting in that person's company, even being attracted to him or her. It is when this spills over into strong, undeniable sexual feelings, coupled, perhaps, with an inability to relate to those of the opposite sex, that we may come to wonder about our sexuality. Sometimes at this stage, we may be persuaded to 'come out', when in fact, we are still very uncertain about our sexuality. This ambivalence is a very natural phase in our teenage years. Most of us, if we are honest, would admit to having had these sorts of feelings during those years.

Remember that there are as many different kinds of gay people as there are heterosexuals. There are couples who lead completely ordinary, even boring, lives and remain faithful to each other just as in a marriage, and there are others who haunt the gay scene of contact bars and clubs. There are gays who are flamboyant about their sexuality and flaunt it; equally there are many gay people who are completely the opposite and no one would know that they are homosexual.

One day, perhaps, people will no longer be labelled according to their sexual orientation and we will all just get on with our lives, but at the moment being gay, despite the name, can be anything but a joyous experience.

Coming out

A child who grows up to be homosexual often realizes at an early age that he or she is 'different' in some way. If the child feels that his or her parents won't understand or sympathize with the difference, the child may feel the need to lead a double existence. There may come a time in your life, however, when you feel that you no longer want to live a lie and you want to live openly. In short you want to come out. This takes a lot of courage.

- Take it gently, test the water first, advises Parents' Friend, a support group for gays and their families (see page 164). Note how your parents or friends react to gay issues on TV, radio or in the papers. Without being too pointed, just mention these in passing and see how they react. If the result is not encouraging, then perhaps the time is not quite right.
- Talk it over with someone sympathetic first, perhaps another gay person who has been through the same experience. Rehearse how you are going to break the news and to whom.
- If you are planning to let it be known generally that you are gay, the first people you should tell are your family. If they hear about it second-hand, it could cause them immense bewilderment and shock. You must give them time to get used to the idea; remember you have had longer to think it over than they have.
- Find one friend or relation you can trust and tell that person first, then discuss how and when you can 'come out' to your parents. Perhaps that person would agree to be nearby at the time.
- Never let the news slip out in the middle of a family row, tell them quietly, marshal your facts. Tell them you love them and no longer wish to live a lie.

- If there are people you do not want told the news, tell your family this as well.
- Do not be surprised if your family tries to sweep the whole thing under the carpet and refuses to face the facts, especially if you do not have, or live with, a regular partner,
- If you do have a partner whom they haven't met, wait a while before introducing them.
- Gather round a support group of friends, gay or otherwise, to bolster you up if you get a bad response from other people you tell. Have someone to turn to if things go wrong. Remember, there are lesbian, gay and bisexual support groups throughout the country (*see page 163*).
- Even if your family or friends say that they want to have nothing to do with you, nothing lasts for ever, and they will almost certainly come round in the end. If you do lose official contact, try to keep in touch via a family friend.

If your child tells you he or she is gay
- Remember that this is probably the most difficult thing your child has had to do in his entire life and that it has taken him a great deal of courage to face you.
- Be aware that even if your child seems calm or even defiant, that underneath he is probably feeling very anxious about how you will react to the news.
- Reassure your child that you still love him. He may worry that you will throw him out of the house and refuse to see him any more.
- Do not waste time beating your head against the wall, asking where you went wrong. It is not your fault.
- Do not think that your child will grow out of it if he has taken the step of telling you. At this point you can be sure that he has thought about it a great deal.
- Remember that you, too, now have to 'come out' and let friends and relatives know about the situation. Think it over carefully and discuss it with your child. Then, when you break the news, do it in a positive manner. People will take their cue from you on how to react to the news.
- If your child has a partner, then try to be as open and friendly to them as you can – it is the same situation, after all, as meeting a prospective son- or daughter-in-law.
- Remember that if your child is loved by someone, even if that person is of the same sex, that is a great bonus.
- Contact a support group (*see page 163*) which will put you in touch with other parents who have been through the same situation.

Lesbian and gay parents
If, after a divorce, you live with a lesbian or gay partner, certain rules apply as far as your children from your previous marriage are concerned.

- Provided you can prove that you are giving the child a stable home, your sexuality should not affect the court's decision. However, it is a good idea to consult a solicitor about the matter. Gay and Lesbian support groups (*see page* 163) can help you.
- If you want your gay partner to take on legal responsibility for your children in the case of your death, you have to get the court to make out a Residence Order in your joint names. The same applies if you, as a lesbian couple, have a child by artificial insemination. See a solicitor about this.
- Gay or lesbian couples are unable to adopt a child as a pair. One of them must apply to adopt as a single person.

Transvestism

A transvestite, or cross-dresser, is someone who has a powerful desire to wear the clothing of the opposite sex. A transvestite is not necessarily gay – in fact, many transvestites are heterosexual men, some of whom like to wear women's underwear under their suits. Not all of them do this for sexual reasons. Their wives may live with them for years without discovering their secret. A full cross-dresser may wear a wig, make-up and women's clothes at weekends or for an hour or so each day. Strangely enough, it does not usually affect the person's sex life, but he needs an understanding partner who does not feel threatened by the tranvestite's need to get in touch with his feminine side. Transvestites do not usually want to alter their gender; they dress this way, from time to time, in order to get the best out of both worlds, male and female.

Transsexualism

A transsexual is someone who is convinced that he (or she) is trapped in the wrong body and that he or she should be the opposite sex. There are thought to be about 25,000 transsexuals in this country, and the phrase 'gender dysphoric disorder' is sometimes used to describe their plight. Many live as heterosexuals, though often in miserable relationships, and many marry and have families.

The person affected may have come to this conclusion at an early age, feeling wrong even as a small boy or girl (it is not unknown for this to happen as young as four or five years old). There are roughly the same number of men and women in this country who have this problem. At puberty, a girl who feels she should be a boy will have a particularly distressing time as she grows breasts she does not want and begins her periods. People in this situation feel distress and discomfort trapped inside the wrong body.

Realizing that you are transsexual can be a lonely experience. If you decide to change your sex you can face rejection from your parents, and, if you are married, rejection from your family. The partner of a man who changes into a woman can face the bizarre situation of being labelled a lesbian, if she continues to live with him after his gender change. Many who decide to have treatment for this problem move away from their homes to another part of the country where they can be accepted as the opposite sex.

Transsexuals say that the law is a quarter of a century behind medical thinking. At the moment, your birth certificate cannot be altered if you change your sex, although in Scotland, it is possible to have a change of name attached to it. You cannot marry in your new role, or have a new passport or adopt children under your new name.

What to do if you need a sex change

This process is now more correctly called 'gender reassignment' and is treated by a mix of hormone treatment and surgery. First see your GP, who should refer you to a Gender Identity Clinic or, possibly, to a psychiatrist who is an expert in gender identity disorders. Be warned: NHS funds for this are very low and waiting lists are long; you may, in any case, have to pay for some of the cosmetic treatments yourself.

If your GP has no knowledge or information on treatments available, then contact a support group such as Gender Identity Consultancy Services (*see page 163*) which can put you in touch with the appropriate professionals, either in the NHS or privately. Going through a gender change is a long and often painful business and needs a great deal of courage, not least of all to face people who have always thought of you in terms of the opposite sex.

If deemed suitable, you will be given hormone treatment in the first instance, and you will be seen regularly by a psychiatrist to help you as you go through your gender change. At this stage a man becoming a woman will need to have electrolysis to remove facial, and possibly chest, hair. Transsexuals have to wait for a minimum of one year, living and working in their new gender role before surgery can be considered – on the NHS there is usually at least a two-year wait for what is called gender confirmation surgery, which transsexuals would say is done to correct a physical handicap not a psychiatric illness. The patient has to get at least two positive psychiatric opinions before any surgery can take place. You may have your testes removed at this stage (orchidectomy) to reduce testosterone levels in your body. A woman becoming a man will probably have a mastectomy and a hysterectomy.

Although there is an operation available to construct a penis it is still very much in the experimental stages, and many women becoming men decide not to have it done. If the person is secure in this new role as a man, he may feel that he need not go through this particular ordeal. A man turning into a woman can be operated on by a urological surgeon who will remove the testes (if this has not already been done), and the penis, shorting and re-positioning the urethra and creating a vagina. On the cosmetic side, the patient may decide to have her breasts enlarged.

SEXUAL DEVIATIONS

Most of us joke at some time or other about kinky sex. But what may start off as fun, a bit of S & M, for instance, can end in trouble. Sexual deviation is a very woolly subject and, as such, is hard to define. Deviant activity could be classified as sexual activity which causes pain or suffering to another person, perhaps because that person is under age or has not given consent, or it could be activity which is against the law.

Is it an illness?

How would you feel if your partner became obsessed with a particular sexual practice that distressed, offended or even hurt you? Anything that happens between two consenting adults is not usually thought of as a problem. It has to be said, however, that people who claim that 'straight' sex is boring and are constantly searching for new diversions may well have some sort of deep-rooted problem in their sex lives.

If your partner becomes more obsessed by the activity than by you, then alarm signals should be raised – a compulsive disorder may be on the way.

A deviation that does not hurt either the deviant or anyone else is harmless enough. If you have to wear rubber in order to become aroused, the rest of us might find it amusing, but it is not doing any harm. Some deviations, however, can cause pain and suffering, and it is then that help is needed. And of course there are those sexual practices which are illegal – having sex in a public place is an example.

When you should get help

- If you become concerned about your own or your partner's behaviour.
- If the activity is a danger to anyone.
- If it is against the law – under the age of 16 a heterosexual person is considered to be incapable of giving consent – under 18 in the case of gays.

Ask yourself if you are fully aware, or if your partner is fully aware of what you want to do. Is your partner an equal, of a similar age and intellect? Do you feel you are acting responsibly towards yourself and your partner?

The law: can I be prosecuted?

To be prosecuted for committing a sexual offence at least one of these things must apply.

- The sexual act took place without the consent of the other person – sexual assault or rape.
- The act was with someone under the age of consent (*see page 157*).
- It is a prohibited act: incest, zoophilia (bestiality), buggery with a female or sex with a 'mentally defective person'.
- It is a homosexual act between two men in public (*see* **Legal**, *page 458*).
- It is a homosexual act by a man who is himself under the age of consent.

Treatment

There are various ways in which these problems can be treated.

Counselling
This is usually the first step. Counselling helps people to come to terms with their own sexuality and to delve into their pasts to see what may have caused the problem. Counselling is available on the National Health Service.

Behavioural therapy
This varies according to the problem and is aimed at making people change their behaviour patterns. It might be used in the case of an exhibitionist or a fetishist. If the behaviour is particularly worrying or dangerous then aversion therapy might be used – pairing the event with an electric shock, for instance.

Drug treatment
Sometimes drugs are prescribed to lower the sex drive. On other occasions tranquillizers are used.

Paraphilia

This word, which comes from the Greek words meaning 'altered love', is a term used by medics to describe certain sexual activities or fantasies. Paraphiliacs can be gay, heterosexual or bisexual. Some practices are considered illegal (*see above*), others are not. The symptoms of paraphilia are regular sexually arousing fantasies, sexual urges or behaviours involving

- Non-human objects (shoes in foot fetishism, for example).
- Suffering or humiliation of oneself or one's partner.
- Sex with children or other non-consenting persons, which is in fact rape.

Some people find themselves unable to be aroused without at least thinking of one or the other of the situations above.

Fetishism comes in three varieties.

* That concerned with parts of the body. You can have a fetish over women's (or men's) feet, hair or legs.
* That concerned with clothing – underwear, gloves or shoes.
* That concerned with the feel of something, such as rubber, leather or fur.

Sado-masochism, also known as S & M, can be experienced in two different ways.

* Sadism is when you get sexual pleasure from hurting or dominating someone by spanking or whipping or, more dangerously, branding them or administering electric shocks.
* Masochism is the flip side of sadism, when you yourself get pleasure from being whipped or hurt by someone else. It also covers the more dangerous practice known as auto-erotic asphyxia.

Auto-erotic asphyxia

Until the bizarre and lonely death of an MP which hit the headlines, most of us had never heard of auto-erotic asphyxia. In fact more than 200 men a year die in this country attempting to reach the ultimate erotic experience, although sometimes it is mistaken for suicide.

A sexual asphysic does not normally get involved with fetishes and other sex games, he – and almost all of them are men – is likely to be a respectable middle-class, often middle-aged pillar of society; part of the excitement for him is that it is done in secret. Sexual asphysics get their thrills from depriving themselves of oxygen, usually to the first stages of strangulation, sometimes by using a plastic bag over the face, to become sexually aroused. They may also be nude, or dressed in women's clothes at the time, and have hard-core pornographic magazines on hand. Death occurs when, in an effort to have the ultimate orgasm, they go too far and are unable to prevent themselves from being strangled or suffocated.

SEX WITHOUT CONSENT

Some people can only get sexual satisfaction out of doing something without the consent of the victim. The commonest form is **rape** or **sexual assault** (*see* **Emergencies,** *page 7*). The predator attacks the victim and only gets satisfaction if it causes terror and pain.

Child abuse or paedophilia is another form of sexual assault. In this case the deviant can only get aroused by molesting children who are just entering the age of puberty or even younger. Paedophiles can be very cunning and infiltrate a family without anyone noticing – offering to babysit, for instance, or to take the child out for the day.

The paedophile plans very carefully, seeking out a sensitive, emotionally vulnerable child, perhaps one who lacks self-confidence and needs extra attention. It may be a child from a family without a father, or where the mother is busy working. He will watch and wait, calculating how to get time alone with the child, afterwards telling the child concerned that 'it's our secret' and assure the child that no one will believe the child if he did say anything. Children who are literally allowed to run wild, in the street, around the estate, are also at risk from paedophiles. In this case the paedophile will target them and literally take a child off the street with offers of sweets or toys.

If your child shows a sudden change of behaviour towards a family friend or relative, starts wetting the bed again and seems distressed, then there is always the possibility that sexual abuse has taken place. Be wary.

Child abuse is against the law and can be punishable under 'gross indecency with a child or indecent assault'. Sex between two underage children is also illegal. Sex with an underage girl is punishable under the heading of 'illegal sexual intercourse'. (*See also* **Children**, *page 254.*)

Indecent exposure and exhibitionism is when the deviant gets pleasure from shocking strangers by exposing himself (or, very rarely, herself) to them. Sometimes the exhibitionist enjoys doing this to children, and has been known to lurk in recreation grounds and on the edge of school playgrounds. This can be prosecuted as 'indecent exposure'.

Necropilia is a sexual attraction to corpses, often featured in horror films but something that does occur in real life. This act of having sex with a corpse or committing a sex act while with it is not illegal in itself. But the deviant could be prosecuted for assaulting the body or trespass if he intruded into an area where the body was kept.

Voyeurism or the Peeping Tom syndrome is another way some people get satisfaction. This involves either secretly watching two people having sex or looking at their sexual organs. The thrill is as much in the risk of discovery as in what they actually see. Anyone arrested for this would be prosecuted for a 'breach of the peace' or possibly 'being a public nuisance'.

Bestiality, now called *Zoophilia*, involves sexually assaulting animals, while **infantilism** is when the deviant wants to be treated as an infant – sometimes to the extent of dressing in baby-like clothes.

Where do I go for help?
There are a number of organizations that treat deviationists and others that will support them (*see page 162*).

SEX: HELP DIRECTORY

Abortion, anti-abortion, birth control pressure groups

- Abortion Law Reform Association, 27–35 Mortimer Street, London W1N 7RJ, (0171 637 7264). Works to promote a woman's right to choose whether or not to continue with her pregnancy.
- Birth Control Campaign, 16 Mortimer Street, London W1N 7RD, (0171 580 9360). Exists to promote the provision of birth control services, including sterilization and abortion within the NHS.
- Birth Control Trust, 16 Mortimer Street, London W1N 7RJ, (0171 580 9360). Campaigns for more research on contraception, sterilization and abortion and more education and information on contraception.
- National Abortion Campaign, The Print House, 18 Ashwin Street, London E8 3DL, (0171 923 4976). Champions the right of women to make their own decisions about abortion and campaigns for adequate abortion facilities on the NHS.
- Newlife, Kay House, 51 Stonebridge Drive, Frome, Somerset BA11 2TW, (01373 451632). Opponents of abortion, concerned with the human rights of born and unborn children.
- Pro-Choice Alliance, 27–35 Mortimer Street, London W1N 7RJ, (0171 636 4619). Campaigns for the easing of the abortion laws and for free abortion services.
- Society for the Protection of Unborn Children, 7 Tufton Street, London SW1P 3QN, (0171 222 5845). Campaigns for the repeal of the Abortion Act.

Birth control, abortion

NB The word 'abortion' is the official medical term for losing a foetus of less than six months. This covers accidental miscarriage as well as therapeutic abortion.

- British Pregnancy Advisory Service, Austy Manor, Wootton Wawen, Solihull, West Midlands B95 6BX, (01564 793225). Helps with birth control and with abortion. It has clinics and nursing homes throughout the country.
- Brook Advisory Centres, Head Office, 165 Grays Inn Road, London WC1X 8UD, (0171 713 9000). Gives confidential help and advice on contraception, pregnancy testing and sexual problems. There are branches throughout the country – look in your local Phone Book. It also has an information line on 0171 617 8000, providing recorded advice on a wide number of topics.

- Family Planning Association, 27–35 Mortimer Street, London W1N 7RJ, (0171 636 7866). The FPA information service will tell you which family planning aids, such as the pill and condoms, are available free under the NHS.
- LIFE, Save the Unborn Child, LIFE House, 1a Newbold Terrace, Leamington Spa, Warwickshire CV32 4EA, (01926 421587). Will help if you want to avoid having an abortion or if you are pregnant and need somewhere to stay. It has a helpline on 01926 311511. This organization, as its name suggests, campaigns against abortion.
- Natural Family Planning Service, 1 Blythe Mews, Blythe Road, London W14 0NW, (0171 371 1341). Provides advice on family planning without the use of contraceptives. It also gives counselling and assistance with infertility, non-consummation and psychosexual problems.
- Pregnancy Advisory Service, 11–13 Charlotte Street, London W1P 1HD, (0171 637 8962). Pregnancy testing, emergency contraception, counselling and help with unwanted pregnancies. It also has a full abortion service.

See also

National Association of Natural Family Planning Teachers (*see page 217*).

Problems with your partner

- Association to Aid the Sexual and Personal Relationships of People with a Disability, 286 Camden Road, London N7 0BJ, (0171 607 8851). Counsels and helps couples who have personal or sexual problems due to disability. It also issues helpful leaflets on the subject.
- The British Association for Sexual and Marital Therapy, PO Box 62, Sheffield S10 3TS. Has a comprehensive list of NHS and private sex therapists. Send an SAE for its list.
- Institute for Sex Education and Research, 40 School Road, Moseley, Birmingham B13 9SN, (0121 449 0892). A private clinic run by Dr Martin Cole. Write to him with a brief outline of your problem to make an appointment. Fees are negotiable.
- Institute of Psychosexual Medicine, 11 Chandos Street, Off Cavendish Square, London W1M 9DE, (0171 580 0631). It has a list of NHS and private doctors trained in psychosexual counselling. Send an SAE for its list.
- The London Institute of Sexuality, 10 Warwick Road, Earls Court, London SW5, (0171 373 0901). Has lists of sex therapists, mainly in the London area.
- The Maudesley NHS Trust, Denmark Hill, London SE5 8AZ, (0171 703 6333). This specialist hospital has a large psychosexual clinic which deals mainly with people who want to have a normal sexual relationship but are unable to do so through physical or psychological difficulties. You can go to the clinic direct, or be referred to it by your GP.

- Resolve: Vaginismus Support Group, PO Box 820, London NW10 3AW, (Fax 0181 883 6571). Advises and counsels women suffering from this condition and puts them in touch with others who have the same problem.
- Sexual Dysfunction Clinic, Department of Psychological Medicine, Western General Hospital, Crewe Road, Edinburgh, (0131 537 1000). An NHS clinic which occasionally takes people without a referral from their GP.

See also Relate (*page 205*).

Sexuality

'Acceptance' Helpline and Support Group for Parents of Lesbians and Gay Men, 64 Holmside Avenue, Halfway Houses, Sheerness, Kent ME12 3EY, (01795 661463). Helps the parents of gay people to come to terms with the fact that their children are homosexual. It runs a telephone helpline from 7pm–9pm, Tuesday to Friday.

- Albany Trust, The Sunra Centre, 26 Balham Hill, London SW12 9EB, (0181 675 6669). Has a personal counselling service for people who are unsure of their sexual identity or are having problems with a partner over sexual needs. Fees are negotiable, depending on what you can afford to pay.
- Beaumont Society, BM Box 3084, London WC1N 3XX. A contact and self-help group for transsexuals and transvestites. It has a telephone information line on 015582 412220.
- Gender Identity Consultancy Services, BM Box 7624, London WC1N 3XX, (01323 641100). Offers help and counselling to transsexuals via a number of groups and puts them in touch with others in the same situation.
- Identity Counselling Service, Beauchamp Lodge, 2 Warwick Crescent, London W2 6NE, (0171 289 6175). Helps and advises gays, lesbians and bisexuals who are having difficulty 'coming out'.
- Jewish Lesbian and Gay Helpline, BM Jewish Helpline, London WC1N 3XX, (0171 706 3123). Gives counselling, support and advice over the phone to Jewish gays and lesbians. It will also put you in touch with other organizations, Jewish or otherwise, which will give sympathetic help.
- Kenric, BM Kenric, London WC1N 3XX. An organization for lesbians which organizes all kinds of social and sporting activities. Write to the above address for details. It also has phone-a-friend and pen-friend schemes.
- Lesbian and Gay Christian Movement, Oxford House, Derbyshire Street, Bethnal Green, London E2 6HG, (0171 739 1249). A Christian organization which runs a network of groups all over the country and has counselling and pen-friend services. It has a helpline on 0171 739 8134.
- Lesbian and Gay Youth Movement, MN/GYM, London WC1N 3XX, (0181 317 9690). Helps young gays and lesbians with housing, legal and health

problems. It also has a pen-friend scheme and runs social events from time to
time.

- Lesbian Youth Support Information Service, PO Box 8, Todmorden, Lancs
  OL14 5TZ, (01706 817235). Helps and supports young lesbians with counselling
  and information. It also has a helpline on the above number.
- London Bisexual Group, PO Box 3325, London N1 EQ, (0181 569 7500). A
  support group for bisexual people. Apart from its helpline, above, it also
  advises and counsels by phone or letter, and can put people in touch with
  groups in other parts of the country.
- London Lesbian and Gay Switchboard, BM Switchboard, London WC1N 3XX,
  (0171 837 7324). A round-the-clock helpline for lesbians and gays. However, it
  is frequently engaged, and you will have to be persistent to get through.
- London Lesbian Line, Box BM 1514, London WC1N 3XX, (0171 251 6911). A
  London-based helpline for lesbians giving advice and information, mainly on
  where to find local groups and what social events are on offer.
- Parents' Friend, c/o VA Leeds, Stringer House, 34 Lupton Street, Hunslet,
  Leeds LS10 2QW, (0113 2674627). Supports and counsels parents, relatives and
  friends of children who have come out. It has a helpline on the number above
  and numerous useful publications.
- Rose's Club, Roundel Street, Staniforth Road, Sheffield S9 3LE,
  (0114 261 9444). Help, support and social club for transvestites and their
  partners.

See also Lesbian and Gay Bereavement Project (**Bereavement,** *page 202*).

Sexual abuse, violence

- London Rape Crisis Centre, PO Box 69, London WC1X 9NJ, (0171 916 5466).
  Counsels victims of rape or sexual violence either personally or through its
  helpline (0171 837 1600).
- Portal Christian Rehabilitation Centres, 5 Junction Road, Romford, Essex RM1
  3QS, (01708 741971). A Christian-based organization which offers care and
  counselling to young men and women who have suffered abuse of all kinds
  during childhood and who have been in long-term care, in psychiatric
  hospitals or in prison.
- Women's Aid Federation (England), PO Box 391, Bristol BS99 7WS,
  (0117 963 3494). Local groups throughout England offer counselling, practical
  help and a refuge for women and children who are suffering emotional,
  mental or physical violence, harassment or sexual abuse. It has a telephone
  helpline on 0117 963 3542.
- Women Against Rape, King's Cross Women's Centre, 71 Tonbridge Street
  London WC1H 9DZ, (0171 837 7509). Offers support as well as practical and

legal advice to women and girls who have been sexually assaulted or raped, helping them through court procedures, welfare and housing problems.
- WASH, Women Against Sexual Harassment, 312 The Chandlery, 50 Westminster Bridge Road, London SE1 7QY, (0171 721 7592). Advises and helps women who have been sexually harassed, especially if it affects their work situation. It will give legal and general advice either over the phone or in person.

4

PARTNERS AND FRIENDS

We all have to learn how to live alongside one another, since this is part of the process of growing up. But close relationships with partners, with relatives and with friends need extra work sometimes. Living together in harmony means a great deal of give and take on both sides, particularly if you have been used to doing precisely what you please, but with willingness and good humour, most obstacles can be overcome.

PARTNERSHIP PROBLEMS

Quarrels

For some couples, fighting is a means of communication or even a form of intimacy. However, they often forget that it is not pretty – indeed embarrassing – for others, especially their friends, to watch. Many people who may be perfectly charming on their own, turn out to be a social nightmare when with their partner. Others need to fight in order to fancy each other. Bickering, too, becomes such a part of some barren relationships that the couple would not have anything to communicate if they had to be civil to each other. In my experience, women do not know when to end the argument, and tend to go on and on about the subject, while men avoid confronting uncomfortable issues and disappear as fast as they can.

It is a case of basic politeness, if not good sense, to look upon your relationship as a stage act or a firm, and close ranks when you are in public. If you cannot go out together without putting each other down, triumphantly interrupting or capping each other's stories or starting a row, then consider socializing separately to avoid embarrassing your friends. It might give your relationship fresh impetus.

If you must quarrel do so constructively. Get something out of it, do not just slag each other off.

- Think before you shout. Never start a quarrel when your partner is half awake, when either or both of you have been drinking or if you have had a beastly day. It will make things worse.

- If it is a major issue, consider writing down the points you want to make beforehand. Then make your points and stick to them, do not drag in other irrelevant issues. Look upon it as a debate, not a fight.
- What are you rowing about? Is it money, sex or the children? Or is it something more mundane like untidiness, lateness and who does the washing-up? It might be a good idea to sit down and work out what can be done about it rather than shouting at each other.
- Do not drag in the past – it is negative and gets you absolutely nowhere. Do not go over old ground again and again. If you find you are getting repetitious it is time for a temporary truce.
- Talk *quietly*. One of the toughest and most effective women executives I know in the media world is five foot nothing and works in a male-dominated area. She puts her point slowly and quietly – and inevitably wins. Try it just once, especially if you are known to be a shouter – you'll be surprised at the effect it has.
- Be open-minded and be prepared to listen, for once, to your partner's point of view. Listen, if you can, until your partner's argument peters out. He will then have lost most of his energy and steam and you will get a fair hearing.
- Do not argue simply to win, especially if you have a sneaking feeling your partner may be right. You'll end up with a Pyrrhic victory – you may come out on top, but you may lose the love of your partner in the end.
- Think in terms of trade-offs. Work out in your own mind which points you are determined to stick to and which ones you might be willing to concede.
- If you are rowing about your children, do not do it in front of them. Children are naturally subversive and may take a certain amount of pleasure in setting one of you against the other. If the row is a serious one, on the other hand, it might frighten them.
- Do not hit below the belt. If you know your partner is ashamed or embarrassed about something – his lack of height or lack of education for instance – homing in on it in a fight is only going to make him feel worse. He might retaliate by telling you something about yourself you'd rather not know.
- Do not sulk. Being accused of sulking will only make you feel wilder. If you are the moody type, withdraw from the scene pretending, at least, that you have work to do.
- Keep your cool. Bursting into tears and stamping your foot will provide a good excuse for your partner to walk away, saying that he cannot deal with you in that state.
- Do not use your partner as a punchbag for other things that have gone wrong in your life. If the children have been impossible or if you have had a really bad day at work, then say so, but do not pick a fight.

- If you have had a major row, do not let your partner overhear you on the phone to friends or relatives about it. If you must tell someone, do it in private when your partner is not around.
- Never let the sun go down on your wrath, as our grandmothers used to say. Try to reach some sort of a truce before you go to bed. One of the saddest stories I know is of a man who had a row with his wife and threatened to leave her just before she went to the airport. She died in a plane crash and he has never been able to forgive himself.

Jealousy

Jealousy is a primitive, destructive emotion, one of the first emotions we experience as a child and if we experience it in adulthood, it indicates that we have never quite out-grown these childhood feelings. If you are a jealous person you are in a no-win situation. It grows inside like a cancer, turning us into irrational, unreasonable human beings. And sadly it may bring the very thing that we dread – rejection by our partners.

What makes a person jealous?

To most of us, the word 'love' involves a sexual partnership. But love also includes warmth, affection, real concern and selflessness. However, love can also be selfish – some people want to grab all the love that his or her partner has and may not want to share the partner with family or friends. The jealous person may harbour resentments against the people their partner works with, the partner's former lovers or, in some extreme cases, the partner's children from another relationship.

Jealousy stems from a lack of self-confidence and self-esteem. A jealous person feels that he is not lovable and not worthy of attention and concern. Often these feelings are rooted in childhood. If you felt that your parents did not love you, or that they loved your brothers and sisters more than you, then you become convinced that you are second-rate. The sad thing is that you will subconsciously bring these feelings with you into any relationship you form.

Because you have such a low opinion of yourself, you cannot quite believe that your partner has actually chosen you. You may search all the time for signs that your partner is attracted to someone else. This can develop into a phobia, where you question every movement, monitor phone calls, letters and search your partner's clothes for evidence.

How to cure yourself of jealousy

You have to get yourself and your feelings under control and take responsibility for your behaviour. You cannot expect other people to bolster your inadequate sense of self-worth, something that your parents should have done for you. Now you have to work on it yourself. Perhaps start by looking at why you feel so insecure.

- Write down a list of your achievements – passing a driving test, getting a job – you will be surprised at what you have accomplished.
- Make a list of things you want to achieve and start work on them. Send off for the prospectus for that course you want to take. Get library books out on something you want to study.
- Stop asking your partner where he has been if he is late. Put it out of your mind. Take a mental broom and sweep the thought into the corner. Each time you do it you will find it is easier.
- Do not quiz your partner or make remarks about people of the opposite sex that he or she sees on a regular basis. By bringing up the person's name constantly and accusing your partner of an affair with that person, you may put the idea into your partner's head. He may reason that if he is being accused of having an affair behind your back, he might as well actually do so.
- When you go out with your partner to parties and social events, do not watch to see what he is doing. Deliberately move away from his side and talk to other people. Do not look back to see whom he is talking to; concentrate on yourself and on the people you meet.

Each time you make the effort to distract your mind from obsessive suspicions and thoughts, you will find it easier and easier to do. It is like giving up smoking: at first it is difficult, but it gets easier after a while.

If you live with someone who is jealous

A person who is always demanding love and asking for assurances of undying love is suffering from low self-esteem. Before such a person can form a real relationship, without jealousy, that individual must first build up a sense of their own self-worth.

- Look upon a jealous person as someone with an illness. If you want a quiet life, be considerate. It is foolish to seek out and flirt with a younger, better-looking person if you know your partner is going to be upset.
- Do not feed yourself to the lions. If you must flirt, do so when your partner is not there.
- If you are quizzed about your movements, answer quietly and calmly, but refuse to be tethered. You must live your own life. Giving in to a jealous person who wants you chained to his side makes his condition worse.
- If you think it will help, talk things over with him, analyse his feelings and why he has them. Decide together what to do about it.
- Show your jealous partner as much love and affection as you can. Praise his efforts, help to build up his self-confidence. Then, hopefully, the jealousy will fade away.

Counselling

Problems with your partner, whether emotional or sexual, can be hard to talk about with friends or family. You may not want your family to know, or you may be too embarrassed to confide in friends. This is when counselling can come in. An independent, trained outsider, someone who will not pass judgement on you or try to lecture you, may be what you need. You can talk over the most intimate details of your life because you know the meeting is confidential. You can also, with a counsellor's help, explore your own thoughts and feelings not just about your problem but about your family background and your past, all of which may have some bearing on your present plight. Find out more about yourself – what your strengths and weaknesses are, what your priorities are – and you may find it easier to deal with the issue at hand.

Where do I find a counsellor?

Ask your doctor to refer you to a health authority clinic. He may also know of private counsellors in your area who could take you on. If you are referred to a health authority clinic, counselling is free, but you may have to wait weeks for an appointment. If you do not want to talk to your GP, or if you find him unhelpful, then a doctor at a Family Planning Clinic – even if you are not a regular patient – should be able to help.

If you are referred to a private counsellor, expect to pay £20–25 for a session. A private counsellor will probably be able to see you in the evening or at weekends. Alternatively, you can contact Relate, formerly called the Marriage Guidance Council (*see page 205*). Sessions are free but contributions are welcome. There will probably be a waiting list.

The top ten reasons why people go to Relate are:
• Lack of communication.
• Financial difficulties.
• Sexual problems.
• Adultery.
• The birth of a baby.
• Redundancy.
• A death in the family.
• Life changes such as growing older and the changes these bring in their train.
• A change of circumstances like moving house or changing a job.
• Children growing up and possibly leaving home.

What happens when I see a counsellor?

You can be seen individually or as a couple. Some counsellors prefer to see each partner individually, then see both of you together. The session will usually last about 45 minutes – perhaps longer for your first appointment. You are usually seen on a weekly basis. The counsellor will put you at your ease, ask you questions about the problem, about yourself and, above all, let you talk.

ADULTERY

Adultery happens in many marriages that are apparently full of love and affection, where the couple have a good sex life. The discovery that your partner is having an affair shatters the trust between you, and sometimes destroys the marriage as well. You suddenly find your partner has been deceiving you, and things are never quite the same again. You feel angry, betrayed and hurt. If you are in a marriage where love has already gone, then the marriage is not likely to survive.

An affair can rock a marriage at any time; just after you have married, after the arrival of the first baby or the moment the children are finally off your hands. But the clue here is that each of these events marks a significant staging post in your life, a time of great stress. In the early years of marriage, we make the transition from being 'madly in love' to being affectionate and loving. We ride out problems, the arrival – or non-arrival – of children and the changes they bring. Immature people find these things difficult to handle. In the later years we may have to deal with boredom. Many women, with more time on their hands, begin to discover themselves and their real needs and their partners may not fit in with this revised image of themselves.

Because women no longer marry for a meal ticket, many refuse to tolerate their husbands having affairs, something which might have been tacitly accepted in Victorian times. And now that more women go out to work, it is much easier for them, too, to commit adultery. People working alongside each other in a pressured environment may be drawn into having an affair, especially if their partners do not understand the jargon, the problems and the pressures that go with the job.

When adrenalin is running high, someone you might not normally fancy may become highly desirable. The couple, who were formally good friends, may now find themselves lovers. And opportunity is often there – working late, going on training courses and staying away overnight. Sex may not even be involved in this close friendship with its own verbal shorthand that excludes others. But this kind of friendship can be just as hurtful to partners as adultery.

Now there is yet another threat to marriage. Redundancy, job losses and money worries can make a partner feel isolated and set apart. He may long to run away from it all and having an affair becomes a substitute.

If you discover your partner is having an affair

Unless your partner has said that he or she is leaving, you have three choices. You can

- Sue for divorce.
- Stand by your partner and go on as if nothing has happened.
- Stay in the marriage, try to see what is wrong and put it right.

There are a number of ways of coping with the difficult news and the emotional turmoil you are bound to feel.

- Try to keep calm, even if you are burning inside. Express your initial rage and misery to a good friend, get the shouting and crying over before you tackle your partner.
- Do not do or say anything you might regret or set a solicitor on him, saying you want a divorce. Wait and think things over calmly.
- Do not be a victim. Do not blame your partner for things other than the infidelity.
- Ask yourself if your partner secretly wants to end the marriage and this is a desperate way of copping out?
- Do not ask for details. The less you know, the easier it will be for you to put the incident behind you.
- Do not tell your children unless you are forced to, especially if they are very young. It is a selfish self-indulgence and places a burden on them that they should not have to bear. It can distress teenagers particularly, at a very vulnerable time of life. If your children are grown up and might find out from another source, it is best to tell them in as matter-of-fact manner as possible. But do not encourage them to take sides.
- Come to terms with the fact that it has happened, nothing will change that. Then decide what to do.
- If this is just one of many relationships, consider seriously if you want the marriage to go on. This might be a good time to see a counsellor.
- Do not rush into bed with someone else. You will not feel any better afterwards.
- Do not tell your partner that he has to stop. Instead just say quietly that if it continues, you will have to consider whether or not you can stay.
- If your partner comes back to you, or keeps vacillating between you and your rival, are you prepared to take this? The answer is no.
- Give your partner – and yourself – some space. You both need time to think.
- Look after yourself. Changing your looks might give you a temporary lift. But changing your inner life, taking up a new consuming interest, joining a group that might fill your 'personal space' and give your self-esteem a much-needed boost is better still.

Someone else's affair

Discovery of an affair is made all that much more humiliating if you discover that friends, sometimes even family members, have known about it all the time. But what should you do if you know that a close friend's wife or husband is having an affair behind your friend's back.

Do not interfere unless you are put in a situation where you are letting the friend down by not telling them. For all you know, they may know of the situation and may prefer not to acknowledge it. If on the other hand, the friend says that she suspects her partner is being unfaithful, then you are put in a difficult situation.

Tackle the culprit directly with what you know and say that loyalty to the victim compels you to tell her, then see what he says. You have to balance the fact that your friend may not thank you for telling the truth, but, on the other hand, will feel betrayed if he or she finds out later that you knew all the time.

If you are having an affair

Ask yourself:

- Is it really worth it? If I am found out, will I be able to take on board my partner's misery and anger?
- Why am I still in the marriage if I feel I need this?
- Why do I want to confess? Some people feel that by dumping their guilt onto their innocent partner they have somehow cleansed themselves of their sins. This is a very selfish thing to do.

If you are the third party in a relationship

A number of questions also arise if you are the third party in a relationship. Does your lover acknowledge you or are you stuck in a hole-in-the-corner affair? Sneaking off to side-street restaurants and avoiding friends and colleagues may be fun, even exciting, for a while, but it soon becomes a subject for deep resentment.

You may well be propping up their marriage. By providing sex and sympathy – if those are the things missing in the marriage – you could well be keeping it going. You must also ask yourself whether your lover is *really* going to leave his family. Statistics show that while women will often make the break, married men very rarely leave when they say that they will. Often the so-called 'weaker' partner – the clinging wife, the wimpish husband – holds the trump cards. And if your lover is really the wonderful person that you think he is, how can he leave someone who is threatening suicide, cries and says she cannot go on without him?

Are you providing a bridge? A lover can be an escape route from a failed marriage, but will be discarded when the partner is finally free to choose someone new.

What about the children? If there are children involved, things can get very sad, stressful and messy. The ecstatic moments you have together now will disappear if you find yourself looking after someone else's mutinous brood every other weekend, and you will be cast in the role of a she- or he-devil. And as all parents know to their cost, children and joyful uninhibited sex just do not mix. And do you want a family of your own? Does your lover want one, the second time around? If you harbour a longing for a child, make sure that your lover does too.

Your lover has told you the marriage is over – but is it? Do the partners still socialize together, go to family and school events and on holiday together? The other side of this question surely must be to ask yourself how much longer you are prepared to be alone at Christmas, Easter and the summer holidays? Might it not be better to make a break and find someone who is free?

Mending the marriage

There is no doubt that once you and your partner employ solicitors the gulf between you will increase. If you want to save your marriage it is worthwhile trying a reconciliation service.

When trust is shattered, it is like a broken plate. You can glue the pieces together but the joins are there to be seen. Your partner has been deceiving you and telling lies. But painstakingly, piece by piece, it is possible to rebuild a relationship if both partners want it to work. Time not only heals, but does lend distance to the event. If you decide that you want to save your marriage, then you need to do some stock-taking and pinpoint areas that need attention and repair.

- Can you *really* forgive and forget? There is nothing more disagreeable than a vengeful partner who is determined to make the culprit pay for the rest of his life. If you cannot resolve the problems, the affair will lurk like a time bomb ticking away, and your relationship may end in divorce years later. Counselling may help.
- Are you bored with each other? Could that have been the cause? Have you drifted apart? If so, what can be done about it?
- Do you really talk? Or is your conversation confined to who is going to take the kids to school or who is doing the shopping?
- Do you spend too little time together – or too much? Both can be damaging to a relationship.
- Are you too involved with your job or the children to consider your partner's needs?
- If your partner says 'It didn't mean a thing' can you believe him?
- Has the desire for sex gone – and can anything be done about it? Can you ever make love again? Sometimes an affair will make you want to show you are as good in bed as your rival – not always a good idea. Or things may go the other way and you may feel unable to have sex without a vision of the other person flashing into your mind, ruining your love-making. For men, this can be a time when impotence happens for the first time.
- What have you got in common and how can you build on it?

If you are the guilty one

- Are you prepared to make a clean break with your lover to save your marriage? You cannot have your cake and eat it.
- Are you prepared to listen while your partner spills out feelings of hurt and anger to you?
- Are you prepared to give your partner lots of assurance and support and tell him or her that he or she is loved while they rebuild their shattered self-esteem.
- Can you put up with your partner's very natural suspicions and demands to know where you have been and with whom?

If the relationship comes to an end

When a relationship breaks up you do, in fact, go through a kind of bereavement (*see page 195*) because you have lost someone who was dear to you. The difference is, however, that the person is still alive and you do not have happy memories of them any more. It may have been a total shock, you may have seen it coming, you may have even instigated the break, but it takes time to get over something like this. Expect to have mood swings, loss of confidence and feelings of disbelief that you are suddenly half of what was a couple. These are normal reactions. Bruised but unbeaten, it is time to take up life again.

Talk to sympathetic friends once then stop. You do not want to sound like a worn tape, played over and over again. And going on about it is like sticking a knife into an open wound – you are stopping yourself from healing. Instead, get in touch with a support group like Dignity or Single Again (*see **Help Section,** page 204*). You will find that you belong to an enormous club, and that you are not the only person sitting alone at home on evenings and weekends.

Do not be afraid to be angry – punch a cushion if it makes you feel better – but better still, channel your anger into some furious house-cleaning or into a sport such as swimming or cycling, preferably in company.

Do not go looking for another relationship at this stage because you are carrying a lot of emotional baggage that needs to be unloaded first. If you take this into a new situation it is likely to fail. Also do not be afraid to confront your ex-partner if you feel you have a genuine grievance over money or some practical problem, but remember, the more distance you put between the two of you, the faster your feelings will heal. Above all, do not blame yourself for what happened.

Finally, the time will come, I assure you, when you suddenly realize that you have not thought about your ex-partner at all. Or better still (as has happened to me) you meet up again and wonder 'what on earth did I see in him?'.

SEPARATION AND DIVORCE

The breakup of a marriage or partnership is always a sad occasion. But you have company: 40 per cent of all marriages end in divorce these days, so you will find yourself in a large club, albeit one that no one wants to join. You may feel that you have come to the point where you cannot go on and that divorce is inevitable. Take care, though, to work out your situation before you act.

Before you sue for divorce

Work out the financial implications before you begin proceedings. Getting a divorce or deed of separation is rather like making out a will and should be considered in the same way. There are a number of questions that should be resolved.

Where are you going to live?
One of you will have to move out of your shared residence. If you own the house:
- What is it worth? The value is usually split 50/50, so you will be left with half the value of the house to spend or possibly a large mortgage.
- Could you sell it easily?
- Whose name is it in?
- Who pays the mortgage at the moment?
- Has one of you paid for major improvements over the years?
  If you rent:
- Whose name is on the rent book or lease?
- Who pays the rent?
- If you take over the rent would the landlord object?

What else must be shared out?
- If you have a car, who owns it?
- If your partner has a company pension do you have any rights at the moment as a widow or widower? Currently research is being conducted into whether a divorced woman should be entitled to a share of her ex-husband's pension.
- Is either of you expecting a legacy under a will?
- What insurances, savings, valuables like jewellery or antiques are there?

Other financial matters
- What will you live on? If you do not have a job, can you get one? If not, how do you plan to survive?
- What will your outgoings be? What will your running expenses be to live on your own? Will you need to buy a car, TV or furniture and how are you going to finance this?

- Will you have to pay maintenance? Will your partner expect maintenance (at present up to 30 per cent of your income)? Do not think you get off scot-free because you are a woman – I was one of the first women in the country to be sued for alimony.
- What money are you entitled to? Would you be entitled to maintenance? If so, how much?
- Will you need help from the state? Find out from your local DSS what you are likely to get in income support, family credit and housing benefit.
- Do you have any joint accounts with a bank or building society? If so, these need either to be wound up or to be given new instructions.

Divorce

Big changes are afoot in divorce law. The blame element for marriage breakdown may be removed and there may be mandatory time scheduled into procedings for conciliation counselling to take place. However, even under current divorce laws, getting rid of your partner is much simpler than it used to be. Basically all you have to prove is that your marriage has irretrievably broken down for one of several reasons.

Your partner has committed adultery and as a result you find it intolerable to go on living together

You do not have to name the co-respondent unless you want to. If you do not know who it is you can say that your partner has committed adultery with a woman whose name and identity are unknown to you. You will have to say where and when the adultery took place. If you both agree to the divorce, the easiest way out is for your partner to make a 'confession statement' saying he has committed adultery at a specific time and place. If you do name the co-respondent then that person has to be served with a petition. If your partner refuses to admit he has committed adultery and you have no proof, the divorce becomes a defended one and could cost a great deal of time and money.

Your partner's behaviour is so bad that you cannot reasonably be expected to go on living together

Unreasonable behaviour on the part of your partner may be difficult to define. The following kinds of behaviour are usually considered unreasonable.
- Violence or serious threats of violence.
- Homosexual conduct.
- Refusal to have children, knowing that you want to have them.
- Refusal to have sexual intercourse.
- Unreasonable financial conduct – serious gambling is an example.
- Persistent nagging.

Remember you will have to convince the court that the behaviour is sufficient to end the marriage. If, say, you are planning to petition on the grounds of violence, then you should keep a diary of dates, times and incidents. You will need a note of recent incidents. If they happened more than six months previously, you will be considered to have condoned them.

Your partner has deserted you and you have been living apart for at least two years

This is a much simpler case. All you need to do is to give the date when your partner left and state that it was without your consent, along with other circumstances surrounding this departure.

You have lived apart for at least two years and your partner agrees to a divorce

This situation makes the divorce a mere formality. Your partner will have to give his consent by filling in an acknowledgement of service when he gets the petition. But you may both have to prove that you lived apart for two years. If you spent some or all of that time under the same roof, then you will have to show, later on in the proceedings, that you slept and ate apart and each did your own housework, washing etc.

You have been living apart for more than five years

In this case you can get a divorce whether or not your partner agrees. Your partner can, however, oppose the divorce on grounds of financial or other hardship.

How soon after marriage can you get a divorce?

You have to have been married for at least one year. In Scotland you do not even have to wait a year.

Starting proceedings

Even if you both agree that you should part, it is not possible for you to apply jointly, someone has to start the divorce proceedings. This partner becomes the petitioner, the other partner is called the respondent. Who plays which role will make no difference to how the court deals with things like maintenance and child custody, but being the petitioner is advantageous because it means that you are in control and can, to some extent, slow down or speed up the proceedings.

To petition for divorce you apply to a County Court that operates as a Family Hearing Centre, or to a Divorce County Court. If you are worried about proceedings being reported in a local paper, there is nothing to stop you applying for a divorce at any County Court in England or Wales provided you live in those countries.

If your spouse is planning to defend or dispute the case then your divorce proceedings may be transferred to the High Court in London which normally deals with difficult cases. If your partner feels so strongly about being dubbed the respondent that he files a petition in retaliation (wasteful in time and money) then the High Court would probably take the case on.

Do I need a solicitor?

A solicitor is not necessary for the actual business of getting a divorce but you may well need to consult one beforehand to check that you have just cause. And if there is going to be a battle about children or money, then a solicitor is vital. The trouble with using a solicitor is that what may start as an amicable agreement to part can turn into a legal fight. Try not to use one to fight your case in court unless it is necessary, since this is when expenses soar. It is better to try and iron out differences privately beforehand. If you do employ a solicitor, it is vital that you choose one who specializes in divorce and family law (*see page 204*). You and your partner cannot share a solicitor, as this is considered a conflict of interest.

A solicitor can
- Take a dispassionate, level-headed view of what is going on.
- Do all your paperwork for you.
- Help fix custody and maintenance orders and agree finances – he has no personal involvement.
- Draw up a settlement.

Or you can simply use him to check that an agreement you have come to is fair.

How do I start to sue?

First you need to get hold of two copies of a form of petition for divorce. You will need a third copy if you are naming someone as a co-respondent as that person will need to be sent a petition too. You can get the forms from any local court that handles divorce cases. On the petition you will have to give:
- Your full name and that of your partner.
- The date and place of the marriage.
- The last address where you both lived together.
- Your present addresses.
- The occupations of both you and your partner.
- The full names of any children under adult age and their dates of birth.
- Details of any previous court proceedings to do with the marriage or with property.
- The reason why the marriage has irretrievably broken down (later on you will have to swear on oath that these statements are true).

You will also need your marriage certificate or, if you have lost it, a certified copy of it obtainable from the General Register Office (*see page 203*). You could also get one from the Superintendent Registrar of Births, Deaths and Marriages for the area where you married, or from the parson of the church where you were married. If you married abroad and your certificate is in a foreign language, you will have to get a translation of it (look for translators in the Yellow Pages) which you will have to take to a Notary Public (Yellow Pages again) to get it authenticated.

If children are involved, you must obtain and fill out two copies of a form called a Statement of Proposed Arrangements outlining your intended arrangements for them. You need to fill both copies in together, and countersign them, keeping one each. Children may be your joint children, your own children, his own children or adopted children.

You will need to pay a fee unless you are on income support, family credit or green form legal aid (*see page 444*) in which case you need to fill in a Fee Exemption Form instead.

All these items are posted or taken to the divorce court you are using (the marriage certificate will be returned to you afterwards). Do not forget to photocopy any papers you are submitting – you may want to refer to them. If you are employing a solicitor, he will help you fill in the form and will have to put in a Certificate of Reconciliation saying whether or not you have been given any advice about reconciliation. This is not necessary, however, if you are getting free or part-aided advice under the green form scheme (*see page 444*).

Undefended divorce

If both partners are in agreement over the divorce, your divorce petition will be sent to the respondent, the non-suing partner. The respondent then has to confirm to the court that he has received it and say whether or not he is planning to defend it. At this stage you will have to produce a sworn statement about the reason for the divorce (*see above*). You must swear this before a Commissioner for Oaths. Your solicitor may be one, otherwise look in the Yellow Pages. If the divorce is not being defended then it is up to you, the petitioner, to ask the court to proceed with the petition. This is all paperwork and can be done by post and you will not have to attend a hearing.

If either of you is claiming maintenance at this stage, then a claim for **maintenance pending suit** is lodged in order to get interim funds until the divorce goes through. If you do not claim at this point then maintenance and other similar claims will be left on one side until the divorce goes through. The court will then consider your petition, together with your sworn statement, and if all is well the judge will grant you a **decree nisi**. Six weeks later you can ask for a **decree absolute** which brings your marriage to an end.

Maintenance and children before proceedings begin

The fact that you cannot start divorce proceedings until a year is up does not stop you from applying for maintenance, child support or custody of any children before this date. You do this at the local Magistrates' Court or a County Court Family Hearing Centre.

Money

The idea of having a 'clean break' divorce is very seductive, especially if you have had a bad time with your partner. This is when you may either offer, or accept, a lump sum, a once-and-for-all payment, rather than ongoing maintenance of any kind. This can be particularly attractive if you want to have as little contact with each other as possible. This transaction may include transferring property from one partner to the other, or selling a property and splitting the proceeds.

If you are thinking of offering a lump sum, check first whether your almost ex-partner is planning to marry again or take up a live-in relationship. In these cases it is better to opt for maintenance payments because your liability may cease if the partner marries again and no children are involved.

You cannot dispose of your assets and then come to court claiming that you have no money to pay a lump sum or on-going maintenance. The court has the power to look back as long as three years previous to see whether you were deliberately trying to get rid of your capital with this in mind.

Maintenance

Maintenance is the money that your partner pays you, or you pay your partner, on a regular basis after the relationship has broken down. This may be decided informally between the two of you, but if there is disagreement, and if your partner reneges on the deal, then you may have to go to court to sort the matter out. Any maintenance order made by the court is enforceable; in other words, your partner can be fined, even imprisoned for not keeping up the payments.

How much will I get?

In making the order, the court will take into account the amount of money you and your ex-partner both earn, and your assets, but above all, the interests of your children will be considered. The court will base its judgement on
- The income, capital and earning potential of both of you.
- The ages of your children and whether they have any disabilities.
- Your needs, your ex-partner's needs and those of the children.

The order can be varied at any time on application by one side or the other, if circumstances change.

Claiming maintenance

Before taking your ex-partner to court for maintenance, talk to your solicitor, particularly if a divorce or some other kind of civil action is pending. To claim maintenance via the courts you will have to first prove that your ex-partner is the father (or more unusually, the mother) of the child – his/her name on the birth certificate will do. The court may give you an interim maintenance order so that you have something to live on until it reaches a final decision.

Any maintenance payments should be made directly to the former partner, not to the children. This is because under new regulations, maintenance payments made to children no longer qualify for tax relief. Maintenance is considered to be income where benefits are concerned. If your partner does not keep up maintenence payments or refuses to make them in the first place, the Child Support Agency may become involved but should only be contacted as a last resort. This organization, which has had a lot of bad press recently, is being reorganized at the moment.

Splitting up if you are not married

Sensible couples who live together or are planning to live together and not marry should set down on paper who owns what. Unfortunately this is seldom done for fear of sounding mercenary. However, it could save a great deal of trouble at a later date. If you have children, then you are treated by law in the same way as a married couple. If you are childless then things are different. If you do split up, then this is the score.

Property

If you own the property you live in, whoever is named on the title deeds is the legal owner but you may have a claim if you are not named as the owner (*see page 484*). The house, like anything large that you bought as a joint purchase, is held as a 'trust for sale' and if you split up, either of you can insist that it is sold and that you get your share. For more details on this look at the entry **Home** (*see page* 462).

Possessions

When it comes to large-scale possessions, you may find yourself in court trying to prove that the car he bought for you is a gift and not just a loan, while he maintains it was bought merely for your use while you co-habited.

Maintenance

As two single people living together, you have no obligation to support each other either during or after the relationship. If you have children, then you are treated as a married couple.

CUSTODY AND ACCESS

Diplomacy is the best way to get access to, and share custody of, your children. But if diplomacy does not work with your partner, then going to court to fight for your rights is not necessarily complex or expensive if you have help from people who have gone through the same experience. Families Need Fathers (*see page 275*) is one such organization and it will deal with mothers, as well as fathers, who find themselves in this situation.

The law concerning custody and access is fairly straightforward and you can conduct your own case if you have to. You must impress the court, and the Family Welfare Officer who holds most of the trump cards, that you are a well-adjusted, positive human being who is concerned about the welfare of your child, and that contact with the child will be of benefit to him or her. You may not succeed in getting access at first, but it is vital that you keep on trying – otherwise your child may feel in later years that you abandoned him or her.

Both sides can apply for legal custody or access to the child (under the Guardianship of Minors Act 1971). You can do this even if the child is being looked after by a third party. First, you make application in the Magistrates' Court, County Court, or High Court and it can be done with legal aid if you qualify for it. If you are the father, you will have to prove paternity. If your name is on the child's birth certificate this is simple to do. If not you may have to take a blood test (*see page 221*).

If you and your partner are in dispute over who should have custody of the child, then the court will consider the interests of the child first, but will also take into account other factors such as the wishes of the parents, the way you have both behaved, and the child's wishes as well if he or she is over 7 years old. The court will rate stability high on the list, so if your child has been living with you, then you are unlikely to lose custody. However, if you are a lesbian mother you might have problems – if so contact a support group (*see page 163*).

What the court can do

The court can make an interim order granting temporary care and control to one parent until a final decision is made. It can also make an order for legal custody to either of you. This gives you the right to make decisions about the child and have it in your care. The court can also order access, giving a parent the right to see the child regularly, or it can make an order committing your child into care (*see page 256*). Alternatively, it might make a supervision order (*see page 256*). If your partner is being violent or threatens violence to you and your children, the court can take out an injunction to protect you (*see page 187*).

Conciliation

If you and your partner are in dispute about the future of your children, some County Courts and the High Court operate a conciliation system, which it may recommend that you use. The dispute is heard informally in the registrar's room rather than the court and a court welfare officer may be there. You, in your turn, may want to have your solicitor with you. If the children are over the age of 7, they can attend, and the welfare officer will interview them separately to get their views on the subject. If conciliation fails to solve the dispute then it may go to the High Court. Conciliation costs money, but this is recoverable via legal aid, if you qualify.

Ward of court

If you suspect that your partner may try to take your child out of the country, you may have to make the child a ward of court. This is a very serious step to take because it means that you give up your parental right to the child and hand it over to the court instead.

To have a child made a ward of court, you must apply in the High Court, although this can be done very quickly and can indeed be completed over the telephone if there is an emergency situation. Your child can still live with you while he or she is a ward of court, provided you ask for care and control. The measure normally lasts for 21 days and you have to apply for it to be extended after that. You, as a parent, are not the only person who can apply for a child to be made a ward of court. Grandparents have the right to apply, as do other relatives. The local authority can also do so, usually if they are planning to remove your child into care (*see page 256*).

WHAT TO TELL THE CHILDREN

However acrimonious things may be between you and your partner, meet to decide in advance how you are going to explain the situation to your children.

- Tell them together, and have the same story. Do not let them hear two different versions. Remember, it is their divorce too.
- Be as honest as you can. Do not try to deceive them with implausible scenarios (Daddy has to work away from home), or suggest that the separation is just temporary, if you know it is not. Children have a way of seeing through deceit of any kind.
- Assure them that they are loved as much as ever by both of you, making it clear that it is in no way their fault. Children often feel it is their fault when their parents split up, thinking that by being naughty occasionally or causing problems that they are responsible for the divorce, especially if they have heard you arguing over their behaviour.
- Emphasize the things that will not change in their lives, that they will stay in the same home, if that is the case, or go to the same school. Children are very conservative and the thought of any upheaval in addition to the divorce will be very stressful to them.

- Do not pretend that you are the best of friends if you are not. But make the effort at least to be calm and cordial to each other in the presence of the children.
- Do not score against your ex-partner or criticize him or her to the children. They will already have torn feelings of loyalty towards you both.
- Try to avoid your children having to go to court, even an informal one. Act like grown-ups and try to settle their future through discussion rather than dispute.
- Fix arrangements for visits and handovers in advance and in private. Do not distress or humiliate your children by arguing over these matters in front of them.
- Try very hard not to break any promises to them from now on, even if it causes you great personal inconvenience. Keep dates to see them, take them on holidays you have promised. They will already be feeling unstable, and being let down will make it worse.
- Above all, do not despair of the situation. Divorce can actually improve your relationships with your children on a one-to-one basis. And things will get better.

Your name

As a divorced woman you can choose to continue using your married name or you can revert to your previous one. What you cannot do is use your former husband's name in a way that implies you are still married to him. If you do, your ex-husband can seek a court injunction to stop you. If, by representing yourself as his wife, you imply that the woman he is married to is not his legal wife, then he can sue you for libel or slander.

AFTER THE DIVORCE

Divorce is the second most stressful thing that can happen in your life – the first is the death of someone close to you. Nobody wins in this situation and women are usually the hardest hit, especially if they have young children to bring up.

Many women say they suffer an identity crisis when they are no longer someone's partner. Your social life is suddenly shunted into a siding. You can feel rejected by friends as well as by your partner. You will probably also feel a mix of anger, relief that it is all over, and confusion too, wondering where you go next. If you have initiated the divorce then you are more likely to have plans for the future than if it was forced upon you.

It is normal to feel anxious about the future. Do not keep your worries to yourself; talk them over with a trusted friend, with a support group or a counsellor. If you are feeling really down, call the Samaritans (on 0345 909090).

If you find you cannot sleep for worrying, make a list of all your problems – they will not look nearly so bad in the morning. Don't be surprised if you have regrets over what might have been.

You may feel grief, too, because a dead marriage, even a bad one, brings its own kind of bereavement. The difference is that you are mourning for someone who is not dead but still around. You may have instigated the divorce but that may not make you feel any better as it may be laced with guilt. But there are things you can do to help you on the road to recovery.

- Take your regrets and worries, visualize them in your head then imagine sweeping them into a corner with a broom and leave them there.
- Take time to make a life plan, working out what you want from life now that you are free. You can have your own dreams and ambitions without someone laughing at them or trampling on them. But you are also going to have to take responsibility for yourself.
- Remember that you were loved at one time and there are people who love you still – your children, parents, relatives and friends and all the new people who will get to know and love you in the future.
- Expect to lose and gain some friends. There is bound to be a realignment of relationships. Friends and relations, his and yours, are part of the baggage you take with you into the breakup, and no one knows quite who will come to the surface. Some friends you expected to continue to see drift off, and others you thought of as your partner's friends become firm allies. The main thing now is not to rake over the past with them but talk about other things – your plans, what you are doing and going to do.
- Do not be afraid to ring people up and tell them that you still value their friendship. They may be embarrassed at first but if, when you meet them, you are resolutely optimistic and do not rake over the old issues, the chances are you will keep them whoever they 'belonged' to. Some relatives will disappear, others not. If there are children involved then obviously you will be keeping in touch with grandma even though seeing her may be a hurtful reminder of what you have lost.
- Make new friends. We all suffer from self-doubt and lack of confidence going into a new situation, including those who appear to be full of self-esteem. Put yourself out and about, but avoid dating agencies; they rarely work and only make you more aware of your plight. Do not think at this stage in terms of sharing life with just one person. Learn to look at life in the round and find a group of good friends instead.

Some people need sex to feel that they are still desirable. When they are not having it they feel they are no longer attractive. The fact that you have been desired should give you enough confidence to go without for a while. But think carefully before indulging in a series of flings. If you are exploiting other people by using their bodies for sex with no interest in them as people, there will be an awful emptiness about the situation.

DOMESTIC VIOLENCE

About a quarter of all reported crime involves domestic violence of some sort or other. And one in ten women suffers from violence, usually at the hands of her husband and these are only the statistics of reported cases. Women can be violent too, of course, kicking and scratching or thumping their partners. So if someone in your family attacks or attempts to harm you in some way, what can you do?

If your partner is violent or has threatened violence to you

You have four choices.

- You can apply for an injunction to get him out of the home. This can usually be done within 24 hours.
- You can go to the Social Services for help.
- You can go and stay with friends or relatives or go to an aid refuge.
- You can contact the police, who are, increasingly, taking a very hard line on domestic violence.

Help

The first thing to do is to remove yourself from the situation. If you are just a couple or have very small children, it is somewhat easier to go and stay with relatives or friends. However, if you have children who are locked into school, say, in the middle of studying for exams, then it needs more thought. In an emergency, your relatives may well be your first stop. It is certainly less traumatic for the children, who will know them and feel more secure.

There is a problem over this, however, if your partner is threatening violence, since he will know where they live and turn up on the doorstep. They may also not have room for you in the long term. In these cases it is best to call a refuge and move in there. Refuges generally have addresses that are kept secret. It would certainly be far more difficult for your partner to track you down, and if he does, there are people at the refuge who are more able to cope with him than your relatives.

If you are a council house tenant and are forced to leave the house do **not** ring the council and say you are giving up your tenancy. If you do that the council can say that you have made yourself intentionally homeless and it will not give you any help in finding another home.

The police

Like all large organizations, police stations vary and the way your local one handles what is known as 'a domestic' may be helpful or not, according to where you live.

The Probation Service

As I have said elsewhere in the book, the Probation Service does not only work with offenders, they can help you in many ways. It has a duty officer on call during office hours who will be able to give advice and refer you to other agencies. The duty officer may also be able to give some legal advice regarding your situation.

Citizens' Advice Bureau

The Citizens' Advice Bureau can help you sort out your rights, possibly finding you a solicitor, but is less able to find you accommodation.

Refuges

If you are really serious about sorting out domestic violence, whether it is aimed at you or your children, then contacting a refuge is the best way to do it. You will be given time to rebuild your self-confidence so that you feel like a person again, not a thing to be battered about. You will get your self-respect back, you may get your home back or the refuge will help you find somewhere else to live. The women who work there have a lot of contacts with local agencies like the DSS and social workers, and they will help you contact the relevant people, perhaps sending someone with you if you go for an interview.

Refuges for battered wives no longer have bare boards and broken furniture, the spartan accommodation they used to offer. They are now a place where you can feel secure and safe. They will protect you as well as look after you, and you will realize that you are not alone. It seems a pity to have to leave your home and go to a strange place but it may only be temporary – the refuge may well be able to get your husband evicted and your home back.

Refuges are either run by the council, by social workers or, more often than not, by a group of independent women. There are more than a hundred of them throughout the country. There are disadvantages to refuges – they are busy and crowded, there is little privacy and you will have to share washing and cooking facilities with other women and children, so think of a refuge as a short-term measure.

It is a sad comment on our society that most refuges are bursting at the seams and your local one may not be able to take you. If that happens, it will always give you the telephone number of one that has got space. They promise that no woman is ever turned away. The important thing about a refuge is that it is just that. Even if you do not need to stay there, you can go to them for help and advice. And if you subsequently move out, they are always on the other end of the phone.

How to find a refuge

Your Citizens' Advice Bureau can tell you where your nearest refuge is, so will the Social Services. The police will also know, and in an emergency they will take you there if you fear violence. Otherwise ring the Women's Aid Federation (*see page 204*) which has the numbers of all refuges throughout the country.

Taking things further

- You can get immediate legal aid for an injunction against your partner if he or she has been violent to you or to get your children back if they have been taken by your partner (*see page 444*).
- The Magistrates' Court will deal with applications for custody of children. This is presided over by lay-people, usually local citizens, not judges and the public is not allowed in (*see page 434*).
- You can apply for an injunction against violence in the County Court (*see page 434*) where a judge will hear your request 'in chambers', that is, in private.

What is an injunction?

You can apply for an injunction against your partner for a number of other reasons than violence or threatened violence. The injunction can order him to do a number of things:

- Stop assaulting, molesting or harassing you. This covers verbal as well as physical abuse, in short anything that stops you functioning in a normal domestic way.
- Stop assaulting any of your children under the age of 18.
- Stop his friends or relatives from doing any of the above.
- Make him leave home and not return. This injunction would usually have a time limit on it – three months for instance.
- Make him keep a certain distance from your home, your workplace and your children's school.
- Stop him damaging or removing any property from your home.
- If you have had to leave the home or he has ousted you, then an injunction can be made to let you back in.

Taking out an injunction is an aggressive act and should not be done lightly. Do not be pressured into doing this if you fear for your own safety and that of your children if you do so.

Getting an injunction

You can apply for an injunction yourself under the Domestic Violence and Matrimonial Proceedings Act 1976, via a county court, but if speed is of the essence it is better to go through a solicitor. You can use the Green Card Scheme to pay (*see page 444*). You can take out an injunction even if you are no longer living with your partner provided the time gap is not too long. The proceedings will be in a county court, in private. Your partner has to be given four days' notice to attend. The court will take into consideration

- His behaviour.
- Where you are living, where he would live if he was made to leave.
- The needs of your children.

If the court does issue an injunction it can also add a 'power of arrest' to the injunction if he has caused you or the children actual bodily harm
or if there is a likelihood that he will do so. The power of arrest means that the police have the power to arrest him if he breaks the injunction, although they are not obliged to do so. If the situation arises, you may have to lean on the police to act.

Stopping your partner from molesting you is not the only way of using an injunction. It may be invoked as part of the proceedings for custody of children, for making a child a ward of court and as part of an action for damages for trespass or assault.

Injunctions in an emergency

In an emergency – if for instance you fear violence and do not want your partner to know that you are applying for an injunction – you can apply for an **ex parte injunction** using emergency legal aid if necessary (*see page 444*). In this case your partner is not given notice to attend the court, but the injunction is only given for seven days, so you can get your act together. It is unusual for somebody to be ejected from their home or threatened with arrest under an ex parte injunction. It provides breathing space while other proceedings take place and before a full hearing is arranged. You can get an emergency ex parte injunction at any time, even over the weekend – ring your local police station to find out where the duty judge is in your area (your solicitor would normally do this for you). If you fear for your life and move to another address, your solicitor can apply for it to be kept secret, in other words, not mentioned on the court papers. This request is usually granted.

What happens if he disobeys the injunction?

Your partner is then in contempt of court. This means that he can be hauled back before the court again and the terms of the injunction may be stiffened. The court has the power to send him to prison but this is rarely done. If he does disobey the injunction, make a note of what happened and when and phone your solicitor. You may have to go back to court to have the injunction reinforced or to have him committed to prison.

If his behaviour is so bad that it is affecting you and the children, but he has not been violent or threatened violence, you can ask for a court order to restrain him or to get him to leave. This can be done while you are staying with friends or in a refuge.

Place of Safety Order

Another measure a magistrate can impose in an emergency is to make a Place of Safety Order. This allows the Social Services to take your child away to a place of safety – usually a children's home or foster home but it could be the police station. The Social Services do this if it has reason to believe that there are grounds for making a care order for the child in the future. A Place of Safety Order lasts 28 days and cannot be renewed; however, the court can supersede it with an interim care order instead.

Interim care order

This is a temporary measure which puts your child into care while his or her future is being sorted out. It has a limit of 28 days and there is nothing to stop the court handing the child back to you once the situation has been resolved, probably with a court case. Depending on the circumstances, the child might be returned to you with a supervision order. This means that the local Social Services will supervise the care of your child, probably by frequent visits. It pays, in general, to co-operate with the social workers even if they seem to you to be dictatorial or patronizing. They have a great deal of power when it comes to negotiating with the local court and will be asked to report on you. For further information *see* **Children,** *page 256.*

Council help

If you have to leave your home because of violence or threats and do not want to return, you can apply to the council for housing as a homeless person. It is their duty, under the Housing Act of 1985, to help women who have suffered violence or threats from someone in the same house. But you will only get instant temporary accommodation if you are thought to be in 'priority need' (*see* **Housing**, *page 489*).

LONELINESS

We are all likely to find ourselves alone at some time in our lives. Over 30 per cent of the population now lives alone and the figure is rising. There are many reasons why we may find ourselves in this situation.

- A partner may die or leave and children grow up and leave home.
- A relationship may come to an end.
- We may retire or be made redundant.
- We may move to a new area and not know anybody (mothers with small babies often come into this category).
- We may be a single parent trapped at home with small children and without the money to afford to go out.
- We may be old.

- We may be ill – illness and disability can isolate us from other people, especially if we cannot get around.
- Those who are HIV-positive or suffering from AIDS can feel especially isolated and frightened and often have to face up to prejudice as well.
- Mental health problems, especially agoraphobia or depression, can bring loneliness in their wake, since both of these illnesses cause us to withdraw into ourselves.
- People from minority ethnic or racial groups may feel desperately lonely if they are away from people of the same background.
- Closet lesbians and gays who are not in a relationship may feel isolated and lonely too.

Then there are all the temporary reasons for feeling lonely – the teenage years can be a lonely time, and middle-aged women who are going through the menopause may feel lonely and depressed, especially if they are having problems within their relationships.

What is loneliness?

Why do we dread being alone so much? We come into the world on our own and leave in the same way. The dread of loneliness can cause panic, like a fear of the dark. To avoid it some people get into the most disastrous relationships. Today, when there is so much emphasis placed on relationships as central to our happiness, loneliness can be experienced as an overwhelming feeling that we are isolated from the rest of society. It is feeling abandoned, unloved, insecure and excluded. It is as if there is a party going on out there and you have not been invited. And you can get these feelings even if you are in a crowd. Some people feel desperately lonely even though they are married or living with family.

Alone is not lonely

The word 'alone' is defined by the dictionary as 'being by oneself without assistance', whereas 'lonely' is described as 'solitary, companionless and isolated'. We can be alone without being lonely. Many people are very content to be in their own company, to the point where they actively seek solitude. Creative people, like writers, painters and poets, can only produce work if they are on their own. And anyone who has to study hard appreciates being left to himself to do so. Those people who have exhausting busy jobs, surrounded by people all the time, long to have time alone and cannot understand why some of us shrink from it. Busy mothers with a brood of noisy children may also wish they could spend more time by themselves. Strangely enough, people who live alone and like it tend to attract lots of friends. And many couples tend to be secretly envious of them.

How to cope with loneliness

Work out why you feel isolated and do something about it.

- Do not seek out or continue unsatisfactory relationships just for the sake of company. Never stay trapped in an unhappy partnership because you are afraid to let go. You are far better off without people who make you feel low.
- Spoil yourself. Take trouble over your meals. If you live alone you can go for quality instead of quantity and take special care with the food you prepare.
- Learn to like your own company. Very often what we are subconsciously seeking is someone who is exactly like us. In your own companionship there is no argument. You can choose to do whatever you want.
- Learn how to combat panic attacks that often come with loneliness. If you feel panicky in crowds or uncomfortable in public, try relaxation or yoga classes and assertiveness training to make you more self-confident and to calm you down.
- Talk to people. Practise on the postman, the people in the corner shop, bus conductors. Get into the habit of initiating conversation, even if it is only about the weather. Do not be afraid of rejection.
- Take up some new interest or activity, something that will stretch your mind and make you work hard. Watch the Open University programmes on TV to get ideas.
- If you are computer-literate, consider joining the Internet, then you can talk to people all over the world, day or night, for just the cost of a local phone call.
- Do not join contact or singles groups where your very singleness will be brought home to you. Instead pinpoint some interest and take it up seriously. At painting clubs, sailing clubs and language classes you can get to know people without feeling you need to socialize with them as well. As time goes by you may meet a new set of friends through these interests.
- If you do not have a special interest, join a pressure group or the local branch of a political party. There you will meet a large cross-section of people of all ages.
- Dining and wine and food clubs are springing up in large cities and are other places to meet people. If there is not one in your area, why not start one?
- Build up your self-esteem by mastering some skill or sport.
- Help others, but at this stage, avoid anything that is going to make you feel down; working with the very sick and the very old can wait until you have enough inner strength to cope with those situations. Helping the disabled or becoming an 'uncle' or 'auntie' to a child in care, on the other hand, can be very rewarding for you as well as for them.
- If you are feeling really low, consider therapy. Talking things over with a psychotherapist may help enormously.

- If you are retired and getting on in years, consider going into sheltered accommodation where there is always a warden around, and plenty of people to talk to in your peer group.
- Find a support group. In the pages of this book you will find groups for many kinds of loneliness. Take advantage of them and get in touch.

Alone on holiday

How to have a happy holiday.

- Consider taking a special-interest trip – a painting course in Tuscany, biking in France or walking in the Lake District. These sorts of holidays are often filled with people travelling alone; if they are not single, the chances are that their partners do not share the same interests.
- Remember there are travel companies that will match people with travel companions and other firms that specialize in women-only holidays (*see* **Help Section,** *page 532*). If you are a single parent there are holidays for you too (*see* **Children,** *page 272*).
- Pick a trip you will really enjoy – do not go in the expectation of meeting Mr/Ms Right.
- Ask your travel agent what sorts of people have booked on the holiday. He should be able to find out.
- If you are going on a singles holiday, choose one that features a large rather than a small group of people – expect there to be far more women than men.
- Avoid going during school holidays when you will be surrounded by families.
- Avoid booking into big impersonal hotels. You are much better off in small family-run places.
- Go on excursions and activities, mix as much as you can. Circulate right from the start and do not latch on to just one person.

UNREQUITED LOVE

You love someone and he or she does not love you. Maybe the person does not even notice you; unrequited love is very hard to bear. At its worst it can become an obsession that ruins your life. It has even led to murder. We all hate rejection, it makes us wonder what is wrong with us, we feel demeaned, downcast and we are convinced that we must be unlovable. And if the object of your affections is in love with someone else and tells you about it, the pain is all the harder to bear. But we cannot *make* somebody love us.

Unrequited love is a negative emotion and if this is happening to you, take swift action.

- Remove yourself as far as you can from the object of your affections. If you work alongside the person, consider changing your job.
- Do not let the person know how you feel. Try to keep it to yourself and in doing so keep your dignity. If you are sure the person does not return your affection, it is better not to say anything.
- Get a life. Fill your waking day with activities, mixing with other people as much as possible. Do not make life hell for yourself by waiting for the phone to ring.
- Do not waste time day-dreaming. Be realistic, think about something else, push the idea from your mind.
- Cultivate the friendships of people who are single and unattached and not in love. Go out and have a good time.
- If the person once loved you and does not any more, treat it like a divorce. It is time to pick up the pieces and move on.
- Think of all the people whom you like very much but do not fancy. There is nothing wrong in that. In fact lovers may come and go, but friends go on for ever.
- Do not let yourself be exploited. Sometimes calculating people sense that they are the object of others' affections and play on this. You may find yourself being a doormat, being made to help with tasks that no one else wants to do.

BEREAVEMENT

Despite the fact that death has been brutalized and cheapened these days by continual exposure to it on TV, the very word 'bereavement' frightens most people. We tend to shy away from the idea, we are unwilling to discuss it, we feel awkward talking about it, and certainly find it difficult to handle the situation.

Meeting a person who has just been bereaved is a situation many people would rather avoid. They may feel they must avoid mentioning the person who is dead, for instance, in case it causes a reaction. But grief is a normal, albeit a heart-rending reaction to loss. We have lost the company of someone who has shared our life in some way. We have to come to terms with the fact that we can never talk to that person again. Things left unsaid and questions left unanswered remain forever in our minds. Many people feel that their happiness has died with the person who has gone. They find themselves having to go out on their own, cook on their own, sit and eat on their own and go to bed on their own.

We have to come to terms with the fact that we are going to have to make a new life with someone missing from it. The heartache and pain seems as if it will never go away. Sometimes, if the relationship was not a happy one, the pain is even worse because it is tinged with regret.

Grief affects us in different ways. Sometimes it makes us focus on our own life and relationships. Some people bottle things up, others are very vocal about their feelings. Sometimes those who are the calmest and most in charge will suffer delayed trauma. We feel as if we are called upon to play the role of a sorrowing partner, relative or friend in public when we would rather keep our intimate grieving to ourselves. Men, in particular, find it difficult to express their feelings and may suffer great stress without showing it, whereas women are usually much better at opening up. It is not unusual to suffer some kind of psychosomatic illness – aches and pains and shortness of breath. We may be unable to eat or to sleep. The reaction to the death of someone close to you, especially if it was unexpected, can prompt a whole host of reactions.

Disbelief

'It cannot have happened, there must be a mistake' . . . this is a common reaction, particularly if the death is sudden. Anything can trigger off memories – clothes left behind or possessions. When a close friend of mine committed suicide, I just could not believe what had happened, I felt as though he had moved back to his native Australia. I kept wanting to send him letters. Planting something in the loved one's memory may help. Watching a tree or a rose grow as the years go by can be a great comfort.

Anger and resentment

These are very normal reactions. Not only can we feel angry that the death has happened, but we can sometimes direct our anger against the person who has died. How could he or she have left us like this? Or our anger may be directed against the doctors who treated the person. You might want to rage against an uncaring god. You may feel resentful towards the world at large and those who are enjoying themselves when you are in such pain.

Guilt

This is another emotion that can strike us. 'I was unkind to him, I never said goodbye properly.' If someone dies after a long and painful illness we may feel guilty for the very natural way in which we had hoped that their suffering would soon be at an end.

Fear

We may be overwhelmed by fear, because the death of someone close makes us conscious of our own mortality. We may also be afraid of trying to cope without the support of that person. If we have lost a child, we may be fearful of letting the other children out of our sight.

Isolation

If you lose a beloved parent or partner, you feel very alone in the world. It seems as if things will never be the same again and that you will never feel happy or want to laugh. Nothing can turn back the clock and return the person you have lost. Life must go on. But you will learn to accept what has happened and that is the new beginning. Dealing with grief is part of a growing process; we emerge from it very often a more tolerant and a more rounded person. Expect mood swings from anger and bitterness to sadness. They show that the healing process is under way.

Decisions

If you have lost someone who has shared your life, do nothing at first. You might later regret an impulsive decision to sell up and move. Go away if necessary, stay with friends, but do not put your house on the market or decide to move to another place until you are absolutely sure what you are doing. The pain of your loss will return from time to time. Sudden reminders will jolt you – something with your loved one's handwriting on it or a film you saw together. But it becomes more bearable each day and you begin to see the way ahead more clearly.

Telling someone the bad news

You may be unfortunate enough to have to break the news of someone's death to the partner, family or friends. Sometimes it is better for a friend or family member to break the news of a death rather than a policeman or a doctor. Although both these professions have experience of doing this, they are not always the best people for the task. There are ways of handling the situation.

Prepare the person for the worst Lessen the shock as much as you can by telling him gently that you have some bad news.

Tell the person in private Take him to one side, do not blurt the news out in front of other people.

Stay with the person Sit with him, hold his hand, put your arm around him.

Remain calm People react to sudden bad news in different ways. Make yourself into a rock that they can cling to through their tears. Do not be surprised and alarmed if the person screams, hits you and refuses to believe you at first. Make allowances for the situation.

Do not feel guilty The death was not your fault, so do not feel that it was.

Listen Listen quietly to what the person has to say. Do not feel that you need to fill a vacuum with useless chat. Do not go on about your own experience of bereavement and how you coped.

Bring in a friend or relative to take over When you feel the time is right, find someone from the family to take over from you.

SUDDEN DEATH

The sudden death of someone you love either through an accident, a heart attack or worst of all, suicide, is always traumatic. We have no chance to prepare ourselves for what has happened. In some cases, in an air crash or fire, we may not even see the body of the person who has died and therefore find it hard to come to terms with the fact that they have actually gone. We may blame ourselves. 'If only I hadn't kept him talking on the doorstep he would not have hit that other car.' or 'He said he didn't feel well that morning, I should have made him stay home.' Perhaps you parted with the loved one on bad terms.

Suicide

The feelings of grief at the suicide of someone you love is partnered with the overwhelming sadness that the person had not been able to communicate his plight to you. None of us can ever know why someone makes a final decision to kill himself. It is interesting to note that very few people who have a terminal or life-threatening illness – something you would imagine would make you want to contemplate suicide – actually do so. Very few suicide decisions are made on the spur of the moment, they are usually planned and well thought out.

Do not look back
There is no point going over old ground, puzzling over why the person did it and what indications there were that you might have missed.

Do not feel guilty
Particularly if the suicide is of someone who was mentally ill, you may curse yourself for having lost patience with him, for not having listened enough, or that you should have offered more help. But few of us have total control over other human beings and the chances are that it would have made no difference. Lovers who rejected the person who killed himself, and wives who have left their husbands who subsequently killed themselves, have a particular burden to bear. But it is likely that the suicide's view of the world was so bleak that no amount of help would have changed it.

The death of a parent

The gap left by the loss of your parents is a large one. Whom are you going to tell now, when something bad happens, or when you've achieved a success? We all need someone to be proud of us, someone to go to for advice, even if we do not take it. The thing about a parent's love is that it is unconditional. Even the closest partner cannot quite fill that space. Often there are many questions we would have liked to have asked – on family history perhaps, or some secret which only becomes apparent when we go through their possessions after their death.

When our parents are very old, we expect them to die sooner or later, but when they do we are often overwhelmed by feelings of guilt – that we did not visit them as often as we should; that we were often irritated by their behaviour, their slowness and deafness, and showed it; that we never lived up to their expectations for us. We may also feel guilty that we took them for granted.

The death of a child

The hardest death to get over is that of a child, a profoundly distressing event that we all hope will never happen to us. From a miscarriage or still birth, to a cot death or terminal illness and accident, the shock and the emotional turmoil are great. There is the sight of a still, cold little body, or a premature child struggling for life in a special care baby unit, then a distressingly tiny coffin, and finally the return home to the nightmare of putting things away, the cot, the pram and the toys. Time does heal, but it does take time. Now, at least, there is counselling and help on offer so you need not suffer alone (*see page 201*). The Child Death Helpline is open 7 nights a week from 7pm to 10pm and on Wednesdays from 10 am to 1pm on Freephone 0800 282 986.

The death of a child is a family affair. If the child is yours, you may find yourself having to console his brothers and sisters who may blame themselves for not having played with the child, perhaps, or loved him enough, or for being jealous of the attention you gave him. If other children are affected they often feel that it is something that they have done which has caused the baby's death. In the case of something unexplained like a cot death – now called a sudden infant death syndrome – you and your partner may not only blame yourselves but each other. This is the time to call for some counselling (*see page 201*).

A child runs out onto a road and is run over. You, as the mother, blame yourself for taking your eye off him for a minute. A child dies while you are at work and you castigate yourself for the very fact that you were not there, even if it would have made no difference. Whatever the reason for the child's death, you are likely to feel guilty. Talk to other people about it, talk it out. Do this by getting in touch with one of the many support groups (*see page 201*).

The loss of a baby brings thoughts not so much of the past but of what might have been. Most of us, when we are expecting a child, day-dream about the life ahead of that child. When this is cut short we are devastated. You may also feel isolated because people surprisingly enough tend to treat the death of a baby as less important than that of an older child. Remarks like 'well you can always try again' are tactless and unintentionally cruel.

Stillbirth is just as traumatic. You may feel a failure. You may feel that there is something wrong with you, that you are not a whole mother because your baby has died. A miscarriage can be almost as distressing, as I know from personal experience. All the initial excitement of knowing that there is a new life on the way, the preparation and feeling it move inside you, suddenly come to nothing.

The devastating news that the baby you are carrying has a severe abnormality is a terrible burden to bear. The natural reaction at first is disbelief – the doctors must have made a mistake. Then the decision has to be made whether or not to continue with the pregnancy. You and your partner will want to think about how it will affect your lives and the lives of your other children. You will also want to consider the quality of life that the baby could expect if it was born.

By law, a baby that is stillborn after 28 weeks must be buried or cremated. If the baby did not survive for that time you still have a legal right to arrange for the baby to be buried, but you must let the hospital know immediately. If a formal burial is not wanted, the hospital can organize things for you. In that case the baby will either be cremated or buried with others in a mass unmarked grave. Some people want to see their baby, even if it was stillborn, to say goodbye to the baby, while others may be frightened if it is their first experience of death.

This is where support systems come in (*see page 201*); being able to talk to someone else who has been through the same experience can be a tremendous help.

Putting your life together

At some stage of grieving after the death of a baby or a small child you come to the realization that life must go on. You must pick up the pieces and go on living if only for your partner or for the other children and your friends. This is particularly hard to do. You will have good days and bad days. The bad days will seem so bleak that you wonder how you can go on. But the good days will give you a glimpse of the world out there and the fact that it is going on around you.

If you marked them on a graph you would find that the bad days gradually become not quite so bad, and the good days increase – in other words, an upward slope would show on the chart. Then you would know that you are on the mend. Then the day comes when you realize that you have not thought about your loss.

Acceptance is the first stage you have to reach. When we can accept what has happened, then the healing process has begun. Tears will be shed. All the other feelings of grief will be present, but at first there may also be bitterness and envy and resentment – why has this happened to me? and why has *she* got a healthy child when mine has been taken from me? You see other women in the street shouting at and slapping their children and hate them. Sometimes we find ourselves turning against our partner, forgetting that he too is suffering.

If you are the father you may feel powerless to help and feel shut out. One of the saddest couples I know lost their only child after an accident when she was six years old. They never spoke to each other about it. He refuses to discuss it as it causes him too much pain. Write about it, if it helps. Write a letter to the baby who has gone, write down your thoughts, or keep a diary.

Bereavement – a postscript

The wish to believe that someone you love is still alive and contactable in another world is a very understandable one. Unfortunately some unscrupulous people put ads in newspapers offering to help grievers get in touch with the dead or even call on them. The Spiritualist National Union says that anyone invading your privacy and grief and offering to put you in touch with the dead should be reported to the police. Any medium who is genuine will say that trying to communicate with a dead person can be nothing more than an experiment; any medium who says he can put you in touch with the dead is fraudulent. If you do wish to consult a medium, the best way to find one is via your local spiritualist church.

PARTNERS AND FRIENDS: HELP DIRECTORY

Bereavement

- Alder Centre, Royal Liverpool Children's NHS Trust, Eaton Road, Liverpool L12 2AT, (0151 252 5391). Counsels and befriends all those affected by a child's death. Has a helpline on 0151 228 9759 from 7 pm to 10 pm.
- Child Death Helpline, (0171 829 8685). Open on Mondays and Thursdays from 7 pm to 10 pm, counselling anyone affected by the death of a child.
- Compassionate Friends, 53 North Street, Bristol BS3 1EN, (0117 966 5202). A support and friendship group that offers counselling to families who have lost a child of any age. Run by parents who have been bereaved. Has a helpful newsletter, runs a postal library and mans a helpline on 0117 953 9639.
- Cruse, Cruse House, 126 Sheen Road, Richmond, Surrey TW9 1UR, (0181 940 4818). With many branches throughout the country, Cruse offers counselling and help to anyone who is bereaved, and a chance to make contact with other people in a similar situation.
- Foundation for the Study of Infant Deaths, 14 Halkin Street, London SW1X 7DP, (0171 235 0965). Has local parent support groups throughout the country and offers counselling and information to bereaved families after the death of a small child. Their 24-hour helpline number is 0171 235 1721.

- Gay Bereavement Project, Unitarian Rooms, Hoop Lane, London NW11 8BS, (0181 455 6844). Gives advice and support to homosexual people on the death of partners. Has a helpline from 7 pm to midnight on 0181 455 8894.
- Institute of Family Therapy, 43 New Cavendish Street, London W1M 7RG, (0171 935 1651). Counsels bereaved families and those with someone in their family who is seriously ill. The service is free but donations are welcome to help other families.
- Jewish Bereavement Counselling Service, 1 Cyprus Gardens, London N3 1SP, (0181 349 0839). This organization has a round-the-clock telephone helpline for bereaved Jewish families. Also has counsellors who will visit families living in north-west and south-west London.
- Lesbian and Gay Bereavement Project, Colindale Hospital, London NW9 5HG, (0181 455 8894). This project runs a helpline for gays and lesbians who have lost a partner through death. Also offers practical help on funeral arrangements, inquests and wills.
- National Association of Bereavement Services, 20 Norton Folgate, London E1 6DB, (0171 247 0617). Can put you in touch with a local bereavement support service.
- National Association of Widows, 54–57 Allison Street, Digbeth, Birmingham B5 5TH, (0121 643 8348). A support, friendship, information and advice group for widows with branches throughout the country.
- Parents Anonymous, 8 Manor Gardens, London N7 6LA, (0171 263 8918). Crisis support and counselling for parents of children who are critically ill in hospital and for parents and family who have lost a child through sudden death.
- Portsmouth Baby Loss Support Group, Rita Fraser, 14b Lovedean Lane, Portsmouth, Hants PO8 8HH, (01705 592958). Offers support and comfort to those who have lost a baby as a result of a miscarriage, ectopic pregnancy, stillbirth or termination for foetal abnormality.
- Red Admiral Project, 15a Philbeach Gardens, Earls Court, London SW5 9EB, (0171 835 1495). Setting up a support group for women bereaved through HIV and AIDS.
- SA MM support against murder and manslaughter, Cranmer House, 39 Brixton Road, London SW9 6DZ, (0171 735 3838). This group offers support and care to parents of murdered children, via letters, phone calls and personal visits. Also puts them in touch with other agencies that can help.
- Shadow of Suicide, (Compassionate Friends), 53 North St, Bristol BS3 1EN, (0117 966 5202). A support group for parents, grandparents and families of children of any age, including adults, who have committed suicide. Has a helpline on 0117 953 9639.

- Stillbirth and Neonatal Death Society, 28 Portland Place, London W1N 4DE, (0171 436 5881). A network of self-help groups throughout the country that gives support and friendship to parents who have lost a child late in pregnancy, at the time of birth or soon afterwards. Also has a number of helpful leaflets on the subject.
- Twins and Multiple Births Association, Bereavement Support Group, PO Box 30, Little Sutton, South Wirral L66 1TH, (0151 348 0020). Offers counselling for anyone who has lost a twin.
- Yad b'Yad, (0181 444 7134). A Jewish child bereavement support group.

See also

Miscarriage Association, Conception (*page 124*).
Natural Death Centre, Death (*page 309*).
Samaritans (*page 19*).
Twins and Multiple Births Association, Conception (*page 216*).

Divorce

Divorce Conciliation and Advisory Service, 38 Ebury Street, London SW1W 0LU, (0171 730 2422). Runs a counselling service for couples, particularly those with children, who are having problems with their marriage and are thinking of divorce.

- General Register Office, St Catherine's House, 10 Kingsway, London WC2B 6JP, (0171 242 0262). The place to go for a copy of birth, death or marriage certificates.
- The General Register Office, Smedley Hydro, Trafalgar Road, Southport PR8 2HH, (0151 471 4200). The address to obtain a copy of birth, death or marriage certificates by post.
- Jewish Marriage Council, 23 Ravenshurst Avenue, London NW4 4EE, (0181 203 6311). Not only counsels couples with relationship problems or who are contemplating divorce, but also runs a marriage bureau for Jewish people. Has a helpline on 0181 203 6211. If you live out of London the reduced rate helpline is 01345 581999.
- National Council for the Divorced and Separated, 13 High Street, Little Shelford, Cambridge CB2 5ES, (0116 270 8880). Runs counselling centres throughout the country for people whose marriages have ended in divorce or separation. Also advises people by post.
- Network of Access and Child Contact Centres, St Andrew's with Castlegate, United Reform Church, Goldsmith Street, Nottingham NG1 5JT, (0115 948 4557). Works with children of divorced or separated parents by providing centres throughout the country where the children can meet up with

the other parent or member of the family who does not otherwise get a
chance to see them.
- Solicitors Family Law Association, PO Box 302, Orpington, Kent BR6 8QX,
  (01689 850227). Can supply a list of solicitors in your area who will adopt a
  reasonable, conciliatory attitude to divorce and represent your interests.

See also
Both Parents Forever, Children (*page 275*).
Families Need Fathers, Children (*page 275*).
Legal Action for Women, Legal (*page 459*).

Domestic violence

Women's Aid Federation (England), PO Box 391, Bristol BS99 7WS,
(0117 963 3494). Local groups throughout England offer counselling, practical
help and a refuge for women and children who are suffering emotional, mental
or physical violence, harassment or sexual abuse. It has a telephone helpline on
0117 963 3542.

Loneliness

Carr-Gomm Society Ltd, Telegraph Hill Centre, Kitto Road, London SE14 5TY,
(0171 277 6060). This society is a housing association which has a large number
of small sheltered flats for lonely people of all ages, of either sex.
- Outsiders Club, PO Box 4ZB, London EC2A 3BX, (0171 739 3195). Counsels
  and helps people, including the disabled, who feel isolated and rejected or
  have a bad self-image. Has some helpful publications and will supply names
  and addresses of other members so you can get in touch with them. Has
  monthly lunches in London and in Birmingham as well as local events,
  weekends and parties.
- Single Again, Suite 33, 10 Barley Mow Passage, (0181 749 3745). An
  organization formed to give advice and support to people experiencing the
  breakdown of a relationship, divorce and bereavement. Publishes a bi-
  monthly magazine and has a women's network that puts women in touch with
  other single women in their area. Has a recorded adviceline on 0891 551212
- Single Concern, PO Box 4, High Street, Goring-on-Thames RG8 9DN,
  (01491 873195). Also known as Person-to-Person and Future Friends, this
  organization for lonely or isolated people has a help service and publishes a
  magazine. It also helps with problems such as depression, divorce,
  bereavement and single parenthood.

Partnership problems

Association for Analytic and Bodymind Therapy and Training, Princes House, 8 Princes Avenue, London N10 3LR, (0181 883 5418). Has weekend and self-help groups to help couples improve communications with each other and mend relationships that are under stress.

- British Association for Counselling, 1 Regent Place, Rugby, Warwickshire CV21 2PJ, (01788 578328). Has a national directory of counsellors with a note of their fees and issues an information sheet on counselling.
- Catholic Marriage Advisory Council, 23 Kensington Square, London W8 5HH, (0171 937 37810). Has 80 centres throughout England and Wales (look under Catholic in your local Phone Book). You can usually be seen within a fortnight and no charge is made for counselling, though donations are welcome.
- Dignity, 16 Brixham Close, Horston Grange, Nuneaton CV11 6YT, (01203 350312 9am to 8pm) (01203 397947 8pm to 10pm) (01203 398452 10pm to midnight). An organization that helps people suffering the distress of suspected or confirmed adultery. Offers advice and counselling and has a newsletter.
- London Marriage Guidance, 76a New Cavendish Street, London W1M 7LB, (0171 580 1087). Offers counselling at the above address and at 30 other centres around London. Some places offer evening appointments and the cost of a session depends on your ability to pay. The waiting list is one to three months.
- Marriage Counselling, Scotland, 105 Hanover Street, Edinburgh EH2 1DJ, (0131 225 5006). Has centres throughout Scotland (look in your Phone Book). There is no charge, but donations are welcomed.
- National Marriage Guidance, Herbert Gray College, Little Church Street, Rugby, Warwickshire CV21 3AP, (01788 573241). Has a series of centres throughout the country (look in your Phone Book). It works with couples, helping them over relationship or sexual problems. Fees are in accordance with what you can afford to pay.
- Relate – Marriage Guidance. Has numerous centres around the country, offering counselling and advice on marriage/partnership problems. You can find Relate listed in your local Phone Book.

5

CONCEPTION

INFERTILITY

It is reckoned that one couple in six suffers some problems conceiving a baby, partly because many people put off starting a family until quite late, by which time the woman (and sometimes the man) is less likely to be fertile – keep in mind the dropping sperm count of men in the western world. And more people than ever are now seeking fertility treatment, a complex maze of diagnosis and treatment that can take many years to complete.

You are generally diagnosed as having a problem if you have tried to conceive for over a year without any success. There are many reasons why this should be. Sometimes a woman fails to produce eggs or they may only be released very irregularly from the ovaries. She may have blocked fallopian tubes, endometriosis or it may be that her cervical mucus is hostile to the male sperm. Only detective work by a doctor can determine the reason.

Male infertility is much more common than is generally thought – in up to half of infertile couples, it could be the man who has the problem. It could be caused by a low sperm count, which in turn can be caused by too much drink or drugs, or smoking, mumps in childhood, or, more commonly these days, simply too much stress.

Fertility tests

If you are concerned about your fertility, you can now buy ovulation prediction test kits, based on a urine sample. The results are somewhat tricky to understand and they are not infallible, but they provide a useful rough guide. Male fertility test kits are also on sale but they tend only to give the sperm count, and not the quality of the sperm which also needs to be taken into consideration.

What can be done

If you are desperate to have children but are having problems conceiving, there are a number of treatments that may help. The main ones are:

IVF (In-vitro fertilization)

As the name suggests, this procedure quite literally means fertilization in glass – in this case, a test tube. The woman is given fertility drugs to stimulate her egg production, ending in a hormone injection to trigger ovulation. She is then given a general anaesthetic and her eggs are collected with an aspiration needle that is introduced into the ovaries via a small probe through a tiny incision. Alternatively, an ultrasound probe is put into the vagina, then an aspiration needle is used to collect the eggs. Surplus eggs can be frozen for future use.

After collection, the eggs are incubated for a short time. Then sperm is added to them and they are incubated for a further 24 to 48 hours. If fertilization takes place, three eggs – the maximum number allowed now, after so many multiple births – are returned to the womb 48 to 72 hours after collection in a procedure that is no more uncomfortable than a cervical smear.

GIFT (Gamete intra-fallopian transfer)

This newer technique is a variation on IVF. In this procedure, the eggs are collected, and mixed with the sperm, but instead of being put back into the womb, the most mature three are transferred back into the fallopian tubes, making it nearer to what happens in a normal pregnancy. This generally has a better success rate than IVF, though sometimes it can be combined with IVF to give a higher success rate.

ICSI (Intra-cytoplasmic sperm injection)

In this procedure the woman is injected with egg-stimulating drugs, mature eggs are collected and injected with sperm via a micro-needle seven times smaller than a human hair. Fertilized eggs are then inserted into the womb.

ICSI is sometimes combined with electro-ejaculation – a way of extracting sperm from men who cannot ejaculate. This technique is used to enable paralysed men to become fathers.

Artificial insemination

This is a much simpler process than the two above. In this case sperm from the man (or sometimes a donor) is simply injected directly into the womb. This is done in cases where there are problems with intercourse, where the man has weak sperm or where the woman has cervical mucus that is hostile to sperm.

If you have treatment with sperm from a donor at a clinic registered by the Human Fertilization and Embryology Authority and are married at the time of the birth of the resulting child, then your husband is the legal father, unless he can prove he did not consent to the treatment. If, however, the arrangement was a private one, then the donor of the sperm is technically the father. But unless he is married to you he does not have 'parental responsibility' (*see page 221*).

Donated eggs

Other techniques may involve donated eggs. The donor has hormone injections, then a scan and finally a minor operation to remove the eggs. Since few eggs are available, treatment with donor eggs may involve a long wait – twice as long for black people because of the lack of volunteer donors.

Taking the treatment

If you decide to go for a course of treatment you will first have an initial consultation. As a woman, you may have a hysterosalpingogram (HSG), a procedure in which dye is passed through the cervix and up into the fallopian tubes under X-ray to highlight any abnormalities. The man will have supplied a sample of semen for testing. Latest figures show that one in three women who have IVF or GIFT treatments can expect to become pregnant. Of those, one in eight will have a full-term healthy baby.

Multiple births

Apart from the expensive IVF programme, many women now have halfway house drug treatments for fertility, often administered by their GPs. These stimulate the ovaries and are mainly responsible for multiple births. These treatments are totally unregulated and do not have the same guidelines as the IVF programme has. An instant family can be an infertile couple's dream but the reality of triplets, quads or even higher numbers of children can be a nightmare and a social disaster. An ultrasound scan will show if a multiple birth is likely, indicating the number of follicles present. If there are a number of foetuses in the womb, the doctor and the mother-to-be then have to decide whether to kill off some of the foetuses by an injection of potassium.

Multiple babies produced in this way are more likely to be sick or disabled than single babies. You may end up with one or two healthy children and a disabled one. The babies will inevitably be premature and, with that, suffer from all kinds of chronic conditions. Many are in special care for months on end. The Human Fertilization and Embryology authority is worried about the situation and some form of control on this technique is likely to be introduced in the future.

Surrogate mothers

Accepting money to have a baby to order for someone else is illegal. However, it is reckoned that more than two thousand women have got round the law by accepting 'expenses' for being a surrogate mother. Although you make a childless couple's life complete, having then to give away a baby you have carried to someone else can have a devastating effect on your life. Many women who have done this have felt they never got over their loss. It is almost as if the child was still-born or given away for adoption. If you are tempted to help someone in this way, think very carefully about what effect it is likely to have on you before you agree.

FERTILITY TREATMENT AND THE NHS

The inability to conceive is felt as a stigma by some women while others can become depressed and isolated, and it can affect their marriage. Yet the possibility of having this very expensive treatment, free on the NHS, is akin to winning the National Lottery – whether or not you get treatment is a lottery of sorts in itself. And patients are now being charged for NHS fertility treatments at some hospitals, notably St Thomas's in London.

What are your chances of getting NHS treatment for infertility? At the moment it depends on which part of the country you live in – only 45 of the 133 health authorities and trusts will pay for IVF treatment at the moment and the numbers are likely to shrink. And you could wait up to five years for it to be done. Some authorities will not pay for treatment for people over the age of 35, in others the age limit is 40. Your GP should be able to tell you what your chances are of having it done in your particular part of the country. Otherwise expect to pay well over a thousand pounds for private treatment.

PREGNANCY

There is a big shake-up underway in the maternity services. The Department of Health's recent report recommended a move away from high-tech hospital-led care in pregnancy and childbirth, recognizing that most pregnant women are not patients but normal, healthy people who are about to give birth. The report recognizes that midwives, rather than doctors, are the best people to look after pregnant women.

Pregnancy tests

With the aid of a simple kit, bought over the counter at the chemist's, it is easy to find out whether or not you are pregnant. They are not totally infallible, however; if the test says you are pregnant, check with your doctor before spreading the news. These tests are so easy to do for yourself that most GPs have stopped doing them for patients, advising them to buy a kit. Your chemist may be able to do the test for you, in which case it may work out cheaper than buying a kit yourself. You may have to wait some days for the result.

Pregnancy: your rights

The Patients' Charter says:

- You should be told the name of the midwife who will be responsible for your care.
- You should have the opportunity to see a consultant obstetrician, a doctor who specializes in pregnancy and childbirth, at least once during your pregnancy.
- You should also have the opportunity to see a consultant paediatrician or paedriatric surgeon, doctors who specialize in the care of children, if your obstretrician anticipates problems with your baby.
- You have the right to see your maternity records and to know that people who work for the NHS have a legal duty to keep their contents confidential. If you want to, you can ask to keep your maternity records during your pregnancy rather than leave them with the hospital, GP or midwife.
- You have the right to be given information on local maternity services including the type of care on offer, where you can give birth – including at home – what pain relief can be offered and what tests you can have and why. You should be given time to consider options before you make your decisions.
- You have a right to be given an explanation of any treatment proposed, including the benefits, risks and any alternatives, before you decide whether you will agree to the treatment.
- Your doctor or midwife should give advice on how you can best look after yourself and your baby while you are pregnant. This includes information on a healthy diet and the effects of smoking in pregnancy.
- Your hospital should give you a specific time for your ante-natal appointments and you should be seen within 30 minutes of that time.

Working benefits

Plans are afoot to change the benefits system for expectant mothers who work. But at the moment if you are planning to return to work after having the baby, even if you work part-time, you are entitled to:

- At least 14 weeks' maternity leave – 40 weeks if you have been with the same employer for two years.
- The right to return to work and statutory maternity pay, provided you have worked for at least six months.

To make sure of and protect your rights, contact the Maternity Alliance (*page 216*) for a copy of *Pregnant at Work Update*.

Antenatal care

You are entitled to paid time off for antenatal care. This includes time needed to travel to your clinic or your GP for appointments. You are entitled to this no matter how few hours you work or however recently you started your job. Antenatal care also includes parentcraft and relaxation classes. You need to tell your employers when you need time off and how long you are likely to be away. Your employers have the right to ask to see your appointment card and a certificate confirming you are pregnant signed by your GP, midwife or health visitor. If you are not paid or are refused time off, you can make a claim to the industrial tribunal within three months.

Your employer's duties

If you are pregnant or have given birth within the last six months or are breastfeeding and at work, new legislation says that your employer must make sure that the kind of work you do and the conditions you do it in will not put your health or your baby's health at risk. You only benefit from this rule if you have notified your employer in writing of your condition. Your employer must then:
- Assess the risks in your workplace.
- Do all that is reasonable to remove or reduce any risks found.
- Give you information on the risks and the measures taken to prevent or reduce them.
- If the risks still remain, your employer should alter your conditions or hours of work if it is reasonable to do so, to avoid the risk.
- If this is not possible, or the risk still remains, your employer must offer you a suitable alternative job or suspend you on full pay until the risk is over.
- If you unreasonably refuse the alternative work offered, you then lose the right to full pay while you are suspended.

Your rights

You are entitled to 14 weeks maternity leave if, as an employee, you write to your employers at least 21 days in advance telling them that you are pregnant and giving them the expected date of childbirth.
- You must also tell your employers the date when you intend to start your maternity leave, though you don't have to put this in writing unless your employers ask for it.
- If you are suddenly called into hospital and cannot give the 21 days notice, you must write to your employers as soon as you reasonably can.

- Your employers are entitled to ask for a copy of your maternity certificate (form MAT B1) which your midwife or GP will give to you when you are about six months pregnant.

What pay do I get?

- You are entitled to 18 weeks of payments called statutory maternity pay. For the first six weeks you get 90 per cent of your average pay, calculated on your gross earnings in the two months before the end of the 15th week before the baby is due.
- After the first six weeks, you are entitled to a basic allowance for up to 12 weeks or the time you go back to work.
- If you carry on working to nearer the time the baby is due you still get the 18 weeks maternity pay.

When can I start my leave?

It is up to you to decide when you want to stop work but the earliest you can take your leave is eleven weeks before the expected week of delivery. If you want to, however, you can work right up until the week your child is due.

However, if you have a pregnancy-related illness and are absent from work in the last six weeks of your pregnancy, your employer may make you take maternity leave from that moment – it depends on his attitude. If this happens, your maternity benefits, rather than sickness benefits, will be paid from that time.

- During your maternity leave all your employment rights – entitlement to holiday, pension rights, use of company car, will continue as though you were still at work.
- You do not need to give any notice of return if you are going back at the end of a normal 14-week maternity leave period.
- If you want to return before the 14 weeks are up, you must give your employers 7 days notice in writing of the date you will be back. If you don't do this, your employers can send you away again until the 14 weeks are up.
- You are not allowed by law to return to work within 2 weeks of the birth of your child, so if the baby is late, and your 14-week leave has run out, it will automatically be extended by 2 weeks from the actual birth of the child.
- If you are sick and unable to return to work when your 14-week leave is up, you should be able to get sick pay from your employers.

Returning to work – extended leave

If you have worked for the same employer for two years or more and the firm employs more than five people, you could qualify for additional maternity absence, provided you work at least until the end of the 12th week before the baby is due. Extended maternity absence can run up to 29 weeks. Your employers may write to you any time from 11 weeks after the start of your maternity leave, asking you to confirm you are going back to work. You must reply in writing within 14 days if you wish to return, otherwise you lose the right to do so. If you do not hear from your employers, you must write to them at least 21 days before you intend to return, telling them the exact date you will do so. You must return to work within 29 weeks after the birth of your child except in the following situations:

- You are ill. You can then delay going back to work for up to four weeks. You must then tell your employers you are extending your leave because of sickness and send them a medical certificate.
- There is an interruption of work because of outside circumstances, such as a strike.
- Your employers have asked you to delay your return and have given you a new date to restart work.
- Because you and your employers have agreed you should delay your return.

Dismissal because of pregnancy and/or maternity leave

It is now against the law for your firm to dismiss you or select you for redundancy for any reason connected with the fact that you are pregnant, have just given birth or are on maternity leave. It does not matter how long you have worked for them, or how many hours a week you work. If you are dismissed under these circumstances, your employer must give you a written statement of the reasons. You should not have to ask for this.

If you believe the reason you were dismissed is related to your pregnancy, contact your trades union or the Citizens' Advice Bureau. They will help you put in your claim to an industrial tribunal. The claim must be made within three months of dismissal. If you feel you have been discriminated against because you are a woman, if you were sacked or suffered a disadvantage like demotion or having your hours cut because you are pregnant or have had a baby, then you can also go to a tribunal.

What if I am self-employed, gave up work or changed jobs while pregnant?

You are then entitled to a maternity allowance provided you have paid full rate National Insurance contributions for at least 26 of the 55 weeks before the week in which the baby is expected. The rate per week depends on whether you are self-employed or unemployed or were employed in the qualifying week. Claim via form MA1 which you can get from your antenatal clinic or Social Security Office. Send it in when you are about six months pregnant, together with a maternity certificate.

CHILDBIRTH

The choices

These should include:

- Seeing your GP during your pregnancy, then a hospital delivery.
- Having antenatal care and delivery at the hospital.
- GP Unit delivery, where there is a midwife attached to your local practice. In this case the midwife goes to your home and then takes you to a GP obstetric unit for the birth of the baby which may or may not be attached to a hospital.
- Domino delivery. In this case you see a midwife during pregnancy then you give birth in the obstetric unit in the local hospital but come out soon afterwards.
- Care from a community midwife with a home delivery. If there are complications, however, you will be taken into hospital.
- You should have the choice whether to have your partner or other friend or relative with you while you are in labour and giving birth. You can decide who that will be.

For safety reasons, your baby is identified by name labels during its stay in hospital. These are put on shortly after the birth. You must be shown the labels as soon as possible, so that you can check that the information on them is correct. You can keep your baby with you in hospital unless there are clinical reasons why you should not. You should also be able to ask for your baby to be put in the nursery if you want this.

Your midwife or doctor should give you information on how to feed your baby. And they should give you support until you are happy with your baby's feeding. Consideration should be shown to your privacy, dignity, religious and cultural beliefs and dietary needs while you are in hospital, and that any confidential discussions with you take place in private. Relatives and friends should be able to visit you at all reasonable times as long as this does not disturb others.

Having a baby at home

Your GP is not obliged to provide you with maternity medical care if you ask for a home birth. However, if he refuses to get involved, you have the right to ask another GP to provide maternity cover for you.

Many women have been intimidated by their GPs when they have asked to have a baby at home, being told they might bleed to death, or that they were putting their baby at risk and might end up with a brain-damaged child. There have even been stories of women being struck off their doctors' lists for daring to suggest the possibility of childbirth at home, say the National Childbirth Trust. There may be many reasons behind this – not least of all that he feels he doesn't have the skills and the confidence to offer care for a home birth.

Being there

If you have your baby in hospital, most maternity units are quite happy to allow your partner to be there. But since the kidnapping of several new-born babies from hospitals, overnight visitors are discouraged as a security precaution. This, combined with the fact of overcrowding, may make it difficult for a man to be with his partner overnight. Before you go in for the birth, find out from your hospital whether or not your partner is allowed to be there all the time. It can be disconcerting and upsetting if he is suddenly sent away, just when you need him most.

Doulas

Doula is a Greek word meaning an experienced woman who helps others, and this name has been taken by an organization from the USA, now in this country too, which provides women with 'birth companions'. They are women who offer practical and emotional advice and support before and during the birth process but do not take any part in the medical processes. Some midwives are happy to have them alongside, others are not. Many women, particularly single or first-time mothers, need extra emotional support at this time. There are at the moment only a dozen *doulas* in this country. If you are interested ask your midwife if there is one in your area.

Post-natal depression

It is believed that at least one mother in ten is affected by the baby blues, as they are called. This mild depression is often caused by hormonal fluctuations just after the birth. Within a few days, things calm down and the baby blues disappear. But in up to 15 per cent of women it can turn into a real depression that warrants attention. If you are feeling unduly anxious or depressed when you come home from hospital, tell your midwife, health visitor or GP at once so that you get help right away. Anyone suffering from post-natal depression, a situation which goes on for months, needs attention, and the much more serious, but rare post-natal psychosis needs specialist treatment.

CONCEPTION: HELP DIRECTORY

Childbirth and pregnancy

- Active Birth Centre, 25 Bickerton Road, London N19 5JT, (0171 561 9006).
  Dedicated to making sure that women have the best experience possible of

pregnancy, labour and birth. It runs special antenatal workshops including those for birth in an upright position or in a water tank, yoga classes during pregnancy, baby massage and many alternative therapies including homoeopathy and acupuncture. It also hires out water pools for birthing.

- APEC, Action on Pre-Eclampsia, 61 Greenways, Abbots Langley, Herts WD5 0EU, (01923 266778). Has a helpline, above. Send a large SAE and 36p stamps for an information pack on the condition and what is likely to happen in a future pregnancy.
- Association for Improvements in the Maternity Services, 40 Kingswood Avenue, London NW6 6LS, (0181 960 5585). Although basically a pressure group dedicated to improving maternity care, it can advise you on your rights, what choices are available to you and where and how to complain if you experience a problem.
- Centre for Pregnancy Nutrition – Eating for Pregnancy Helpline, University of Sheffield, Dept of Obstetrics and Gynaecology, Clinical Sciences Centre, Northern General Hospital, Herries Road, Sheffield S5 7AU, (0114 243 4343). Gives advice to pregnant women on nutrition and healthy eating. Its helpline number is on 0114 242 4084.
- Maternity Alliance, 5th Floor, 45 Beech Street, London EC2P 2LX, (0171 588 8582). Can advise you on your legal rights during pregnancy and birth and give you information about the maternity services. Send an SAE plus an extra first-class stamp for a copy of *Pregnant at Work Update*.
- National Childbirth Trust, Alexandra House, Oldham Terrace, London W3 6NH, (0181 992 8637). Supports and counsels anyone worried about having a caesarean birth.
- SATFA, Support after Termination for Abnormality, 78 Charlotte Street, London W1P 1LB, (0171 631 0285). Gives information, counselling and support to expectant mothers whose baby is found to be abnormal and who are faced with the decision to terminate the pregnancy or not.
- Twins and Multiple Births Association, PO Box 30, Little Sutton, South Wirral L66 1TH, (0151 348 0020). Support group for parents of twins, triplets or more. It runs Twin Clubs throughout the country and gives special counselling on bereavement, single parenthood, etc. It has a helpline on evenings and weekends on 01732 868000.

Infertility

- Child, Charter House, 45 St Leonards Road, Bexhill-on-Sea, East Sussex TN40 1JA, (0181 893 7110). Gives practical advice and help to women suffering from infertility. Call the number above for 24-hour over-the-phone help. It also has a full range of leaflets on all aspects of infertility and medical advisers who will answer queries by post.

- COTS, Childlessness Overcome Through Surrogacy, Loandhu Cottage, Gruids, Lairg, Sutherland IB27 4AS, (01549 402401). Gives general help and advice on surrogacy via its helpline above.
- ISSUE, The National Fertility Association, 509 Aldridge Road, Great Barr, Birmingham B44 8NA, (0121 344 4414). Aimed at helping infertile couples in their choice of treatments, ISSUE has a complete information service, backed up by fact-sheets and a 24-hour support line (see above).
- National Association of Natural Family Planning Teachers, NFP Centre, Liverpool Women's Hospital, Crown Street, Liverpool L8 7SS, (0151 526 7663). Runs clinics which help women to become pregnant using natural methods. It also advises on birth control by natural methods.

See also

British Pregnancy Advisory Service, Birth Control (*page 161*).

JAFA, Jewish Association for Fostering Adoption and Infertility, Fostering (*page 271*).

6

CHILDREN

CHILDREN'S RIGHTS

According to the UN convention on the rights of the child, all children must have:
- A standard of living adequate for their physical, mental, spiritual, moral and social development.
- The highest attainable standard of health.
- The provision of appropriate and equal opportunities for cultural, artistic, recreational and leisure activity.
- They should be protected from all forms of physical or mental violence.
- Detention and imprisonment if it is needed should be used only as a measure of last resort and for the shortest appropriate period of time.

Unfortunately reality falls somewhat short of this ideal, with many families facing an endless struggle to manage with poor food and poor housing, polluted air and few safe places to play. Other countries – Norway and Australia are two examples – have appointed children's ombudsmen or the equivalent to watch over children's rights. There is no sign so far of similar action being taken in this country despite efforts being made by the RSPCC and the Save the Children Fund.

The Children Act of 1989 says that Social Services must provide help for a child whenever it is assessed as being 'in need'. Officially, a child in need is one who is unlikely to achieve or maintain a reasonable standard of health or development until Social Services provides him with support and service. This statement can cover a number of situations:
- Children in families with very little money.
- Children whose families are homeless.
- Children who are living in poor housing conditions.
- Children who are separated from one or both parents because of divorce, imprisonment or immigration problems.
- Children who have to bear some inappropriate caring responsibilities within the family.
- Children suffering social deprivation and isolation.
- Children who may be neglected or abused, children with emotional difficulties or children with disabilities may also come under this heading.

More rights and responsibilities

Under the Children Act and the Children and Young Persons Act
a child can:
- Be convicted of a criminal offence from the age of 10, if it can be proved that the child knew he was doing wrong.
- Be convicted of rape, assault, or intent to commit rape or unlawful sexual intercourse with a girl under 16, from the age of 14.
- Be given a custodial sentence, with certain restrictions, from the age of 15.
- Consent to sexual intercourse from the age of 16, if a girl.
- Can marry from the age of 16, with consent from parents or a court.
- Apply for his or her own passport from the age of 16.
- Join the armed forces, if a boy, from the age of 16 with parental consent.
- Change his or her name by deed poll from the age of 16.
- Get a part-time job, with some restrictions, from the age of 13.
- Leave school at the age of 16 and work full-time.
- Officially leave home at the age of 16.
- Buy a pet from the age of 12.
- Buy fireworks from the age of 16.
- Buy or hire a firearm and ammunition, or a crossbow, from the age of 17.
- Drink alcohol in private from the age of 5.
- Go into a pub, but not buy or drink alcohol from the age of 14.
- Drink beer, cider or wine with a meal in a restaurant, including that of a pub or hotel, from the age of 16.
- Ride in the front of a car if in a strapped cot or with an appropriate child restraint. After the age of 12, or when he or she reaches 1.5m (5ft) in height, can ride in front with an adult seat belt.
- Hold a licence to ride a moped or pilot a glider from the age of 16. Hold a pilot's licence from the age of 17.
- Hold a licence to drive most vehicles from the age of 17.
- Pay full fare on trains and on buses and tubes from the age of 16.

At 18, a child officially becomes an adult. He has the right to vote, marry, own land, buy a house, open a bank account and make a will. He can also buy alcohol and place bets. Criminal charges will be dealt with, from then on, in adult courts, but he may be sent to a young offender's institution. However, under the age of 21 he cannot become an MP.

PARENTS' RIGHTS

The Children Act defines parents' responsibility as 'all the rights, duties, powers, responsibilities and authority which by law a parent of a child has in relation to the child and his property'. As a parent, you have the right to:

- Have your children with you and to make decisions about them.
- To consent to their adoption.
- To choose their names.
- To decide where they are to live.
- To choose their religion.
- To choose their schools.
- To see that they go to school between the ages of 5 and 16.
- To administer discipline to them when necessary.
- To apply for a passport on their behalf.
- To represent them when necessary.
- To consent on their behalf to medical treatment and to see that they have it.
- To appoint a guardian for them in the event of your death.
- To consent to a child's marriage if she or he is under 18 (but over 16).

Parental responsibility

The Family Law Reform Act of 1987 now gives both partners parental rights over a child, whether they are married or not, provided the father applies to court for them, whereas before only the mother had all the rights. A father who is not married to the child's mother must apply to the court under section 4 of the act to share parental rights even if his name is on the birth certificate. Normally this is done with the consent of the mother, but, if there is a dispute, he may have to prove that he is the true father of the child, which might involve a blood or DNA test if the situation is disputed and he has not got a maintenance assessment against him.

Other ways of acquiring parental responsibility include marrying the mother, if a court makes a Residence Order for the child to live with him, or if he makes a Parental Responsibility Agreement with the mother. Even if he does not apply for parental rights, an unmarried father still has a duty to maintain his child and may have a Maintenance Order made against him. The fact that he is paying maintenance, however, does not give him parental responsibility unless he has claimed it. In the event of his death, the child is entitled to inherit from him as if it were a legitimate child.

An unmarried father, on the other hand, has no automatic right to see his child unless he has parental responsibility or a court has made an order to that effect. Parents who share parental responsibility but live apart can still share the care of their children. Each one takes over responsibility while the child is with them (*see also* **Custody and access,** *page 183*).

If you have responsibility for a child under 16, or under 19 in full-time education, you can claim **child benefit** which can be paid directly into your bank or building society account if you have one, or by cash via the local Post Office. You may also be eligible for **Family Credit,** a weekly tax-free cash payment for working people bringing up children.

If you are receiving Family Credit and you have a child under the age of one who is not being breast-fed you can buy milk at a reduced price from your maternity or child health clinic. If you are on Income Support, children under the age of five can get free milk and vitamins – ask for leaflet AB11 from your local DSS office. You may be able to get help with school uniforms for older children – ask at your local Education Office. Remember that children under 16 or under 19 in full-time education automatically get free prescriptions, sight tests and vouchers for glasses. Young people under 18, or 19 in full-time education also get free dental treatment.

Look out at your local Post Office for a Family Credit claim pack, a wallet full of leaflets that gives you details on how and what to claim.

REGISTERING A BIRTH

Registering a birth is quite a simple formality. It must be done within 6 weeks in England and Wales and 3 weeks in Scotland.

If you are married

Both parents are responsible for registering the birth. One parent goes to the Registrar of Births and Deaths (address in the Phone Book). It seems incredible, but you do not need any proof that the baby has been born. And you can give the baby any first names or surnames you wish. You are then given a certificate. There are two versions available, one which gives full details of the names of the parents and a short one from which it is impossible to tell whether the child's parents are married or not.

If you are not married

The mother has to register the birth of the child if you are not married. If the father wants his name on the certificate he must also be present. Or he must give her a sworn testimonial (done in the presence of a solicitor) to give to the Registrar. Or he can ask for this to be done in a letter supported by a Parental Responsibility Agreement between you or a Parental Responsibility order.

He can also be put on the birth certificate if you are armed with a letter from him agreeing, supported by a court order requiring him to make financial provision for the child – but not a Child Support Agency assessment for maintenance. If the father does not want his name to appear on the certificate, the space will be left blank. The inclusion of the child's father's name on the certificate does not give him automatic parental rights.

Can the certificate be altered?

Yes, in the following circumstances.

- You want to change the child's name. This can be done at any time within a year, either by producing a Christian baptismal certificate in the new name or by filling in a form on the spot, given to you by the registrar.
- If you marry the child's father and you want the child to have his surname or hyphenate his surname to yours.
- If you give the child up for adoption, a new registration certificate will be made out.

Citizenship

A child born in this country today does not automatically qualify for British citizenship unless one parent is a British citizen or is settled in the UK at the time of the birth. If the parents are not married, only the nationality of the mother is taken into account. If the child is born here and stays here for at least 10 years without being abroad for more than 90 days in any one year, he can apply at the end of that time to become a British citizen in his own right.

If the child was born abroad and the mother is a British citizen – or his father, if you are married, then the child will be a British citizen too. The only exception could be if you were not British but now have British citizenship – contact the Home Office over this. If your child is born abroad and you want him to take on the nationality of the country concerned, you need to contact the authorities in that country or their embassy or consulate abroad.

Passports

If you are British, you can apply to the Passport Office via a form from your local Post Office to have your child's name added to your passport. Or you can, if you wish, get a separate passport for your child.

LONE PARENTS

What is a single parent?

A single parent is someone who looks after children on his (but more usually, her) own. The phrase lumps together a whole host of people from the girl who has chosen to have a baby and bring it up without a partner, to a widow who has lost a much-loved husband or a man or woman who is struggling to look after the children after a divorce. There are a lot of lone parents out there – the figures have almost trebled since 1971 and single parents now form at least 21 per cent of the population. More than 90 per cent of that group, not surprisingly, are women.

Bringing up a child without a partner, even if you have chosen to do so, has its downside. Often, it can be the end of your career opportunities, for the time being at least. Your social life can take a knock too, and you could find it difficult to make new relationships, swamped, as you are, by family ties. On the other hand, you do have complete freedom to bring up your family any way you wish and you do not have to struggle with an adult involvement or have disputes over how the children should be brought up. You often have a much closer relationship with them too.

If you are bringing up children on your own, in addition to child benefit, you might also be able to claim **one parent benefit** or a **guardian's allowance, child care charges** and **education welfare benefits**. You may be eligible for family credit, housing benefit, income support, and free NHS treatment depending on your situation. If you are a lone parent you can choose for your benefits to be paid weekly rather than monthly.

The Child Support Agency

At the moment this agency is undergoing changes after widespread criticism. There have been stories of miscalculations, distress and even suicides resulting from the agency's pursuit of maintenance. If you are receiving DSS benefits, then the agency will almost certainly contact you to find out if, and how, the father is supporting your children. You will be required to apply for a child maintenance assessment. As you are in receipt of benefits you are required to co-operate with them.

But if you think that giving the agency authority to recover maintenance from the absent parent will lead to harm or undue distress for you or any of the children living with you, you can ask the agency to agree you do not have to give this authority. The Child Support Agency's leaflet then says in a rather sinister manner 'The agency's staff will want to discuss this with you'; that is where, it seems, the trouble starts. In working out child maintenance the agency takes into account:

- The day-to-day cost of maintaining a child.
- The income of the parent with care and that of the absent parent, after making allowance for tax, National Insurance and basis expenses including rent or mortgage costs.
- Any other children either parent may have.

New partners of either parent, however, are not expected to pay anything towards the maintenance of a child that is not their own. The assessment is supposed to ensure that you and any second family have enough to live on, but obviously if there is not enough money to go round, someone is going to lose out. As an absent parent, once you have paid the basic maintenance requirement and still have money left, you are asked to pay money on top of the basic rate at a certain rate in the pound. If you have any queries, ring the Child Support Agency Enquiry Line on 0345 133 13.

Being a single mother

Single mothers often find that family discipline is the most difficult thing to maintain without the backing of a father. Often the best way to deal with this is to run the family as a co-operative with rules made by negotiation.

Single parents need a support network, so set about building one around you. Not just babysitters but people whom you can phone if you are feeling down. Do not be afraid to get official help too. A health visitor can usually be relied on for practical assistance at the baby stage. If there are problems of a serious social kind, bear in mind that you can go unofficially to your local Probation Service for help and advice rather than taking your child to the police for stealing or drug abuse.

Single parents are almost inevitably short of money, since there is often only one income coming in. Children go through a stage when they are forever repeating, like a mantra, 'but all my friends have Nike running shoes, Levis, compact disc players, computers, etc'. Play it straight with them. Explain to them that there just is not enough cash to go round at the moment. If they are old enough, involve them in working out a family budget.

Being a single father

Apart from the purely domestic problems of having a full-time job and a home to run, single fathers often find they encounter prejudice because society is geared to children being looked after by women. However, most of them do a splendid job in difficult circumstances.

Many lone fathers may find it difficult to express their finer feelings and to have a really close relationship with their children. If you have a daughter, the problem becomes even more complicated because you will need to tell her what will happen to her body as she grows up. In this case it is often best to get a sympathetic female relative or close friend to do it for you – or even your ex-wife, if you are in regular contact. But you should make it clear to your child that you know about the changes she is going through and that she will need extra cash to buy sanitary towels for instance.

Single fathers will also find that most single parent groups are for, and composed mainly of, women; things are changing and more men are joining in. Maybe you should start one of your own.

How to be a happy single parent

- Make time for yourself. Take some time every day – even if it is only a quarter of an hour – when you concentrate solely on yourself and your own needs.
- Do not become isolated. It is all too easy to withdraw into your shell and involve yourself solely with survival. Join a local support group for single parents, involve yourself with the parent-teacher organization at school, get out and about.
- Do not try to be Superman or Superwoman. Make a priority list of things you have to do in the day and let the rest go hang. Juggling too many things will exhaust you.
- Ask for help from neighbours, friends and relatives. Do not feel guilty about doing so. Get all the help that you can from the system too – health visitors, for instance.
- Remember you are the most important person in your child's life. It is quality rather than quantity of time that counts. Set aside a while every day to sit and talk and play with your children, let the housework wait.
- Involve the children from an early age by getting them to help in the house with simple tasks like setting the table and making their own beds. If you catch them early enough they take a pride in doing these things, after that the tasks become a habit.
- Say sorry if you feel you have been unfair to them. Be big enough to apologize if you realize you have been wrong. Explain that you were overtired, stressed. Even very young children can understand a heartfelt apology and are usually very forgiving.

ADOPTION

At its most basic, adoption is a practical way of providing a new family for a child when its own parents are not able to do so. To adopt a child you have to get an adoption order made by a Magistrates' Court, County Court or High Court, which takes away legal parental responsibility from the original parents and gives it to you. You will also need a certificate of adoption from the Registrar General. This takes the place of the child's birth certificate from then on for all legal purposes.

Once these two steps have been taken, the adopted child becomes a full member of his new family with the same rights as any other children – to inherit money from you, or become a British citizen if one of you is a British citizen, even if Britain is not the child's country of origin. If you wish to adopt a child from abroad, it is vital to go through an accredited agency such as Childlink to avoid possible distress or even prosecution if you attempt to take a child out of a foreign country.

If you marry your child's father after the child's birth there is no need for him to apply for an adoption order. On your marriage the child immediately becomes legitimate as though you were married when he was born.

Rules and regulations

New rulings are in the pipeline but in order to adopt a child in this country at the moment, these are a number of qualifications which must be met:
- First of all, you must live in Britain, even if you are not British by birth. If you are living abroad, then you must be British.
- If married people adopt a child, the adoption must be in both their names.

Those are a legal requirement, but when you come to actually try and adopt a baby, the following rules will probably apply:
- You must have been married at least three years.
- You must not have been married for more than ten years.
- You must be healthy.
- You must be unable to have a child of your own.
- You must be of the same race as the child you want to adopt (there are exceptions to this rule).

Things that may go against you

Few agencies would consider placing an adoptive child with an applicant who:
- Is 45 years older than the child in question. This means that if you were adopting a child aged 10, for instance, you would have to be under 55 years old.
- If you are living in temporary accommodation or accommodation that is not suitable for bringing up a child.
- If you have any kind of criminal conviction.
- If you have large dogs or any other domestic animals that could endanger the health and/or safety of the child.
- If you smoke or drink heavily or take drugs. Drink and drugs are obviously bad habits in a prospective parent but smoking is taken very seriously too – one woman was turned down because she smoked between five and ten cigarettes a day.
- If you have a serious or life-threatening medical condition or suffer from mental illness.
- If you are undergoing a programme of fertility treatment that has not been completed. Most societies would expect you to agree not to have a baby of your own until the adoptive child has settled well into the family first.

What happens when you adopt a child

Adoption costs nothing. If you are not adopting as a relative or step-parent, you must go to an adoption agency approved by the Secretary of State for Health. Agencies are not allowed to charge for this service. It is particularly important to go through the proper channels if you are planning to adopt a child from abroad – remember the story of the couple who tried to smuggle out a Romanian orphan and ended up in jail. Apart from the legal issues, if you go through an unscrupulous middle-man, you will never know whether the mother genuinely wanted to part with her baby or whether she was bribed or bullied or, indeed, if the child was stolen.

First, you have to be approved as a prospective parent. You will be asked to provide references and health documents and you will be checked to see if you have fallen foul of the law. A social worker will come and see you to assess your situation.

If you pass that hurdle, then you have to be matched with the right child. This decision is very much in the hands of the agency, usually via an adoption panel. Things like race, religion, personality and any special needs of the child have to be matched with those of the family. If you have been very specific about what kind of child you want then you may have to wait longer than if you were willing to accept a wide range of age and ability. Increasingly, agencies are showing prospective parents a video of a child before the first meeting. There are not enough babies to go round, but there are a lot of older children, children with handicaps or problems who need homes. Your chances of adopting are greater amongst this group, and rules may be bent to accommodate your case.

The child will then be placed with you for a probation period of at least three months, possibly more. There must be a period of at least 13 weeks before you can make an application to adopt. Sometimes this happens after an introductory period, when you meet the child at his present foster home and get to know the child first. Then, if all goes well, once a legal agreement has been made with the original parents, you will be free to apply for an adoption order.

Once this has been made, the agency has no legal right to interfere with the way you bring up the child. But most of them offer useful support, sometimes financial, as well as emotional. If the child has relatives, many agencies will encourage some kind of contact with them through the exchange of letters and photos, perhaps.

You can actually apply to adopt your own child, which sounds a curious thing to do. It is done on occasions to sever all legal links between the child and its father and his family. If this happens then the father is not liable to pay maintenance. If you marry, or remarry, your new husband can apply to adopt your child by a previous relationship. But the court will have to take into account the situation which exists with the child's natural father. It may grant a Residence Order to you both, instead, giving you the right to bring up the child together.

Handing over

Get as much information as you can about the child's habits before you take on the role of parent, so that things go as smoothly as possible in those crucial first few days. This is especially important if you are adopting a small baby. You need to know about feeding times for instance, the size of bottle and teat the baby has been accustomed to, the brand of baby-milk used and whether the baby has had any solids. You should also know about the baby's sleep pattern and what he or she has been used to sleeping in – carrycot or cot – and whether the baby is used to having a light in the room. You also need detailed background information on the child. You need to know if the child has had any health problems and whether he or she has been immunized or has any allergies.

A fostered child

If the child is a toddler or older and is in a foster home, then the situation has to be handled with delicacy. The child will probably treat his foster parents as his real parents. Make the changeover smoother by visiting the child as much as you can during the long handing-over process. Simply taking the child away from its former background may make him feel that he has been abandoned by the foster parents – and if the child knows he was abandoned by his original parents, then he could well feel terribly distressed. The foster parents should be on your side over this, telling the toddler, when the time is right, that you want him to go and live with you. If the child has already visited your house and seen the room he will sleep in, the change-over should go more smoothly.

The child is going to need comfort and reassurance. He needs to feel that whatever unpleasant things that may have happened in his past are now over and will not ever happen again. Let the child talk about the past if he wants to, and provide security and understanding.

Placing your child for adoption

If circumstances are such that you decide you have to place your baby for adoption:

- First make contact with the adoption section of your local Social Service department.
- If you are married, both parents must give their consent.
- If you are not married and the father has no official authority (parental responsibility, a Residence or Custody Order) then you do not have to get his consent to the adoption. However, the court will want to satisfy itself that he

does not intend to apply for one of these orders. If he does have parental responsibility, a Residence or a Custody Order then you will have to get his permission.

- If your child is in care, then the local authority can, in some circumstances, decide to put the child up for adoption. If you refuse consent, then they can apply to the court. If this situation arises, get advice from the Family Rights Group (*see page 266*).

If you do decide to have your baby adopted, expect to go through a period of emotional pain and adjustment. Most natural mothers who have given up a baby for adoption suffer real trauma. Unlike the loss of a child through death, which fades in time, your thoughts about the child may intensify over the years even if you go on to have a happy marriage and other children.

Some people deal with the loss by denying to themselves that they have had a baby and avoid any mention of the subject of adoption. You may have a great need to know how your child is, and that need to know may not go away. So-called open adoption is becoming an increasingly attractive alternative to the traditional kind. In open adoptions, the natural mother keeps in touch with the adoptive parents and has visiting rights to her child. This calls for a great deal of trust on both sides and care must be taken that the child is not disturbed by the situation. Making contact, if it has not been organized before, is usually initiated via letter to the family through the social services. Or sometimes contact is maintained via the grandparents.

The adopted child: finding your parents

Adoption practice, as we know it today, started in 1926. At that time it was normal for both birth parents to know the people who took over their children. The whole idea of secrecy did not come onto the scene until the 1950s when the identity of the natural parents was kept secret to protect the adoptive parents from the stigma of infertility as it was then thought to be.

Since the 1970s, however, the Adoption Act allows an adoptive child access to his or her birth records. The natural mother, on the other hand, does not get any help in tracing her child, and can only take passive steps by putting her name on a register. Anyone over the age of 18 who has been adopted now has the right to get a copy of their original birth certificate from the Registrar General. You can do this at an earlier age if you know what your original name was. From this certificate you will be able to get your natural mother's name and, possibly, that of your father, depending on the circumstances and where your mother was living at the time.

To trace your parents, get in touch with the Adoption Contact Register. It works one way, giving you, as an adopted child, details of where your blood relatives are.

It does not tell them where you are and it may not be able to help; however, there are other organizations that may assist you (*see page 270*).

BEING A STEP-PARENT

This is the age of the complex family. With so many marriages ending in divorce – and one in three marriages is in fact a remarriage – the numbers of families with step-parents and children is growing each year. Once, most people remarried because of the death of their partner, now the reasons are different. The family could be less clearly defined, too; mum could have a live-in boyfriend, while dad may have remarried and started a second family.

Many people who never dreamed they would become a step-parent find themselves in this situation today. It is believed that more than two million children are affected this way. You become an instant step-family if you or your partner have children from a previous partnership. It also affects grandparents who find themselves with step-grandchildren – a situation they sometimes find difficult to handle. And if both partners remarry, the children could find themselves with four lots of grandparents instead of two.

Remarriages may start off with the highest hopes and the best of intentions. You may be besotted by your new partner, but taking on someone else's children involves a great deal of patience, goodwill and give and take. You may suddenly find yourself with an instant family at a relatively young age, or perhaps a step-daughter or son only a couple of years younger than you are.

Think before you act

Remember that you are taking a big step but not taking it in isolation. There are other people involved – children principally, as well as new in-laws and various sets of grandparents.

- If you harbour the slightest dislike or resentment towards your prospective step-children, you should question whether it is right for you to marry their parent.
- If you are planning to marry someone whose partner has died, can you cope with the ex-partner who may by now have been elevated to near sainthood by the family?
- Can you face up to possible problems and pressures from ex-husband or ex-wife on both sides? You may not be the cause of the break-up but you are likely to be tarred with the same brush.
- Do you and your prospective partner agree on how the children should be brought up? Make sure you hammer out the ground rules beforehand.

- If you have no children of your own and feel reluctant to take on a ready-made family, then it is probably better that you do not.
- If you feel pangs of jealousy over the time and affection your prospective partner gives the children then think very carefully about whether or not you can deal with these feelings.
- If your prospective family has teenagers in it, the going is likely to be harder than if they are young. How do you feel about late nights and loud music from ghetto-blasters? Remember, insecure children tend to behave very badly at times. And it is all too easy to interpret their normal teenage insolence or moodiness as an act against you personally.

In any case, it pays to have a dummy run to see what it might be like to be a step-parent; going on a family holiday together could be one way to try it out. Camping would be a good crash course in parenting – if you can survive that you can survive anything!

How to be a happy step-parent

Step-parents have a lot to live down; from Snow White to Cinderella, step-mothers, in particular, have had a bad press. You are going to need a great deal of patience, an open, flexible mind and a loving heart. In addition you will need a great deal of energy and a great deal of resilience. It is hard work being a parent. It is even harder work being a step-parent. You do not have a biological link with your step-children so it makes it more difficult to love them unconditionally. There will also be times when you will feel excluded from a tightly-knit family group.

- Do not rush your fences. Unless the children are very young, do not attempt to act as a parent; content yourself with being a friend. Above all, do not expect them to call you mummy or daddy.
- Allow time for your step-children to adjust to you. Remember, you and your partner have chosen each other, but the children have not chosen you. They have to get to know you before they can love you. Also remember that the children may be playing pig in the middle, and being in the middle of a situation like this is uncomfortable.
- Be pleasant but firm. Children can be very manipulative and can find ways of getting round their natural parent while getting at you at the same time.
- Whenever you can, leave the natural parent to discipline their own children. Assert authority by all means, but let your partner dole out any punishments at first. It is unfair of mothers who find it difficult to control their sons to expect a new partner to take over the task instantly, since it will cause immediate antagonism.

- Make time to be alone with your partner. Organize a babysitter, or take advantage of times when the children go to see their other natural parent. If you are newly married, you need time and space to be together and get to know each other.
- If there has been a divorce, your new step-children, particularly the older ones, are having to come to terms with the fact that mum and dad are never going to be together again, and that will be hard.
- Talk things through. Bring problems out in the open and discuss them as a family, especially if there are teenagers involved. But keep rows with your partner strictly private. The children are probably already feeling insecure and if they see you arguing they may feel that this marriage, too, is on the rocks.

YOUR CHILD'S EARLY YEARS

Many of us simply do not know what it is to have sleepless nights or to be sick with worry until we have a child. The arrival of a first baby can reduce even a trained nurse to a trembling worry-wracked wreck.

Breastfeeding

Some women find it very easy to breastfeed their babies. Others have difficulty, while still more find they need to supplement breast milk with formula baby milk.

It has now been found that breast milk contains certain complex fatty acids essential for brain and eye development. The problem is that babies cannot take these fatty acids in formula baby milks which are composed of cow's milk boosted with vegetable fats, until they are about six months old. Formula milk cannot provide certain enzymes that help digestion, and the antibodies to ward off infection. So if you can manage to partially breastfeed for the first six months, you will be giving your baby a better start.

Inoculations

The Health Education Authority recommends the following schedule of inoculations for children.
- **2–4 months:** diphtheria, tetanus, whooping cough/pertussis (DTP), polio and HIB (Haemophious influenza Type B meningitis blood poisoning).
- **12–15 months:** measles, mumps, rubella (MMR).
- **1–15-year-olds:** hepatitis A if visiting areas outside northern and western Europe, North America or Australasia.
- **3–5 years:** diphtheria, tetanus, polio booster.

- **10–14-year-old girls:** rubella.
- **15–19-year-olds:** tetanus, polio.

Reactions and side-effects

The HEA says that the risks of harmful effects from the diseases are much more serious than from the inoculations. However, you should talk to your GP about any worries you might have. Your child should not be inoculated if:

- He is unwell or has a fever the day he is to have the inoculation.
- He has had a serious reaction to any previous immunizations.
- He has had a previous severe allergic reaction after eating egg.
- He is taking medicine, especially steroids.

After an inoculation, it is wise to keep a close eye on your child for any adverse reaction. If your child seems very unwell, has a temperature, becomes jittery or screams continuously after an injection, call the doctor. Serious side-effects such as convusions and high fever are possible after DTP triple vaccine and from MMR. A small red swelling, about the size of a milk bottle top, appears in one child in ten after HIB immunization and should disappear within 4 to 8 hours.

SAFETY FIRST

The Royal Society for the Prevention of Accidents says that the commonest cause of death among children between the ages of one and five is accidents rather than health problems.

Safety in the home

- Remove ribbons or cords on baby clothes that could accidentally strangle the child.
- Never use a pillow in a cot or pram during a baby's first year.
- Never leave a small baby unattended or propped up by itself on a settee or bed.
- Lock away medicines, poisons, household cleaners and garden sprays.
- Do not give children peanuts, hard sweets or small objects they could choke on.
- Turn handles of saucepans towards the centre of the cooker, do not leave them sticking out.
- Keep dangling kettle or iron flexes out of reach. Take care with electric flexes which can be chewed. Use safety guards on electric sockets.
- Check any area where a baby is to be for small objects like buttons and pins. Make sure anything sharp or breakable is out of reach.
- Keep all plastic bags well out of the way, do not leave spare ones lying around when you unload the shopping.

- Always use a safety gate on the stairs. Protect the lower halves of glass doors or panels by fitting safety film over them.
- If you have an open fire, always use a fireguard.
- Check brakes on prams and pushchairs regularly.
- Make sure your child is well clear when you fold up a pushchair
- Run cold water into the bath first, before the hot.
- Never leave a baby alone near water or in the bath even for a moment. If you have a fish tank or aquarium put it out of the baby's reach.
- Keep hot drinks and liquids out of reach in the centre of the table. They can still burn a child even if they have been standing for twenty minutes.

CRYING BABIES

It is estimated that from a quarter to a half of all babies are what the Americans call 'fussy' and cry for no obvious reason. Crying is a baby's first means of communication, its way of saying 'I want' or 'do not want'. But even when food, sleep and warmth are provided some babies may go on to cry endlessly. Do not feel that you have failed, or that you are incompetent; you are just unlucky! If you are faced with a constantly crying baby, try to remember that this is only temporary, however much it may drive you to distraction.

There are certain reasons why some babies may cry more than average: birth complications; wind pains – probably due to the fact that the baby's digestive system is still developing; premature birth; and some babies need soothing surroundings, peace and quiet in order to sleep, while others do not.

How to cope

Babies cry because they are hungry, thirsty or in pain. They may also cry if they are too cold or too hot, have a wet or soiled nappy or be suffering from nappy rash. All these things are relatively easy to deal with. Sometimes babies simply get lonely and want to be held and comforted. Sometimes they get overtired and fight against going to sleep. Gentle rocking, a change of bed from cot to pram or vice versa, a soothing baby-tape on cassette or the gentle ticking of a clock may help to get them off. But what do you do if your baby cries constantly for no apparent reason? The sound of an incessantly crying baby can be very upsetting, especially since we are genetically programmed to respond to the baby's cry. What about you?

- Get someone to look after the baby while you get right away from the sound – go for a walk or a swim, go to the shops even, but get right away from time to time. In short, grab all the help you can get.

- Do not go by the book, follow your own instincts. Pick up your baby and feed him when you feel it is right to do so.
- Do not over-stimulate your baby by waving toys in front of him or by introducing new faces. Keep your daily routine serene.
- If you feel so fraught that you are almost tempted to hit the baby, put the baby to bed and quietly walk away into another room and close the door. Stay away until you have calmed down – phone a friend.
- Take turns with your partner to be on baby-watch at night, so that you take it in turns to sleep out of earshot. Keep the baby's cot by the bed so that you do not have to keep getting out and padding to another room, but do not take the baby into the bed unless you really have to.
- Try holding it securely to you and rocking it. Try gentle, soothing massage too. Massaging a baby's tummy gently can help get rid of colic.
- Try keeping the baby's afternoon sleep short if he has difficulty in getting off at night. This sometimes works but could have the reverse effect if the baby is overtired. It will then be more difficult to get him to sleep in the evening.
- Try to establish a calm routine for bed-time even if he won't go to sleep at first. Put the baby to bed, leave the room, let him cry for up to 5 minutes, then return, tuck him in and leave the room again. Do this over and over again until he finally goes to sleep.
- If the problem is really bad, mimic the baby's own sleep pattern – when he sleeps, have a nap yourself.
- Keep a diary of the baby's crying/sleep/feeding habits for a week. Studying them may give you a clue as to what is causing the trouble.
- If the problem continues, check the baby's diet with a health visitor or with your doctor.
- Try not to take the child into bed with you because it will all too soon become a habit, ruining your sleep and your sex life, and cause siblings to feel jealous.
- Join a support network (*see* **Cry-sis,** *page 270*). Remember, there are other mothers out there with the same problems.

Is your baby comfortable?

Babies do not like:
- Being held with their heads or backs unsupported.
- Being held at arm's length.
- Being gripped too tightly.
- Being picked up very suddenly.
- Being tossed in the air or subjected to rough play.
- Being shaken – his head is heavy compared to the rest of his body so will move with great force. Shaking, even in fun, could cause a brain haemorrhage.

If the situation continues, and your doctor has found nothing wrong, it may be worthwhile consulting a cranial osteopath. All babies who are born vaginally, rather than by Caesarian, have their heads distorted during birth while passing through the birth canal. This is perfectly normal and the plates of the skull are not fused at this age, making this passage through the birth canal possible. There is now a theory that some babies' heads may have been temporarily distorted during birth, to the extent that it causes them to suffer from a wide range of medical problems from colic to headaches. Other babies may suffer because they lay in an uncomfortable way in the womb. A growing number of child cranial osteopaths are helping affected babies. Some have found that gentle manipulation of the skull to release pressure has solved the problem (*see* **Help Directory,** *page 270*).

Finally, cheer yourself with the thought that there is light at the end of the tunnel and babies quickly grow out of this phase. How normal is normal? Expect anything up to two and a half hours of crying a day. Crying starts in earnest at two weeks and increases to a maximum at six to eight weeks. After three or four months, unless you are very unlucky, your baby should start to quieten down.

ILLNESS

When to get urgent help

Call the ambulance if:
- Your baby has apparently stopped breathing, goes blue or has a fit.
- If you cannot wake him.
- If he seems unaware of what is going on, his eyes are glazed and he is not focusing as he normally does.
- If he has had a serious fall or injury.

Symptoms that may need urgent attention

- The baby suddenly takes very little fluid.
- If he brings up green vomit.
- If there is a large amount of blood, not just a streak in his nappy.
- If when he draws a breath a hole, or deep dent, appears between his lower chest and upper tummy. This is known as 'indrawing' and means that the baby has a breathing difficulty. The hole appears quite naturally when the baby hiccoughs or cries very loudly.
- If there is a bulge in his groin or scrotum that gets bigger when he cries.

Some reasons why you should take your baby to see the doctor

- If the baby 'just doesn't look right'. Use your own instinct, you know your baby better than anyone else. Does he seem floppy, listless, is he pale all over, not just in his face?

- If he vomits large amounts of food after several feeds in a row.
- If he is covered in a rash.
- If he has a temperature of 38.3°C (100.8°F) or higher. Wait an hour or two, cooling the baby off with a damp flannel, then check his temperature again.

Phoning the doctor

- If you are talking over the phone, have the child by you. If your child has a rash, for instance, the doctor may want a detailed description of the spots or want you to press the skin.
- Have a list of questions written down, including the important question, how long should this last?
- Have a pencil and paper ready to write down instructions – if you have been in a state of panic you may not remember whether it was 1 ounce of water every 20 minutes or 20 ounces of water every hour.
- The younger the baby, the quicker things happen – under 3 to 4 months the situation can change very quickly – you need to be anxious about a high temperature.

CHILDREN WITH SPECIAL NEEDS

See also Special educational needs (*page 329*).

Slow to talk

Do not be surprised if it takes your toddler some time to talk clearly. Up until the age of five a number of children are difficult to understand; it is only after that age that you may consider getting professional help. The fact that they are talking is all that matters at this stage. If they are children from bilingual parents, or with English-speaking parents living in another country, hearing two different languages, they can be expected to take at least six months longer to talk than other children.

Stuttering and stammering

This can be a temporary state of affairs when a child is, perhaps, under stress, or it could be a situation that needs the help of a speech therapist. Some stuttering is perfectly normal in the development of speech in some children; often they are thinking faster than they can talk and may get muddled. However, more serious stuttering later on may require professional help. If your child tends to stammer:

- Listen carefully to him, concentrate on what he is saying, not how he is saying it.
- Do not look away from him when he stammers.
- Slow down your own rate of talking. Children try to keep up with their parents' speed of speech.
- Reduce the number of questions you ask and make sure you give your child time to answer one before asking another.
- Praise him for things he does well to build up his confidence.
- Evolve a less hurried lifestyle, a regular routine and structured environment, with plenty of sleep and a healthy diet. It has been found that many stammerers respond well to this.

The hyperactive child

Doctors are divided over what causes Attention Deficit Hyperactivity Disorder (ADHD) . Some think it may be a chemical disorder in the brain, others think it could be genetic and still others believe it may be linked to diet. They are equally divided over how it should be treated – experiments with a drug called Ritalin, which is commonly used in the United States for this disorder, are now in progress in this country. If your child is hyperactive and you are not getting the help that you need from your GP or psychiatrist, join a support group (*see page 267*) because more is being found out about this condition all the time, and the group may have news of something that can help.

CHILD CARE

Your rights

If you are receiving Family Credit, a Disability Working Allowance, Housing Benefit or Council Tax Benefit you should be able to have child-care charges up to a certain sum, offset against your earnings when your entitlement is worked out. To take advantage of this, your child must be with a registered approved child-minder, nursery or playgroup scheme. For further details ring freeline Social Security on 0800 666 555.

If you decide to go back to work after the birth of your child, and need to hire someone to care for your child, this could be the moment when you discover for the first time what it is like to be an employer. You will also find that a great deal of the money you earn is going to be swallowed up in hired help. Before deciding to go back to work, it is as well to get some idea of what your employer's attitude will be to enforced days off when your child is ill, or the au pair does a runner back to France, and to the fact that you will probably not be able to work overtime. Remember, too, that childminders and nannies will have statutory days off, and holidays to be fitted in, and they will want to be paid for them. When you go away on holiday you may have to pay a retaining fee to the nursery or to the childminder to retain your child's place with them.

The question of whether you have someone in your home or take your child to someone outside your home to be cared for has pluses and minuses on both sides. The big advantage of having help at home is that if your child is ill, the carer in your home will be able to continue to look after the child. But before taking on live-in help in the home, ask yourself: am I going to mind losing some space and my privacy? If you are on your own, this might be an advantage, if you are a couple there is no doubt that having a stranger to live with you can cause stress in the relationship at times.

There is an experimental scheme being proposed whereby parents will be offered £1000 worth of vouchers for their children to take up places in pre-school nurseries. At the moment this experiment only covers 10 per cent of England, but there are plans to extend it to cover the whole of the country by 1997. This will not only mean that more people are able to put their children in nurseries, but that more nurseries will open up to cope with the demand. However, if you cannot afford to top up the government hand-out, the money will only pay for just over two months' nursery care at present rates if you have to go to a private nursery.

If your child goes to a day nursery, play-group, or anywhere where it is in contact with other children, you can expect him or her to catch childhood ailments like colds and chickenpox earlier than if he had waited until starting school where he would be in contact with a lot of children. If the child is ill, you, or someone else, will have to stay home to look after him.

From your child's point of view – and yours – a sense of security is everything; being taken or left with one stranger, then another, can be very disturbing for a small child so ad hoc arrangements are to be avoided if possible. The best way to assess any out-of-home care facility is to visit the nursery or the minder when they are in operation. You will soon discover whether the children there seem happy and contented or not.

Full-time help at home

Nannies

Nannies do not come cheap, whether they are trained or not. They may live in or they can come to you on a daily basis, which is often more desirable if your house is small. She will still expect to be fed during the hours she is working for you. Real nannies do not expect to do any housework, though they may relent and do some shopping for you. They expect to have their own room, of course, with TV. They do not expect to have to baby-sit more than one or two evenings a week.

Some nannies expect to be able to have the use of a car. Few, if any of them, want to wear uniforms, but they may demand certain types of equipment for their charge. In anything but the grandest houses, nanny usually eats with the family, but she may prefer to take a tray up to her own room.

If you do not wish to have someone living in your house, you might consider hiring a live-out nanny. She will come in every day to care for your children in your own home and you will not have to give up your privacy. However, live-out nannies are more expensive than those who live in.

There are no official regulations for nannies; you have to make your own mind up as to whether the one you choose is competent. Remember that in spite of a fistful of diplomas, if the nanny is very young, she may not have much practical experience of dealing with children. The great advantage of a nanny, if you can afford one, is that your child gets her sole attention.

One way of spreading the cost of a nanny is to share one with another mother, deciding between you which house becomes, in effect, a day nursery. Most nannies work around 50 hours a week – it is vital to get the hours sorted out in advance. If you employ a proper nanny you may be liable to pay National Insurance and deduct tax on her behalf.

Where to find a nanny Look for a nanny through any reputable agency, through word-of-mouth or through an advertisement in a publication like *The Lady* which lists domestic posts or *TNT*, a magazine for Antipodeans. Most of these will cost you money. For daily nannies try an ad in the local paper.

Points to watch Be sure to suss out a prospective nanny's views on child-care in general and things like feeding and potty-training. You will want to know why she left her last job (though she may lie to you) and, if you take up references, check them out by phone. You should also check out whether or not she smokes, whether she can stand animals, if you have any, and whether she seems to have basic common sense and some knowledge of first aid. Cover yourself, if you are not completely sure about her, by taking her on for a trial period.

Mother's helps

Considered a notch below nanny in the below-stairs hierarchy, mother's helps are not usually trained and have the advantage that they will do housework and cooking as well as looking after the child. You will probably have to pay for their NI stamp and deduct Income Tax from their pay-cheque (contact your local tax office). Paying them in cash without doing this could leave you liable to prosecution.

Where to find them See nannies, above. You could also try your local Jobcentre.

A relative

If granny can be persuaded to help out on a regular basis, this can be the best of all worlds, even if it is a temporary arrangement while you find the right girl to take over. If an aunt or a cousin is out of work at the time, there is always the possibility that they may be willing to do a stint. It is not fair to expect a relative to work for nothing, however. If they refuse payment then you should give them regular generous presents.

Au pairs

Like them or loathe them, many families with a working mother would not be able to survive without the help of an au pair girl. They are a useful option, a half-way measure between full-blown domestic help and coping on your own. I attribute every crow's foot, every line on my face to one or other of the 32 au pairs I had to help me survive parenthood. They ranged from Cecille, who said she was one of the last of the Hapsburgs and could I bring her breakfast at nine, to the lovely Gretta Mole from Trømso whose version of Incy Wincy Spider in Norwegian, I can still perform, if asked, at parties.

Au pairs are not hired help. They are guests in your house and they are here to learn English – even if most of it is picked up in all-night discos. The latest Home Office guideline says:

- Au pairs cannot legally be asked to work for more than 4 hours a day, 25 hours a week.
- They should also not be asked to baby-sit for more than two nights a week.
- This is in return for food and lodging, plus £35–40 pocket money and a chance to learn English.
- They are also not to do more than light housework and taking care of children.

They must also have their own room and two free days a week. You will be expected to provide items like soap, shampoo, as well as their meals and to fork out for their phone calls, unless you make a specific arrangement beforehand. Remember that the girl may well feel homesick at first so go out of your way to find her friends among other au pairs.

Where to find them Look for an au pair through a reputable agency, via your local church or by putting an advertisement in a newspaper of the country of your choice.

Points to watch Most au pairs, from my experience, claim to love children and to speak good English – they really need some basic knowledge to be able to do things like answer the phone. The former statement you have to take on trust, though a girl who comes from a large family is more likely to be used to children than an only child. The easiest way to test her English is simply to phone her up!

Sharing care

If you have a close and trusted friend with a baby around the same age as yours and part-time jobs, you could organize to take it in turns to look after both the children. This might work on the job front too if you have a part-time job you share with another mother. It is a cheap method of child-care that has a lot of advantages. If your child is of school age, it could be that another mother would be willing to take your child home with hers and look after him until you return from work, perhaps in return for occasional baby-sitting or care of both children during holidays or weekends.

Where to find them Via your local well-baby clinic, nursery or school.

Help outside the home

Child-minder

Child-minders are now more carefully regulated since the Children Act came into force. Under this act, local authorities have to keep a register of all carers of children under the age of 8, even if they only do it part-time. Child-minders, who are usually mothers themselves, will accept children during working hours, roughly 8.30 am until 6 pm or thereabouts. They usually arrange a set weekly fee, but might charge by the hour.

Where to find them No doubt there are still many unofficial child-minders that the authorities do not know about, but to make sure you get one that is registered, and therefore inspected regularly, you should ask the local Social Services Department for a list. Your local library or health clinic may also have addresses.

Points to watch What is the house like? It may not be tidy but it should be clean. Are there things to play with? Is she near enough for it to be convenient as a drop-off place on the way to work? Does she smoke? Are there large dogs or pets around? Is she properly insured? Have you met her own children? Do they seem to be well-behaved? It would be an advantage if there was somewhere secure out of doors where the children could play. Registered child-minders are only allowed to take on three children at any one time.

Crèche

This can mean a full-time nursery, mainly for babies, or one attached to the organization for which you work. When assessing what it has to offer, follow the guide-lines for a day nursery below.

Day nursery

If your children are assessed as children in need, then the Social Services must provide day-care in a nursery and supervised activities out of school for them. Some day nurseries are council-run while others are private. Council nurseries usually charge on a sliding scale according to what you can afford – in some circumstances it might be free – but they are all usually difficult to get into and it is a good idea to enquire well in advance. Some nurseries charge extra for your child's mid-day meal, others include it in the price. Almost all day nurseries operate five days a week.

Where to find one The easiest way to find out about nurseries is to contact your local Social Services office, which should be able to give you a list. The best way to find a good one is by word-of-mouth, so ask around.

Points to watch Is it officially registered? Is at least one helper an SRN or suitably qualified to deal with emergencies? Are there things for the children to play with? One of the advantages of a day nursery is that there should be a wide range of facilities available for the children. Avoid groups where there is a mix of older and very young children if your child is a toddler. Boisterous older children playing in the same area may knock him over. If your child is excessively shy he may find a day nursery an overwhelming place compared to a smaller group of children with a child-minder.

After-school schemes

Some enlightened primary schools, realizing that many mothers work, now run informal supervised play-group care for children after the witching hour of 3.30 pm when official school closes.

Where to find one The school should be able to tell you if there is one in operation; alternatively, it may know of a support group or other organization that could collect your child from school and look after him until you come home.

Points to watch Reliability is the key word here. Ask other mothers who are using the scheme to make sure it does all it says it will do.

Crisis care

There will always come a time when the best-laid care plans can go awry. So have a list of people to hand whom you can call on in an emergency. They could include neighbours, relatives, members of a child support group you belong to, the baby-sitter or a commercial emergency child-care agency of the kind you might find in the Yellow Pages.

BABY-SITTERS

All parents deserve an evening out without the children from time to time, but when your children are young, in particular, it is bound to be tinged with worry about how the baby-sitter is behaving and coping.

How to find and keep a baby-sitter

- Never employ anyone under the age of 14. it is unfair to burden anyone younger than that with the responsibility of small children.
- Organize the hours and the pay well in advance. Ask around to find the local rate. Pay the baby-sitter promptly in cash at the end of the evening and thank her.

- Cancel going out if your child is ill. It is not fair to expect someone else to look after your ill child.
- If the child has to have some medicine, either give it yourself or write down careful instructions.
- Tell the sitter everything you can think of about the child's habits and how he normally goes off to sleep. Tell the sitter whether your child likes a bed-time story, whether he has a snack and whether there should be a light on in the room.
- Leave the phone number of where you are so that you can be contacted if necessary. Write it down yourself. It is sometimes wise to leave the number of a reliable neighbour or friend as well.
- If you are running late, phone and say so. Pay the sitter extra.
- Always take the baby-sitter home unless he/she has their own car.
- If you are going to be very late, consider having the baby-sitter stay overnight.
- Leave telephone numbers for emergencies, the doctor and a neighbour. Make sure the sitter knows about dialling 999.
- Give the baby-sitter a basic fire drill – emergency exits if there are any.
- Show the sitter how to work the TV, radio and central heating.
- Do not expect the baby-sitter to bathe or feed the baby before he goes to bed. By all means let the sitter join in, but do not delegate the job to the person unless she is known to you and the baby and would like to do it – otherwise it is too much of a responsibility.
- Do not expect the baby-sitter to wash up or clear away anything other than dishes she has used.
- Leave food and (non-alcoholic) drink out for the sitter.
- Lay down the ground rules about whether or not she can have a visit from a friend.
- Check that the house is secure but that the sitter knows how to get out in an emergency. Get her to put the door on a safety chain if you have one. Be sure to tell her if anyone might call.
- Tell the sitter not to let anyone in. If someone calls at the door, tell the sitter to talk to them through the letter box or via the safety chain.

The British Red Cross runs a special training programme for would-be baby-sitters. If you know anyone who would like to take part, tell them to contact their local branch of the Red Cross – the number should be in the Phone Book.

Home alone

One of the most difficult aspects of being a parent is finding someone else to keep an eye on the children for you from time to time. It is tempting to pop out to the shops for something, assuming that quite small children who are playing happily at home will be safe for a few minutes. It is estimated that one in five primary school children goes home to an empty house after school, but the NSPCC say:

- Never leave a baby alone, not even for a few minutes. Apart from risks such as the baby being sick and choking or fire, for a small baby, 15 minutes is a long time to feel abandoned and left to cry alone.
- Young children should also never be left alone, not even for a short time. An hour without you or another caring adult can be very lonely and distressing. And there are many safety risks for a curious, exploring child.
- Most 9- to 12-year-olds may seem self-reliant but are not mature enough to be left on their own for more than a very short while; certainly not every day. Before you decide, make sure your children feel happy and confident about being alone and that they know where you are and exactly what to do in an emergency.
- It is not fair to expect older children who are not mature themselves to look after a young child.
- It is never safe to leave your children alone at night, even if they are asleep. What if they woke suddenly from a bad dream and came looking for you? The dark can be terrifying and there are too many possible dangers. It is just not worth the risk.

Out alone

The NSPCC says that in most situations:

- Children under about 8 years old should not be out alone, especially in busy towns. Even when out playing with other children, they need to be kept in the care and sight of an adult or much older child who is mature and trustworthy.
- You should never leave young children in unsupervised play areas in shops and car parks. And do not leave them alone in the car or outside a shop, not even for a few minutes.
- If you are in a crowded place, keep children in a pram or buggy, hold hands tightly or use reins. Do not walk far ahead of small children who cannot keep up. Remember it only takes a moment for a toddler to wander off.
- As soon as children are able to understand, teach them their full names, address and telephone number. Practise these with them until they are sure.
- Tell them clearly that they must never go off with anyone, not even someone they know, without asking you first.
- In busy, public places arrange somewhere safe to meet in case you get separated, like a cash desk or information desk.

If things become really difficult, bear in mind that under the Children Act, the Social Services are obliged to provide temporary help for you if you face situations such as going into hospital, if you are suffering from severe short-term stress and have no one within the family to care for the children. They will probably take the children into short-term care and draw up a written agreement for you to sign. This should tell you what they have agreed to do for you and you should read it carefully before you sign. However, you have the right to remove your children from their care at any time unless a Residence Order or an Emergency Protection Order of Care is in force.

PROBLEMS

From the age of around two, children suddenly discover that they have tremendous power over their parents. From then on tantrums and other troubles start and it is downhill all the way. When the child is very small, distraction rather than punishment is the best way of dealing with a tantrum. If you can distract his attention you are more likely to get results.

Food fads

One way in which a child may exercise this new-found power over you is by refusing to eat. This can be distressing but seldom goes on long enough for the child to become ill.
- If he starts playing up at meal-times when he has an audience, try feeding him by himself.
- Try *cuisine minceur*. Put small portions on the plate, make the food look as attractive as possible – use pieces of carrot, greenery to make a face with eyes, a nose and a mouth, for instance.
- Do not force him to eat foods that he obviously dislikes; most of us dislike something.
- If he absolutely refuses meals for the moment, leave out enticing snacks that he can help himself to, such as pieces of peeled fruit.
- If he is old enough, encourage him to feed himself, however inexpertly.

Bed-wetting

This is more common in boys than in girls. Many children take a long time to be dry at night – it is not uncommon to find this problem in five- or six-year-olds. Anxiety will sometimes cause a child to revert to wetting the bed. Another cause may be the arrival of a baby brother or sister. Resign yourself to the situation for the time being. Buy a good plastic or butyl cover for the mattress and invest in drip-dry bed linen. Go back to nappies or trainer pants at night if you need to. You could also try putting the child on the pot just before you go to bed at night. The child does not even have to be fully awake to do this. Show your appreciation when the child manages to make it through the night with a dry bed, but do not make too big a deal out of it.

Jealousy

Also known as sibling rivalry, jealousy can erupt at any time. It can be a simple primeval emotion over toys or it can be more serious. We can understand a toddler's nose being put out of joint by a new arrival – which often results in a relapse into baby behaviour. But that is relatively easily dealt with by giving him special time, or by bringing in granny to make a fuss of him.

Continued jealousy among younger children needs looking into. Could it be that you are, in fact, favouring one child over the other, or showing one child off as clever or pretty, to relatives and friends. Children can be jealous of their mother's or father's relationship with a step-parent. This needs tactful handling. Explain to the child that it makes no difference to your relationship with them which is just as strong as ever. Praise the jealous child lavishly if he shows kindness towards his hated rival. Make sure there are fair shares of everything. And keep your cool – before long they will band together to gang up on you.

Violence

We expect our children to bicker and quarrel with each other, but sometimes it gets out of hand. Children can be violent little animals at times and girls are just as bad as boys – I can remember my little sister biting me quite viciously. Sometimes it is an excuse for confrontation with a parent, so punishment is not the best option. Handle it by saying firmly that the child is not allowed to hurt his brother. It is important to point out, if such is the case, that the child is bigger and stronger and could do real harm. Show that his behaviour is making you sad and hope that his better nature will prevail. Make it a family rule that no one is allowed to hit anyone else, under any circumstances, with any sort of weapon, even a slipper. If a fight breaks out, the best thing to do is to separate the two protagonists, sit each one down and talk things through.

Video violence

There are a lot of arguments going on about whether violence on the TV screen can affect children's behaviour. What kind of videos are your children watching, not just at home but at their friends' homes?

The law

By law it is a serious criminal offence to supply a video that is not classified when it should have been – the main categories that are exempt are educational, sport, religion and music. The classifications are:

Uc which means that the film or programme has a universal category and is suitable for everyone, especially for children. Many of the films in this category have been made specially for young children. If it has a number such as 12 on it, this means it is most suitable for children over the age of 12.

U means that the film is suitable for all the family, but again it may have a figure after it suggesting the minimum age of children who might watch.

PG These initials stand for Parental Guidance and it is up to you, as a parent, to decide whether the film is suitable for a child to watch. The video industry is now putting a note on the sleeve of most videos to give some idea of the theme or content.

More serious problems

Sometimes a perfectly happy-go-lucky child becomes unaccountably unhappy, withdrawn, tearful or lethargic. There could be many reasons for such a sudden change, which may be accompanied by sleeplessness or complaints about not feeling well even though the doctor can find nothing wrong. It is easy enough to dismiss this as just a phase the child is going through. But there may be one of several underlying reasons for this:

- Could something be wrong at school? The first thing to investigate is the nursery, play-group or school the child attends. Is he being bullied? Picked on by a teacher? Perhaps the school has noticed that something is wrong.
- Is there some sort of family conflict going on that the child could have tuned in to? Could he have become anxious after overhearing you discussing money worries or is there a divorce in the offing?
- If he will not sleep at night, has he seen something frightening on TV?

Are you planning too much activity for your child? A new syndrome has arrived – the stressed toddler. The Maudesley Hospital in London is treating an increasing number of children under the age of five for stress and counselling parents who are disappointed that their child is not achieving as well as they would like.

Many small children have diaries that are overplanned, being rushed from toddler groups to dancing classes and French lessons to computer classes at the age of two. If your child refuses to nap in the afternoon, the chances are that he or she is not relaxed enough, but hyped up by the morning activities. The experts all agree that small children need personal space, time to play and potter about, perhaps just looking and listening, rather than learning.

Getting help

The first person to go to is your GP, especially if your child is suddenly listless and easily fatigued. If he cannot find anything wrong, then he may suggest you take your child to a local counselling centre, which may be called, variously, a child guidance clinic or a family service unit, perhaps involving psychotherapy. The therapist may want to talk to the child alone to try to get to the bottom of the problem.

How to be a happy parent

- Set clear limits of behaviour and define what will, and will not, be tolerated so that your children know where they stand.
- Show your children plenty of love and affection, build up their self-esteem.
- Do not forget to praise and encourage them as much as you scold them.
- Tell them what you do want them to do as well as what you do not want them to do.
- Make sure that what you are asking a child to do is within his ability.
- If you do have to punish your child, make sure that he knows why he is being punished.
- Make rules but be flexible enough to break them now and then.
- Play it for laughs at times. A well-placed joke can often diffuse a tense situation, provided that joke is at your expense rather than the child's.
- Try to avoid shouting and smacking since both of these things show that you, as a parent, have lost control.
- Try looking at things from your child's point of view.
- Listen attentively to what they say, make time to do this.
- Do not use sarcasm. Small children do not understand it and older children find it wounding. In both cases, it fails to make the point.
- Present a united front, otherwise the canny child will play one parent off against the other.

BAD BEHAVIOUR IN TEENAGERS

Teenagers have a hard time. They have to come to terms with physical changes in their bodies: for girls, growing breasts and starting their periods; for boys, voices breaking, facial hair and an increasingly active penis. They must also learn to be able to judge situations and make decisions for themselves, the beginning of responsibility for their own lives. Teenagers must also face up to sexual maturity, to eventually having to support themselves and finally, to leave home and survive.

What kind of parent are you?

Is your thinking out of date? The world of teenagers has changed, the world moves on, fast. It is totally unrealistic, for instance, to believe that your child will not experiment with sex and possibly with drugs. A teenager might say a perfect parent is someone who leaves them alone. Left to their own devices, however, they would feel uneasy and unhappy because their lives would have no boundaries – they would be forced to take grown-up decisions before they want to. They would also feel that you were not interested in them.

Be assertive, not aggressive. Aggressive parents are no better than passive ones – they make a lot of noise and achieve little. Teenagers will revolt against you if you are too heavy-handed. By being assertive, you put your point of view to them but at the same time are willing to discuss and negotiate. Be prepared to face up to conflict – they are flexing their verbal muscles and practising on you.

Parent's rights

You have the right to be treated with respect and not as a bumbling senile idiot from the dark ages. But you, in your turn, must respect your teenage child's right to make some decisions that you know are wrong, and to stand back and watch him take the consequences. You have the right to make family decisions, but these should be open to discussion. You also have the right to get on with your own life.

Young people often feel they are facing problems which no one else in the world has ever had to handle before. It is a good idea to remind them that adults have problems too, and give them some idea what yours are, so you can discuss them. Do things together – if you cannot get them to go out with you, even just watching TV together is better than nothing. Encourage rather than discourage them to bring their friends to the house; however irritating and disruptive it may be, it is good for you to meet and know their friends in order to build up a picture of your child's life.

We would all like our teenagers to turn out to be happy fulfilled adults, but the most we can hope to do is to create a healthy, secure family environment where they can develop their potential. As teenagers learn to take responsibility for their own actions, we sometimes have to stand back and watch them make mistakes in order that they may learn from those mistakes.

Parents have a certain amount of power but it is simply not possible to take someone and mould them into the kind of person you would like them to be. One minute you believe you have brought up a reasonably behaved child, the next he seems to have turned into a teenage monster. Common problems that parents complain of, but which teenagers would consider to be normal behaviour, are:

- Staying out late at night.
- Skipping school lessons, with a nose-dive in exam results.
- Playing loud music.
- Behaving aggressively.
- Refusing to talk – sitting slumped, answering in grunts and scowling.
- Wearing outrageous clothes and hair.
- Mixing with undesirable people.

- Swearing.
- Staying in bed all day whenever possible.
- Refusing to help around the house.
- Using the phone for hours at a time.

Parenthood involves a learning curve – but by the time you think you have got it sorted out, the birds are longing to fly the nest. Overnight, it seems, you have a stranger living in your own home. When trouble erupts, initial attempts to take things calmly and offer bribes and rewards degenerate into shouted orders and threats. At this stage you find, to your surprise, that it is quite possible to love your children but not actually like them. Your children, in turn, feel grown up but do not have enough money, enough knowledge or enough skills at this stage to survive on their own. They know they have to depend on you and they resent it. With teenagers in the house, the ground rules change.

What is not your responsibility

- Homework. Whether or not your teenager does it, at this stage, is his decision and he will be answerable to the teacher, not you.
- Friends. You cannot choose your child's friends any more than he can choose yours. Your teenager may be enamoured of a group that swear, smoke, are in trouble with the police and take drugs, but there is little you can do about it except to provide a home environment he will measure his friends against and, hopefully, find them wanting. Making friends that parents do not like is one way to demonstrate teenage independence. You may feel these friends are taking your child away from you. Indeed they are, but only temporarily, we hope. What you can do, however, is to stand your ground and make basic rules about when and how often they come to your house.
- Bedroom. The state his room is in is not your concern. Just shut the door and forget it. Nagging will not achieve anything except exhaust you.

The confrontation

Inevitably things will come to a head and a certain amount of antler-clashing will go on. Try, if you can, to look upon the incident as a business discussion rather than a personal slanging match. The main objective is to keep the lines of communication open

- Deal with the problem immediately. Decide what it is, exactly, that you want from them. Wallpapering over a conflict is not a good idea. However, if you are in a rage, calm down first.
- Stay calm, even if your stomach is churning at the prospect of a confrontation. A calm person is much more effective in putting over his point than one who shouts. The child then feels he is like a wave dashing himself against something solid like a lighthouse or a rock.

- Write it all down first if it helps. Prepare yourself for the onslaught. Write down everything you resent about your teenager's behaviour, what angers you, what is worrying you. Having got it all out of your system you can then study the list and choose what to say and what to leave unsaid. Or, if you prefer, you can talk to the teenager in his absence, getting it all straight in your head.
- Do not start with an accusation. Instead say 'I see that . . .' or 'I've noticed that . . .' do not say 'how could you . . .' or 'you never . . .', or 'you always . . .'.
- Tell your teenager what it is you want him to do, not what you do not want him to do. 'I want you in before midnight' not 'I do not want you staying out after midnight'. If he says that all his friends are allowed out all night, just observe that perhaps their parents do not care about their children as much as you do – there is no answer to that. Make it quite clear what you are willing to do or to put up with and what you are not, so there is no room for doubt. 'I want you to take your friends up to your own room, not into the living room', for instance, or 'I want you to ring me if you are going to be late' and so on.
- Do not make personal remarks. Do not be tempted to drop in snide comments about his appearance or habits, that are irrelevant, stick to the subject in hand.
- Listen to his side of the story. While he is having his say, do not interrupt. If he is in a rage, let him get it all out before you reply, then say 'Let's discuss this'. If he starts hurling insults, stay implacable, even if you are shaking underneath.
- Do not make empty threats. State calmly what the consequences will be if he refuses to cooperate then stick to it. Give him time to think over your proposal and say you want an answer at a given time.
- Take things one step at a time. Deal with one specific problem, do not hurl general accusations about other things that annoy you since that will muddy the waters unnecessarily.
- Show him how his behaviour affects your life. Point out that you cannot watch what you want on TV, for instance, and that you are stuck with piles of washing up after he and his friends have left.
- Treat him as a grown-up. Go through things point by point in a businesslike way. Copy the way politicians behave when they are cornered during a debate; keep repeating, over and over again, a key phrase like 'I want you in early tonight'. Repeat it until it sinks in.
- Ask his opinion. If you cannot solve the problem yourself, involve him by asking what suggestions he can come up with.
- Do not be the meat in the sandwich. Make him responsible for what he does. If, for instance, he has been playing pop music at mega-decibel levels, or revving up a motorbike late at night and the neighbours complain, put him directly in touch, walk away and let them get on with it.
- Never show that you have won. Do not crow over the fact that you are victorious. You can afford to be generous if you have gained ground.

- Sort out territorial rights. If he tends to take over the living room with friends, scattering dirty coffee cups and cigarette ash all over the place, negotiate set times when they can use the room and make it clear that part of the deal is that they clear up afterwards. See if something can be done to make his own room more attractive – it might pay to invest in a second-hand TV set to go in it.
- If your teenager lets you down, do not be a doormat, stand your ground if he reneges on an agreement. Repeat what you want from him and what he has agreed to do. Do not lose your temper at this stage, save that as the ultimate weapon; above all, do not take the more-in-sorrow-than-in-anger tack.
- Keep your self-esteem going. You may be told you are totally useless as a parent, but that is par for the course, we have all heard that one. Do something that makes you feel like a human being again. Have a personal creative project on the go and make time for it. Get out and about and talk to other people about things unconnected with children. If all else fails, put on a talk channel on the radio to reassure you that there is another world out there. Then settle down with a good book, some music or have a long hot bath.
- Have someone to moan to, other than your partner who gets enough of that anyway. Trade places with another parent, share experiences and see the funny side of things – but do not whatever you do let the children overhear you doing it. Take your troubles out of the house to air them.
- Do not pry into his personal life. Reading diaries and letters is simply not on. Any material that you discover cannot be used without indicating, that as a parent you have betrayed his trust.
- Thank your teenager for his cooperation even if you feel you could thump him. If he has conceded a point or said he is willing to do something, then you have gained some ground. If he clears up a mess or comes in on time, show you have noticed and approved.

Serious trouble

Sometimes things get out of hand and your child gets into serious trouble, perhaps falling foul of the law. If this happens, make sure that you get your facts straight and that you understand what is said to you. I remember my sister freaking out overhearing her child talk about 'having cold turkey' and jumping to the conclusion that she was trying to come off drugs, when in fact she actually meant having cold turkey to eat.

Having discovered your child has done something terrible, the first thing to do is to try to find out the reason why. Is it because he wanted to experience the thrill of taking risks or because it was fun, or because all his friends were doing it. He could be bored or may want to appear grown up. Your support at this stage is vital; your child has to know that you still love and care for him whatever he has done. But do not minimize the seriousness of his actions – point out the legal implications if there are any.

If you need help with the problem, then ask for it. Talking things over with another person, best of all, a stranger, helps to put things in perspective. There are support groups now on every subject that you are likely to come across. Probation officers can often be very helpful in an unofficial way (*see page 224*).

Teenagers and sex (*see page 145*).

CHILD NEGLECT AND ABUSE

What is child abuse? The NSPCC defines several kinds of abuse.

Physical abuse

When parents or adult deliberately inflict injuries on a child or, knowingly, do not prevent the child from being harmed. It also includes using excessive force when feeding, changing or handling a child and giving him poisonous substances, inappropriate drugs or alcohol.

Warning signs: unexplained bruises, cuts or burns, refusal to undress in front of other people, bald patches, fear of medical examination and fear of physical contact with anyone.

Emotional abuse

When parents continuously fail to show their child love or affection, or when they threaten, taunt or shout at a child, causing him or her to lose confidence and self-esteem, so that he becomes nervous or withdrawn.

Warning signs: sudden speech disorders, over-reaction to mistakes, neurotic behaviour such as rocking, hair twisting or self-mutilation.

Sexual abuse

When an adult forces a child to take part in a sexual activity, using the child to satisfy his own sexual needs. This includes exposing children to pornographic videos, books and other material. People who abuse children in this way often inflict added stress by telling the child that this is a secret that he or she must not tell anyone.

Warning signs: there could be medical problems like chronic itching of the genitals. The child may exhibit knowledge about sex inappropriate to his age, sudden regression to thumb-sucking, being withdrawn and depressed. A child may also show sudden fear of being left alone with someone he knows well, he may start wetting the bed or be worried if someone tries to help him take his clothes off.

Neglect

This occurs if a parent fails to meet a child's basic needs, such as providing food and warm clothing, or constantly leaves children who are too young to look after themselves alone or without proper supervision. Neglect is just as serious as other forms of child abuse because the effects can be just as damaging and long-lasting.

Warning signs: constant hunger, unkempt dirty appearance, emaciated look, untreated medical conditions.

What to do

If you know of a child who is being neglected or left alone, think first about how you could help the family, perhaps by offering to baby-sit occasionally. If you cannot help, or if you think the child's situation is serious, contact the police, Social Services or the NSPCC at once.

If you suspect a child is being abused, share your worry first with someone who knows the family – a neighbour, relative or teacher. If you are still worried, contact the NSPCC Child Protection Helpline (*see page 265*) or the Social Services. Social workers and the police are under a statutory duty to investigate when there is concern that a child has been or is being abused or is at risk of significant harm. An investigation may lead to the child's name being placed on a Child Protection Register and could involve child-care proceedings and a criminal prosecution. The child may be taken into care, as a result, or even adopted.

What to tell your own child

Most children are innocent and trusting and are easily taken advantage of, so you need to teach them to be street-wise.

- Tell them to trust their own feelings if they feel uneasy about someone.
- Instil a sense of pride in their own bodies and emphasize that their bodies belong to them and they can choose whom they want to kiss and hug.
- Tell them they have the right to say no if an adult or older child tries to touch them or to do something that makes them frightened or that they do not like.
- If older children have to walk alone after dark, tell them to choose a busy, well-lit route and never take short cuts through parks or secluded places. They should also tell you where they are going, whom they are going with and when they will be coming home.
- If anyone does attack them they should be instructed to yell, kick, bite and do anything that will help them to escape.

YOUR CHILD AND THE SOCIAL SERVICES

Children in care

You often hear stories about children being taken into care, but not many people know that you, as a parent, can apply for this to be done. Once called Voluntary Care, this name no longer exists. Instead, if your child needs to be looked after, the Social Services have a duty to place them in 'accommodation' in the short-term as part of emergency arrangements, or in the longer term, if your problems will take time to sort out. Accommodation could mean in a foster home, a children's home or a residential school. You then make a 'voluntary arrangement' with the authorities. You are only likely to consider this serious step if your relationship has totally broken down, if you are threatened with violence or if you are ill, and it seems that the only solution is to hand them over for the time being to the Social Services.

There were instances in the past when parents who, in desperation, had handed their children over, found that they could not get their children back again, but new legislation makes this far less likely to happen.

Why might my children go into care?

The local Social Services, the NSPCC or the police can apply for an order taking your child into care for a number of reasons.
- Your child's health or development is being neglected.
- The health or development of another child in your household was neglected and they are afraid it will happen to the present child.
- Someone in your household has been convicted of offences against children.
- Someone you are about to take into your household has been convicted of offences against children.
- Your child is in moral danger.
- You are unable to control your child.
- Your child is not getting a proper education and is not attending school.
- Your child has committed an offence.
- You are not able to give the child the care and control that he needs.

The local council Social Services can get an Emergency Protection Order to remove your children from your home or keep your child in a safe place. Any child up to the age of 17 could be made the subject of a care order.

Child protection procedures

If anyone thinks that your child may be in danger or that you are having problems looking after your children, child protection procedures may be brought in. This is usually done if it is suspected that the child is suffering from abuse or neglect – see above.

The professionals – social workers and police – will only start an investigation if they believe the risk to your child is 'significant'. This could be because there are unexplained marks on the child's body, the child has talked to someone about his worries, a professional is worried about the child or the child has been removed from your care. The investigation, which comes first, can last for several weeks, and you may have meetings with several people about it. During this time you have the right to complain if you are not happy about what happens and you can ask questions.

Will my child be taken away?
Under government guidelines a child is usually only taken away from his parents if there is a risk to the life of the child or likelihood of serious injury. Only if it is believed that the child is in immediate danger can they consider taking that child away from home. This does not mean that the child will go into care. The child could be in accommodation elsewhere, perhaps with the local authority.

What is the next stage?
There will be a **Child Protection Conference**, which is a meeting held by social workers and other professionals to discuss their worries about your child to see if any special action is needed. By law you have to be told about the conference beforehand, and you have the right to attend – it is a good idea to take someone with you for moral support. If you do not have a friend or relative, try to get someone working for a local law centre or the Citizens' Advice Bureau or, if necessary, someone who speaks English better than you do. If you are not invited, then talk to the Social Services about it.

The conference is usually held in the Social Services office. Your child may or may not be invited to come, depending on the circumstances and the child's age. The conference makes decisions on:
- Whether to put your child's name on the Child Protection Register.
- Whether or not the child was abused, and what kind of abuse the child suffered.
- Who the child's keyworker will be, the person with whom you will have direct contact.

They will then decide what to do about the situation, what help they can give and, in some circumstances, if the child should be taken away from the parents and possibly put into care. This does not happen as often as you think: out of every hundred children who are the subject of a conference of this kind, only 17 are likely to be taken from their homes.

An Emergency Protection Order

This is usually applied for by the Social Services or the NSPCC or the police, who may or may not give you warning that they are going to do so. If you are given notice, you have the right to be present at the Magistrates' Court hearing. Go and see a solicitor right away. Get someone who is on your local Law Society Child Care Panel to come with you (ask your local Citizens' Advice Bureau about this). You now have, under the Children Act, an absolute right to Legal Aid whatever your circumstances are.

If the order is granted they have the right to take your child immediately from your home. An Emergency Protection Order lasts up to 8 days and can be extended only for a further week. At the end of this time, your child may be able to come home and live with you again, or the Social Services may apply for a Supervision Order or an Interim Care Order.

Supervision Order

A Supervision Order lasts for a year but can be extended to three years. There are three different kinds of supervision order:

• An ordinary Supervision Order means that you and your child will be visited from time to time by someone from the Social Services, and may be called in for medical or other examinations.

• An Education Supervision Order is sometimes taken out when a child is not going to school regularly either because you do not send him, or because he is playing truant. This does not apply, of course, to parents who are educating their children at home (*see page 324*).

• A Criminal Supervision Order may be made if your child has been found guilty of a crime in the Juvenile Court.

Interim Care Order

The first Interim Care Order lasts up to eight weeks, when your child will be in the care of the Social Services, probably in a foster home or a children's home. After that he may be returned to you, or the Social Services may apply for a Care Order.

Care Order

Although you still have 'parental responsibility' for your child, you now share this with the Social Services who will put him in a foster home, children's home or residential school. This is an open-ended decision, but by law the case has to be reviewed regularly, and at any time the Social Services can decide to allow the child to come and live with you for short periods or visit or eventually be returned to you.

They must allow you to have 'reasonable contact' with your child and they can help you with the cost of visiting that child if it would cause you 'undue financial hardship' to make the journey. Do everything you can to keep in touch with the

Social Services during this time, show them how much everyone in the family is concerned about the children's future. Make sure that the children take with them some favourite toys, photographs or tapes.

While your child is in care

If your child is taken into care you are bound to feel depressed and distressed and guilty that it has happened. But your child's interests have to come first. Do not waste time, and perhaps make yourself ill by going over what went wrong. Work instead towards making things right for the future. It is vital to make your child realize that you still love and care about him. There are many support groups for parents in this situation (*see page 266*); get in touch with one, you will find that it helps.

Adoption of children in care

The Social Services may start making moves towards adopting your child if:
- You die and there is no one else to look after them.
- If there is reason to believe that you have abandoned your children. They are considered to be abandoned if you have disappeared and had no contact with them for a year after they went into care.
- If you are considered an unfit parent – either because of your way of life or because you are ill or disabled in a way that makes it impossible for you to look after them.

When a mistake is made

Mistakes can be made, and to be wrongly accused of abusing your own child is one of the most nightmarish situations a parent can face. It could be that the school or nursery, even a neighbour, may notice something about a child's behaviour that makes them think the child may be being abused, and the next thing the parent knows is the arrival of a police officer and a social worker on the doorstep.

Parents Against Injustice, the charity that specializes in giving advice and support to those who may be mistakenly involved in investigations of child abuse (*see page 265*), says that it is difficult to comprehend the feeling of isolation and the helplessness that parents feel at a time like this. The effect on the children is so great that it is almost as bad as if they had been abused. If this situation happens to you or you are threatened, get expert help.

How to complain

It can be very difficult to make a complaint against officialdom. You may be afraid it will be used against you or your child, or that the council will not investigate their own workers properly, but it pays to persevere. You have the right to complain as a parent:

- About the services – or lack of services – provided by the local authority.
- If you feel the arrangements made for looking after your child are not satisfactory.
- If you feel that you have not been treated properly.
- If the contact arrangements for you and the various officials are not satisfactory.

Send your complaint in writing or make a statement to the local authority, who must appoint an independent person to look into the complaint. They have to do this within 28 days. You should then receive a letter from them, after they have consulted the independent person, giving you their decision. If you wish to appeal against that, they then have to organize an outside panel and an official hearing.

If you are not satisfied with what is going on, do not forget the power of the press. Write down what has happened and take your case to your local paper. A mere whiff of a reporter on the premises might well make the council act.

Coming out of care

Nine out of ten children who are put in the hands of the Social Services, for whatever reason, do eventually return home, three out of four before six months is up. It can be a stressful time when children return. If you, as a parent, have been worried whether you will ever get them back, this anxiety may spill over to the time when they do indeed come back home to live. It may be that they have already been visiting you at weekends which will make the hand-over easier, but everyone will need time to settle down. Do not get upset if the children seem like strangers at first. Expect there to be arguments from time to time; the main thing is that you should talk things through together to clear the air. If you feel you cannot cope, ask the social worker for help and advice.

MISSING/ABDUCTED CHILDREN

There are two laws in this country covering child abduction; under the Child Abduction Act kidnapping a child is technically a criminal offence. Under the act, any parent who takes a child out of the country without the prior written permission of the other, or permission of the court, may be committing a crime. It is not an offence, however, if a court has agreed to the child being removed from the country.

In certain circumstances, if the parent holds a Residence Order, that parent may take the child out of England and Wales for a holiday of up to one month without the other parent's permission. Even if your partner has custody of the child, a court can make an order to stop him from taking the child abroad, particularly if abduction is feared. Then failure or refusal to return the child to the United Kingdom could be considered a 'wrongful retention' of the child under the Hague Convention. A useful free booklet called *Child Abduction* is available from the Child Abduction Unit (*see page 275*).

If you are afraid your partner may abduct your child

- Alert the police, make a statement to this effect.
- Apply to the court to make a Prohibited Steps Order or a Residence Order which would state that the other parent could not take the child abroad without your prior consent or the court's permission.
- Fax, telephone or write to the Passport Office (*see page 18*) asking the agency not to grant passport facilities to the children. The agency will probably need to see a Custody, Residence, Prohibited Steps or Wardship Order. This is not necessary, however, if you are an unmarried mother or father.
- If your partner or ex-partner is not a British national, contact the embassy or consulate of his country asking it not to issue a passport to your child. It is not obliged to comply with this, but may do so anyway. Even if it refuses, you may at least know whether or not a passport has been requested.
- Alert your solicitor; you may have to take fast court action.

If your child has already been abducted

See **Emergencies**, *page 17*.

If your child is taken abroad

As border restrictions are lifted and it becomes easier to move from one country to another, and more and more of us marry people from other countries, so the number of international child custody disputes increases.

Both of you, as parents, may believe you have the right to have your child living with you, or to have contact with the child. But if your partner takes your child to another country, it is the courts of that country which will decide who should have custody. Every country has exclusive jurisdiction within its own territory. The British courts cannot force the courts of another country to decide the case or enforce the law in a certain way. Similarly a court order giving you custody is not usually enforceable in another country. There are two internationally agreed legal procedures to help return a child that has been abducted. The following countries obey either or both of these rules: Argentina, Australia, Austria,

Bahamas, Belgium, Belize, Bosnia Hercegovina, Burkina Faso, Canada (most provinces), Chile, Croatia, Cyprus (Southern), Denmark, Ecuador, Finland, France, Germany, Greece, Honduras, Hungary, Israel, Luxembourg, Macedonia, Mauritius, Mexico, Monaco, Netherlands, New Zealand, Norway, Panama, Portugal, Poland, Republic of Ireland, Romania, St Kitts and Nevis, Slovenia, Spain, Sweden, Switzerland, USA.

Algeria, Morocco, Egypt, Iran, India and Pakistan are not signatories to these procedures. If your child has been taken to one of the countries listed, then you should do the following:

- Contact the Child Abduction Unit of the Lord Chancellor's Department (*see page 275*) if you live in England or Wales. This unit will take brief details over the phone and send you a form. Complete this as soon as possible, together with photocopies of any relevant court orders and photographs of the missing child and the abductor if you have them, and any other information which might help in locating them.

To get help under the International Conventions:

- The child must be under 16.
- Habitually resident in the UK.
- You must have normal rights of custody.

The Child Abduction Unit will fax or airmail a formal application, translated if necessary into the language of the country it is going to, asking for the return of the child or enforcement of your right of access or contact with it. The Child Abduction Unit will then act as a point of contact between you or your solicitor and the authorities abroad. It will do everything it can to get the matter dealt with quickly and will keep you or your solicitor informed of what progress has been made.

How much does it cost?

Consult the Child Abduction Unit. Generally speaking, you should not have to pay. However, in the case of some countries you may have to satisfy a means test, or be asked to pay something if costs are not covered by their own legal aid system. In the case of the United States, there is no legal aid system but the authorities will make an effort to provide help either at a reduced rate or free of charge.

What if my child has been taken to a non-convention country?

This is when the problems start. You may have to start legal proceedings in the courts of the country concerned. You cannot get legal aid for this. However, you may be able to get it from the country in which your child has been taken. Get a lawyer in the country concerned for immediate legal advice on the laws and practice there. Find out what your rights are under local law. Then contact the Consular Department of the Foreign and Commonwealth Office (*see page 532*).

What the Consular Department can do

- It can give you a list of local lawyers who can correspond in English.
- Ask the local authorities in the country concerned for help in tracing your child.
- Once the child is located try to get a report on his or her welfare – but this can only be done with the other parent's consent and at your own cost.
- Ask the local court to handle the case as quickly as possible.
- Pass letters between you and the child and arrange for a place where you can spend time together privately – but only with your partner's consent.
- Draw to the attention of the local court to any UK court orders you have obtained. Although such an order has no binding force overseas, it may be taken into account by the court there.

What the Consular Department cannot do

- Neither it nor the British consuls abroad can give legal advice or act as your representative.
- If your child is a national of the country concerned by birth, then the courts there are not obliged to allow consular staff to make any representations about the child at all.
- The foreign court cannot pass down judgments which go against their own law. They are usually unwilling to oppose family, religious or cultural traditions and often the law is based on these. Women, in particular, may not have the same rights as they do in England.

If you do not know where your child has been taken

- Alert the local police by telephone and then go there in person and give a statement. They do not need a court order to act, just a statement from you giving evidence of your rights to the child and your objection to his or her removal.
- The police will then circulate the child's name to all UK points of departure.

What you will need: a checklist

All of the following would be of help to the authorities if they are trying to find your child:

- The full name of your child.
- His date and place of birth.
- His passport number if he has one and the date and place of issue.
- A good physical description of the child.
- The most up-to-date photographs you have (ask family and friends if necessary for these).
- The full name, any aliases and maiden name, if it is a woman who has taken the child.

- The abductor's date and place of birth.
- The abductor's passport number if you have it, and date and place of issue (a point to remember if you fear abduction).
- The person's occupation.
- The date you think the person is likely to try to leave the country or did leave the country.
- Any clues as to flight information or registration number of car.
- Any details of ties to a foreign country – family, friends, business contacts. Or somewhere where they have habitually gone for a holiday.
- Photographs of the person.
- Copies of any agreement or court order you hold relating to the child.
- The child's birth certificate.
- The name and address of your solicitor if you have one.

What else can I do?
Contact Reunite, National Council for Abducted Children (*see page 275*). In addition to help with legal problems, raising money, if necessary, and getting assistance in bringing the child back they offer a counselling service.

CHILDREN: HELP DIRECTORY

Behaviour problems

- Centre for Fun and Families, 25 Shanklin Drive, Knighton, Leicester LE2 3RH, (0116 270 7198). Helps families whose children have behavioural difficulties. It can offer information packs.
- Enuresis Resource and Information Centre, 65 St Michael's Hill, Bristol BS2 8DZ, (0117 926 4920). Gives advice, information and support to parents of children who are habitual bed-wetters.
- Michael Palin Centre for Stammering Children, Finsbury Health Centre, Pine Street, London EC1R 0JH, (0171 837 0031). Gives help and advice to parents of children who stammer. It has a useful video for parents.

See also CRY-SIS Support Group (*page 270*).

Child abuse

- Childline, 2nd Floor, Royal Mail Building, Studd Street, London N1 0QW, (0171 239 1000). It operates a freephone national helpline on 0800 1111 for children and young people in trouble or danger. A counsellor is available round-the-clock and the service is confidential.

- Childwatch, 206 Hessle Road, Hull, North Humberside HU3 3BE, (01482 325552). A campaigning organization for more awareness of child abuse. It will also answer queries on the subject.
- Foundation for Women's Health Research and Development, 38 King Street, London WC2E 8JT, (0171 379 6889) F 836 1975. Is particularly concerned with the mutilation of young girls caused by female circumcision.
- National Children's Home, 85 Highbury Park, London N5 1UD, (0171 226 2033). Has a network of child abuse treatment centres throughout the country.
- Kidscape, 152 Buckingham Palace Road, London SW1W 9TR, (0171 730 3300). Campaigns for children's safety, does programmes in schools and has useful literature for both children and parents to read.
- National Society for the Prevention of Cruelty to Children (NSPCC), 42 Curtain Road, London EC2A 3NH, (0171 825 2500). A long-established organization which has teams and inspectors throughout the country combating child abuse and neglect. Also helps families where children are at risk. It has a round-the-clock National Child Protection Helpline on 0800 800 500.
- Ormiston Trust, 10 Abercorn Place, London NW8 9XP, (0171 289 8166). Works with children under the age of 12 who are at risk and their families. It has projects throughout the country.
- Parentline, Endway House, The Endway, Hadleigh, Essex SS7 2AN, (01702 554782). A counselling service for parents under stress, particularly where children are at risk as a result. There are groups throughout the country, helplines and drop-in advice and information centres. It has a helpline on 01268 757077.
- Parents Against Injustice, 10 Water Lane, Bishop's Stortford, Herts CM23 2JZ, (01279 656564). The only national charity that operates a help and support service for parents and families whose children have been mistakenly thought to be at risk or to have been abused.
- Parents Anonymous, Manor Gardens Centre, 8 Manor Gardens, London N7 6LA, (0171 263 8918). It offers confidential counselling and help, including over the phone via its helpline above, to parents who have been tempted to abuse their children or who have done so.

Child care

- The Parent Helpline on 0171 837 5513 is a national helpline which will give you details of child-care facilities in your area.

- British Association of the Experiment in International Living, Otesaga, West Malvern Road, Upper Wyche, Malvern, Worcs WR14 4EN, (01684 562577). Arranges homestays for overseas youths in British homes on an au pair basis.
- International Catholic Society for Girls, St Patrick's International Centre, 24 Great Chapel Street, London W1V 3AF, (0171 734 2156). Runs a placement service for au pairs in this country placing girls with Catholic families.
- Kids' Clubs Network, Bellerive House, 3 Muirfield Crescent, London E14 9SZ, (0171 512 2100). Helps parents who want to set up out-of-school activities for their children, such as holiday clubs.
- National Childminding Association, 8 Masons Hill, Bromley, Kent BR2 9EY, (0181 464 6164). It has an advice line on 0181 466 0200.
- National Council of Voluntary Child Care Organizations, Unit 4, Pride Court, 80–82 White Lion Street, London N1 9PS, (0171 833 3319). Puts families in touch with other organizations which will give them specialist help and advice.
- Parents at Work, 77 Holloway Road, London N7 8JZ, (0171 700 5771). Gives information and advice to working women. It has a number of local groups throughout the country.
- Pre-school Playgroups Association, 61–63 King's Cross Road, London WC1X 9LL, (0171 833 0991). Worth approaching if you are trying to find out what facilities are available in your area for pre-school-aged children.
- Sailors' Families Society, Newland, Hull HU6 7RJ, (01482 342331). Gives residential care to children of sailors in need. It also has hostels for teenagers and children with learning difficulties and sheltered accommodation for elderly sailors.

Children in care

- Family Rights Group, The Print House, 18 Ashwin Street, London E8 3DL, (0171 923 2628). Helps families whose children are in care or involved in court proceedings. It has an advice line on 0171 249 0008.
- First Key, National Leaving Care Service, Oxford Chambers, Oxford Place, Leeds LS1 3AX, (0113 24413898). Advises and helps children who are about to leave or who have left care, helping them find accommodation.
- Grandparents Federation, Room 3, Moot House, The Stow, Harlow, Essex CM2 3AG, (01279 437145). Works through a series of local groups throughout the country, counselling grandparents whose grandchildren are in care.
- National Association of Young People in Care, 23 New Mount Street, Manchester M4 4DE, (0161 953 4041). Gives advice and help by phone or post regarding young people in care or after-care.

- Parents Aid, Hare Street Family Centre, Harberts Road, Harlow, Essex CM19 4EU, (01279 452166). Gives practical help, advice and support via groups throughout the country, to families whose children are taken into care or adopted without their consent. It publishes a useful guide to the Social Services.
- Shaftesbury Homes and Arethusa, 3 Rectory Grove, London SW4 0EG, (0171 720 8709). Runs residential homes for teenagers in care, for homeless teenagers and also for single parents.
- Voice for the Child in Care, Unit 4, Pride Court, 80–82 White Lion Street, London N1 9PS, (0171 833 5792). Has helpful leaflets for young people in care.
- Who Cares Trust, Kemp House, 152–160 City Road, London EC1V 2NP, (0171 251 3117). This organization runs a magazine for children in care and gives information and help to them as well.

Children with special needs

- ADHD Family Support Group, c/o Mrs G. Nead, 1a High Street, Dilton Marsh, Westbury, Wiltshire BA14 4DL, (01373 826045). Helps parents of hyperactive children. Send an SAE for information.
- AFASIC – Overcoming Speech Impairments, 347 Central Market, Smithfield, London EC1A 9NH, (0171 236 3632). Helps and advises parents of children with speech impairments.
- Allergy-induced Autism Support and Self-help Group, 3 Palmera Avenue, Calcot, Reading, Berks RG31 7DZ, (01734 419460). A support group for families with autistic children. It offers counselling over the phone, personally and by post. It also puts parents in touch with local families who have autistic children.
- Association for All Speech-impaired Children, 347 Central Markets, Smithfield, London EC1A 9NH, (0171 236 3632). Has an information service for parents of children with speech impediments and gives advice. It also runs activity days and weeks for children.
- Association for Brain-damaged Children and Young Adults, Clifton House, 3 St Paul's Road, Foleshill,Coventry CV6 5DE, (01203 665450). Specializes in short-stay care and holidays for brain-damaged children. It also gives advice and support to parents.
- British Institute for Brain-injured Children, Knowle Hall, Knowle, Bridgwater, Somerset TA7 8PJ, (01278 684060). Helps parents to treat brain-injured children in the home. It also monitors the child's progress and gives specialist treatment where necessary.
- Contact a Family, 170 Tottenham Court Road, London W1P 0HA, (0171 383 3555). Encourages families of children with special needs to help

and support each other. There is a network of groups all over the country. It holds conferences and training sessions.

- Forest School Camps, 110 Burbage Road, London SE24 9HD, (0171 274 7566). Runs adventure holiday camps and activity breaks for children, including those who are mentally and/or physically handicapped.
- Handicapped Adventure Playground Association, Fulham Palace, Bishops Avenue, London SW6 6EA, (0171 736 4443). Has a service offering advice to parent self-help groups that want to set up an adventure playground. The association also runs five playgrounds in the London area, not just for handicapped children but also those with emotional or behavioural problems.
- Handicapped Children's Pilgrimage and Hosanna House Trust, 100a High Street, Banstead, Surrey SM7 2RB, (01737 353311). Provides practical and financial help for handicapped children to make visits to Lourdes in France, where they stay in specially adapted accommodation.
- Hyperactive Children's Support Group, 71 Whyke Lane, Chichester, West Sussex PO19 2LD, (01903 725182). Helps, advises and supports families of hyperactive children with information of all kinds, including diet.
- In Touch, 10 Norman Road, Sale, Cheshire, M33 3DF, (0161 905 2440). A support group for parents of mentally handicapped children, helping them to make contact with others in a similar situation. It also helps parents find professional care and has a telephone and post enquiry service.
- Invalid Children's Aid Nationwide, Barbican City Centre, 1–3 Dufferin Street, London EC1Y 8NA, (0171 374 4422). Supports families who have disabled children, with help, advice and information. It also runs several residential schools, one for asthmatic children, others for those with speech and language disorders as well as a college for severely physically disabled students.
- Isle of Wight Deaf Projects, 8 Victoria Court, Freshwater Bay, Isle of Wight PO4 9PU, (01983 754140). Works with deaf children, not just on the Isle of Wight but nationally, with mobile workshops, especially on performing arts for the deaf. It concentrates particularly on children from ethnic minorities and poor families.
- KIDS, 80 Waynflete Square, London W10 6UD, (0181 969 2817). Helps the families of children with special needs in every way – those with learning difficulties, physical or mental handicap. It works with parents at home, counselling them and helping them set up educational programmes that suit their child. It also runs outings and play groups and has a wide range of other activities.
- Kith and Kids, 404 Camden Road, London N7 0SJ, (0181 810 7432). A practical help group for parents of handicapped children with counselling, baby- and child-sitting services and holiday schemes.

- National Autistic Society, 276 Willesden Lane, London NW2 5RB, (0181 451 1114). The society has an advice and information service for parents and carers of autistic children, as well as a diagnosis and assessment service. It also runs a number of schools for autistic children.
- Society for the Autistically Handicapped, 199 Blandford Avenue, Kettering, Northants NN16 9AT, (01536 523274). Runs a round-the-clock helpline for parents and carers of autistic children.

See also Disability (*page 127*).

- Treloar Trust, Froyle, Alton, Hants GU3 4JX, (01420 22442). A charity which runs the Lord Mayor Treloar Residential College which takes severely disabled children from the age of 8 up. It also has sheltered employment schemes for older children and teams take part in the Duke of Edinburgh's Awards and the games at Stoke Mandeville.

See also

Lady Hoare Trust for Physically Disabled Children (*page 104*).

National Federation of Families with Visually Impaired Children (*page 107*).

Sense (*page 107*).

The Charity for Incontinent and Stoma Children (*page 121*).

Vision Aid (*page 108*).

Network '81 (*page 346*).

Ravenswood Foundation (*page 346*).

Womens Aid Federation (*page 164*).

Children's rights

- Child Poverty Action Group, 5th Floor, 1–5 Bath Street, London EC1V 9PY, (0171 253 3406) Fax 0171 490 0561. A pressure group that will take up the cause of families denied benefits to which they are entitled.
- Children's Legal Centre, The University of Essex, Wivenhoe Park, Colchester CO4 3SQ, (0120 687 3820). Gives advice by post or by phone on children's legal rights. In some cases it will take up a legal case on a child's behalf.

Early years

- Association of Breast-feeding Mothers, 26 Holmshaw Close, London SE26 4TH, (0181 778 4769). Has support groups around the country to counsel mothers with breast-feeding problems.
- BLISSLINK, Baby Life Support Systems, 17–21 Emerald Street, London WC1N 3QL, (0171 831 9393). Has a support service for parents whose babies are in special or intensive care.

- Cleft Lip and Palate Association, 1 Eastwood Gardens, Kenton, Newcastle-upon-Tyne NE3 3DQ, (0191 285 9396). A support group for parents of new-born babies suffering from this condition.
- CRY-SIS Support Group, 27 Old Gloucester Street, London WC1N 3XX, (0171 404 5011). Runs a network of self-help groups throughout the country, giving practical advice and emotional support to mothers of babies who cry incessantly and have sleep problems.
- Diaphragmatic Hernia Support Association, 36 Langney Drive, Bridewell, Ashford, Kent TN23 2UF, (0233 641911). Helps families whose children were born with this congenital condition, both at the time of surgery and for the months afterwards.
- Home-Start UK, 2 Salisbury Road, Leicester LE1 7QR, (0116 233 9955). Can put you in touch with a local Home-Start scheme which gives advice, support and friendship to families with children under the age of five.
- La Leche League of Great Britain, 27 Olde Gloucester Street, London WC1N 3XX, (0171 242 1278). Has a round-the-clock helpline for mothers having problems breast-feeding their babies.
- Multiple Births Foundation, Queen Charlotte's and Chelsea Hospital, Goldhawk Road, London W6 0XG, (0181 748 4666). A support and advice service for families who have twins, triplets and multiple births. It runs a special clinic in London.
- Naevus Support Group, 58 Necton Road, Wheathampstead, St Albans, Herts AL4 8AU, (01582 832853). Gives out information on all aspects of birthmarks. It runs support groups and sends out a regular newsletter on the subject.
- National Childbirth Trust, Alexandra House, Oldham Terrace, London W3 6NH, (0181 992 8637) F 5929. Counsels mothers with breast-feeding problems and provides support to new mothers via a newsletter.
- National Early Years Network, 77 Holloway Road, London N7 8JZ, (0171 607 9573). Gives help and information to families with small children.
- Osteopathic Centre for Children, 4 Harcourt House, 19A Cavendish Square, London W1M 9AD, (0171 495 1231). Can give information on osteopathy for babies and small children.

Fostering, adoption

- The General Register Office, Adoptions Section, Smedley Hydro, Trafalgar Road, Birkdale, Southport PR8 2HH. This office keeps the Adoption Register.
- British Agencies for Adoption and Fostering, Skyline House, 200 Union Street, London SE1 0LX, (0171 593 2000). Has an advice service and an exchange placement scheme for children with special needs.

- Catholic Children's Society (Westminster), 73 St Charles Square, London W10 6EJ, (0181 969 5305). Acts as an adoption agency for the Westminster and Brentwood areas. It also gives support to families in bed and breakfast hotels and counselling to families in need.
- Childlink (Church Adoption Agency), 10 Lion Yard, Tremadoc Road, London SW4 7NQ, (0171 498 1933). Counsels parents who are thinking of putting their child out for adoption, families thinking of adopting a child and people who have themselves been adopted. It also places children for adoption.
- Children First in Trans-Racial Fostering and Adoption, 37 Warner Road, London N8 7HB, (0181 341 7190). This group has been formed to try to stop authorities and agencies from banning children of one race from being adopted by a family from another.
- Children's Family Trust, Maracas, Church Road, Farnham Royal, Slough, Bucks SL2 3AW, (01753 642137). This organization takes children into care, especially brothers and sisters, placing them in its own Trust-run homes.
- Independent Adoption Service, 121–123 Camberwell Road, London SE5 0HB, (0171 703 1088). This agency deals especially with difficult-to-adopt children; brothers and sisters, black children and older age-group children within the greater London area.
- JAFA, Jewish Association for Fostering, Adoption and Infertility, PO Box 20, Prestwich, Manchester M25 5BY, (0161 773 3148). Gives advice and help on fostering, adoption and infertility. Will put you in touch with other relevant groups.
- National Children's Home, 85 Highbury Park, London N5 1UD, (0171 226 2033). As well as running children's homes and special schools, this organization also runs a fostering and adoption service and works with homeless young people and young offenders in a network of centres all over the country.
- National Foster Care Association, Leonard House, 5–7 Marshalsea Road, London SE1 1EP, (0171 828 6266). Provides information and help on fostering children.
- National Organization for Counselling Adoptees and Their Parents, 3 New High Street, Headington, Oxford OX3 7AJ, (01865 875000). Give counselling and help over the phone to grown-up children who have been adopted and to their adoptive and natural parents.
- Norwood Child Care, Norwood House, Harmony Way (off Victoria Road), Hendon, London NW4 2BZ, (0181 203 3030). Runs an adoption agency helping Jewish children and foster families too. It also helps with mentally and physically handicapped children.
- Parent to Parent Information on Adoption Services, Lower Boddington, Daventry, Northants NN11 6YB, (01327 260295). A nationwide service that collects and passes on information about adopting a child, including those

with special needs. Can give names of locally based adoption agencies. It also helps people who are thinking of adopting, or have adopted, a child.

- Parents for Children, 41 Southgate Road, London N1 3JP, (0171 359 7530). Specializes in placing disabled and older children with families for adoption.
- Post-Adoption Centre, 5 Torriano Mews, Torriano Avenue, London NW5 2RZ, (0171 284 0555). Gives help and support to three groups of people: those who have been adopted, those who have adopted children and those whose children were adopted.
- Thomas Coram Foundation for Children, 40 Brunswick Square, London WC1N 1AZ, (0171 278 2424). Places children with special needs with families for adoption, runs residential and non-residential centres for young people who have been in care. It also works with families who are living in temporary – bed and breakfast – accommodation.

Lone parents

- Christian Family Concern, 42 South Park Hill Road, Croydon, Surrey CR2 7YB, (0181 688 0251). This Christian-based organization offers help and support for needy mothers and their children. It runs a bedsit scheme, mother-and-baby home, a drop-in care centre and day nursery.
- Gingerbread, 49 Wellington Street, London WC2E 7BN, (0171 240 0953). A long-established support group for single parents with a network of clubs across the country. Apart from counselling and information, it gives practical support with day-care schemes for children of working single parents. It also gives advice over the phone.
- National Council for One Parent Families, 255 Kentish Town Road, London NW5 2LX, (0171 267 1361). This well-known organization and pressure group gives advice on legal matters, benefits and the rights in general of lone parents. It has a regular newsletter.
- One Parent Family Holidays, 1 Kildonan Courtyard, Barrhill Girvan, Ayrshire KA26 0PS, (0177 688 9500). Organizes holidays for one-parent families. You have to pay, but you are sure to be in the company of other people who understand your particular problems.
- One Parent Families, Scotland, 13 Gayfield Square, Edinburgh EH1 3NX, (0131 556 3899). Helps lone parents with practical or emotional problems. Has leaflets and booklets.

See also Single Concern Group (*page 204*).

Miscellaneous

- Association of Interchurch Families, Interchurch House, 35–41 Lower Marsh, London SE1 7RL, (0171 620 4444). A Christian organization offering help and advice to families of any denomination.
- Barnado's, Tanners Lane, Barkingside, Ilford, Essex IG6 1QG, (0181 550 8822). This famous organization still runs a few foster homes but has widened its scope to help a wide range of disadvantaged groups: from children with special needs, young offenders, drug abusers and families under stress.
- Children Need Grandparents, 2 Surrey Way, Laindon West, Basildon, Essex SS15 6PS, (01268 414607). A help and support group for grandparents who are refused access to their grandchildren for whatever reason.
- Children Country Holidays Fund, 42–43 Lower Marsh, London SE1 7RG, (0171 928 6522). The Fund provides a fortnight's summer holiday to thousands of disadvantaged London children each year.
- Community Action Projects, Students Union, Goodricke College, University of York, Heslington, York YO1 5DD, (01904 433133). Runs holiday camps and out-of-school projects for disadvantaged children in the York area.
- Children's Society, Edward Rudolf House, Margery Street, London WC1X 0JL, (0171 837 4299). Church of England-based organization that helps children in many ways. It has safe houses for teenage runaways, places for teenagers leaving care and will find homes for children with special needs. It also has houses for disabled children and works with the police and probation service to offer alternatives to prison for children in trouble with the law.
- Day Care Trust, 4 Wild Court, London WC2B 4AU, (0171 405 5617). Gives help and information to parents, by phone or by post, over bringing up their children.
- End Physical Punishment of Children, 77 Holloway Road, London N7 8JZ, (0171 700 0627). Campaigns for the end of physical punishment of children. Has advice and information for parents on the subject.
- Exploring Parenthood, 4 Highbury Place, Treadgold Street, London W11 4BP, (0171 221 4471). Has a helpline for parents, counselling families under stress. It works with single parents, those with a disability in the family and step-families. It has a special service for black parents.
- Family Welfare Association, 501–505 Kingsland Road, London E8 4AU, (0171 254 6251). Helps families on the poverty line by running support centres such as day care for people with mental problems and has an advisory service for educational grants etc in the London area.
- Mother's Union, Mary Sumner House, 24 Tufton Street, London SW1P 3RB, (0171 222 5533). Church of England-based association which gives help to people with emotional problems via its network of clubs throughout the

country. It runs holiday breaks for stressed families and has a message service
for teenage runaways who don't want to phone home directly.

- National Children's Home, 85 Highbury Park, London N5 1UD, (0171 226 2033).
  A charity which helps children and their families in many ways: there are child
  sexual abuse treatment centres all over the country, projects for young people
  leaving care and homeless young people. It also works with young offenders,
  acting as go-between for estranged children and their families. It also runs an
  adoption and fostering service.
- Parent Network, 44–46 Caversham Road, London NW5 2DS, (0171 485 8535).
  Helps educate and support parents over the daily problems of family life in
  groups throughout the country and aims to help them and their children feel
  better about themselves and each other.
- Parent Resource and Mother Support, Churchgate House, 96 Churchgate,
  Stockport, Cheshire SK1 1YJ, (0161 477 0606). Runs an information and
  support service for parents with a phone helpline and counselling.
- Royal Gardeners' Orphan Fund, 48 St Albans Road, Caldicote, Hitchin, Herts
  SG4 8UT, (01438 820783). Helps orphaned children of professional gardeners
  with grants, counselling and education.
- Save the Children Fund, 17 Grove Lane, London SE5 8RD, (0171 703 5400) F
  703 2278. Runs family centres and works with disadvantaged young people,
  with disabled children, the children of travellers and with prisoners'
  families.
- Send a Child to Hucklow Fund, 41 Bradford Drive, Ewell, Epsom, Surrey
  KT19 0AQ, (0181 393 9122). Backed by the Unitarian church, this Fund runs a
  holiday centre at Great Hucklow for needy children in groups, whatever their
  religious beliefs.
- Women's Royal Voluntary Service, 234–244 Stockwell Road, London SW9 9SP,
  (0171 416 0146). This long-established organization works with and helps all
  types of people from the elderly to the handicapped, running clubs and
  serving meals on wheels. It also works with young families and arranges
  holidays for disadvantaged children. In many areas it has mother-and-baby
  clubs. Works with people in the Forces and, of course, comes into its own
  when an emergency arises.

Missing/abducted children

- The Child Abduction Unit, The Lord Chancellor's Department, Official
  Solicitor's Office, 81 Chancery Lane, London WC2A 1DD, (0171 911 7127)
  general enquiries, (0171 911 7047) direct line. Acts as a central clearing house
  for processing searches and applications for the return of an abducted child.

- Both Parents Forever, 39 Cloonmore Avenue, Orpington, Kent BR6 9LE, (01689 854343). Advice on how to prevent your child being abducted and what to do if it happens. Help for parents and grandparents on children's rights after divorce, separation or care proceedings.
- Families Need Fathers, 134 Curtain Road, London EC2A 3AR, (0171 613 5060). A self-help group that gives support to couples with custody problems or who are denied access to their children.
- REUNITE, National Council for Abducted Children, PO Box 4, London WC1X 3DX, (0171 404 8356). Information, support and advice service to relatives, parents and friends of abducted children. It gives practical help over national and international law, and lawyers at home and abroad who have experience of child abduction work and who speak English. Also has contacts with child abduction organizations overseas. It will tell you how to raise money if you need it and how to get help in bringing your child back.

Sick children

- Acorns Children's Hospice, 103 Oak Tree Lane, Selly Oak, Birmingham B29 6HZ, (0121 414 1741). Gives support and counselling to families in the West Midlands that have a child who is terminally ill. Also offers bereavement counselling.
- Action for Sick Children, Argyle House, 29–31 Euston Road, London NW1 2SD, (0171 833 2041). Offers help and support via local groups to parents whose children are sick either in hospital or at home.
- Association for Children with Life-threatening and Terminal Conditions, Institute of Child Health, Royal Hospital for Sick Children, 65 St Michael's Hill, Bristol BS2 8BJ, (0117 922 1556). Offers advice, support and information.
- COPE Children's Trust, COPE House, 6 Tower Street, Leicester LE1 6WS, (0116 254 9346). Works mainly with children and young people in the East Midlands who are suffering from life-threatening illness. It has a respite hospice in Loughborough.
- Evalina Children's Family Trust Ltd, 115–122 Snowsfields, London SE1 3SF, (0171 955 4780). Provides accommodation for families referred to them by the hospital, of children who are seriously ill and being treated at Guy's Hospital, London.
- Heart Line Association, 40 The Crescent, Briket Wood, St Albans, Hertfordshire AL2 3NF, (01923 670763). A society concerned with children with heart disease. It also has a bereavement support group.
- Helen House Hospice for Children, 37 Leopard Street, Oxford OX4 1QT, (01865 728251). This organization has other children's hospices in Yorkshire, Birmingham, Manchester and Cambridge, with more planned.

- Rainbow Trust Children's Charity, Surrey House, 31 Church Street, Leatherhead, Surrey KT22 8EF, (01372 363438). Has a team of mobile counsellors who will give total help in the family home when a child is dying. It also has accommodation for short stays.
- REACT, 73 Whitehall Park Road, London W4 3NB, (0181 995 8188). Works with children and young people suffering from serious illnesses that could result in death.
- Sick Children's Trust, 1a Doughty Street, London WC1N 2PH, (0171 404 3329). Provides temporary accommodation for families whose children are in hospital with life-threatening illnesses near hospitals in London, Kent and Yorkshire.
- Sick Children's Trust, Tadworth Court, Tadworth, Surrey KT20 5RU, (01737 373773). Based on Tadworth Court Hospital and School, the Trust works with children who are chronically sick, disabled, have serious learning problems and those with head injuries.
- The Starlight Foundation, 8a Bloomsbury Square, London WC1A 2LP, (0171 430 1642). Tries to grant the wishes of critically ill children.

Step-parenthood

- Step-Family, Chapel House, Hatton Place, London EC1N 8RU, (0171 209 2460). Counsels, offers help and advice to step-parents who are encountering problems. It also runs self-help groups throughout the UK and has therapists on tap. It has a helpline on 0171 209 2464.

The teenage years

- Youth Access, Ashby House, 62d Ashby Road, Loughborough, Leicester LE11 3AE, (01509 210420). Helps and counsels teenagers who have problems at centres throughout the country.

7

THE THIRD AGE

WHAT DOES IT FEEL LIKE TO BE OLD?

We are all getting older day by day, that is a fact of life. More than two million of us are now over 80, which is not surprising given that the average human life expectancy in this country has been increased by 25 years during this century. By the year 2029, one in four people will be drawing state pensions – if such things still exist.

Better housing, better education and better nutrition mean that many of us will live longer, more productive lives and enjoy reasonable health. Verdi composed his best works at 70 and Sir Winston Churchill ruled the country at the same age. Picasso painted in his old age and Sir John Gielgud had some of his best acting roles at 90, the age when actress Jessica Tandy was still making films. No one dared to patronize them. My mother, at the age of 94, told me she was sorry for the 'old people across the road', who were, in fact, 25 years younger than she was. This book has been written by an old-age pensioner.

Most people think that getting old means wearing out, as if their bodies are machines that are running down. Some people moan about their aches and pains and stiffness, while others will go on blithely, only pulled up short when they find that they cannot run as they used to, or dash up the stairs in quite the same energetic way. It is a fact that we lose more brain cells per year when we are relatively young, than when we are older – the greatest loss comes when we are around 40, often the time when we first notice our memories are not all that they should be. This explains why children can work computers and puzzles much better than grown-ups can.

We are at our sporting peak in our early twenties, but scientists have found that although technical prowess may lessen, physical endurance does not decline much with age. That is why so many septagenarians take part in marathon runs.

How to have a happy third age

A recent survey found that 50 per cent of people over the age of 75 said they did not feel old. We need to look upon our third age as a time when we continue to develop – and to have fun, doing those things we did not have the time for earlier in our lives. Most alert, active people feel much younger than they actually are until they look in the mirror. But while some elderly people go on behaving much as they did twenty years ago, there are many more who decide that they are 'old' at some stage in their life. This often happens when they become of pensionable age – sometimes even before. They then start underrating their capabilities, throwing in the sponge and settling into inactivity, both of the mind and of the body.

From 60 on, the chances of having some kind of disability do rise. Eyesight may deteriorate, hearing can be less than perfect, and arthritis and rheumatism may appear, often on the site of a former injury (*see* **Health,** *page 20*). Some people resign themselves to aches and pains as part of getting old while others, more sensibly, get help. Go to the doctor, be persistent, make sure that there is no medication that can relieve the situation. Arthritis sufferers, for instance, who are perhaps waiting for a hip replacement can lead a near-normal life with the aid of anti-inflammatory drugs. But one man's disability is just a nuisance to someone else. This is the time to become inventive and find a way round the problem.

Fending off the years

- Get regular check-ups from the doctor, the optician and the dentist. Have your feet attended to regularly – chiropody is supposed to be free to pensioners, although waiting lists are long.
- Have a healthy life-style. Eat properly and do not miss meals.
- Do not smoke.
- Drinking too much brings its own problems, not least to the heart and the liver, to say nothing of accidents. If you are drunk, you are much more likely to fall down and are also much more likely to damage yourself than when you were younger.
- Keep flexible; find a form of exercise that suits you and stick to it. Make a point of walking as much as you can, even if you have a free bus pass. Cycle or swim – aquasizes (exercising in water) are much easier on aching limbs, and most health centres have sessions.
- Keep your brain active – it needs exercise just like any other part of the body.
- Accommodate yourself. Find ways round things that bother you. If your memory starts playing tricks, write things down, make lists or keep a diary of what you plan to do and what shopping you need. Make a habit of putting everyday things such as your handbag, the newspaper and the dog's lead in the same place. Hang spectacles around your neck and keep your car keys on a special hook.
- Give your memory a rest from time to time by doing something that does not require acute intellectual input – gardening, listening to or playing music and painting all fall into this category.

- If walking tires you easily, organize your day so that you have sit-downs from time to time. If your sight bothers you, watch less TV and listen to more radio instead.
- Safeguard the future, then forget it. If you have the cash to spare it might pay to take out insurance in case you need to go into a home. There are a number of packages on offer and you can start a policy usually any time up to the age of 75. There are also schemes for people who need care immediately or who are already in care. Some policies require a lump sum to start, as well as monthly premiums. Most of them pay the nursing home direct. If you are considering taking out this type of insurance, check that the policy covers you indefinitely, not for a limited time only. See if there is a scheme that increases your benefits in line with inflation, particularly if you are buying well ahead.

Cashing in on old age

- Make sure you have your free travel card if your local authority issues one. You usually get it via the local Post Office on production of proof of age and a photo and proof of address.
- Check out admission fees. Museums and cinemas have special deals for OAPs, and some hairdressers offer special prices too. Swimming pools and fitness centres also cater for older people with special rates.

Sheltered accommodation

It is tempting to give up an old house that is getting to be too much for you and move into a brand-new well-designed flat. You will save on heating bills because of the modern insulation and double glazing, and all exterior maintenance and gardening will be taken care of as well. And if the flat comes with some sort of support system for your old age, then it may be a wise move. If you are planning to go into sheltered accommodation, as it is called, bear in mind that you need to do so while you are still relatively fit – some developments will not take people who appear frail or ill.

There are various grades of sheltered accommodation and 'retirement flats' on offer. Some have a house manager only, while others offer nursing care of some sort or other. There are also 'extra care' sheltered housing schemes which have a more comprehensive support system and are half-way to becoming residential homes. Some sheltered schemes offer extra services such as meals and domestic help. All should have a security entry phone system, smoke alarms, a house manager and a 24-hour emergency system.

Extra services like this do not come cheaply, and you must be careful to look for any hidden charges. Also, ask yourself whether you want to live in a ghetto of elderly people – might you not be better off in a mixed community? You may prefer to buy a 'sheltered' flat now and let it until the time comes when you feel ready to 'join the club'. It pays to shop around and see whether it is possible to find somewhere that is charity-aided (*see* **Help Directory**, *page 312*). If you are a council tenant, ask whether the council has sheltered housing into which you could transfer.

If you are thinking of buying, go to the development, talk to the other residents and ask questions.

- Is there someone on hand 24 hours a day? If not, is there a good alarm system? The Code of Practice for sheltered housing says there must be some form of alarm.
- Does the development keep changing wardens? If so, it may not be a happy ship.
- How high are the service charges? And do they keep rising? Service charges for this kind of accommodation are bound to be steep since they cover the warden's pay and living costs.
- What are the other residents like? Do they seem to be people you could get along with?
- Is the accommodation thoughtfully planned? Are sockets easy to reach and window catches easy to open? Are there hand grips in the bath and other practical aids around? You may not need them now, but they will come in handy later on. Check whether there is enough room to house your favourite furniture and if there is non-slip flooring.
- Will I be thrown out if I get ill? Some developments have a clause in the lease giving them the right to move you out if you become very ill or frail. Others have additional services available for the bed-bound.
- How far is it from the shops? And is it on an easy, level site.
- How is the security? Is there an entry phone system? Are there smoke detectors fitted?
- What communal facilities are there? Is there a launderette, a TV and sitting room or even guest suites for visitors?

Staying in your own home

If you are planning to stay where you are, a lot can be done to make the house easier to live in and manage.

- If the house is large, could it be converted to one-floor living? Think laterally, consider changing the living accommodation. It is relatively easy now to turn a spare bedroom into a bathroom.
- Could things be made easier? It does not cost much to have floor sockets moved to waist-height, or to have lighter handles put on doors.
- Could the lighting be improved? Remember that strategically placed table lamps give much more light than a 150-watt bulb at ceiling height. Make sure there are no trailing flexes, however.

- Have you got all the labour-saving machines you can afford? A dishwasher might make all the difference. You can buy tabletop models that avoid the problem of having to bend down to load them.
- Is the house warm enough? This might be the time to install night storage heaters or central heating.
- What about fire hazards? Should an open fire be replaced by an electric heater?
- Would some of the aids and modifications for the disabled be useful (*see* **Disabled**, *page 75*)?

THE OLD-AGE PENSION: YOUR RIGHTS

At present you have the right to a basic retirement pension if you have paid sufficient National Insurance contributions. You become eligible at age 60 if you are a woman and 65 if you are a man, although the plan is to make the age 65 for everyone by stages. If you are a married woman and have paid reduced contributions, you must wait until 65 to get your pension. If you are separated from your husband you can still claim the pension. If you are a divorced woman, however, you can claim your pension at 60.

What if I do not qualify?

If you have not paid enough National Insurance contributions then you go onto income support instead. But by the time you reach 80, provided you have lived in the UK from the age of 60, you qualify for a proper pension. In addition to the above, you may qualify for an **Attendance Allowance** or a **Disability Living Allowance**. Or if you are caring for someone old you might be able to claim an **Invalid Care Allowance.** Ask the Benefits Agency for leaflet FB32 *Benefits after Retirement*, which tells you what other benefits you can claim as a pensioner.

How your pension is paid

You can draw your pension in cash at your local Post Office or have it paid directly into a building society, giro or bank account. If you go to live abroad you are still entitled to claim your pension, in which case your pension can be paid directly into your UK bank account or into an overseas bank.

Two booklets well worth reading are *Your Pension Matters, a Guide Through the Pension Maze for Women*, obtainable free from the Equal Opportunities Commission (*see page 314*), and *Benefits after Retirement, What You Could Claim as a Pensioner*, published by the Benefits Agency, which tells you of 20 or more benefits you might be entitled to; your local branch will most likely have a copy.

The year 2010

Anyone who is coming up to retirement age should know that there are some proposed pension changes for the year 2010 and on.

- From 2010 on, the state pension age for women will gradually be increased so that by 2020 it will be age 65.
- The present arrangement which allows married women to get a pension based on their husband's national insurance contributions will be extended to men.

At this stage these are only proposals and are subject to parliamentary approval.

Private pensions

See **Finance,** *page 378.*

HEALTH PROBLEMS

A report by the Medical Research Council on data from the USA says that 'those people who insist on staying in control of their own lives – the wilful and the cantankerous – live longer than the more compliant "sweet old folk" who make good patients'. So if you want to receive a 100th birthday telegram from the Queen, according to the Council, you should stay in command, be informed and be 'thoroughly obstreperous in refusing to be fobbed off with second-rate care'.

It is believed that given proper screening and improved diet we should all live longer than the allotted 72 years for men and 78 years for women. A five-year trial is going on at the moment to see if this is true. And with new discoveries into what actually makes us age, the prognosis is that we may make 104 in the next century. Meanwhile either we or the older people we care for should obey some simple rules to keep as fit as possible.

- Have a yearly health check; it is your right as an old-age pensioner.
- Eat a balanced diet, do not feel that it is too much trouble to prepare fresh vegetables and salads or to buy fruit.
- Take moderate exercise – get in the habit of walking to as many places as possible in an effort not to seize up.
- Lonely and depressed people tend to neglect themselves. Make sure that you keep in touch with friends and family.
- Get your brain into gear; it needs exercising too. Bored people often become depressed.

Day-to-day problems

It is often the irritating small things rather than major illnesses that can make being old so debilitating. Being overweight, having painful feet or having a problem with breathlessness – all these things can make you drift into becoming a permanent invalid. But often something can be done to relieve creaking limbs, insomnia and difficulties in seeing or hearing properly.

Deafness

If you find yourself going deaf, your first stop is a visit to your GP. But be aware that your sudden deafness may be caused by something as simple as impacted wax in the ear, so get it checked out. There are two kinds of deafness: basic loss of hearing and another type when the ear has difficulty in focusing sound. Some of us, as we get older, especially if we live on our own in relatively silent surroundings, may be able to hear, but have difficulty in filtering out background sounds when listening to a specific conversation.

Young parents are used to living in an environment of constant noise. The TV or radio may be on in the background, the children may make a din and there may be street noises. They are able to decipher all the sounds and filter out what is unnecessary, but older people, especially those living alone, may lose this facility. Younger people also have a tendency to mumble and may not bother to pronounce consonants clearly. If you are dealing with a deaf person, face him when you speak and pronounce the words clearly but not in an exaggerated way which will only humiliate the person.

A hearing aid might help. But even the best hearing aids tend to amplify all sound, not just what you want to hear. They work perfectly on a one-to-one basis, but can be horrendous in a noisy place, when you are with a group or in a restaurant, distorting the sounds coming from all directions (*see also page 70*).

Eye problems

Glaucoma is a condition that can cause blindness but can be treated easily in its early stages. So always ask for a glaucoma test if you are not offered one by your optician. He can give you a simple test (basically puffing air at your eyes). Always go for a check if you notice any disturbance in your sight. Cataracts are now treatable. The first sign that something may be wrong is if bright lights dazzle you more than usual when driving. Strong lighting will help, but not so that it shines in your eyes.

Insomnia and how to beat it

We are said to need less sleep as we grow older, but outright insomnia is wearing and depressing. You are suffering from insomnia if you have difficulty staying awake during the day. Waking and not getting off to sleep again can become a habit that is hard to break. Research has shown that you can make up for lost sleep the following day without any ill effects.

- Try to avoid taking sleeping pills – some people become addicted to them after a hospital stay. Try natural remedies instead.

- Switch to having a hot milky drink instead of tea or coffee last thing at night – they are both stimulants.
- Avoid having an over-full bladder. If you wake up in the night to go to the toilet, you may find it difficult to get to sleep again.
- Keep your alcohol input down. Three or four stiff drinks may ensure you get off to sleep, but you are bound to wake up about 4am.
- Make sure that you are pleasantly tired. Do not go to bed until you feel sleepy.
- If you cannot get to sleep within ten minutes or so, get up and read or watch TV.
- If you do wake up in the middle of the night, do not look at the clock.
- Have a hot bath last thing at night to relax you.
- Take a boring book to bed, not an exciting one.
- If you have an alcoholic drink in the evening, make it last thing – if you drink early in the evening, you may fall asleep in front of the TV.
- Make sure the bed is warm and comfortable – if you do not have an electric blanket, get a hot-water bottle.
- Make sure the room is not stuffy or overheated.

Other problems: warning signs

Keep an eye on yourself or anyone elderly for whom you are caring.
- Unusual fatigue needs checking out. It could be a sign of diabetes, heart disease, anaemia, thyroid problems or cancer.
- A persistent headache could be insufficient sleep, bad ventilation, or sight problems if it comes on after reading. If it does not go away, get expert help. It could be caused by hypertension and there is a remote possibility that it could be a brain tumour.
- Shortness of breath after mild exertion needs checking out, so does a pain in the chest, especially if it spreads down the arm. It could be a heart problem such as angina which can be kept under control with medicine.
- A persistent cough, especially one that is worse at night, needs looking into. So does a wheezy chest or a cough that will not go away.
- Constipation may be caused by bad diet or inactivity. If it comes on suddenly for no reason or alternates with diarrhoea it should be reported to the doctor. No one should take laxatives on a regular basis.
- Backache can be caused by physical injury such as slipped disc but could well be caused by poor posture. Unusual strenuous activity can set up all sorts of aches and pains in unused muscles. Sometimes doing some physical task while stressed or worried can also cause the back muscles to seize up.

Dizziness

At least 50 per cent of people over the age of 70 suffer from this frightening experience which can be caused by a number of things – problems with the balance of the inner ear, circulatory problems, an alteration in the heartbeat rhythm, sight difficulties or blood pressure changes. Check it out with the doctor.

If you are looking after someone elderly and the person has a fall, tell the doctor, especially if it happens more than once or if there was no object to cause the person to trip. Research has shown that a lot of falls in elderly people, often resulting in broken hips, are caused not by tripping or not seeing properly but by some kind of circulatory malfunction that causes dizziness and faintness. Regular check-ups will help prevent this happening. The fall may also be caused by a mini-stroke. If this condition is caught in time and treated, it can be kept under control.

Everyone who is elderly should learn how to get up after a fall. Roll over onto one side – your strongest side. Using your elbow as a lever, begin to rise and grab the leg-rung of a chair if there is one nearby, and get onto your knees. Then, using a chair as a lever, rise to your feet.

Stroke: the signs
Everyone fears that they may have a stroke, but remarkable work is done now to help people make a full recovery. Many people have minor strokes without realizing what it is. Look out for:
• Sudden loss of speech or difficulty in speaking.
• Paralysis down one side of the body or face.
• Loss of feeling in an arm or leg.
• Sudden visual problems.

Incontinence and how to handle it
This is another embarrassing problem that can strike in old age. Stress incontinence may occur when we suddenly sneeze, laugh or run. There are many possible causes, all of which can be helped medically: an enlarged prostate, a prolapsed womb, stretching caused by constipation, a stone in the bladder, an infection or the side-effects of a diuretic drug are all possibilities. See your doctor, who may then refer you to a urologist. You could be suffering from a simple lack of muscle control, which can be cured by doing specific exercises or by using a pessary. There are other causes that are not treatable such as the after-effects of stroke, spinal injury or some kinds of brain disorder.
• Do not restrict your intake of fluids, as this could cause a urinary infection.
• Switch to poly-cotton bedclothes that can be laundered quickly and easily without ironing. Protect your mattress with a plastic or rubber sheet.
• Make sure that there are toilet facilities close to hand. This may mean investing in a commode – you can buy quite a fetching Lloyd Loom chair with this facility.
• It is also possible to buy incontinence pants. Look for advertisements in the back of Sunday papers.

Depression

Depression, which can be treated, can have some of the same symptoms as early Alzheimer's disease – withdrawal and confusion are common to both illnesses. As a result, many elderly people are misdiagnosed as having the onset of Alzheimer's instead of depression which is easier to treat. The warning signals to watch out for are:

- Lack of concentration.
- Loss of interest in food.
- Loss of interest in current affairs and the family.
- Sometimes agitation and restlessness.
- Inability to sleep, particularly in the early morning.
- An air of hopelessness and emptiness.
- Exaggerated concern over minor health problems such as constipation.

Depression can often be cured with a mix of counselling and drugs like the new Prozac (*see page 89*).

Paranoia

Often considered a bit of a joke by younger members of the family, this state is more likely to occur with grandma than grandpa. Typical signs of paranoia include viewing everyone with mistrust, sometimes outright hostility and insisting that people are doing things to annoy them (my mother-in-law was convinced the man next door had a machine against his wall to interfere with her TV reception). This situation can be treated with drugs, but check first that there is no physical reason that is depriving the sufferer's brain cells of oxygen. Make sure that the person is not alone too much – any of us can suffer delusions if we are in total isolation for any length of time.

ALZHEIMER'S DISEASE

One person in five over the age of 80 has the risk of suffering from Alzheimer's disease, which used to be called senile dementia. Not only is it difficult for the sufferer, but it can leave a family in turmoil. Each day in this country 42 people are diagnosed as suffering from Alzheimer's; some of them, it must be said, are between the ages of 18 and 60. However, it is reckoned that 20 per cent of people diagnosed as having Alzheimer's are probably suffering from another form of dementia – only by examining the brain tissue can anyone be sure.

Alzheimer's is a degenerative disease brought on by physical changes in the brain tissue. The brain itself shrinks and develops plaques or dark spots, while a tangling of the neurofibrillary system stops surviving cells from communicating with each other.

Dementia alert: the symptoms

- Endlessly repetitive conversation.
- Restlessness.
- Inability to recognize people.
- Lack of motivation to do anything.
- Lapses of memory.
- Sudden loss of inhibitions.
- Aggression.
- Night disturbance, possible incontinence and falls.
- Personality change.
- Child-like behaviour.
- Inability to carry on a logical conversation.
- Loss of short-term memory.
- Disorientation, confusion.
- Inability to think or reason.
- Inability to do simple tasks.

Alzheimer's starts with forgetfulness and making mistakes while working, and is sometimes mistaken for stress. It is the reverse of growing up; the patient gradually becomes baby-like again. In later stages the sufferer cannot sign his name, is unable to understand what has happened, becomes restless, agitated and incontinent. However, it is important not to over-react should you feel you are suffering from some of these symptoms. If you are on holiday away from the usual routine, you may be hard put to remember which day it is and what time it is. An elderly person who lives alone may exhibit these symptoms simply from lack of stimulation.

If you care for someone with Alzheimer's

While some conditions of old age, such as Parkinson's disease, can now be treated, there is no cure for Alzheimer's at present. It is thought that in the next 5 to 10 years, drugs will be developed that will slow down the progression of this distressing disease. Meanwhile the Alzheimer's Disease Society (*see page 312*) has a free phoneline with recorded information on the disease on 0800 318771. If the sufferer is under 65 years old, the National Hospital for Neurology and Neurosurgery has a helpful support service called CANDID (Counselling and Diagnosis in Dementia) on 0171 837 3611, extension 3855.

- Find out all you can about the condition. See addresses in the Help directory.
- Join a local support group. Knowing that you are not alone will make you feel better about it.
- However badly the person is affected, do not discuss his condition in front of him. It is difficult to know how much he would take in.

- Get advice from your local community psychiatric nurse. Your doctor will put you in touch.
- Make sure that the house is as safe and secure as possible.
- At some stage the sufferer may forget who he is. Keep family photos around as a reminder, make sure there is a large clock on the wall that works and a calendar close to hand.
- Make sure the person has his name and address written down and carried in a pocket, perhaps. He may wander away at some stage and become lost.
- Maintain eye contact with the person when you speak to him, and try to be as calm as possible and not lose your temper.
- Show the sufferer old family photographs and mementos. Talking about the past can sometimes bring on a temporary remission.
- Look upon the sufferer as if he was a child. Remove keys from locks and bolts from doors in case he locks himself in, the stopper from baths and sinks in case he leaves taps on. You are safer with electric rather than gas cookers.
- If the person is confused and gets up in the middle of the night, thinking it is day-time, do not confront him, go along with him and perhaps give the person a hot drink. Talk to the person.
- If he is aggressive or tries to push you away when you are washing and dressing him, go away for a few moments, then try again.
- Do not force-feed the person if he refuses to eat. It is possible to get liquid food like Complan from the chemist that will give him the nourishment he needs. Check that ill-fitting dentures or decayed teeth are not the cause.

Reality orientation is a technique that is used with some success with Alzheimer's patients to help them stay in touch with reality in the early stages of the disease. This involves telling the person the date and what the weather is like, what he is going to have to eat and what is happening in the world outside, in an effort to keep the person in touch. If he has difficulty finding his way around the house, simple symbols pinned to the door of the bathroom and his bedroom can help. Many Alzheimer's sufferers respond well to music.

LOOKING AFTER SOMEONE WHO IS OLD

Many of us will find ourselves responsible for elderly parents or partners at some point in our lives. However, many people in their eighties are surprisingly fit with alert minds, and most of them fiercely resist the idea of leaving their homes. All they may need is a regular eye kept on them and a watch out for anything unusual. And an efficient fail-safe system is easy to install in case they have a fall or a stroke. First assess what is needed. Can the person cope on his (but more likely her, since women live much longer than men) own at home and do they prefer to do so?

Can she look after herself?

First check that the house is as easy to run as possible, then ask yourself these questions:

- Might it be possible for her to take in a lodger or let a room in return for someone keeping an eye on her? Or what about swapping homes? If you live in a flat and she is rattling round in a large house, could you switch?
- Can she shop and cook for herself, or can you organize someone to do this? Can she wash herself and her clothes? A laundry service may be available – ask the Social Services.
- Can she keep the place reasonably under control? Here again help may be forthcoming.
- Is the lavatory easy to reach in the middle of the night? Ideally it should be no more than 15 paces away. Can it be flushed easily? It is worth knowing that motorized lavatories can now be installed almost anywhere in the house, without the need for conventional plumbing.
- Is there an alarm system in case she has a fall? They are relatively easy to install.

Watch her walk round the house and look for hazards that could be eliminated, note places where strategically placed hand holds can help; up the stairs and by the bath are two logical spots. Does she need a bath seat? You can buy a removable one that sits rather like a soap rack across the bath. Get the Social Services to help you over this – it may even pay for the work to be done, since it is as anxious as you are for old people to be independent. Ask yourself these questions about the house.

- Does the house need insulation? It is possible you could get a grant for this.
- Is the house too expensive to heat? She may be tempted to turn the heating off. Make frequent calls in cold weather to make sure she is warm enough. Signs of hypothermia include being unusually quiet and withdrawn.
- Is the lighting efficient enough for her to see her way around after dark?
- Does she smoke? If so, install smoke detectors and fire extinguishers and make sure she knows where they are and how to use them. Check that her clothes and the furnishings are fire-resistant. It is possible to spray some things to make them flame-resistant.
- Does she have unsafe heaters – paraffin stoves and open fires are hazards for elderly people. Try to replace an open fire with an electric one with a guard.
- Does she have to stand on a chair to reach anything? Are her kitchen food cupboards at the right height? Install more at waist-level.
- Is the flooring safe – slippery ceramic tiles or polished wood could be covered by plastic flooring. Get rid of rugs.

- Does she need a walking aid? She might find a tripod walking aid a boon and much safer than a stick. For other ideas, *see* **Disabled,** *page 75.*
- Is her bed too high and too difficult to climb into? If she is fond of it, get the legs shortened to make life easier for her – or would she be better sleeping downstairs? If so, get her a divan that can be made to look like a settee by day with the aid of a cluster of large cushions – it is demoralizing to have a full-blown bed in your sitting room. It makes you feel like an elderly invalid.
- Is her bed warm enough? An electric blanket, if she has not got one, could be a solution – the stopper of a hot water bottle can be difficult to undo in old age. Impress on her that she must not use a hot water bottle and an electric blanket together. If she has an electric blanket, get it checked for safety if it is an old one.
- Is the bathroom warm? If you install an electric heater, make sure it is securely fixed and out of reach, with a pull cord to switch it on and off.
- Make sure that the run from bed to bath is clear of obstacles and well-lit with light switches that are conveniently placed. Make sure that the lavatory is not too cold – a tubular heater might be the answer here. And install a vertical hand rail by the lavatory so she can haul herself up. An easy-to-clean plastic mat or floor covering is a good idea, especially if the aged relative is a man and might miss the target.
- See that she has comfortable shoes – trainers are ideal if you can persuade her to wear them. If she has difficulty in doing up her shoes, get ones with Velcro fastenings.
- Has she got some friends? Lonely and depressed people tend to neglect themselves. Make sure she keeps up her friendships, and has some stimulation.
- If all else fails, could you build an extension to your own home as a 'granny flat'? Local planners are much more flexible than they used to be and this solution would increase the value of your property.

Community Care Services

The number of NHS long-stay beds for the elderly has been slashed by 40 per cent over the last five years. Instead, there is supposed to be more care available in the community. Since 1993, local authorities have had a duty under the NHS and Community Care Act to assess people who appear to need care services which the authorities should then provide. Many local authorities are still unable to do this, but if you feel you or the person you care for needs help which the authority might be able to arrange, then you have the right to ask the local authority for an assessment of their needs.

The list below indicates what *should* be on hand via the Social Services, but many areas have waiting lists or a rationing scheme so that only the really desperate get attention. Social Services departments are struggling to spread what money is available over an ever-growing demand. Many have funding crises, many are trimming back the levels at which people are assessed as being in need because the authorities simply cannot pay. However, it is always worthwhile finding out what is available in your locality; you might be lucky.

- **Home helps** to assist with cooking, cleaning and shopping for elderly or disabled people living alone.
- **Meals on Wheels** for the elderly who cannot cook for themselves.
- **Laundry services** for those who are too old or too ill to do their washing, or who are incontinent.
- **Care attendants** to bathe disabled and elderly people, to do their washing and odd jobs around the house.
- **Night-time carers** for people who need help during the night.

Many areas now have day hospitals where elderly people can take a bath with assistance, have their hair done, and have occupational and physiotherapy. They serve as halfway houses between hospital proper and the community. If you are not satisfied with what you are offered after an assessment, then make a complaint through the local authority's complaints procedure – they have to tell you about this.

Home alarms

Hardly a day goes by without reading about some elderly person lying undiscovered for days after a fall. It is now possible to have a personal alarm system, triggered off by a device worn round the neck or wrist of the elderly person, which will either alert a helper or a central alarm centre. Some enlightened local authorities are issuing them free to aged people or selling them very cheaply. If you are buying one for a relative, check it out yourself.

- Is it easy to use, especially if you are in a panic or in pain.
- Can you cancel it easily if you press it by mistake?
- Does it give a warning that the battery is running low?
- Is it easy and comfortable to wear?
- Does it have a reasonable range?

Cold weather care

Every winter a number of elderly people die of hypothermia. Quite often their relatives have been shocked by the death. If you are keeping an eye on a relative or a neighbour and cold weather comes, there are a number of points to keep in mind.

- Make sure that she has at least one hot meal and plenty of hot drinks every day.
- Ensure that she wraps up warmly before going out, no matter how short the trip. Several thin layers are better than one thick one. She should also wear something on her head – a surprising amount of body heat escapes from your skull.

- Make sure that she keeps moving and gets a little exercise every day. Even if she is chairbound she can still exercise her arms, legs, hands and feet.
- Take her emergency food stocks in the form of cans, packets, UHT milk and frozen food in case bad weather makes it difficult to get out to the shops. Remember, bread freezes easily and there is always space in the ice compartment of the fridge for a few slices.
- Hang heavy curtains over her front door to help keep the heat in – a blanket will do.

LIVING ALONE AT HOME

There may come a time when it becomes clear that you cannot leave granny or grandpa on their own.

Warning signs

- Has she suddenly become untidy, when she used to be well-organized?
- Is there a smell of urine in the house?
- Does she leave unwashed clothes and bedding around?
- Does she wear the same clothes all the time?
- Is she taking pills? Old people tend to go on taking medicine for a condition even after it has been cured. Have a pill check from time to time with the doctor.
- Is she sleeping properly?
- Does she seem tired all the time?
- Is she eating properly?
- Is she finding it difficult to make decisions?
- Is she no longer interested in anything?
- Does she spill drinks and food when carrying them?
- Does she take a long time to climb the stairs, with rests between the steps?
- Has she become very forgetful – with a danger of leaving gas and water taps on?

There are many reasons why old people may have to give up living alone; ill health may be one reason or because a regular daily visitor can no longer call; perhaps the person has lost her partner or may have just come out of hospital after an operation. People take their elderly relatives in for many reasons, but mainly because they feel they owe their relatives a debt. Or it could be because the person does not want to go, or cannot be got, into a home.

People from other cultures are much more caring about the older generation than we are. In Germany, families are by law responsible for arranging care for their relatives. Statistics show that in this country, while more than 46 per cent of people over 60 years of age who are classified as 'white' are in homes of various sorts, the figure for black people is less than 1.6 per cent. At one time it was unthinkable that anyone but the family should look after an old relative, but today with both partners in full-time jobs and the stresses and strains of modern life, things are different. Divorce has made things more difficult. New obligations created by second and step-families may over-ride our plans to look after elderly relatives. An ex-mother-in-law cannot expect her ex-daughter-in-law to take her in. And divorce late in life is becoming more of a threat than death, for it means that the partner who might have cared for you will not be around.

Around six million frail, disabled and elderly people are being looked after at home at the present time. A few of these have paid carers but mostly care is done by family and friends who save the country an estimated bill of £34 million. There is no law that daughters rather than sons should do the caring or that the eldest rather than the youngest should do it. But, unfortunately, even in this day and age, the unmarried eldest daughter is in the hot seat.

Taking someone into your home, whether the person is old or not, is bound to involve a change, and more than likely, some sacrifice in your way of life. You may, of course, have no option, but never take on caring on impulse – think it through before you make the offer. Sometimes it pays to ask a third party for neutral advice on the subject to help you make a realistic assessment. You should also ascertain what your aged parent feels about the situation. Some elderly people are happy to live in the bosom of their family, oblivious to the stresses and strains it may bring, feeling it is their due as your parent. From their point of view, it is also an upheaval. They are losing their independence and their self-esteem as well as losing their home and taking on the unknown.

Will it work?

- Can you care for your parent without neglecting your family and making them resentful?
- Is your family with you in this decision? Inserting Granny into a resentful household will result in unhappiness all round.
- What will happen if you are taken ill? Is there anyone who can replace you?
- Try having your relative to stay for a holiday to see what the implications are. Until you have actually lived with the person, you do not really know what is involved, or how your family will react to someone taking over some of their territory.
- How much are you prepared to give up? Your life-style is bound to change.

- How is your own health? You need mental and physical stamina to care for the elderly – and a sense of humour.
- Are you prepared to put up with their rituals of many years' standing? It is not right to try to make elderly people change the habits of a life-time, whether it is wearing a vest all summer or watching TV soaps.
- Can your finances stand the extra guest? Her pension will not cover everything.
- Will you resent having all this extra work to do? Are there ways you can get help?
- Will you get any breaks, or holidays? Build them in.
- Is the house safe and suitable? How will you cope if she becomes incontinent or wanders round the house at night? Old houses with twisty stairs and uneven floors can cause problems.

Making it work

Start as you mean to go on. Draw up guide-lines to make sure that you can continue to lead your own social life. You do not want to feel like a human sacrifice. The 'Martha' syndrome makes for a tight-lipped carer and those who are being cared for feel only too well that they are a burden. The result? Unhappiness all round.

Work out a roster beforehand with other members of your family so that, as part of the deal, she stays with them from time to time and you get a break. Be firm with your siblings, make them do their share – the fact that they have a family to look after and you may not is no excuse. Never mind if your aged parent grumbles at being sent away, you have your own life to live. You might try to find out how long she might be with you? See her doctor. Old people are entitled by law to a yearly health check. Have a quiet word to get some idea of how your relative is and what the future is likely to hold.

Make things as easy as possible for her and for you by getting all the aids you can. She may have difficulty getting out of the bath. If that is the case, a vertical handrail should be fitted beside the bath and the base of the bath should not be slippery – buy a rubber mat which clings to the bottom by suction. It is even possible to get a hoist to lift anyone old or handicapped in and out of the bath. Try to get regular help in the house, perhaps with the laundry, for instance, to cut your workload. Social Services might organize this.

Take regular breaks – see if your local authority has any kind of facility for respite care. If not, organize something with other members of your family.

Getting along together

What makes an old person difficult to get along with? Inflexibility is one thing. Many elderly people seem to have fixed ideas on everything. Pessimism is another trait you often find in the old; so is selfishness – there is a theory that the selfish part of the brain is the first thing to develop in a baby and the last thing we lose. In addition many elderly people develop acute forms of their already undesirable traits – the careful spender may become outright mean and the heavy drinker, a near alcoholic. How, then, can you cope?

- Be encouraging.
- Do not harp on about her mistakes and misdemeanours, but at the same time do not go along with her delusions.
- Do not become over-protective or too sympathetic, be positive instead.
- Do not keep reminding the person that she is old. She knows that fact all too well.
- Make life as pleasant as possible, place her bed or chair by the window, for instance, so she can see out.
- Treat the person as an adult, not a child – how many of us have been patronized in hospital by nurses calling us by our Christian names?
- Give her jobs and some responsibility in the house, even if it is only peeling the potatoes, or listening to a grandchild's reading home-work. Involve her with the family, do not make her feel like a hospital patient.

Your rights as a carer

You should be entitled to tax relief if your relative is declared to be your dependant. If your relative qualifies to be registered disabled or partly disabled, you should be able to get financial help for aids like a wheelchair, walking frames and even a free radio. Ask your local Social Services or contact the Disabled Living Foundation. You could be eligible for grants towards the cost of adapting your home – making electricity safer and moving switches. Ask the DSS. There may be heating grants available too – again ask the DSS.

If you are a carer who is looking after someone who gets an attendance allowance for more than 35 hours a week, you should enquire about the **invalid care allowance** to which you may be entitled. If you are on Income Support or some other welfare benefit, it could be that you qualify for a **carer premium.** If your charge is disabled or registered blind, you might also be able to get a special badge for your car which enables you to park free or on single yellow lines in some places. If you are a married woman and your partner has to go into a home, you are now entitled to keep half of his occupational pension if he has one.

WHERE TO GET HELP

There is a whole support system available via the NHS. Your GP or, in some cases, the Social Services can refer you to a wide range of people who will give you practical help and advice – ask the receptionist at your surgery.

- **Social workers** come to you via the Social Services Department. They can guide you through the maze of what is available to you as a carer.

- In some areas there are **Care Managers** to deal specifically with your kind of problems – general social workers have a heavy case-load of other categories of people. Care managers should also be able to organize respite care – someone to either come in or take your charge somewhere while you have a break.

- **District nurses** specialize in treating people in their homes. She, or her assistant, will give baths (often a two-person job), and change dressings. She is also a useful source of information on equipment that might be of use and where to get it. There should also be a **night nurse** available to help if your relative is very ill or, if you are nursing the person day and night, to give you a break.

- **Practice nurses** may be attached to your GP practice if it is of any size. She will do routine health checks and injections. She can give you general advice and may visit your home.

- **Health visitors** are usually thought of as people who deal with babies and small children but their scope is now being widened to deal with the elderly and the disabled too.

- **Physiotherapist and occupational therapist** can help in two ways: a physio can suggest simple exercises to do to keep mobile and can give massage for painful limbs. The occupational therapist can be of immense help in suggesting ways of dealing with basic tasks like getting dressed and washing for someone who is disabled. She will also help with advice on aids and equipment.

- **Chiropodist** Old-age pensioners are entitled to free foot care and you should be able to find a chiropodist to visit your home. However, waiting lists are usually long.

- **Dieticians** can be a great help if your relative has, say, diabetes or some other condition that needs a special diet. She may also refer you to a **speech therapist** if the patient has difficulty in swallowing her food or in eating.

- **Psychiatric helpers** may be of assistance if your charge is mentally confused or suffering from actual mental illness. You may be able to call on the services of a **psychiatrist** or a **psychotherapist**. You, yourself, could ask for counselling if the situation is causing you problems or tipping you into depression.

Do we have to pay?

You, as a carer, cannot be charged for any of these services unless you are a 'spouse', in which case you might be asked to contribute. Your charge, however, will be means-tested and may have to make a contribution to certain types of help.

Looking after yourself

It is vital that you take care of yourself and your own health if you are caring for someone else.

- Make sure you have a reasonable diet.
- Give yourself 'treats' from time to time – buy a box of chocolates and have your hair done.
- Do not neglect your own body. Avoid backache. Do not attempt to lift a heavy person with your back bent; bend your knees instead – remember what they told you at antenatal classes.
- Get enough sleep. If your charge is restless at night, treat her as you would a baby, in other words, when she takes a nap during the day, do the same.
- If it all gets to be too much; try to avoid the danger of becoming addicted to tranquillizers, drink or sweets just to get by – if this happens then get help and advice (*see* **States of mind**, *page 39*).
- Do not become a granny-basher. If you watch a parent become totally forgetful and verbally silly, you find yourself assuming the role of parent and irritability may set in. You may find yourself verbally abusing them and you may well feel you want to hit them. Find a sympathetic friend you can have a good moan to, and join a support group (*see page 308*). If the problem becomes serious, ask for counselling.
- Keep up old friendships – people, alas, tend to shy away from someone who is looking after an elderly relative, preferring not to get involved. This means that you may have to make an extra effort to keep in touch with friends. You might well make new friendships too, with people in the same situation you find yourself, via a support group (*see page 308*).
- Keep your morale up – could this be the time to take an Open University course that you can do at home (*see page 340*)? It now does short-term as well as degree courses.

Coming out of hospital

There are occasions when you might find yourself a carer without any warning – this may happen when an aged relative is discharged from hospital. There are stories of granny-dumping – old people being left on their own doorsteps to fend for themselves, and, it must be said, the other way round, where despairing relatives leave an old person in Accident and Emergency and flee. If the hospital is threatening to release someone to you and you are worried about the person's state of health:

- Talk to the ward sister, find out all you can about the nature of the illness or disability and what care is needed.

- Find out if a nurse can visit you at home to help, even if it is only for a few days.
- Are you going to need special equipment? Or you might need something like a hoist to get the person in and out of the bath. Ask to see the occupational therapist at the hospital and talk it through with her.
- You should be told what help is available to you in the community – speak to the hospital social worker.

GOING INTO A HOME

There may come a time when you are no longer able to cope and your aged relative will have to go into a home. We may feel guilty about this but it may be the only solution. Many women, in particular, find themselves caught in a trap between the needs of a parent and of their growing family, and have to make a choice.

Residential and nursing homes have become one of the big business booms of the era, raking in about £2 billion a year. Half a million people are currently in long-term places and only a small minority of these have all their fees paid by the state. Instead, because they do not qualify for aid, the elderly are using up their savings and selling their homes to pay nursing home fees. Expected legacies, money that children might have hoped to inherit, are eaten up as old people struggle to stay in nursing homes. What state support there is for long-term care fees is now paid by local authorities and is means-tested.

To qualify for full support the patient must have less than a total of £3000 in capital and assets. Those with between £3000 and £8000 will have to pay part of the cost on a sliding scale. People with more than £8000 of capital, even if it is tied up in a house they cannot sell, are on their own, having to rely on friends and family or pay care fees out of their money until it runs out. However, they will still have any attendance and disability living allowances to put towards the cost of care. And if their house is also occupied by someone getting disability allowance or an elderly spouse with nowhere to go, the council would not make them sell the home.

If you want to avoid spending all your money and your assets on care in the home, with nothing to leave for your children, you should consider creating what is called a 'beneficial life tenancy' in your home. You then give your house away to your children but have the legal right to live in it as long as you wish. This must be done at least five years before you are likely to need residential care. Ask your lawyer about it.

What happens when the money runs out?

If you think you are going to need help from public funds, under new legislation you must now have an assessment by the local authority of your care needs before going into a home. Your local Social Services Department should be able to supply details. Otherwise contact Age Concern (*page 311*). If you are already in a home and the money runs out, then the local council will be liable to house you. Unless you have agreed with them beforehand, you might be moved to another residential home. If you are worried about the long-term implications for yourself or the person you are putting into a home, ask for an assessment as above. If you are assessed as needing residential or nursing care, they can arrange a home for you, with you paying the full fees until your savings are reduced to £8000.

Choosing a home
There are two kinds of homes to choose from.
- **Residential homes** are usually privately run, though some may be administered by a charity and a very few are run by the local authority. Inmates get all their meals plus some help with washing, dressing themselves and feeding. Residential homes may or may not accept people with Alzheimer's or similar conditions and unless they house fewer than four people, they have to be registered with the local authority.
- **Nursing homes** cost more than residential homes and are usually run by private organizations. They give nursing care by qualified nurses for people who are ill, infirm or suffering from an injury. The fact that nursing is available round-the-clock is what makes them different from residential homes.

How to find a home
At their best, old people's homes can be bright, lively places, where inmates are given loving care. At their worst, these homes can be bleak and silent, where the occupants have no dignity and are treated roughly and unkindly. There have been stories of old people being left for as long as an hour on the lavatory, and of them being punished for silly things. Most aged people in this situation would become so demoralized that they would be unlikely to make a fuss. *The Good Homes Guide* by Shena Kennedy (Simon & Schuster) has descriptions of more than 2,000 homes and also discusses the financial implications as well.

So, how to find a good home? The most reliable advice comes from word of mouth, so ask friends and neighbours if they know of anywhere they could recommend. Failing that, the Registration Officer for Care Homes at your local Social Services department, and the Registration Officer for Nursing Homes at your local District Health Authority should be able to give you lists of names. Social workers are also a good source of information. Many charities also have

lists of suitable homes. From then on, it is a case of touring round and finding out
if there is a suitable vacancy.

How to choose

Age Concern says you should bear the following points in mind when looking at
care homes.

- Does the home encourage its residents to do as much as possible for
  themselves, and to make choices about as many aspects of their daily lives as
  they can?
- Do they have a choice of single or shared rooms? If they share, do they have
  any say about whom they share with?
- Can they bring personal possessions with them – pictures, plants or furniture?
- Can they choose what and when they will eat. Are special diets catered for?
  Can residents eat privately with guests from time to time? Can they prepare
  any food and drink for themselves?
- Are you free to see them when and where you choose?
- Can they use a telephone in privacy for incoming and outgoing calls?
- Can they get up and go to bed when they choose? If not, are the arrangements
  reasonable?
- Are they ever taken out on outings, to the shops, to the theatre, to a place of
  worship or for entertainments?
- What physical activities are there for residents?
- Is there more than one living room, so that there is a quiet room as well as one
  with television?
- Are books and newspapers available to residents? Do residents visit the library
  or does a mobile library come?
- How near is it to family and friends?
- Do residents have their own doctor?
- Do the managers of the home ask about how the residents would like to handle
  money or medicines?
- Is there a residents' committee? And does the home encourage residents to say
  how they feel about living there and provide written information on how to
  discuss a problem or make a complaint?
- Are toilets available in all parts of the home, fully equipped with handles and
  other helpful aids?
- Can wheelchairs go everywhere within the home? Is there a lift?
- Are there areas for smoking and non-smoking?
- What happens if a resident requires more or less care than they currently have?
  Might they have to leave?
- Can residents help in ordinary activities of the home if they want to – cleaning,
  cooking, gardening or looking after pets?

- See if it is possible to have a trial period in the home, since many of them offer this.

Having found a suitable home, there are still questions to be asked about the fees.

- Who signs the contract? If you are required to sign on someone else's behalf, as a relative, get legal advice to see what you are committing yourself to.
- Is a deposit required? Is this returnable and what is it for?
- How much is the weekly fee and what exactly does this provide?
- How many weeks in advance must you pay?
- What are the extras, if any – laundry, hairdressing and newspapers? And exactly how much do they cost?
- How much notice will the home give you if they have to raise their fees?
- What fees do you have to pay if you take the patient away for a short time, say on holiday or if they go into hospital?

LOOKING AFTER SOMEONE WHO IS DYING

Most people who know they are going to die, perhaps from cancer, wish to do so at home. A last illness can be long and tedious but now should not be painful – great strides have been made in pain control with drugs. But a dying parent may feel keenly the loss of dignity when roles are reversed and they become the child and you the parent. They may feel embarrassed that they are incontinent or are causing a great deal of work for those around them.

At some time in our lives we may find ourselves looking after a partner or a relative who has been sent home from hospital to die. If you find yourself in this situation, get help, do not shoulder the burden alone. Get help from friends and relatives, set up a shift system so that you are able to get out from time to time. Small children are often unconcerned by the sight of someone who is near death and will sit on the bed happily chatting away to them.

Keep an eye on your charge's day-to-day health, watch out for things like bed sores. Go to the patient's GP and find out what services are on offer. You may need to get medical help on pain control. You may need to call on the help of district nurses, or, if the patient is suffering from cancer, from Macmillan nurses or the Sue Ryder Foundation which help people in their homes (see page 109). You may need to get help from the council Social Services over, say, a laundry service for bedclothes or from the Red Cross for the loan of equipment and the church, if the patient would like a visit. Do not get dragged down by the situation, get all the help that you can.

Hospices not only take in people to die, they can give help and advice with pain control, and will take in a dying person for a 'holiday', so that the carer can have a short break. They also help look after the emotional needs of relatives and friends.

Should the dying person go into a hospice?

There are now more than a hundred hospices in this country offering people with terminal illness the care they need, usually for short periods of time while their medication is balanced to make them as free from pain as possible.

If you are finding it difficult to cope and there is space available at a local hospice, you will know that your charge will get first-class nursing and pain relief. At a hospice, visiting hours are usually much more flexible than in a hospital and the atmosphere is more positive and welcoming. Some, but not all, hospices have a religious background but people of any faith are accepted.

Euthanasia

The word euthanasia comes from the Greek *eu thanatos*, meaning a good death. Suicide with someone's help, or voluntary euthanasia, is against the law in this country. No one wants anyone to have a prolonged and painful death and doctors freely admit to helping unofficially, probably with an opiate or sedative overdose to put the person out of his misery. Advances in medical science mean that people who might have died within a few days from pneumonia or a cancer are kept alive by machines. If you want to have more control over your dying, making a Living Will is one way to ask that your life will not be unduly prolonged. It is a simple document stating that you do not wish the dying process to be prolonged under certain conditions which you specify (*see* **Legal,** *page 456*).

DEATH

(*See also* **Sudden death, Emergencies,** *page 8*, **Bereavement,** *page 195*.)
We in the West are frightened of death and we tend to deny it. Many people have little contact with those who are dying; children may be told where babies come from, but death is rarely explained to them.

What to do

(*See also* **How to tell if a person is dead, Emergencies,** *page 8*.)
If you are sure that the person is dead:
* Phone the doctor. If the doctor has seen the person during the previous fortnight, or has been treating him for the illness he died from, then the doctor will come and write out a death certificate for you. If this is not the case, you may have to phone the local Coroner's Office. If the death is unexplained or accidental, the Coroner might decide to hold a post-mortem. In that case you will eventually need a pink form from the Coroner to register the death.

- Phone your local hospital at once if the deceased wished his organs to be donated. If the Coroner is involved, you will have to ring that office first to get permission. As a relative, you do have the right to refuse this donation. And if the person was over 55 years old, only the eyes may be of use.
- Once the person has been certified dead, the body is usually laid flat, with the arms across the chest and the eyes closed. The deceased is sometimes washed. If you feel you cannot touch the body, then a district or practice nurse can be fetched to do it.
- Look for the will, tell the trustees and see if the funeral has been pre-paid or space booked in a graveyard. Then contact an undertaker if you are using one (*see below*). He will not be able to fix the funeral until the Registrar or Coroner's certificate, if there is to be one, has been issued. He will also need official permission from an executor of the will or if there is no will, the official next-of-kin. The undertaker will take the body away to await the funeral, unless you want it to remain in the house.
- Register the death within 5 days at your local Registrar of Births, Marriages and Deaths (address in your local Phone Book) unless a post-mortem is being held. You will have to fill in a form giving:
- The date and place of death.
- The full name and address of the deceased. In the case of a married woman, her maiden name too.
- Occupation, or name and occupation of the husband.
- The date of birth of the surviving widow or widower.
- You also need to take along any official pension and any other benefit books, and NHS card.

The Registrar will give you:

- A death certificate which you may need to produce in connection with the will, insurance policies and pension claims, savings certificates and premium bonds.
- A Certificate of Registration. You will need this when you are returning any pension or benefit books.
- A Certificate for Burial or Cremation. Your funeral director will need this.
- Take the Registration Certificate to the local DSS office, if you are eligible for a death grant, a widow's payment or a widow's pension.
- If there is no will, then a solicitor will have to get letters of administration for you. Someone will also have to give financial and legal advice over any taxes.
- Contact the person's relatives, if you are a friend. You will also need to tell the bank, the solicitor, if he is not a trustee, credit card companies, mortgage companies and anybody else who has had regular financial dealings with the person who has died.
- Finally, return any pension or benefit book to the DSS. The person's passport, driving licence and membership cards need to be returned.

- Tell relatives and relevant friends of the time of the funeral and stipulate details like whether you want flowers to be sent (usually direct to the undertaker) or whether you would prefer donations to a charity.

HOW TO ARRANGE A FUNERAL

There is no legal requirement for you to have a funeral service when you die. All that the law requires is that your death is registered and a death certificate is issued. After those obligations have been fulfilled then you can have a ceremony if you choose or go without one. You can postpone your funeral by leaving your body for research. In that case, you will eventually be buried or cremated and your relatives will be invited to attend. However, medical schools will not take the body of anyone who has had cancer or has had their organs removed for transplants or has had an autopsy.

The cost of the most basic funeral at the moment ranges from £300 to £725, depending on where you live. This normally covers the cost of removal of the body to the funeral director's premises, a hearse, a coffin and the undertakers' fees. Undertakers are supposed to conform to a code of practice which means that they must show you a clear price list. Do not be embarrassed to ask for it, however distasteful you may feel it to be at a time like this. This should also tell you how much the actual charges for the burial or cremation itself will be.

On top of the funeral director's charges, you will have to pay 'disbursement' fees to the minister who conducts the service, and if it is at a crematorium, the fees of the two doctors who will have to see the body before cremation. The National Association of Funeral Directors (*see page 311*) has a code of practice.

If a cremation is planned, you need to get a certificate signed by two doctors or a coroner, and by the crematorium's own doctor. The executor or next-of-kin has to give official permission for the cremation and has to say what is to be done with the ashes – a point to remember. You can take the ashes home with you, then do what you like with them. The ashes could be scattered on the water, on the garden or a favourite place. Or they can be buried.

A free funeral

The DSS has a leaflet FB29 which will give you details of what benefits are available when someone dies. If you are a widow under the age of 60, for instance, and your husband had paid his National Insurance contributions to date and was not getting his state pension, then you are entitled to a Widow's Payment of £1000.

A funeral can be paid for by the DSS if the person responsible for burying the body is on Income Support or Family Credit or Housing Benefit although that person's money over £500, or £1000 if they are over sixty, will be used towards the costs. Also any money in the estate of the deceased will also go towards the costs. To check out the details ask for Leaflet SF200. You have to make a claim before the funeral or within three months after.

What if there is no one to make burial arrangements? If you discover a neighbour with no living relatives dead in their flat, then your local authority is obliged under the Public Health – Control of Disease Act to arrange for the disposal of the body. In that case the Social Services department will arrange the funeral and register the death in the name of the council.

Paying for your own funeral

You can plan and pay for your funeral in advance either by a lump sum or a series of sums over up to five years. The money you pay is put into a trust fund and the interest from that money will take care of inflationary price rises in the future. The advantage from the point of view of the family is that the arrangements, which they might find distressing to make, are already in place and the undertaker chosen. Make sure that it also covers what are called 'disbursement fees', charges for the actual burial or cremation that must be paid to the church or crematorium. And the problem that some families face of having to pay for the funeral up-front before they receive any money under probate, does not occur. The other option is to take out an insurance policy in trust that will pay up a lump sum quickly after your death, on receipt of the death certificate.

However, there are snags – hard-sell techniques by some of the insurance companies can be unpleasant. The Office of Fair Trading is currently investigating what it considers to be a danger that some unscrupulous companies may get into the business; there needs to be some mechanism which will protect the customer if the company concerned goes out of business.

To avoid a problem, choose a firm that is a member of either the National Association for Pre-paid Funeral Plans or the Funeral Planning Council, both of whom have a code of practice. Failing that, choose a firm that protects your money by putting it in the hands of an independent trustee such as a major bank. Make sure that it also covers everything – see the comments on 'disbursement fees' above.

Do-it-yourself funerals

If you are planning any sort of funeral that deviates from the norm, say, handling it yourself or having a non-religious service, then the Natural Death Centre (*see page 309*) can offer all the advice and back-up you need. It has a useful book called *The Natural Death Handbook*.

Arranging a non-religious funeral
You can ask the undertaker to organize a non-religious ceremony but you can arrange a humanist funeral, as a ceremony without religion is called, yourself.

This could be a simple gathering of friends to celebrate the life of the person who has died with poetry readings and speeches. The British Humanist Association and the National Secular Society and the Natural Death Centre (*see page 309*) can all help you plan a suitable ceremony.

- You do not need to enlist the help of an undertaker to run a funeral. You can do it yourself, buying the coffin from a wholesaler – or even make one from chipboard and timber. There is even a cardboard coffin available (*see page 308*). And some crematoria and cemeteries will accept a body in a body bag rather than a box.
- Remember that a dead person weighs a great deal, so enlist the help of several friends to help carry the coffin. There is no need to have a hearse – a normal-sized coffin should go into the back of an estate car.
- If the deceased is being cremated, most good crematoriums should be able to supply you with a leaflet called *Information and Specifications for an Interment or Cremation Arranged Without the Guidance of a Funeral Director*, giving guidelines.
- Remember that funerals at a crematorium tend to be conducted on a conveyor-belt principal, with one lot of mourners coming in through one entrance while those from the previous service leave at another. If you are planning to hold the funeral yourself, then it pays to book the last slot in the day as you may not be as professional about timing as an undertaker would.

Burial

All you need is a document from the Registrar of Births and Deaths or a coroner to officially register the burial. Fill in and tear off a slip to say where the burial took place and return this to the Registrar of Births and Deaths.

- You do not have to be buried in a conventional cemetery. According to the Department of the Environment there is nothing in law to prevent a burial in ground other than a cemetery unless there is a specific health risk, such as pollution draining into a water supply. In short you can be buried anywhere as long as you have the permission of the owner of the land.
- Some owners of nature reserves and woodlands are now allowing burials on their property, and one or two enlightened councils are now setting up 'green' burial grounds too. You can even be buried alongside your pet. There is usually no headstone, instead it is usual for a tree to be planted for each grave.
- You can be buried in your own garden, provided there is nothing in the property deeds which says you cannot do so.
- Your grave can be any depth – except in town where the Local Authorities Cemeteries Order specifies it must be at least 24in (60cm) deep if the soil is clay or 36in (90cm) deep if the soil is sandy.

- You do not need to have a service or a headstone to mark a grave. But if the land is sold, the buyer must be made aware of the fact that someone is buried in it.
- You do not have to be buried in a coffin, you could be put in a bio-degradable cardboard box, or you could be wrapped in a cloth. And you can be buried in any position you wish, including standing up.

Burial in your own garden

Having a body buried in your back garden will, according to estate agents, reduce the value of your property by up to a half, so if there is plenty of space available, it would be better to fence off a piece of it as a burial ground before you sell the house. Planning permission is not required for the burial of one or two people, say a husband and wife, but permission might be needed if more bodies were involved. You should not make a grave within 800ft (250m) of a water source such as a well or a stream. When the house is sold, the vendor is obliged to disclose to would-be purchasers that a body is buried in the garden.

Burial at sea

All you need for a burial at sea is a boat, but there is a lot of red tape attached to the process in order to discourage people from doing so. First you need a licence from the Marine Environment Protection Department at the Ministry of Agriculture, Fisheries and Food (*see page 308*), then you need a Coroner's Out of England Form (Form 104) which you get from the Registrar and send to the local coroner. There are certain rules about the burial itself.

- The coffin must be made of something biodegradable, therefore not made from any synthetic, hardwood, lead, zinc or copper.
- It must be weighted with at least 3cwt of iron, steel or concrete. and it must have large holes in it so that it will sink quickly.
- The body should be weighted and should not be embalmed. It must have a plastic tag around the ankle with the name and date of burial of the deceased in case the body is eventually washed ashore.
- A certificate of Freedom from Fever and Infection should be obtained from your GP.

Once it is all over

If the deceased owned or rented a house, check your rights or those of people mentioned in the will. Then there is the sad job of sorting and disposing of the person's belongings. Get other people to help you, and do not throw things like clothes, books and bits of furniture away – there are many charity shops who would be glad to have them.

THE THIRD AGE: HELP DIRECTORY

Burial

- The Association of Nature Reserve Burial Grounds, c/o The Natural Death Centre, 20 Heber Road, Cricklewood, London NW2 6AA, (0181 208 2853). Can advise you of farmers or, possibly, a local authority in your area that has established a burial ground. Currently there are some near Wolverhampton, Rugby, Burton-upon-Trent, Carlisle and Brighton with more being opened every month.
- The Cremation Society of Great Britain, Brecon House, 16–16a Albion Place, Maidstone, Kent ME14 5DZ, (01622 688292). Compakta Ltd, The Old White Cottage, 2 Newbold Road, Desford, Leics LE9 9GS, (01455 828642). Can supply cardboard coffins direct or through your funeral director.
- James Gibson Funeral Services, 342 St Helen's Road, Bolton, Lancs BL3 3RP, (01204 655869). Sells a cheap basic coffin including handles and lining.
- Ministry of Agriculture Fisheries and Food, Whitehall Place, London SW1A 2HH, (0171 270 3000). Grants the licence for a body to be buried at sea.
- Westminster Packaging, New Road, Sheerness, Kent ME12 1NB, (01795 580051). Has ecological cardboard caskets. These can be arranged through the funeral director.

Carers

- Association of Crossroads Care Attendant Schemes, 10 Regent Place, Rugby, Warwickshire CV21 2PN, (01788 573653). Provides respite for carers. There are over 200 schemes throughout the UK – all are affiliated to the national association.
- British Red Cross Society, 9 Grosvenor Crescent, London SW1X 7EJ, (0171 235 5454). Has services for carers such as a Home from Hospital scheme, equipment loan and respite services.
- Carers National Association, 20/25 Glasshouse Yard, London EC1A 4JS, (0171 490 8818), (Carers' line 0171 490 8898 Monday to Friday 1 pm to 4 pm). Offers advice and support to anyone who is caring for a sick, elderly or disabled relative or friend.
- Caring Costs, Room 604, Charity Base, 50 Westminster Bridge Road, London SE1 7QY, (0171 721 7653). Campaigns for an independent income for carers.

- Hospice Information Service, St Christopher's Hospice, 51–59 Lawrie Park Road, Sydenham, London SE26 6DZ, (0181 778 9252).
- Keep Able, Fleming Close, Park Farm, Wellingborough, Northants NN8 3UF, (01933 679426). Supplies equipment to elderly or disabled people. It stocks over 2000 items, ranging from cutlery to large powered items.
- National Back Pain Association, 16 Elmtree Road, Teddington, Middlesex TW11 8ST, (0181 977 5474). Provides information and a carer's guide to back care. Also leaflets on back problems.
- Princess Royal Trust, 16 Byward Street, London EC3R 5BA, (0171 480 7788). Provides information, support, counselling and advice to all types of carers, not only those who look after the elderly. It has centres throughout the country.
- SEMI Care Trust, University Settlement, 43 Ducie Road, Barton Hill, Bristol, Avon BS5 0AX, (0117 9559219). Has a telephone information and advice service for families and carers of old people.

Caring for someone who is dying

Ananda Network, Buddhist Hospice Trust, PO Box 123, Ashford, Kent TN242 9TF, (0181 789 6170). Although Buddhist-based, this group offers companionship to the dying or the bereaved of any religion, or those with no religion.

- The Befriending Network, 11 St Bernards Road, Oxford OX2 6EH, (01865 512405). Consists of a network of volunteers throughout the country whose aim is to improve the quality of life of those who are terminally ill and their families, giving carers a break while volunteers look after the patient.
- Hospice Information Service, St Christopher's Hospice, Lawrie Park Road, London SE26 6DZ, (0181 778 9252). Can help you find a hospice not just in Britain but anywhere in the world.
- The Natural Death Centre, 20 Heber Road, Cricklewood, London NW2 6AA, (0181 208 2853). Aims to improve the quality of dying. It gives information and help to families looking after dying people at home. It also has an information pack on organizing alternative funerals. Please send six first-class stamps for a copy.
- Voluntary Euthanasia Society, 13 Prince of Wales Terrace, London W8, (0171 937 7770). Apart from campaigning for a change in the law over euthanasia, it can also provide a declaration form for patients to sign asking not to be kept alive when treatment offered only prolongs the process of dying.

Death

- British Organ Donor Society, Balsham, Cambridge CB1 6DL, (01223 893636).

Acts as an advice, support and self-help group to families who are involved in organ donation, and to patients who receive a donated organ. It also has a commemorative tree scheme: a tree is planted in remembrance of the person who, after death, donated an organ and to give thanks on behalf of whoever received it.

- London Anatomy Office, Department of Anatomy, Charing Cross and Westminster Medical School, Fulham Palace Road, London W6 8RF, (0181 846 1216). The office to contact if you wish to leave your body to medical research. Otherwise, contact the medical school of your local large hospital.

See also Bereavement (*page 195*).

Financial help

NB When compiling this list, the author quizzed the meaning of 'gentlefolk' which appears several times. It is apparently a euphemism for someone from one of the the professions.

- The Association of Charity Officers, c/o the RICS Benevolent Fund Ltd, 1st Floor, Tavistock House North, Tavistock Square, London WC1H 9RJ, (0171 383 5557). Over 240 member funds for professional, commercial and occupational groups. For advice on which fund to approach, contact the Association in writing, giving details of your family background and career pattern.
- Distressed Gentlefolk's Association, 1 Derry Street, Kensington, W8 5HY, (0171 396 6700). Has residential homes for elderly 'gentlefolk' of both sexes, and will give financial help where necessary, as well as clothing and food to the elderly living in their own homes.
- Guild of Aid for Gentlepeople, 10 St Christopher's Place, London W1M 6HY, (0171 935 0641). Gives financial assistance to 'men and women of gentle birth or good education'.
- Royal United Kingdom Beneficent Association, 6 Avonmore Road, London W14 8RL, (0171 602 6274). Will grant annuities to elderly professional people who find themselves in financial difficulties. It also helps find places in residential accommodation or sheltered flats.
- National Benevolent Institution, 61 Bayswater Road, London W2 3PG, (0171 723 0021). Gives financial help in the form of annuities and one-off payments to 'distressed gentlefolk'. Has accommodation in various parts of the country including self-contained flats for 'retired ladies'.

Funerals

- British Humanist Association, 14 Lamb's Conduit Passage, London WC1R 4RH, (0171 430 0908). Can provide information on non-religious funerals.

- National Association of Funeral Directors, 618 Warwick Road, Solihull, West Midlands B91 1AA, (0121 711 1343).
- Indian Funeral Service, Chani House, Alexander Place, Lower Park Road, London N11, (0181 361 6151). Does ritual Hindu and Moslem services.

General

- Age Concern England, Astral House, 1268 London Road, London SW16 4ER, (0181 679 8000). A very helpful organization which aims to improve life for older people and offers information and advice.
- Age Endeavour Fellowship, Willowthorpe, High Street, Stanstead Abbots, Nr Ware, Herts SG12 8AS, (0920 870158). Working from the premise that old people are happier if they are active, it has Employment Fellowship centres throughout the country offering all kinds of work and leisure activities.
- Age-Link, 29 Penbury Road, Norwood Green, Southall, Middx UB2 5RX, (0181 571 5888). Aims to improve the life-style of old people by bringing them together with a younger age group via visits, trips and outings.
- Contact, 15 Henrietta Street, London WC2E 8QH, (0171 240 0630). Concentrates on social life for elderly people who live alone by offering group tea parties and other activities in the houses of volunteer hosts.
- Fellowship of Cycling Old-Timers, 2 Westwood Road, Marlow, Bucks SL7 2AT, (01628 483235). Puts keen cyclists over 50 in touch with each other and offers help.
- Help the Aged, St James's Walk, London EC1R 0BE, (0171 253 0253) (Helpline 0800-289404, Monday to Friday, 10 pm – 4 pm). Gives advice over the phone and by post to elderly people and their families. It also has a number of social projects all over the country.
- Pre-Retirement Association of Great Britain and Northern Ireland, 26 Frederick Sanger Road, Surrey Research Park, Guildford, Surrey GU2 5YD, (01483 301170). Runs courses for people approaching retirement. It also has a list of pre-retirement groups throughout the country.
- Standing Conference of Ethnic Minority Senior Citizens, 5 Westminster Bridge Road, London SE1 7XW, (0171 928 0095). Supports, helps and advises families and friends who care for the elderly from ethnic minority groups.
- University of the Third Age, 1 Stockwell Green, London SW9 9JF, (0171 737 2541). Contact this organization to find out about educational courses etc. for the retired.

Health

- Alzheimer's Disease Society, Gordon House, 10 Greencoat Place, London SW1P 1PH, (0171 306 0606). A support system for families of victims of Alzheimer's disease, formerly called senile dementia. It gives information on what the health and social services, voluntary groups can do to help. It also gives members news of new treatments and the results of research into the disease.
- Coloplast Advisory Service, Freepost, Peterborough PE2 6BR, (0800 622124). Has leaflets on incontinence and a freephone service will put you in touch with your nearest Continence Adviser.
- Continence Advisory Service, Continence Foundation Helpline, Disability North, Castles Farm Road, Newcastle-upon-Tyne NE3 1PH, (0191 213 0050, Weekdays 2 pm–7 pm).
- Continence Foundation, 2 Doughty Street, London WC1N 2PH, (0171 404 6875). Has an incontinence helpline, Monday to Friday, 9 am – 6 pm on 0191 2130050.

See also
Disabled (*page 66*).
Deafness (*page 70*).

Housing help/residential homes

- Abbeyfield Society, Abbeyfield House, 53 Victoria Street, St Albans, Hertfordshire AL1 3UW, (01727 857536). Specializes in building or adapting houses or bed-sitting rooms for the elderly and extra-care homes for those who are in need of extra care.
- Brendoncare Foundation, Brendon, Park Road, Winchester, Hants SO23 7BE, (01962 852133). Has a number of residential and nursing homes in the south of England looking after frail and elderly people in need of care and nursing.
- British Federation of Care Home Proprietors, 852 Melton Road, Thurmaston, Leicester LE4 8BN, (0116 2640095). Can provide lists of member homes nationwide, together with advice and guidance. Members have to adhere to certain standards of care and are independently monitored in accordance with national guidelines. It has a code of practice as a pre-condition of membership.
- Central & Cecil Housing Trust, 2–4 Priory Road, Kew, Richmond, Surrey TW9 3DG, (0181 940 9828). Runs residential homes at Teddington and Richmond near London for elderly people, and bed-sitter accommodation in Ealing. It also has three centres in central London offering accommodation for homeless women.

- Dresden Homes, Dresden House, 18 Albany Villas, Hove, East Sussex BN3 2SA, (01273 732173). Runs a residential home for needy elderly ladies.
- Elderly Accommodation Counsel, 46a Chiswick High Road, London W4 1SZ. Main Enquiries (0181 742 1182). A very useful organization that maintains a database of all forms of accommodation for the elderly nationwide. Can provide advice on top-up funding.
- House of Hospitality, Grace and Compassion Benedictines, Holy Cross Priory, Cross-in-Hand, Heathfield, Sussex TN21 0TS, (01435 863808). The nuns run some residential accommodation; also sheltered flats and bed-sitters for the elderly.
- Key-Change, 43 Westminster Bridge Road, London SE1 7JB, (0171 633 0533). A Christian-based organization that runs homes for the elderly, homeless and ex-offenders, also holiday homes and clubs throughout the country.
- Methodist Homes for the Aged, Epworth House, Stuart Street, Derby DE1 2EQ, (01332 296200). Nationwide organization providing residential care and sheltered housing for any elderly person in need, whatever their personal beliefs.
- National Care Homes Association, 5 Bloomsbury Place, London WC1A 2QA, (0171 436 1871). More than 70 member associations of private residential care and nursing homes; will offer advice on any matters regarding such care.
- National Free Church Women's Council, 27 Tavistock Square, London WC1H 9HH, (0171 387 8413). Run by the United Free Church, the Council has branches throughout the country which provide homes for old people, also mothers and babies.
- Registered Nursing Home Association, Calthorpe House, Hagley Road, Edgbaston, Birmingham B16 8QY, (0121 454 2511). Provides information on registered nursing homes in the UK and the Republic of Ireland which conform to certain standards and which have been visited by the Association.
- Relatives Association, 5 Tavistock Place, London WC1H 9SS, (0171 916 6055). An organization of relatives and friends of older people in residential care, nursing homes and long-stay hospitals, aiming to improve the quality of life. Provides advice, service and local groups.
- Royal Surgical Aid Society, 47 Great Russell Street, London WC1B 3PA, (0171 637 4577). Runs some residential and nursing homes in this country for the elderly and mentally infirm.
- Servite Houses, 2 Bridge Avenue, London W6 9JP, (0181 563 7090). Has an accommodation network in the south-east of England for the elderly and the mentally handicapped, including residential homes.
- Catholic Women's League, 164 Stockwell Road, London SW9 9TQ, (0171 738 4894). Runs flats and homes for the elderly at a number of places

including Newcastle, Leeds, Ealing and Torrington. It also helps refugees and
victims of war.

- Field Lane Foundation, 16 Vine Hill, London EC1R 5EA, (0171 837 0412). Runs
residential care homes, nursing homes and sheltered flats for the elderly.
- Friends of the Elderly and Gentlefolk's Aid Association, 42 Ebury Street,
London SW1W 0LZ, (0171 730 8263). Has a number of retirement homes
throughout the country and also gives grants to help the aged stay in their
own homes. Its welfare department can help funding for nursing homes where
there is a shortfall in the money needed for fees.

See also

Association of Jewish Ex-Servicemen and Women (*page 424*).
Association of Jewish Refugees in Great Britain (*page 424*).
Cheshire Homes (*page 128*).
Sons of Divine Providence, (*see* **States of Mind,** *page 139*).
Sue Ryder Foundation (*page 110*).
Salvation Army (*page 18*).

Pensions

- Equal Opportunities Commission, Overseas House, Quay Street, Manchester
M3 3HN, (0161 833 9244). Has a useful booklet *Your Pension Matters!* which is
a guide through the pension maze for women.
- Newcastle Pensions Customer Service Unit, Room 137D, DSS Longbenton,
Newcastle-upon-Tyne NE98 1YX, (0191 225 7879). Has a useful leaflet FB32
called *Benefits After Retirement*.
- Newcastle Pensions Directorate, Newcastle-upon-Tyne, NE98 1YX,
(0191 213 5000). When phoning with queries give your full name and address
and benefit reference number.
- Pensions Ombudsman, 11 Belgrave Road, London SW1V 1RB, (0171 834 9144).

Rights

- Counsel and Care, Twyman House, 16 Bonny Street, London NW1 9PG,
(0171 485 1566, Monday to Friday, 10.30 am–4 pm). Gives help and advice
ranging from going into a home and rights, to welfare benefits for the elderly
(60+). It also offers financial help on occasions and can advise on how to
adapt a house to suit the aged. It will consider charitable organizations.

Sheltered housing

- Anchor Housing Trust, Anchor House, 269a Banbury Road, Oxford OX2 7HU,
(01865 854000). Runs sheltered accommodation all over the country for the

elderly, some with day-care, and also has a Stay Put scheme where it helps older people to repair and adapt their homes for permanent residency.

- ASRA Housing Association Ltd, 58 Earl Howe Street, Leicester LE2 0DF, (0116 2558121). Works in the West Midlands offering a sheltered housing scheme for elderly Asians within the community.
- Fellowship Houses Trust, Clock House, 192 High Road, Byfleet, Surrey KT14 7RN, (01932 343172). Has several warden-assisted housing schemes for the elderly in the south of England.

See also

Field Lane Foundation (*page 314*).
Methodist Homes for the Aged (*page 313*).

Staying put

- Care Alternatives, 206 Worple Road, London SW20 8PN, (0181 946 8202). Helps and encourages elderly people to stay in their own homes.
- Care and Repair Ltd, Castle House, Kirtley Drive, Nottingham NG7 1LD, (0115 9799091). Helps elderly or disabled house owners to stay in their own homes rather than going into a residential home. Local groups will help organize the money for repairs and adaptions to the housing.

See also Friends of the Elderly and Gentlefolk's Aid Association (*page 314*).

8

EDUCATION

In these days when there is so much competition for jobs, it is vital that our children get the best education they can. Never underestimate the importance of parent-power – your active interest in the schools they attend can often make all the difference. This section gives a survey of what is on offer and what you, personally, can do to support and encourage your child.

YOUR RIGHTS

You and your child have a certain number of rights (and responsibilities) when it comes to education, and first among these is the right to a free school place for your child between the ages of 5 and 16, and a school or college place from the ages of 16 to 18. Your child also has the right to a good education. This means that you can expect the school to do its best to make sure that every child does as well as he or she possibly can. According to the Department of Education, your child has a right to 'broad and balanced studies which promote spiritual, moral, cultural, mental and physical development and prepare him or her for adult life'.

You, in your turn, have a duty to make sure that your child goes to school until he or she is 16 years old. If your child habitually plays truant, you could be prosecuted, and the child could have an Education Supervision Order put upon him or her.

A place at school

You have a right to a place in the school of your choice unless all the places at the school have been given to pupils who have a stronger claim to a place at that school. Your local education authority can tell you which schools in your area have vacant places. Your right to choose is qualified by the phrase 'as long as the admission is within the general policy'. This means that you may be restricted by:

- The sex of the pupils (you cannot insist on sending a girl to an all-boys school).
- The child's ability, if some form of academic selection is used by the school concerned.

- The child's religion, as in the case of a voluntary school which encourages a particular set of beliefs, an all-Catholic or all-Muslim school, for instance.

In reality, the school of your choice may be full and your child will have to go on a waiting list. There may be only one school within reasonable travelling distance – parents have been known to move house in order to get their children in somewhere.

At school

Once your child is at school, you have the right to receive a written report on your child's progress at least once a year. From now on you should receive a summary of a report from the Office for Standards in Education (OFSTED) at some stage. All state schools are inspected by them at least once every four years.

If your child has special educational needs (*see page 329*), your child has the right to an education that meets those needs. This will be in an ordinary school where possible, otherwise your child may attend a special school – see below.

While your child is at school he or she has the right to advice about the options that may best suit his or her needs at 14, and you have the right to be consulted too – probably at special parents' evenings. And after 16, your child has the right to receive information, advice and guidance about educational and employment choices. This will be provided by the school and the local careers service. Young people are entitled to continue their education and training beyond 16, moving to a college as a free full-time student or combining part-time study with a job, perhaps through a Youth Training Scheme. They can also be given the new Youth Credit Vouchers which they can exchange for part-time education or training leading to a recognized qualification.

Types of state schools

- **Standard schools** are now divided between those that are run, in effect, by the local council and those that are self-governing or grant-maintained and run themselves.
- **Voluntary schools,** also known as church schools, are those that encourage a particular set of beliefs.
- **Technology colleges** are schools which run the National Curriculum but devote extra time to technology, sciences and maths; 14- to 16-year-olds follow a full course in technology rather than the short course required by the National Curriculum.
- **City Technology Colleges,** known as CTCs, are a new type of secondary school set up mainly in large towns and cities through partnerships between government and business. These concentrate mainly on technology and science. All of these schools teach the full National Curriculum so that all pupils have a broad-based education.

- **Selective schools** are those that only admit more academically able pupils. Some schools offer places to pupils with an aptitude in a particular subject. They are the equivalent of the old-fashioned grammar schools.
- **Special schools** are for children with a disability or learning difficulty. In this case your child will be assessed first, or you can ask for him to be assessed. The local council pays for the place if the school charges fees.
- **Independent schools** charge fees but the government does offer assisted places in nearly 300 independent schools to children of parents with low incomes. Under the Assisted Places Scheme, all or part of the pupil's fees are paid, depending on parents' income.

THE NATIONAL CURRICULUM

All state schools, but not private schools, must now conform to the National Curriculum. The subjects that your child must study are: English, maths, science, technology, a foreign language in secondary schools, history, geography, art, music and PE. However, rather surprisingly, history and geography are not compulsory after the age of 14, and neither are art or music, so it pays to keep a beady eye on the policy of the school you are planning to send your child to.

Each subject in the Curriculum is divided into attainment targets. These could include speaking and listening, reading, writing, spelling, handwriting and so on. Each target is divided into ten possible levels of attainment. To reach level one in reading a child should be able to recognize familiar words or letters. At level ten they would be au fait with literature and poetry. Unless you choose otherwise, your child must be given sex education in secondary school, but you can choose to withdraw your child from those lessons.

Tests and exams

With the arrival of the National Curriculum comes the controversial assessment tests. At the ages of about 7, 11 and 14, and again at 16, your child will be tested in the basic subjects of English, maths and science. At secondary school they will be entered for GCSEs or other public examinations including vocational qualifications when they are 16. Many children will then go on to do A-levels or GNVQs – General National Vocational Qualifications

HOW TO CHOOSE A SCHOOL

Start well ahead – a year is not too early. Begin by asking to see brochures or prospecti from several schools. By law, all schools must now issue some sort of prospectus showing their achievements and what they have to offer. The prospectus will explain which rules a particular school follows in deciding who will be offered places there. It must state clearly how it decides who is offered places if there is not room enough for everyone. For example, one school may give priority to children who live nearest, another to those with a brother or sister at the school. But there are a number of other things you can do as part of your investigation of schools.

- Ask to see the school magazine if there is one.
- Talk to parents and pupils at the school gate.
- Contact the parent-teacher association. The problems that it is tackling will give you a good idea of what the school is like.
- Ask to see round the school, look at the work the children are doing and what is on display, and look at the notice boards. At primary schools in particular, there should be an atmosphere of fun.
- Assess the relationships between the teachers and the pupils if you can. Teachers should be firm but friendly. Are the children well-behaved in class?
- Check the school in the annual performance tables which not only show what their exam results are compared with other schools, but also give details of things like rate of truancy, etc. Bear in mind, however, that the ratings are unfair since schools in an area with a large number of immigrants or deprived families are bound to have lower results.
- Find out about the school's arrangements for sex education and careers education and advice, what facilities are available for gifted children, and, if it interests you, what moral and spiritual guidance it gives. All these things should be in the prospectus.
- Find out too what it teaches in addition to the National Curriculum.

Methods of teaching

Schools sort their pupils out in various ways. Some are **mixed ability** establishments – this usually happens at primary level. Children are grouped together mixing below-average, average and above-average achievers in the same class. Or the school may go for **streaming**. In this case your child is put into a stream according to his general ability. If the school operates this system, find out what arrangements there are for a child to switch if the child is discovered to be in the wrong group. Then there is **banding** which is basically another form of streaming.

A more flexible type of selection is **setting** – your child is put into a particular group for each subject and may therefore be rated below-average in one subject, and be with an above-average group in another subject.

Racial discrimination and schools

Schools and colleges must see that everyone has fair access to what is taught. They cannot discriminate in entry rules, in the type of education they give, or in the measures of discipline they impose on the grounds of race, colour or creed. They must also provide teaching in English as a second language if required. One way in which schools may sometimes discriminate is by asking would-be parents to write a detailed letter on why they want their child to attend the school. This is sometimes seen as a way of 'weeding out' parents who cannot speak or write English very well and are therefore marked out as immigrants. But this is against the law.

  If you think that your child has been discriminated against by not being sent to the school of your choice, you should first complain to the Department for Education, the Welsh Education Office or the Scottish Education Department. The department may agree to act on your complaint and tell the school or the college that it must take your child. Meanwhile go to the local racial equality council if there is one in your area or the Commission for Racial Equality for advice. If they do not back you within two months, you can take the case to court (a county court in England or Wales or a sheriff court in Scotland). You must do this within six months of the incident, though this can be lengthened if the minister took some time to consider it. In this case you are able to get legal aid if you qualify.

Teachers

Over a number of years, the teaching profession has seen the erosion of much of its power, which has been taken over by the local authorities instead.

As a result, teaching is now a beleaguered profession that is scrutinized all the time by governors, inspectors of all kinds (including Her Majesty's inspectors who can come and make lightning checks at any time), parents and parent-teacher associations. No other profession – not even doctors or dentists – has to take this kind of scrutiny. All of these people consider themselves experts on the subject of teaching. Why? Because they all went to school!

How to influence what goes on at your child's school

Once your child is in school, it is important to keep abreast of what is going on, and, when necessary, to voice your discontent and be able to do something about it. You can achieve this in a number of ways, including:

- Standing for election as a parent-governor. Governors have a great deal of influence on key issues at their school, especially over how money is spent on equipment and that sort of thing (*see page 321*).

- Join the Parent-Teacher Association – or start one if your school has not got one. The National Confederation of Parent-Teacher Associations (*see page 347*) can tell you how to start a group.

Becoming a school governor

If you really want to influence what goes on at your local school, have a say in the appointment of teachers, and how money is spent, consider becoming a governor. School governors are drawn from four different sources.

- You can put your name forward to be a parent-governor. Do this by contacting the head and requesting to be considered.
- Local authority nominees are appointed via the local branches of the three political parties. Be active in your local party and then ask to be nominated from there.
- Co-opted governors are found from among local business people, interested members of the public and ex-policemen. Go to the school and say you would like to do the job. Most schools find it very hard to get enough people for the governing body and may well welcome you with open arms.
- Teacher-governors are elected by the teachers.

Governors have considerable powers including the right to suspend a child or not – overturning a teacher's decision if they want to; they can appoint teachers, including deciding who should be dismissed or made redundant, and set all teachers' pay; they can direct budgets and fix the curriculum.

Governing bodies are often broken down into special committees – Finance and General Purposes, Curriculum, Personnel, Premises, and Exclusions and Expulsions. Someone who has building experience might well want to serve on the Premises Committee, someone else with experience of the law might be more interested in the Exclusions and Expulsions Committee, while an accountant would gravitate towards finance. If you are attached to, say, a large comprehensive school in a busy city area, then expect to attend committee meetings, and perhaps other meetings, about once a week.

School problems

If your child has a problem at school and attends a large comprehensive, ask to see the pastoral teacher, a senior staff member who may have a better overall picture of your child than the specialist subject staff. Or ask to see the school counsellor if there is one.

PUNISHMENT

State schools, unlike private schools, are no longer allowed to administer any sort of corporal punishment (the cane) to naughty children. Instead if a child persistently or seriously misbehaves then he or she can be 'excluded'. This means the child is banned from the school, usually for a few days. The number of exclusions has tripled in the last three years, some of this is a knock-on effect from the pressure that league tables put on a school's performance. A child can be permanently excluded, or expelled. But he must then be offered a place in another school, or one of the new neighbourhood education centres that are being set up, or in some exceptional cases, he may be educated via home tuition. If your child is excluded you have the right to appeal (*see below*).

HOW TO COMPLAIN

There are a number of circumstances that may cause you to want to take further action and to complain. If the local council or the school's governors do not offer you a place in the school of your choice they must remind you about your right to appeal and how to use it. Sometimes bizarre decisions are made by schools; one which reached the newspapers recently involved twins being parted. If they do not inform you of your rights, then get the Department For Education's booklet on admission procedures (*see page 347*) which sets out what you should do.

But school admission problems are not the only reason why you might need to complain.

- If the head teacher decides for some reason your child should not follow the full National Curriculum for the moment and you disagree, then you should appeal to the school governors. Failing that, go to the Secretary of State for Education.
- If you disagree with decisions about your child's special educational needs; if, for instance, the local council will not fund a place for your child at a special school you can now appeal to a new tribunal which deals with all appeals against local councils (*see page 346*).
- If your child is excluded, suspended or expelled, then the head teacher must tell you why this has happened. You then have a right to put your case to the governing body and, in the case of expulsion, take things further with an appeal to a special committee dealing with these cases.
- You can also complain if you believe your child has been given an exam grade that does not do justice to his ability (*see ACE page 346*).

PRIVATE EDUCATION

What can private education give your child? Individual attention is the short answer. There is no doubt that private schools have the staff and the facilities to get the best out of a child who might founder in the state system. Classes are smaller and if the child boards, distractions are fewer. But can you afford the fees? And if so, do you want to?

There is no child more unhappy than one who has been educated in the private system then suddenly switched to the state system because family fortunes have foundered, perhaps because his father has been made redundant. So if you intend to educate your child this way, you should make adequate safeguards to be able to finish the job.

Boarding schools

In the last five years, the number of children going into boarding education has dropped by 20 per cent, with many more children now going to private day-schools instead. There may be many reasons why children board – marriage break-down, far-flung or scattered families may mean that the only way a child can get a stable education is by attending boarding school. Indeed you can get state help for your child to board under certain circumstances. Some children thrive in an institutionalized atmosphere, others do not. There is no doubt that over a period of time, your boarding-school child can become very self-reliant but may also become a remote stranger.

The costs of educating a child at an independent boarding school are enormous, and in the case of the average family, would involve a real sacrifice. If you have several children the figures multiply since it would not be fair to send one and not the others. But there is no doubt that private education does give the less academically able child a better chance. Many parents who send their children to private schools say they do so because they feel that state education is under-funded and under-staffed and is not demanding enough. Many parents object to the large class numbers in many state schools. Others say they send their children there because it has always been a family tradition to go to private school.

If you cannot pay

There is an assisted-places scheme in more than 300 private schools run by the government on a means-tested basis. You can get details from the Department for Education (*see page 343*).

The independent school system

- **Pre-prep schools** take children from the age of 3. Some are junior departments of the prep school which the child would attend later on.
- **Prep schools** may take children as young as 5, but most start at 7 or 8. They may be co-educational, mixing girls and boys, or single-sex.

- **Grammar or direct grant schools**, once part of the state system, normally take children from the age of 11. Pupils may go on at the age of 16 to a state sixth-form college, or stay on to do A-levels.
- **Senior schools**, some of them known as public schools, take pupils at 12 or 13 sometimes via the Common Entrance exam. Most are still single-sex schools but some of the better-known public schools for boys now allow girls into the sixth-form.
- **Special schools** If your child has a particular talent, you may be able to get him into a special school, often via a scholarship or bursary. Many abbeys and cathedrals have choir schools, for instance, and there are ballet, music and stage schools too. If your child's present school cannot help over special education, then try going to an educational consultancy for information (*see page 343*).

Choosing a private school

Be realistic when putting your child's name down for schools. To get into the very top public schools your child will have to have been to a high-flying prep school which will coach him for the examinations. Make a choice of three or four schools, and in the case of secondary schools, include one with less tough entry conditions in case your child's exam results are not good. Then go around and visit each of the schools.

- Let your child help choose once you have found a selection of schools that suit you.
- Make a visit to the schools of your choice with your child – my daughter voted with her feet at one school I took her to, and ran away while we were being shown round.
- Find out how often they are allowed home. For some children weekly boarding is the best bet.
- If your child is very bright and cash is short, see whether you can get help with the fees from the Department for Education (*see page 343*).
- Find out who your child would be able to go to for help if he was feeling home-sick, or had any worries. Most boarding schools are divided into houses, and frequently the housemaster's wife fulfils this role.
- Choose a school that is not too far away.
- Take a particular note of what subjects they teach – private schools do not have to comply with the National Curriculum.

EDUCATING YOUR CHILD AT HOME

There are many reasons why you may decide you want to educate your child yourself. The local facilities may not be up to scratch, your child may be a school refuser due to bullying by teachers or other children, or your child may have special needs and the personal attention you feel he or she requires is not being provided. The law is simple and straightforward. As a parent you have a primary right and duty to educate your child. This task is usually delegated to the local authority or to a private school. You also have a duty to educate the child full time and efficiently, in a manner appropriate to the child's age, ability, aptitude and any special needs. You are also required to prepare your child for life in this society. This should include the ability to mix with his or her peer group.

If you decide to educate your child yourself, you will probably have a visit from a local Educational Welfare Officer or Educational Social Worker. Whatever they may tell you, Anne Wade of Education Otherwise (*see page 342*) says:

- You do not have to follow the National Curriculum.
- You do not have to have a timetable.
- You do not have to have a special room set aside to work in.
- You do not have to designate a set minimum number of hours a week for the purpose.

Most home-educated children find it best to go on eventually to a local college or tech.

Encouraging your child at home

It pays to encourage your child to read. The single most important skill he is likely to acquire in the course of education is the ability to read fluently, with ease, understanding and enjoyment. Surround your child with picture books from an early age, read lots of stories, act them out as you read them. If you do not have the money to buy books, go to your local library; most have excellent children's sections. Buy story cassettes which have accompanying picture books so that children get to associate the sounds with the words.

Carry on reading to your children from time to time, even if they can read themselves.

SOCIAL PROBLEMS

Bullying

Ever since Tom Brown's school days, bullying has made many a school child's life total hell and there have even been reported suicides as a result of it. Now the subject is finally being taken seriously by teachers, parents and the police. Not long ago three schoolboys who attacked a fellow pupil, punching and kicking him as he lay helpless on the ground, were each sentenced to three years' custody. But children are still unhappy to 'grass' to parents or teacher if they are being bullied.

And bullying can leave, in its wake, anxiety, depression, shyness, low self-esteem and poor academic achievement, all spilling over into adult life.

It is reckoned that one in four primary school children has been bullied at some time or other. Famous names like Frank Bruno, Neil Kinnock and Tom Cruise all say they suffered from it during their school days. Bullying breeds on secrecy and the victim is often terrified to tell because he has been warned that if he does tell, the bully will 'come and get them'. But condoning bullying by saying it happened to you and did not do you any harm, and that the child will just have to learn to stand up for himself or that he must hit back, only makes things worse.

What is bullying?
According to the children's charity Kidscape (*see page 341.*) bullying takes five forms:
- Physical: pushing, kicking, hitting, pinching and other kinds of violence.
- Verbal: name-calling, spreading rumours, persistent teasing and sarcasm.
- Emotional: sending a child to Coventry, hiding his school books, ridiculing and humiliating him. This kind of bullying is often very difficult to prove.
- Racist: racial abuse, taunts, graffiti and gestures.
- Sexual: unwanted physical contact or abusive comments of a sexual nature.

Bullying by teachers
Children who are naughty or disruptive in class can expect to be rebuked by their teacher. But very occasionally a teacher can continually pick on a child, humiliating him in front of the class. This situation needs to be handled with a certain amount of tact. The best thing to do is to talk privately to the teacher concerned to see what the problem is and if that fails, see somebody senior in the school about the situation, possibly at a parents' evening.

Who gets bullied?
Usually the children who are 'different' – in their speech, their looks and their abilities. The victim is usually someone who does not 'fit in' with the herd, perhaps considered a swot, too smartly or bizarrely dressed, too timid or a loner. Fat children, undersized children and those who wear specs are frequent targets, as are very clever children. The bullying can range from verbal abuse to actual physical assault. The child's possessions may be stolen, hidden or destroyed, his school work sabotaged. Strangely enough, some of these same attributes – of not fitting in, for instance, can often be found in the person who is doing the bullying. They, too, often find it difficult to be accepted by the rest of the herd. They may also have problems at home.

Warning signs
- Does your child suddenly want a lift to school when he can easily walk there? Or has he started taking a different route to school?

- Has he started complaining of minor illnesses in the hope of being allowed to stay home?
- Has your child's school work suddenly deteriorated?
- Has he started stammering or become very withdrawn?
- Has your child begun to have nightmares, or found it difficult to get to sleep?
- Is he continually 'losing' his dinner money?
- Are his clothes torn, has he got unexplained bruises?
- Has he started playing truant?

What to do
- Try to coax the names of the culprits out of your child and any reason why they acted that way.
- Your first stop is the school itself. Schools now take bullying extremely seriously and quick action will probably result. If you are a lone parent and feel nervous about tackling the situation, take a friend, male or female, with you for moral support. Talk to the head of year or head teacher. If you do not get any satisfaction, make a formal complaint to the school governors or the Local Education Authority.
- It is worth while raising it with the Parent-Teacher Association too.
- Give your child all the support and back-up you can. You cannot fight the child's battles for him but what you can do is give him the emotional ammunition he needs to handle the situation.
- If all else fails, change schools.

What to tell your child to do
Kidscape suggests you tell him:
- Try not to show that he is upset or angry.
- Do not fight back unless you absolutely have to. It is better to lose your pocket money as that can be replaced.
- Make a joke of it if you can, whatever you feel like inside. That reaction will put the bully off balance.
- Ask the bully to repeat what he said – this can sometimes take the wind out of his sails.
- Avoid being alone in places where you may get picked on, and stay with a crowd.
- Tell a friend what is happening, ask for his or her support.

Is your child a bully?
If you discover that your child is bullying others, then nip it in the bud. Unchecked, a bully who finds he can get away with violence, aggression and threats, frequently ends up involved in crime – more than 80 per cent of offenders in institutions have been involved in bullying in some form or other during their

school-days. Bullies are not born, they are made. Many of them learn it at home from violent parents, older brothers or at their first schools. Quite often, bullies are people who have difficulty in making friends. Having said that, not all bullies come from unstable deprived homes.

What to do

- Stay as calm as possible on hearing the news.
- Avoid becoming angry or defensive when dealing with teachers, other parents or people in authority.
- Find out exactly what your child has been doing and to whom.
- Ask if this is the first time or if it has happened before.
- Talk to the staff, tell them that you are tackling the situation and that your child is making an effort to improve his behaviour.

Then talk to your child; see if he can tell you why he is doing this, and what he thinks might help it to stop. Tell him that you still love him but that his behaviour is making you unhappy. Bullies sometimes attack because:

- They do not understand the victim.
- They are jealous of the victim for some reason.
- They are envious of the victim because they want to be like him.
- They like to feel powerful.
- They want to try to feel 'big'.
- Or they may themselves be having problems at school.

Try to get the reason for your child's behaviour and you are halfway to solving the problem. Your child should be encouraged to:

- Make amends to the victim in some way, and to try, at any rate, to understand him and make friends with him.
- Take up some martial art, perhaps judo or karate which both have strong ethical guidelines, as a physical outlet if he has difficulty in controlling his temper. At the very least he should take up a sport.

Truancy

Truancy is often caused by something more personal than problems at school. It could be the child's appearance. He could be being taunted for being fat, clumsy or having to wear spectacles. It is possible that he is being harassed because of his ethnic origin. Truancy can also be triggered off by a family crisis. Children are often more upset than they seem about disputes between parents and threats of divorce. Personal problems with a specific teacher might be another cause, or difficulty over lessons. The longer truancy goes on, the more difficult it is for your child to return to normal attendance. Work is missed, his absence has been noticed and he is in trouble.

Refusal to go to school

There are many reasons why children refuse to go to school, and they may not tell you what the reasons are. It could well be that the child is being bullied either by another pupil or by a particular teacher. It could be that there are family problems and the child is afraid to leave the house because the father's threat that he is going to leave might come true while the child is out. It could also be that he has difficulty in reading, writing or comprehension and needs special help.

In the cases of truancy and refusal, the first thing to do is to sit down with the child and try to find out what is causing his behaviour. If this does not work, then a visit to a children's clinic might be the answer – a sympathetic professional may be able to find out what the root of the problem is by gentle questioning. Family therapy may be suggested, in which the whole family talks over the problem. Finally, it may be that a change of school is the best way of solving matters.

Suspension/expulsion

If a decision has been made to suspend or expel your child, you should get a letter from the head of the school stating the fact. The letter will also say for how long the child is excluded, why this action has being taken and what your rights are. If the child is being suspended for more than five days, you will be invited to school to discuss the situation. You have a right to appeal against the decision to the governors or the Local Education Authority.

SPECIAL NEEDS

One in five children has special educational needs at some time or other. It can be devastating to discover that your child has some sort of handicap or disability. The problem may be discovered at birth by the parents or by an alert heath visitor. Or it may not surface until the child goes to a play-group or to school. Sometimes parents suspect but deny there is anything wrong.

What is 'normal'? One child will be running around but not talking at 18 months while another can talk but not walk very well. By the age of five, these things will have evened out generally, unless the child needs some sort of special help.

Do not delay

Get help right away, a child's early years are among the most important ones. Even if he has not started school the Local Education Authority (LEA) will be willing to discuss the situation. If your child is over 2 years old and you think he has learning difficulties, you can ask your LEA to make an assessment of his special educational needs. Even at an early age the LEA may be able to help you by sending a teacher to your home, especially if the child has hearing or sight problems. A trained home visitor may be able to suggest activities that will encourage your child to develop his skills. Or the LEA may suggest a specific playgroup or opportunity group that can help your child develop through play.

Be persistent

You know your child better than anyone else. If you are told there is nothing wrong, but you are sure there is, stand your ground and insist on tests.

Make a list

Keep a careful list of symptoms that worry you. Produce them when the child is being assessed.

Ask 'why not?'

If you are told that specialist help or tests are not necessary pin the doctor down. Ask why he thinks so.

Ask for a second opinion

You have the right to do this. The sooner the situation is sorted out the sooner help will be to hand. If there is a problem the younger the child is when it is tackled, the better.

Get outside help

There is a a vast network of support groups now for every conceivable condition, no matter how rare it is. Indeed, Contact a Family (*see page 268.*) has issued a directory of family support networks for more than 200 conditions.

Special needs and education

The Department for Education says that all children with special educational needs have a right to a broad and well-balanced education, including as much work as possible under the National Curriculum. And you, as a parent, have a right to take part in any decisions made about your child's education and to be kept in touch at all stages.

Who has special needs?

Anyone who has learning difficulties, behaviour problems or physical disabilities is rated as a child with special needs. If the child finds it much harder to learn than most children of the same age that would be considered a special educational need and he would be entitled to help known as special educational provision. The learning difficulties could be caused by something physical, a problem with sight, hearing or speech for instance, a mental disability or a health problem. It is vital that you find out at an early stage.

A study of three-year-olds found that one in 12 had 'potentially significant language problems' and may have difficulty in expressing themselves. It is believed that one child in every school class is likely to be dyslexic, getting b's and d's mixed up in reading and words reversed – another symptom of dyslexia can be poor co-ordination. But for all these problems specialist teaching with structured exercises can go a long way to improving things. In the case of dyslexia specially tinted lenses can help to clarify the messages the eyes receive from the brain. MENCAP (*see page 124*) has a useful book called *Facing the Future* which helps parents of children with learning difficulties.

If your child has special needs, the school should then draw up an individual education plan, if necessary, which will set targets for your child to achieve. Deaf children may need to go where there is someone who is fluent at BSL – basic sign language. You may be asked to work on this with the child at home. If necessary the school will call in specialist help and advice from outside. If still more help is needed it may ask the LEA to make a statutory assessment.

A statutory assessment

This is a detailed examination to find out exactly what your child's needs are and what special help is required. This will probably be done in committee, involving your doctor, any professional who has been in involved with the child and people from the school. You have the right to go with your child to any interview, medical test or other test during this assessment. At some stage the committee may ask to see your child alone because children often act quite differently when their parents are not there. If you do not want to go, you can ask for a 'Named Person' to help you and express your views. Your Named Person can come from a parents' support group, be a professional of some kind, a friend or a relative.

The LEA may then make a statement of special educational needs , a document that sets out your child's needs and the special help he should have. If a change of school is involved it will send you details of all schools that are suitable for children with special educational needs. You have a right to express a preference for the school you want your child to go to, providing the school is suitable for your child's age, ability and needs and that his presence there will not affect the efficient education of other children already at the school. You may be offered a special school which takes children with particular types of special needs, if there is one in your area.

From then on the LEA must check your child's progress regularly – at least once a year – and make sure that the statement continues to meet the child's needs. When your child reaches 14 the LEA will do a special review and produce a Transition Plan for his move into adult life. Education for children with special needs does not stop at 16, places can be found for them at colleges of further education, on a full- or part-time basis, and at other special schools.

If your child is sick

Sometimes a child is temporarily assessed as having special educational needs because he has been ill over a long period of time or has to go into hospital. You should then contact your LEA which will make sure that your child is given help, either at home or in hospital (*see page 345*). If the child has to take an exam or an assessment, this can be done at home or in the hospital.

How you can help your child

- Keep in close contact with your child's teachers to find out about his progress. Find out from the school the name of the teacher who is responsible for children with special educational needs and make contact with her. Show that you are a concerned parent.
- Tell the school anything that might be useful about your child's health and development when it was younger; for instance, how he behaves at home, the possible causes of the difficulties and any other information that might help.
- Make sure that your child works on any special programmes the school may set.
- Make sure that he has help, if he needs it, from spectacles, hearing aids and that he takes any medication that has been prescribed at the right times.
- When your child starts proper school or moves to a new school, tell the new teachers about the kind of special help that has been provided by the previous school, by the health or social services. If you move to another area you should let your LEA know so it can pass on the necessary records and papers.

How to complain

If you are unhappy about the help your child is getting at school you should first speak to the teacher and head teacher about it. Ask for a meeting with them, and write down what is worrying you beforehand, if you find that useful. It may be a good idea to keep a diary of events. If you do not get any satisfaction, then you should contact the LEA, and then, if you are still not happy, you can complain to the Secretary of State for Education – use the services of your support network, if you belong to one, to help you with this.

If you have asked for a statutory assessment to be done and the LEA decides not to take you, then you have the right to appeal to a Special Educational Needs Tribunal which consists of three people, one of them a lawyer. Ask your LEA for the address of your nearest tribunal.

THE GIFTED CHILD

Gifted children often have a hard time at school especially in the early years. They can feel bored and lack stimulation and this can lead to behavioural problems. Like children with special needs they can be difficult to bring up. Indeed sometimes they are mistaken for children with special needs. The bright child does have special needs but those needs are not, of course, the same. Gifted children can sink into depression if their minds are not fed. In large classes in an under-resourced school, children at either end of the spectrum – those who are extra-bright and those with special needs – can be left to their own devices while the harassed teacher deals with the middle band.

Is yours a gifted child?

The National Association for Gifted Children (*see page 342*) says a gifted child can be one who:
- Never stops asking questions.
- Walked and talked early, and has a wide vocabulary.
- Has never needed much sleep.
- Is very demanding and has great physical and mental energy.
- Possesses a vivid imagination.
- Likes to take the lead when playing with friends.
- Could read from an early age, always has his nose in a book.
- Pays extraordinary attention to detail.
- Loses interest when asked to do more of the same.
- Has a lively mind, quickly grasps a new idea.
- Shows surprising powers of concentration when interested.

Very few bright children will show all these traits – indeed some of them will be found in children who are not particularly able. But they are pointers which may indicate that special provision might be needed for your child.

Gifted children show a great thirst for knowledge and, says the association, it is vital that this need is recognized as early as possible so that parents and teachers can give them plenty of opportunities to develop their talents. In school classes where adequate provision is not made for them, gifted children tend to become bored because not enough is demanded of them. This leads to switching off, day-dreaming, to trying to avoid school, or disruptiveness – they may play the clown or be truculent with teachers. You may need to get advice on how to handle the situation from a trained educational counsellor, particularly if the child has a talent for, say, music or art.

It may be possible to send the gifted child to a special school (*see page 342*).

Get a copy of *Help with Bright Children* from the National Association for Gifted Children (*see page 342*) which gives practical advice, information and suggestions on raising and educating a super-bright child.

The funding in many state schools can be affected by how many succeed in keeping pupils into the sixth form. The less scrupulous schools, it is said, may therefore actively discourage senior pupils from going on into college, preferring them to stay so that their funding stays at a good level. Bear this in mind if your child, gifted or not, is being urged to stay on at school rather than go on to a specialized college; get the facts and make your own mind up.

EXAMINATIONS

As your child makes his way through the school system, exams loom large on the horizon. Children are being crammed for exams as never before, with some state schools running Easter revision courses for GCSE and A-level pupils, something that the independent schools have done for some time. Some are even starting revision at Christmas. Exam failure, or the threat of it, can cause enormous stress, leading to anxiety attacks and even suicide. It is estimated that nearly a third of exam entrants fail to get the grade they should because their performance is affected by stress.

Homework – how to help

- Do not freak out if there is music coming from his room. The fact that the radio is blaring away does not mean that he is not doing his homework. Most children have the ability to study and listen to loud music at the same time, even if we could not cope under those circumstances.
- Make sure the room where he studies is warm enough but not too warm. An electric or gas fire roaring away may make the child feel drowsy.
- Has he got a comfortable chair to sit in? A second-hand typist's chair might make all the difference and can often be picked up cheaply.
- Do not expect your child to toil away for hours. As with work at a computer, it is reckoned that two hours at one stretch is long enough for intensive study. After that he should stop for a while and do something physical.

Exam stress

Keep a watchful eye on your child if he or she:
- Changes his or her eating habits, particularly if the child will not take any food.
- Stops pursuing usual interests or hobbies.
- Makes excuses not to meet friends.

These could all be warning signs that the child is studying too hard. Instead, try to get him to get up early and go to bed early. Early morning is a better time for revision than at the end of the day. Avoid talking about the subject of exams if you can. But if your child has specific worries, get him to talk to the teacher concerned. Or encourage him to ring a support network like Parentline (*see page 265*) who will counsel him over the phone. You can also make sure that your child switches off at times, either by watching TV, going to the cinema, a football match or a disco. Help your child work out a revision timetable so that the work is divided into manageable sessions. Finally, make it quite clear to your child that you love him dearly, whatever results he gets. Do not pass on your own fears about the outcome.

Failure

You can appeal against an exam result if there are mitigating circumstances – the child was unwell at the time the exam was taken or has a history of illness. The appeal should be made via the school. If you think the marking has been unusually severe, you can appeal for a check that the marks were added up properly. This takes some time and there is a fee for this, although sometimes a school may ask for this to be done on behalf of several pupils. You can ask the school to contact the examining body concerned and question the result. If that fails to appease you, you can get the school to go to the Independent Appeals Authority for School Examinations. It can only do this, however, if there has been some flaw in the procedures.

You do, however, have the right to enter or re-enter your child for any examination, whether the school supports you in this or not. If you do this without the school's support, you will have to pay the exam fee.

GOING TO UNIVERSITY

There has never been such a wide choice of university courses, particularly since many of the old technical colleges now have university status. You can take a degree in anything from ballet to consumer protection or equine studies, with a choice of more than 100 universities. The average entry requirement is now 2 A-levels, but some places will take less. You no longer have to stay on in the sixth form for an extra year and take a separate entrance exam to get into Oxford or Cambridge, selection is now done by interview.

About a third of all 18-year-olds now go on to take a degree, but one in eight university students either fails his degree or never completes the course, says educational consultants Gabbitas (*see page 343*). In some institutions the figure is over 20 per cent. What has gone wrong? Sometimes it can be financial pressures, personal problems – some people find they are simply not cut out for university study, or health problems. Often though, it is disappointment with the courses they have chosen. Many students simply do not spend enough time studying their options and thinking about what they want to do.

First do your homework

In your first sixth-form year start researching what choices there are available for the subjects you want to take. Check the grades that are required for your chosen courses and consider realistically if you have a hope of getting them. Hedge your bets by picking a university which needs lower grades as your alternative choice. Then ask yourself these questions:

- Are you going to stay home or move away? Staying home is cheaper but cuts down your choices.
- Do you want a university in a city or out of town?
- How much is accommodation going to cost? Do you want to live in hall or in rented digs? If you are planning to live in hall, find out whether you have to share a room, how many meals you are entitled to, how far out of town it is and whether there are shops nearby.
- Would it be better to take a degree in two subjects for more flexibility?

Applying for university

Your school will help you do this. Basically, you apply to the central agency for degrees called the Universities and Colleges Admissions Service (UCAS). It sends you an entry form which you then use to apply to the institution of your choice. Via your school or college or from UCAS itself, you get a handbook, an application form with an instruction sheet on how to complete it and an acknowledgement card.

Filling in the form

- Make several photocopies of the form to practise on. Do not attempt to fill in the form itself at this stage. Those responsible for looking at and acting on the forms say that many students make silly mistakes, for example, putting the day's date against the words date of birth which rather spoils the impression they are trying to make.
- Be neat and tidy, accurate and legible – after all, you want to look as though you are well-educated. All these things will score points for you.

The Further Information section is the selling part. Fewer and fewer universities are calling people for interview so it is what you write here that counts. This is the only part of the form where you have an opportunity to say what you have been doing and what your aims are, and it is the only place where the examiners can see what actually makes you tick. What singles you out from all the rest? That is what you need to show.

At the moment, you and your teacher have to predict what your A-level or similar results are likely to be. Here it pays to be honest, otherwise when the results do come through at a lower level, it looks as though you have not attempted to reach your potential.

You now have six choices of university. To avoid disappointment apply across a good spread, apart from the high-flying university you may hope to get into, in case your results are bad. A choice of only high-achieving universities, teamed with unexpectedly low results might result in either a last-minute scrabble to get in somewhere, or worse still, a year's wait.

What happens next

Your form has to be with UCAS by January, long before you have taken your final exams. By spring you will hopefully have had an offer from one or more universities. These will be conditional on your exam results. If you have several offers you may decide to reject some at this stage. August is the crunch month, when your results come through. If your grades are close to those demanded by your first-choice university, ring up and see if it will take you.

Clearing

If you have had no offers, or your grades are too low, you then enter the clearing system at the end of August. You should receive your Clearing Entry Form (CEF), known as a 'passport', with your Clearing Entry Number, which you must quote when talking to universities. Then:

- Check the up-to-date official vacancy lists, then look up the courses in your UCAS handbook to see what the courses involve. Look in advertisements in papers like *The Guardian* for advertised vacancies at universities.
- Phone or fax the university and ask to speak to the admissions office. Have your clearing number and your grades at the ready.
- If it offers you a place, send off your CEF to the admissions office immediately, or better still take it in person. Speed is of the essence. You can only apply to one university at a time.
- If the university gives you a firm offer, check that it is for the course you want.

You need to be available for interview and you must keep in touch. If you do not get what you want, you can always resit exams or apply again next year.

Universities abroad

If you have an award from your LEA for a higher education course in the UK and are interested in studying for part of the time in another country, you may be able to have your award paid while you are abroad, and you may also be eligible, in certain circumstances, for supplementary allowances. If you are thinking of studying abroad, get hold of *The European Choice*, a useful booklet issued by the Department for Education (*see page 347*) which gives a run-down on opportunities for higher education in Europe, together with information on grants and allowances.

Taking a year out

You have the option of deferring entry to university. This means applying for a course with the intention of taking a year out to work or travel. You have to give your reasons for doing this and you need to outline the plans you have for that year. You will also need to check that the institution you want to go to will accept a deferred entry.

Finance

The National Union of Students claims that one-third of all students have money worries. Ever since grants were cut by 10 per cent in real terms, students have found it more and more difficult to survive. As a student you can get a certain amount of money via grants, which may be topped up by loans, money from parents and part-time jobs.

Grants are paid by the LEA in three instalments. If you leave your course before the end you may be asked to repay some of the grant. Your grant is now generally considered too small to live on and few students qualify for the full amount as grants are means-tested on the 'residual income' of your parents. Residual income means the money left after mortgage payments and other similar outgoings have been met. A grant is reduced, if you, as the student have any help from a scholarship.

Loans are administered by the Student Loans Company (SLC) on an annual basis and students must apply for them before 31 July in the academic year for which they are needed. The loans are interest-free. Your college or university decides whether or not you are eligible but this is not usually a problem. Call the SLC on its Freefone number 0800 405010 for details. Loans have to be repaid by monthly instalments after your course is completed. You may be able to defer payment if your income after graduation is below a certain level.

How to budget

Money is bound to be tight when you are a student.

- Buy a season ticket rather than a daily travel pass if you have to travel to and fro.
- Look for own-brand foods in supermarkets, as they are always cheaper.
- Do not shop when you are hungry.
- Buy as much as you can at students' discount shops.

- Go to charity shops such as Oxfam, for basic clothes; you are bound to find bargains.
- Buy as much equipment and as many books as you can, second-hand.
- Open a student bank account that has special rates, discounts or free overdrafts.
- Save your phone calls for cheap times of day.
- If you have to pay separately for heating, turn it down and wear warm clothes instead.
- Organize a holiday job well in advance to bring in extra cash.

RETURNING TO EDUCATION

More people are returning to education in later years – indeed mature students now outnumber the young. Yet many universities are still geared towards school-leavers. However, as more places become available the situation is set to change. So whether you are returning to work and need to update your skills or simply want to enrich your life by studying, there should be something for you.

Mature students

What is a mature student? Normally someone aged 21 or over when entering higher education. If you have a good group of O-levels under your belt, you should not need to take A-levels to get in. But some universities may want to reassure themselves that you have studied recently, via the Open University or at evening classes.

How to apply

Contact UCAS (*see page 347*) and ask for advice on becoming a mature student. Do not be put off by your lack of qualifications. Most universities operate a CATS (Credit Accumulation and Transfer) or APEL (Accreditation of Prior Learning) scheme which takes into account your previous learning experience, even if it did not result in qualifications. The National Union of Students has a useful advice booklet (*see page 347*).

Finance for mature students

The grant and loan system is geared to young people who have a family to fall back on. The older student allowance has now been abolished, although you may be able to get a free overdraft from your bank. However, if this is your first degree, your university fees are automatically paid by the government. You should be able to get a basic grant from your LEA, which is means-tested but is unlikely to keep you. Look, too, in a copy of the *Grants Register* (edited by Lisa Williams, Macmillan) in your local library; this publication lists organizations which provide grants to mature students.

If you are under 50 you can apply for a student loan from the government. If you are over 50 you may be able to negotiate something with your bank, but you will have to pay interest. You are not, however, eligible for housing benefit or income support while studying full-time. You may be able to claim a dependant's allowance if you are a single parent. You also cannot sign on as unemployed, or claim sick pay. But you will not normally have to pay council tax or National Insurance contributions.

Open University

Studying in your own home may be the most attractive or, indeed, the only option you have; the Open University which links a postal course with help by radio and TV can help (*see page 342*). It takes six years to take a degree this way and a disciplined attitude to work. But along the line you will make many good friends via summer schools and have a great sense of achievement. It suits almost everyone, because you can choose the hours when you work. And for relatively little cost you can take a degree over as many years as you choose.

Access courses

Enquire from your LEA or college to see what access courses are available to you. These are designed as a bridge to get you into a degree course. Through access courses and part-time A-levels and study at further education colleges it is possible, eventually, to get into university. But they are equally useful for studying some life-long interest.

NVQs: learning while you work

National Vocational Qualifications (NVQs) are administered by the Business and Technology Education Council and are awarded on a practical assessment of what you do at work. They are available across a wide range of occupations, from agriculture to confectionery, and you achieve them in your own time at your own pace. There are no barriers of age, previous experience or qualifications.

You can work towards an NVQ in several different ways, depending on your ability, needs and experience and also the facilities available where you work. NVQs are made up of separate units which are assessed one at a time, building up to the whole qualification. They may be gained through an organization like City and Guilds or via your employer, if you work for a large concern. Contact your local Training and Enterprise Council for details if your employer cannot help, or call the NVQ enquiry line on 0171 718 1914.

Other options

Learning by correspondence course is now known as 'distance learning' and the Association of British Correspondence Colleges (*see below*) offers a wide range of courses including A-levels and GCSEs which you can do from home.

The Open College of the Arts, which is affiliated with the Open University, specializes in courses which range from painting and sculpture to writing and even garden design. If you want a less structured learning course, consider contacting the University of the Third Age which has branches all over the country. Finally, remember that your own local authority will also have a wide range of evening and day-time courses to choose from, some of which will be free to pensioners.

EDUCATION: HELP DIRECTORY

Bullying

- Anti Bullying Campaign, 10 Borough High Street, London SE1 9QQ (0171 378 1446). Has a helpline, above for parents.
- Kidscape Campaign for Children's Safety, 152 Buckingham Palace Road, London SW1W 9TR, (0171 730 3300). Has a free parent's guide to bullying and child abuse in schools.

Further education

- Association of British Correspondence Colleges, 6 Francis Grove, London SW19 4DT, (0181 544 9559). Can supply you with details of correspondence colleges for 'distance learning', as it is now called.
- BTEC, Business and Technology Education Council, Central House, Upper Woburn Place, London WC1 0HH, (0171 413 8400). Has fact sheets on business and technology courses.
- Council for the Accreditation of Correspondence Colleges, 27 Marylebone Road, London NW1 5JS, (0171 935 5391). Has a list of accredited correspondence colleges.
- National Council for Vocational Qualifications, 222 Euston Road, London NW1 2BZ, (0171 387 9898). Has an information helpline on 0171 728 191 which can give you details about vocational qualifications.

- National Federation of Women's Institutes, 104 New King's Road, London SW6 4LY, (0171 371 9300). Runs some educational courses.
- National Institute of Adult Education, 21 De Montfort Street, Leicester LE1 7GE, (0116 2551451). Runs an information service for people who want to return to education.
- Open College of the Arts, Houndhill Lane, Worsborough, Barnsley, South Yorkshire S70 6TU, (01226 730495). Affiliated to the Open University, the college runs courses with local tutorial support on a wide range of subjects, from garden design to video production, music and painting. Ring its information line on 0891 168902 for a copy of its guide to courses.
- Open University, Central Enquiry Service, PO Box 200, Milton Keynes MK7 6YZ, (01908 274066). Contact it for details of courses and a prospectus.
- Townswomen's Guilds, Chamber of Commerce House, 75 Harborne Road, Edgbaston, Birmingham B15 3DA, (0121 456 3435). Has educational courses.
- University of the Third Age, Third Age Trust, 1 Stockwell Green, London SW9 9JF, (0171 737 2541). Can put you in touch with branches all over the country, and has information on many different educational courses.
- Woman Returners Network, 8 John Adam Street, London WC2N 6EZ, (0171 839 8188). Has a directory of places where women can take up further education or training for a job. It also advises and helps women who want to return to work.

Gifted children

- Gifted Children's Information Centre, Hampton Grange, 21 Hampton Lane, Solihull B91 2QJ, (0121 705 4547). Gives telephone counselling, arranges assessments for gifted children, also those who are dyslexic, left-handed or handicapped. It also has a legal section which can advise and help parents who are having problems with schools.
- National Association for Gifted Children, Park Campus, Boughton Green Road, Northampton, Northants NN2 7AL, (01604 792300). Counsels and helps the parents of gifted children, especially on educational matters via self-help groups throughout the country.

Home education

- Education Otherwise, PO Box 7420, London N9 9SG, (0891 518303). Gives help and advice via its helpline, above, if you want to educate your child yourself, at home. Send an A5 size SAE for information.
- World-Wide Education Service, St George's House, 14–17 Wells Street, London W1P 3FP, (0171 637 2644). Helps parents, often those who live abroad, who want to educate their children at home. It runs the WES Home

School which sends out National Curriculum teaching programmes, course books and gives tutorial help for children from the ages of 3 to 11. It is also possible to get material on single subjects.

Private education

- Department for Education, Mowden Hall, Darlington DL3 9BG, (01325 392157). Contact the department for details of assisted places at private schools.
- Gabbitas Educational Consultants Ltd, Broughton House, 6–8 Sackville Street, Piccadilly, London W1X 2BR, (0171 734 0161). Has a free school selection service for parents looking for a private school for their child. It also counsels parents seeking detailed guidance on a choice of school and will act as guardians for pupils from overseas.
- Independent Schools' Information Service (ISIS), 56 Buckingham Gate, London SW1E 6AG, (0171 630 8793). Can give information on independent schools throughout the country.

Projects for young people, youth service

- Air Training Corps, RAQF College Cranwell, Sleaford, Lincolnshire NG34 8HB, (01400 261201). The Air Training Corps takes boys and girls from 13 to 22 with an interest in flying and possibly the RAF, and gives them spare time training. It runs summer camps and flights at RAF stations here and overseas.
- Army Cadet Force Association, E Block, Duke of York's Headquarters, London SW3 4RR, (0171 730 9733). This organization takes boys and girls who are thinking of an army career or joining the Reserve, and gives them adventure training based on army lines. Among the subjects covered are first aid, rifle shooting and sport. There is an annual summer camp.
- British Association of the Experiment in International Living, Otesaga, West Malvern Road, Upper Wyche, Malvern, Worcs WR14 4EN, (01684 562577). Runs an au pair service sending British teenagers to Canada and the USA.
- Cirdan Trust, Fullbridge Wharf, Maldon, Essex CM9 7LE, (01621 851433). Offers training in sailing large vessels, mainly sailing barges, off the coast of England and the Continent.
- Duke of Edinburgh's Award, Gulliver House, Madeira Walk, Windsor, Berks SL4 1EU, (01753 810753). Has a programme of activities for young people, including those who are handicapped, for ages 14 to 25, culminating in bronze, silver and gold awards. The scheme is administered through youth clubs, schools and other similar organizations.
- Health Projects Abroad, PO Box 24, Bakewell, Derbyshire DE45 1ZW, (01629 64051). Organizes short-term health projects in mainly Third World

countries which take volunteers from the ages of 18 to 28. The work involved includes building new health centres, sanitation facilities, etc.

- Project Trust, The Hebridean Centre, Isle of Coll, Argyll, Scotland, PA78 6TB, (01879 23 0444). Sends young school-leavers between the ages of 17 and 19 abroad for a year to work as assistant teachers, social workers or on farms. The destinations are Africa, Australia, the Caribbean and Central and South America, the Middle East and Far East.
- Raleigh International, Raleigh House, 27 Parsons Green Lane, London SW6 4HZ, (0171 371 8585). Works with young people between the ages of 17 and 25, running eight international expeditions each year around the world, with the aim of developing their self-confidence and independence.
- Sail Training Association, 2a The Hard, Portsmouth, Hants PO1 3PT, (01705 832055). Takes young people between the ages of 16 and 24 on two-week adventure trips aboard two sailing ships. It also takes part in the Tall Ships Race each year.
- Sea Cadet Corps, 202 Lambeth Road, London SE1 7JF, (0171 928 8978). This organization gives spare-time sea training to boys and girls from 12 to 18, some of whom go on to join the Navy. Apart from subjects like meteorology and boatwork, they do rifle shooting and other sports. Also runs summer camps and training courses on Navy ships.
- Sea Ranger Association, HQTS Lord Amory, Dollar Bay, 631 Manchester Road, London E14 9NU, (0171 987 1757). Gives nautical training to girls and organizes sports activities too. Takes part in the Duke of Edinburgh's Award scheme.
- The Daneford Education Trust, 18 Cheverell House, Pritchards Road, London E2 9BN, (0171 729 1928). Sends students on teaching projects abroad, mainly in Third World countries. It has an advice line on 0171 739 4690.
- Trident Trust, 14b St Cross Street, Saffron Court, London EC1N 8XA, (0171 242 1616). Organizes community projects and work experience for young people aged 14 to 18, and personal development courses to help them decide on a career.
- Young Enterprise, Ewert Place, Summertown, Oxford OX2 7BZ, (01865 311180). Gives business experience to teenage boys and girls between the ages of 15 and 19 by helping them set up and manage model companies on their own, with business advisers on hand to help.
- Young Explorers' Trust, c/o Royal Geographical Society, 1 Kensington Gore, London SW7 2AR, (01623 861027). This organization gives advice and encouragement to groups or single young people, including those who are disadvantaged or disabled, who are planning expeditions to remote places either in the British Isles or abroad.

Sick children

- National Association for the Education of Sick Children, 18 Victoria Park Square, London E2 9PF, (0181 980 8523). This organization has a national directory listing what provision is made by Local Education Authorities and hospitals for the education of sick children. It will also give advice and help to parents who are having problems over educating a sick child.

See also Children and Disabled sections (*pages 218, 66*).

Special educational needs

- Bridges, New Street, Ross-on-Wye, Herefordshire HR9 7DA, (01594 834120). A pressure group acting on behalf of people with learning disabilities. It can give advice and information and put you in touch with local groups.
- British Dyslexia Association, 98 London Road, Reading, Berks RG1 5AU, (01734 668271). Gives out general information on dyslexia. Has a useful information pack, please enclose a 38p SAE.
- Brothers of Charity Services, Lisieux Hall, Whittle-le-Woods, Chorley, Lancs PR6 7DX, (01257 266311). A Catholic organization which helps people with learning problems to lead as normal a life as possible. Has residential and day centres and will help to organize a learning programme for those who have difficulties in education. It also gives out information on what services are available.
- Camphill Village Trust Ltd, Gawaine House, 56 Welham Road, Malton, North Yorks YO17 9DP, (01653 697105). Runs a number of communities for adults which also cater for people with learning difficulties.
- Citizen Advocacy Alliance, 6 Lind Road, Surrey SM1 4PJ, (0181 643 7111). Working in the south-west London area, the Alliance provides mentors for people with a learning disability, helping them to improve their quality of life. It will also represent their rights and interests where necessary.
- Dyslexia Institute Ltd, 133 Gresham Road, Staines, Middx TW18 2AJ, (01784 463851).
- Helps and advises the parents of dyslexic children. It also has teaching and assessment centres throughout the country.
- Haringey Association for Independent Living Ltd, 732 Lordship Lane, Wood Green, London N22 5JN, (0181 888 9022). Works in north London, giving help and advice to people with learning problems and their families with a round-the-clock care service. It also runs some permanent residential accommodation.

- Helen Arkell Dyslexic Centre, Frensham, Farnham, Surrey GU10 3BW, (01252 792400). Gives help to dyslexic children and their parents with remedial education, speech and language therapy. The initial consultation is free.
- National Association for Special Educational Needs, Natham House, 4/5 Amber Business Village, Amber Close, Amington, Tamworth B77 4RP, (0182 731 1500). Has a parents' forum to discuss the development of children with special educational needs.
- National Council for Special Education, 1 Wood Street, Stratford-upon-Avon, Warwickshire CV37 6JE, (01789 205332). This council has branches all over the country looking after the education and welfare of children and young people with any kind of special educational need.
- Network '81, 1–7 Woodfield Terrace, Stansted, Essex CM24 8AJ, (01279 647415). Supports and counsels parents of children with special educational needs and advises them of their rights.
- One-to-One, 404 Camden Road, London N7 0SJ, (0171 700 5574). Runs a personal service in hospitals and in the community, supporting people with learning problems on a one-to-one basis.
- Paget Gorman Society, 3 Gypsy Lane, Headington, Oxford OX3 7PT, (01865 61908). Helps the parents of children who have difficulty in communicating, using a special signed speech system.
- Parents in Partnership, Unit 2, 70 South Lambeth Road, London SW8 1RL, (0171 735 7735). Gives support, information and advice to parents of children with special educational needs. It can put you in touch with your local self-help group.
- Rathbone Society, 77 Whitworth Street, Manchester M1 6EZ, (0161 236 5358). Has an advice line for parents of children with learning difficulties and gives help to grown-ups with the same problems, helping them via training, employment and residential homes.
- Ravenswood Foundation, Broadway House, 80–82 The Broadway, Stanmore, Middx HA7 4HB, (0181 954 4555). Has residential centres both in Berkshire and in London, caring for and educating people with learning problems and their families.
- United Response, 162–164 Upper Richmond Road, London SW15 2SL, (0181 780 9686). Supports and helps people with learning problems or mental health difficulties. It has residential homes and day centres throughout the country and an information service.

State schools

- ACE, Advisory Centre for Education Ltd, 1b Aberdeen Studios, 22 Highbury Grove, London N5 2DQ, (0171 354 8321). Gives free and independent advice to parents of children in state schools. Will advise in a dispute with a child's school or education authority and answer questions about education. It also has leaflets and books.

- National Confederation of Parent Teacher Associations, 2 Ebbsfleet Industrial Estate, Stonebridge Road, Gravesend, Kent DA11 9DZ, (01474 560618). Gives advice to parents by letter or telephone on anything to do with the co-operation of parents and schoolteachers.

University

- Department for Education, PO Box 2193, London WE15 2EU, (0171 925 5000). Has a free booklet on student grants and loans.
- Educational Grants Advisory Service, Family Welfare Association, 36 Goldhawk Road, London W12 8DH, (0181 742 9209). Provides advice on grants and publishes a guide *Money to Study*.
- National Union of Students, 461 Holloway Road, London N7 6LJ, (0171 272 8900). Has information on all aspects of being a student.
- Universities and Colleges Admissions Service, UCAS, PO Box 28, Cheltenham, Glos. G150 3SA, (01242 227788). The organization to get in touch with over university admission. It also gives advice to mature students.

9

EMPLOYMENT

Gone are the days when you could leave school, join a firm and expect to be there until you retired. The world of employment and work has changed out of all recognition with the dawn of the technological age. Most of us can expect to be made redundant at some point in our working lives and can be expected to retrain in order to find other work. However, some things do not change – presenting yourself well when looking for a job and doing the best job you can when you have a job, are as important now as they ever were.

APPLYING FOR A JOB

Be business-like, be brief, do not sound desperate and be enthusiastic – those are the important things to bear in mind when applying for a job. Remember that you are your own public relations officer, the way you sell yourself is vital to success.

The letter

- Always type letters of application (unless you have been specifically instructed not to), even if you have to get a friend to do it for you.
- Make sure your application matches the description of the job, do not stray off the subject.
- Keep it short. Make sure that it does not go over more than one sheet of paper. Do it in draft, then see how much you can trim in the way of excess wordage and florid phrasing.
- Attach a CV. Instead of putting all the information about your past career in the letter itself, enclose your CV on a separate sheet (do not forget to put your name and address on the CV in case it becomes detached from the letter).
- State which job you are applying for. Many companies have multi-advertisements at any one time.
- Say where you heard about it. If you are replying to an advertisement, refer to the ad, the publication and the date.
- Say why you are interested in the job.

- Explain briefly why you are qualified to do the work. Say what is going to single you out from all the rest and make you worth interviewing.
- Do not lie about what you have done or can do, you will almost certainly be caught out.
- End on an up-beat note, saying that you are looking forward to hearing from them. Sign it yours faithfully.
- Check your spelling (if you use a computer run a spell-check through it).
- Read it out loud to see if it sounds right.

If you are not replying to an advertisement but writing 'cold':

- Write to a specific person, if possible (ask the switchboard operator).
- Ask if he will consider you for a job.
- Give brief reasons why he should employ you.
- Ask for an interview or a few minutes of his time.

Preparing your CV

It goes without saying that a CV should always be typed, even if you are forced for some reason to send a hand-written letter with it. Ideally, it should take no more than one sheet of paper, unless you have an impressive list of qualifications. Keep it short and snappy – it makes you look more efficient. A CV usually starts at the present time and works backwards to your school days. If you are middle-aged and your school record was not very impressive, there is no reason to include it. If you are in your twenties, however, you will need it. There are many books on how to write a CV. If you find it difficult, borrow one from the library. The CV should give:

- Your name.
- Your date of birth.
- Your age.
- Your home address.
- Your telephone number.
- Education and exams passed.
- Any academic qualifications or technical training.
- All the jobs that you have held to date – unless you are middle-aged, in which case some of the earlier ones could be dropped.
- If you have some consuming spare-time interest or hobby – if you are a member of the Territorial Army, work for charity or are a first-class golfer, then it is worth mentioning.
- Your qualifications.
- Your work experience in reverse order, starting with your last job.
- Other achievements that are work-related.
- Ability to drive and whether you have your own transport.

- Special skills or languages.
- Significant leisure interests.
- The salary and benefits you last received.
- Names of two referees.

The interview

Remember, if you have been called for an interview then you have a good chance of getting the job – be positive. Remember, too, that the interviewer is on your side – you want the job, he wants to fill it. Be yourself; do not try and put on a false personality or accent, it simply will not work. But do look bright, keen and eager. Rehearse the interview beforehand in your mind. Be prepared to answer questions like 'Why do you want to work here?' and 'What makes you think you are right for the job?' or 'What have been your greatest accomplishments?'

Do your homework before going for an interview – find out all you can about the firm. The fact that you know it is opening a new branch in Huddersfield shows that you are au fait with what is going on. Many larger companies have prospecti that they issue to shareholders. You could ring up and ask for one. Know what the company does, who its main customers are and who its main competitors are. Is your prospective firm the off-shoot of a bigger organization? If so, find out about that too.

Arrive in good time for the interview. To be safe, catch an earlier train or bus. It is better to kick your heels in the waiting room for a while than turn up flustered and breathless. Look clean and tidy – check your fingernails and polish your shoes. These are small details but ones that interviewers will notice. If you have long hair, tie it back. Recent research shows that people wearing spectacles are taken more seriously. If you are desperate for a job that demands that you look sober and industrious, it might pay to invest in a cheap off-the-peg pair, especially if you are female. It works in other areas too – there was a case recently of a 21-year-old hairdresser who wanted to lease some premises and was thought by the landlords to be 'too young and silly'. Next time she saw somewhere to rent, she conducted negotiations wearing a long skirt, spectacles and carrying a briefcase – she got her shop and a grant from a training and enterprise council!

Do yourself justice but do not exaggerate your skills, it could back-fire.

If you are asked if you have any questions, do not query hours of work or holidays – you can find that out elsewhere, and it gives a bad impression. Instead ask positive things like 'When would you want me to start?'

IN WORK

Having landed the job and mastered it, you need to keep your eye on the next rung of the ladder.

How to improve your prospects of promotion

- Take your job seriously, even if it is a lowly one. If you are asked to make tea, make it and serve it with care, do not slam the cup down in front of people.
- Believe in yourself and other people will believe in you.
- Develop your own career. Sign on for all the training courses you can get, consider going to adult education college to improve your skills. Not only will you keep up to date with your job but you may well make useful contacts who could be of help if you find yourself job-hunting.
- Be versatile and willing, work hard at your own job and help others in theirs if you are asked.
- Dress seriously for the job, if you are in an office, casual clothes will not make you promotion material.
- Control your work flow, be organized and efficient and deliver on time.
- Learn to like and understand your bosses, be aware of the pressures they are facing.
- Be confident, assert yourself without being overbearing. Mice never get anywhere.
- Be ready to grab any opportunity that is going. Do not be put off by lack of qualifications. In the work place it is enthusiasm and energy that counts.
- Do not be cynical and negative, be positive, even on bad days. Never bad-mouth your boss.

PROBLEMS AT WORK

Sexual harassment

Sexual harassment implies unwelcome physical attention of some kind or other, often the boss – male or female – forcing their attentions on a junior colleague. It is believed that claims for sexual harassment may rocket in this country following the European Court of Justice's decision to lift the ceiling of £11,000 for pay-outs in sexual discrimination cases. Now for the first time men are complaining about it too.

In this country sexual harassment comes under the heading of sex discrimination, and cases have been rising steadily. Many more people put up with harassment because they are too scared of repercussions to speak out. The price is high in terms of the trauma you may go through – you may be branded a trouble-maker, there may be unwelcome publicity, you may even lose your job – but most people who have done it feel that in the long run it was worth it.

What to do if you feel you are being harassed

- Keep a diary, of what has gone on and when, and whether there were any witnesses.
- Complain to the perpetrator formally in writing and keep a copy, so that you have a record.
- If there is someone trustworthy in your work place, confide in that person. You may need the person to give evidence.
- Go to the Equal Opportunities Commission (*see page 314*) or to your local Law Centre (the Citizens' Advice Bureau can tell you where it is). Tell them what is happening and get their advice.
- If you decide to take the case to an industrial tribunal, you must apply within three months of the last incident. You will be given a form to fill in and send to the person who has been harassing you.

Sexual correctness in the office

If you want to be squeaky clean:

- Avoid personal comments. Even a compliment can be misinterpreted. The impression you intend to give may not be the one that the recipient perceives.
- Do not call anyone darling or dear or other similar names.
- Do not tell anecdotes or jokes of a sexual nature. Teasing, ribbing, cracking of semi-rude jokes are not advisable.
- Do not touch fellow employees. Physical contact can be wrongly interpreted. A friendly hand on a shoulder can be misconstrued even if the recipient is of the same sex.
- Avoid conspiratory winks and nods.
- Socialize as little as possible outside the office unless you are with your partner. Even a friendly invitation to 'come for a drink' after work to a subordinate can be interpreted as a command – and that can be interpreted as harassment.

In short, behave as if you are being monitored by a TV camera and respect other people's 'personal' space.

Sexual discrimination

Under the Sexual Discrimination Acts of 1975 and 1986, it is now unlawful for an employer to treat anyone, on grounds of sex, less favourably than a person of the opposite sex is, or would be, treated in the same circumstances. In employment, or any advertisement related to employment, it is also unlawful to discriminate against anyone because they are married.

What is sexual discrimination?

There are two kinds of sexual discrimination. Direct discrimination means treating a woman less favourably than a man because she is a woman or vice versa. Indirect discrimination is when conditions are applied to everyone which favour one sex more than the other, for example, an advertisement that insists on candidates being more than 6ft tall, which will rule most women out. Your employers may not discriminate against you because of your sex either in their recruitment of you or their treatment of you. The ruling also holds for promotion or training opportunities. They are no longer allowed to label jobs 'for men' or 'for women' or for 'single people only'. The only exception is if the person's sex is a 'genuine occupational qualification' such as a part in a film or play. If you feel you are being discriminated against in this way, contact the Equal Opportunities Commission (*see page 314*).

OFFICE STRESS

British workers suffer more stress-related illnesses than any of our European counterparts – a recent survey showed that 60 per cent of British workers complain of stress compared with a European average of 54 per cent.

Research shows that one in five of us has taken time off work due to work worries, and in 1994 a former social worker became the first person to successfully sue his employers for ill-health caused by overwork. A survey found that most office staff felt unappreciated, had little confidence in their superiors and felt insecure in their jobs.

Work stress can cause headaches, long-term tiredness, backache and stomach pains as well as the more obvious depression and anxiety. Now it is being linked by some physicians with more serious things such as asthma, skin conditions like eczema and psoriasis and even diabetes.

Are you suffering from work stress?

Among the first signs are:
- Finding the simplest things an effort.
- Losing your sense of proportion – the smallest problems become something you cannot surmount.
- Having feelings of panic, and that you cannot cope.
- Losing your normal sense of humour.
- Sleeping badly, waking early.

According to doctors, these things may lead to tangible physical changes such as high blood pressure and even an alteration of cholesterol levels in the blood.

How to survive stress at work

- Keep your skills up-to-date, so that you can be on top of things. Be aware of

what is going on in new technology. It will also make you more marketable if
you find yourself having to look for a new job.

- Realize that these days a job is no longer for life. Be aware of the fact that in a
few years' time you may need to re-think your career.
- Take regular exercise – swimming, running, playing tennis, walking – you do
not have to work out in a gym. Do not push yourself too far. It is now
recognized that physical exercise does help to relieve stress.
- Have outside interests, something that gives you another kind of identity, as an
artist, musician, writer, gardener, dog breeder – anything that is a contrast to
what you do during the day.
- If you have a partner, think in terms of your joint careers. Might it be better for
one of you to push ahead a career while the other one marks time, taking on a
more domestic role?
- Discuss your work problems with someone you trust. Talking things through
can often help solve problems. Make sure you pick someone sympathetic –
talking to someone who does not want to hear will make your stress even
worse.
- Leave your work problems behind you when you go home. Do not brood. Write
down the way you feel on paper, then destroy it.
- After a hard day at the office or factory or on the road give yourself time and
space to relax, do not just flop into bed, exhausted.

Try to set aside 20 minutes a day to really unwind, listen to music, lose yourself in
a book or even try meditating. Try relaxation techniques: lie down, relax each part
of your body in turn, starting with your feet. Then visualize your problems as a
series of layers, imagine yourself rising up through them to the surface again.
See also **States of mind,** *page 39.*

CHANGING YOUR JOB

If you decide to change your job, you will need to plan carefully. The best way to
leave is when you have another job lined up. If you leave your employment
without other work in prospect you cannot rely on unemployment pay as you may
be considered to have made yourself deliberately out of work. Ask yourself:

- Why do I want to leave? It could be a career move or it could be that you are
bored in your present employment. Work out your motives, be honest with
yourself.
- Are there jobs available in my field? Take a look at advertisements in the
papers and ask employment agencies.
- Can I use my skills elsewhere? It could be that your skills are so narrow that
they are only of use to your present employer. In that case you need to retrain.

- Can I stand a period of unemployment?
- Am I prepared to move? You might find you have to relocate.
- Are my ideas on pay levels realistic?
- How will my company pension be affected?

LOSING YOUR JOB

Everyone these days is frightened of losing their jobs – with good reason. Redundancy can happen now to anyone (I've been made redundant three times) and many of us face the sack. Losing your job at a time of high unemployment is a terrifying leap into the unknown and, if you have people who depend on you, then things seem even worse.

If you are being made redundant you are joining the largest club in Great Britain, with members of all ages. At one time a career in a bank was considered safe but not anymore. This area, too, is subject to job cuts. Other safe havens like the civil service, local authorities and big companies like British Telecom are all shedding staff too. No longer can you join a large company with the thought that you will progress up the ladder and have a job for life. The paternalistic boss is a thing of the past. Short-term contracts are more likely in the future. So we must keep flexible and take charge of our own careers.

If you suspect you are going to lose your job.

- Never leave of your own accord, however hard you are being pushed or however unpleasant life is made for you. Hang on in there, being made redundant brings certain special benefits with it.
- Find the contract you signed, the letter you got when you were first employed. You may find you are entitled to something you had forgotten about.
- Take advantage now of any company benefits like private health care – get a free check-up while you can.
- Sharpen up your skills. If you can go on a computer course at the company's expense, do so, hastily. Or find out how to work one via other employees.
- Survey the job market, get the trade magazines, take note of what is going in your field and start planning a CV and letters.
- Check out your finances. Do not take on any large loans, move house or buy a new car – put everything on hold.
- If the company talks about early retirement, do not volunteer unless you have another job to go to. It sounds seductive, but enforced unemployment at a relatively young age is demoralizing. Once the heady experience of not having to get up in the morning has worn off, you feel as if you are on the scrap heap.

- Do not volunteer to go unless the company comes up with a good financial package, otherwise you may lose money.

Redundancy – your rights

If you have worked for the same employer for two years or more, you should be eligible for a set redundancy payment on a sliding scale according to your salary and the number of years you have worked. If your employer cannot make redundancy payments – if the firm has gone into liquidation – then the state will pay you instead, up to a maximum sum for each week.

Leaving the firm

- Do not shout at your almost former boss or say anything you may regret – you may meet up with him again in another work-place some day.
- Take the news with as much dignity as you can muster and walk away. Remember that the person who is firing you, if he is half human, will be feeling pretty bad too. I once heard of a personnel manager who was given the task of making twenty people redundant, then was called in and fired by his boss.
- Do not flounce off; serve out your period of notice, otherwise you might lose benefits.
- Find out what you are entitled to. If the business has been taken over and you now have a new owner, your rights may not be the same as they were. Check it out with your union or with a solicitor.
- Bargain for anything that might be of use – if you are being made redundant and have a company car, they may let you go on using it for a while or sell it to you at a knock-down price. The same thing goes for a computer if the office is selling up.
- Get these promises in writing – out of sheer embarrassment your boss may murmur things about 'seeing you right' or 'helping you out' – get the facts from him right away.
- Ask for time off. If you have worked for the company for more than two years and it is making you redundant, then you should be given paid time off to look for other jobs and go for interviews.
- Check out your holiday entitlements, either take the time or money in lieu. Your employer should pay you for any annual holiday you are owed.
- If you are offered another job in the company and refuse it, you may be penalized from the point of view of benefits. But you are usually allowed a month to try it out without that happening. Check your situation with your trade union or the personnel department.
- If you are made redundant and manage to get another job right away, try to get your new employer to wait until your period of notice has been worked out, or

you may lose your redundancy benefits. Otherwise see if your existing firm will agree to let you go without your redundancy rights being affected.

- If you are given a lump sum, get financial advice – any large amounts of money you get could be taxed. The Inland Revenue is looking at the technical aspects of redundancy and finding more and more pretexts to charge tax. Take advice before you pay off your mortgage or buy a car for cash with the money. You may need it as a salary to tide you over until you get the next job, or to invest in starting a new business.

You will probably be eligible for a rebate from the Income Tax authorities. Get its IR41 leaflet *Income Tax and the Unemployed* from your local Tax Office. The money will usually take months to come through, but if you are in a desperate situation you may be able to get it more quickly.

Coping

Losing a job can affect people like a death in the family. There is a numbness, you cannot believe what has happened and you need time for the implications to sink in. And, as with a death, you will probably have to go through a period of adjustment. Expect to feel low – it will take a while to recover your bounce. You may feel hurt and bitter. Your self-esteem takes a knock and suddenly you have no status. You need to let go – your old job has gone and you have to put it behind you, not mull over it. Find someone sympathetic to talk to. Consider counselling if things are really bad. Ask your doctor what is available, although you may have to pay. Otherwise contact the British Association for Counselling for addresses (*see page 136*).

If your partner is sacked or made redundant

In some ways it can be harder for you as you cannot take direct action. You may feel shocked, but it is vital to keep a calm exterior.

- Support your partner and work out a plan together.
- Do not keep harking back to the past. What is done is done.
- Sort out your finances first, working out what you have to live on.
- Listen, let him talk, give him your full attention, do not fiddle or do other things at the same time.
- Be upbeat and positive even if you are feeling sick inside.
- Do not blame him even if you suspect it is his fault.
- Be loving. Do not be upset if he does not want to respond in a sexual manner, make do with cuddles instead.
- Be encouraging.
- Be constructive, try to understand what he is feeling.
- Above all, keep the lines of communication open, talk things over.

- Show him that there is a life after employment.
- Be tolerant if he seems snappy and down. Gently but firmly make it clear that you are not going to be used as a human punch-bag.
- Give him space, but look for warning signs of clinical depression and, if necessary, get help.
- Remember that men in particular feel that they are on the scrap-yard if they lose their jobs. Women have fewer problems because they usually have another role as a mother, daughter, sister, and are usually better at talking through their problems
- Find someone trustworthy and discreet to 'unload' your own feelings onto.
- Remember you are in this together.

YOUR NEW LIFE STARTS HERE

For the time being think of yourself as the managing director of a one-person firm.
- Do not take a holiday if your mind is in turmoil – think about what you are going to do first or you will not enjoy it.
- Do not waste mental energy on bitterness. Negative thoughts are a waste of precious time.
- Do sort out your finances. List all the things you own outright – the car perhaps, which you can sell if you need to. Go through your outgoings – household help, insurance and savings, mortgage, rates – putting them into two columns, one for essential things and one for things you could, at a pinch, do without. Look through your bank statements to see what standing orders and direct debits you have and decide which of them you should keep.
- Do not be tempted to use your credit cards lavishly on the principle that something will turn up and you will be able to pay them off – it may not happen for some time.
- Do not be upset if you cannot shoulder the burden on your own, share your fears with your partner, your family or close friends
- Take stock: do you want a change of direction? Do you want to move to another part of the country? Do you want to retrain? Involve your partner and family from the start in your future plans.
- Look at what you have accomplished in life and feel proud of it.
- Look at your spare-time interests – could you capitalize on one of those as a living?
- Structure your days even if your appointments list only involves going out for the papers and walking the dog. Get up in the morning, do not slop around in a dressing gown or old track suit, it will make you feel unemployed.

- Be business-like. Make a work-area in your house. Keep a diary – make a note of firms who tell you to apply again later.
- Have a filing system even if it is only for rejection letters, use cardboard boxes or plastic bags. Make brief notes of each interview, with names and how it went; you might want to refer to it again.
- Set targets for yourself tackling jobs and interests you never had time for before.
- Work out your aggression in exercise – cycle, swim or dig the garden.
- Network – put yourself about, go to the pubs where people in your field drink at lunch time etc.
- Learn something: update your job skills and your hobby skills. Go to the library and read, sign on for the Open University – it does specialist courses now as well as degrees.
- Consider helping others. Voluntary work can heal. Aiding people who are in a worse situation than you are can put your own problems into perspective.

What to do next

If you were made redundant, the Department of Employment has a free advice helpline for you on 0800 848489. Go to the Jobcentre as soon as you can and sign on for your entitlement to unemployment benefit. You are entitled to receive unemployment pay for up to a year and claims are not always backdated. Take with you your P45, details of mortgage payments, savings, your dependants and any other income in the family, everything that might be relevant. This will save you having to make a return visit.

A Jobseekers Allowance is planned to replace Unemployment Benefit and Income Support for unemployed people. If you are what is called 'non-employed' or not available for work, you will continue to get income support as before. To get the Jobseekers Allowance you will have to prove you are available for, capable of and actively seeking work. Your partner can be working up to 24 hours a week before your entitlement to this allowance is lost. There is also a Back to Work Bonus Scheme in the offing. Ask your local Benefits office for further details.

The sooner you apply for benefits the better, as housing benefit in particular is a notoriously slow procedure, so start it before you have trouble with the mortgage company. Signing on also means that your National Insurance contributions, which you need to keep up for your state pension, will be paid for you.

If you are planning to work for yourself in future the DSS will be able to tell you about retraining and enterprise schemes to help you. It will tell you what benefits you can claim for and how to get them. The DSS Helpline is on 0800 666555. Check out at your local library to see what concessions are available to you as an 'unemployed person'. There may be free entry to a community sports centre, for instance, or swimming pool.

Working while on unemployment pay

You are allowed to do a certain amount of work without having to sign off and start again. Check with your Jobcentre for the latest situation. However, you will not get unemployment benefit over this period.

GETTING BACK TO WORK

If you have been made redundant in middle age, it seems at first that it will be more difficult to survive in the job market. Employers tend to have doubts about older workers – will they take to new technology or retrain easily, are they fit? How long will they want to work? But happily things are changing:

- The upper age limit for the Department of the Employment's Training for Work Programme has been raised from 59 to 63.
- Jobcentres have been instructed to resist advertisements with a bar on age. They have also been told to send people for interviews who match all requirements apart from their age.
- In May 1994 an industrial tribunal accepted redundancy on the grounds of age as unfair dismissal, which has changed the attitude of many employers.
- There is no such thing as state retirement age. You can collect your state pension and continue to work for as long as you like if you can find a job.

Job-hunting if you are older

- Take stock of yourself. Sum up your strengths and weaknesses.
- Work out your financial needs – could you manage on a smaller salary?
- Consider what motivates you and what your interests are. Then see if there are any gaps in your skills and see how you can fill the gaps. Enquire at your local Jobcentre, get details of training schemes.
- Do not mention your age unless you are specifically asked for it.
- Appear flexible on hours and consider doing shifts, if necessary.
- Do not underestimate your experience. Many of the skills you have developed in the workplace and outside are what employers are looking for. Do not just think about your former job, take into account spare-time activities and interests too – perhaps you are a good organizer, for instance.
- Do not be dismayed if the interviewer looks younger than you.
- At interviews keep your dignity, and do not launch into a diatribe against your previous employers.

- Your age gives you special qualities. Older people tend to be more reliable, more dedicated, with a more mature approach to the job. You are also likely to have a high degree of commitment.
- Research now shows that older people learn new skills just as readily, often more readily than young people. Show prospective employers that you are prepared to learn. Sign on for courses.

Professional help

There are many places you can go to for help. In some cases you have to pay for it, in other cases you do not.

- **Your local Jobcentre** should be your first stop. It should be able to offer you a variety of alternatives including a Job Review Service, guidance and back-to-work plans. Many run Job Search Seminars and Job Review workshops for those who have been out of work for at least three months – your fares will be paid to attend these. There may be Restart counselling after 6 months of unemployment. Others may have a Job Interview Guarantee system – work experience with an employer who guarantees to give you a job interview, but not necessarily a job at the end. This is confined to people who have been jobless for more than six months. Many Jobcentres also run job clubs – worth going to as a way of networking. Ask for a copy of its booklet called *Just the Job*.
- **Outplacement agencies** can come up with a structured programme to help you develop new job skills and a CV. But it will cost you.
- **Career counsellors** do tests which will highlight your aptitudes and abilities. The British Psychological Association can give you lists of accredited counsellors. Ask them to specify what their programme offers.
- **Employment agencies** do not charge you but the employer, so they are worth a try. Many of them specialize in, say, jobs in publishing or engineering. Look in trade journals in the library to find out where they are. Some of them offer temporary work – a good way of getting into a firm.
- **Your trade union or professional organization**, if you belong to one, may well be able to help you in your job hunt.
- **The government** now has a Career Development Loan scheme administered via the banks, which is intended to help people who want to retrain for a new job. For details ring the free helpline on 0800 585505.

Financial advisors

If you are given a lump sum on your redundancy, you may decide to get advice on how to invest it. Keep your money somewhere flexible for the time being while you sort things out. Before hiring anyone and, possibly, spending several thousand pounds check out:

- If the firm or advisor has a vested interest? Is he going to try to sell you life insurance?
- Is the firm a member of an accredited association? There used to be two called LAUTRO and FIMBRA. These organizations have now merged but the letters may still be on the firm's letterhead. If you are not sure, check with the Securities and Investment Board (*see* **Finance**, *page 405*).
- Should you get your employer to top up your pension to the statutory limit from your redundancy payment? They have to do that, not you. But remember your money will then be tied up until you retire.
- Should you pay off your mortgage? Bumping up your capital assets this way might penalize you for income support. Also tax relief on mortgages, although shrinking, would be lost if you start work again.
- Should you sell your endowment policies? There are companies that specialize in buying these but this should only be done if you need to raise cash as you will lose their full value.

Job-hunting consultancies

If you have lost your job and are pushing 50 and panicking, the advertisements in the paper may look tempting. Some say 'Trust in us, we have the inside information, we'll help you find a job'. Their claim that they can unlock a hidden job market is used as a carrot to tempt the unwary. You think you are paying the entrance fee to an Aladdin's cave of jobs. But they want your money up-front – something that even solicitors do not ask for. If you are over 50, view with deep suspicion any agency that assures you it will get you back in a job with ease. Some people end up wasting their redundancy money, paying £6000 for little more than a new CV. A real job consultant will help you with job ideas, taking a dispassionate view of your talents, often suggesting directions you have never thought of. He will point you in the right direction, but will not offer to retrain you, that is not part of his job.

All consultants, good and the bad, use psychometric tests – pencil and paper or computer-based questions – to assess you. But it takes a skilled counsellor to interpret them. One who knows what he or she is doing should be able to tell you whether you are suited to a particular vacancy and to give an opinion of your talents in the round.

How to find the right consultant

There are no formal qualifications for this work, no letters after anyone's name, so you need to be careful.

- Pick a firm that belongs to an official body like CDOA – Career Development and Outplacement Association. CDOA also has an official complaints procedure so you know that if things go wrong you should be able to have some redress.
- If it is not a member of CDOA, look at the general background of the firm. Has it been in business long?
- Ask for personal references.
- Ask for an initial chat to see exactly what it has to offer you.
- Be realistic. If you are middle-aged or more, if you have no particular skills or have been trained to do something that is no longer needed, then finding another job is going to be a long hard haul and you may need retraining.

STARTING YOUR OWN BUSINESS

The number of people working from home, many of them using high technology, has doubled in two years. The idea of working for yourself sounds very seductive, but needs careful thought.

How to set up a business

If you are thinking of running your own business there are a number of start-up schemes around at the moment. It is worthwhile contacting your local Training and Enterprise Council or Business Link, if there is one, to see if they can offer help. The Citizens' Advice Bureau (in your local Phone Book) can also be a good source of free help. Try too the Greater London Business Centre (phone them on 0800 222 999) which despite its name covers the whole of the UK and the Rural Development Commission (phone 01722 336255).

Your business name

You can use your own name as a business name without any problems. If you use a name that is not your own, the law demands you show the name and address of your business, both on the premises where you work and on your stationery. To check whether the name you want to use is already taken, contact Companies House on 01222 388588. Avoid names that sound like something official or connected with royalty or you may need the approval of the Secretary of State. Check with Regulations SI 1685/1981S1 and 1653/1982 from the Stationery Office (*see page 372*). A useful leaflet to read is *Notes for Guidance on Business Names and Business Ownership* from the Department of Trade.

Income tax

The Inland Revenue has some useful leaflets if you are planning to set up business by yourself:

- IR57 *Thinking of Working for Yourself?*
- IR28 *Starting in Business.*
- IR56 *Employed or self-employed?*

If you cannot get copies locally, contact the Inland Revenue in London (*see page 372*).

As soon as you work for yourself you count as self-employed and come under Schedule D which has some advantages as you can deduct certain expenses against your income. However, you may not qualify if:

- You are working as an outworker for a single supplier.
- You are solely answerable to one company for your work.
- If the company supplies some of the equipment you use.
- If you have borrowed money to invest in the business and some other person holds the collateral.
- If someone else is also responsible if you make a loss.

If in doubt, ask your local Tax Office.

What you can deduct

- Heating, lighting and cleaning expenses for your work space.
- The cost of raw materials including stationery.
- Business telephone calls (ask British Telecom for an itemized bill to help you sort them out).
- Postage.
- Subscriptions to professional or trade organizations.
- Subscriptions to trade magazines and newspapers.
- Payment to helpers.
- Advertising and publicity.
- Business travel expenses and hotels.
- Proportion of the running costs of your car.
- Interest on business loans or overdrafts.
- Business insurance.
- Repairs and maintenance to equipment or work premises.
- Depreciation on equipment.

You need to continue to pay National Insurance. Get leaflet NP18 or N127A if your income is going to be very small, from your local Social Security office.

Setting up a company

There is no advantage in setting up a company unless you are planning a large business that will expand. It costs money to set one up and someone has to be made company director, someone company secretary. You have to submit audited annual accounts to Companies House and you lose some tax advantages as you have to pay yourself a salary or a dividend and become in effect an employee.

Banks are no more likely – probably less likely – to lend an unknown company money than an individual person. If they do you will still have to provide collateral – probably your house – against a loan. The only advantage of having a company is that you, personally, cannot be made bankrupt. But if the company goes down, anything you have pledged against a loan will be taken from you. For more information on forming a company, contact the Companies House on 01222 388588.

A partnership

Partnerships should not be entered into lightly. If you take on a partner in a formal partnership then you are 'jointly and severally responsible'. This means that if either of you reneges, the other has to settle any of his or her debts, even if you did not know about them.

Borrowing money

Even if you are able to start out without any borrowed money, there may come the time when you have a cash-flow problem. This is the time to see your bank manager, who, if he feels you are a secure prospect, may offer you:

- **An overdraft** which is the most flexible way to borrow. You just take out what you need at a given time. The disadvantage is that the bank can call in the debt whenever it likes. Your overdraft will have a ceiling and if you want to go over it you will have to renegotiate with the bank.
- **A formal loan** is a more secure method of borrowing as a set sum of money will be lent to you over a set period and you pay it off at a fixed rate of interest over a year or more. However, you may be asked to guarantee it by taking out a second mortgage on your house or lodging share certificates with the bank. At the moment the government is operating a **Loan Guarantee Scheme** with banks to help small businesses – ask your bank about it. It is backed by the Department of Employment which guarantees 70 per cent of the total and helps small firms with a viable business plan to get finance after they have failed in their attempts to raise money elsewhere. It enables banks to lend up to £100,000 to new or existing businesses over two to seven years. It is reassuring to know that the Sock Shop and Waterstone's bookshops were both helped to get off the ground in this way. The Loan Guarantee Scheme is only available if you cannot get a conventional loan perhaps because you do not have any security to offer, or any track record. *See page 372* for a list of banks that are participating in the scheme.

Your business plan

Your bank will want to know all about your business and your plans for it, so draw up a business plan before you see the bank. giving the following details:
- A brief run-down on yourself and your business.
- The potential market for your product or service.
- A survey of the competition.
- A cash-flow forecast of what money will be coming in and what has to go out on materials, expenses and salaries.
- A budget for the year ahead.

Where else to get a loan

If your bank turns you down it is not the end of the world; there are other ways of borrowing money. First of all get the booklet *Finance without Debt* from the Department of Employment (*see page 373*) which is a guide to sources of venture capital. You might also qualify for help from a regional development commission or enterprise board – ask your local Citizens' Advice Bureau. Or a body like the Training and Enterprise Council might advise you, train you and pay you a small sum a week while you learn.
- **Moneylenders** should be avoided at all costs. If you are tempted by an advertisement in the paper, talk it over first with your solicitor.
- **Friends** If you decide to borrow from friends, you must get a proper agreement drawn up by a solicitor. How much interest are they expecting? Do they want any active involvement in your business? These are points to check out.
- **Hire purchase** can be a useful way of buying capital equipment you need. But be sure you can afford the monthly payments. If your equipment has a domestic angle to it – a sewing machine or a computer – you may find that there are interest-free credit deals going with major stores.
- **Credit cards** can also be used to buy large items. Check the actual interest you will pay and compare it with any possible hire-purchase deals.

Trade marks and patents

If you want to make a particular symbol your own, then you might need to register it as a Trade Mark or a Service Mark, giving you sole right to use it. Ask for booklets *Applying for a Trade Mark* and *Applying for the Registration of a Service Mark* from the Trade Marks Registry (0171 438 4700) which sets out what you need to do and how much you have to pay. If you have an idea that needs patenting, you will need a professional patent agent. Get in touch with the Chartered Institute of Patent Agents (0171 405 9450).

Working from home

Before the Industrial Revolution almost everyone worked from home, hence the term 'cottage industry'. Now, at the end of the millenium, we are tending to revert to this idea either through redundancy or by the nature of our work, especially if it involves computers. Many large firms are 'down-sizing' by encouraging workers to take their work and do it from home. But think it over before you decide

The advantages

- There is no commuting.
- You have more flexible hours.
- You do not have to wear special clothes, you can stay in a track suit and slippers all day, if you choose.
- If you are running your own business, you have no rent to pay.

The disadvantages

- The risk of constant interruption. People think that because you are at home you are not working and may phone or call.
- A feeling of isolation.
- There is no one to encourage or motivate you. You have to do it yourself.

Do not attempt to work from home if you

- Tend to make most of your friends at work.
- Need to bounce ideas off people.
- Hate being alone.
- Are easily bored.
- Lack staying power.
- Cannot make a separate work space for yourself, however small; otherwise you will live in your 'office'.
- Need planning permission for your work.

Do I need planning permission?

You may need planning permission in the following cases. Check out with your local Planning Department first.

- If you need to add a room or a workshop or convert your garage in some structural way.
- If you are obviously changing the use of the premises – starting a restaurant or a cattery.
- If you are changing the structure of the house – turning it into a hotel, for instance.
- If you are planning to make or repair things in a very large and noticeable way.
- If you plan to sell things from your house on a day-to-day basis or give some sort of service. You need to get permission for constant visitors and car

parking. Occasional selling parties, such as Tupperware, do not count. But a hairdressing or beauty salon would need permission.

- If you are going to use noisy machines or produce industrial odours.
- If you need to display a large permanent sign of any kind. A 'no vacancies' board in the window would not count.
- If you live in a built-up area or estate and your work would involve activities that do not fit in – lorries arriving with supplies for instance.

Any of the activities above could be construed as a 'change of use' of the premises. You should not need planning permission if:

- You are running a business from home rather than producing something, if the work is telephone based or uses a computer.
- If you still live at home and the house still looks like a residential building.
- If most of the house is residential with just one room as a workroom or office.
- If you do not use more than a reasonable number of machines. One or two computers or sewing machines would be fine. Five or more might bring in the planners.
- If your business callers are sporadic.

Insurance: points to watch

You must tell your insurance company that you are running a business from home or your policy could be declared invalid if, say, there was a fire. You need public liability insurance if people are coming to your home on business or if you employ someone. Otherwise if they fall or injure themselves you could be liable. You need special insurance against theft if you are storing other people's possessions in your house, perhaps jewellery that is being repaired. You need to tell your car insurers if you are delivering or collecting things in any quantity. If you plan to employ people in your home, then you need to know about the Employers' Liability (Compulsory Insurance) Act. Contact the Health and Safety Executive (0171 243 6000) for details.

The best way to work at home

- Plan your day, give it some structure.
- Find out when you are at your working best and plan your work schedule around this time.
- Deal firmly with interruptions. Take your work seriously then others will do the same. This applies especially to your family.
- Give yourself coffee breaks, especially if you are working at a computer. It has been found that two hours at one stretch is as much as the average person can take, staring at a screen.

- Build in social breaks, meet someone for lunch once a week, go out in the evening to the cinema to meet people and to eat out.
- Let off steam by doing some kind of activity – walking, swimming or cycling.
- Do not take your job to bed with you, learn to switch off when evening comes.
- Invest in wall charts, notebooks, paraphernalia that will make you feel as though you are in a 'real' office or workshop.
- Do not finish a job completely at the end of the day, leave one thing to be done. That will get you going in the morning.

NB This book was written from home.

EMPLOYMENT: HELP DIRECTORY

Agencies specializing in helping older people

- Age Works, South Bank Techno Park, 9290 London Road, London SE1 6LN, (0171 717 1559). Specializes in finding employment for the over 40s.
- Careers Continued, 14 Trinity Square, London EC3N 4AA, (0171 680 0033).
- City Women's Network, PO Box 353, Uxbridge, Middx UB10 0UN, (0181 569 2351). A networking organization for senior executive women.
- Forties People, 11–13 Dowgate Hill, London EC4R 2ST, (0171 329 4044).
- Recruit Plc, Recruit House, 45–47 High Street, Hemel Hempstead, Hertfordshire HP1 3AG, (01442 233550).
- Third Age Challenge Trust, Anglia House, 115 Commercial Road, Swindon SN1 5PL, (01793 533370). Helps set up work and training projects for older workers.

Careers for women

Blackburn House Centre for Women, Hope Street, Liverpool L1 9JB, (0151 709 4356). Gives training courses in new technology, electronics, telecommunications.

- National Women's Register, 3a Vulcan House, Vulcan Road North, Norwich NR6 6AQ, (01603 406767). A national organization that helps women who want to develop their own particular talents, also a support and contact group.
- Society of Women Writers and Journalists, 110 Whitehall Road, London E4 6DW, (0181 529 0886). Fee-paying membership. Upholds standards of women writers and offers advice.

- Women and Manual Trades, 52–54 Featherstone Street, London EC1Y 8RT, (0171 251 9192). A useful source for any woman who wants to train for, or work in, what are called the manual trades, many of which are traditionally male-dominated. It gives help and advice to enquirers and sends out a newsletter.
- Women in Management, 64 Marryat Road, London SW19 5BN, (0181 944 6332). Runs training and development workshops for women who are in, or are aiming to be in, management.
- Women in Medicine, 21 Wallingford Avenue, London W10 6QA, (0181 960 7446). Has a useful leaflet *Planning and Pitfalls: Careers for Women in Medicine* aimed at medical students in their third year.
- Women into Information Technology Foundation Ltd, Concept 2000, 250 Farnborough Road, Farnborough, Hants GU14 7LU, (01252 528329). Gives help and advice to women who are planning to make a career in information technology.
- Women's Engineering Society, Imperial College of Science and Technology, Dept of Civil Engineering, Imperial College Road, London SW7 2BU, (0171 594 6025). Promotes the education, training and practice of engineering among women, ensuring that the voices of women engineers are heard. Offers bursaries.
- Women's Farm and Garden Association, 175 Gloucester Street, Cirencester, Glos GL7 2DP, (01285 658339). Advises and helps women and girls who want to make a career in agriculture or horticulture.
- Women's Media Resource Project, 89a Kingsland High Street, London E8 2PB, (0171 254 6536). Helps women who want to make a career in sound engineering, audio-visual and recording techniques, with introductory courses in the subject. Send SAE for information.
- Women's National Commission, Level 4, Caxton House, Tothill Street, London SW1H 9NF, (0171 273 5486).
- Women's Radio Group, 90 de Beauvoir Road, London N1 4EN, (0171 241 3729). Runs courses for women on all aspects of radio, from appearing on programmes to production. It can also give you information on jobs and opportunities that are available.

Choosing a career/training

- British Association for Counselling, 1 Regent Place, Rugby, Warwickshire CV21 2PJ, (01788 578328). Send an A4 SAE for information.
- Housing Employment Register and Advice, 2 Valentine Place, London SE1 8QH, (0171 928 6141) 401 2938. Runs a housing employment agency offering jobs in the industry.

- Marine Society, 202 Lambeth Road, London SE1 7JW, (0171 261 9535). Can give grants to young people who want to make a career at sea.
- National Council for Voluntary Youth Services, Coborn House, 3 Coborn Road, London E3 2DA, (0181 980 5712). Professional association for youth workers.
- Service Away from Home Trust, 12B Asylum Road, London SE15 2RL, (0171 358 0690). Helps young people to make the break from living with the family with youth training schemes and accommodation throughout the country.
- Springboard, 727 Old Kent Road, London SE14, (0171 639 1007). Helps young people starting out with youth training schemes and advice.
- Youth Development/Youth Workers Association, Old Vicarage, Mossley, Lancs OL5 0QY, (01457 834943). Runs a careers advice service for young people.
- Youth Workers Association, CVYS Building, 122 Rochdale Road, Oldham OL1 1NT, (0161 626 9948).

Employment for disabled/mentally handicapped people

- British Printing Society, BM ISPA, London WC1N 3XX, (0252 26771). Helps printers who are either elderly or disabled (as well as able-bodied), using primarily traditional techniques, in both a practical and psychological way.
- CARE, 9 Weir Road, Kibworth, Leicester LE8 0LQ, (0116 2793225). This organization has residential workshops throughout the country for people with mental handicaps. These handle a wide range of occupations from pottery crafts and printing to outdoor occupations like horticulture and agriculture.
- Royal British Legion, 48 Pall Mall, London SW1Y 5JY, (0171 973 0633). Helps ex-service men and women who find themselves in difficult circumstances. Its activities include convalescent and residential homes for the ill and the disabled. Also has a small business advisory service and loan service.
- General Welfare of the Blind, 37–55 Ashburton Grove, London N7 7DW, (0171 609 0206). The association runs special factories where blind people can work, with hostels and houses where they can live in London and Luton, both while working and after retirement.
- Law Society Group for Solicitors with Disabilities, The Law Society, 50 Chancer Lane, London WC2A 1SX, (0171 242 1222). Helps law students and solicitors with disabilities and those looking for jobs in the legal profession.
- Outset, Drake House, 18 Creekside, London SE8 3DZ, (0181 692 7141). Has a number of projects in London and in the Midlands giving vocational training and employment opportunities to the disabled.

- Papworth Trust, Papworth Hall, Papworth Everard, Cambs CM 3 8RF, (01480 830341). Employs many disabled people in the seven businesses it runs, giving them vocational assessment and training. It also runs a housing association with properties that include sheltered housing for the disabled and the elderly, and also hostels for people with more severe disabilities.

See also Disabled (*page 127*).

Problems at work

Autogenic Training Centre, 100 Harley Street, London W1N 1AF, (0171 935 1811). Teaches autogenic training for stress relief.
- Advisory Conciliation and Arbitration Service (ACAS). Clifton House, 83 Euston Road, London NW1 2RB, (171 396 5100).

See also International Stress Management Association (**States of Mind**, *page 138*).

Starting your own business

- Fresh Solutions, Haultwick Farm, Haultwick, Nr Ware, Herts SG11 1JQ, Inland Revenue, Somerset House, London WC2R 1LB (0171 438 6420). (01920 438001). Suppliers of training and consultancy in the teleworking field.
- Ownbase, 68 First Avenue, Bush Hill Park, Enfield EN1 1BN, (0181 363 0808). A useful support group for those who work from home. It gives advice and information and can put you in touch with other people who are also home-based.
- H.M. Stationery Office, Publications, PO Box 276, London SW8 5AT (0171 573 9090).
- Wren Telecottage, Warwickshire Rural Enterprise Network, Stoneleigh Park, Stoneleigh, Warwickshire CV8 2RR, (Freephone 0800 616008).
- Banks currently lending money under the Loan Guarantee Scheme: Allied Irish Banks, Bank of Credit and Commerce International, Bank of Ireland, Bank of Scotland, Bank of Wales, Barclays Bank, Clydesdale Bank, Co-operative Bank, Hill Samuel, Lloyds Bank, Midland Bank, National Westminster Bank, Northern Bank, Northern Investors Loan Finance Ltd, Royal Bank of Scotland, TSB Group, Ulster Bank, Yorkshire Bank, Yorkshire Enterprise Ltd.

Unemployment

- Bootstrap Enterprises, 18 Ashwin Street, London E8 3DL, (0171 254 0775). Gives people who are out of work positive help to get back into the job market with counselling and training.

- Fairbridge, 1 Westminster Bridge Road, London SE1 7PL, (0171 928 1704). Works with unemployed young people (14–25) keeping up their morale, training them in skills leading to employment, giving them adventure-style outdoor activities.
- Employment Department, Moorfoot, Sheffield S1 4PQ, (0114 2753275).
- Industrial Common Ownership Movement, Vassalli House, 20 Central Road, Leeds LS1 6DE, (0113 2461737) 244. The organization to contact if you are planning to set up a job co-operative. It offers legal advice, training and consultancy and will help you apply for grants from the European Commission.
- Instant Muscle Ltd, Springside House, 84 North End Road, London W14 9ES, (0171 603 2604). Helps people find jobs with training and counselling, but more important, encourages people who have decided to become self-employed or who are working under the Enterprise Allowance Scheme and are about to move on to the commercial world.

Voluntary/charity work

- Charity Appointments, 3 Spital Yard, London E1 6AQ, (0171 247 4502). Recruits salaried personnel for charity organizations. It charges a placement fee.
- Charity Recruitment, 40 Rosebery Avenue, London EC1R 4RN, (0171 833 0414) F 833 0188 contact. Places salaried senior middle management in non-profit charity organizations. It does charge a placement fee.
- National Association of Volunteer Bureaux, St Peter's College, College Road, Saltley, Birmingham B8 3TE, (0121 327 0265). Initial contact should be made with your local bureaux (telephone numbers found in your Phone Book). If unable to find this information then telephone above number.
- National Centre for Volunteering in Scotland, 80 Murrary Place, Sterling FK8 2BX, (01786 479593).
- REACH, Bear Wharf, 27 Bankside, London SE1 9ET, (0171 928 0452). Helps put together people who have business and professional skills with organizations who could utilize them on a non-fee-paying basis.
- Volunteer Development Agency, Annsgate House, 70–74 Ann Street, Belfast, Northern Ireland BT1 4EH, (01232 236100).

Your rights

- City Centre, 32–35 Featherstone Street, London EC1Y 8QX, (Helpline 0171 608 1338). Works on behalf of office workers over their rights, welfare, health and safety. It will give advice over the phone and by interview.

- Lesbian and Gay Employment Rights, St Margaret's House, 21 Old Ford Road, London E2 9PL, (0171 704 8066). Supports and advises lesbian and gay people who may be faced with discrimination at work.
- Low Pay Unit, 27–29 Amwell Street, London EC1R 1UN, (Helpline – 0171 713 7583; Admin 713 7616). Has an information service which will tell you what your rights are over pay.

See also Equal Opportunities Commission (*page 314*).

10

FINANCE

As Mr Macawber said so succintly, to be free from money worries is to be happy indeed. But most of us find ourselves at some time of life, with what is politely known as a 'cash-flow problem'. This section tells you when and where you can get help from the state, from banks and from other institutions. It also shows you how to keep out of financial trouble and, if all else fails, how to survive.

BENEFITS: YOUR RIGHTS

It is estimated that over £1.6 billion in state benefits are left unclaimed each year by people who are entitled to them. One in three eligible families, for instance, do not realize that they can get family credit. Some benefits are based on contributions you make – National Insurance is one such benefit – others depend on the situation you find yourself in. Go through the checklist below to see if you might qualify.

Income support

If you are on a low income you may qualify for income support. This is payable if you work for less than 16 hours a week in paid employment and you have less than £8,000 capital. If you are on income support you also get:
- Free NHS prescriptions.
- Free dental treatment on the NHS.
- Travel paid to hospital for NHS treatment.
- Help with the cost of spectacles.
- Access to housing benefit.
- Help, if necessary, from the Social Fund (*see page 377*).
- If you are a single parent you can claim for a **Family Premium** and the **Lone Parent Premium** on top of your allowance.

Low earners may also be entitled to **child care charges** and **Housing Benefit,** as well as **Child Benefit**. For more details *see* **Children,** *page 218.*

How to claim income support

If you are not working, go to an unemployment benefit office and fill in form B1. Otherwise you will be given an A1 or SP1 according to your circumstances.

Family Credit

If you have children and a very low income, you may be eligible for **Family Credit.** It is a weekly tax-free cash payment for working people bringing up children where either parent works 16 hours or more a week and together you have less than £8,000 capital. You will be given a number of 'credits' according to your earning status and the ages of your children. You continue to get Family Credit for six months, whatever happens to your earnings. Get a Family Credit claim pack from the Post Office or phone free on 0800 500 222 for one.

Other help that is available

- If you are out of work you should be able to claim **Unemployment Benefit.**
- If you pay rent or own your house and pay rates, you might be able to claim **Housing Benefit** and **Council Tax Benefit**.
- If you are pregnant and have been paying National Insurance you may qualify for **Statutory Maternity Pay** or a **Maternity Allowance**. For details of parent and child benefits *see* **Children**, *page 218.*
- If you are ill and off work for at least 4 days and have paid National Insurance you could get **Statutory Sick Pay** or **Sickness Benefit**. If you are ill for a long time, or disabled, you may qualify for **Incapacity Benefit** or **Severe Disablement Allowance** or a **Mobility Allowance** too. If you are disabled *see page 67* for a full list of benefits you can claim. If you are over 65, you may also be able to claim an **Attendance Allowance**. For full pensioners' rights *see page 281.*
- A **Disability Working Allowance** and a **Disability Living Allowance** are two other benefits that are available.
- If your injury or disease is work-related, investigate industrial injuries disablement benefit.
- If you are a carer looking after someone who gets an attendance allowance for more than 35 hours a week, you should enquire about the **Invalid Care Allowance** to which you may be entitled. Other benefits that may be available to you, depending on your circumstances, are **Child Benefit**, **Council Tax Benefit**, **Home Responsibilities Protection**, **Housing Benefit**, **Income Support** and free NHS treatment.
- If you are widowed, you may be entitled to a lump sum called a **Widow's Payment**. If you are still caring for or are expecting your deceased husband's child, you can get a **Widowed Mother's Allowance**. And you may be entitled to a **Widow's Pension**. You may also qualify to receive **Industrial Death Benefit**, **War Widow's Pension** and **One-parent Benefit**.

The Social Fund

If you are hit by a sudden expense such as funeral costs or a new baby while you are on Income Support, or if you are trying to avoid going into residential care, you might qualify for a grant or loan from the **Social Fund**. It is there to help you with any one-off expenses that you would find difficult to meet out of your weekly benefit. It could be for something essential like a cooker or a bed. The Social Fund does not normally give outright payments but loans. You will have to pay it back out of your weekly benefit – bear that in mind before you apply.

Payments from the Social Fund come in several different ways. You can ask for a **Budgeting Loan** to help you with important intermittent expenses. Then **Crisis Loans** are available to everyone, not just those on income support, for expenses that arise in an emergency or as a consequence of a disaster – if you are a victim of flooding or fire, for instance.

A Community Care Grant is the only money from the Social Fund which does not have to be repaid. Aim at trying to get this, rather than a loan, if you are in trouble. It is discretionary – in other words you are not entitled to the money, you have to persuade the Social Fund Officer that you are a deserving case. It is a very limited fund – each local office has a budget. A Community Care Grant is given on the following grounds:

- You are trying to re-establish yourself in the community after being in institutional care.
- To keep you in the community so that you do not have to go into institutional care.
- To ease exceptional pressure on you or your family.
- To help you with your travel expenses to, say, visit a sick close relative or attend their funeral, or to see your child if he is with your ex-partner, pending a custody action.
- To help you move or to buy vital items of clothing such as shoes for yourself and your family if you are in need.

How to apply

Get a form SF300 from your local DSS office and fill it in. You cannot appeal against its decision if you are turned down, but you can ask for an independent review of the case – go to a Law Centre for help on this.

Remember that benefits regulations are changing all the time. To find out the latest situation call the Benefits Agency Freeline (*see page 403*). Make sure that you are getting all you are entitled to. The DSS has taken such a drubbing that it is actually eager to help you claim what is yours by right.

How to complain

If you are unhappy with the treatment you get from your local Benefits Agency or at a decision it makes, get the leaflet *How to Appeal* from your local office and ask to see the Customer Services Manager. Your case may come up before an adjudication officer and then go on to the Social Security Appeal Tribunal. If you do not get satisfaction then go to your MP – you might even qualify for compensation if you have been wrongly denied a benefit.

PROVIDING FOR THE FUTURE

How to have a happy retirement

We can no longer rely on the state pension for a basic living income and its value is likely to fall even more. It would be unwise to assume that the pension from your job will be all you need, either, so start saving now if you are able to. Invest as much as you can through additional voluntary contributions via your firm's scheme. But check first to see how it works, all schemes must have a booklet which spells out the rules. Or take out a personal plan which you may get tax relief on. Take a look at what National Savings are offering in safe index-linked or tax-free schemes, and see what the building societies are offering. But be careful about putting money in high risk investments even though the rewards appear tempting. If you have a large amount of money to invest, consult an accredited financial adviser (*see page 405*).

Private pensions

If you are paying into a firm's pension plan and are dissatisfied with the way the scheme is run, talk to the trustees. If you belong to a trade union, get the representative to do so for you. If you do not get satisfaction, go to the Occupational Pensions Advisory Service (*see page 405*). If that fails, your last opportunity for redress rests with the Pensions Ombudsman (*see page 314*).
If you were persuaded to leave a company pension scheme and take on a personal pension plan and are worse off as a result, you may be able to claim compensation through the Personal Investment Authority's Pension Unit (*see page 405*).

Providing for care in old age

If you have assets worth £8,000 or more, the state will not pay for you to go into a home if you need care. So, if you have regular money coming in or if you have some put by, it might pay to take out an insurance policy that will pay care fees for as long as they are needed either by a single payment or regular premiums. These policies are relatively new. Consult an independent financial adviser to see if it would be worthwhile in your case.

INVESTING MONEY

It pays to get professional help if you have a large sum to invest, but proceed with caution. I speak from personal experience here as my mother asked me to sit in on a meeting with a 'nice man from the bank' who advised her on investing her money. I felt that he was risking too much on the stock market but was overruled. Six months later the stock market crisis occurred and overnight her investments more than halved.

- Get information from at least two, better still three advisers, one of whom should be an independent – not linked to a bank or with an insurance company.
- Ask whether he belongs to a professional association. An adviser should be registered on the Securities and Investments Board's Central Register (*see page 405*); ring and check up on the person.
- Ask questions. If you do not understand what he is talking about, ask him to explain in plain language. Better still, get him to write it down so you can study the proposal at your leisure.
- There is no such thing as a guaranteed fortune. If you are offered a return on your money that is much higher than what seems to be available everywhere else, you may be putting your savings at risk. Get a second opinion.
- Remember that if you buy life insurance, a pension or unit trusts there is a 'cooling off' period by law in many cases (but not all) which gives you the right to cancel within 14 days. Ask whether this is so in your case if you feel you are being pressured.
- Check the charges, find out whether you can call in your investment early, and if so, whether there are any penalties.
- Do not assume that a well-known well-advertised name is going to give you a better deal than a small one. Read the small print.

If things go wrong

Whenever you invest your money in anything other than outlets like National Savings, you take the normal risk that the value of your investment may go up or down over time, especially if your investment is linked with the stock market. But if you place your hard-earned money in the hands of a professional adviser, there is also a risk that you may be badly advised. In addition, if your adviser defrauds you or goes bankrupt, there is an additional risk that you may lose your money.

However, if your investments were made since the end of 1986, you may be able to get compensation. Most accountants, solicitors, insurance brokers and actuaries have their own compensation schemes for a situation like this. Some professional associations are listed on *page 404*.

GUARANTEEING A LOAN

Sometimes a friend or a member of your family may ask you to guarantee a bank loan for them. Think carefully if you do this and consult your solicitor first, because, depending on how the guarantee is worded, you could be committing yourself for life to a liability for someone else's debts with no way of escape. If the person you are guaranteeing finds that they cannot meet the loan repayments, the bank may well have the right to make you pay off all the debts immediately.

If you are asked for a guarantee, take these simple precautions:
- Make sure the amount of money you are guaranteeing is clearly stated.
- Never guarantee a sum of money that you could not repay if you were asked to.
- Check the agreement thoroughly to see if there are any penalty clauses for late repayment of the loan – you could be liable for these as well if the borrower is unable to meet the debt.
- Remember that even if you are guaranteeing something jointly with someone else, you could still be liable for the full amount of the debt if the other person absconded or was unable to pay up.
- Be sure to attach a copy of the guarantee to your will so that if you die, your executors know that there is a claim on your estate.

INCOME TAX

Your rights

Under the Taxpayer's Charter, the tax man should help you in 'every reasonable way' to obtain your rights and to understand your obligations under tax laws. But you have to supply the full facts to help them give you the information you need. They should be courteous, considerate and prompt at all times, and the tax you owe should be decided impartially and be no more than is due according to the law. Information about your tax affairs should be treated in strictest confidence and used for lawful purposes only. The Tax department must have regard for how much it costs you to deal with your tax affairs and for the need to keep these costs to a minimum.

How to deal with the tax man

If you think you are being asked to pay too much tax:
- Ring the Inland Revenue enquiries line at your local Tax Office to ask what justification it has for charging you the amount in question.

- If you find you get no response from your local office, write to the District Inspector, and if nothing happens, contact the Regional Controller with your complaint.
- If you get a Notice of Assessment you must appeal against it **in writing** within 30 days of the date on the notice.
- Write to the address on the Notice of Assessment saying you wish to appeal and why you are appealing. Keep copies of everything you send.
- At the same time you should ask the Inspector to postpone that part of the assessment you think is excessive 'until such time as the quantum of the assessment is agreed'. You should pay him something on account, say what you think the assessment should be, as evidence of good intent and to avoid interest charges.

If you cannot reach an agreement, ask for your case to be dealt with by the Commissioners of Tax, or if you feel that the commissioners come to the wrong decision, you can take the case to the High Court. To do this you must let the Commissioners' clerk know in writing within 30 days of the decision. You can claim back money you think the Revenue owes you going back six tax years – and it can do the same to you. It can also go back as far as 20 years if it thinks you have been cheating them.

Remember that the Inland Revenue will charge interest on any money you owe and have not paid, starting on outstanding tax not paid within 30 days of the date of assessment. If you cannot pay the sum it is demanding but have no reason to believe it is unreasonable, tell them immediately. They may be able to agree to a scheme for a series of payments instead. If you are under suspicion of evading, rather than avoiding, payment of tax, the Inland Revenue has wide-ranging powers – it can even have your phone tapped. Whether it has reason to suspect you or not, the Inland Revenue has the power to look through your bank and building society accounts. It can also insist that you, your partner and/or members of your family hand over documents which it believes contain information it needs. However, it must give you notice of this in writing.

Ways to cut your tax

Check with your local Tax Office to make sure you have the right tax code. If you are married, elderly, bringing up young children, registered blind or recently widowed, you get a higher tax allowance. If you are married and you are earning less than the married person's tax allowance, think of transferring the whole of the allowance to your higher-earning partner to get full relief. Check whether you should be getting any tax relief on your mortgage and/or on any maintenance payments you have to make.

MORTGAGES

If you are borrowing money from a building society or bank to buy your home, they then have enormous power over your life. A mortgage company can take you to court, technically, even if you are only £1 in arrears. It can also make your life a misery with demands for payments. Check the various offers carefully. Some of those that offer tempting interest rates may place restrictions on you and impose heavy penalties if you want to give up the mortgage, re-mortgage or switch to another lender.

How to have a happy mortgage

Take it for the shortest possible time
Repaying a mortgage over 25 years is an expensive strategy, so go for 15 years instead if you can. At one time it was sensible to get a house as soon as possible and take on as large a debt as you could because the value of your house was likely to rise along with your salary. Now the opposite is the case. We can no longer assume that we will be earning good money in the later stages of a 25-year loan nor that the value of the house will appreciate. So if you can afford to do so, approach the building society to see if you can shorten the term of your mortgage.

Go for a repayment mortgage
Then you are paying off capital and interest simultaneously. Your monthly payments cover some interest and something off the original debt. You know then that by the end of the term the debt will be cleared. With a mortgage linked to an endowment policy, you are paying interest only to the building society and separate insurance premiums which aim to produce enough money to pay off the loan at the end of the term. But you could get into the negative equity trap (*see page 383*).

Do not tell them you are pregnant
You could be refused a loan if you are pregnant. You do not have to be a single mother – the same thing is happening to couples who have applied for a joint mortgage when the woman is on maternity leave. Building societies have been known to insist that the loan is based on the husband's income only until she returns to work. In other cases, pregnant women asking for mortgages in their own names have been refused unless their husbands acted as guarantors. Clearly the arrival of a baby puts a strain on the family's resources but research shows that only 7 per cent of arrears are caused by this and in those the problem is only temporary.

Basically, if you are over 6 months, in some cases only 3 months, pregnant, insurers do not like to take on the risk, even if you are earning more than your husband. The National Council of Women advises you not to mention that you are pregnant unless there is a pertinent reason. If you are in this situation, get onto the head office of the building society you are proposing to approach and find out what its attitude is likely to be.

Take out mortgage payment protection insurance

This will cover you if you cannot make your payments due to unemployment, illness, or accident. The building society can probably offer you a scheme but it pays to shop around as you might get cheaper premiums elsewhere. A mortgage protection insurance will usually pay out monthly benefit if you are taken ill or have an accident and cannot work, or if you become unemployed. The policy will usually pay out for up to 12 months, and there may be an 'excess' period of 60 days before it starts paying out.

Mortgage problems

Negative equity

Negative equity is the nightmare of the nineties. It means, basically, that you owe more on your house than it is now worth, having bought at the top of the market. You may think that you are covered by mortgage guarantee insurance, but you may be called upon to find the money yourself (see below). Endowment loans are often to blame for negative equity. On a repayment mortgage, the amount of capital you borrow goes down each year. On an endowment loan it is paid off at the end. The problem is that over recent years money invested in the stock market, as many policies are, has not yielded the interest that was hoped and far from giving you a tax-free nest egg, as happened at one time, the surrender value may not even cover the sum borrowed. Support groups are now being started up for victims.

What if I lose my job and cannot pay?

Legislation which came into effect recently makes it clear that if you take out a mortgage, lose your job and end up on income support, you do not get any help with the payments for nine months. If your partner has left you and has stopped paying the mortgage and you are on income support, you are entitled to claim provided you are still living in the property. Thereafter you will get help only with the interest part of the mortgage payment – the DSS says that it is not in the business of helping people to amass capital. So you will have to arrange with your building society to accept interest-only payments on the house for the time being. If you have an endowment mortgage, the DSS will not pay the insurance premium and you may have to re-negotiate your mortgage.

Mortgage guarantee policies

If you have a large mortgage, one of the conditions may be that you take out a mortgage guarantee policy. You might well think that this covers you if you are unable to make your mortgage payments but this is not the case. It is designed to pay the building society – not you – if you fall behind with your payments, the house is sold and the sale does not repay your loan. And the company who issued the policy to you is within its rights to pursue you to get its money back.

What if the building society threatens to repossess my home?

If you hit mortgage troubles and repossession looms, remember you are better off putting the house on the market yourself. You are bound to get a more reasonable price for it that way. At the word 'repossession' potential buyers tend to knock off thousands from the asking price.

Go immediately to see the Debt Counsellor at your local Citizens' Advice Bureau (address in the Phone Book). If it does not have one, it will pass you on to a special Money Advice Centre which will not only advise you on what to do, but probably negotiate with the building society or bank on your behalf.
The building society has to get a Court Order before it can put you out and negotiating with the building society at this stage may result in the Order being suspended.

If all goes against you and the building society is adamant about repossessing the property, you will have to leave your home – the date will be given in the Order. You will then be in the position of having to keep up your mortgage payments or run up a further bill, until the house has been sold.

Giving up on your mortgage

You are out of work, you have been struggling to keep up your mortgage repayments, and, at the same time, the value of your house is now less than the lump sum you owe. It is at times like this that the temptation to cut and run is almost overwhelming. Before you hand over the keys, however, take this into account:

- You still have to meet the mortgage repayments until the house is sold.
- If the house is sold for less than the amount you owe, you are liable for the difference.
- If you took out a mortgage indemnity policy, remember it covers the lender, not you. And you could still be sued for any shortfall.
- Building societies want to get the best possible price for houses that have been repossessed. It is a well-known fact that many of them are 'sitting' on their housing stock, releasing properties for sale in small dribs and drabs so as not to depress the market, or holding on to them until things pick up. Meanwhile you have to keep on paying.

- If you volunteer your house for repossession, any thoughts that the council might rehouse you go down the drain because you will have made yourself 'voluntarily homeless' and therefore it is not legally bound to find you accommodation.

YOU AND YOUR BANK

Your rights

The Banking Code of Practice says that terms and conditions should be expressed in plain language and give a fair and balanced description of the relationship between you, the customer, and the bank. Details of charges or interest you have to pay should be sent to you when you open an account. Banks will now have to give you no less than 24 days notice of the amount they are going to deduct from your account for their charges. Current interest rates should be on display in branches, and should also be available via leaflets and possibly a personal notification to you. Your bank must have a procedure for handling complaints fairly and quickly and it should tell you about this and tell you how you can complain. No bank should disclose details of your personal account or, indeed, your name and address to a third party. If it is asked to give information about you to a credit agency then it should give you at least 28 days notice of this, though it does not always happen.

How to get the best out of your bank

Pick a large bank rather than a small one – it will take less of an interest in your account if it dips into the red. Make a point of dealing with the same member of staff if possible, building up a friendly relationship with the person. This is useful if you get into a mess and need help.

Opening a bank account

You may have to fill in an application form to open an account but you are more likely to simply see a personal banker. The bank will want to see
- Proof of your identity – a driving licence or passport.
- Proof of your income – pay slips, tax returns, a letter from your accountant if you run your own business.
- If you are switching accounts, recent bank statements. If you are changing banks you will probably need to sign an 'authority to transfer form'.

You and your cheque book

Writing a cheque

Cheque frauds are on the increase, so take these simple precautions when you make out a cheque:

- Write the word 'only' after the name of the person the cheque is made out to. Do the same after writing out the sum involved – one hundred pounds only.
- Having written out the amount, draw a line through the rest of the space.
- If the words 'or order' appear on the cheque, cross them out and initial them.
- Write 'not transferable' across the cheque.

  The bank should pay you compensation if you write out a cheque crossed 'Account payee' or A/C payee only and it is fraudulently cashed. Few shops and other retail organizations will accept your cheque without the backing of a cheque card which your bank should give you. Cheques sent through the post, however, do not have to be backed by a card, but the goods are unlikely to be sent to you until the cheque has cleared. Debit cards such as Delta or Switch are now often supplied by banks. They save the slog of writing out a cheque but work in the same way, debiting the money to your account.

Missing or stolen cheques

If you lose your cheque book, phone the bank immediately. It is then liable for any cheques that a thief might forge. If you find the cheque book again, tell the bank immediately. It may ask you to destroy that cheque book and give you another one. If you try to write cheques using the old book, they may bounce. If you forget to tell the bank your cheque book is missing and someone forges cheques from it, then you are liable.

Stopping a cheque

If you wish to stop a cheque you should ring the bank immediately, giving it the cheque number. The bank will probably want confirmation in writing. Ask how much it will cost to put a stop on it – it could be more than the value of the cheque in question. However, if the shop has written your cheque card number on the back, then you are not able to stop it – a point to bear in mind, as most shops ask you to do this. Do not proffer your cheque card unless asked for it.

Paying in

When you pay a cheque into your account, you will have to wait several days, usually about four working days, for it to 'clear', that is, for your bank to collect the money from the account on which it is drawn. This period may be longer in the case of small banks and building societies, but is always quicker if you pay the money into your own branch. This interval is needed by the bank to 'collect' the money or to get the cheque back again marked unpaid. So you cannot withdraw that money right away. If you pay in cash, the money should be available immediately.

Standing orders and direct debits

These are arrangements where you tell your bank to pay someone a certain sum at certain intervals – it can be yearly but is more likely to be on a monthly basis. If you want that sum changed, then you have to instruct the bank accordingly and get the bank to confirm that it has done this. One of the easiest ways for money to 'leak' from your bank account is via direct debits and standing orders that you have forgotten about and which take money from your account.

Check your account carefully to see what standing orders you have going out at a given time, and ring your bank if you are not sure what you have. Remember to include them in your budget if you are doing your sums. A standing order is simply an order to pay a certain sum to the account of a certain person or company on a certain date. When you sign a direct debit arrangement you authorize someone to collect so much a month from your account. It is possible for them to vary the amount but if they do so they have to let you know in advance. You very often pay for gas, electricity or central heating fuel in this way. If you can get away with a standing order, rather than a direct debit, then you are more in control of your affairs. But some organizations – including clubs – will only deal with you on a direct debit basis.

The bank need not honour a standing order or a direct debit payment if there is insufficient money in your account to pay it. But if it considers you to be generally credit-worthy then there should not be any trouble.

You and your overdraft

Bank overdrafts are usually available to customers aged 18 and over. An overdraft is usually for an amount up to half your monthly income after tax.

If your account is overdrawn, interest is charged on a daily basis and added to the sum you owe. This can mean that a relatively small sum can escalate into a terrifying figure. Most overdrafts are agreed for one year, but the bank has the right to call them in at any time.

Always agree an overdraft in advance. If you are not well known to your bank you will probably be asked to fill in a form with personal and employment details, how much you earn and whether you own your house. It may also ask you to fill in a 'budget planner' showing your monthly income and expenditure. And you may be recommended to take out overdraft protection insurance – something worth considering anyway. If you run into an unauthorized overdraft, you may be charged higher interest and possibly extra charges.

Your bank: how to complain

Banks are headed by humans, even in this technological age, and they can make mistakes. These are the top problems spotlighted by the Banking Ombudsman:

- Bouncing cheques after it told you the cheque would be honoured.
- Imposing higher charges than it had told you it would make.
- Transferring money from your account without your authority.
- Changing a rate of interest after specifying a sum on an account application form.
- Selling you a financial plan that would not benefit you in any way.
- Giving out details of your financial or personal affairs without your permission.

If you have a complaint against your bank, you should try to sort it out with the local branch first:

- Make your complaint as speedily as possible, while the incident is still fresh in everyone's mind.
- Make sure you target the right person – ring up if necessary, and find out whom you should contact. And make a note of the name of the person you speak to.
- Follow up your verbal complaint with a letter; if possible, type it out. Make sure to date it and head it up with your account number. Make it brief.
- Keep careful records of your complaint, copies of letters, statements, bills etc. in a special file so you can lay your hands on the evidence immediately.

If all else fails and you have had no satisfaction, take your case to the Banking Ombudsman who can make awards of up to £100,000 in compensation. He is there to deal with complaints about all kinds of banking business, about bank credit cards and some executor and trustee services. He cannot help you, however, until you have reached the end of the road in trying to obtain satisfaction through the bank's own complaints procedure. This usually means taking your complaint as far as the bank head office – though you can write to the Ombudsman if you feel your complaint is being ignored or has got bogged down.

The bank should tell you when your complaint has reached deadlock at the highest level. If you then decide to take it to the Ombudsman, you must do this within six months.

What happens next?
The Ombudsman will check that your complaint is one he can deal with and that deadlock has been reached.

- He will then ask you to send any relevant letters and papers.
- If he agrees to your complaint he will then authorize the bank to give him any relevant information that it has.
- He will then try to sort out your complaint informally, pointing out any misunderstandings.
- If that fails, he may ask for more formal presentations of the case from both sides and then make his recommendation.
- During all this time you still keep your right to go to court instead if you want to.

HOW TO KEEP OUT OF FINANCIAL TROUBLE

- Be grown up: keep all receipts, tickets from cash dispensers, credit card vouchers, and fill in your cheque stubs. Check them against your statements.
- Switch any surplus cash into an account that pays interest – unless you have a current account that does so. Or consider topping up your pension.
- Make sure you have all the tax allowances that you are entitled to.
- Try to pay your credit cards off in full within the time limit allowed. Remember that some card companies do not charge an annual fee. Use those.
- If you are planning to buy something very expensive, negotiate a loan from the bank or building society rather than running up a credit card debt.
- If you are earning good money, do not be tempted by a low start mortgage. Try to pay off as much as you can now.
- Check out your insurance policies for the house and for the car each year instead of automatically renewing them. You might get a better deal elsewhere.

CREDIT CARDS

Banks and building societies all issue credit cards now under either Access or Visa schemes with which you can pay for a vast number of services – train and airline tickets, hotel and restaurant bills, and you can use them to make purchases. You can also use your card to get cash 'out of the wall' or over the counter. You will be sent one with a ceiling on the amount you are allowed to charge, which varies according to how much the lenders think you are worth. You are sent a bill each month and have 25 days after that to pay. You have to make a minimum payment but can otherwise choose how much to pay back and when.

They are an all-too-easy way of borrowing money but if you do not pay them off in full each month they can cost you dearly. If you buy an expensive dishwasher costing £450 with your card and take three months to pay back the money, at current rates you will have paid £464.74 for it – an extra £14.74. It pays, therefore, to settle large credit account bills from your savings account if you have one, since interest rates are so low at the moment. Some credit cards offer a degree of consumer protection. Some cards charge an annual fee, some do not – check it out before applying.

Gold cards

Gold cards are normally only issued to people who earn more than £25,000 a year. Their advantage is that they offer a higher spending limit and many have an overdraft facility of up to £10,000 at an advantageous interest rate. They also often offer comprehensive travel insurance and other facilities. You have to pay a yearly charge for your gold card. The disadvantage of it is that it is a convenience, not a credit card but a debit card since you have to pay off the sum that you charge the following month. Not all gold cards offer consumer protection. It is wise to check this out before you sign up for one.

What if my limit is too low?

Most credit card companies will raise your credit limit automatically if you use your card often, charging it to the hilt. Alternatively you can ask them to do so, and if you have a good track record of payment there should be no difficulty, otherwise they might want a bank reference. If you know that you have a large payment coming up – say, a holiday payment – you can ring the customer service line and ask to have your credit increased. In most cases they will do so. You may inadvertently go over your credit limit without realizing it. In most cases if this is only a small amount, the credit card company will allow you that leeway when the shop rings through to check. It all depends on your track record.

What if I lose my card?

Phone the card company right away (*see page 6*); the number to ring will be on a copy of your bill. If your card is Access or Visa you get some protection under the Consumer Credit act. If someone finds it and uses it, the most the company can charge your account is £50. But swift action after you discover its loss can avoid that happening. If you have a gold card, the ceiling is usually £25.

If you have a debit card or a store charge card these are not covered by the Act, so it is even more vital to let the company know if one goes missing.

If you have a lot of credit cards it definitely pays to take out insurance in case you lose them. There are many companies that do this – most credit card companies have a scheme.

How to look after your card

Keep your card in a secure place and do not carry your pin number with you. If you cannot remember it then bury it as a fake phone number in your phone book. Do not let anyone else use your card or pin. Do not throw away receipts at the cash machine with your number on them. Keep all receipts, including those from electronic terminals and cash dispensers, until you get your statement. Check it carefully; if there is any wrong transaction shown, phone the credit card company immediately. Do not carry your card in a handbag or pocket together with keys or coins, the magnetic strip may get scratched. For the same reason do not put two cards in your wallet back to back. Electrical equipment like washing machines and dishwashers can also interfere with the magnetic strip on credit cards so keep your cards away from them.

Which Magazine advises that to be extra secure, when you sign a credit card voucher, you should ask for the carbons as well, or see that they are destroyed. Thieves can use details on discarded carbons to buy things on your card by phone.

Debit and cashpoint cards

Your bank may offer you a debit card called Visa Delta, Switch or Connect. You can use it to pay for things without having to write out a cheque. The money for the purchase is then automatically taken out of your bank account. You can spend as much as your current account can take. The other advantage is that you can use these cards in many shops that will not take ordinary credit cards. If your cashpoint card is stolen, however, you could be liable for any money taken before you report the theft – check this out with your bank.

Store charge cards

Most major stores and some chains like Marks & Spencer offer credit cards of their own. If you pay your bill off each month and take advantage of special in-store promotions to cards holders, they are a good thing to have. However, if you run up credit on them, the charges are usually higher than those for ordinary credit cards and you may not be covered by the Consumer Credit Act – again, check before you acquire one.

Credit card protection

If you have bought something on your credit card costing between £50 and £15,000 and used less than £15,000 credit, it should be covered against theft, loss or accidental damage for 100 days. Check with your card company to see if this is so before you make the purchase, for there are some cases where the credit card company can wriggle out of the deal – in the case of travel, for instance, if you book your holiday with a 'third party', a travel agent instead of with the company direct.

How to cancel your card

The credit card company has the right to ask you for your card back and to cancel it if you keep defaulting on payment. The company may also ask you to stop using it temporarily if you are behind with your payments. However, you may decide to give it up of your own accord. If so, this is how you set about it.

- Cut the card in two and send it back to the company with a letter saying you want to close your account. The company may ignore this at first.
- At the same time, cancel any other payments you may have made, say, for card insurance.

The idea of taking out a loan to clear credit card debts is seductive. You can come clean with the bank and ask it to lend you money at a lower interest to pay off the debts. If you are a well-thought-of customer it will not ask for security. If the bank talks about a second mortgage on your home, think again – you could lose it if you fall behind on payments. The only problem with this wheeze is that it enables you to continue to use your credit cards and run into even more trouble.

BEST WAYS TO BORROW

Unexpected calls on your cash can make problems – you may have a major repair bill on your car, need a new washing machine, or have to fund a family funeral. Or you may be moving house and have suddenly realized you have some unexpected outgoings to go with it. What is the best way to raise the finance?

Interest-free credit
If it is household equipment you need, then take a look at what the big stores are offering. Many of them have interest-free credit deals on major items like washing machines. But check the actual cost of the piece of equipment concerned – it may be priced much higher than the same item in cut-price shops like Argos.

Controlled use of a credit card
If you have a credit card and have 'money to spend' on it, then paying for an inexpensive item this way may be a solution. You will have to be strict with yourself – pretend you are asking the bank for a loan and make a plan to pay it off in large chunks over a small period. The APR rate (Annual Percentage Rate) of credit cards is terrifyingly high. If you are making a large purchase, it might be worthwhile asking the bank how much it would charge to lend you the money over a short period and compare this with what you would have to pay the credit card company.

A second mortgage or mortgage increase
If you need the money for some ambitious plan like a new kitchen, an extension or a garage, it may pay you to increase your mortgage if it is a relatively low one. Any mortgage increase or so-called 'second mortgage' may be charged at a higher rate than the mortgage you are already paying.

A personal loan

Both credit card companies and banks offer money which is repaid over a shorter period of time than that of a mortgage. The facts are usually set out simply and clearly in leaflets that often come in the same envelope as your monthly credit card bill. But personal loans usually cost more than straightforward bank loans. So if you are on good terms with your bank, it is better to borrow money through the bank direct.

A loan on your insurance

If you have life insurance, you may be able to borrow from the company a sum of money that is equal to the cash-in value of your policy. You may well find to your surprise that this is a very small sum, unless you have been paying for years.

Being refused credit

If you make a request for credit – filling in a hire-purchase agreement form, for instance – and are turned down, it can be embarrassing and frustrating, particularly if you do not know why you are not considered credit-worthy. Virtually all of us are credit-rated by one or other of the main credit reference agencies, with details of any late payments or defaults we may have made.

Your rights

- If you are trying or have tried to get credit for up to £15,000, you have a legal right to know the name and address of any credit reference agency that the lender has consulted for details about you.
- If you are turned down for credit you have 28 days to ask the lenders whether it used a credit agency to check up on you and if so, which one. The lender is legally bound to give this information within 7 working days.
- You can then write to the agency and ask for a copy of your file (a small charge is made) and if necessary dispute the information contained in it. The names and addresses of the main credit agencies are given on *page 405*.
- You do not have to be refused credit to see what information credit agencies hold on you. You can write to them at any time to ask for a copy of your file.
- If you have reason to believe that you have been turned down for credit because of racial discrimination, contact the Commission for Racial Equality (*see page 420*).

Borrowing money

Credit – your rights

If you are taking out a loan of any size, make sure of your rights before you sign on the line. It is possible to pull out of some credit deals if you change your mind, but not all of them. According to the Office of Fair Trading, if you change your mind and want to cancel a credit deal, you should be all right if:

- The deal was made within the last few days *and* you talked to the lender or supplier in person, not on the telephone *and* when you signed the credit agreement you were not on the lender's or supplier's business premises, including an exhibition stand. Agreements signed in shops are not normally cancellable, but agreements signed at home usually are.
- If you change your mind and the lender has not yet signed the agreement, you have the right to withdraw from a credit deal.

When you sign, you should be given a copy of the credit agreement which sets out your cancellation rights. You should also receive by post a second copy or a notice of your cancellation rights. If you can cancel there should be a cancellation box on your copy of the agreement telling you what to do. Act quickly as there are tight time limits. The goods you were buying through the credit agreement will then have to go back. It is the shop's responsibility to collect them.

HOW TO COPE WITH A CASH CRISIS

All kinds of things can land you suddenly in debt – you may lose your job, there might be a sudden rise in the cost of your mortgage or you might suddenly find you are fending for yourself after the breakdown of a relationship. If this happens to you:

- Act quickly. Do not ignore the problem and hope it will go away. The longer you leave it, the worse it will get.
- Make a list of what you owe in order of priority. Decide which bills you must pay, not in order of how much money is involved but the consequences for you. Some debts affect your actual way of life – to have the gas, electricity or phone cut off, to have the house repossessed or to be thrown out into the street by a landlord, matters more than a credit card bill or hire-purchase on a car.
- Do not be knocked off balance when you make this list, or put the creditors that are likely to make the most noise at the top. Some companies as a matter of practice send out heavy letters for even the smallest unpaid bill. And in order to get the money from you, they will have to take you to court which involves a long wait.
- Do not ignore threatening letters – reply to them. Otherwise if you get taken to court you might find that you not only have to pay your bills but may have to pay costs as well.
- Do not surrender a life insurance policy early to raise cash unless you really need to. You are very unlikely to get back all the money you put in.
- Contact your creditors and talk to them. Be calm. Explain what has happened and how you plan to put it right. If the first person you speak to is unhelpful, ask to speak to somebody more senior who may be able to agree to what you

say. If you speak to them over the phone and they agree to be co-operative, ask them to put it in a letter and send it to you.

- If you feel you cannot do it face-to-face or over the phone, write them a letter – go to your Citizens' Advice Bureau and get them to help you do it if necessary. On your gas and electricity bills there are numbers that you can call if you have difficulty over paying. Most large utilities have been so pilloried by the newspapers and TV for coming down heavily on people that they have become much more receptive if you ring and say you cannot pay and have a good reason why. Many of them have budget schemes which spread the lump sum over a number of weeks.

- In the case of other creditors, work out a reasonable offer to repay the money you owe. Do not worry if it seems very small if that is really all you can afford. Creditors prefer you to pay a small amount regularly than make an offer you cannot keep up. Do not give up trying; even if creditors are difficult, they might capitulate in the end.

- Do not borrow money to pay off your debts unless you can get it from friends or family. Never go to a money lender.

- If you have lost your job, or are off work because of illness, go to your local Department of Social Security Benefits Agency (listed in the Phone Book) and see whether you are entitled to any benefits, and if not, when you can claim (*see page 403*). If you have a mortgage, check whether your payments are covered by mortgage or credit insurance schemes.

- Work out how much you need to survive. Deduct that from the money that you have coming in and see how much is left over for repayments. Make a personal budget showing what your expenses are and what you have coming in. You can then show this to the court, if necessary.

- If you receive court papers, fill in the reply forms and send them back. Let the court have all the facts. Photocopy the forms so you have a record of what you said.

- If you are asked to attend a court hearing, be sure to go. You are not a criminal, this is a civil matter.

Where to borrow in a crisis

Try your family and friends

Be business-like, tell them how much you want and what it is for. Tell them how long you will take to pay it back and how you intend to do so. And offer them an interest rate that is less than the bank would charge but still attractive to them. The downside of borrowing from people who are close to you is that it does put a strain on your relationship. And you may be surprised and rather hurt if they turn you down. Some people think that because they have lent you £100 to get you out of a scrape, they have bought your soul. So it is up to you to decide if it is worth coping with this in order to borrow cheaply.

Get a guarantor

Another way family and friends could help without actually parting with cash is to act as a guarantor for a loan from somewhere else – probably the bank. This is useful if you have not had the time to build up a good enough track record with the bank to borrow from it direct, but if you default, then whoever guaranteed the loan would have to pay the bank back, so they have to be able to trust you.

Ask the bank

Banks make money by lending money. If you have a good relationship with your bank, you should not have any trouble asking for a loan. This could be through a loan account or a temporary overdraft. In the case of a loan account, the manager will want it to be over a fixed period and money will be deducted from your account on a monthly basis – though in some circumstances the bank might give you respite for a month or two so that you do not start repaying right away. Banks are not in business to be charitable, however, and you will have to pay dearly for the money. A bank loan is usually at least one per cent over the current bank rate.

Try your firm

If you work in a well-established job with a large or prosperous company, try asking the personnel manager if the company would lend you the money. It is more likely to do that if you want it for some life-enhancing purchase, than to get yourself out of a financial mess. Many years ago, needing an operation which meant a long wait on the NHS, I asked my employers to lend me the money to have it done privately. They agreed and gave me an interest-free loan because they knew it was in their interest for me to be as fit as possible.

Loan sharks and cowboy lenders

If the bank turns you down and you have no friends to help you out do **not** panic and be tempted to answer one of those ads in the paper which offer you instant cash – up to £10,000 credit now, no questions asked etc. You may even have someone knocking at the door from time to time offering you a loan. If someone approaches you and offers a loan without you having contacted them first, you are allowed five full days after receiving a copy of the agreement in which to change your mind. If you go into an office and sign up, however, you are not so lucky. If you take out a secured loan you will have to offer the lender some kind of security – which often means your car or your home. If you do not repay then they can apply to the court to sell it. If you take out an unsecured loan you will not have to provide any security but the rate of interest is bound to be higher and if you fail to pay up, your creditor could apply to the court to sell your assets to cover it.

If you are committed to a loan that later appears to be a complete rip-off, you might be able to get a court to release you. Always get a written quotation and READ THE SMALL PRINT. If it is secured on your house, remember it is the same as a mortgage and if you cannot pay up you could lose your home. If you think a loan looks dodgy or too good to be true, get a second opinion from your local Citizens' Advice Bureau or consumer advice centre. Remember, if you borrow again you are paying interest on interest.

How to pawn something

If you are desperate for instant cash in an emergency or have a short-term cash-flow problem, you could consider pawning something. You leave something of value, a piece of jewellery or silver, perhaps, with a pawnbroker and borrow money against its value. You get the item back when you have paid off the loan and the interest charged. If you do not repay the money after a period of time, then the article will be sold.

Pawnbrokers usually lend between a third and a half of the value of the item and give you a contract, whereby you pay around 5 per cent interest each month. Contracts usually last about six months and if you cannot redeem your pledge (pay off the money at the end), the article will be sold, but you are usually given some extra time to come up with the cash. How do you find a pawnbroker? Some shops have the familiar sign – three balls – hanging outside, otherwise read the lettering on shop-fronts of antique shops and second-hand jewellers; many of them act as pawnbrokers.

Dealing with creditors

Make them an offer to pay off the debt (*see above*) on a monthly basis if possible. Never be persuaded to pay off more than you can manage at one time or you will fall into debt again. If they refuse your offer and demand more:
- Start paying the amount you have offered anyway as evidence of good will.
- If other creditors have accepted your offer of credit and frozen the interest, write to the creditors who have refused and tell them this.
- If this fails, contact the National Debtline (*see page 404*) for advice on your next step.

What can I do if they harass me?
If your creditors threaten or harass you to make you pay, they may be committing a criminal offence. It is illegal for a lender to keep demanding payment by
- Phoning you late at night or repeatedly at work.

- Parking a van marked 'Debt Collector' outside your home.
- Displaying your name on a board as a non-payer.
- Contacting your employer.
- Or trying to make you think you can be prosecuted in the criminal court because you have not paid your debts – you cannot.

If any of these things happen, get in touch with your local Trading Standards Department or Consumer Protection Department (both in the Phone Book) right away.

What if my creditors take me to court?

If your creditors take you to court:

- You will receive a 'default summons' telling you how much the creditor says you owe.
- The summons has a reply form for you to write down your offer of repayment. Fill this in and send it to the creditor – called the plaintiff – with a copy of your personal budget.
- If you do not agree with the amount of the claim, say so on the form and send it back to the court.
- If the creditor accepts your offer you will receive an order to pay that amount each month.
- If the creditor does not accept your offer, the court staff will write and tell you what it has decided you should pay each month.
- If you do not agree with the amount the court says you must pay, you can ask for a hearing to explain your offer to the District Judge – you must do this within 14 days of getting the order.
- The court will give you a hearing date. You must go to the hearing. Take a copy of your personal budget (*see above*) with you.
- If the hearing is too far away for you to attend, ask for it to be transferred to your local court instead.

Once your case is in the process of being heard by a county court, the court will stop interest being charged on most credit agreements. This means that the amount you owe is now fixed and cannot increase.

What if my circumstances change?

If you have a problem over your payments – if, for instance, you are made redundant or sacked from your job, ask the court for a reduction. Get form N245 from the local County Court office to do so. Many people are frightened of courts and feel like criminals because they owe money. But the County Court which handles money matters is not there to judge whether you are guilty or innocent, but to settle disputes about money owed and how to repay it. Remember the courts are not there just to serve the interests of your creditors.

Why is it better not to go bankrupt?

If you can come to a private agreement with your creditors, instead of going bankrupt

- You have more control over your own life. There is no trustee taking over your affairs.
- You have more say in how your assets are dealt with and how payments are made to creditors.
- You may be able to persuade any creditors who have the right to repossess your home or your car to let you keep them. Both could go if you are made bankrupt.
- You avoid restrictions on trading and on getting credit.
- It will cost you less, because the fees and expenses charged in bankruptcy proceedings can be quite high.

If you are on the verge of bankruptcy, there are several things you can do. First, write to all your individual creditors to see whether they will accept payment in instalments – give them a timetable showing what this is likely to be.

If one or more of your creditors has already got a court judgment against you and your total debts are not more than £5,000, you could ask the County Court to make an Administration Order, provided you have enough income to make regular weekly or monthly repayments which would include a small fee charged by the court for doing this. Getting an administration order is cheaper than going bankrupt and may well stop your creditors from pressing for you to be made bankrupt. However, if you do not keep up the payments the order could be cancelled and you might have the same restrictions put on you as if you were bankrupt. So if you suddenly find you cannot make the repayments, you must apply to the court at once and ask for the terms of the order to be changed.

You can find an Insolvency Practitioner (the court will give you names of local ones) and ask him to get an Individual Voluntary Arrangement for you with your creditors. You will have to pay him for this, so find out first what he plans to charge. The arrangement means that you make a formal proposal to your creditors to pay off part or all of your debts, something that has to be done via a local County Court. Companies can do the same thing – in 1994 a chain of bookshops, faced with receivership, sought a Company Voluntary Arrangement which allowed the company to continue trading for a limited period without being pursued by its creditors. Your Insolvency Practitioner will apply to the court for an Interim Order – this stops your creditors taking bankruptcy or other action against you. He tells the court what you propose and he usually holds a meeting with your creditors who vote whether or not to accept your proposition. If enough creditors (together owning more than 75 per cent of the value of your debts) are in favour, then you go ahead with the arrangement and are saved from being made bankrupt. At the worst, it gives you a breathing space before an actual bankruptcy order is made.

GOING BANKRUPT

If it is really impossible for you to pay your debts, you may have to go bankrupt – this decision may be taken for you by one of your creditors who can apply to the court for a bankruptcy if you owe them at least £750 and they have not been able to get any of it back from you. Alternatively, if you decide to go bankrupt you can ask the courts to do so. But, ironically, you have to find a considerable deposit and you will need money for court fees. Despite stories in the papers about companies losing millions, becoming bankrupt, then starting all over again, becoming personally bankrupt is not a happy experience. The good news is that you will not have to pay all those debts hanging over you once you are discharged. The bad news is that you lose control over your personal affairs.

How are you made bankrupt?

A court will make a bankruptcy order against you only after a petition has been presented either by creditors who are owed at least £750 or by you. A bankruptcy order can be made even if you refuse to acknowledge or agree to it. So if you dispute your creditors' claims, you should try to reach a settlement with them before the bankruptcy order is made. If you try to do so afterwards it is difficult and expensive.

At which court is the bankruptcy order made?

Bankruptcy petitions are usually presented either at the High Court in London or a County Court near to where you live or trade. A petition can be presented against you even if you are not in the country at the time, provided that you normally live in, or have had 'recent residential or business connection with', England and Wales.

Who will deal with my case?

An officer of the court called the Official Receiver will act as trustee of your estate. He will investigate your financial affairs for the period before and during your bankruptcy and report the results to your creditors. In some cases, instead of dealing with you himself, after consulting with your creditors, he may appoint an Insolvency practitioner to look after you. This is usually an accountant or solicitor appointed by the court who is then responsible for disposing of your assets and paying your creditors. His job is to sort out and settle your debts or decide how much in the pound you can pay your creditors and how you are going to pay them back. He is also there to keep your creditors off your back. He will also arrange for basic services like gas and electricity to be reconnected if they have been cut off.

What happens next?

You will have an interview at the offices of the Official Receiver where you will be asked exactly what has happened to cause your situation. You will then have to give him, within 21 days of the bankruptcy order being made:

- A full list of your assets – possessions and money in the bank.
- A full list of what money you owe and to whom.
- Your books, records and bank statements relating to your financial affairs.

He will also hold a meeting of creditors to discuss the situation and you will have to attend. At this he will tell the creditors, who may include the Inland Revenue and Customs and Excise for VAT, how much money, if any, there is to be shared out. It is up to them then to put in their claims. His payment list gives first priority to secured debts, then his fees and the trustees fees, then the Inland Revenue, VAT and Social Security, after that employee wages and finally, unsecured creditors. If you are running a business he will normally close this down and dismiss your employees, who then also join your list of creditors if they are owed any wages. But in some circumstances he may try to find another buyer for the business.

How will bankruptcy affect me?

You must stop using your bank, building society and similar accounts and you must not attempt to obtain credit, nor make payments directly to your creditors. You may be also asked to go to court and explain how you got into debt. If you do not co-operate you could be arrested.

Your trustee will take control of most of your assets. He will dispose of them, probably by selling them, and use the money to pay his costs and to pay creditors. He also has the right to recover anything you may have disposed of in a way which was unfair to your creditors, for instance, if you sold your car to a relative for less than its worth. You are, however, allowed to keep some assets – tools and other pieces of equipment and books necessary for your use in employment or business. You might be able to keep your car or van if it is necessary for your business or to get you to work if there is no public transport. You are also allowed to keep your clothing, bedding, furniture household equipment and other basic items you and your family need in the home. He would leave the washing machine, but if you had several luxury TV sets, some of these might go.

You cannot obtain credit of more than £250, even together with another person, without telling the person you are borrowing from that you are bankrupt. This includes any kind of hire purchase agreement. You cannot carry on a business – either directly or through someone else – in a different name from that in which you were made bankrupt without telling everyone the name of the business with which you were made bankrupt. You cannot start a company without the court's permission whether you are made a director or not. Breaking these rules can be considered a criminal offence and you could go to jail.

You are also debarred for holding certain 'public offices' – check with the court. The Official Receiver will also take a look at your regular income if you are in work and may order you to pay part of it to him for distribution to the creditors if he thinks you have money to spare. Your creditors will stop asking you for money directly and will deal with the trustee instead. However, if you have a mortgage, or pay rent, arrangements will have to be made for you to pay it. The same goes for any outstanding court fines or family maintenance orders. The electricity, gas, water and telephone companies may not approach you for settlement of outstanding bills but they may ask you for a deposit for payment in advance for further supplies.

What happens to my home?

It will probably have to be sold to help pay your debts. However, if you are married, your husband or wife, even if they are not a joint owner of the property, may be able to get the sale put off for up to a year. This is to give them time to find somewhere else to live or perhaps get a relative or friend to buy the property to prevent a forced sale. As the housing situation is currently in recession, the trustee may not be able to sell your home. In this case he may decide to obtain a 'charging order' on it which is like a second mortgage. This will be the total sum you owe in the bankruptcy, including his and other costs, which will have to be paid, with interest, from your share of the profits when the property is sold.

Once you are discharged from bankruptcy, the trustee can, in some circumstances, still sell your home if you have debts outstanding. If you rent your home, then the trustee cannot do anything about it. But you will still have to find the money for the rent and the trustee may decide to tell your landlord that you are bankrupt, particularly if you owe him back rent which you cannot pay.

What am I allowed to do?

You can open a new account with a bank or building society, but you must tell them when you do so that you are bankrupt, which may mean they will impose conditions and limitations. But you cannot ask for an overdraft or write cheques which you know will put the account in debit. Your trustee will also keep an eye on the account and if there are larger amounts in it than you need, he can claim them to help pay your creditors.

How long does bankruptcy last?

If you manage to pay your debts and expenses in full, then the court will annul your bankruptcy order. Otherwise you are usually 'discharged' – freed from bankruptcy – after three years. If you have made yourself bankrupt and owe less than £250 it may be after two years. Discharge releases you from most of the debts that you owed at the time you were made bankrupt (*see above*). The only ones that might be outstanding were any that related to fraud, or certain crimes or court fines. And the court would have to make up its own mind whether you should still have to pay items such as outstanding maintenance to an ex-husband or wife.

Once you are discharged then the slate is wiped clean. You can borrow money, start a business or be a company director if you wish. But be warned – if you should go bankrupt again, then you will not get an automatic discharge this time. You can only apply for it after five years and the court may refuse or delay the decision.

FINANCE: HELP DIRECTORY

Bankruptcy

- Insolvency Service, 21 Bloomsbury Street, London WC1B 3SS, (0171 637 1110). Has a useful booklet *A Guide to Bankruptcy*.
- The Money Advice Association, (0171 236 3566). Can give you details of centres offering money advice services.

Banks

- The Banking Ombudsman, 70 Grays Inn Road, London, WC1X 8NB, (0171 404 9944).

Benefits

- To obtain DSS Information leaflets, call Freephone 0800 666555.
  The Benefits Agency of the DSS has the following free helplines:
  Benefit enquiry line 0800 882 200.
  In Chinese 0800 252 451.
  In Punjabi 0800 521 360.

In Urdu 0800 289 188.

Welsh 0800 289011.

Northern Ireland 0800 616757.

If you have a disability: 08002200.

There is a Social Security Freeline 0800 666 555.

There is also a London Emergency Office:

- Benefits Agency, London Emergency Office, Keyworth House, Keyworth Street, London SE1 1HP, (0171 620 1456) This line is only available after 3 pm daily. Ring for numbers in your area. Open Monday to Friday 6 pm to 10 pm, Saturday 9 am to 10 pm, Sunday and public holidays (except Christmas Day (2 pm to 10 pm).

Credit cards

Telephone lines for lost credit cards (*see* **Emergencies,** *page 6*).

Debt, dealing with creditors

- National Debtline, Birmingham Settlement, 318 Summer Lane, Birmingham B19 3RL, (0121 359 8501). Has a telephone advice service for people who are in debt.

Income tax

- Chartered Association of Certified Accountants, 29 Lincoln's Inn Fields, London WC2A 3EE, (0171 242 6855).
- Institute of Chartered Accountants, in England and Wales, Gloucester House, 399 Silbury Boulevard, Central Milton Keynes MK9 2HL, (01908 248100).
- Revenue Adjudicator, Haymarket House, 28 Haymarket, London SW1Y 4SP, (0171 930 2292).

Investment, insurance

- Institute of Actuaries, Staple Inn Hall, High Holborn, London WC1V 7QJ, (0171 242 0106).
- Insurance Brokers' Registration Council (IBRC), 15 St Helen's Place, London EC3A 6DS, (0171 588 4387).
- Insurance Ombudsman, City Gate One, 135 Park Street, London SE1 9EA, (0171 928 7600). Handles cases where you are in dispute with your insurer.
- Investment Management Regulatory Organization (IMRO), Broadwalk House, 6 Appold Street, London EC2A 2AA, (0171 628 6022).

- Personal Insurance Arbitration Service, Chartered Institute of Arbitrators, 24 Angel Gate, 326 City Road, London EC1V 2RS, (0171 837 4483). Arbitrates over insurance problems.
- Personal Investment Authority, 1 Canada Square, Canary Wharf, London E14 5AZ. Has a consumer helpline on 0171 538 8860.
- Securities and Investments Board, Gavrelle House, 2–14 Bunhill Row, London EC1Y 8RA, (0171 638 1240). Ring 0171 929 3652 to check whether your financial adviser is authorized and on this register.

Mortgages

- Building Societies Ombudsman, Grosvenor House, 35–37 Grosvenor Gardens, London SW1X 7AW, (0171 931 0044).
- Council of Mortgage Lenders, 3 Savile Row, London W1, (0171 437 0655).

Obtaining credit

- Association of British Credit Unions Ltd (ABCUL), Unit 307, Westminster Business Square, 339 Kennington Lane, London SE11 5QY, (0171 582 2626).
- Data Protection Registrar, Complaints Dept, Wycliffe House, Water Lane, Wilmslow, Cheshire SK9 5AF, (0625 535777). Contact this office if you wish to complain that you have been unjustly refused credit.
- Director General of Fair Trading, Office of Fair Trading, Field House, 15–25 Bream's Buildings, London EC4A 1PR, (0171 242 2858).
- National Federation of Credit Unions, Suite 1.1 & 1.2, Howard House Commercial Centre, Howard Street, North Shields NE30 1A, (0191 257 2219).

Credit reference agencies
- CCN Systems Ltd., Consumer Affairs Dept, PO Box 40, Nottingham NG7 2SS, (0115 941 0888).
- Equifax Europe Ltd, Consumer Affairs Dept, Spectrum House, 1A North Avenue, Clydebank, Glasgow G81 2DR, (0141 951 1253).

Private pensions

- Occupational Pensions Advisory Service (OPAS), 11 Belgrave Road, London, SW1V 1RB, (0171 233 8080).
- The Personal Investment Authority's Pension Unit, Hertsmere House, Hertsmere Road, London E14 4AB, (0171 417 7001). Will give advice to anyone who left a company pension scheme to go into a personal pension plan and is now claiming compensation.
- Registrar of Pension Schemes, Occupational Pensions Board, PO Box 1NN, Newcastle-upon-Tyne NE99 1NN, (0191 225 6394).

11

ETHNIC MINORITIES

YOUR RIGHTS

There is said to be a racially motivated attack on somebody, somewhere in Britain every 15 minutes. People who are going about their everyday business are assaulted because of the colour of their skin or because of their origin. And they are not even safe in their homes; their houses are set on fire, flaming rags or animal excreta are pushed through their letterboxes along with threatening messages.

No company or educational establishment is allowed to let anyone using racist abuse get away with it. Dealing with members of the public in general is more difficult. Words hurt, whether they are shouted at you in the street, scrawled on a wall or pushed through your letterbox. It is small comfort to think that the people who do these things are ignorant and uninformed. It is not only black people or Asians who are insulted, Jews and Irish people have to face up to abuse from time to time. Racial attacks are a crime and racial discrimination is against the law but there is no special legislation to deal with it. It comes under the general heading of violence, despite the fact that you are being singled out because of your race. However, when a judge in a trial has been given evidence that someone was attacked because of their race he can impose a longer sentence. Under the Public Order Act, it is an offence to use threatening, insulting or abusive words or behaviour with the intention of stirring up racial hatred.

It is certainly illegal for someone to hit you or make you fear he will attack you. This behaviour can carry a charge of assault. The same goes if someone spits at you, throws a stone at you or sets a dog on you. It is also illegal if someone threatens you with a knife, a broken bottle or a hammer in his hand – all of which could be construed as offensive weapons. Using threatening, abusive or insulting words or behaviour towards you is also illegal, especially if it is meant or likely to stir up racial hatred. Criminal damage to your property or possessions such as breaking windows, snapping off car aerials and daubing paint on doors is also illegal as is putting racist leaflets through your door.

What to do if it happens to you

Keep your dignity, which may be difficult in the circumstances. Let them know that you do not like what they are doing, but do not let them see you lose control.

- Make a careful record of what is happening.
- Try to get some witnesses.
- Contact the police.
- If you have been injured, see a doctor who can write a report on how badly you have been hurt. It is a good idea to have a photograph taken of any injuries.
- If there is any evidence around, such as a broken window, leave it untouched until the police have seen it.

Going to the police

The police have a duty to keep the peace and this includes protecting you and your family against racial harassment or attack. It is important, therefore, that any crime of this kind is reported right away. Many police forces now have special units to tackle race crimes which are logged now as 'racial incidents'. Contact the police as soon as possible. If you have difficulty understanding what they say because English is not your first language, take someone with you. There are organizations that can help (*see page 420*). Tell them that you are reporting a race attack.

- Write down (or get someone else to do so) what happened, who did what, when, the names of the people who attacked you, if you know them, or what they looked like.
- Give the police the names of any witnesses.
- If the police take a statement from you, ask for a copy.
- Make a note of the name of the policeman who interviewed you and any other policemen who were involved and the date you reported the incident to the police. Let the police see you doing this.
- If you are not happy about the way you are being treated, ask to see the most senior officer on duty.

Afterwards, bolster your courage by going to a support group (*see page 420*) if you have not done so before. Not only may it take up your case for you, but support groups provide useful places for you to let off steam. If nothing seems to be happening, do not give up; continue to fight for yourself, pester the police, your firm and the council, if necessary. Go to your local Law Centre or see a solicitor and ask him to follow up your complaint with the police. Or go to your local race unit – most towns now have racial equality councils. If you cannot locate one, ask your local Citizens' Advice Bureau. If all else fails, make an official complaint against the police (*see* **Legal,** *page 432*).

IMMIGRATION

Some people have the 'right of abode' in the United Kingdom. Apart from British citizens, those who are Commonwealth citizens with one parent born here, or women from the Commonwealth who married men with right of abode before 1983, may have the right of abode.

Entry clearance

If you are planning to come to the United Kingdom from another country, for anything other than a visit – emigrating, coming to stay permanently or for the purposes of work or business – you must obtain entry clearance before you arrive. This is permission from a British Consulate, Embassy or High Commission in your country of origin which will stamp your passport. You cannot get this when you arrive in the UK; it must be done before you set out.

If you are a national of a European Community country, however, you can come here for work, business or self-employment and to 'provide or receive services'. The exceptions to this are Spanish and Portuguese citizens who are not able to come here to work at the moment. On arrival, your passport will be stamped again by the immigration officer at the airport or sea port giving you 'leave to enter'. This stamp will set out any restrictions placed upon you as to how long you can stay, what kind of work or business you can do and whether you need to register with the police. You could be deported if you disobey these restrictions. If you need to extend your stay, you can apply to the Home Office for leave to remain.

Seeking asylum

There is no official procedure either in this country or at UK consulates abroad for those seeking asylum, but airlines and shipping companies can be fined heavily for bringing in someone without a correct visa or passport. Any refugee who does manage to reach the UK should ask for asylum immediately from the immigration officer. At the same time the refugee should ask to see someone from the UK Immigrants' Advisory Service Refugee Unit, or if landing at Heathrow, the Refugee Arrivals Project at Heathrow Airport.

The government has recently toughened its stance on immigration under the Asylum and Immigration Appeals Act which has been condemned as racist, and will result in more and more people being turned away. Amnesty International has highlighted what it calls a 'game of human pinball' with asylum-seekers. Under the 1993 Asylum and Immigration Appeals Act, the Home Office is allowed to return asylum-seekers to so-called 'safe third countries' – countries through which the refugees may have passed in transit to the UK and where, in the view of the Home

Office, they should have sought asylum. In other words, if someone fleeing from Iraq arrives in this country via France, the Home Office can send him back to France rather than giving him asylum here. The obvious lesson is that anyone planning to seek asylum in this country should try to come here direct, rather than transiting through another country.

If you are discovered to be an illegal immigrant and detained, you will probably be deported. Due to overcrowding, illegal immigrants often have to be held in solitary confinement for some time in police cells designed for a 24-hour stay with insufficient washing facilities.

Partners

There are stringent rules in operation for fiancé(e)s, husbands and wives which, according to the National Council for Civil Liberties, appear to be aimed specifically at Asian immigration from the sub-continent, for the Home Office tends to view the arranged marriage system with suspicion. If you are an incoming fiancé(e), husband or wife, you have to prove:

- That you met your partner or would-be partner before you applied for your entry clearance.
- That you intend to live permanently with your partner.
- That the marriage is permanent and not a ruse to come to the UK.

Be prepared to face long delays before you get the permit you need.

Relatives

The newly introduced DNA system of testing, which helps in proving family relationships, should make it easier for parents, grandparents and children of immigrants to enter the country. Aged parents, when one parent is over the age of 65, and widowed mothers of any age who can prove they are dependent on their son or daughter in the UK and have no relatives in their own country to look after them, should be able to get permission to live here. Other younger relatives would probably not be given permission.

Children under the age of 18 who are joining both parents should have no difficulty in coming to this country. But if the parents are separated or divorced, or the children are under the care of a guardian, things can become more complicated. And if the child is adopted, he will only be allowed in if it can be proved that his biological parent is unable to look after him.

Visitors to this country

Anyone who can show, either by themselves or via friends and relatives, that they can pay their way without claiming benefits is permitted to enter the UK for up to six months. You may have to satisfy the immigration officer that you intend to leave at the end of your visit by showing a return airline ticket. You should never suggest in any way that you are looking for work or for marriage to a UK citizen. You are, of course, allowed in for private medical care.

Overseas students in this country

To stay in this country as a student, you must show proof that you have been accepted for private or further full-time education for at least 15 hours of daytime lessons. You also have to show that you can pay your fees and living expenses and that you intend to leave at the end of your course.

Male students can bring a wife and children with them, but owing to an archaic and unjust rule, female students may not bring a husband and children with them. If you are coming in on a government or British Council scholarship, you may not be allowed to do any paid work, neither will your wife – check with the organization who gave you the scholarship. Otherwise you might be able to get permission to work from the Department of Employment and your wife may be permitted to work too. Doctors and dentists doing postgraduate study are usually allowed to work. It is always important to check out the rules before accepting any sort of part-time job.

Working in the UK

Although a large number of immigrants to this country are known to be working without permits, officially, if you come from abroad and wish to work in this country, your employer must obtain a work permit from the Department of Employment before you apply for your entry clearance to come to the UK. Even this does not guarantee you the job. If it is felt that false representations have been made, or that you are not actually taking up the job, or that the job is no longer available, you may be refused permission to enter the UK. Once in this country, if you want to change your job you need permission from the Department of Employment.

Au pairs

Au pair girls are an exception to the rule above. They must be between the ages of 17 and 27, be female and be single. They must also be West European and be coming to England to learn English by living with a family and doing light work in the house for a set number of hours a week. They are not allowed to stay more than two years. Au pair boys are now banned.

Working holidays

Technically, any Commonwealth citizen can apply to come to the UK as a working holidaymaker. But permission for this tends to be restricted to white Commonwealth citizens, says the National Council for Civil Liberties. Like au pairs, their stay is restricted to two years.

Other entrants

Unless you are an artist or a writer, you must have at least £200,000 of 'disposable' capital or for those who are of 'independent means', not less than £20,000 a year income in order to live in this country. Nevertheless, you are forbidden to take paid work and you must 'demonstrate a close connection with the UK' or the immigration authorities must feel that your admission would be 'in the national interest'. There are tough rules for business people or those who are self-employed who want to settle here. They have to pass a test of 'investment capacity' and show that their business will create new jobs for people already settled in the UK.

Writers and artists, on the other hand, do not have to take income or capital tests but they need to show they can pay their own way from their own writing or art.

Extending your stay

There are no hard and fast rules about being allowed to stay on in this country, only guidelines; you have to rely on the 'discretion' of the immigration authorities.

- If you come from abroad, then marry in this country you can apply to stay on as a spouse.
- If you are a student and need to take another course you would probably be allowed to do so as long as it was a logical development of the original course.
- You must make application to the Home Office for further leave before your existing leave expires. Post your application by recorded delivery so that the Home Office has a record that it was actually posted by you.

What if I am refused entry?

You could be refused entry to this country for a number of reasons.

- If you have certain medical problems.
- If you have a criminal record.
- If you have a current deportation order.
- If your exclusion is 'conducive to the public good' perhaps on political grounds.
- If you do not have entry clearance.

In all cases you should be allowed to telephone friends, relatives and your high commission. In some cases 'temporary admission' may be given to you. If a friend or relative phones from the airport to say they are being refused admission to the country, you should immediately get advice and help (*see page 420*).

How to appeal

If you ask for entry clearance from a British embassy, high commission or consulate in your own country and are refused, you have three months in which to appeal against the decision. If you did not come to the country with entry clearance and were sent back, you have to appeal against the decision within 28 days of leaving the UK. If you arrived with entry clearance but were refused admission, you can appeal within 14 days while you are still in the UK. You cannot get legal aid to cover the appeal but you might get financial help with the solicitor's advice and preparation of your case.

Being deported

A deportation order means that you cannot apply to come back to the UK until the order is revoked. This is not done, except in exceptional circumstances, until three years has lapsed since your departure from the UK. You can be deported at any time, usually because you have been found to be an illegal immigrant or because of a court order against you. If you are to be deported, notice of intention will be sent to your last known address, but you do not have to receive it in person. Dependent members of your family may also be deported at the same time if they do not have the right to remain on some other basis. You have 14 days to appeal, but unless you arrived in the UK more than 7 years previously or you are seeking asylum, you can only challenge the facts of the case and no compassionate circumstances can be taken into consideration.

RACIAL DISCRIMINATION

The Commission for Racial Equality points out that under the Race Relations Act there are three kinds of discrimination:

Direct discrimination
This occurs when someone is treated less favourably than others on racial grounds. The word 'race' covers colour, nationality and ethnic or national origin. For example, if the police fail to provide adequate translation services for a Bangladeshi woman who has been attacked but finds it difficult to express herself in English, this would be considered direct discrimination.

Indirect discrimination
This sort of discrimination is more subtle. It occurs when a rule which seems to be quite fair, because it applies to everyone, actually puts people from certain ethnic groups at a much greater disadvantage than others. An example of this might be a Neighbourhood Watch letter that asks people to look out for any

gypsies in the area. Gypsies are defined as a racial group under the Race Relations Act.

Victimization

The Act also protects anyone who is victimized for having taken a case of racial discrimination to the courts or having supported someone else's case. It would be considered victimization if an Asian prisoner who has brought a complaint that there is no reading material available in Hindi is subsequently not allowed to use the prison's education and training facilities.

Being stopped by the police

Research studies by the Commission For Racial Equality show that if you are black you are more likely to be:

- Questioned, stopped or arrested by police on suspicion of committing a crime.
- Charged with a criminal offence rather than cautioned.
- Remanded in custody rather than allowed bail.
- Sentenced to jail at the end of the trial.
- Given the dirtier and more humiliating jobs when in prison.

Some judges have been accused of giving longer sentences to some men just because they were black. Certain groups in authority, such as the police, the courts, immigration officers and so on, can do things which might appear to add up to discrimination under the Race Relations Act, but which cannot be stopped. However, no one can discriminate in the service they provide. If the police refuse to help a black family whose house has been burgled, this would be considered to be unlawful.

Discrimination happens in many ways. A recent survey found that half of all passengers searched by Customs and Excise officers at ports and airports were black, even though figures from the department show that white suspects are three times more likely to be carrying drugs.

How to complain

- Get legal advice from a solicitor, Law Centre, Citizens' Advice Bureau or Racial Equality Council before you lodge a complaint.
- You can get an individual or an organization to make a complaint on your behalf if your knowledge of English is not good, but you must give them written consent to do so.
- You can make a complaint in person but it is better to put it down in writing, making it as brief as you can. Keep a copy of what you say.
- Give the name and the rank of the person you are complaining about if you can.
- You can only complain about the conduct of specific police officers, you cannot make a complaint about the police in general.

- Send your complaint to the Chief Constable of the force where the person you are complaining about works.

Housing

The Racial Discrimination Act protects you against discrimination when you rent, buy or sell a house. You cannot be refused accommodation because of your race, colour or ethnic origin or offered worse terms and conditions than others. This covers council property, housing associations, hostels, private landlords, estate agents and accommodation agencies, property developers and managing agents and owner-occupiers. It also covers banks and building societies who might be involved in lending you money to buy a house.

In short, discrimination in housing is against the law. It is an offence for anyone to refuse to let you a flat or sell you a house because of your race. It is equally against the law for an estate agent to warn white house hunters to avoid certain areas because there is a large population of black people or to refuse to give particulars of houses for sale in 'white areas' to black people.

It can be very difficult to prove that you have been discriminated against over housing because this act is very easy to disguise. If you feel that you have been treated in this way, get in touch with the Commission for Racial Equality at once, but it will need hard facts before it can act. If, for instance, you think that an estate agent or landlord has refused you a property because of your colour or race, it may be that you will have to set a trap and get a white friend to enquire about the same property. If your friend is offered it, then the person concerned would have some difficulty in putting up a defence against the Commission for Racial Equality.

Exceptions to the law

Lodgings are not always covered by the law. If the landlord, owner or a near relative lives on the premises and shares facilities with lodgers, they are allowed to choose whom they will share with which may result in discrimination. The same applies to people who take someone into their home as one of the family – fostering, perhaps, or caring for an elderly person.

Harassment

If you are a council tenant and are being racially harassed by your neighbours, then as well as going to the police about it, you should report the situation to the council's Housing Department which should take action to help you. It may take out a legal case against the offenders or it could evict them. You could also, if you wanted to, ask the council to rehouse you somewhere else.

Education

Analysis of the official census shows that black Africans are now the most highly educated members of British society and are twice as likely to hold jobs in the professions as barristers and doctors than white people. More than a quarter of adults hold qualifications above A-level, compared with about one in eight in whites. Chinese people come next, Indians from Africa and the Asian sub-continent are third. Yet they still face discrimination in education.

Your rights

Schools and colleges must see that everyone has fair access to what is taught. A school or college cannot racially discriminate in entry rules, in the type of education it gives or in the measures of discipline it imposes. The Commission for Racial Equality says:

- A school uniform should not ban turbans or enforce skirts for girls.
- Entry requirements should not depend on parents writing detailed letters, often a problem if the parents have difficulty in writing in English.
- Schools should offer English as a second language.

If you think you have been discriminated against

Go to the Commission first or the local Racial Equality Council in your area, if there is one. They will tell you whether your case is valid and give you advice. You must first complain to the Department for Education in England, the Welsh Education Office or the Scottish Education Department (*see* **Education**, *page 347*). The department may agree to act on your complaint and can tell schools and colleges what to do. If you do not have a response from the department within two months, you can take the case to a County Court, or a Sheriff Court in Scotland. You may get legal aid for the case but you must take your case to court within six months minus one day of the incident – though if the Department of Education took a long time to consider it, you may be allowed extra time.

Bullying

If any of your children are racially harassed or bullied at school or on the way to or from school, you should tell the Education Department of your local Council and inform the school. Many schools now have very firm policies on bullying of any kind (*see also* **Education**, *page 341*).

Employment

It is a fact that young black school-leavers tend to be stuck at the back of the jobs queue, even behind the disabled. The Employment Department has commissioned a survey to find out why so many black men and those from Asian communities are out of work. Its findings will form the basis of government policy in the future. Meanwhile it is a case of every man for himself.

Have you been discriminated against over a job?
Sometimes a less qualified and less experienced white worker is chosen over a black one, or promoted unfairly. There can be discrimination over pay as well – having an all-white day shift and an all-Asian or black night shift, for instance, and paying the day shift overtime but not the night staff.

If you face discrimination or racial insults at work
If you think you have been discriminated against at work because of your race or colour, get help and advice as soon as possible. If someone in authority – a teacher, policeman, someone in your firm – behaves this way then go to the manager, the head teacher, or the police station and make your complaint. If you go on a training course and are denied work experience while whites around you are sent out to local employers, take the matter up with whoever is in authority. There have been cases of black people being trapped in a workshop while white trainees go out for practical experience. Go straight to your trade union, if there is one, or Law Centre, Racial Equality Council or the Citizens' Advice Bureau.

You may see a job advertised in a shop window, for instance, and were told it had gone, only to find that a white person who went in after you was offered the job. Racial discrimination is difficult to prove so get expert help as soon as you can. Time limits are very strict – if you leave your complaint for more than a fortnight you may run out of time. However, it can often be months after you were refused a job or promotion before you found out that someone less able than you got it. In this case, tribunals will usually let the time limit run from the moment you found out.

Think over carefully what happened. Can you be sure you were treated unfairly on the basis of your colour, race, national or ethnic origin? A hunch is not good enough, says the Commission for Racial Equality. You must have some hard facts. Make the person concerned aware of the fact that his remarks are insulting and distressing to you, even if they are said in a joking way. Words like 'black bastard', 'Paki' and 'Yid' are considered by tribunals to be insulting even if they are said in jest. If the person does not stop, go to the personnel manager about it. If that does no good then you should contact an Industrial Tribunal. You may be entitled to damages for the way you have been treated.

If you are making a complaint
- Make it formal by putting it down on paper. Get help if necessary to do this.
- Keep a record of all incidents of discrimination and copies of all correspondence.
- Get the advice of a good employment lawyer. Your local Racial Equality Council or Citizens' Advice Bureau should help you here.

Exceptions to the law

- Racial discrimination rules do not apply in the case of people employed in private homes. So a private household can legally refuse to hire you on racial grounds.
- Some small firms are also outside the law. In partnerships where there are fewer than six partners, the rules do not apply.
- If a firm is hiring people for jobs that involve working outside Britain most of the time, it is allowed to discriminate on racial grounds.
- Some official 'British' bodies like the British Museum, the British Council and the Bank of England are allowed to discriminate against people by birth, nationality, descent or residence, but they are not allowed to discriminate by race or colour.
- Certain people can advertise for someone from a particular group if it is necessary for the job – hiring a black actor to play a black person on stage, for instance. The same applies to Indian restaurants which are allowed to hire only Indian waiters.

Health

It is a fact that when people from ethnic minorities become mentally ill, they are more likely to suffer rough treatment at the hands of the psychiatric services, partly through ignorance and partly through racial prejudice. The Council for Racial Equality says that people from ethnic minorities are far more likely to be:

- Removed by the police to 'a place of safety' under the Mental Health Act.
- Detained in hospital against their will.
- Kept in a locked ward.
- Given high doses of medicine.
- Given ECT treatment (*see page 452*) without their consent.
- Remanded in custody for psychiatric reports.
- Subjected to restriction orders.
- Detained in higher degrees of security for longer.
- Moved from a prison to a 'regional secure unit' or special hospital like Broadmoor.
- Less likely to get early treatment such as psychotherapy or counselling and 12 times more likely to end up diagnosed as schizophrenic than white people.

What to do

If you think that you, a member of your family or a friend is or has been treated unfairly in hospital, they can complain under the Race Relations Act. You can also lodge a complaint with the hospital, then with the Commission for Racial Equality if the patient cannot speak English and no efforts are made to supply an interpreter or if no effort has been made to cater for the kind of food that the person normally eats.

The community

Abuse from neighbours

Neighbours who habitually insult you or make your life hell because of your race can face a civil action which could end in a fine or, if they live in council accommodation, in eviction from their home.

Abuse and attacks in public

Under the Public Order Act, racial abuse in a public place can be an offence. If you are insulted in this way you must have witnesses to make your case stick, so get names and addresses of anyone who saw what went on. The court can then make your aggressor pay compensation to you or a fine to the court. And, if you live in England or Wales, they can be bound over to keep the peace. If the incident happens at a football match in England and Wales, the person may be prosecuted under the Football (Offences) Act 1991, but you must have witnesses.

Pubs and clubs

Under the Race Relations Act it is against the law for:

- A pub to put up a sign saying 'No Travellers' since this would exclude Gypsies more than anyone else.
- A pub or restaurant to impose a 'no hats' rule as this would exclude turban-wearing Sikhs.
- A company running a leisure complex to instruct staff to keep black or Asian customers out and to sack its employees if they do not adhere to the instructions.
- A hotel hiring out a room to tell people using it that they must not allow in people from ethnic minorities.
- A club or restaurant to refuse entry to people because of colour or racial origins.

However, it is within the law to set up a club where the main object is to allow the benefits of membership to be enjoyed by those of a particular racial or national group so long as this is not done on grounds of colour. Therefore clubs like the London Irish Association and the Bradford Pakistani Club are both within the law.

What to do if you think you are being excluded

- Contact the Commission for Racial Equality, your local Racial Equality Council or Citizens' Advice Bureau as soon as you can.
- If you think a club is discriminating against you, try to get some evidence you can show to other people. If you are black, see if you can get someone who is white to also apply to see if that person is accepted while you are turned down.
- If you have an Asian name and are turned down, send in another application in an English name. It will not necessarily prove discrimination, but it will help reveal whether or not there is a problem.

- Get help and take your case to court if necessary. You may be able to get legal aid.

What is the Commission for Racial Equality?

The Commission was set up by the 1976 Race Relations Act. Funded by the Home Office, but working independently of government, it is run by Commissioners appointed by the Home Secretary. The CRE, as it is known, works towards the elimination of racial discrimination, promotes equal opportunities and good race relations. It is therefore concerned with all victims of racial discrimination irrespective of their colour, race or nationality.

How it can help you
- It can give advice and information.
- You can report incidents to it and it will give you legal advice.
- If you have been racially attacked, harassed or abused, the Commission will put you in touch with the best people to advise you on action.
- It also helps organizations develop equal opportunities for their staff.

The Commission for Racial Equality can only help you if your case is covered by the Race Relations Act. Its complaints officers will help you as much as possible with advice but they are not your representatives. It is only if and when they make a firm offer of legal assistance that they will act as your representative. Until then it is up to you to do your paperwork and attend any preliminary hearings.

ETHNIC MINORITIES: HELP DIRECTORY

General

- AFFOR, c/o Foundry School, Foundry Road, Birmingham B18 4LP, (0121 523 8076). Campaigns for better education for black youths.
- Black Female Prisoners Scheme, Brixton Enterprise Centre, 444 Brixton Road, London SW9 8EJ, (0171 733 5520). Supports black women in prison and after their release by helping their families and themselves.
- Black Women for Wages for Housework, King's Cross Women's Centre, 71 Tonbridge Street, London WC1H 9DZ, (0171 837 7509). Gives help and advice on black women's rights to welfare, housing, immigration. It also helps over health and disability problems, and counsels victims of rape, racism etc.

- Commission for Racial Equality, Elliot House, 10–12 Allington Street, London SW1E 5EH, (0171 828 7022) F 630 7605. Works towards the elimination of racial discrimination.
- Federation of Black Housing Organizations, 374 Grays Inn Road, London WC1X 8BB, (0171 837 8288). Works to encourage black people to join more tenants' and housing associations.
- Institute of Race Relations, 2–6 Leeke Street, London WC1X 9HS, (0171 837 0041) F 278 0623. Gives information and advice on race problems. It will refer you to the appropriate organization.
- International Social Service UK, Cranmer House, 39 Brixton Road, London SW9 6DD, (0171 735 8941), F 582 0696. Traces long-lost parents, relatives abroad. It also has an advisory service on marriage to foreigners and assists immigrants who wish to return home.
- Local Authorities Race Relations Information Exchange, 41 Belgrave Square, London SW1X 8NZ, (0171 259 5464). Can give you the name and phone number of the local Race Relations worker in your area.
- National Association of Community Relations Councils, 8–16 Coronet Street, London N1 6HD, (0171 739 6658). Can put you in touch with your local Community Relations Council.
- National Convention of Black Teachers, PO Box 30, Pinner, Middx HA5 5HF, (0181 866 1682). Offers support to black teachers, especially against racial discrimination. It also has an advice service for parents.
- Pascal Theatre Company, 35 Flaxman Court, Flaxman Terrace, London WC1H 9AR, (0171 383 0920). Offers encouragement to playwrights and writers of the ethnic minorities, presenting new plays, helping with publication.
- Sex, Race and Class, Black and Third World Women's Discussion and Study Group, King's Cross Women's Centre, 71 Tonbridge Street, London WC1H 9DZ, (0171 837 7509). A centre for support and discussion to help bring together Asian, African, Afro-Caribbean and other black women of all ages.

See also Homeless Action and Accommodation Ltd (**Home** *page 493*).

Immigrants, refugees

- Asylum Aid, 244a Upper Street, London N1 1RU, (0171 359 4026). Helps refugees who are applying for asylum in this country, helps them present their claims or appeals against a Home Office decision, intervening when necessary. It also gives help over housing, welfare rights etc.
- Campaign Against Racist Laws, 15 Kenton Avenue, Southall, Middx UB1 3QF, (0181 571 1437). Helps immigrants who are facing the threat of deportation.
- Joint Council for the Welfare of Immigrants, 115 Old Street, London EC1V 9JZ, (0171 251 8706). Takes up cases of immigrants facing deportation with the Home Office, gives legal advice.

- Medical Foundation for the Care of Victims of Torture, 96–98 Grafton Road, London NW5 3EJ, (0171 284 4321). Provides medical advice and counselling to people who are suffering injury after torture via self-help groups.
- Ockenden Venture, Ockenden, Constitution Hill, Woking, Surrey GU22 7UU, (01483 772012). Provides a home for Vietnamese refugees from Hong Kong and long-term care for handicapped refugees of any nationality.
- Refugee Action, 240a Clapham Road, London SW9 0PZ, (0171 735 5361). Counsels newly arrived refugees, giving information on social services, housing, employment etc. Recently it has been dealing with Bosnian refugees.
- Refugee Arrivals Project, Room 2005, Queen's Building, Heathrow Airport, Hounslow, Middx TW6 1DL, (0181 759 5740). Gives a completely independent advice and information service to refugees arriving at any of the main airports in the south: Heathrow, Gatwick, Stansted, Luton or London City. The Project helps refugees over health, financial, housing, educational or legal problems before handing them on to local agencies after their first weeks in this country.
- Refugee Council, Bondway House, 3–9 Bondway, London SW8 1SJ, (0171 582 6922). Works to help and counsel refugees to this country with short-term hostel accommodation and advice and practical assistance over job training. It has a telephone helpline on 0171 582 1162.
- Refugee Legal Centre, Sussex House, 39–45 Bermondsey Street, London SE1 3XF, (0171 827 9090). Advises refugees on legal problems.
- Immigration Advisory Service, County House, 190 Great Dover Street, London SE1 4YB, (0171 357 6917). Advises immigrants in this country on rights, helping them with language problems. The organization has offices at both Heathrow and Gatwick airports and in most major cities and will act for immigrants at tribunals or make representations to the Home Office, the Foreign and the Commonwealth Office.
- Urban Trust, c/o Carib Housing, 58 Kennington Park Road, London SE11 4RS, (0171 735 2443). Can give grants and loans to black people, in particular those living in deprived inner city areas, to help them over housing problems.

Individual minority groups

African

- Adun Society, 62 Bedford High Street, London SE8 4IT, (0181 694 1951). Aims to keep alive African cultural heritage among young Africans in this country. The society gives help with child-care, training, employment, health, immigration, housing, and over legal problems. It also runs courses for women in fashion design and business development.

- African Refugee Housing Action Group Ltd, 2nd Floor, St Margarets, 25 Leighton Road, London NW5 2QD, (0171 482 3829). Gives help to African refugees in this country over both short-term and long-term housing, with their DSS claims etc. It also campaigns for the rights of immigrants and refugees.
- Akina Mama wa Afrika, c/o London Women's Centre, Wesley House, 4 Wild Court, London WC2B 5AU, (0171 405 0678). Gives advice to African women living in this country and especially gives help, via its African Women Prisoners' Project, to African women who are in British prisons.
- East London Black Women's Organization, Clinton Road, London E7 0HD, (0181 534 7545). Organizes workshops, counselling sessions, cultural events and self-help groups for black African women in that part of London.
- Ghana Welfare Association, Greater London House, 547–551 High Road, London E11 4PB, (0181 558 9311). An umbrella organization offering support to Ghanaians in this country, advising them over welfare rights, housing benefits and counselling over immigration problems. It also has a large social and cultural programme.
- Mbaaku-Black Women's Group, 21a Groveway, London SW9 0AH, (0171 793 0106). A support and shelter organization for black and minority group women in south London. It advises over jobs, housing and there is a crèche for children of working mothers during the school holidays.

Afro-Caribbean

- Afro-Caribbean Education Resource Centre, Wyvil Road, London SW8 2TJ, (0171 627 2662). Is concerned with making sure that Afro-Caribbean heritage is represented in schools and develops materials for use in primary schools in particular. It also runs an annual young black writers' essay competition and has a library of published material relating to the experience of being black in this country.
- Afro-Caribbean Educational Project, Women's Centre, 603 High Road, London E10 6RF, (0181 556 4053). Runs a national advice and information service for Afro-Caribbean women, with training courses and local projects.
- Afro-Caribbean Library Association, Community Services Team, Shoreditch Library, Pitfield Street, London N1 6EX, (0171 729 3545). Promotes black history and heritage, and works to make sure that black communities are given all available information on racial equality.
- Afro-Caribbean Resource Centre, 339 Dudley Road, Winson Green, Birmingham B18 4HB, (0121 455 6382). Gives help to Afro-Caribbean people in the Birmingham area, especially over poverty and hardship via retraining projects, communication skills and education. It also supports local community associations.

- Caribbean Community Centre, 416 Seven Sisters Road, Manor House, London N4 2LX, (0181 802 0550). Works locally providing accommodation for homeless young black people. It also offers counselling to local West Indian families, visiting young mothers with children and old people, schools and prisons.
- Standing Conference of West Indian Organisations in Great Britain, 5 Westminster Bridge Road, London SE1 7XW, (0171 928 7861). Represents West Indians in this country, gives general information, runs a counselling and legal advice service.
- West Indian Women's Association, William Morris Community Centre, Greenleaf Road, London E17 4JF, (0181 521 4456). Aims to help young people in particular to develop their mental, physical and spiritual potential and to encourage the study of their West Indian heritage.

Armenian
- Centre for Armenian Information and Advice, 105A Mill Hill Road, Acton, London W3 8JF, (0181 992 4621). The centre offers help and support to Armenian refugees living in this country, looking after their welfare rights, organizing English lessons, supplying interpreters for attendance at court, doctor's surgeries and hospitals.

Asian
- Bangladesh Association, 5 Fordham Street, London E1 1HS, (0171 247 3733). Does social and welfare work for Bangladeshis.
- Bangladesh Women's Association, 22 Stanley Road, London N15 3HB, (0181 365 7498). Offers help to Bangladeshi women and their families over their rights to pensions, social security and unemployment benefits. It also deals with health and immigration problems.
- Confederation of Indian Organizations (UK), 170 Tolcarne Drive, Pinner, Middx HA5 2DR, (0181 863 9089). Aims to help Indians to live in harmony in this country without losing their cultural identity. It also offers help with translating/interpreting in the Greater London area.
- India Welfare Society, 11 Middle Row, London W10 5AT, (0181 969 9493). Hindu-based organization that looks after the affairs of Indians in this country, with counselling services for families, with particular attention to the elderly.
- Indian Workers' Association, 112a The Green, Southall, Middx UB2 4BQ, (0181 574 6019). Looks after the welfare of immigrants, advising them on immigration, housing, education and racial problems.
- Maternity & Health Links, The Old Co-op, 42 Chelsea Road, Easton, Bristol BS5 6AF, (0117 9558495). Provides an interpreting service in the Bristol area for Asian women during pregnancy and in their general dealings with the

NHS. It also has a home tuition scheme, teaching English and basic health education.
- Pakistan Welfare Association, 46 Quicks Road, London SW19 1EY, (0181 544 1644). Works to keep Pakistani culture and tradition alive in Britain by organizing festivals and educational classes. It also advises locally based Pakistanis on racial, immigration and educational problems.
- Wandsworth Asian Community Centre, 57–59 Trinity Road, London SW17 7SD, (0181 871 7774). Works with local Asians, running crèches, classes, counselling sessions.

Chinese
- Camden Chinese Community Centre, 173 Arlington Road, London NW1 7EY, (0171 267 3019). Although based in north London, this centre looks after the interests of all Chinese people, giving advice on rights and benefits, housing, immigration.
- Chinese Information and Advice Centre, 68 Shaftesbury Avenue, London W1V 7DF, (0171 836 8291). Helps Chinese people in this country over immigration, employment, benefits, and also counsels them over domestic problems.

Greek Cypriots
- Cypriot Advisory Service, 26 Crowndale Road, London NW1 1TT, (0171 387 6617). Advises and counsels Cypriots in this country. It also runs a translating and interpreting service.
- National Federation of Cypriots in Great Britain, 4 Porchester Terrace, London W2 3TL, (Mobile phone 0956 849094). Supports and advises Cypriots in Britain and encourages them to keep links with their culture.

See also Standing Conference of Ethnic Minority Senior Citizens (**The Third Age**, *page 311*).

Jewish
- Anglo-Jewish Association, 5th Floor, Woburn House, Upper Woburn Place, London WC1H 0EP, (0171 387 5937). Gives grants to Jewish students from abroad to study in this country.
- Association for Jewish Youth, AJY House, 128 East Lane, Wembley, Middx HA0 3NL, (0181 908 4747). Works with young people to promote voluntary service within the community.
- Association of Jewish Ex-Servicemen and Women, Ajex House, East Bank, London N16 5RT, (0181 800 2844). Helps Jewish ex-servicemen and women with problems by giving both support and financial aid. It runs a housing association for the elderly and organizes social activities for the disabled.
- Association of Jewish Refugees, 1 Hampstead Gate, 1a Frognal, London NW3 6AL, (0171 431 6161). Helps Jews who were victims of Nazi oppression,

offering sheltered accommodation and help while they are waiting to go into residential homes.

- Board of Deputies of British Jews, Commonwealth House, 1–19 New Oxford Street, London WC1A 1NF, (0171 543 5400). Works to administer Jewish affairs and combat anti-semitism in this country.
- Central British Fund for World Jewish Relief, Drayton House, 30 Gordon Street, London WC1H 0AN, (0171 387 3925). Helps Jews from any part of the world who have come to this country to escape persecution.
- Institute of Community Relations, 2–4 Amhurst Park, London N16 5AE, (0181 800 8612). Works towards racial understanding between Orthodox Jews and other nationalities and religions.
- Jewish Lads and Girls Brigade, 3 Beechcroft Road, South Woodford, London E18 1LA, (0181 989 8990). Works with young Jews, with community and social work, sports, camping.
- League of Jewish Women, Commonwealth House, 1–19 New Oxford Street, London WC1A 1NF. A contact organization that does a great deal of voluntary work with groups throughout the country.
- Union of Maccabi Associations in Great Britain and Northern Ireland, Gildes Game House, 73 Compayne Gardens, London NW6 3RS, (0171 328 0382). An association of Jewish youth clubs co-ordinating social and sporting events which culminate in the Jewish Olympics in Israel.

See also

Jewish Association for Fostering Adoption and Infertility (**Fostering**, *page 271*).
Jewish Bereavement Counselling Service (**Bereavement**, *page 202*).
Jewish Care (**Disabled**, *page 128*).
Jewish Lesbian and Gay Helpline (**Sexuality**, *page 163*).
Jewish Marriage Council (**Separation, Divorce**, *page 203*).

Latin American

- Latin American Women's Rights Service, Wesley House, Wild Court, London WC2B 5AJ, (0171 831 4145). Gives information and advice to women from Latin American countries living in the Greater London area. It also organizes social events.

Muslims

- League of British Muslims, Eton Road, Ilford, Essex IG1 2UE, (0181 514 0706). Based on a community centre in Essex, the League advises and helps Muslim youths, families over immigration and welfare problems, and also elderly people.
- Union of Muslim Organisations of UK and Eire, 109 Campden Hill Road, London W8 7TL, (0171 229 0538). A support organization for Muslims living in this country. It runs camps for young people and a marriage guidance service, speaks up on behalf of their religious rights.

Sikhs

- Sikh Cultural Society of Great Britain, 88 Mollison Way, Edgware, Middx HA8 5QW, (0181 952 1215). Gives out information and answers queries about the Sikh religion.
- Sikh Divine Fellowship, 46 Sudbury Court Drive, Harrow, Middx HA1 3DD, (0181 904 9244). A religious centre which has meetings for meditation and yoga.

Turkish Cypriots

- Turkish Cypriot Cultural Association, 14a Graham Road, London E8 IDA, (0171 249 7410). Does welfare work among the Turkish Cypriot community in London, especially the elderly. It helps young people, women and single parents particularly.

Turks

- Turkish People's Cultural Centre, 84 Balls Pond Road, London N1 4AJ, (0171 923 1202). Advises Turkish-speaking workers in Britain, helping them over rights and welfare issues, offering translation and interpreting services, English language courses and cultural and sporting activities.
- Turkish Women's Centre, 110 Clarence Road, London E5 8JA, (0181 986 1358). A back-up organization for Turkish women living in this country advising them and giving help with translating or interpreting. It also runs a number of social and sporting programmes.

Vietnamese

- Vietnamese Refugees Community in Southwark, Employment Training and Enterprise Centre, 9 Pear Court, East Surrey Grove, London SE15 6PF. Helps Vietnamese settle in this part of London. It advises on education and training and helps those who want to start a business.
- Young Vietnamese Association, 43–45 Broad Street, Teddington, Middx TW11 8QZ, (0181 943 4842). Helps young Vietnamese people, particularly those who have been in care, with housing and counselling at its drop-in centre at Teddington.

12

LEGAL

Most of us find ourselves face to face with the law at some point in our lives, sometimes falling foul of it and sometimes as victims. This section helps you through the maze of rules and regulations and gives you an indication of what happens in situations such as an unscheduled court appearance.

DEALING WITH THE POLICE – THEIR RIGHTS AND YOURS

The Criminal Justice and Public Order Act

This act has given the police and the courts new powers. One new ruling allows the courts to sentence young people between the ages of 12 and 14 who have committed three imprisonable offences or who have breached or offended during a supervision order to detention in new institutions called secure training centres which are presently being built.

Other changes include a provision for a reduction in sentence if you plead guilty to an offence, and a change to the right of silence. From now on, although you cannot be committed for trial solely on the grounds of failure to reply to police questioning, the ruling says the court may 'draw adverse inferences' from your failure to mention facts when questioned or charged, or to give evidence at a trial or account for objects, substances or marks present at the time of your arrest, or for your presence at a particular place or time. In effect, this is the abolition of the right to remain silent.

Under this ruling the police now have extended powers to take samples – swabs and DNA samples – for all recordable crimes which theoretically includes offences such as fare-dodging and shop-lifting. Their powers to use 'reasonable force' to do so is also extended. Also, when a senior police officer has reasonable grounds to believe that serious incidents of violence may take place, he can order his men to stop and search pedestrians and vehicles for offensive weapons or dangerous articles within a specified area.

There are also two new offences: you are now guilty of an offence if you are in possession of an article 'in circumstances giving rise to a reasonable suspicion' that it is intended 'for a purpose connected with commission, instigation or preparation of acts of terrorism'; you are also guilty of an offence if you are found to be collecting or possessing without authorization 'any information which is of such a nature that it is likely to be useful to terrorists'.

Male rape is now an official offence, but the gay age of consent has been lowered from 21 to 18. There is a new offence of aggravated trespass that could affect many of us (*see page 520*). The police also have the power to end outdoor festivals (*see page 521*). Squatters and tenants who refuse to leave are now affected by a new law which allows landlords to evict them.

Stop and search

The police have a right to stop and search anyone who they think is carrying drugs, guns, knives or any kind of offensive weapon, stolen goods or tools used for burglary. They can also stop you if they think you are in possession of a protected species of plant or bird life, including birds' eggs. You are not obliged to stop or give your name and address to the police, but if you do not co-operate, there is likely to be further trouble. While the police are questioning you, you have the right to ask the officer conducting the questioning for his number and which station he comes from.

You have the right to ask why the police have stopped you to ask for your name and address in the street or while you are driving your car. They may also ask you where you are going or where you have come from, or whether you know somebody. You also have the right to refuse to answer any questions without your solicitor being present (*but see* **Right of silence**, *page 427*). You can be arrested without a warrant for a large number of suspected crimes, both major and minor, including:

- Indecent assault.
- Murder.
- Smuggling.
- Refusal to take a breath test.
- Obstructing a highway.
- Being drunk and incapable.
- Assault.
- Being an illegal immigrant.
- Refusing to give your name and address when you are legally bound to – after a car accident, for instance.

You should not be arrested merely because of your appearance – if you are dressed in a certain way or are black.

What about racial discrimination?

There is strong evidence that if you come from an ethnic minority group you could be discriminated against (*see page 413*).

Being searched

Before searching you, the policeman must:

- Identify himself by showing you his warrant (identity) card, giving you his name and that of his police station.
- Tell you why he wants to search you.
- Tell you what he is looking for.

A search in public means you will be asked to take off your top garments (coat or jacket) and gloves, if you are wearing them. Any further search than that should be done in a van or at the police station. However, if you are 'out of public view' (in a pub or restaurant lavatory) the police may go as far as getting someone of the same sex to strip and search you. This was the case in a high court action not so long ago when two teenage girls received compensation for being treated this way.

If you are searched you do not have to give your name and address; the police must either arrest you or allow you to leave. If you are not under arrest, you do not have to go to a police station, although they may ask you to. If you are in a public place and they think you have a mental disorder and are in need of care or control they can take you to 'a place of safety'. You can be held there at the most for 72 hours until an approved social worker and a doctor have assessed you. The police are not allowed, under their own code of practice, to arrest a person who is mentally handicapped or make them sign a statement unless someone responsible for their care is present. This can be a close relative, their carer or someone who is experienced in dealing with mentally ill or mentally handicapped people.

See also

Emergencies (*page 3*).
Lesbian and Gay rights (*page 458*).

SHOPLIFTING

The Portia Trust, which is the support group for shop-lifters (*see page 461*), says that every year there are more than 50 suicides following allegations, some of them false, of shoplifting. However, it must be said that shops are also up against well-organized gangs of professional shop-lifters who steal goods to the value of millions a year. You can be prosecuted for taking something from a store or shop without paying for it, even if you did so by mistake. More than once, in a distracted frame of mind I have put something into my shopping bag rather than the supermarket basket; fortunately, I have discovered it before I got to the checkout. So I have the utmost sympathy for someone else who makes the same mistake.

If you are stopped in a store, suspected of shoplifting, the shop has to prove that you did not intend to pay for the goods in question. That is why security people usually wait until you are out in the street before they stop you. However, in some stores, the mere fact that you have gone to another floor or department may be enough for a detective to stop you. If you want to take something and look at it in daylight or to match it to another article, ask an assistant first. Make a note of her name (usually on a lapel badge) or, better still, get her to go with you.

When buying something, always retain your receipt even for very small purchases. You may need it to prove you have bought the item in question. If you are absent-minded or under stress and not thinking what you are doing, or perhaps distracted by small children in tow, make sure that any bags you have with you are kept zipped up right until the moment you reach the checkout or cash point. Remember that store detectives, or security officers, as they are officially known, are not policemen. In fact, last year 2,700 of them were found to have previous convictions themselves. They are making a citizen's arrest, not an official one. Although they have the right to prosecute you, most stores prefer this to be done by the police. However, some large supermarkets have their own legal departments which handle prosecutions, working very closely with the police who 'process' them.

Remember, security officers have no power except to make a citizen's arrest. They must not put their hands in your shopping bag or handbag and they have no power to search you. They are committing an offence if they even attempt to do so.

What happens if you are stopped

You will probably be taken to an office in the store for questioning. In making a citizen's arrest, a store detective can question you. He may search your person and your possessions for any incriminating evidence, although he is not legally allowed to do so. If you are very young or very old or very hysterical and distressed and admit you have stolen, they may decide to take matters no further, demand payment for goods and blacklist you from the store.

- You have the right not to give your name and address. In that case they will probably send for the police.
- Ask immediately to phone your solicitor. If you do not have one, ask to be taken to a police station where under your legal rights they are bound to find you a duty solicitor. If you admit guilt and there are extenuating circumstances, the police may give you a verbal caution (*but see* **Cautions**, *page 436*) and leave things at that. Otherwise you will be left waiting for weeks, possibly months, to see whether a summons is delivered to your home, ordering you to attend magistrates' court (*see page 434*).

- If you need help, get in touch with the Portia Trust (*see page 461*).
- Remember that if you plead not guilty and are acquitted, you can claim against the store for malicious prosecution.
- Make sure that your fingerprints and photograph, if they were taken, are destroyed in front of you. You are allowed one month to have this done.

DRINKING AND DRIVING

No one should drink and drive. There is no 'safe' limit for the amount of alcohol you can take in before getting behind the driving wheel. Officially, if you are a man and drink more than 3 units of alcohol or a woman and drink 1-2 units, then drive your car, you are in danger of being charged with a drink-drive offence.

On average your liver processes alcohol at the rate of one unit an hour which will give you a rough idea of the time lapse you should allow before thinking of taking to the road. But how we react to alcohol depends on our size, weight and state of health, and the time of day we take a drink. So what is a safe interval for one person could be over the top for another. The legal limit of alcohol allowed in the blood is 80 milligrams per 100 millilitres of blood – beyond that figure you can be charged for a drink-drive offence. Plans are being discussed to lower that amount. The police also have the right to prosecute you for drink-driving, even if you are under the official limit, if they feel that alcohol has affected your ability to drive.

A police officer in uniform can stop you and breath-test you if he has reasonable grounds to suspect you are driving or are in charge of a car, on a public road or other public place, with alcohol in your body. You can also be breath-tested if you have been involved in an accident or have committed a 'moving traffic offence'. And you do not have to be actually driving to be charged, people who have decided not to drive but to wait in their car until the effects of drink have worn off or have a nap in it can also be breath-tested and prosecuted. So if you feel you have had too much to drink, hand the car keys to someone else and keep well away from the vehicle.

If you are stopped, the policeman will ask you to take a roadside breath-test which must be taken at least 20 minutes after you say you last had a drink. If you fail this test or refuse to take it, you will be arrested. Refusal can lead to a large fine and automatic disqualification. Even if you are obviously drunk and unfit to drive, you cannot be arrested without taking the test. The police can also follow you into your home to test you. You will be taken to the police station where another, more accurate, breath-testing machine will be used. You will be asked to give two breath samples and the lower reading of the two will be used. This will give a print-out which can be used as evidence in court.

If the reading is over the limit but on the borderline – say, 50 micrograms per 100ml of breath (the official level is 35 micrograms but the police rarely prosecute below 40 micrograms) you can choose to have either a blood or urine test instead. You can also opt for a blood or urine test if there is some medical reason for not taking the breath test – chronic asthma may be one reason.

Drink-driving and the law

If you are convicted you will automatically be disqualified from driving for at least a year, even if there are good reasons why you should keep your licence. You may also be fined heavily and could even be sent to prison. If you commit a second drink-driving offence within ten years you can be disqualified for 3 years and there is even the likelihood of being sent to prison, especially if you were involved in an accident where death or injury took place. If you already have a history of two disqualifications or are more than $2\frac{1}{2}$ times over the limit, you can have your driving licence taken away until it is decided you are fit to drive again and you may have to retake a driving test.

QUESTIONING AND ARREST

The sequence of events is fairly straightforward – you are arrested, you are charged, then you appear before the local magistrates when you will either be detained in custody pending a trial, released on bail or released altogether if the magistrates feel there is no case to answer.

See also
If you are arrested (**Emergencies**, *page 3*).

THE POLICE: HOW TO COMPLAIN

If you feel a policeman has behaved wrongly or badly, you are entitled to make a complaint. First decide exactly what was wrong.
* Was the police officer rude to you?
* Did he or she damage your property?
* Or injure you unnecessarily?
These are all situations about which you have a right to complain. There are various ways of doing this:
* You can go to any police station and tell the duty officer you have a complaint to make. An officer will take down the details from you.

- You can go to your local Citizens' Advice Bureau who will listen to your complaint and tell you whether your complaint is valid, and if so, how to go about making it.
- You can go to a solicitor and ask him to act for you.
- You can get a friend or a member of your family to put in a complaint on your behalf as long as you give them a signed letter agreeing that they can do so.
- You can write a full account of what happened and send it to the Chief Constable of the force that the policeman belongs to.
- You can write to the Police Complaints Authority (*see page 460*) which will pass your complaint on to the right place.

What happens next?

The next step depends on your complaint. If it is a minor incident, you may feel that an apology is all you need. This may come either from the officer or from his police force. However, you may find there was a reason for the way the officer behaved and be satisfied with an explanation – it is up to you to decide whether or not you are happy for the complaint to be dealt with in this way. If this is not acceptable to you or if the complaint concerns a serious matter, there will be a full investigation.

The police will appoint a senior officer to find out what happened. He will talk to you to find out exactly what your complaint is. He will also talk to the policeman involved and to any witnesses. There is no specific procedure but the officer may apologize to you on behalf of the policeman involved if he has admitted misconduct, or, in some circumstances, even if he has not. If you are not satisfied by this you can ask for your complaint to be formally investigated by the police force. If it is a really serious offence, involving death or injury, the Police Complaints Authority takes charge. This is a totally independent public watchdog – no police officers are members.

Your complaint – a checklist
You should say:
- What exactly happened.
- When it happened.
- Where it happened.
- What was done.
- What was said.

You should also say:
- Whether there were any witnesses.
- Where they can be contacted.

You will also need:
- Proof of any damage, witnesses' statements, photos of the scene and damaged objects.

Suing the police

Even if you have made a complaint to the police direct, you still have the right to take them to court and sue if you feel you are owed compensation – if the police have damaged your property, for instance. This is called a civil action and you can find out how to go about it via the Citizens' Advice Bureau or a solicitor. If you take out a civil action, the complaint you made to the police direct will be held up until the court hearing has been completed. Remember, the police have the right to bring a civil action against you too.

TYPES OF COURT

The Magistrates' Court

deals with child custody orders, small crimes and driving cases. It also hears and commits people charged with major crimes to the Crown Court. Some Magistrates' Courts have separate sessions in which they deal with domestic matters. In a Magistrates' Court you will be asked to go into the witness box and speak, but before you do so, you will have to swear an oath, depending on your religion. This will be read to you and you repeat the oath after the clerk, or you are given the oath on a card to read.

The Juvenile Court or Youth Court

is used for hearing cases against children under the age of 17. This court is also used for care proceedings if proceedings are being brought by the local authority.

The County Court

is where you go if you are applying for an injunction against somebody, applying for custody of your children or dealing with property disputes. You are not likely to be called on to speak at a County Court. Most of the work is done from affidavits, written statements which you then swear are true. The County Court also handles disputes over tenancies and undefended divorces.

The County Court is also the **Small Claims Court**. This is the cheapest way to get justice, since even if you lose and have costs awarded against you, the costs will be small. If you win, you will also get back your court fee and if you ask for it, your expenses. Find out if you have a valid case by going to your local Citizens' Advice Bureau which should be able to tell you.

- Get a form from the court and fill it in. You will have to say how much you are claiming, why you are claiming it and whom you are claiming it from. You can get an explanatory booklet from the court which will help you fill it in or the staff at the court will help you.

- The court will then send a summons to the defendant, who has 14 days to reply. If the court does not receive a reply, it may make a ruling in your favour there and then.

- If the case is defended, the court will probably order a pre-trial review when you will have to turn up with the relevant papers – letters, bills and so on.
- There will then be a hearing, which should be within six months of the start of your action. It will take place in private and the judge will normally give a ruling right away. He will then deal with expenses, so keep a note of lost earnings, travel etc. to make sure you get them back.

The Crown Court

used to be called the Assizes or Quarter Sessions and is used almost entirely for serious criminal cases. But it also handles appeals against decisions handed out by the Magistrates' Court. The Crown Court is presided over by a judge and cases often involve a jury.

The High Court

is the court of appeal against decisions made by lower courts. It is also used to make a child a ward of court. For your case to be heard in the High Court you have to be represented by a barrister.

The Coroner's Court

is where inquests are held into deaths, whether unlawful, accidental or unexplained. If someone dies and the doctor is not sure what the cause is, a post-mortem examination may be done and an inquest held on the result.

GOING TO COURT

You will receive a summons ordering you to appear in court at a given date and time. You must turn up unless you can produce a doctor's certificate saying you are too ill to appear. This must be sent in advance of the hearing date. Alternatively, your solicitor may be able to rearrange the hearing if you have another good reason for changing it. Take a friend or relative with you if you can. Get there in good time, allowing ten to fifteen minutes to find out which court you are listed for, then wait outside until your name is called. You may have to wait hours, if earlier cases drag on. If you begin to feel panicky or distressed, the Portia Trust suggest you ask to speak to a probation officer who should be sympathetic and helpful.

When your name is called, you will be ushered into the courtroom and told where to stand. You will then be asked to give your name and address and whether you have a solicitor with you. You will also be asked whether you are willing to have your case tried there and then or whether you wish to go for trial before a judge and jury at a Crown Court, something that is usually reserved for more serious cases. You will then be asked whether you plead 'guilty' or 'not guilty'. If you plead guilty the case will continue immediately. Someone – a policeman or prosecuting solicitor – will outline the case against you and you will be asked whether you want to challenge the evidence or say anything in your defence.

If you decide to speak, you will be asked to repeat an oath to 'tell the truth and nothing but the truth'. If you give evidence under oath, the prosecution has the right to question you. Try to be as calm as possible if this happens. In British law an accused person is innocent until he is proven guilty and the onus of that proof rests with the prosecution. They are not allowed by law to give any hint that you have any previous convictions. These are not disclosed until after you have been found guilty, if that is the case. When the court announces its verdict, you can say immediately that you wish to appeal if you want to do so. You must confirm this by letter saying so, addressed to the Clerk of the Court. The letter must give your name and address, the date of your conviction and your reasons for appealing against it. Otherwise you have up to 28 days to appeal against your sentence. An appeal would be heard by the Crown Court.

Verdicts

A caution
This is not actually done at the court but at a police station. If you are offered this, it is no panacea. In order to receive a caution you have to say, in effect, 'I am guilty'. If you are not guilty, you may be tempted to take a caution to be spared the ordeal of going to court. But a caution goes on your record and lasts for three years. If you are picked up for something else during that time, it can be taken into account if you are sentenced. The caution also stays on the police computer for ten years.

Not guilty
If the magistrates find you not guilty you are free to go.

Absolute discharge
This goes one step further than being judged not guilty. In this case, the court feels the offence is so trivial, and the prosecution's case so weak, the evidence so scanty, that there is no case to answer. In this case no record is made of the alleged offence and you do not have to refer to it when filling in forms such as job applications. The slate is clean.

Conditional discharge
In this case you are told that provided you are not convicted of another offence during a stated period, perhaps a year, no further action will be taken. But if you offend again, the case will be taken into account when sentence for the second offence is passed.

A fine

If you are fined, you can ask for time to pay. The court will take into account your circumstances. If your child is fined, then you, as a parent, are liable to pay over the money. You may also be asked to pay costs, but these should never exceed the amount of the fine.

A community work order

A community work order is sometimes ordered instead of a fine. In this case you will be ordered to do a certain number of hours' community work, possibly helping elderly people.

A probation order

This is sometimes given instead of a prison sentence. It means that you will be put under the care of a probation officer who will try to sort out your problems. You will report to him on a regular basis for a set number of months.

Referral to another court

You could be remanded on bail or in custody for a hearing at a higher court.

Attending court

People are often intimidated about going to court. There is a mystique about it and it can be particularly traumatic for victims and witnesses of crime, especially if they do not know what the procedures are. Victims of crimes are often not told that a case is coming to court or even how the investigations are going; the first notice may be when a summons comes in the post asking them to give evidence. They are often not told what the charges will be, whether the defendant is likely to get bail, or what the dates are for subsequent hearings.

Witnesses and victims are often summoned to court, wait for hours then are not required to give evidence or find that the case is adjourned. Sometimes they have to share waiting rooms with defendants and their supporters or face hostile questioning by the defendant's lawyer.

If you are called to court

The first intimation that you are needed in court will be the arrival by post of a Witness Order. The first thing to check is the date – you may be given very short notice – Witness Orders have been known to arrive as late as the day before the hearing. If you have difficulty in understanding the wording, ask the court staff about it. Check that the starting time is given and that you have the address of the courtroom.

The Witness Service

If you have problems, ask if you can see someone from the Witness Service which is staffed by trained volunteers who are available now in more than half the 76 Crown Courts in England and Wales for victims and their families.

- If you have never gone to court before, it can arrange for you to visit the Crown Court Centre and perhaps look around a courtroom before the hearing.
- It will tell you about court procedures and answer your questions.
- It will find you somewhere to wait before you are called to give evidence, away from where the defendants and their relatives are waiting.
- It will give you emotional support before, during and after the hearing.
- It can supply someone to go with you into the courtroom when you are called to give evidence.
- It will help you with things like filling out expense forms.

What the Witness Service cannot do is to discuss your evidence with you or give you legal advice – though it can put you in touch with someone who will.

A Process Server

A Process Server is a servant of the court whose job is to serve papers, perhaps a summons on you, either at your home, your place of work or even in a police cell. It may be a demand for payment, a threat of bankruptcy proceedings, an ousting order or an injunction. He has to put the papers into your hands and get you to sign for them.

An identity parade

If you are the victim of a crime you may be asked to attend an identity parade at your local police station. This is a line-up of innocent people called in off the street and the suspect. You will probably be given a cup of tea and told what is going to happen – some police stations show an explanatory video. There is a screen between the line-up and you and the people in the line-up cannot see you.

JURY SERVICE

Jury service is mandatory in this country for anyone whose name appears on the electoral register who is over 18 and under 65 and has lived in the UK for at least five years. There are some exceptions.

- Those who are mentally ill or mentally handicapped.
- Those who are employed by the prison service.
- Those who are part of the legal system – barristers, court officials, magistrates.

- A monk, nun or minister of any religious denomination.
- A police officer or special constable or employee of a forensic lab.

Jurers are picked at random and can expect to get a month's notice and to have to serve on the jury for about ten working days. If you receive a summons to attend and ignore it, you can be fined up to £400 for not turning up. You can ask to be excused but not barred from service if:

- You are a practising doctor, dentist, nurse, midwife, vet or pharmacist.
- You have done jury service during the past two years.
- You are a member of the armed forces.
- You are an MP, a peer or a member of the European Parliament.

There are also other valid reasons you can give for not doing jury service at the time you are asked to attend.

- You are sitting an examination.
- You are moving house.
- You have booked a holiday.
- You no longer live in the area.
- You are the parent of a young child and have to care for him.
- You are unable to read or write.
- You do not speak English very well.
- You are looking after a sick relative.
- You are in poor health or deaf or blind.
- You have suffered a bereavement.
- You run your own one-man business or have heavy work commitments.

If one of these conditions applies to you, you must say so on the summons form and return it within seven days. You may be disqualified from jury service if you have a criminal record.

NB The conditions and numbers are different in Scotland and Northern Ireland.

What happens when I do jury service?

When you get to the court, an official will explain what will happen at the trial, what you have to do and what expenses you can claim. More jurors are called than are actually needed and twelve of you will be picked. At this stage you may be asked to drop out, perhaps because you have some link with the case, because the defendant or the prosecution may object to you for some reason or because the trial is likely to last a long time and this causes a problem for you.

You will be sworn in either on the New Testament or another holy book according to your religion. Or you will be asked to 'affirm' instead. You will then sit in a special place in the court during the trial. The jury will then retire to a special room and elect one member to speak on their behalf. You then see whether you can reach either a majority (at least ten of you) or a unanimous verdict. If this is not possible, you will be dismissed as jurors and the case retried.

Expenses

As a juror you are entitled to claim for:

- Loss of earnings up to a certain sum.
- Subsistence allowance if you are away from home for up to five hours.
- The cost of travel.
- The cost of a child-minder if you do not normally have one.

YOUR RIGHTS AS A PRISONER ON REMAND

You are allowed a minimum of $1\frac{1}{2}$ hours of visits every week, and up to three adults and your children are allowed on each visit, but they must all come at the same time. Your visitors may have their hand baggage and pockets searched. If they refuse the prison may refuse the visit. Your visitors can hand you cigarettes or tobacco, but they cannot give you sweets or food or phonecards. They may be allowed to give you radio batteries. They can also bring in clothes for you and take away your washing.

If your visitors are close relatives in receipt of benefits such as income support, they may be able to get help with their travelling costs and possibly an overnight stay. Close relatives include a partner who was living with you for four months or more before you came into prison or someone who is the other parent of a child of yours. If your children are in care, in a children's home or foster home, you can apply for your children to have a private visit or for you to visit them every three months.

You are allowed to send out two free letters a week and as many as you like at your own expense. Your letters will not normally be read but the envelopes will be opened to make sure they do not contain anything that is not allowed. The prison will pay for letters connected with the defence of your case, for urgent business matters or family problems if you have no cash. You can buy special prison service phonecards from the prison shop and there is usually no limit on the number of calls you can make. You are allowed to make free phone calls on the official phone if you need to get in touch with your lawyer urgently. A random number of phone calls may be listened to by prison officers.

YOUR RIGHTS AS A CONVICTED PRISONER

You are allowed a minimum of two 30-minute visits every four weeks. To get these you must send out a Visiting Order to the people you want to visit you. You can save up these visits if you wish and ask for visits in advance.

You can apply to have a 'special visit' if you are seriously ill, if there is a family crisis or if you need to sort out urgent business or legal matters.

Visitors cannot normally hand in anything to you except letters. If smoking is allowed they can offer you cigarettes to smoke during the visit. If there is a coffee bar they can buy you things to eat and drink during the visit. Your visitors will have their hand baggage and pockets searched. If the prison has reason to think they are trying to smuggle something in, they can call in the police to do a strip-search.

If your children are in care, in a foster home or children's home, you can ask to visit the children at their home if they are not able to come to you. Close relatives receiving benefits may be able to get help with travelling costs and with the cost of an overnight stay. Close relatives include a partner who was living with you for four months or more before you came into prison or the mother or father of your child.

You are allowed to send out one free letter every week and to buy extra letters from the prison shop with your earnings or with private cash. Your letters will not normally be read but the envelopes of letters you receive will be opened to make sure they do not contain anything which is not allowed. You can ask for an extra free letter to write to your probation officer, if you have family problems, if you have just been convicted and need to sort out business problems, if you are appealing against your sentence or taking other legal action, or if you are arranging a job or somewhere to live on your release.

You can buy phonecards from the prison shop and there is normally no limit on the number of calls you make. In some prisons if you are not getting visits you can ask to have a free phone call instead. A random number of phone calls may be listened to by prison officers.

LAWYERS

Do you really need a lawyer?

Many people are put off taking legal action because they fear the costs involved. But do you really need a solicitor? Before going to that expense, try one of the following:

- The Citizens' Advice Bureau may be able to sort things out for you free of charge.
- A Consumer Advice Centre which may help on consumer disputes.
- Your local Trading Standards department for consumer affairs.
- A local Law Centre which will give free or low-cost legal services.
- A trade arbitration scheme if you are in dispute with a person or organization that is a member of a trade association.

- Check your insurance policies. If the case involves your car or your home you may find that you are covered for legal costs.
- Or it could be that you can take your case to a small claims court (for claims of £1,000 or less) which has very low fees and where you can represent yourself (*see page 434*).

Solicitor

A solicitor is a lawyer who deals with all aspects of the law whether buying a house, forming a company or being arrested. He is the first person you turn to if you are in trouble with the law or involved in any kind of legal action. If you are using a solicitor for any transaction you are within your rights to ask him how much he will charge for this work and how long he thinks it will take.

- If you think you may qualify for legal aid (*see page 444*) then you must pick a solicitor who operates the Legal Aid Scheme – not all do. Otherwise you may be able to do a conditional fee deal (*see page 445*).
- If yours is an emergency of some kind, you must pick a solicitor who specializes in this kind of work.
- If it is a domestic dispute or divorce you must, again, choose a solicitor who specializes in this subject. The same applies if your problem concerns immigration.
- If you have been injured in an accident and need a solicitor, ring the Law Society's free Accident Line on 0500 19 29 39. They will put you in touch with a specialist solicitor who will give you a consultation free of charge.

How to find a solicitor
The best way to find a solicitor is to ask the advice of someone who has been through the same situation you find yourself in. Ask friends who have been divorced, for instance, whom they used. Otherwise, ask your local Citizens' Advice Bureau or consult the Law Society's Regional Directories of Solicitors practising in the area, which you will find in the reference department of your public library. This directory shows which categories of work they do.

How do I find a legal aid solicitor?
Ask your local Citizens' Advice Bureau or ask for the legal aid solicitors list at your local library. Or enlist the help of a support group involved in your particular problem.

Dealing with your solicitor
Solicitors have their own 'Client Care Code' which says, among other things, that you have to be told who will be handling your case and what is going on. It assumes that you are unfamiliar with the law and lawyers, and that you need to understand what is happening. After the first consultation he should send you a

letter telling you who is handling your case and also give you some idea of costs. If this does not happen, ask for one. Remember if you are in dispute with someone, your solicitor or his firm cannot act for both parties under the Law Society's Solicitors' Practice Rules.

Do not be overwhelmed by your solicitor and by the legal jargon he uses. Ask for explanations and, if necessary, ask why there is a delay – after all, you are paying him, even if it is through legal aid. Keep your costs down when using a solicitor by doing as much of the donkey work yourself as possible. Solicitors make a charge for their time at interviews, for telephone calls and for letters, so it pays to have all the papers with you, and to know all the dates and names; do not be vague – it costs money. Remember that you have the right not to take his advice and that you are entitled at any point to ask how your case is going and how the costs are building up. Remember that any dispute in court is going to cost money, so try to settle things out of court if you can.

Can I change my solicitor?

You can change your solicitor, but it delays proceedings for you have to get the old solicitor to pass all the papers in the case to the new one. He will probably not do this unless he is paid and if you are using legal aid there may be months of delay. If you have a query about some point of law and cannot get a satisfactory answer from your solicitor, you can telephone the Legal Practice Information Department of the Law Society on 0171 242 1222.

Barrister

A barrister or counsel is a specialist lawyer with a different type of training who deals with one particular subject. A QC or Queen's Counsel is a senior barrister appointed by the Lord Chancellor. As the law stands at the moment you cannot go to a barrister direct, you have to go through a solicitor. But there are proposals to change this situation. Your solicitor may decide to hire a barrister to present or defend your case in court if your case is very complicated or has serious implications, for instance, if you could go to prison for a long time. Your solicitor may also suggest you take 'counsel's opinion' on your case, probably to find out if you have a chance of succeeding.

A barrister costs a great deal of money so unless you have some form of legal aid (*see page 444*) you need to think things over carefully and get an estimate of the fees involved before hiring a barrister. At present it is impossible to get compensation from a barrister for professional negligence even if he fails to turn up to the hearing or gets the facts wrong.

LEGAL AID

Set up in 1949 to make sure that every British citizen has an equal right to justice, the intention of legal aid is to help people pay their legal costs. Help is the operative word – if you are earning anything at all you will be expected to contribute on a sliding scale according to your income. You will usually be able to pay these contributions in monthly instalments over a year. Less than 50 per cent of people who apply for aid actually get it. When it is common for someone earning as little as £12,000 a year to be disqualified, it seems grossly unfair to read of millionaires and magnates being given legal aid to the tune of millions of pounds. They do this by minimizing their assets, putting properties in the names of family members and hiding their cash in foreign bank accounts. In short, they are more than a match for the legal aid board officials.

In theory, if you have more than £3,000 in assets other than the equity in your family home (up to £100,000), your furniture and tools of your trade, or more than about £142 fixed a week disposable income after deducting housing costs allowances for dependants, and other amounts which are not taken into account you are ineligible for full legal aid. If you have a disposable income of between £48 and £142 a week then you should get help on a sliding scale. Anyone who qualifies for income support, however, should usually qualify for legal aid of some kind. There are three main kinds of legal aid.

Legal Advice and Assistance
covers advice only and is known as the Green Form Scheme. To be eligible you must have a low disposable income and capital.

Civil Legal Aid
is for cases that go to civil courts. To be eligible for this you must pass a merits test showing that you have reasonable grounds for taking or defending the court action. You also have to be assessed to see whether you qualify financially.

Criminal Legal Aid
is for criminal offences. If you have been charged with a criminal offence the upper financial thresholds for legal aid are higher because the test is whether you need help in meeting your legal costs, but you may still be liable to make contributions.

How to get legal aid

Getting legal aid is no picnic – many people give up when they see the form they have to fill in. It is very complex – the financial statement alone runs to 12 pages. You will need a solicitor to help you fill it in and he can charge you for this service. It is said, by the way, that lawyers can be very influential in deciding who is granted legal aid.

You will have to disclose what your income is, if any, what benefits you are receiving, and if you are working, your employer will have to give details of how much you earn. In civil cases where you recover or preserve money or property but do not fully recover all your costs you will have to meet them from your 'winnings'. In some cases, collection from you can be postponed by the Legal Aid Fund administrators putting a charge on property. This means that if you then sell the property, you must pay back some of your legal aid. If, however, you buy another house to live in with the proceeds, the Legal Aid Board will probably let the charge be transferred but you cannot be sure of this.

The whole process of getting legal aid can take months, and your solicitor will wait to get approval before he starts work. If you are successful you will be given a legal aid certificate. Is all the trouble worthwhile? Yes, if you are involved in a dispute that could escalate and take months, even years of wrangling in court. No, if it is a relatively straightforward case.

Emergency aid

If you have an emergency – perhaps you have to take out an injunction against someone – you can get an Emergency Legal Aid certificate via your solicitor who should be able to obtain it over the telephone. You will then have to apply for a legal aid certificate in the usual way. If you do not get this, you will have to pay for the cost of the work done under the Emergency Certificate. An Emergency Certificate is a useful way to get instant help if you do not have any cash but do not qualify for legal aid. At the worst it gives you a breathing space to get the money together before you are asked to pay.

The Green Form Scheme

This is a modified form of legal aid which pays for you to have 'advice and assistance' from a solicitor. To do this you have to sign a green form which is far less complicated than a full legal aid form. For this you can get two or three hours' work from a solicitor, so go well prepared to get the most of it with dates, times and all the background information in order. Your income is then worked out and you will have to pay a contribution. This is costed on how much net income you have and how many dependants you have. It is worked out on a sliding scale and the rate changes each year. If you are on Income Support or Family Benefit you will not have to contribute anything. Your solicitor will be able to work out right away how much you are likely to have to pay. It is worthwhile asking him, at the same time, how much he would charge to give you an interview session – some solicitors have a small fixed fee which makes the Green Form Scheme unnecessary.

Conditional Fees

A new way to get legal help, called Conditional Fees, has been introduced. Under this scheme you can agree with the solicitor that if you do not win your case you owe him nothing. But at the same time you agree to pay him extra if you do win. However, unlike in America, your lawyer cannot take a share in any compensation you win. The Conditional Fee scheme applies to personal injury claims, if you are the liquidator or trustee in bankruptcy of a person or a company or if you are taking a case to the European Court of Human Rights or the Commission.

Points to watch

Conditional Fee agreements cover the fees of your own solicitor. But there could be other costs if you lose your case. You might have to pay the winning side's costs and you might also have to pay bills from expert witnesses or barristers used on your case. There may also be court fees and other expenses. If you are an accident victim, however, you do not need to worry. The Law Society's insurance scheme will cover the legal costs of the winning side if you lose your case. You do not need to take out the insurance scheme Accident Line Protect, until you see a solicitor.

If you wish to complain about your solicitor

- Your first step is to complain to him directly about his service.
- If you get no satisfaction, you should write to the Solicitors Complaints Bureau (*see page 460*) putting your complaint succinctly and clearly in writing. It has a useful booklet on the subject called *How and When?*, and a helpline on 0171 834 8663.
- If you have done this and you are not satisfied, contact the Legal Services Ombudsman and ask him to investigate whether your complaint was considered fully and fairly. You must do this within 3 months after the Solicitors Complaints Bureau has given you its decision. The Ombudsman will not normally get involved if the Bureau is still considering your complaint.

What happens then?

If the Ombudsman thinks you have a case, he may recommend that the Solicitors Complaints Bureau should reconsider your complaint, or should pay you compensation because of the way your case was handled. Or he may say that the offending solicitor should pay you compensation and that the Complaints Bureau or the solicitor concerned should repay some or all of your expenses in taking your complaint to the Ombudsman. When he has made this recommendation, the solicitor or the Bureau must tell him within 3 months what they are doing or have done about it. If they do not contact him or if they refuse to co-operate, the Ombudsman can publicize details of your case in the local paper and recover the costs of the advertisement.

How to contact the Ombudsman

Write or telephone (*see page 460*) and ask for a form to complete and return. He will then decide whether or not to take up your case. If he does and needs more information he will contact you. The same procedure is used if you wish to make a complaint about a Licensed Conveyancer over the way he handled your house sale or purchase, or against a barrister who represented you in court. See the relevant addresses in the **Home** section (*page 462*).

COMPENSATION AWARDS

Awards for victims of disaster, criminal and personal injury vary widely. There are no set figures for the loss of a limb or any other physical injury suffered as a result of an industrial or road accident. Awards are usually agreed through out-of-court settlements and depend on how much your life has been changed by the injury. This is a situation which definitely requires a lawyer (see the details on conditional fees, above).

Compensation for crime

If you or someone close to you is the victim of violence, you may be able to get compensation for personal injury from the Criminal Injuries Compensation Board. Injury while trying to stop someone committing a crime or injury while chasing a suspected criminal may also be eligible for compensation. The Criminal Injuries compensation scheme, on the other hand, has a set list of payments ranging from £1,250 for a dislocated finger to £100,000 for the loss of both legs. Compensation can also be claimed for someone who dies from another cause, such as a heart attack, after a crime of violence.

The request for compensation can be made by the victim, a married partner or co-habitee if you have lived together for more than two years. In the case of death there is a flat rate award which can only be claimed by a widow, widower or parent.

How to claim

Get a claim form from the Criminal Injuries Compensation Board (*see page 458*) as soon as possible. You do not have to wait until someone is arrested. You must claim within three years of injury or death but the sooner you do so the more likely you are to succeed.

POWER OF ATTORNEY

One day you may find yourself in a situation where you have to give or be given power of attorney. This is a document which gives someone the power to sign or act on someone else's behalf. This is done by a deed which should be, but is not always, signed in the presence of two witnesses. You could want someone to sign documents for you on the sale of your house while you are abroad, for instance, or to use your bank account in some way. Often it is used when someone is too ill, either physically or mentally, to cope with their affairs. You can grant power of attorney to anyone who is not bankrupt and is over the age of 18. Consult your solicitor about this or write to the Court of Protection (*see page 460*) for help.

Do you really need it?

If you only want someone to act on your behalf in a straightforward way, it may not be necessary to take out power of attorney. You can simply write a letter to your bank authorizing someone else to have access to your account. And if it is a case of collecting child benefit or pension, your local Society Security Office should be able to give permission for someone else to do it on the beneficiary's behalf.

CHILDREN AND THE POLICE

The first inkling you may have that your child is in trouble with the law may be a phone call from the station or a visit from a police officer. If your child is caught stealing, he will almost certainly be taken straight to the police station to be interviewed. At this stage, if he is under 17 a child must, by law, have a 'responsible adult', a parent, a solicitor or a social worker present, unless the delay will involve an immediate risk of harm to others, or serious loss or damage to property.

It may be that the police officer will just give the child an unofficial warning depending on the seriousness of the offence he is supposed to have committed. The police officer can do this whether the child agrees he is guilty or not. The police may give a formal caution, which the parents must attend, and which is marked on the child's record. This will only happen if the child has pleaded guilty and the victim of the offence does not want to press charges. If the offence is too serious for this, then the police will pass the papers to the Crown Prosecution Service who will decide whether or not to take action. If your child is to be hauled into court, then you need to consult a solicitor as soon as possible.

Your child and legal aid

Children can apply for legal aid. The arrangements for each kind vary but for civil legal aid your finances are not taken into account (so that most children qualify). Applications are usually made by the child's parent or guardian.

What if my child is taken to court?

If he is under 17, he will go to a youth court presided over by magistrates, which is not open to the general public. The case may take weeks or even months to come up so you should make sure that all the events surrounding the case are written down and, if the child is pleading not guilty, that witnesses' names and addresses are recorded.

When the hearing comes up, as parents you must be present. Newspaper reporters may be there but they are not allowed to publish the child's name or give any other clues to his identity. Once the evidence has been given, your child and you, as his parent, will be given an opportunity to speak and to give your side of the story. If your child says nothing, the magistrates may incline towards thinking he has something to hide. If your child has pleaded guilty, anything positive he has done to redress the crime, repairing damaged property, saving towards a fine or an apology to the victim will be taken into account before the magistrates make up their minds. If your child has pleaded not guilty, you will probably need a solicitor to represent you and to call witnesses.

What the magistrates may do

Your child may be given an absolute discharge, a conditional charge or a fine (*see page 436*) and he may be made to pay **compensation** to the victim if, say, he has damaged property. An offer on your part to do this might make a fine against him less harsh. Magistrates also have the right to defer the sentence for up to six months on certain conditions. These could involve a change of life-style, starting a new job or attending an education centre. If the child complies with these conditions, it is possible that the final sentence will be lower than what would otherwise be expected.

If your child is found guilty

The magistrates will probably call for reports from the school, a doctor, probation officer, social worker and anyone appropriate. If it will help, then it is a good idea to organize these yourself. If the reports are not available, the case may be adjourned until they are, which means another court appearance.

An Attendance Centre Order

may be imposed on your child instead of imprisonment if he is under 21, or if he does not comply with an order such as paying a fine on time. Attendance centres are police-run and their aim is not just to deprive offenders of their leisure time but also to try to teach them some constructive kind of recreation. These sessions usually take place in school buildings out of hours and at weekends and your child will be told when and where to report – usually for a two-hour session. If he does not do so, he will land up in court again, so it is in your interest to see that he goes along.

A Supervision Order

means that your child will be monitored by a social worker for a certain length of time. It may also mean that the child will have to take part in group activities and perhaps go into some kind of residential establishment away from home for a short period. Supervision orders vary according to the severity of the crime and among their requirements is regular attendance at school.

Youth Custody

is, in effect, prison. If the offence is a serious one, a boy over the age of 14 and a girl over the age of 15 can be detained in this way.

Community Service Order

is a relatively new measure. A child over 16 can be ordered to do some form of service in the community for a set number of hours over a period of 12 months. This is supervised by a probation officer and can only be put into action if the child agrees.

Being Bound Over

is another option the magistrates may use. In this case, you as a parent will be bound over for a certain sum to, for instance, guarantee your child's good behaviour or regular attendance at school. If your child reneges you lose the money.

MENTAL INCAPACITY AND THE LAW

People may be unable to look after their own affairs for a number of reasons including alcoholism, psychological illness, severe personality disorder or senile dementia. If someone close to you is unable to look after their own affairs:

- Write to the Court of Protection (*see page 460*) and get a form CP3.
- Get a certificate from the doctor confirming that the person is incapable of administering his property and affairs or get the doctor to fill in the relevant part of the form.

- If the patient is considered to be capable of understanding it, the court will then send someone to hand the patient a notice telling him that it proposes to appoint a receiver. This person might be the local GP.
- The Court of Protection will appoint a receiver to act as the patient's agent – this could be a friend, a local GP or a solicitor. This person will deal with problems like bills.

If the person is not mentally ill but severely ill physically and cannot cope with his affairs, he can appoint someone to act as a trustee, giving the trustee Power of Attorney. The use of this is only valid as long as the patient is able to keep mental control over things. If the person's mental powers fail, then after a mental test by the patient's doctor, the Court of Protection takes over – it is at this stage that the trustee, if he or she is untrustworthy, frequently misuses the patient's money, a point that the family should keep an eye on if they have reason to doubt this person's honesty.

The Mental Health Act: your legal rights

These days, with more and more of the mentally ill being released into the community, getting into a mental hospital is not as easy as it was. But if you are considered to be mentally ill and potentially dangerous to yourself or to others, your social worker or a relative may decide that you need to be committed. The last thing mental hospitals want is more live-in patients since it costs so much, so committal is only used in serious cases. In order to be committed, there must be approval from two doctors, one of whom must be approved by the local authority as having experience in dealing with mental disorders. They will then recommend the detention unless there is an emergency situation, in which case one doctor will do. If these requirements are met, the person can be taken to hospital by force, if necessary. The patient can be admitted for assessment or admitted for treatment.

Assessment is a short-term committal – you cannot be detained for more than 28 days and the application cannot be repeated. It is used when the doctor needs time to decide if the patient needs long-term treatment. If you disagree with this, you have the right to appeal to a Mental Health Review Tribunal within 14 days of your admission. Admission for treatment can either be done in the case of someone in hospital for assessment or on the advice of an approved social worker after consultation with relatives. In some cases the social worker can apply to the court for the relative's rights to be removed.

Mental hospitals: your rights

If you have been detained against your will, you still have certain rights. The hospital has the right to take action against your will to save your life or prevent a serious deterioration in your condition or prevent serious suffering. It can also take action if you need to be stopped from endangering yourself or others. But:

- They can only give you psychosurgery, a leucotomy or a lobotomy, if you consent and if they have a certificate from the doctor.
- While you have to take the medication they prescribe for the first three months, after that they need your consent.
- You can refuse to have other treatment like ECT (electro-convulsive therapy) but you could be overruled by a second opinion from a doctor appointed by the Mental Health Commission.

The points above refer to your mental condition. They do not cover treatment for any physical illness you may have. You also have the right to ask for a second opinion from a qualified doctor. If this is involved with an appeal or legal action, his fees may be covered by legal aid.

Supposing I admit myself?

The doctor can keep you in for up to three days for treatment. A nurse is only allowed to keep you in for six hours. If you are a voluntary patient, the hospital has to explain the nature, purpose and likely effects of what they plan to do to you. You then have the right to refuse this treatment. But, if it is necessary to do it to save your life (after a suicide attempt for instance) then you could be over-ruled.

Supposing I disagree with the decision?

Then make an objection in writing to the local Social Services authority.

If I am admitted, how long must I stay in hospital?

Either the doctor or a near relative can arrange for your discharge at any time. But this may be over-ruled if you are considered to be potentially dangerous to yourself or to others. If you want to discharge yourself against medical advice then you may be asked to sign a statement to that effect.

Can I appeal?

A relative can appeal on your behalf to a Mental Review Tribunal which consists of a doctor, a lawyer and someone with experience of social work, for your release within 28 days. You should have some advice over this and be represented at the tribunal. Contact MIND or the Law Society (*see page 460*) and ask for details of a solicitor with experience of this via the scheme Advice by Way of Representation which he can do under the Legal Aid Act.

Where do I get an application form?

You can get an application form from the hospital, the Tribunal's office or the Local Health Authority. The 'admission for treatment' lasts for 6 months. After that the doctor can renew it if necessary for another 6 months. After that it can be renewed by the year.

What power does the Tribunal have?
It can discharge you if you have appealed against detention for assessment or treatment and it is satisfied that you are not suffering from a mental disorder severe enough to justify keeping you in, or that the detention is not necessary for your, or anyone else's, health and safety.

Where is the Tribunal held?
It is usually done in private at the hospital where you are being kept. The medical member of the panel will examine you beforehand and find out what treatment you have been having and why. You are entitled to hear the doctor and social worker's evidence, to question them and to call witnesses. Their travelling expenses will be paid by the Tribunal. If you want an independent psychiatric and/or social work report, a solicitor can arrange this for you – it qualifies for legal aid.

What if I want to make a complaint about my treatment?
Start with the manager of the hospital where you are, then try the Health Service Commissioner. If that does not give you satisfaction, then you or someone acting on your behalf must contact the Mental Health Act Commission (*see page 460*). It will investigate your case, interview you and, if necessary, get a second opinion. The Commission has no 'teeth', however; all it can do is investigate the case and make a report on it.

Will my case be monitored?
Yes, by law the hospital must refer your case to the Mental Health Review Tribunal for assessment within 6 months of your admission for treatment. In the case of long-term stay, the Tribunal must consider your case every three years (every year in the case of patients under 16).

Can the hospital let me out?
If the hospital considers it safe to do so, it can give you leave of absence, either indefinitely or for a specific period. If you have been on leave for six months and at the end of that time have not run away, you are automatically discharged.

What happens if I run away?
You face arrest and return to the place where you were detained. If, however, you are absent for more than a month, you are automatically discharged.

MAKING A WILL

If you die intestate (without having left a will) whatever you leave is divided according to the intestacy laws and your relatives cannot do anything about it. Basically your married partner, if you have one, gets the first £40,000 of your estate and the income from half of any money left over. But the rest of the capital itself goes to your children.

You can make a will before you marry as though you are married (when you are engaged) provided you make it clear in that will that you are planning to marry. It is called 'a will made in contemplation of marriage'.

Your will, separation and divorce

If you and your partner **separate** and you have made out a will leaving everything to him or her, nothing is changed unless you take steps to do so. So if the separation seems permanent, and you do not want to leave the person any money, get to a solicitor right away to change your will. If you **divorce** your will is immediately affected. Any bequests you leave to your now ex-partner are automatically cancelled and he can no longer be named as your executor. This can very much alter the balance of your will, for, if you have left the 'residue of your estate' to a distant relative, if your partner's bequest is removed, the distant relative could inherit a surprisingly large sum.

What if I am left out of my partner's will?

If your partner leaves you out of his will, or if a bequest to you is cancelled by divorce, you can appeal. You have six months to lodge a claim from the time probate is granted, provided you have not remarried. But you have to convince the court you are suffering from financial hardship. It will then take into account your financial circumstances and those of other people mentioned in the will as well as the amount that your ex-partner left and what was said in the divorce settlement.

If the boot is on the other foot, how can you stop your ex-partner from making a claim against your estate? Make sure that when the divorce goes through, any settlement you make is conditional upon your ex-partner being barred from making any future claim against the estate. Reinforce it by writing a letter, at the same time as you make your will, explaining why you have left your ex-partner out of it. If your partner tries to make this proviso against you when the divorce is going through, you can tell the court that the financial proposals still leave you dependent on your partner and it would be unjust to block a claim. Or you can get your ex-partner to take out a life insurance policy naming you as a beneficiary on his death.

What should go in my will?

Quite apart from stating who will get the house and the money, there are other things to decide.

- Where and how you want to be buried/cremated.
- Whether you want to leave money for your friends to have a memorial party for you.
- Do you want to nominate someone as a guardian for your children if you and your partner should die before they are old enough to look after themselves?
- Do your children need protection from themselves via a trust, so that they cannot waste their inherited money?
- What do you want done with 'moveable goods and chattels', clothes, furniture? Do you want to leave any special thing to an individual?
- Do you want to leave all or any part of your body to science?

Writing your own will

You can buy DIY forms to make your own will from any stationers. The danger of using a form is that it has definite lines on which to write and an unscrupulous heir could forge insertions between the spaces. If you want to do it yourself, use the form as an *aide-mémoire* by all means, but write your will out yourself, by hand. You can also draw up your will via your bank, via an insurance company or other companies. If you do it yourself bear it mind:

- It can be written out by hand or typed.
- The pages must be numbered (a safeguard to make sure no one inserts anything afterwards).
- You must start with the words 'this is the last will and testament of . . . and give your name in full, including your maiden name if you had one.
- It must be dated and you should say it revokes all previous wills – even if there are no others. You should give the full names of people you want to inherit your money or leave something to.
- As you do not know exactly how much money you will have to leave, put it in proportions rather than actual sums – two thirds, one third etc.
- If you are leaving property, give the full address of the house concerned.
- You need two witnesses to co-sign the will with you. They cannot benefit from the contents and must give their names, addresses and occupations.
- You should appoint two executors (who can be beneficiaries of the will) to act for your estate, paying out any outstanding bills, getting money out of banks etc. You can use a lawyer for this, but doing so will slow up the speed with which the will is executed after your death and cost money, so it is better to use two beneficiaries – your children, for instance.

- Finally you and two witnesses should sign every page including the bottom of the will as a safeguard.
- You can then lodge the will with the Principal Probate Registry, so there is no danger that it will be lost – but you need to tell your family you have done so.

Using a solicitor

Why pay a solicitor anything up to £100 or more to draw up a will for you when you can do it yourself? What a solicitor will do is ask you questions about things that might not have occurred to you, and the final will will be much more comprehensive. He will also act as a trustee, if you want him to, and keep a copy of the will on file so that your heirs will know where to get it. Go to a solicitor you know or one recommended by a friend. Do not be afraid to ask him what he will charge.

Where there is a will . . .
Check your will every seven years at least. If you marry or remarry it will need re-drafting because in these circumstances any existing will is automatically revoked by law.

If you are an executor
Get a copy of *How to Obtain Probate* from the Lord Chancellor's Department. This leaflet explains what your duties are and how to go about them.

A LIVING WILL

A Living Will is not a kind of self-inflicted euthanasia (*see page 309*) nor is it a licence for doctors to put you out of your misery. It is an instruction to the doctor or the hospital caring for you not to prolong the dying process once you have got to a stage where it is uncomfortable and distressing to live. No one knows what the manner of their dying will be, most of us dread the idea of lying in a coma, paralysed by a stroke and unable to speak, and above all being unable to communicate with your carers. In an excess of zeal, some hospitals bring people back from the brink of death time and time again. But who wants to end their life in pain and distress wired up to monitors with uncomfortable tubes, or on a life-support system? Apart from our own feelings, there are those of our distraught relatives to consider.

Under present law, a Living Will cannot be legally enforced, all we can hope is that the doctors will take notice of our wishes. It takes the form of a document signed in front of two witnesses, with one copy given to your GP to file away, the other handed to your closest relative or friend. You should also, of course, tell all your family about its existence. If you are suffering from terminal cancer or AIDS, then the end may unfortunately be clear. If you are not, you may need to update your remarks as cures are found for conditions which at one time would have been considered terminal.

The Natural Death Centre (*see page 309*) and the Terence Higgins Trust (*see page 97*) have forms of living will which you can study. If you are interested, send them a stamped addressed envelope for details. Living Wills are not legally enforceable and doctors do not have to comply with your request, but they usually do.

HOW TO CHANGE YOUR NAME

You can change your name without any formality at all – unless it is for the purposes of fraud. Simply start using your new name and that is that. However, certain people need to be told including your bank, so you can be issued with a new cheque book, National Insurance, Income Tax authorities and any other official bodies so that their documents can be altered. But for some purposes – including getting a new passport or a driving licence – you will have to produce evidence of a change of name. This can be done in three ways.

Deed Poll
is a written statement of your original name and the one you wish to use, drawn up by a solicitor. Register a copy at the Passport Office and it will give you a passport in your new name only, otherwise both names will appear. There is a fee for this.

Statutory Declaration
involves simply swearing before a solicitor that you are using another name. It is cheaper than a deed poll.

Advertisement
is the cheapest way of all to change your name. You simply put an announcement in your local paper that you are adopting a new name. If you wanted to keep it quiet, you could put the ad in any local paper you choose – one a hundred miles away from you. Keep copies of the ad to produce when necessary for official purposes.

Changing your Christian name

There is nothing to stop you calling yourself whatever Christian name you like, but it is much harder to change your Christian name formally. The only way to do so officially is by an Act of Parliament. But it can be changed by a bishop if you are being confirmed or, if a child is adopted, the new parents can add a fresh Christian name to the child's original one.

Taking someone else's name
If you go to live with someone and want to take that person's name, then you can change your own name by the three different ways above – although you might not want to advertise. Do not forget to get official documents altered.

See also
Divorce, **Partners and Friends** (*page 176*).
Renting and Buying Property (*pages 475, 463*).

LEGAL: HELP DIRECTORY

Arrest

Gays and Lesbians
- GALOP, Gay London Policing Group, 38 Mount Pleasant, London WC1X 0AP, (Helpline 0171 837 7324). It has a 24-hour answerphone line for those in trouble with the police.
- GLAD, Gay and Lesbian Legal Advice, 7 pm–9.30 pm Monday to Friday, (0171 976 0840). London 24-hour Lesbian and Gay Helpline (0171 837 7324).
- LAGER helpline, (0171 704 8066) for lesbian women, (0171 704 6066) for gay men.

Compensation awards

- Criminal Injuries Compensation Board, Morley House, 26–30 Holborn Viaduct, London EC1A 2JQ, (0171 936 3476).
- Criminal Injuries Compensation Board, Tay House, 300 Barr Street, Glasgow G2 4JR, (0141 331 2726). Deals with claims from victims of crimes of violence via the Criminal Injuries Compensation scheme. Write or phone for a copy of its explanatory leaflet.

Drinking and driving

- Campaign Against Drinking and Driving, 83 Jesmond Road, Newcastle-upon-Tyne NE2 1NH, (0191 2811581). Apart from campaigning against drunken driving, this organization gives support and help to the families of people killed in these circumstances and victims who survived.

General

- Legal Action for Women, King's Cross Women's Centre, 71 Tonbridge Street, London WC1H 9DZ, (0171 837 7509). Offers support and advice to women facing all kinds of situations, from being prosecuted for prostitution or threatened with deportation to problems over divorce, child custody, compensation for injuries or dismissal. It also advises and helps victims of rape and domestic violence.
- Liberty, National Council for Civil Liberties, 21 Tabard Street, London SE1 4LA, (0171 403 3888). Can advise you on a wide range of problems from arrest to racial harassment and your rights under the Mental Health Act.
- Rights of Women, 52–54 Featherstone Street, London EC1Y 8RT, (0171 251 6577) 608 0928. Gives free legal advice to women over legal problems.

Going to court

- INTERIGHTS, 33 Islington High Street, London N1 9LH, (0171 278 3230). Experts in Human Rights law, it will advise you of your rights in international courts.
- INQUEST, Ground Floor, Alexandra National House, 330 Seven Sisters Road, London N4 2PJ, (0181 802 7430). Gives legal advice to anyone facing a problem in connection with an inquest. It will also suggest a suitable solicitor to represent you in a coroner's or other court. It will also put you in touch with other people who have suffered a similar problem.
- JUSTICE, 59 Carter Lane, London EC4V 5AQ. Takes up the cases of, and helps, people who feel they are victims of a miscarriage of justice.
- Victim Support, England, Wales and Northern Ireland, Cranmer House, 39 Brixton Road, London SW9 6DZ, (0171 587 1162). An organization that helps victims of crime, giving practical help, information and emotional support. It can also assist with advice about compensation, insurance, police procedures, attending court and crime prevention.
- Victim Support Scotland, 14 Frederick Street, Edinburgh EH2 2HB, (0131 225 7779). *See above.*

Lawyers: how to complain

- Chartered Institute of Arbitrators, 24 Angel Gate, 326 City Road, London EC1V 2RS, (0171 837 4483). Runs a solicitors arbitration scheme. However, it will only act if your solicitor agrees to go to arbitration.

- General Council of the Bar, 3 Bedford Row, London WC1R 4DB, (0171 242 0082). The organization to write to if you have a complaint against a barrister.
- Law Society, 113 Chancery Lane, London WC2A 1PL, (0171 242 1222).
- Law Society, Solicitors Complaints Bureau, Victoria Court, 8 Dormer Place, Leamington Spa, Warwickshire CV32 5AE, (01926 820082).
- Legal Services Ombudsman, 22 Oxford Court, Oxford Street, Manchester M2 3WQ, (0161 236 9532). Investigates complaints made by the public about services they have received from solicitors, barristers or conveyancers.

Mental incapacity and the law

- Court of Protection, Protection Division of the Public Trust Office, Stewart House, 24 Kingsway, London WC2B 6JX, (0171 269 7300). Appoints a receiver to handle the affairs of anyone who is unable to do so. Contact the Chief Clerk for a form CP3.
- Mental Health Act Commission, 2nd Floor, Maid Marion House, 56 Houndsgate, Nottingham NG1 6BG (0115 950 4040).

The police – how to complain

- Police Complaints Authority, 10 Great George Street, London SW1P 3AE, (0171 273 6450).

Prison

- Aldo Trust, 92 Chesterfield House, Chesterfield Gardens, London W1Y 5TE, (0171 491 1242). Gives financial help to people in prison to encourage their education and spare-time interests. It also works with people who are in detention awaiting trial.
- Apex Trust, Battersea Park Road, Battersea, London SW11 4ND, (0171 627 3726). Helps people who have been in prison to get jobs with training and support and finds them work opportunities.
- Bourne Trust, Lincoln House, 1–3 Brixton Road, London SW9 6DE, (0171 582 1313). Helps prisoners, ex-prisoners and their families.
- Bridge-Builders National Association for the Education and Guidance of Offenders, c/o Robins Wood House, Robins Wood Road, Aspley, Nottingham NG8 3NH, (0115 9293291). Works with people in prison and ex-prisoners to help them with education and job training.
- Help and Advice Line for Offenders' Wives, 30 Blackford Street, Winson Green, Birmingham B18 4BN, (0121 523 4898). Gives support and help not just to prisoners' wives but their families as well. The counsellors are themselves

relatives of prisoners. They will also work on your behalf with the prison service or the social services and dealing with court appearances.

- Langley House Trust, 46 Market Square, Witney, Oxon OX8 6AL, (01993 774075). Christian charity working for the care and support of ex-offenders. It has a number of residential homes throughout England, including two drug rehabilitation projects.
- National Association for the Care and Resettlement of Offenders, 169 Clapham Road, London SW9 0PU, (0171 582 6500). Works with people who are newly out of prison helping them over housing, training for new jobs, employment. It also helps the families of prisoners.
- Prisoners Abroad, 82 Rosebery Avenue, London EC1R 4RR, (0171 833 3467). Works to help UK residents imprisoned abroad and their families. It will also give information, support and advice.
- Prisoners Advice and Information Network, BM Pain, London WC1N 3XX, (0181 542 3744). Answers enquiries from prisoners and their families during their confinement.
- Prisoners' Families and Friends Network, 106 Weston Street, London SE1 3QG, (0171 403 4091). Helps friends and families of people in prison in a practical way, with advice and information. It also makes some personal visits in the London area.
- Rainer Foundation, 89 Blackheath Hill, London SE10 8TJ, (0181 694 9497). Works mainly with young people between the ages of 13 to 26, offering alternatives to custody for young offenders. It also helps young mothers and those who are homeless.

Shoplifting

- Crisis Counselling for Alleged Shoplifters, PO Box 147, Stanmore, Middx HA7 4YT, (0171 722 3685 & 0181 202 5787). Helps anyone who has been accused of shoplifting with legal medical advice or counselling. It also works with children accused of the same offence.
- Portia Trust, The Croft, Bowness-on-Solway, Cumbria CA5 5AG, (016973 51820). A support group for people accused of shoplifting or stealing a child. Send an SAE for the leaflet *If You are Accused of Shoplifting*. It may also be able to send someone, not a solicitor, to court with you to speak up for you.

13

HOME

One of the most important decisions we take in life is where we are going to live. This section helps you through the hurdles whether you are buying, selling or renting a home. It also deals with all manner of problems that could arise, including fire, flood and theft.

YOUR RIGHTS

Your home may be your castle, but a surprisingly large number of people are allowed to enter it without your permission.

The police have the right to enter your house in certain circumstances – if they have reason to believe that someone is in danger of being seriously hurt is one example. Armed with a warrant they have the right to search the house, whether or not you are there, for wanted people or stolen goods, and the right to take away items for which they must give you a receipt. If they have forced entry while you are out they must leave a copy of the warrant behind and make the premises secure.

Government and local council officials have the right to enter your house forcibly in an emergency – gas leaks, flooding or fire. Environmental Health Officers with a warrant can enter if, for instance, there is a rat infestation and Building Inspectors may enter if dangerous building work has taken place.

Utility services – gas, water, electricity – if armed with a magistrate's warrant, and after having given 24 hours notice, can enter your home to disconnect services because of non-payment of a bill. They also have the right to break in if there is a gas leak or any similar emergency.

Bailiffs can enter your home without your permission, but only if they are in possession of a court order. However, they are not allowed to force entry, and must only come in through unlocked doors or windows. Once they are in they are allowed to break down inner doors and cupboard doors and to force their way out again having selected and taken away goods. They must let you keep essential clothes, bedding and work tools.

TV Licence Inspectors can get a warrant to enter and search your house if they suspect you own a TV and have not got a licence or have a black and white licence for a colour set.

Customs and Excise Officials and VAT men have the right to enter your home to search for smuggled goods or to check up on VAT returns they suspect have been falsified. If they come at night, however, they must bring a policeman with them.

Tax Inspectors are also allowed into your home at any time, armed with a warrant. They are also allowed to break in with the help of the police.

Social Workers, armed with a court authority, have the right to enter and inspect your premises if they believe a mentally disturbed person is being ill-treated or is unable to look after themselves or a child is in danger. They can also enter a home where a child is being fostered.

Letting people into your home

- Always ask for proof of identity if someone is seeking to enter your house. Do not be embarrassed about it since it is plain common sense.
- Do not take a uniform as proof that the person is genuine. If you have any doubts, phone the department that the person says he has come from.
- Ask to see the court order or warrant if they are attempting a forcible entry. Make sure it is properly completed and signed by a magistrate, sheriff or judge. The warrant will tell you what they are allowed to do.
- Remember that anyone apart from the officials listed above who enters your home without your permission is trespassing. You can evict them and sue for compensation for any damage they do.

BUYING A HOUSE

Owning your own home is not the seductive idea that it used to be, but despite that 70 per cent of us own our own homes. As most of us have to take out a mortgage to buy a house and with tax relief on the decline, it is vital to work out your actual costs before saddling yourself with payments for most of your working life. It is the biggest financial commitment you are ever likely to make.

Having once decided you want a property, you are on a roller coaster that does not stop until it is finally yours − or not − as the case may be. Many deals fall through and you can suffer great disappointment and stress if things do not go well. You are also facing a complicated organizational project before you finally send out those change-of-address cards − juggling with estate agents, mortgage companies and solicitors who never seem to move fast enough. Then there is the packing, unpacking and organizing services like gas, electricity and telephone. So know what you are in for and plan well ahead.

Step one: financial planning

- Work out how much you can afford to spend.
- If you are selling a house first, how much cash will there be left?
- What is the maximum amount you can borrow without putting yourself in financial difficulties? Remember tax relief on mortgages has been reduced and will probably be reduced still more.
- Have you any savings to add to these sums?
- Do you need to deduct a sum for furniture and furnishings?

Simple addition should give you the answer to these questions, but do not forget to set money aside for the following things:

Estate agent's commission of $1-2\frac{1}{2}$ per cent which comes off the amount you get for the house you are selling. Ask in advance what he charges.

Solicitor's fees, both for your own transaction and for the building society. Solicitors can charge what they like. Ask in advance what these charges are likely to be.

Stamp Duty on the house purchase. If the house costs less than £60,000 there is no duty; above that it is on a sliding scale according to the price.

The Land Registry fee comes on a sliding scale according to the value of the house.

The searches – your solicitor will include them in his bill.

The building society's legal fee is cheaper if your solicitor acts for you both.

The building society's valuer's fee.

The Surveyor's fee if you decide to have a full survey done for yourself.

Building insurance – many building societies make you pay in advance for this and insist that you take up their schemes.

Mortgage insurance is something new. Ask your building society about it.

Mortgage arrangement fee – most building societies charge one so ask them what it will be.

Step two: viewing properties

- Make up your mind about what kind of house you want.
- Tell the estate agent whether you want an old or a new house. If you want an old one, say whether you want one that has been restored or one that needs work on it.
- Decide how many bedrooms you need, how much garden you want and whether you must have a garage.
- What services do you want nearby – buses, schools and shops?

Be frank with the estate agent about the price range. You are wasting his time and yours looking at 'dream homes' above your price level unless the agent thinks the seller will come down. Remember that although the estate agent appears to be on your side when you say you want to try a lower offer, he is acting for, and will get, commission from the seller. And the more he can sell the house for, the more money he will get.

You and your estate agent: how to complain

Remember that the Property Misdescriptions Act means that it is a criminal offence for an estate agent to make a false or misleading statement about the property he shows you. However, estate agents are not saints but businessmen and are not averse to sharp practices. Watch out for:

- Pressure to use their mortgage and insurance services (which nets them more commission).
- Attempts to sell you unnecessary insurance, especially life insurance.
- Attempts to discourage anyone else making an offer on your house, if you have someone interested. This spreads the buyers around.
- Attempts to persuade you to put your price unreasonably low to get a quick sale.

If a house deal falls through or there is some other problem, you may have the right to make an official complaint. If your agent infringed your legal rights in some way, treated you unfairly or was guilty of maladministration or inefficiency or delay which caused the deal to fall through, then you have reason to complain. You also have grounds for complaint if he did anything that caused you to lose money or suffer inconvenience.

If the agency is a member of the Ombudsman for Corporate Estate Agents Scheme – which all well-established agents are – you should tell your agent that you wish to complain to the head of the firm about his behaviour via the firm's own internal complaints procedure. If you get no satisfaction this way then you should write to the OCEA Ombudsman (*see page 492*) setting out details of your complaint. The Ombudsman will then ask the agency for full details and make a decision. The agency could be liable to pay you compensation up to £100,000 in full and final settlement of your complaint so it is well worthwhile complaining.

Viewing

Normally the estate agent will want to come with you to view the house or if it is empty he may lend you the keys. Take a pen and paper to jot down notes and take a Polaroid camera with you if you have one. The measurements of the rooms should be on the particulars you are given.

Be your own surveyor

If you are not having your own survey done, get a copy of a free leaflet *The Property Doctor* from the Royal Institution of Chartered Surveyors (*see page 490*). There are a number of things to look out for when viewing a property.

- Are there stains on the ceilings and are they sagging and cracked?

- Are there marks on the wall that might be rising damp? Ask if the building has a damp course.
- Are there any cracks running diagonally across the walls? This could be settlement.
- Have part of the walls or ceiling been painted recently? They could be covering something up.
- How are the window frames – are they in good condition or are they rotten?
- Cross the road and look at the roof: are there loose or slipping tiles or slates?
- Do the walls bulge at all?
- Is there crumbling or unpointed brickwork or missing guttering – all signs of neglect.

If you are keen on a house, it pays to get the owner's permission to send in an accredited dry rot and woodworm specialist (*see page 490*) and, if necessary, a damp proof course installer to give you a free survey. They will be able to tell you about the condition of the respective parts of the house.

You should also ask the owner:

- What council tax band are they in.
- What fixtures and fittings are included – some people will even take light bulbs and door handles with them when they go.
- Ask about grey areas such as curtain tracks, fitted bookshelves, built-in cupboards, wardrobes, kitchen units, TV aerials, shrubs and trees in the garden.
- Is the property freehold or leasehold – would you own the land it actually stands on or in effect be renting the ground for a set number of years? The estate agent's particulars should tell you that.

If you are selling and your house is on view

- Insist that the estate agent accompanies any prospective buyers and does not allow complete strangers into the house alone.
- Have a log book ready showing what has been done to the house and when.
- Empty cupboards if you have no time to tidy them – tip the contents into plastic sacks and store temporarily in the garage.
- Buy cheap bunches of fresh flowers and put them around the house.
- If the garden looks bad in midwinter, produce photos, if you can, showing it in bloom.
- Put on the central heating, switch off the TV and play soothing music instead.

Buying a flat

If you are buying a flat, check whether things like the communal heating system, the roof, the exterior paintwork and walls have been overhauled and repaired in recent time. Otherwise you might have an unpleasant shock after moving in, with a demand for your share of the cost of building work. Ask what the service charges have been over the years – you can see then whether the rises have been gradual or steep.

If you are buying your own council flat, the Department of the Environment (*see page 529*) has a useful booklet *Your Right to Buy Your Home*. Bear in mind that if you sell your council flat or house within three years, you may have to refund a proportion of the loan.

Buying an old house

If you are planning to buy and improve an old house, go to the planning department of the local authority and ask if permission is needed to do what you have in mind. Check if it is a listed building. That fact should be shown on the estate agent's particulars. Houses officially rated of special historic interest may have restrictions placed on them. However, you may qualify for a grant, but money is thin on the ground and it is quite difficult to get one. So do not be taken in by glowing promises of grants from the seller or the estate agent – check and see.

There are house renovation grants available for some houses, but not those used as second homes or built or converted less than 10 years ago. Not many of them are handed out and the regulations change all the time. If you are disabled, however, (*see page 66*), or have income-related benefits and need to do minor repairs you might qualify. In most cases the grant would cover only a percentage of the 'eligible expense of the cost of improvement'. To find out more, get a copy of the free booklet *House Renovation Grants* from the Department of the Environment (*see page 529*).

Buying a new house

A house on a new estate may be a tempting proposition, particularly if you are stuck with a property you cannot sell. Many companies have mortgage schemes offering up to 100 per cent credit. Others may offer to take your own home in part-exchange, but, as with part-exchanged cars, the trade-in price of the property may be lower than on the open market.

If you are buying a house that is in the process of construction, you may be asked to pay for it stage by stage. In this case, you should tell the building society at the beginning as they will want to send a surveyor to inspect the work before handing over the money. Check that the builder is a registered member of the National House Building Council. This means you are covered for the repair of faulty work in the first two years and it will also give you eight years' cover if main structural faults develop. Also, if the builder goes bankrupt before the house is finished you will get back your deposit or the cost of the completion of the building up to a certain value.

Buying a repossessed house

Many building societies, banks and other mortgage lenders sell off repossessed houses, sometimes at a low rate. The system is the same as buying from someone privately. But bear in mind that they may not know or even have seen the house, so the onus is on you to check the property over very carefully.

Buying a council house

There is currently a 'Right to Buy' scheme where a tenant can buy the council house or flat he or she is living in at a large discount depending on how long the person has been there or been a council tenant elsewhere in the district. Ask for the leaflet *Your Right to Buy Your Home* from the Citizens' Advice Bureau. You must have lived in the property for at least two years and the discount rises according to how many years you have been there. Enquire also about the many schemes which involve part-renting, part-buying or an option to buy in the future.

Using a surveyor

Having a private survey done is an expensive business but may save you in the long run if you are buying an old property. Anyone in this country can call himself a surveyor, so pick someone who is accredited in some way – a chartered surveyor, perhaps (*see page 490*). But bear in mind that, even if things go wrong, as long as the surveyor has used 'reasonable skill and care', as the law stands, you have to prove that he is negligent. You can only claim the difference between what you paid for the house and its true value when the defects are taken into account. Every surveyor has to carry professional indemnity insurance but should there be a dispute, the surveyor has to agree to go to arbitration and there is not as yet an Ombudsman scheme.

Buying a house together if you are not married

If you are buying a house with your partner but you are not married, and the property is going to be in one person's name, you should draw up a written **express trust** between you. This is called a trust deed. This document would save any disagreements over the property by clearly stating each party's share and what is intended to happen to that share in the event of death or separation.

The trust deed can divide the value of the property into shares of, say 50/50, 75/25, and it can give you a right of occupation. If the house is in your partner's name, you cannot automatically stop a sale or mortgage or other loan being raised but there is afforded protection for your interest. An additional safeguard to the trust deed is to register your interest under the Land Registration Act 1925, or the Land Charges Act 1972 – either effectively gives notice to any/all parties of your interest in the property. Consult a solicitor about this.

Another option is for the two of you to own the property as 'tenants in common' with the personal stakes you make in the property written down. This form of co-ownership was abolished in law by the Law of Property Act 1925 but exists in equity behind a trust for sale. Consult your solicitor about this.

Step three: making an offer

It used to be generally accepted that the seller asked for more than he thought he would get for his house and bargaining would go from there. But these days sellers are so anxious to off-load their property that they are likely to advertise it at the most attractive price they can. In other words the bluff and counter-bluff that went on in the days when the market was buoyant does not happen as much as it did.

Work out how much needs doing to the house and how much you can afford. Take into account how much similar properties are going for, how panicky the owners are about selling and above all, how much you want it. If you do not have a property to sell, and if you have finance organized, say so because it may sway the owner to accept a lower price.

Then make an official offer to the estate agent 'Subject to Contract'. This means that if you cannot raise the money or the survey is unsatisfactory, you can opt out. Also, if the searches reveal something worrying or if you just decide against the property, you are covered. If you are at all suspicious about your estate agent, confirm the offer in writing to the vendor. Some estate agents may ask you to give a deposit at this stage as a token of goodwill. This will be returned without question if you withdraw. The agent will ask you for the name and address of your solicitor. If you have one and plan to use him then that is quite straightforward. If you do not have a solicitor, then you might consider using a firm of conveyancers instead. These are people who specialize in property only and are usually faster than solicitors who are usually grappling with other cases as well.

You should be shopping around for a mortgage if you have not done so before. Let your mortgage company know what your offer is and whether you think it is likely to be accepted. Get their valuer organized to go round and see the building. If the property is old and in a bad condition, a building society could retain part of the mortgage money until work is done on it – this happens just when you need the cash to do the work. If this is likely, then talk to the bank about a bridging loan to help you through.

If you have a house to sell first

To save disappointment and distress, put your house on the market before you look for something else. DO NOT EXCHANGE CONTRACTS ON A PROPERTY IF YOUR HOUSE IS STILL UNSOLD. To do so is to head for bankruptcy, for you could be locked into an expensive bridging loan from the bank – if indeed they would let you have one – for a year or more.

Step four: view the house again

If you first saw the house at night, go during the day and vice versa.

Step five: if the offer is accepted

Alert your building society – get it to send its valuer to look at the property. Confirm your offer once again subject to contract. Also get your solicitor to act as quickly as possible; if you are getting the house for less than the asking price, the estate agent is legally bound to pass on other offers right up to the moment when contracts are exchanged. If you have beaten the price down, it is now a more attractive proposition.

Your solicitor or conveyancer will now get busy making his searches from the local council and preliminary enquiries about things like boundaries. If you are in a hurry it is possible to pay extra to have a fast personal search done. Your solicitor will send a list of questions to the seller's solicitor who will draw up a draft contract. Tedious though they are, these searches are vital – for all you know there might be plans to put a motorway through the back garden. If your solicitor is satisfied with the information he gets, if the funding is in place and the contract drawn up, then comes the next stage.

Step six: exchange of contracts

You and your seller both sign the contract and at this stage it is usual to hand over 10 per cent of the purchase price. If this is difficult your solicitor may be able to get theirs to agree to a lower amount; otherwise the bank will usually lend you the money. At the signing of the contract the final Completion Date has to be agreed. At this stage, book a removal firm unless you are planning to do it yourself. Once you have both signed the contract, neither side can back out.

Step seven: completion

This usually takes place between two weeks and a month after the exchange of contracts. It is a matter to be decided between you and the seller. On completion date your solicitor will transfer the funds by telegraphic transfer. The owners will have to be out of the house and hand over the keys. The deeds of the house will be handed over – probably to the building society unless you paid in cash.

Things to do before completion

- Organize to take over the electricity, gas and water. They need at least seven working days' notice. Arrange for meters to be read on moving day.
- Try to arrange to take over the existing phone line. It will cost you much less than if there is a break in the service and you have to be reconnected.
- Get a post redirection form from the Post Office; you can have letters sent on for up to a year or more, if necessary. You need to give them a few days' notice.
- If the electrical wiring in the house is ancient and you are not sure about it, get the Electricity Board to test the wiring of the house and report on what needs

doing. It will make a charge for this, according to the size of the building, but it is worthwhile having it done. If you want a gas supply and there is not one already in existence, call your local British Gas office or showroom. It will probably make a charge for any piping that has to be laid through your front garden and, in some cases, for piping along the road too, if it has to come a long way.

Insuring your house

Your building society may insist that you insure your house with a specific company. If this is not the case:

- Shop around and get quotes from several companies. Do not pay for a quote if you go through a broker since this should be free.
- See whether you are eligible for any kind of no-claims discount; they can reduce premiums by 25 per cent or more.
- If you have approved home security – a burglar alarm installed by a member of NACOSS (*see page 493*) for instance – you should get a reduction in your premium. If your insurance company says no, try someone else.
- Do not under-insure the contents of your house – if you have to make a claim the payment may be scaled down accordingly.
- If you opt for voluntary excess and pay, say, the first £200 of the claim, you should get a reduced premium
- If you take out contents and building insurance with the same company you should get a reduction.
- Enquire whether there are age-related discounts – usually for the over fifties.
- Insure your home for the full rebuilding cost, not its market value which also takes the value of the land into account. Rebuilding costs should cover permanent fittings such as central heating and unexpected items like demolition costs. Most insurers offer index-linked policies so that the sum insured goes up in line with rebuilding costs.
- If your contents policy is on a 'new for old' basis, you will be paid the full cost of repairing damaged items or replacing them at current prices – this may not apply to clothing, however. Some companies offer basic 'indemnity' cover which means that they will deduct a sum for wear and tear.
- Keep copies of receipts for all major household purchases, almost all companies will require receipts for goods you claim on.
- If you have valuable items like jewellery or antiques, you will need a professional valuation for them.
- It never pays to be under-insured. Make sure that your contents insurance is enough to enable you to replace all your possessions if they are destroyed. If you do not have adequate cover, the insurance company can refuse your claim.

Other ways of buying a home

Housing associations

There are a number of house-buying schemes through housing associations where buildings are converted or houses are built for joint ownership. Now many are also running a do-it-yourself ownership scheme; if you cannot raise all the money yourself, the housing association owns a percentage of your property which it rents out to you. After a year you can start buying out the association until you own the property entirely. The highest priority goes to homeless people and applicants have to have enough income to be able to pay the mortgage and rent each month. Enquire about this from the Housing Corporation (*see page 494*).

Buying the freehold of your flat

It is now technically feasible to buy the freehold of your flat via an act passed in 1993. But if your flat is in a block, you cannot do it on your own; all the tenants have to band together to apply. The new legislation is very complicated but the Enfranchisement Advisory Service (*see page 492*) can advise you.

MOVING IN

Mover's checklist

Do not forget to tell:
- Your bank.
- The Driver Vehicle Licensing Centre, Swansea (*see page 492*). It is against the law to have a driving licence with the wrong address.
- Stores with whom you have accounts.
- Credit card companies.
- Doctor and dentist.
- Local council rates department.
- Benefit agencies like the DSS if you draw benefits of any kind – pensions, child benefits etc.
- Income tax officials.
- The Post Office.
- Investment companies.
- Pension scheme companies.
- House and car insurance companies.
- Standing orders and direct debits.
- Loan, hire purchase and rental companies.
- Schools – give them as much notice as possible.
- Subscriptions to magazines, clubs.

- TV licence office.
- Your employers.
- Do not forget to cancel the milk and the papers in good time.

ALTERATIONS, RENOVATIONS AND REPAIRS

Before you attempt to do anything radical with your house you need to contact the local council and make sure that you do not need planning permission. If you are on Income Support or certain other benefits, you could be eligible for a grant towards the cost of draught-proofing and insulating your home. Contact the Energy Action Grants Agency (*see page 492*). There is also a Staying Put Scheme which might help you renovate your house if your income is low – enquire from your local council offices. You can also apply to your local council for a Renovation Grant to help with insulation or a Minor Works Assistance Grant if you are receiving benefit.

Getting the work done

Unfortunately, some of the most lucrative ways of making money – double glazing, roofing, installing burglar alarms, damp proof courses and woodworm treatments, attract cowboys, smooth-talking operators who offer to do the work for you at a 'special price' and who may do a shoddy job. The best way to avoid this is to check them out against a professional association. And it goes without saying that both gas and electricity are potentially lethal and must be installed in a house by someone who knows what they are doing. Under the Control of Pesticides Regulations, wood treatment firms have a statutory duty to tell you what kind of treatment is going to be carried out. Woodworm only needs treating if it is still active, which is why you need an expert survey. And anyone who is elderly or who has breathing problems should stay out of the way while the work is done.

In the case of dry rot, which, despite its name, is caused by moisture, there is no way of telling how far the rot has spread before the work begins, so it is difficult to know how much you are going to have to pay. You must have an operator you can trust. Most of the people listed in the Help Directory (*see page 490*) insist their members have at least three years' experience in the job and have a code of practice. They often arbitrate if there is a dispute, but only if it is with one of their members.

Finding a builder

Any kind of building work is expensive and it is dangerous to skimp. A bad builder may start cheap, but end up being more expensive than an apparently dear one, leaving work behind them that needs redoing. Choose a builder that you can get on with. As with marriage, if you are at all uncertain, do not proceed. Go by personal recommendation if you can. Be sceptical of 'flyers' from builders pushed through your letter box. Even in these days good builders do not need to advertise. If you cannot get a personal recommendation, get the name of a client from the builder you are planning to hire and ask the client if his work was done well, cleanly, on time and to the price quoted on the estimate.

Before he starts, write a detailed description of the job and make sure you get an equally detailed estimate in writing. You should cover preparatory work, any associated repairs and when the work should begin and end. You should also specify that the site should be left clean and tidy with all rubbish and unused materials removed. If you get quotes from more than one builder, give them all exactly the same job description.

Talk things over in detail with the builder. If it is a major job, find out what is going to happen and how it will be done. What time will they start work? Is it going to make a great deal of noise? If you are home all day, or if you are having scaffolding put up outside the bedroom window with work starting at 7 am, you might want to go away for a few days or move into another room.

Having got your builder, take his advice but do not be rail-roaded into anything you do not want, especially flooring or materials he is trying to sell you 'cheap'. Do not use builders who offer to do work VAT free. They may be unqualified, inexperienced and are certainly on the fiddle. If the VAT inspectors find out they will shut down the builder so he may not even finish the job for you. Do not forget to cost in the VAT, currently at 17.5 per cent, when calculating the bill.

Also make sure you get any local authority permission you need to do the work or grants for which you might be eligible. Make sure your builder has insurance and let your insurance company know that work is being done. Sort out the order in which the work will be done and clear out rooms where necessary to make the job easier. Your builder should tidy up afterwards. Try to avoid extras as they may well cost you dear. If you want other things done, start from scratch again and get an estimate.

Walk round the work when it is finished and inspect it with the builder. If you are unhappy with it, put your comments in writing. If any problems come up after the work is done, the builder should make it good for no extra cost. Your builder may ask for some money up front; this is reasonable if he has to buy materials, but do not be persuaded into paying large amounts in advance. Space it out – builders have been known to pocket the cash and disappear.

RENTING

More and more people are renting rather than buying now. It makes sense to rent if you are likely to have to move in the near future because of your job, or while a house is being built for you, or if you simply cannot make up your mind what to buy. Before entering into an agreement, check it over carefully. How easily can you get out of the arrangement? Are there any restrictions over, say, keeping pets? What outgoings are there apart from the rent? Ask around to see if the rent is a fair one.

Check whether you are responsible for repairs and whether these cover the inside of the house or flat or the fabric of the building. If your landlord does not give you an inventory, draw up one of your own and get him to sign it. That way there will be no dispute over what you leave behind you when you go.

HOW TO GET A COUNCIL HOUSE

The main ways to get a council house are to apply officially and go on a waiting list, or by being homeless. How long you are on a council waiting list depends on where you live; the length of time varies tremendously. It will also depend on the accommodation you want – a house, a flat, a house with a garden, and how many bedrooms are needed. The council will assess you according to the conditions in which you are living when you make application. You are more likely to get a council house if you have a local connection. This means:

- You have lived in the area for six months during the last year or three years out of the last five.
- You or someone in your household has a permanent full- or part-time job in the area.
- You have close family living in the area and they have lived there for at least five years.
- You have some special reason. Circumstances that would be taken into consideration are people in the area who can speak your language if you come from an ethnic group; or if you want to return to the area where you lived or were brought up.

Your right as a tenant

Having once been allocated a council home you have some security. The council cannot make you leave without applying to the County Court for a **possession order.** To get this it has to prove that there are justifiable grounds, such as not paying the rent for a long time. Before it can take you to court, the council must serve you with a notice telling you of its intention. If this happens, go straight to a solicitor or your local Law Centre find one through a Citizens' Advice Bureau.

Changing houses

If you are a council house tenant, you can, if you want to, move home in several different ways.
- By asking the council for a transfer to somewhere else. This may take time.
- As a housing tenant you have a right by law to a private exchange, finding another tenant who is willing to swap with you. This system sometimes works well if your job is taking you to another part of the country.

Advertise in the local paper. Both of you then have to apply to your local councils for permission, which is usually given. However, it may be withheld if the person you are swapping with is in trouble with their council over rent arrears, or if the accommodation is not suitable, or if the house has been specially adapted or sited for some reason, say, for disabled people.
- If you have to change to another part of the country because of your job or the need of relatives, you can apply under the National Mobility Scheme for a transfer. Ask your local council for details.

LETTING YOUR PROPERTY

If you are not successful in selling your home and you have to move out of the area, you could recoup some of your mortgage payments by letting.
- You will need to get permission from your mortgage company if you want to let your house. Sometimes it will ask for references from the prospective tenant. Sometimes it will increase your mortgage rate, so find out in advance.
- If you rent out the property, you can no longer claim mortgage relief against your tax.
- To protect yourself, go for a shorthold fixed-term tenancy of six months to start with. If the property is unfurnished, however, you may have to let it for a longer period.
- Be business-like, even if you are letting to friends. Blame your 'old-fashioned solicitor' if necessary.
- Draw up a proper lease and get it checked by a solicitor.
- Ask for four weeks' rent in advance .
- Get references – from a bank or building society, or from a previous landlord. Personal references can be faked but official ones cannot. Ask to see the original copy, however, not a fax or a photocopy since both of these can be forged.

- If you are letting the property furnished, make a proper inventory and get the
  tenant to sign it.

If you do not want to find your own tenant, you can go through an agent who will
either charge you a one-off fee for finding someone or a percentage of the rent –
usually about 15 per cent.

Problems with tenants

If a tenant refuses to pay the rent then he or she is in breach of the agreement and
you will have to begin possession proceedings. Use a solicitor to do the job. You
may have to get a court order to get the tenant out. Details of solicitors
specializing in landlord and tenant matters can be obtained from the Law Society
(*see page 460*).

Lodgers, bed-and-breakfast

Another way of making money from your home is to take in lodgers or, if you live
in a suitable area, to do bed-and-breakfast. A useful publication to consult is
Letting Rooms in Your Home which you should be able to get from your local
Citizens' Advice Bureau or direct from the Department of the Environment (*see
page 529*). Success in this enterprise depends on the reaction of the family. If they
are against sharing the house with strangers you could be doomed to failure.

- Only one bathroom in the house? Do not take on more than two tenants.
  Installing a second bathroom if you have the space would not only ease the
  pressure but also increase the value of the property.
- Will you have to buy new bedding or equipment? Buy cheap and cheerful bed
  and household linen and replace it frequently. If you are doing bed-and-
  breakfast, buy bedding in a cotton/polyester mix that dries quickly and does not
  need ironing. If you are letting bedsits, look around at car boot sales for second-
  hand cookers and fridges which are often very cheap.

HOME SECURITY

There is a burglary in this country every 30 seconds. Most burglaries – 80 per cent
– happen when the house in empty, more often than not in the afternoons. And the
fact that a house has been burgled does not mean it will not happen again – some
houses seem particularly inviting to thieves and may get 'done' time after time.

Burglars want to work quickly. They do not want to spend too much time or
make too much noise breaking into a house, so the aim of home security is to
make life as difficult as possible for them. The more force a burglar has to make
to get in, the more evidence the police will have at the scene of the crime. The

police are happy to advise you on how best to secure your house. Each police station has a crime prevention officer who will come and see you – enquire via your local Neighbourhood Watch. Check out the most vulnerable parts of the house.

The front door

An automatic light which comes on as you near the front door is a useful deterrent and easy to fit. Avoid planting trees and shrubs in the front garden that obscure the front door from the street and keep hedges low. A Yale lock is not enough; you should have a deadlock too, preferably a mortice lock which carries a kite mark of British Standard 3621. This can only be opened with a key, which means that if you are out and the burglar gets inside, he will not be able to get out of the front door. The letter box should have a cage behind it. That way the burglar cannot get his hand in through the slot and at the locks from the inside.

The door itself should have strong hinges, and it is worthwhile fitting bolts which will help hold the door in place if someone tries to ram or charge it. Fit a peephole on the door so that you can see who is there before opening it. Have a chain on the door so that you can open it a little and prevent anyone from pushing in.

Back doors

A favourite place for burglars to use, back doors should have a mortice lock on them too. If the door has glass panels in it, they should be shatter-proof. If there is a cat flap, make sure it is not sited in such a way that the burglar could put his hand through and grab keys. If you have sliding patio doors, these can be levered off their runners. To prevent this you should have a locking bolt on them.

Windows

You can get special locks for all kinds of windows now, even decorative fanlights. Two out of three break-ins are made through the windows, so fit them with screw locks – if the thieves have to break the glass it will make a noise and draw attention. Double-glazing plus window locks are the best deterrents but remember to have the keys somewhere accessible inside the house in case of fire as you will be unable to smash the windows to get out.

Louvred glass windows are a present to thieves because they are very easy to take out of their frames. They should be glued in place with an epoxy resin or replaced with a fixed glass window. Remember that a burglar can get in through a gap in a window only slightly larger than his head. You can fit locks which let you open the window a little, but make sure that the opening is narrow enough – ask a crime prevention officer.

Security grilles

If you have a lot of valuables or if you are in an area that is considered to be burglar-prone, and if you live in a basement flat, then security grilles may be necessary. Apart from bars in the windows you can now get wrought-iron patterns that are rather more pleasant. Alternatively, you can get security roller shutters that can be pulled down and locked when you are out.

Garage and garden

Close and lock the garage door before you depart. An empty garage shows that you are out. If you are away for several days, persuade a neighbour to park their car in your driveway so it looks as though someone is at home.

The garage is a favourite place for the burglar to find a few handy tools and a ladder with which to burgle your house or someone else's, so remember to keep it locked. If you store your ladders out-of-doors or in a garden shed, they should be padlocked to a bracket on the wall. Keep trees and shrubs in the garden itself well pruned since they make good hiding places. A broken-down back gate or one that is swinging open is also an invitation to burgle. Trellis on top of walls or fences, especially with prickly roses growing over it, makes it difficult for a burglar to climb into your garden – and deters cats!

More ways to beat the burglar

Burglar alarms act as a deterrent, even a false burglar alarm box fitted on the wall will deter a burglar. It is important to check with your insurance company to find out whether it will recognize a DIY-fitted alarm. There are two British Standards: BS 4737 for professionally fitted ones, and BS 6707 for DIY-fitted alarms. It is worthwhile getting a quote from several firms to do the job. If you are alone a great deal, they will also fit a 'panic button' by your bed which you can press if you hear someone breaking in.

- A light on a time switch is a useful deterrent. Programme it so that it comes on at different times on different days or change its timing from one week to another. If you are going out for several hours, leave the radio or TV on.
- Mark your valuables. Your local Crime Prevention Officer should have post-coded property stickers that you can use to mark your possessions with your postcode.
- Do not display antiques, paintings, TV and videos where they can be easily seen from the street.
- Do not keep large quantities of cash around the house – especially in the teapot. If you must have a pearl necklace or a roll of banknotes on hand they are better stored under an empty baked bean tin which has been opened at the bottom and has its label intact.

- Have gas and electricity meters fitted so they can be read from out-of-doors.
- Join Neighbourhood Watch. Not only will you have stickers on your window, but you will have the comfort of knowing that someone is keeping an eye on things while you are out. You will also have someone to tell that you are going away for any time.
- If you are selling your house and have a board to advertise the fact, do not allow in callers at the door; they could be burglars, muggers and rapists. Make them go through the estate agent.
- If you are moving in, change the locks or check with the mortice lock company to find out how many keys were issued and to whom.
- If you have an answerphone, do not say that you are out, say you are unable to take their call at the moment or that you are busy.

Practical Ways to Crack Crime is a free handbook which you should be able to get from your local police station. Otherwise write to Crack Crime, PO Box 999, Sudbury, Suffolk CO10 6FS, for your copy.

FIRE

All sorts of things cause fires – the main cause is cigarette smoking, but portable heaters placed too near furniture, fan heaters on which something has been draped and electric blankets that have not been serviced for years can all be the cause. It takes no time at all for a fire to take hold in your house. You may have three minutes, perhaps no more than five, to escape.

If you have any kind of open flame in your house such as gas jets, or people who smoke, or if your electrical wiring is old, it is vital to fit smoke alarms. They cost no more than a few pounds and are easy to fit. Be careful how you site them as it is easy to set one off by burning toast or by an over-hot frying pan. How many you install depends on the size of your house but there must be at least one upstairs and one downstairs.

- Make sure that you replace the batteries regularly – once a year is usual – and check they are working properly every month.
- When buying new or, more importantly, second-hand upholstered furniture, make sure the filling is fire-proof.
- If you are deaf you can get a smoke detector called Deaf Alert made by Zettler (*see page 493*) which is especially useful at night when many undiscovered fires start. It can easily be installed without having to call in an electrician. It comes in two parts: one is placed on the ceiling at the head of the stairs or by the bedroom, the other, a disc that vibrates to raise the alarm, goes under the sleeper's pillow.
- Keep a modern version of a rope ladder (available in stores like Ikea) in the top floor of the house.

- If you have window locks, keep the keys somewhere where you can find them instantly, preferably on the top floor, while door keys should be downstairs.
- Have a family evacuation plan so that everyone knows what to do in an emergency.

If you are in doubt about the safety of your home, ask for the local Fire Prevention Officer to come and see you. He is based at your local fire station. Your furniture may be dangerous. It is not the actual flames that kill most people in a fire but fumes – either smoke or poisonous gasses from upholstery, especially in furniture bought before 1988 when new regulations came in regarding safety.

How to avoid a fire

- Have all equipment that could cause a fire serviced regularly – boilers for instance.
- Get your wiring checked if it is more than 15 years old.
- Have electric blankets checked every three years by the manufacturer. Never sleep on an electric underblanket when it is still switched on.
- Buy a fire extinguisher.
- If you do a lot of frying or use a chip pan, buy a fire blanket. Get one that conforms to British Standard 6575, hang it on the wall near the cooker.
- Do not overload power points with too many extension leads or adapters, especially if the wiring is old.
- If you have open fires, get the chimney swept every year. Always use a fire guard if there are children around.
- Avoid hanging curtains near to cookers or draped over the back of the TV set.
- Do not store potentially flammable things like old newspapers, cloths and things like furniture polish under the stairs. In the event of a fire they would go up like a torch and possibly cut off your retreat down the stairs. Put them in the garage instead.
- Never smoke when using an aerosol and do not spray them near an open flame or electric bar fire. Do not store aerosols on sunlit window sills.
- Never leave clothes to dry near an open or electric bar fire or blow heater.
- Never leave matches or lighters around on tables where children could reach them.
- Make sure that boilers and stoves, whether gas or solid fuel, have adequate ventilation or gases could build up.
- Shut all the doors in downstairs rooms when you go to bed. If a fire does start it will not spread so quickly.
- If you smell gas, call the Gas Board immediately. Switch off any gas appliances you may have.

See also **Emergencies** *page 9.*

What to do after a fire

If you are unlucky enough to have a fire, clearing up afterwards can be a long and messy business. The fire brigade may have had to break windows or open walls and ceilings to check for hidden flames.

- Contact your insurance company immediately. Most have an emergency contact number. Do not do or dispose of anything until the assessor has been.
- If windows and doors have to be boarded up, ask the police or the fire brigade to give you the name of a company who will do this for you.
- If you have had a chimney fire, do not attempt to light the fire again for at least 24 hours and get the chimney cleaned as soon as possible.
- Open up the house as much as possible. Smoke from a fire leaves thick layers of strong-smelling dust that takes time to eradicate.
- If they have used hoses in upstairs rooms, check with the fire brigade's building control officer whether you have to make holes in downstairs ceilings to let water out.
- Ask the brigade to lend you waterproof salvage sheets to protect immovable furniture if this has to be done.
- Get de-humidifiers from your local hire shop and use them to help dry the house out.
- Vacuum curtains and furniture to get as much soot off them as possible before you attempt to wash them as soot can stain.
- Use sugar soap to wash down paintwork since ordinary cleaners may not do the job well enough.

STORM DAMAGE

Fierce rain storms and high winds can all wreak havoc with your house, especially the roof. If your house has been badly maintained you may not get as much on your insurance claim as you need. So check over the house from time to time with this in mind. *See* **Emergencies** *page 11*.

The roof

This is the most vulnerable part of the house. Check it for loose tiles and corroded nails holding the tiles in place. Check the chimney stack – if it blows down it can cause a lot of damage or even kill someone. Make sure aerials and satellite dishes are firmly fixed. Look for defective flashing and cracks in joints in the eaves.

Fences and walls

These may not be covered by your insurance. Check that brickwork is in good repair and that fence posts are firm.

Trees

If you have large old trees in your garden, get them checked out by a tree surgeon from time to time. If one came crashing down it could do untold damage.

What to do after storm damage

- Do not attempt to turn on the gas or electricity. If there has been flooding, do not drink tap water before checking that it is safe to do so.
- Ring the insurance company's emergency help line, since it may want to come and inspect the damage.
- If you are unable to lock the house because of damage, tell the police.
- If there are holes in the roof or walls, cover them with something to keep out the weather – tarpaulin, hardboard or plastic.
- Clear gutters that may have rubble in them.

FLOODS

Whether from burst pipes or natural causes, flooding can be traumatic. But there are ways to avoid domestic disasters.
- Know where your stop-cock is. It is often under the kitchen sink.
- Lag cold water pipes in the loft and the cold water tank to stop them from freezing in winter.
- If you go away in cold weather, leave the heating on low and open up the hatch into the loft so warmth will penetrate from down below.
- If you are going away for a long time, drain the plumbing system and turn off the mains.

What to do after a flood
See **Emergencies,** *page 11*).

If you are made homeless
Call your local Social Services and ask for emergency accommodation.

CLAIMING ON YOUR INSURANCE

- Act immediately; get your claim in as fast as you can, while you still remember the details clearly.
- Put your claim in writing. Head your letter up with your policy number.
- Photograph or keep the evidence. If your house or car has been damaged for instance, photograph it. If things are broken, keep them for inspection.

- Keep a diary of phone calls and get the name of the person you spoke to. Use faxes as much as possible as a record.
- If you are going for compensation then say how much you want and why. Note down your expenses.
- Give the company a date as a deadline for its reply. After that start pressing for a response.
- If it offers you a sum in 'full and final settlement' remember it means just that and you cannot go back for more.
- If you do not get any satisfaction, go to the Insurance Ombudsman (*see page 404*).

HOUSING PROBLEMS

When a relationship breaks down

If you are married you have an automatic right to a share of the home you own, no matter whose name is on the mortgage. In essence both spouses have the right to occupy the matrimonial home unless/until a court order dictates otherwise.

If you are not married, but are living with someone and have done so since before April 1989 and the property is not in your name, you have to establish an 'interest' in the house. Your lawyer will tell you how to go about it. Unless the property is in your name or your joint names, you may not be able to stay there or to benefit financially from its sale even if you have lived together there for years, and have a family. Only the legal owner has the right to occupy the property. You would need to take your case to court to decide what your share is in the home, whether it should be sold and when it should be sold. For a claim in the property you need to establish an interest, for example showing you have made mortgage payments.

If the house is in his name and you are not married, you have no automatic right to live there if he asks you to go. If you have children, you could claim a share on behalf of those children. If you have no children, you do not necessarily have the right to any share of the proceedings if he sells the house. However, if you have contributed to a large extent to the conversion, furnishing or upkeep, you have a good case – see a solicitor. The following information applies to those who are not married.

Taking action

If you think your partner may be trying to sell the house without your knowledge or agreement and you want to protect your interest in it, you can **register a caution** if the property is, as most are, on registered land. Under the Land Charges Act you can register a **class F charge** in the Land Registry to protect yourself. This means that if he does try to sell the house, this matter will have to be cleared up before a new owner takes the house on.

Proving an interest

Although your partner may be the sole owner of the property, if you have signed a trust deed (*see* **Buying a House**, *page 468*) then you have right of occupation. If you have not signed an express trust deed, you may be able to prove that you have an interest in the home via an implied trust. If, for instance, you paid for improvements in the home. Both these procedures are likely to be lengthy and possibly expensive.

You can also try to prove that you have a **contractual licence,** that is to say, an understanding that does not necessarily have to be written down, that in return for living in the house you contribute by paying the household bills for instance. A contractual licence does not confer any rights of ownership, merely occupation. Always keep a record of any payments that you make as a matter of prudence, even if the relationship is not under threat.

If you can show that you were officially engaged to be married, even if you have not married, you can apply to the court under the above act for a 'declaration of ownership of the property'. Property that is purchased in preparation for a marriage which is later cancelled will be treated as co-owned. If the couple cannot reach agreement over the proceeds of the sale, the court will decide to award each party an amount that reflects that party's contribution. The court can also make:

- An order for the property to be sold and the money divided between you.
- An order to postpone the sale if your ex-partner is embarking on one. This is usually only done if small children are involved.

Buying your partner out

If you have an interest in the property and want to stay there, you could offer to pay your partner his share and buy him out. Go to a building society or bank and state your case. You may be able to raise the money needed to buy out your partner's share by getting a loan or a mortgage. If you are earning an income someone will possibly lend you the money.

When the home is owned jointly

In this case, you and your partner have an equal right to live in the home and neither side can sell it or borrow money using it as collateral, without the permission and signature of the other one. There is no way you can exclude your ex-partner from a property that is partly his apart from buying him out, unless he has been violent to you, or threatens to be (*see page 187*). If you agree to sell the property, you cannot then go to the council as a homeless person – it may say you have done it intentionally. If the court orders the sale of the property or if the mortgage lenders foreclose and order a sale, then you may rank as homeless.

If you own the property

You can ask your ex-partner to leave if you own the property and give him notice to do so. If violence is involved, you can do this quickly (*see* **Injunction,** *page 187*). If, on the other hand, he makes your life such a misery that you are forced to leave your own home, the council will not rehouse you unless he has been, or threatens to be, violent towards you. Even then the council's responsibility is limited and temporary unless you fall into a 'vulnerable' group by being pregnant, disabled or a pensioner.

You can serve a 'notice to quit' on your partner which must state the date by which the property is to be vacated. If this does not produce the desired result, then get professional advice on taking possession proceedings through the County Court or with an eviction order. Either way, you are still responsible for the mortgage until other arrangements are made.

The threat of eviction

People can find themselves suddenly threatened with being made homeless for dozens of reasons – a disaster of some kind or other, a violent domestic dispute or a financial problem.

If your partner is a council tenant and he leaves

Your rights are restricted. You are, technically a licensee, not a tenant, in that you are there with your partner's permission. This means that you, personally, are not legally responsible for the rent. If you are married you can compel the council to accept rent from you instead. If you are not married, you cannot compel the council to accept your rent unless you had a joint tenancy. However, as a licensee you are not liable for any rent arrears.

If your partner leaves you, the council can give you notice to quit and refuse rent payments from you. In practice this seldom happens, especially if there are children and they will usually let you pay the rent – even though in order to do so you may have to apply for Housing Benefit. To qualify for Housing Benefit, the tenancy agreement or rent book usually needs to be in your name. So you need the tenancy to be assigned to you and to get permission from the council. If you have lived there for some time and have children, you are in a strong position to get the tenancy transferred to your name. If you are not married, you may have to go to court for this to be done – contact a solicitor or your local Law Centre.

If you have no dependants then it is highly unlikely that you qualify for a council house unless you have special circumstances such as being pregnant or disabled or an elderly pensioner. If you lived with your partner for at least twelve months and he is willing to do so, he should be able to 'assign' the tenancy to you. To do this you may have to get the council's permission – look up the tenancy agreement as it may have a clause about sub-letting or assignment. You will then have to get a solicitor to draw up a 'deed of assignment' transferring it to your name. But sometimes the local council or housing association have their own standard deed of assignment which is acceptable to them, so ask them first and save money.

If your partner tries to evict you

If your partner wants you out he must give you 'reasonable notice' to go depending on how long you have lived there – usually about 28 days. Once the time is up, technically, you have no right to live in the home.

What to do

Go to the local council housing department and apply to be considered a homeless person. Since the recent changes in the law now state that to be 'homeless' means to be 'roofless' your first visit to the council will be to tell them of your present situation and likely future position. They will then be able to advise you about various other agencies who may also be able to help (*see page 493*) or may be able to refer your case to a housing association.

Once you are homeless, the council have a duty to give you advice and assistance. However, most councils now operate on a priority need basis and their 'advice and assistance' can vary dramatically from giving you directions to get to a hostel to actually providing temporary, and in some cases, permanent, accommodation. If your partner threatens violence or is violent, you can take out an injunction to exclude them from the home (*see page 187*). Even if your partner is the tenant and you are the licensee, if you are a married couple the issue of whose name is on the rent book is virtually irrelevant.

If the tenancy is in your name only

Then your partner becomes the licensee and you can give him notice (usually 28 days) to quit. If he does not go after the time limit has expired, go to a solicitor or Law Centre to get advice on the best way to handle the next step. If he is or has been violent towards you or threatens violence, then you could take out an injunction against him (*see page 187*).

If you are joint tenants

You both have equal rights to live in your home if you are joint tenants so you cannot get your partner to go without his consent, unless he has been violent or threatened violence to you (*see page 187*). If your partner leaves you, you can apply for Housing Benefit. Legally, as joint tenants you are held to be 'jointly and severally liable' for all costs of the property, irrespective of any personal arrangement you may have made. So if he goes, you are responsible for all the rent – and that includes any arrears, though if it is council property the council may make a concession and make you liable for only half the sum. You will need to ask them to 'exercise their discretion' in this matter and to take half the arrears from your account and chase your ex-partner separately for the rest.

If your partner goes and you have children, you can ask a court to transfer the tenancy to your sole name (see a solicitor). If you do not have children, you cannot apply for this. However, continue to pay the rent. Once the landlord has accepted the payment it could be difficult to deny that you – the rent-payer – are a lawful tenant unless he can establish that he genuinely believed that the original tenant was still in occupation and you were merely acting as his agent in paying the rent. If the landlord is successful in denying that you should have the tenancy, then it can be argued that any money you paid in rent, after the departure of your partner, must be returned.

Rehousing

If you are a joint tenant with children, you can ask for the council to rehouse you – perhaps into another area or a smaller home. First, find out whether they will agree to do this, and *get it in writing*. With the council's agreement in your hand, you can then issue a Notice to Quit to the council (get a solicitor to do this). Never, ever issue this without the council's written agreement to a new home, otherwise you could find yourself homeless. Once you have been given and have formally accepted an offer of an alternative tenancy, both you and the council are contractually bound and you can give notice to quit. Make sure that the date of quitting is either the same or preferably overlaps, the date of the start of your new tenancy.

If you are a private tenant

Check out your agreement if you have one. If your landlord does not live on the premises and does not provide things like clean bed-linen or meals, and if you and your partner, if you have one, have a room of your own then:

- If you have been in the tenancy since before 15 January 1989, you are probably a **protected tenant** or **protected shorthold tenant**.
- If you moved in after 15 January 1989, you are an **assured tenant or an assured shorthold tenant.**

All these things matter if you are faced with eviction or if your partner leaves and the tenancy was in his name or in your joint names. The new Criminal Justice and Public Order Act allows a landlord to evict you in some circumstances. If your partner leaves and the tenancy is in his name, the first thing to do is to persuade the landlord that you can take over the tenancy. The best way to do this is to continue to pay the rent regularly after he leaves and then approach the landlord – you are in a stronger position to argue if he has already accepted money from you. The landlord is not likely to notice that the situation has changed if he does not live on the premises. If you have an official tenancy agreement it can then be either assigned or transferred to you. You can claim Housing Benefit, if you qualify, to pay the rent once the tenancy is in your name.

Homelessness

What is a homeless person?

You are not considered to be homeless from the council's point of view if:

- You deliberately did something or failed to do something (pay the rent) which made you without a home.
- The council believes, and can prove, that it was reasonable for you to stay in your former accommodation.

If you are homeless and it is not your fault, then you may qualify for priority housing. Contact the Homeless Person's Unit, or Emergency Housing Unit of your local council – you can also apply in another area if you choose. The Unit will interview you to find out why you are homeless and you will probably have to sign a statement to say that everything you have told them is true. By law, in an emergency the council has to make instant arrangements for you and then ask questions afterwards.

What rates as priority need?

You are deemed to be a priority case if you are homeless and:

- You have children under 16 years of age.
- You are pregnant; it may want confirmation of the fact.
- You have children over 16 but under 19 who are in full-time education or training and are unable to support themselves.
- You are an old-age pensioner.
- You have become homeless through a disaster like flood or fire.
- You are registered as disabled.
- You are mentally ill or mentally handicapped (a doctor's letter would be needed for this).
- You are almost of retirement age and are in bad health.
- You are a battered partner or have been threatened with violence (*see page 187*).

In any of these cases the council should be able to give you some sort of temporary accommodation overnight. The council will also sometimes give priority to teenagers 'at risk' and single women who have been living with someone who is violent and have had to leave because of the violence.

What will the council do with me?

You may be given a room in hostel accommodation run by the council, sharing a kitchen and bathroom with other families. You may be put into bed and breakfast accommodation with shared facilities, possibly in a type of hotel. In this case you will not be able to cook, but will have to buy meals out and there may be a rule that you have to be out of your room for a given number of hours each day.

You may go to a refuge if you are homeless because of violence by your partner.

You may be sent to a mother and baby home run by a matron, if you are young and expecting your first child. Here you will be expected to help with the housework and, perhaps, cooking. You may also be allocated a run-down flat or house that is waiting to be demolished or converted. If this happens, stick with it, however depressing the conditions, because it means that you are on the road to getting a council house or flat of your own.

HOME: HELP DIRECTORY

Architects/surveyors

- Architects Registration Council of the United Kingdom, 73 Hallam Street, London W1N 6EE, (0171 580 5861). Can check on the credentials of an architect.
- The Architectural Association, 34–36 Bedford Square, London WC1 3ES, (0171 636 0974). Runs an association and school for architects. Being a member of the AA does not necessarily mean the person is a qualified architect.
- Institution of Structural Engineers, 11 Upper Belgrave Street, London SW1X 8BH, (0171 235 4535).
- Royal Institute of British Architects (RIBA), 66 Portland Place, London W1N 4AD, (0171 580 5533). Has a leaflet explaining how an architect works; also runs an advisory service.
- The Royal Institution of Chartered Surveyors, 12 Great George Street, Parliament Square, London SW10 3AD, (0171 222 7000). The Professional Practice Department is the place to send complaints.

Building work/conversions

- The British Wood Preserving and Damp-Proofing Association, 6 The Office Village, 4 Romford Road, Stratford, London E15 4ED, (0181 519 2588). Does spot checks, arbitrates and runs a guarantee scheme so that even if the installer goes bankrupt or out of business your guarantee is still valid.
- Building Research Establishment, Bucknall's Lane, Garston, Watford WD2 7JR, (01923 676612 – Administration Office), (01923 664664 – Advice Line). Will test materials used in your house for condensation, infestation, damp proofing, etc if there is a dispute. It charges a fee for this service.
- Building Centre, 26 Store Street, London WC1E 7BT, (0171 637 1022). Will give advice regarding building materials.

- The Building Employers Confederation, 82 New Cavendish Street, London W1M 8AD, (0171 580 5588). Runs a guarantee scheme – for 1 per cent of the contract money you are covered against shoddy work or if the company stops trading. It also covers structural defects for 2 years.
- Confederation for the Registration of Gas Installers, 4 Elmwood, Chineham Business Park, Crockford Lane, Basingstoke, Hampshire RG24 8WG, (01256 707060). Assesses members for competence and makes spot checks on their work. Look up your local office under CORGI in the Phone Book.
- The Electrical Contractors' Association, ESCA House, 34 Palace Court, Bayswater, London W2 4HY, (0171 229 1266). Has lists of members and guarantees their work.
- Federation of Master Builders, 14–15 Great James Street, London WC1N 3DP, (0171 242 7583). Has a register of Warranted Builders – people who have been approved by other members in the area.
- Gas Consumers Council, 6th Floor Abford House, 15 Wilton Road, London SW1V 1LT, (0171 931 0977). Have a free Gas Cost Calculator.
- The Glass and Glazing Federation, 44–48 Borough High Street, London SE1 1XB, (0171 403 7177). Has a code of practice and members must also conform to British Standards and Technical Trade Standards. It offers some protection.
- Institute of Plumbing, 64 Station Lane, Hornchurch, Essex RM12 6NB, (01708 472791). Has a list of trained plumbers and a complaints procedure.
- National Association of Plumbing, Heating and Mechanical Services Contractors, 14–15 Ensign House, Ensign Business Centre, Westwood Way, Coventry CV4 8JA, (01203 470626). Has a code of practice, warranty scheme and list of members.
- National Federation of Roofing Contractors, 24 Weymouth Street, London W1N 4LX, (0171 436 0387). Has a list of trustworthy contractors. Also gives technical advice and will take up and investigate complaints against its members.
- The National Inspection Council for Electrical Installation Contracting, Vintage House, 37 Albert Embankment, London SE1 7UJ, (0171 582 7746) (0171 735 1322 technical enquiries). Lists properly qualified contractors – you should find the list in a public library. It also investigates complaints.
- Scottish and Northern Ireland Plumbing Employers' Federation, 2 Walker Street, Edinburgh EH3 7LB, (0131 225 2255). Has code of practice and arbitration scheme; warranty, insurance in plumbing and domestic central heating.
- Scottish Building Employers Federation, 13 Woodside Crescent, Glasgow G3 7UP, (0141 332 7144). Operates a similar service in Scotland.

- The Society for the Protection of Ancient Buildings, 37 Spital Square, London E1 6DY, (0171 377 1644). Advises on ancient buildings.
- Solid Fuel Advisory Service, Victoria House, Southampton Row, London WC1B 4DH, (0171 405 0034).

Buying a house

- Enfranchisement Advisory Service, 8 Maddox Street, London W1R 9PN, (0171 493 3116). Can advise on buying the freehold of a property you rent.
- Leasehold Enfranchisement Association, 10 Upper Phillimore Gardens, London W8 7HA, (0171 937 0866).
- National Association of Estate Agents, Arbon House, 21 Jury Street, Warwick CV34 4EH, (01926 496800).
- The Ombudsman for Corporate Estate Agents, Beckett House, 4 Bridge Street, Salisbury SP1 2LX, (01722 333306).
- Motor Vehicle Licensing Centre, Swansea SA6 7JL.

Energy conservation

- A Winter Warmth Line is open from mid-October to the end of March each year giving free advice to anyone experiencing problems because of the cold. Ring: 0800 289404 if you live in England or Wales, 0800 838587 if you live in Scotland, 0800 616757 if you live in Northern Ireland.
- Energy Action Grants Agency, PO Box 1NG, Newcastle-upon-Tyne NE99 1NG, (Freephone 0800 181667). Gives grants to disadvantaged people towards the cost of draught-proofing and insulating.
- Friends of the Earth, 56–58 Alma Street, Luton, Bedfordshire LU1 2YZ, (01582 482297). Has a 48-page booklet *Take the Heat off the Planet*, with tips on how you can cut your energy use by a third. It costs £3.45.
- Heating and Ventilating Contractors Association, ESCA House, 34 Palace Court, London W2 4JG, (0171 229 2488). Can give details of a scheme run by the Energy Saving Trust, where you may be able to get a subsidy towards the cost of a new gas condensing boiler which is more economic and efficient than the old style.
- Neighbourhood Energy Action, St Andrews House, 90–92 Pilgrim Street, Newcastle-upon-Tyne NE1 6SG, (091 261 5677). Gives practical advice on home insulation and cutting down on fuel costs for people on low incomes.

Home security

- Master Locksmiths Association, Units 4/5, The Business Park, Woodford Halse, Daventry, Northants NN11 3PZ, (01327 262255).

- The National Approval Council for Security Systems, Queensgate House, 14 Cookham Road, Maidenhead, Berks SL6 8AJ, (01628 37512).
- Zettler Ltd, Zettler House, Pinner Road, Northwood, Middx HA6 1DL, (019238 26155). Makes fire alarms for deaf people.

Homelessness

- Alone in London Service, West Lodge, 190 Euston Road, London NW1 2EF, (0171 387 6184). Advises and helps young people who are homeless. It has a hostel and helps inmates find long-term housing, helps financially when necessary. It can also counsel parents whose children have run away, but cannot liaise with them without the full agreement of the child concerned.
- Catholic Housing Aid Society, 209 Old Marylebone Road, London NW1 5QT, (0171 373 4961). Helps people who are homeless or are living in poor accommodation.
- Centrepoint Charity for Young Homeless, Bewlay House, 2 Swallow Place, London W1R 7AA, (0171 629 2229). Offers overnight and emergency accommodation for young people. It also has a long-stay hostel and some flats and bedsitters.
- CHAR Housing Campaign for Single People, 5–15 Cromer Street, London WC1H 8LS, (0171 833 2071). Works for better conditions for people who are single and homeless.
- Crisis, 7 Whitechapel Road, London E1 1DU, (0171 377 0489). Works with the homeless, especially those who are alone at Christmas, via projects all over the country.
- English Churches Housing Group Ltd, Sutherland House, 70–78 West Hendon Broadway, London NW9 7BT, (0181 203 9233). Has housing accommodation of all kinds throughout the country including sheltered housing for the elderly and hostels for single people.
- Girls Alone Project, 76 Oakley Square, London NW1 1NH, (0171 383 4103). Works with young homeless women referred to it by the Social Services or equivalent bodies, with a long-stay hostel. It also tries to settle them eventually into permanent self-contained flats.
- Homeless Action and Accommodation Ltd, 52–54 Featherstone Street, London EC1Y 8RT, (0171 251 6783). Runs houses in London accommodating homeless women who are referred to them by the Social Services and who may have particular difficulties in being housed. It welcomes in particular women from ethnic minority groups, those suffering from HIV or AIDS and lesbians.
- Homes for Homeless People, 90–92 Bromham Road, Bedford MK40 2QH, (01234 350853). Helps single homeless people throughout the country via emergency and short-stay accommodation and day centres.

- Housing Associations Charitable Trust, 175 Grays Inn Road, London WC1X 8UP, (0171 278 6571). Helps self-help housing associations on their building projects and gives financial aid for schemes that do not come under government grants.
- Piccadilly Advice Centre, 100 Shaftesbury Avenue, London W1V 7DH, (0171 437 1579) (Advice line 0171 434 3773, 2 pm to 9 pm). Counsels and advises young people, especially those who have just arrived in London, over finding somewhere to live. It is open every day of the year, including Christmas Day.
- Shelter Housing Aid Centre London, Kingsbourne House, 229–231 High Holborn, London WC1V 7DA, (Advice Line 0171 404 6929 10 am to 1 pm) (Public Services 0171 404 7447). Runs a telephone advice line helping people who are homeless, those who are in trouble over their mortgages, and also both landlords and tenants who face legal problems.
- Shelter, 88 Old Street, London EC1V 9HU, (0171 505 2000). Helps anyone who is homeless or threatened with eviction.
- Simon Community, PO Box 1187, London NW5 4HW, (0171 485 6639). Works with the homeless in London, especially those who are sleeping on the streets, with medical help and accommodation. It has a night shelter and hostels.
- Society of St Vincent de Paul, Damascus House, The Ridgeway, London NW7 1EL, (0181 906 1339). A Catholic organization that works among the homeless offering shelter, the mentally ill, and counsels those who are lonely, bereaved and elderly. It runs holiday camps for deprived children and also visits people in hospital and in prison.
- Stonham Housing Association Ltd, Octavia House, 235–241 Union Street, London SE1 0LR, (0171 401 2020). Gives accommodation and financial support to people with special problems who face housing difficulties. Among the groups it works with are ex-prisoners, those with mental problems, women escaping from violent relationships, single parents and young people leaving care. Most of the accommodation it offers is temporary but there is some permanent family accommodation.

Housing

- Girls Friendly Society and Townsend Fellowship, Townsend House, 126 Queen's Gate, London SW7 5LQ, (0171 589 9628). Has a scheme for young women featuring shared accommodation in houses.
- Housing Corporation, 149 Tottenham Court Road, London, (0171 393 2000).
- Housing for Women, 353 Kennington Road, London SE11 4QE, (0171 582 7605). Aims to provide homes at a realistic rent for women who are

unable to rent something otherwise. Many of them are referred to the
organization by social workers.

- Institute of Housing, 9 White Lyon Street, London N1 9XJ, (0171 837 4280).
- Over Forty Association for Women Workers, Mary George House, 120–122
  Cromwell Road, London SW7 4ET, (0171 370 2556). A London-based
  organization, working within the London area to provide flats and bedsitters in
  large houses for single women over 40 who are working in the capital and
  cannot afford accommodation.
- Residential Boat Owners Association, 3 Duck's Walk, Twickenham, Middx
  TW1 2DD, (0181 892 5086). Fights for the rights of houseboat owners on rivers,
  canals and coasts of Great Britain and will give advice on safety or legal
  matters and negotiate with the authorities on behalf of members.
- Resource Information Service, The Basement, 38 Great Pulteney Street,
  London W1R 3DE, (0171 494 2408). Helps people who are in need of housing
  by advising them on what services are available both in London and on a
  national basis.
- Society of Action for Children in Tower Blocks, 62 Chelsea Reach Tower,
  Blantyre Street, London SW10 0EG, (0171 352 5135). Fights for the rights of
  tower block tenants and their families; gives information and advice on their
  entitlements.
- Young Women's Christian Association of Great Britain, Clarendon House, 52
  Cornmarket Street, Oxford OX1 3EJ, (01865 726110). A Christian-based organization that has residential accommodation for young women.

See also
Abbeyfield Society (**The Third Age,** *page 312*).
Anchor Housing Trust (**The Third Age,** *page 314*).
ASRA Housing Association Ltd. (**The Third Age,** *page 315*).
Disabled Housing Trust (**Disabled,** *page 127*).
Elderly Accommodation Counsel (**The Third Age,** *page 313*).
Federation of Black Housing Organizations (**Ethnic Minorities,** *page 420*).
Fellowship Houses Trust (**The Third Age,** *page 315*).
Royal British Legion (*page 371*).
Habiteg Housing Association Ltd (*page 128*).
Sue Ryder Foundation (**Health,** *page 110*).

Insurance

Association of British Insurers, 51 Gresham Street, London EC2V 7HQ,
(0171 600 3333). Has a free booklet (send an SAE) on home contents insurance.
Also deals with insurance problems.

Your rights

National Council for Civil Liberties, 21 Tabard Street, London SE1 4LA, (0171 403 3888). Works to defend the right of individual privacy. It also works to protect women and minority groups against discrimination.

14

COMMUNITY

PROBLEMS WITH NEIGHBOURS

Noise

Burglar alarms and car alarms, barking dogs, blaring ghetto-blasters and thudding hi-fis, DIY sounds like drilling, sawing and hammering, neighbourly noises like babies crying and loud sex are all on the increase, especially in modern crowded housing estates. Noise has become a growing menace that can ruin the quality of life, while prolonged exposure can affect your mental health too.

People have committed suicide and murder because of noise – not long ago a policeman was beaten to death by the man who lived in the flat above because he could not stand the classical music the neighbour was playing. Noise has even been used by the police as a weapon – a man who held a woman hostage for two weeks in Hull finally released her after police played loud rock music to him all through the night. Last year complaints about noise in this country rose by more than 10 per cent. Two-thirds of the complaints are about loud music late at night, with revving car engines, car alarms and horns coming a close second. The trouble is that, legally speaking, it is a civil not a criminal matter and something that is difficult to prove. And many people are afraid to complain.

Building work can be noisy too, with drills and cement mixers roaring away. It is possible, if you contact the local council, to get a restriction placed on the hours in which work is carried out.

Who polices it?

Environmental Health Officers (EHOs), not the police, are responsible for tackling noise problems. Strapped-for-cash local authorities cannot afford to enforce noise laws, since most EHOs work office hours, so no one is normally available when most of the noise happens – at night and at weekends. Some councils, however, are now recruiting 24-hour teams to cope with the situation. Many councils run a mediation service for neighbourhood disputes. Many are now getting tougher in their dealings with culprits: many new council tenants have to go through a probationary period of one year when they first move in, during which time they can be evicted for unsocial behaviour.

What can you do about noise?

Speak to the people concerned. Try to be calm and reasonable. They may be unaware of the fact that they are driving their neighbours mad. Sometimes it is just thoughtlessness and just a simple thing like closing the windows can keep the sound down. If it happens on a regular basis, keep a detailed diary of the disturbances that are causing you distress, giving the times and dates. Get other neighbours to do the same if possible, or get written statements from them to back you up. If it is affecting your health get a note from your doctor. Keep this up for two or three weeks and then act.

If the source of the noise comes from someone who is black and you are in danger of being accused of racial discrimination, try to find another black neighbour who is also suffering, and get him to complain too.

Wait and see if the sound abates; if not, call your local council and ask to speak to the Environmental Health Department. Persuade other neighbours to do the same – the more people who complain, the more notice will be taken of the situation. What you are aiming to do is to prove that the noise is a 'statutory nuisance', that it stops you from enjoying your own home or is affecting your health. If he cannot solve things informally, the Environmental Health Officer can issue a statutory noise abatement notice to your neighbour preventing him from continuing to make the noise, or restricting it to certain times of day or days of the week. If the neighbour does not comply with this, he can be taken to court and heavily fined, with a further fine for each day on which the nuisance continues after conviction.

If you live in a private block of flats, check your lease. Most of them contain a provision that you must not annoy your neighbours. If this is so you can approach the freeholders about the problem.

If all else fails, call the police, especially if the noise comes from a motorbike or a car. The offender can be fined if his vehicle exceeds noise limits set down in the regulations. You can also take your complaint directly to the Magistrates' Court (Sheriff Court in Scotland), which will issue an abatement notice if they are satisfied with your evidence. To do this you must have all the facts and figures to hand. If you need to get an injunction to restrain your neighbour from making the noise, you can take your case to a civil court. The court may also award you compensation. If you take either of the routes above, it pays to talk to a solicitor first, to make sure you have a case. This procedure can be expensive and it also takes a long time. It is better, normally, to get the Environmental Health Office to do the prosecuting for you. If the authorities fail to help, you can take your case to a local government Ombudsman. In a case in 1994, a local council (Southwark) was ordered to pay £2,500 compensation to a householder plagued by noisy neighbours because their environmental health and housing officers failed to help.

Alarms

The police and the environmental health office have now got the right to de-activate a car alarm if they are unable to find the owner. (This law does not apply in Northern Ireland.) Under the Environmental Protection Act, Environmental Health Officers, rather than the police, can enter a house and disconnect a burglar alarm that keeps going off. Plans are afoot to make owners of house burglar alarms fit cut-off devices to them and to give the names of keyholders to the police.

Commercial noise

If you have an on-going noise you can do nothing about – perhaps a motorway nearby – then consider putting in double glazing which helps deaden sound. If you are in a block of flats where ordinary everyday noises come through paper-thin walls, think about sound proofing, It is possible to put sound insulation panels on existing structures. If it arises from a newly-built or enlarged road, contact the local Highway Authority. You might be entitled to grants for sound insulation and also for compensation for loss to the value of your house.

If the offending sounds come on a regular basis from a factory, a club or a pub, check with the planning department of your local council to see whether any conditions about noise were set when planning permission was given. There could be a ruling about levels of noise or hours when it can be made, which is being broken. Then it is up to the local authority to enforce the rule.

Aircraft noise

If you move to live near an airport then you would expect a certain amount of aircraft noise. Most noise comes from planes taking off, when they need maximum power, and people find that night flights are the worst problem. Insulation and double glazing can help and if a new airport or a new runway is opened up near you, you should be eligible for a grant to do this.

If you are complaining about a specific incident, you need to know what the plane was doing at the time, either landing or taking off, and which airline it belonged to. If you are not sure, try calling the airport concerned. Complaints should be sent in writing to the Airport Director of the airport at which the plane took off or landed.

Noisy dogs

It is the suddenness, loudness and irregularity of a dog's bark that drives us all mad. Dogs bark mainly out of boredom or because they are left alone for long periods, and some breeds are yappier than others. Incessant barking now comes under the heading of 'a statutory nuisance' and owners are deemed responsible for their dogs' actions (cat owners are not). If your neighbour's dog barks incessantly and you can show that this is interfering with the 'enjoyment' of your property, the council can order the owner to stop or limit the noise at the risk of a heavy fine.

- Talk to the owner about it, and see if you can come to some amicable conclusion.
- If not, report the matter to the police or the local dog warden.
- If you have reason to believe the dog is barking because it is being left alone for hours or is being ill-treated, then call the RSPCA.
- If the barking dog is yours, consider taking it to a pet behaviour counsellor.

Dangerous pets

If you want to keep a dangerous wild animal or a poisonous snake in your home, you have to get a licence from your local council who must be satisfied that the animal is kept secure and has a reasonable area in which to exercise.

The Dangerous Dogs Act

Four breeds of dog are affected by the Dangerous Dogs Act of 1991. They are:

- Pit bull terrier – the onus is often on the owner to prove that the animal is not a pit bull terrier if it looks like one.
- Japanese Toza.
- Fila Braziliero.
- Gogo Argentino.

If you own or are planning to own one of the four dogs above, you must have:

- An exemption certificate with particulars of the dog lodged with the local police.
- Insurance; if this lapses even for one day the dog can be put down immediately.

The animal must also be tattooed, micro-chipped and castrated. It must be kept on a lead and muzzled at all times when it is in a public place and that includes inside your car. Alsatians, Dobermanns and Rottweilers are not affected; however, if any breed of dog behaves in a potentially dangerous way the owner can be fined a large amount of money and possibly disqualified from owning a dog for a set time.

If you own a guard dog, then you must post a warning notice of the fact on the entrance to your property. The dog must also be kept secure. It is a legal requirement that all dogs wear collars inscribed with their names and addresses. If your dog wanders onto someone else's property and causes damage, then you are liable for this. If it messes their garden they can, technically, claim trespass against the animal. Neither of these rules apply to cats, however.

Dog attacks

If you are attacked by a dog you should report the attack to the police immediately, unless the owner can claim you provoked the dog in some way. If someone sets a dog on you in any public place they are committing a criminal offence. You may be able to claim compensation. If the dog is found to be 'dangerous' the local court can order that it is kept under control or destroyed. If it kills or injures livestock, the dog owner is liable to pay compensation for the animal concerned. Livestock owners have the right to destroy a dog that they think is worrying or about to worry their livestock.

More trouble with neighbours

What can you do if your neighbour insists on parking his large mobile home in his drive, clads the house with mock stone or wants to build an ugly extension? The answer is not a lot at the moment unless he happens to live in a listed building. Your neighbour is also entitled to paint his house red, white and blue all over if he so chooses. However, increasingly, house builders are asking owners to sign covenants which restrict their rights in an effort to protect the appearance of a development. This means that if any one owner wants to do something which breaks the rules, they have to consult the other owners first.

If your neighbour's tree, hedge or bush overhangs your property you can cut it back to the boundary but no further. Any clippings, fruit or prunings you take are not yours technically but they are hardly likely to appreciate a fistful of branches thrust into their hands.

Mediation

An increasing number of mediation centres are being set up all over the country (*see page 530*). They are usually free and act as an impartial middleman helping you come to an agreement with your neighbours over any dispute between you. They have no power to impose a decision on either of you but they can take the heat out of an argument.

CRIME PREVENTION

More than one person in four is likely to have been the victim of a crime. Statistics show that you are most likely to be targeted if you are middle-aged, of a higher income group, own your own house and car and live in the south of England. However, we can all help beat the burglar. The police say that local people are in a unique position to help reduce local crime because living or working in the area means they know it better than anyone.

Neighbourhood Watch

More than 5 million households are now covered by this scheme which is built on the idea of householders banding together to look after each other and the neighbourhood in general. It is well worth joining a scheme or helping to set one up – statistics show that in some areas they have been known to reduce burglaries by three-quarters within a year.

A Neighbourhood Watch group varies in size depending on the area. It is led by a voluntary co-ordinator and run by a committee which meets regularly to plan any action. All Neighbourhood Watch groups are closely linked with the local police and usually have an officer who looks after them and tips the group off about any trends in local burglaries. As a member, you look out for and report anything suspicious in your street and at the same time step up the security of your own home. You are given a sticker to put in your window and have free advice from the police who will visit you and tell you what needs to be made more secure.

Street Watch

This is a newer scheme taking Neighbourhood Watch a step further replacing, in some ways, the policeman on the beat. Members of Street Watch regularly walk over specific routes in their area that have been chosen beforehand in co-operation with the police, keeping an eye open for anything untoward. Street Watch is particularly successful in stopping vandalism and minor street crimes. The watchers are not a vigilante group; they do not 'have a go'. In some areas street watchers will escort vulnerable or elderly people who are afraid to go out by themselves. If you want to join or form a scheme like this, contact your local police station.

Self-defence

How far can I go to defend myself or my property?
If you are faced with what appears to be a violent criminal you can protect yourself and/or your property by using 'reasonable force'. If the assailant is injured or killed, however, you could land up in court faced with a criminal charge or a civil action. It will then be up to the magistrates to decide whether your actions were justified.

What is reasonable force?
And how far can you go? This is a grey area as far as the law is concerned. It means reasonable force 'in the circumstances' and what your feelings were at the time is important. If you had genuine reason to believe that your life was under threat, you would be allowed to use more force than if you merely disturbed a burglar. Creeping up after a burglar who has not actually attacked you and batting him over the head with a vase, could be construed as using 'unreasonable force' in a court of law. The same goes if you throw something at someone who is running away with your possessions.

Could I go to prison for standing up for myself?

Yes, you could, but courts have become more sympathetic towards members of the public who are brave – or foolhardy – enough to do this. Doing something like shooting or stabbing someone, however, could land you in trouble. Deterring burglars by doing something like wiring up your front door or car to give intruders an electric shock, however mild, is against the law.

Can I arrest a criminal myself?

You could make a citizen's arrest, but this is rarely done because if the person you arrest has not committed a crime, you could face legal action for having done so.

MUGGINGS AND STREET CRIME

To be the victim of a street crime can be terrifying. People react in many ways and although few of us suffer long-term harm, we may feel angry, frightened or confused. After a mugging it is quite normal to suffer sleepless nights with nightmares and flashbacks, mood swings and difficulty over walking in the same area again. But it is worthwhile remembering that in general the mugger is not after you personally, but your money.

Girl gangs

Do not think you are safe in the street if there are only women around. A new and disturbing trend is for people to find themselves mugged by girls, as actress Liz Hurley found. There has been a startling 70 per cent increase in what the police call 'female crimes' in the last ten years. There is a tendency among disadvantaged, jobless girls or disillusioned schoolgirls who cannot see the point of education because they have no job to go to, to hang around the streets in gangs – one of the most notorious is the Ghetto Girls of south London. These gangs, who may also be taking drugs, usually pick on their own age group. But they have been known to target the elderly.

If you are in a potentially dangerous area and see a gang of girls, or, indeed, youths sitting on a wall, hanging around together, avoid walking right through them – cross the street instead. They tend to use heavy pieces of wood and bricks rather than knives to attack their victims. Be wary, too, of giving two or more people a lift in your car, whether you are a man or a woman.

See also **Emergencies** (*page 5*).

Pickpockets

There is nothing more upsetting than putting your hand in your pocket or handbag and finding your wallet has gone. Most people do not realize they have been robbed for some time after the event. Pickpockets work in busy places, on underground railways and trains, in stores and crowded supermarkets. At stations they are at their most active in the rush hour, in stores at sales time.

- Be on your guard if someone stands unnaturally close to you on the platform, on an escalator or on a train.
- Be especially wary if that person has a bulky coat draped over his arm; he may use it to hide what his hands are doing underneath – picking your pocket.
- Keep your credit cards under cover; do not flash them around when opening your wallet to pay or get a card out for a machine in the wall.
- Use a 'bum bag' or body wallet if you are carrying a large amount of money, wear it under a sweater or inside a coat.
- Be especially careful if there is a lot of shoving and pushing going on around you, it could be a cover for theft.

SAFE TRAVEL

On the train

- Know exactly where you are going before you set out – do not end up standing in the station forecourt consulting a map. If you are being met, arrange a specific meeting point – many stations have several entrances and car-parks.
- Check your train times and bus connections before you go, plan your journey to avoid having to hang around on stations too long.
- If you are travelling alone any distance, have a system to let someone know you have arrived safely when you get there.
- If you are using a car to get to the station, leave it in a well-lit area as near the station entrance as possible. If you are leaving it in daylight try to think what the area will be like in the dark and avoid secluded places.
- If you are going by taxi, use only a reputable taxi or a minicab firm that you or your friends know. Do not accept lifts from strangers
- If you have to wait at a bus stop or station, try to keep to a well-lit area and, if possible, wait with other people you know or recognize.
- If you are travelling on a near-empty bus or train, sit somewhere where there are other people or a conductor/guard nearby. If necessary get out at a station and change carriages.
- Choose a seat next to the aisle or corridor.

- Be streetwise, notice who is around you on the station and in the train just in case something happens and you need to give evidence to the police.
- Do not carry more luggage than you can handle. Be cautious if a stranger offers to help carry your case. Keep your luggage close at hand. Keep your keys separate from anything with your address on it.
- Make sure you know where the emergency handle is located and use it if possible in an emergency. Remember help can be given more easily at a station than in the middle of nowhere.
- Take precautions in crowds, especially if you are strap-hanging. If you are a woman, keep your handbag closed in front of you, with the fastening towards the body. Keep your hand on a zip fastening if possible.
- If you are returning to your car, have the keys ready hidden in your hand by the time you alight from the train. Check the car is secure and that no one is hiding in it **before** you get in. If it is dark use a torch.
- If you are unhappy walking through a car-park, try to get someone you know to walk with you. If station staff are around, ask them to watch you walk to your car.

Hitch-hiking

There cannot be anyone now who is not aware of the dangers of hitching a lift. Getting into a vehicle with a driver you do not know could end in robbery, rape or even murder. If you find yourself forced to hitch-hike for some reason there are some basic precautions you can take.

- If you are hitching a lift at a service station, pub or roadside pull-up – anywhere that has a phone – call a contact number before you take the lift, giving that person the registration number of the vehicle.
- Tell the driver you are being met at the other end.
- Whenever possible, hitch with a friend rather than on your own.

Out and about

- Avoid taking shortcuts along poorly lit paths, subways and alleyways, especially after dark.
- Always walk on the outside of the pavement, especially at night.
- Walk facing the traffic, so that a car cannot pull up behind you without your noticing. Carry your bag on the side away from the road.
- If you are wearing expensive-looking jewellery, hide it with gloves and a scarf when walking in the street.
- Keep your handbag hugged close to your body with the clasp side inwards.

- Keep your house keys separately – perhaps in a pocket if you are going out in an area where mugging is rife. That way if your handbag is snatched you can still get into your home.
- If you are going out for the evening in a potentially dangerous area, leave your credit cards and unwanted money hidden somewhere at home. Do not take them with you.
- A personal alarm is a good idea but having to rummage in your handbag for it may waste vital moments. Buy one that you can wear round your neck instead – you can get a version that is slim enough to fit under a sweater and emits a loud decibel siren when the snatch cord at its base is pulled (*see page 529*).
- Have a list of emergency numbers for the credit card companies to hand so you can contact them right away if you are mugged or lose your cards.
- Appear purposeful and confident and look as though you know where you are going. Stride along. Wear sensible clothes, especially shoes, that do not hinder your walking.
- Keep money stowed deep in your bag or in an inside pocket or leave your handbag behind altogether and take necessary possessions in an ordinary supermarket bag.
- Have your house and car keys handy so you can let yourself in quickly.
- Carry a phone card and change for the phone at all times.
- Never leave both ends of a scarf dangling behind you – they could be used to temporarily throttle you.

In the car

- Make sure your car is locked and store valuables out of sight. Make sure you know the car's registration number – it is amazing the number of people who do not.
- If you are driving, lock yourself in the car and do not leave valuables, such as a handbag, lying on the passenger seat while you fill up at a service station. Lock the car when you go in to pay for petrol.
- Do not drive with an open window and your handbag on the seat – anyone could put an arm in at the traffic lights and steal it.

Protecting your car

Almost half a million cars are stolen in this country each year, nearly three-quarters of them are taken by joyriders or people who have missed the last train home. The rest are probably taken by professional thieves – many of the more expensive models are stolen to order and exported under false number plates within 24 hours of going missing. The cars and motorcycles most at risk are the flashy, sporty ones; for some reason Japanese cars such as Nissans, Hondas and Toyotas are less likely to be stolen, Volvos do not appeal to thieves either.

Speed is of the essence to the car thief, so a good steering wheel lock or a mechanical or electric immobilizer which locks the car in reverse, increase your chances of keeping your car. Car alarms go off so frequently for no reason at all that they are often ignored, but one that is combined with an immobilizer may deter a thief.

- Always lock your car, even when paying for petrol.
- Have a car alarm fitted.
- Scratch the car's registration number on the car radio and have the registration number etched on the car windows.
- Do not park somewhere vulnerable. At night try to park close to street lamps.
- To keep your car as safe as possible in a public car park, try to use one that has an attendant, even if you have to pay a little more. Park in a well-lit place as near as possible to the ticket office.
- Fit a radio or tape player to your car that clips in and out.

Protecting yourself

- Keep the car doors locked when driving, especially at night or in slow-moving traffic.
- If you do a lot of driving on your own, invest in a mobile phone.
- Join a breakdown service. If you are not a member, they will come out if you say you will join on the spot.
- Make sure you know where you are going before you leave. Write the route down and clip it to the dashboard. Do not stop on the side of the road or in a lay-by to consult a map – go to a garage forecourt or outside a shop.
- Be suspicious of other drivers making signals that something is wrong with your car or that they need help. Drive to a safe place before stopping to check your car or to call for breakdown assistance for someone.
- Never give lifts to strangers.
- If you think you are being followed by another car, make sure the windows are shut and the doors locked, slow down and pretend to use your mobile phone if you have one. Drive to the nearest police station or garage forecourt and see what happens.
- If someone pulls in front of you and forces you to stop and then gets out of his car and comes towards you, reverse away from him. If you cannot do this, turn on your hazard lights and sound your horn to attract attention.
- Carry a spare can of petrol in the boot.
- Do not allow yourself to get boxed in, especially when you park. Leave enough space between you and the car in front so that you can drive out easily.
- If you are harassed by another driver, attract attention by pressing the horn and flashing your lights. Do not get out of the car.

- If you are really worried, carry a large sign in the back of your car saying 'Help, get the police' and some blu-tack so that you can stick it onto an inside window.
- If you are parking and returning to the car at night, put it in a well-lit place. Park near to the entrance or exit of a multi-storey car park (*see page 504*).
- Have your keys ready in your hand as you approach the car (*see page 505*).
- Do not leave objects visible in the car, put them in the boot where they are out of sight. If you are a woman, do not leave anything that makes it obvious you are female – high-heeled shoes on the floor or a woman's magazine on the seat.
- If your car breaks down, switch on the hazard warning lights. Get help via the mobile phone if you have one. Lock the doors and shut the windows.
- If a stranger approaches, slide over to the passenger seat – this gives the impression that you not alone but waiting for the driver to return.
- Do not open the window more than a few inches to speak to anyone.

If you have a bike

- Mark the frame with your postcode. Your local police station or Neighbourhood Watch may be able to give you a sticker that says the bicycle is coded in this way.
- Fill in a 'recorded cycle' form at your local police station. They can then match the bike up if it is found – thousands of cycles stay unidentified each year because the police have no idea where to contact the owner.
- Buy a really solid lock made entirely of metal – chains are easily cut.
- Lock your bike to something immovable, such as a railing.

SECURITY INDOORS

If you are a woman living on her own, do not advertise the fact. Use only your surname and initials in the Phone Book and above the door bell. Make sure your house is adequately secure and keep doors locked if you are at home alone and live in a danger area (*see page 501*). If you think someone suspicious is prowling around, indoors or out, do not attempt to investigate, dial 999 immediately.

Do not give out your number when you answer the phone – it could be a burglar checking whether you are in or not. Or if the caller claims to have got the wrong number, ask what number they require. If you are going away for some time and are worried that a pile of post might attract unwanted attention, take advantage of the Royal Mail Keepsafe scheme. For a small fee they will hold all your post safely for you for up to two months. When you return, the post will be delivered on the day of your choice. Get a Keepsafe application form from your local Post Office and send it, with the correct payment, to your local Keepsafe address (*see page 529*).

Malicious calls

Malicious or obscene telephone calls are now taken seriously in law and attract up to £5,000 fine or imprisonment for six months. With the arrival of the last-number recall system which operates out of most exchanges (you dial 1471 to find out the number of the telephone used to make the call) these are likely to lessen. If you are making the call and do not want the recipient to know where you are calling from, all you have to do is dial 141 before the number you are ringing.

What to do

If you are plagued by a telephone pest, report all calls immediately by phoning BT on 0800 66144. Then perhaps the caller can be traced and the offender dealt with. The BT Malicious Calls Bureau says that most people who make nuisance calls tend to do so either to a large number of people or on a persistent basis, so you are helping others if you report it. They can now pick up on calls from all sources including mobile phones. Tests are being done with new technology which will make callers even easier to trace.

- Do not get into conversation with the caller. If he keeps ringing back, put the receiver down on the table, cover it with a cushion and leave it there for a while. In extremis, blowing a whistle down the phone can be very effective.
- If you are alone and the call has upset you, call the National Anti-stalking and Harassment Support Group on 01926 334833.

What to do after a burglary
See **Emergencies,** *page 4.*

CONSUMER PROBLEMS

How to complain

When making a complaint to anyone about goods or services, it is vital to put it in writing. Make sure you address your letter to the right person; if necessary, call the switchboard of the firm concerned to find out. Remember that revenge is a drink best served cold. Screaming and shouting gets you nowhere – you are probably yelling at the wrong person anyway. Think it through, write it down and post or fax your complaint instead. If you have a serious complaint, then go right to the top, address your letter to the managing director or chief executive. That way your letter will get some attention. If the complaint is a serious one, send it by recorded delivery.

Shoddy goods

The Office of Fair Trading says that, under the Sale of Goods Act 1979, any goods that you buy from a commercial trader, even if they are second-hand, must be as they are described in terms of size, colour and material from which they are made.

The goods must be of **satisfactory quality** in terms of their appearance, finish, safety and durability, and must be free of defects unless these have been brought to your attention by the seller, perhaps described as shop-soiled. It is a criminal offence for a trader to say something untrue about the goods offered for sale. If you feel you have been misled you should tell your local Trading Standards officer.

The goods must be **fit for their purpose** including any particular purpose mentioned by you to the seller; if you ask for something waterproof it must be just that. The item must be **as described** by the seller or on the package. In other words, if you are told that a shirt is made of cotton, it should not turn out to be a cotton/polyester mix.

These are your statutory rights and cover all goods bought or hired from a trader, including shops, market stalls, mail order catalogues or door-to-door salesmen. Remember you have some extra protection if you pay for goods by credit card (*see* **Finance,** *page 389*).

Sale goods

The above rules also apply to goods bought in sales. Take no notice of signs saying that there are no refunds on sale goods, it is actually against the law for the trader to display a notice like that.

Returning goods

If you find there is something wrong with what you have bought, contact the seller as soon as possible, phone them if you are unable to get to the shop within a day or so. Make a note of the name of the person you spoke to. If you do this you have not legally 'accepted' the goods and you can still reject them. You are deemed to have 'accepted' the goods if you keep them without complaint for a 'reasonable time'. This is no fixed period, but generally gives you enough time to take the goods home and try them out.

If you realize you have made a mistake and want to return something that is not faulty, however, then you have to rely on the goodwill of the shop concerned to take it back. You have the same rights even if you lose your receipt; however, a receipt is useful evidence of when and where you bought the object and can save a lot of argument, so make a practice of keeping them. You are not legally obliged to return faulty goods to the shop having rejected them. If the item in question is heavy or bulky, ask the shop to collect it.

When you return faulty goods the firm may offer you a replacement, free repair or a credit note rather than your cash back. You do not have to agree to any of these offers. You can insist on having your money back in full. However, if you have kept the goods for some time and have therefore accepted them initially, you can only claim compensation, not your money back. Do not be put off by the shop saying it is the manufacturer's fault; it is their responsibility to deal with your complaint.

If someone gives you something as a present and you want to change it or get the money back, you are not legally entitled to take it back to the shop; the donor must do that.

How to complain

If you have problems over the return of something faulty, put your complaint in writing and keep a copy of your letter. Address it to the head office if the shop is part of a chain; send the letter to the chairman, not the complaints department.

Mail order

More and more of us are buying by mail order. It is convenient and relatively hassle-free, but sometimes things go wrong. Whether you buy goods from a catalogue or from an advertisement in a newspaper or magazine, you have the same rights as if you were buying from a shop; if the goods are faulty or do not match up to their description you are entitled to return them and to get your money back including your return postage.

Examine the goods carefully when they arrive. Do not throw away the packaging as you may want to reuse it. If the goods come to you by post and you sign for them, this does not mean you have signed away your rights, above. You still have reasonable time to examine the goods. If you are offered a free gift, as sometimes happens with mail order offers, it must be sent to you. If it is not as described, then the company may be breaking the law under the Trade Descriptions Act – contact your local Trading Standards officer. If the goods do not arrive within a reasonable time, say, 28 days, or by a date specified in the catalogue or advertisement, you can cancel the order and ask for your money back.

Delivery

If something you have ordered by mail arrives in a damaged condition, contact the mail order company. In most cases they will replace it free of charge. If not, you may have to claim against the Post Office. If the parcel is lost in the post you may have to claim from the Post Office. If you order something by mail order for a specific date, such as Christmas things from a Christmas catalogue and they do not arrive in time, you have the right to reject them and get your money back. Technically, if their failure to arrive on time resulted in your having to pay more for something similar elsewhere, then you could ask the mail order company to pay the extra cost involved.

Buying from newspapers and magazines

Money you send in advance in response to an advertisement should be refunded without question if you return the goods undamaged within seven days of receipt or if the goods are not delivered within 30 days and you decide you no longer want them. The exception to this would be anything that is made-to-measure.

Sending an order
- Check that the newspaper, magazine or catalogue is up to date.
- If you are buying through a newspaper or magazine, check whether you are covered by a protection scheme such as MOPS.
- Do not send cash by post, use a credit card number, a cheque or a postal order. Make sure you keep the stub or counterfoil and that you have a note of where, exactly, you sent it. If you fill in an order form it is a good idea to make a photocopy of it.
- Be careful about giving out credit card details by post or by phone. Make sure you are dealing with a well-known company and that you have its business address and phone number. Do not send money or credit card details to a box number.
- Be sure to include your name and address on your order.
- Keep a copy of the advert or catalogue.
- Read the small print, especially if you are joining a book or record club; you may be agreeing to take expensive items on a regular basis and it can be difficult to pull out of the deal.

Unsolicited goods
If you receive goods through the post that you have not ordered, you are under no obligation to accept them. If you do nothing and do not hear any more from the trader for six months, then the goods become yours. If you contact the trader and say the goods were unsolicited and they do not collect them from you within 30 days, then they also become yours.

Complaint checklist
If you are writing to a mail order company with a complaint, be sure to include in your letter:
- The reason for your complaint.
- The date of the advert and the publication in which it appeared.
- The date of your order.

- What goods you ordered.
- How much you paid and whether you paid by cheque, postal order etc.
- If you have a receipt, say so, but keep it and send a photocopy instead.

Car boot sales

Car boot sales have graduated from being amateur clearing-out-the-garage sales to something much more sophisticated; professional traders have now muscled in. If you buy something from a car boot sale and can prove it is from a trader, rather than a private transaction, then you should be entitled to the same rights as if you bought it in a shop, but it is much more difficult to get repayment or compensation if things go wrong.

If you buy something from a private individual rather than a trader, the only right you have is that the goods should be as described; in other words, if a fridge is described as in working order it should be just that. If, as in the case of a fridge, radio or any other electrically powered equipment, you cannot check it out on the spot, be wary; at the very least get the name and address of the seller. Electrical goods should come complete with a handbook of instructions on how to use them.

Be wary of buying second-hand cassettes, videos and computer software; if they are from a genuine private owner, fine, but if they are from a trader they could be poor quality fake recordings. It is illegal for a trader to pose as a private seller, either through car boot sales or advertisements in the local paper. They attempt to do this because they know your rights are then restricted. If you suspect someone is doing this, contact your local trading standards officer.

One-day sales

Sometimes you see signs for sales at a local hotel or town hall, for 'bankrupt stock'. Treat them with caution, especially if the auctioneer in charge whips up the audience to a frenzy. It could be people have been planted in it to pretend to buy, thereby generating enthusiasm in the crowd. Go along, by all means, for fun, but if you are buying anything serious – household equipment like electrical goods, for instance – insist on paying with your credit card, which will give you some protection.

Buying mobile phones

There is a lot of heavy selling of mobile phones at the moment, with apparently cheap deals on offer. Mobile phones take a great deal of money to set up and whoever sells you one has to cover himself either by charging high rates for calls or by tying you up with a contract that is expensive to break. Read the small print before you sign on. What is the rental? How much is the cancellation fee? What kind of contract have you got and can you get out of it?

Buying antiques

Antique dealers are the most difficult people to sue. When buying, especially from a market stall or car boot sale, get a receipt with a full written description of what you are buying. Get the seller's address and telephone number and always fill in your cheque; do not leave them to fill in their name. If by chance you have bought stolen property, you need to prove that you did so in good faith and that you are not a receiver. Remember that the Trade Descriptions Act does not cover anyone who is trading unofficially, as a hobby for instance, so your rights are then reduced. A real antique dealer will have a VAT number and proper printed stationery.

Buying and selling a car

If you are selling your car through a small ad in the local paper, do not part with it unless the buyer pays by banker's draft, with a building society cheque or in cash. A personal cheque might well bounce.

If you are buying a car privately, see it at the seller's home; be suspicious if the number plate is newer than the car and check the registration document for an official watermark. Remember anyone can register a vehicle in someone else's name. Make careful enquiries from HPI (*see page 528*). More than a quarter of all cars that are written off after accidents make a reappearance on the street. But a write-off is not necessarily a wreck, it can be that the vehicle is so old that it is not worthwhile doing even minor repairs to it or the owner may have a new-for-old policy. Write-offs are sold to specialist salvage buyers who can choose either to use them as scrap, for spare parts or put them back on the road.

If your car is stolen, then sold onto another driver who is completely innocent, the police may impound it while they sort out the question of ownership. You may need the help of a solicitor to get it back. If you buy a car that turns out to be stolen, you could lose both it and your money. Once the car is spotlighted as a stolen vehicle, you have no right to keep it, even if you bought it in good faith. Technically, you need to sue whoever sold it to you to get your money back. If the original owner still owes money on it on hire purchase, you are considered to be the owner and the company who lent the money has to get the remaining instalments back from them. However, if it is a car that has been leased or hired, you have no protection.

SERVICES

Most of us take services like water, gas, electricity and the phone for granted until the day comes when we either forget to, or cannot, pay the bill. How long have we got?

Electricity

If you do not pay your bill, it usually takes up to three months from the receipt of your first account for you to be cut off. You will get a final reminder, then a warning about a month later, then notice that you will be disconnected – the company has to give you at least 48 hours' notice. To do this the electricity company has to get a Right of Entry warrant. To regain your electric supply you may have to pay over a hundred pounds and some companies will demand you pay something in advance.

Gas

The formula here is similar to that of electricity, though the reconnection cost is usually lower. The gas company is supposed to give you seven days' notice before cutting you off. Both the gas and electricity companies usually offer you some way of spreading your payments in order to avoid having to cut you off.

Water

It is very unusual for someone to have the water supply cut off, but in the days of private supplies anything could happen. It usually takes about two months for things to come to a head and you can expect to be disconnected about five or six months after the initial bill. You will probably receive a final notice giving you seven days to pay, then a summons, then 14 days' notice that you are going to be cut off. A reconnection fee will be charged.

Telephone

After a final demand and a warning, British Telecom is likely to disconnect you after about six weeks. It usually sends a final notice giving you seven days to pay. It is expensive to be reconnected, so if you are threatened with disconnection, ring BT (your bill has a helpline number) and explain why you cannot pay. Private phone companies such as Mercury tend to cut you off faster than BT.

NB If you find yourself unable to pay the bill for one of the above essential services, go immediately to your local Citizens' Advice Bureau or the DSS for help and advice.

ROYAL MAIL

Your post

The Post Office has a large range of domestic delivery services ranging from registered post for valuables, recorded delivery proving that your letter has been posted and special delivery guaranteed to reach the recipient the following day. There are also a variety of services for parcels. Any complaints you have about late delivery of letters should be directed to your local Customer Service Unit of the Royal Mail – you will find its address in the Phone Book. If a letter has been delayed, send a photocopy of the envelope with the postmark visible. Royal Mail is supposed to acknowledge your complaint within a week.

You are not entitled to compensation for late delivery, no matter how much inconvenience it caused you. If you paid for something to go by special delivery of any kind, all you are entitled to, if it arrives late, is a refund of your postage. If something that you posted is lost or damaged in the mail, Royal Mail is legally liable to pay compensation up to a certain sum, provided you have proof of posting. This does not mean that you have to send the letter by special delivery of some kind. You can ask for a 'certificate of posting' free of charge from your local Post Office when you send the letter. However, if you send items such as cash or jewellery through the ordinary post and they are lost, you are not entitled to compensation.

Posting a letter or parcel

The services available are:

Certificate of posting
You can demand the Post Office gives you a certificate of posting when you buy stamps for a letter or parcel at the counter. This proves that you have sent the letter or parcel.

Recorded delivery
You pay extra for this service which needs a signature at the other end to prove that the parcel/letter was delivered.

Registered post
Use registered post if you are sending goods worth over £500, money or valuables like jewellery or small works of art. You can get up to £2,200 cover by paying a fee on a sliding scale on top of the first-class postage range.

Consequential loss insurance

You can pay extra for this if you are sending something by registered post. You pay on a sliding scale for extra cover. It is useful if you are sending vital legal documents and might lose an important contract if they were lost.

If you have something of great importance to get somewhere quickly, consider using a local messenger service or a taxi to deliver the letter or parcel if you cannot take it yourself.

TRAINS

British Rail as we used to know it, is now in a state of flux due to privatization. It is being broken up into separate networks, which makes complaining about the service you get much more complicated than it used to be.

- You have no automatic right to a seat on the train because you have bought a ticket. You only have this right if you have reserved a seat.
- Your best bet, if you have a complaint, is to talk to the station staff about the problem in the first instance, then the main line station if one is involved.
- If the train is late, British Rail has only limited responsibility to you if the delay is caused by something beyond the control of the carrier – a cow on the line or bad weather – then they have no obligation to compensate you.
- If, on the other hand, the delay is directly the fault of the company or its employees, it is worthwhile trying to get compensation. Ask for a complaints form and fill it in.
- If you do not get any satisfaction, contact the Transport Users' Consultative Committee in your area or the Customer Relations Manager, British Railways Board (*see page 531*).

BUYING SERVICES

When you buy a service rather than goods from, say, a dry cleaner, hairdresser, shoe repairer or builder you are entitled to a certain standard of work. Whoever performs the service, says the Office of Fair Trading, must do it with 'reasonable care and skill' within a 'reasonable time' and for 'a reasonable charge' if no price has been fixed in advance; if the price was agreed beforehand then you cannot complain later that it was unreasonable.

If you feel you need to complain, contact the company concerned and give it a chance to put things right. If you are not satisfied, put your complaint in writing, say what you want done and set a deadline. If all else fails you can go to court to sue for the return of your money or for compensation, but go to a solicitor or your local Law Centre first, to see if you have a case. The Office of Fair Trading has a helpful information line on 0345 224499.

Dry cleaners

It always pays to go to a dry cleaner who belongs to a trade association, because if things go wrong you have a better chance of satisfaction. If the garment has been damaged or lost, you are entitled to claim the cost of replacing it from the cleaner. If the dry cleaner, on the other hand, thinks that the damage was caused by fair wear and tear or a fault in the manufacture, it may refuse to pay up. This is the moment when you may have to go for arbitration. If your cleaner is a member of the TSA, then contact this body. It may suggest that the garment is sent to an independent laboratory for analysis. If the cleaner is not a member of a trade association, then your only recourse is to go to the small claims court.

- If you stain something, do not try to tackle it yourself if you think it will need professional cleaning. Many dry cleaners say that they could have made a better job of getting a mark out if someone had not attempted to tackle it with detergent and hot water.
- Take the garment in as soon as you can so the stain does not have a chance to set.
- Point out any stains on a garment you take in to the cleaner, tell the cleaner what caused it.
- If the cleaner has not succeeded in getting it out properly, ask that it be cleaned again.

Restaurants

If you book a table in a restaurant, the management must give you 'reasonable time' to arrive. However, if you are running late, it is advisable to ring and tell them. If you arrive on time and, despite booking, the restaurant has no place for you, then you could sue for travelling expenses and any other costs you incur because it has not given you the promised table. However, if you book a table in a restaurant and do not turn up, the restaurant can technically sue you for not doing so. Many popular restaurants now ask for your telephone number when you book.

- A restaurant is not bound to accept credit cards or cheques in payment for a meal. But if it does not do so, it must display a prominent notice, saying so.
- Many trendy restaurants may try to hustle you and move you on quickly after you have had your meal, so that it can get more customers in. You have a right to spend a 'reasonable amount of time' over your food. If you feel that you are being harried, complain and do not leave a tip.

- If you have a problem with a dish you have ordered or the table you have been allocated and cannot solve it with the waiter, ask to see the manager. Take him on one side and explain the situation. Do it quietly and discreetly and do not make a fuss.
- Always check whether service has been added to the bill, especially if paying by credit card, when the restaurant may leave the total blank on the form, hoping you will add some more.
- If you have a reasonable complaint about the food – if the steak was too tough to eat, for instance, and if you cannot get any satisfaction from the staff – deduct the cost of the dish from the bill. Leave the rest of the money, together with your name and address. It will then be up to the restaurant to take action against you to recover the rest of the money.
- It may threaten to call the police if you do not pay in full. The police cannot get involved, however, unless the restaurant can prove you were planning to leave without paying for no reason at all, or if you became violent.
- If a waiter spills food over you during the course of a meal, you are entitled to claim the cost of dry-cleaning from the restaurant, perhaps by deducting it from the bill. If the garment is ruined, then you should claim for its value.
- If you become ill after eating a restaurant meal, go to your doctor to establish the fact that you are unwell, then contact your local Environmental Health Officer, who will then investigate the matter. You may or may not get compensation from the restaurant but these cases are difficult to prove.

THE ENVIRONMENT

Pressure groups

There may be something going on in your neighbourhood that you are not happy about, perhaps plans for a new motorway or a factory estate. This is when you may want to form a pressure group to try to stop this happening. The advantage of joining together to protest for or against something is funding. As a group you are able to afford to pay for professional help and get the council to take notice.

Forming a pressure group

Advertise for like-minded people with letters to your local paper, cards on notice boards in places like the local church, schools, colleges and the public library. Target local celebrities who might help. Get together and work out your objectives, your policies and the reasons for forming the group. Refine it, then write it down succinctly on paper. Find out what local opinion is and what your support is likely to be by submitting another letter in your local paper.

Become an expert on your subject. If possible co-opt a legal expert on your committee. If you are fighting a planning proposal, for instance, study the plans minutely, the way the land is now and what is proposed. Do your homework to find out exactly who, in the council, you need to target for your cause. If it has to do with traffic, you will need the Highways Department. Dirty beaches are the province of the Environmental Health Officer, so are rubbish and pollution. Parking problems come under the Highways Department. Remember that local councillors are split up into specific committees so, apart from the council official, you need to find out which councillors are involved.

Prepare your case, get it looked at by a legal expert if you can. Take photographs if it will help. Do not forget to write to your local MP and to tell the media what you are up to. You will also have to find some way of raising funds. Remember you will need money for things like mailings and photo-copying.

Protest groups

There are many reasons why ordinary citizens decide to protest – a local school or hospital may be due for closure and the local people decide to do something about it. Liberty (The National Council for Civil Liberties) says we all have a fundamental right to protest. Although international human rights law gives us a clear right of peaceful assembly, no such guarantee exists in British law. In our country a right to protest is balanced against a requirement to 'maintain public order'. New legislation means you could be charged with 'aggravated trespass'. This is aimed at hunt saboteurs and animal rights protesters (*see page 428*).

Making a protest

Plan ahead. Give people as much notice as possible of what you are planning.

Decide what form your protest will take – a march, a demonstration outside the premises. Are you going to have loudspeakers, music or banners – all these things need to be thought through at this stage and checks made that you do not need permission. Do you need to call in any special speakers? If so, are they free?

Choose the site where the protest is to be held – is it going to be on public or private land and do you need to get permission? Any meeting in the open air is known as a 'public assembly'. Check with your local council that it is all right to hold a meeting in the park. A meeting held on private land with the permission of the owner has less restrictions than one held in a public place. If you are holding a protest meeting in a hired place, a room in a pub or a village hall, you have to comply with their terms and conditions, probably about fire risk. If the protest is going to be a large one, is there somewhere where protesters can park their cars or even buses?

Make sure you get as much publicity as possible. Alert your local radio, newspaper, TV stations in good time. Tell them what you are doing and why, and who will be there. Remind them nearer the date.

Tell the police about your plans – remember it is part of their duty to uphold your right to protest, not to stop you. If you are planning a march, under the Public Order Act, you must give the police at least six days' clear notice. They will want to know the date, the time and the venue. Someone should be delegated to liaise with the police and give them the name and address of a contact. The police may want to reroute a march, on the grounds of traffic problems, or because it is planned to go through an area where violence might erupt.

Remember that co-operation with the police is essential as they do have powers to impose conditions on marches or meetings or to ban them altogether. But they have to have really substantial reasons for doing so. If the march or meeting is a large one, then appoint stewards, people to help control the crowd and prevent violence.

It is an offence under the Public Meeting Act to try to break up a public meeting. You could be arrested by the police.

PROBLEMS IN TOWN

Air pollution

Old-fashioned smog which gave our cities pea-soupers in the past came mainly from coal fires when coal was the main source of heat. Nowadays sulphur dioxide, its main ingredient, comes from a few factories and power stations. The largest and most lethal kind of pollution today comes from traffic – smoke from diesel fuel, carbon dioxide and carbon monoxide, most toxic of all from cars. Air pollution is deemed to be the cause of the huge increase in asthma and many other respiratory conditions. How can you help?

- Do not use your car for short journeys around town. Walk or cycle whenever you can – it is healthier.
- Make sure your car is serviced regularly and is not emitting smoke.
- Unleaded petrol is just as toxic as leaded petrol unless your car has a catalytic converter. Cars sold since 1993 have this, but if yours is an old banger, you should have one fitted to your exhaust.
- If you see a lorry or car belching out filthy black smoke, make a note of its registration number and report it to your local Traffic Area Office. The number is in your Phone Book.
- Do not make bonfires. Put paper out in the dustbin, or better still, recycle your newspapers and magazines in special paper-collecting bins and make a compost heap of garden refuse.

Litter

Litter is not only unsightly, it is downright dangerous – the King's Cross Underground fire is supposed to have started that way. It is also a hazard – boxes and bags left on the pavement can cause the elderly or people with poor vision to trip over them. In the country, wild animals can be trapped or injured by things like plastic netting and broken glass.

It is illegal to drop litter in the street; you can be fined for this offence, but very few people are prosecuted because it is difficult to catch them actually doing it. Businesses like take-away shops which sell food in packaging also cause litter and are now responsible for the litter that their customers discard.

- Try to avoid buying heavily packaged things. Refuse wrappings if you can. Take a plastic carrier bag with you and reuse it.
- Abandoned cars – the most unsightly street litter of all – are the responsibility of the local council. If they cannot find the owner, they will put a notice on the car warning that it will be taken away (usually a signal for thieves to strip it down). Your local authority is also responsible for abandoned supermarket trolleys.

PROBLEMS IN THE COUNTRY

There are very few places now in this country which are not owned by someone, albeit an organization like the National Trust. But you do have the right, in certain circumstances, to walk over their land.

Trespass

The warning sign 'Trespassers will be prosecuted' is not worth the board on which it is printed because you cannot normally be prosecuted for walking on private land, unless it is owned by the Ministry of Defence or British Rail. In fact it is an offence for a private landowner to put up that particular sign. If you walk through somebody's land other than along a public right of way, you are, technically, a trespasser. The owner has the right to order you off his ground, and in doing so, he has to show you the way to the nearest public footpath or road. He is allowed to use 'reasonable force' to get rid of you if you refuse to go.

The owner can sue you for trespass if you have caused damage to crops or to animals. If a right of way is obstructed, on the other hand, first contact the owner and tell him what has happened. Help keep our footpaths open by joining a pressure group like the Ramblers Association or the Open Spaces Society (*see page 530*).

TRAVEL AND HOLIDAYS

Tips for travellers

The Foreign and Commonwealth Travel Advice Unit has a series of helplines (*see page 532*) that gives you advice on countries you may be planning to visit.

Before you go
- Make sure your passport is still valid.
- Make sure you do not need a visa, especially if you come from a non-EC country and are planning to go to Europe.
- Make sure you have enough insurance to cover every eventuality including death, health problems, car theft, valuables, the lot.
- Take enough money to cover your stay. If you are not using credit cards, take traveller's cheques instead of large amounts of cash. Note down the numbers somewhere and keep them apart from the cheques themselves.
- If you are taking credit cards make sure you know the PIN numbers and that they are not going to expire when you can use them in the country you are visiting. VISA, American Express and Mastercard are the most popular.
- Buy a return ticket or keep funds on one side to pay for your return.
- When you get there, put most of your money in the hotel safe, only walk around with what you need at the time.

You and your local consul

If you are a victim of violence, fall ill or lose your passport abroad, then go to the local British Consul. Most people, alas, mindful of the imposing message in the front of old passports, think that the British Consul is like Father Christmas. He is not. He is not usually interested in car accidents, muggings, lost luggage. He will not:
- Lend you money to get home except in really exceptional circumstances.
- Give you legal advice.
- Get you into a local hospital of your choice.

What he can do, however, is to give you a replacement passport or papers to get you home, if yours has been lost or stolen.

How, then, can you look after yourself while abroad? Take out good, comprehensive travel and health insurance and if you are going on an active holiday such as skiing or sailing, then get a policy that applies to that particular sport. Choose your own policy rather than taking one that goes with the package. Read the small print, see what excess the policy has, how much you personally have to pay before it shells out. If you are going by car, check that the policy includes theft of goods left in the vehicle. If you are taking a computer or any other special piece of equipment, make sure that it is covered too.

Claiming on your travel insurance

Collect every piece of paper you can relating to your claim, especially things like doctors' and hospital bills and taxis receipts before you leave your holiday resort – it is much more difficult trying to get things by post afterwards.

- Do not carry cash in excess of the limit shown on your travel policy – if it is stolen you will not get the extra money.
- Put anything remotely valuable in the hotel safe. Leaving a Rolex watch on the beach while you swim would be construed as 'not taking due care' if it is stolen.
- If you have been mugged or your hotel room ransacked or your luggage stolen, contact the local police as fast as possible. Get something in writing from them. There is a clause in some policies that says you must do this within 24 hours.
- Ring the insurer's emergency helpline immediately after the incident and involve them in your plans.

Holidays: your rights

When you book a package holiday, you enter into a contract with a tour operator. You have to pay the agreed price and it is legally bound to provide you with a holiday as described in its brochure. If the tour operator fails to provide the holiday as promised then you are entitled to claim compensation. However, there are a lot of grey areas involved – if you book a very cheap holiday, just how good can you expect your hotel room to be? And what constitutes an unacceptable delay to your flight?

If you have reason to complain, contact the local representative at the resort, get him to sort it out. If he offers you a cash payment on the spot, do not sign any form of waiver in return. Write to the tour company concerned while you are still abroad; better still, fax them, making your point. Take photographs if you can, then complain within 28 days to an official body like ABTA (*see page 531*) or go to your local Citizens' Advice Bureau for help. Tell the travel agent through which you booked the package.

Cancelled holidays

Sometimes it is a good idea to pay for your package holiday by credit card. Under section 75 of the Consumer Credit Act you may then be able to claim your money back from the card company. Check with your credit card company before you book to see exactly what the conditions are.

Lost luggage

If you are travelling by air, especially if you have to change planes, always carry a basic survival overnight kit in case your luggage goes missing. If you are taking any form of medication, pack it with you in your hand luggage. The carrier, or 'handler' in the case of international airlines, is held responsible for losing your luggage and should compensate you for your loss. This is done, rather surprisingly, on a basis of weight, in other words the larger and heavier your case, the more you will get, ignoring what was actually in it. If you are stranded without luggage and make a fuss, some airlines will give you a small amount to cover overnight things like shaving kit and toiletries. However, if your suitcase contained expensive items such as jewellery and electronic devices, you may have difficulty in getting compensation for them. If you travel in this manner, always have adequate travel insurance.

Holiday health

Most countries in Europe, Australia and New Zealand have a reciprocal agreement with the UK whereby you get medical treatment virtually free of charge if you fall ill. In some cases you have to bear a small part of the cost.

To take advantage of this, you must get a form E111 from your local DSS office. You may find that you have to pay for your treatment at the time and claim it back.

Customs

It is interesting to know that almost four times as many black people are stopped by British customs as whites and more white people are convicted, pro rata, for smuggling offences than black people.

Duty-free goods

Each time you travel to another EC country you are entitled at the moment to buy these quantities of duty-free goods from duty-free and tax-free shops:

- 1 litre of spirits or strong liqueur or 2 litres of fortified or sparkling wine.
- 2 litres of still table wine.
- 60cc/ml of perfume or 250cc/ml toilet water.
- £71 worth of all other goods including beer, gifts or souvenirs.
- 200 cigarettes, 100 cigarillos or 50 cigars or 250g of tobacco.

If you are coming in from a country outside the EC:

- 1 litre spirits or 2 litres sparkling or fortified wine.
- 2 litres of table wine.
- 60cc/ml of perfume or 250cc/ml toilet water.
- £32 worth of gifts, souvenirs or up to 50 litres of beer.
- 200 cigarettes or 50 cigars or 250g tobacco.

Children under the age of 17 are not entitled to an allowance of alcohol or tobacco. Under EC law, duty-free and tax-free shops, including those on the ferry, cannot sell you more than these quantities each time you travel to another EC country. But you can buy them on each journey you make and bring them back to the UK as long as they are for your personal use. So, in effect, provided you buy half on the way out, you can bring back double the amounts shown above on a return visit from this country to one in the EC, except for the £71 money allowance.

The EC countries are Austria, Belgium, Denmark. Finland, France, Germany, Greece, the Irish Republic, Italy, Luxembourg, the Netherlands, Portugal, Spain, Sweden, the UK.

NB The Canary Islands and the Channel Islands are not included.

Illegal goods

There are certain items that cannot be brought back to this country, including:

- Offensive weapons such as flails, firearms, flick knives and explosives (this includes fireworks).
- Obscene magazines, videos and films.
- Illegal drugs such as cannabis, heroin and cocaine.
- Certain plants, fruit, vegetables.
- Foods such as meat, poultry, eggs and milk.
- Dogs, cats and other animals, and live birds.

In addition to the above you are not allowed to import from countries outside the European Community, articles made from many animals and plants without a licence beforehand. These include carved ivory, fur coats and crocodile-skin handbags for which licences will probably not be given. If you are coming from an EC country you do not need a licence but the customs officials may check on the origin of the goods. It is illegal to sell articles made from endangered species without special permission.

How to go through customs

If you are coming to the UK from another EC country you do not need to go through a red or green channel, but will usually go through a separate blue exit for EC travellers. Otherwise always go through the red channel if you think you may be over the limit on duty-free allowances. If not, use the green channel.

Keep receipts for anything bought abroad that might be liable for duty – cameras, watches, electronic equipment, jewellery or antiques, for instance. Remember that if you do have to pay, customs will not take credit cards; you will need cash or a cheque book.

Do not carry parcels through customs for anyone

In some countries there are death penalties for drug smugglers and you might have difficulty in proving you did not know what was in the suitcase. At best you could languish in jail for four years or more waiting for your case to come up. As an innocent 15-year-old, travelling alone to Holland, I was persuaded by a Dutchman to carry a wadge of banknotes through customs at a time when there were currency restrictions – he told me he did not have enough room in his case for them.

If things go wrong

If a customs officer opens your case, you are expected to repack it yourself. Check that he has not broken anything fragile. If any of your baggage is damaged or lost while being examined by customs you are entitled to compensation if you can prove that it is their fault. If you are caught trying to evade paying duty, the goods concerned can be impounded. You then have the choice to pay the penalty they demand or go to court. If you do not claim the goods within six months, they may be disposed of, though customs should let you know that this is going to happen

Body searches

A customs officer may ask to search you or anything you have with you if he reasonably suspects you are carrying any item which is liable to excise duty or tax which has not been paid or any item which is prohibited or restricted from being imported or exported. You can ask what you are suspected of and he must tell you. But he does not have to tell you why you are suspected.

Why should they decide to search you? The reasons range from frequent unexplained trips abroad, the fact that you have arrived from a particular destination or are dressed in a certain way can lead to their suspicions. If you are detained in this way the customs officer must tell you what he suspects you of. Being searched does not mean you are under arrest, it means you are detained while a search is carried out. If they then decide to arrest you, you must be told. However, if you decide to run away before being searched you could be arrested.

There are several types of search: a pocket search when you are asked to empty your pockets; a rub down, when you are frisked, as sometimes happens when you go through airport security; or a strip search or intimate search. If you are subjected to a strip search, this must be done in a private room by someone of the same sex. The room should display a notice telling you of your rights. If an intimate body search (of your orifices like mouth, ears, anus or vagina) is done, then it must be done by a qualified medical person, either a doctor or nurse, not by a customs official.

In the case of a strip search, you have the right not to be completely naked at any time; the top and bottom halves of your body can be searched and re-clothed in order. If you are required to be naked, however, you have the right to have a blanket or similar covering given to you while your clothes are examined. If you are arrested, you have the same rights as at a police station. You can demand to see a solicitor and to tell someone that you have been detained. If you feel you have been unfairly treated, ask to see someone in charge.

How to complain

If you feel you have been badly treated in some way by Customs and Excise, you now have the right to complain and to an independent adjudication and appeal. First ask to see a senior officer. If that does not satisfy you, then complain to the Collector, the overall person in charge. You should do this in writing. If you need to go to a higher authority, write to Customs headquarters (*see page 532*). Always get the name of the individual officer involved at the time the problem arose. If in doubt ring 0171 202 4227 for further advice.

COMMUNITY: HELP DIRECTORY

Consumer

- Advertising Standards Authority, Brook House, 2 Torrington Place, London WC1E 7HW, (0171 580 5555). The authority to complain to about misleading advertisements.
- Consumers Association, 2 Marylebone Road, London NW1 4DF, (0171 734 7005). Information and pressure group, fighting on behalf of consumers. It has a wide range of useful publications, including *Which* magazine.
- Hire Purchase Information, Dolphin House, PO Box 61, New Street, Salisbury, Wilts SP1 2TB. Has a used car information line on 01722 422422. It keeps lists of cars that are subject to hire purchase or rental agreements, stolen cars and cars that have been written off. You pay a fee to enquire about a specific second-hand car. It is not, however, totally infallible, and occasionally cars do slip through the net.
- MOPS, Mail Order Protection Scheme, 16 Tooks Court, London EC4A 1LB, (0171 405 6806). Go to this organization if you have problems with something bought by mail order through a newspaper or a colour supplement.
- Office of Fair Trading, Field House, Breams Buildings, London EC4A 1PR, (0345 224499). Has a consumer information and public liaison line on the above phone number.
- Retail Motor Industry Federation, 201 Great Portland Street, London W1N 6AB, (0171 580 9122). Has an arbitration scheme for car buyers.
- Society of Motor Manufacturers and Traders, Forbes House, Halkin Street, London SW1X 7DS, (0171 235 7000). Operates an arbitration scheme.

- Textile Services Association, 7 Churchill Court, 58 Station Road, North Harrow, Middx HA2 7SA, (0181 863 7755). Contact this association to find a dry cleaner who is one of its members and, therefore, adheres to its code of practice. It has a helpline on 0181 863 8658 which can put you in touch with a cleaner for specialist fabrics such as antique or hand-decorated materials.
- Vehicle Builders and Repairers Association, Belmont House, Finkle Lane, Gilderssome, Leeds LS27 7TW, (0113 258333). The association to go to with complaints over car repairs.

Crime prevention

- Audio Optics Ltd, PO Box 3033, Wokingham RG11 4QQ, (07134 734422). Makes personal alarms that hang round your neck. Available from it direct or from major retail stores.
- Crime Concern, Signal Point, Station Road, Swindon, Wilts SN1 1FE, (0793 514596). If you are thinking about setting up your own Neighbourhood Watch scheme, contact this organization.
- Royal Mail Keepsafe, 6 St Pancras Way, London NW1 1AA, (0171 239 3293). Will send you a leaflet about its Keepsafe service, under which it will hold your mail for you while you are away.

The environment

- Association for the Conservation of Energy, 9 Sherlock Mews, London W1M 3RH, (0171 935 1495). Can give advice on energy conservation.
- The Civic Trust, 17 Carlton House Terrace, London SW1Y 5AW, (0171 930 0914). Can advise on community action to improve the environment.
- Conservation Foundation, 1 Kensington Gore, London SW7 2AR, (0171 581 1253). Can give advice on conservation issues or put you in touch with local groups who can.
- Council for the Protection of Rural England, Warwick House, 25 Buckingham Palace Road, London SW1W 0PP, (0171 976 6433) (01938 552525 for Wales). Can help over countryside issues.
- The Countryside Commission, Postal Sales, PO Box 124, Walgrave, Northampton NN6 9OL, (01604 781848). Can send you a copy of the Countryside Access Charter.
- Department of the Environment, 2 Marsham Street, London SW1P 3EB, (0171 276 0900). The ministry to contact over environmental matters.
- Friends of the Earth, 26 Underwood Street, London N1 7QJ, (0171 490 1555). Can give information and advice on protecting the environment.

- Greenpeace, Canonbury Villas, London N1 2PN, (0171 354 5100). Can put you in touch with a local group.
- Her Majesty's Inspectorate of Pollution, Romney House, 43 Marsham Street, London SW1P 3EB, (0171 276 4152). The office to contact on pollution issues.
- National Rivers Authority, 30 Albert Embankment, London SE1 7TL, (0171 820 0101). It has a free phoneline on 0800 807060 where you can report pollution or flooding.
- Open Spaces Society, 24a Bell Street, Henley-on-Thames, Oxon RG9 2BA, (01491 573535). The society to consult over footpath and commons rights.
- The Ramblers, 1–5 Wandsworth Road, London SW8 2XX, (0171 582 6878). The group to join to help maintain right of access to footpaths and the countryside in general.

General

- Federation of Independent Advice Services (FIAC), 13 Stockwell Road, London SW9 9AU, (0171 274 1839). Has a list of almost a thousand specialist advice centres on a wide range of subjects, including housing, in this country, some with solicitors on their staff.
- Liberty, National Council for Civil Liberties, 21 Tabard Street, London SE1 4LA, (0171 403 3888). Can give information and advice on all aspects of civil liberty.

Neighbourhood problems

- Blue Cross, Shilton Road, Burford, Oxon OX18 4PS, (01993 822651). Has animal hospitals and clinics throughout the country, giving free treatment to animals if owners cannot afford the fees.
- Mediation UK, 82a Gloucester Road, Bristol BS7 8BN, (0117 924 1234). Runs community mediation schemes handling disputes between neighbours and groups. It can send you details of your nearest centre.
- National Canine Defence League, 17 Wakley Street, London EC1V 7LT, (0171 388 0137). Finds homes for unwanted dogs or takes them in via its 15 rescue centres throughout the country.
- Noise Abatement Society, PO Box 8, Bromley, Kent BR2 0UH. Postal enquiries only. Can give information on noise pollution.
- Pets Advisory Committee, 1 Dean's Yard, London SW1P 3NR, (0171 799 9811). Can advise on issues like fouling of pavements, by-laws relating to animals.
- Petsafe, The Old Brewery, Priory Lane, Burford, Oxon OX18 4SG, (01993 823833). Makes Freedom Fence, an electronic system for keeping dogs within boundaries of your property.

- PDSA, People's Dispensary for Sick Animals, Whitechapel Way, Priorslee, Telford, Salop TF2 9PQ, (01952 290999). Will treat pets free at their countrywide clinics if the owners cannot pay.
- The Right to Peace and Quiet Campaign, PO Box 968, London SE2 9RL, (081 312 9997). Send a large SAE for information.
- RSPCA, Causeway, Horsham, West Sussex RH12 1HG, (01763 838329). The organization to contact to report suspected cruelty to animals and for advice over keeping pets.

Services

- Customer Relations Manager, British Railways Board, Euston House, 24 Eversholt Street, London NW1 1DZ, (0171 928 5151). At the moment it is still handling rail complaints.
- Broadcasting Standards Council, 5–8 The Sanctuary, London SW1P 3JS, (0171 233 0544). For complaints about programmes on the grounds of taste, decency, sex and violence. Ask for the Broadcasting Complaints Commission if you have appeared on TV and feel unhappy with the way the interview came over on screen.
- Gas Consumers Council, 15 Wilton Road, London SW1V 1LT, (0171 931 0977). See your gas bill for local office to complain about gas supply, bills or gas appliances. Otherwise contact the above council.
- OFFER, Electricity Consumers Council, Hagley House, Hagley Road, Birmingham B16 8QG, (0121 456 2100), Scotland (0141 331 2678). The council to complain to about problems with your electricity bill.
- OFGAS, 130 Wilton Road, London SW1V 1LQ, (0171 828 0898). A place to complain about gas problems.
- OFTEL, Export House, 50 Ludgate Hill, London EC4M 7JJ, (0171 634 8700). The place to contact over general telephone problems.
- OFWAT, Centre City Tower, 7 Hill Street, Birmingham B5 4UA, (0121 625 1300). Where to complain about water services and supplies.
- Post Office Users National Council, 6 Hercules Road, London SE1 7DN, (0171 928 9458). The place to go with complaints over service. Otherwise call your local Customer Service Unit listed in the Phone Book.

Travel, holidays

- ABTA, Association of British Travel Agents and Tour Operators, 55–57 Newman Street, London W1P 4AH, (0891 20252) Enquiry line. The organization to complain to if you are unable to get satisfactory compensation over a ruined holiday. It is bound by a code of conduct to respond to your letter within 14 days of its receipt.

- AITO, Association of Independent Tour Operators, 133a St Margaret's Road, Twickenham, Middx TW1 1RG, (0181 744 9280). Represents the smaller tour operators.
- The Foreign and Commonwealth Office, King Charles Street, London SW1A 2AH, (0171 270 3000). Its Travel Advice Unit has an information and advice service on 0171 270 4129-79 on travel to any part of the world. It also has 'do's and don'ts' leaflets on 25 most-visited countries and other advice. It now runs a travel helpline: for up-to-date travel advice on: Egypt, the Gambia, India, Israel, Jamaica, Kenya, Nigeria, Pakistan, Russia, South Africa, Turkey and the US call 01374 500900. For information on travel to Croatia call 0171 829 9010.
- HM Customs and Excise, (0171 202 4227). Ring the number above for advice on your treatment at the hands of customs officials.

INDEX

AIDS, 65–6, 96–7
abortion,
— availability, 149–50
— grounds for, 150–51
— post-abortion blues, 152
— procedure, 151–2
— help directory, 161–2
accidents,
— compensation awards, 447, 458
— first aid, 13–16
— in the home, 233–4
— hospital admission, 29
— medical, 25
— road traffic
 animals killed or injured, 3
 damage only, 2
 death or injury from, 1
 insurance claims, 2–3
 raising alarm, 1
 witness's action, 1
addictions,
— addict defined, 80
— gambling, 94–5
— identifying addicts, 80–81
— see also alcohol; drugs; tobacco
adoption, see children
adultery, see divorce; marriage and partners
air pollution, 521
aircraft noise, 499
albinos, 97
alcohol,
— cutting consumption, 91–2
— dealing with problem drinker, 91
— drinking and driving, 431–2, 458
— effect of, 89–90
— signs of alcoholism, 90
— teenage drinking, 92
— help directory, 97–8
— see also cars
allergies, 103
alopecia, 103
alternative medicine,
— acupuncture, 51, 98–9
— Alexander technique, 51, 99

alternative medicine (*continued*),
— aromatherapy, 51, 99
— autogenic training, 52
— ayurvedic medicine, 52, 99
— biodynamics, 52
— biofeedback, 52
— chiropractic, 52, 99
— colonic irrigation, 52
— colour therapy, 52, 99
— diathermy, 52
— faith/spiritual healing, 52, 99–100
— herbalism, 52–3
— holistic medicine, 53, 100
— homeopathy, 53, 100
— hydrotherapy, 53
— hypnotherapy, 53, 100–101
— iridology, 54
— kinesiology, 54
— meditation, 54, 101
— naturopathy, 54, 101
— nutritional therapy, 54
— osteopathy, 54, 101–2
— psychotherapy, 48, 54–5, 102
— radiesthesia, 55
— recovered memory, 55
— reflexology, 55, 102
— relaxation techniques, 55, 102
— Shiatzu, 55, 102
— Siddha medicine, 55
— Unani medicine, 55, 102
— zone therapy, 55
Alzheimer's disease,
— caring for sufferer, 287–8
— meaning of, 286
— prevalency of, 286
— symptoms, 287
amphetamines, 81, *see also* drugs
amyl/butyl nitrate, 81–2, *see also* drugs
anabolic steroids, 82, *see also* drugs
animals kiled or injured on road, 3
ankylosing spondylitis, 103
anorexia, 103–4
antiques, 514
Apert syndrome, 104

citizenship, 222
cleft palate, 111
cocaine, 82–3, *see also* drugs
coeliac disease, 111
colostomy, 111–12
community, *see* crime prevention; dogs;
        environment; neighbour problems;
        sale of goods
Community Service Orders, 450
Community Work Orders, 437
compensation awards, 447, 458
complaints,
— banks, 387–8
— Customs and Excise, 528
— dentists, 37
— doctors, 24–5
— dry cleaners, 518
— estate agents, 465
— goods and services, 509, 511, 512–13
— hospitals, 25
— mental treatment, 453
— restaurants, 518–19
— schools, 322
— services, 517–18
— solicitors, 446–7, 459–60
— trains, 517
— *see also* ethnic minorities; police
complementary medicine, *see* alternative
        medicine
conception,
— fertility tests, 206
— infertility treatment,
        artificial insemination, 207
        donated eggs, 208
        GIFT (gamete intra-fallopian transfer),
        207
        ICSI (intra-cytyoplasmic sperm
        injection), 207
        IVF (in vitro fertilization), 207
        and NHS, 209
        help directory, 216–17
— multiple births, 208, 216
— pregnancy,
        ante-natal care, 211
        changing jobs while, 213
        employee's rights, 211–12
        employer's duties, 211
        maternity leave, statutory and
                additional, 211–13
        mortgage applications and, 382–3
        Patients' Charter on, 210
        self-employed, 213
        teenage, 146
        tests, 209
        unfair dismissal, 213
        working benefits, 210

conception (*continued*),
— problems with, 206
— surrogate mothers, 208–9
— help directory, 215–17
— *see also* childbirth
convicted prisoner's rights, 440–41, *see also*
        prisons
cosmetic surgery, 112
— advisability of, 58
— non-NHS treatment,
        camouflage, 60
        collagen injections, 59
        dermabrasion (chemical peeling), 59
        electrolysis, 59
        laser treatment, 59
— plastic surgery on NHS,
        blepharoplasty (eyelid surgery), 57
        breast augmentation, 57–8
        breast reduction, 57
        face lift (rhitidectomy), 56
        liposuction, 58
        nose reshaping, 57
        octoplasty, 57
— qualified practitioners, 55–6
council houses,
— marital breakdown and, 486–8
— purchase of, 475–6
— rehousing, 488
counselling, 136
County Courts, 434–5
courts,
— barristers, 443
— children and, *see* children
— compensation awards, 447
— Court of Protection, 450–51
— identity parades, 438
— jury service,
        duties as to, 438–9
        expenses, 440
        procedure, 439
— procedure,
        attending, 437
        at hearing, 435–6
        as witness, 437
— process servers, 438
— types of, 434–5
— verdicts,
        absolute discharge, 436
        community work orders, 437
        conditional discharge, 436
        fines, 437
        not guilty, 436
        probation orders, 437
        referral to another court, 437
— Witness Service, 436
— help directory, 459

pain,
— painkillers, 26–7
— help directory, 126
parents, *see* children; teenagers
Parkinson's disease, 126
passports,
— children's, 222
— loss of, 13, 18
pawnbrokers, 397
pensions,
— books, loss of, 6
— private, 378, 405
— State retirement,
    additional benefits, 281
    changes from 2010, 282
    payment methods, 281–2
    qualification requirements, 281
    help directory, 314
pensions, *see* pensions
pets, *see* dogs
phobias, 96
pickpockets, 504
place of safety orders, *see* domestic
        violence
police,
— arrest,
    bail, 4
    charge procedure, 4
    period of detention, 4
    silence, right of arrested person, 3
    help directory, 458
— arrest procedures, 3–4, 432
— cautions, 430, 436, 448
— children and, *see* children
— civil actions against, 434
— complaints against,
    checklist, 433
    grounds for complaint, 432
    investigations into, 433
    procedure, 432–3
    help directory, 460
— Criminal Justice Act, 427–8
— in domestic violence cases, 188
— and ethnic minorities, 407–87
— fingerprinting powers, 3
— identity parades, 438
— motor accidents, 1–3
— powers,
    generally, 427–8
    stop and search, 428–9
— Public Order Act, 427–8
— racial discrimination and, 413
— rape procedure, 7–8
— reporting crimes to, 5
— road traffic accident investigations, 1–3
— search powers, 3

police (*continued*),
— transport, 5
— *see also* courts; legal aid; legal matters;
        prisons
polio, 126
Post Office,
— delivery services available, 516–17
— late or non-delivery, 511–12, 516
pre-menstrual tension, 134
pregnancy, *see* conception
pressure groups, 519–20
prisons,
— letters to, 440–41
— remand prisoners' rights, 440
— telephone calls
— visitors, 440–41
— youth custody, 450
— help directory, 460–61
Probation Service,
— community service orders, 450
— in domestic violence cases, 188
— probation orders, 437
process servers, 438
protest groups, 520–2'
psoriasis, 134
psychiatry, *see* mental illness

RSI (repetitive strain injury), 134
racial discrimination, *see* ethnic minorities
rape,
— counselling, 8, 19, 164–5
— procedure following, 7–8
— *see also* sex
refuges, *see* domestic violence
religious cults, 136
repairs receipts, loss of, 6
restaurants, 518–19
retirement, *see* finance; pensions; third age
rights of way, 522

St John Ambulance, 13, 18
sale of goods,
— antiques, 514
— car boot sales, 513
— cars, 514–15
— complaints, 509, 511, 512–13
— damaged in transit, 511
— late delivery, 511–12
— mail order, 511
— mobile phones, 513–14
— from newspapers, 512
— one day sales, 513
— purchasers' rights, 510
— returning goods, 510–11, 512
— unsolicited goods, 512
— help directory, 528–9